Comparative Reading

The international team of contributors is comprised of

JOHN DOWNING, *University of Victoria,* Victoria, British Columbia, Canada.

MARY AUSTIN, *University of Hawaii,* Honolulu, Hawaii, USA.

FRANZ BIGLMAIER, *Pädagogische Hochschule,* Berlin, Germany.

GASTON BLOM, *University of Colorado,* Denver, Colorado, USA.

M. ALAN BRIMER, *University of Bristol,* Bristol, England.

D. B. ELKONIN, *Academy of Pedagogical Sciences,* Moscow, USSR.

DINA FEITELSON, *Hebrew University of Jerusalem,* Jerusalem, Israel.

ELIZABETH GOODACRE, *University of London,* London, England.

MOGENS JANSEN, *Danish Institute for Educational Research,* Copenhagen, Denmark.

O. K. KYÖSTIÖ, *University of Oulu,* Oulu, Finland.

CHE KAN LEONG, *University of Saskatchewan,* Saskatoon, Saskatchewan, Canada.

KIYOSHI MAKITA, *Keio University School of Medicine,* Tokyo, Japan.

EVE MALMQUIST, *Teachers College of Linköping,* Linköping, Sweden.

CHINNA OOMMEN (nee CHACKO), *Central Institute for Indian Languages,* Mysore, India.

BERTA PERELSTEIN DE BRASLAVSKY, *Universidad Nacional de la Plata,* Argentina.

PAUL RUTHMAN, *Southern Connecticut State College,* New Haven, Connecticut, USA.

TAKAHIKO SAKAMOTO, *Noma Institute of Educational Research,* Tokyo, Japan.

LAWRENCE WIBERG, *University of Colorado,* Denver, Colorado, USA.

Comparative Reading

Cross-National Studies of Behavior and Processes in Reading and Writing

JOHN DOWNING

THE MACMILLAN COMPANY *New York*
COLLIER-MACMILLAN LIMITED *London*

372.4
D 751

Acknowledgments

IN addition to the specific acknowledgments that will be made in appropriate chapters in this book, we wish to thank the numerous other people who have helped us to complete this book. In particular, we want to recognize the valuable help given by several of the secretaries at the University of Victoria. They had an unusually difficult task in preparing the final manuscript because of the (to them) foreign names and words that appear so frequently in the text. Often the orthographies were different from any with which they were accustomed. The work, therefore, was often tedious in its detail. The excellent finish of the final typescript was a great credit to the ideal secretarial patience of Heather Beston, Linda Cleough, Neela Cumming, and Colleen Hills.

We would also like to thank Marianne and Rupert Downing for their help in proofreading.

J. D.

THE MACMILLAN COMPANY
866 Third Avenue, New York, New York 10022

COLLIER-MACMILLAN CANADA, LTD., Toronto, Ontario

Library of Congress catalog card number: 77-182447

Printing: 1 2 3 4 5 6 7 8   Year: 3 4 5 6 7 8 9

Contents

About the Author and Contributors   vii

PART ONE

CHAPTER

1 The Rationale and Scope of Comparative Reading
                                         JOHN DOWNING   3

2 Methodological Problems of Research   M. ALAN BRIMER   13

3 Cross-National Comparisons of Reading Achievement
                                         JOHN DOWNING   32

4 Bases for Comparison   JOHN DOWNING   65

5 Attitude Content in Reading Primers
                        GASTON BLOM and LAWRENCE WIBERG   85

6 Cultural Expectations   JOHN DOWNING   105

7 The Teacher Variable   JOHN DOWNING   128

8 Other Extraneous Factors   JOHN DOWNING   169

9 Linguistic Environments: I   JOHN DOWNING   181

10 Linguistic Environments: II   JOHN DOWNING   217

11 The Future of Comparative Reading   JOHN DOWNING   244

PART TWO

12 Argentina   BERTA PERELSTEIN DE BRASLAVSKY   259

13 Denmark   MOGENS JANSEN   285

14 Finland   O. K. KYÖSTIÖ   308

15 France   PAUL RUTHMAN   319

16 Germany   FRANZ BIGLMAIER   342

17 Great Britain   ELIZABETH GOODACRE   360

18 Hong Kong   CHE KAN LEONG   383

19 India   CHINNA OOMMEN (NEE CHACKO)   403

20 Israel   DINA FEITELSON   426

21 Japan   TAKAHIKO SAKAMOTO and KIYOSHI MAKITA   440

22 Sweden   EVE MALMQUIST   466

23 United States   MARY AUSTIN   488

24 USSR   D. B. ELKONIN   551

    INDEX OF NAMES   581

    INDEX OF SUBJECTS   587

About the Author and Contributors

JOHN DOWNING has been a professor of education at the University of Victoria, British Columbia, since 1970, when he moved to Canada from the University of London, England. He has been a visiting lecturer at many universities in different parts of the world, including a one-year term at the University of California at Berkeley (1967–1968). He began his career in education as a classroom teacher after his initial training in education at Oakley College, Cheltenham, England. From the University of London he obtained his Ph.D. and B.A. degrees in psychology. He was the first president of the United Kingdom Reading Association, a national affiliate of the International Reading Association, on whose International Development Committee he currently serves. He has published eleven books and more than 150 articles on various educational and psychological topics, mostly related to problems of learning to read. His publications include also a basal reader series, *The Downing Readers,* and a series of English dictionaries, *The Pyramid Primary Dictionaries.*

MARY AUSTIN, formerly a classroom teacher, received her Ed.D. from Syracuse University, Syracuse, N.Y., where she majored in educational psychology and reading. She was lecturer on education and director of the Harvard-Carnegie Reading Studies in the Graduate School of Education at Harvard University (1955–1963). She then returned to Western Reserve University as a professor of education, an institution in which she had served as an associate professor and as director of the Reading Improvement Center from 1948–1955. Since 1969, she has been a professor of education and director of the Reading and Language Arts Center in the College of Education at the University of Hawaii. Her publications include numerous articles in professional journals and *The Torch Lighters: Tomorrow's Teachers of Reading*; *The First R: The Harvard Report on Reading in Elementary Schools,* with Coleman Morrison; *Reading Evaluation,* with Clifford L. Bush and Mildred Huebner; a chapter in the NSSE Yearbook, *Innovation and Change in Reading Instruction,* on the professional training of reading personnel; and *The Sound of Poetry,* with Queenie B. Mills. She is co-author of the *Sheldon Basic Reading Series.* A past-president of the International Reading Association and of the National Conference on Research in English, Dr. Austin is currently serving on the IRA Commission on High Quality of Teacher Education.

FRANZ BIGLMAIER is a professor of education at the *Pädagogische Hochschule* in Berlin. He has been a teacher and psychologist in various public schools as well as at the university level. He received his degrees in education and psychology at the University of Munich and in 1950–1951 and 1967 studied in the United States as a Fulbright scholar. He has published numerous articles in German on testing and the teaching of reading in that language.

GASTON E. BLOM, M.D., is a professor of psychiatry and education at the University of Colorado Medical Center. Trained as a psychoanalyst and as an adult and child psychiatrist, he has been interested in psychoeducational approaches to handicapped children, particularly those with emotional disturbances and learning difficulties. He has published in various special education and psychiatric professional journals. He was a member of the National Advisory Committee on Dyslexia and Reading Disorders of the Department of Health, Education, and Welfare, and was a participant in Project Literacy.

M. ALAN BRIMER, after being graduated with a major in English from Cambridge University, England, and training as a teacher at Bristol University, studied psychology at Leeds University. He taught English in a state secondary school before joining the National Foundation for Educational Research in England and Wales. At the NFER he was concerned with, among other activities, the construction of tests of reading and with the inquiry conducted by Joyce Morris into the teaching of reading in Kent. Subsequently he joined the University College, Ibadan, Nigeria, as senior lecturer in educational psychology and published an experimental study of reading speeds of Yoruba students and adapted English and Yoruba versions of a reading test. Since 1963, he has been head of the research unit in the School of Education, University of Bristol, and has published various articles and reviews on studies of reading. He became a member of the International Committee of IEA (International Educational Achievement studies) on reading comprehension and will be responsible for the report of the international study in its implications for the English sample. He is a member of the Governing Board of the UNESCO Institute for Education and is a consultant to UNESCO (IBE) on various themes of cross-national study. His book written in collaboration with Professor L. Pauli, *Wastage in Education: A World Problem,* was published in English and French by UNESCO in September 1971.

DANIEL BORISOVICH ELKONIN is a professor of educational and child psychology at the Academy of Pedagogical Sciences of the USSR and director of the Department of Child Psychology in the Institute of General and Pedagogical Psychology of the Academy of Pedagogical Sciences of the USSR. He also holds the position of professor in the Moscow State University. He entered this field as a pupil of the leading Soviet psychologist Lev S. Vygotsky. His publications include six books on child psychology as well as numerous articles in this field. His main research contributions have been in the following areas: the psychology of reading and writing, the early development of speech and thought, and children's play. In 1958 he organized an experimental school in which a number of new programs were developed, including the new methods of training auditory discrimination in early reading that are described in this book.

DINA FEITELSON started her career as a first-grade teacher in Israel. She was the author of the study of causes of scholastic failure among first-graders that was awarded the Israel Prize for Education for 1953. This investigation triggered major changes in the teaching of beginning reading in Israel. She served as a member of the task force set up by the Israeli Ministry of Education for the development of these new strategies in reading instruction. She has also written a number of theoretical articles on reading, including an important chapter in the forthcoming UNESCO handbook on reading, and a monograph on improving the teaching of the mother tongue in primary schools. Currently she teaches at the Hebrew University of Jerusalem and is serving as a member of the Committee on Reforming Language Curriculum set up by the Israeli Ministry of Education. She was a visiting scholar at the University of Chicago, 1964–1965, and a research associate at Harvard University, 1970–1971.

ELIZABETH J. GOODACRE is the tutor to the course on the psychology of literacy at the London University Institute of Education. A trained infant teacher and educational psychologist, she is the author of several reports of research on the teaching of beginners undertaken by the National Foundation for Educational Research in England and Wales. She has also written a textbook for training teachers—*Children Learning to Read*. Her articles and research reports in professional books and journals are numerous. They have dealt with such diverse areas as "hearing" children read, national comparisons of reading practice and attainment, and the evaluation of current research in Britain. She is particularly concerned with the developmental psychological processes involved in reading.

MOGENS JANSEN is research director of the Danish Institute for Educational Research and president of the Danish National Association of Reading Teachers. His professional training is in two fields, education and psychology (Copenhagen University). He has published several books and numerous articles on language teaching in Danish and about classroom analysis.

OIVA K. KYÖSTIÖ, M.A., Ph.D., has been a teacher in various schools in Finland (1935–1947), a school inspector (1947–1952), and a reader in education at the University of Jyväskyla (1953–1964). Since 1964, he has been a professor of education and dean of the Teachers College at the University of Oulu. He served as a UNESCO adviser in 1967 and in 1968–1969. His publications include ten books or monographs and about one hundred articles on different fields of education. His publications in English have included the following topics: indicators of vocational fitness, reading research at the kindergarten level, teacher role expectations, reading and forgetting among young children, the Finnish school in transition, attainment in coeducational and segregated schools, and reading levels among 15-year-old boys and girls.

CHE KAN LEONG was educated in Hong Kong and in Australia, where he did postgraduate work in educational psychology and child guidance as a UNESCO fellow. After a brief period of secondary school teaching, he worked for twelve years with the Education Department in Hong Kong, first as a lecturer in educational psychology in the Northcote College of Education and later as a research and guidance officer. In this capacity he carried out research into the teaching of the Chinese language and devised and standardized achievement tests. Since 1969, he has been an assistant professor with the Institute of Child Guidance and Development, University of Saskatchewan, Saskatoon, Canada. His main interest is in the psychology of language as related to exceptional children and comparative reading.

KIYOSHI MAKITA received his M.D. and *Igaku Hakushi* (cf. Ph.D.) from the Keio University School of Medicine, Tokyo. Currently he is an associate professor of neuropsychiatry at Keio University and the director of the Children's Psychiatric Service. In 1956 he served as an assistant psychiatrist at the Johns Hopkins Hospital in the United States as a Rockefeller Foundation fellow. He was president of the Third Annual Meeting of the Japanese Child Psychiatric Association in 1962. He has served on several committees and boards concerned with child psychiatry and related disciplines. His several books and articles are in the field of child psychiatry. He also serves in a number of editorial capacities in the same area of scholarly research.

EVE J. MALMQUIST is a professor of education at Teachers College, University of Linköping, Sweden. He received his Ph.D. degree in education at the University of Stockholm. He has served as a member of the board of directors of the International Reading Association and as a member of many of its committees. He was co-chairman of the World Congress on Reading, Copenhagen, Denmark, in 1968 and chairman of the World Congress on Reading, Sydney, Australia, in 1970. He has published some thirty educational measuring instruments, two series of textbooks and workbooks in reading for grades I–VI, eighteen books on studies within the areas of psychology and education, and about 240 articles on different psychological and educational problems, mostly within the field of reading.

CHINNA OOMMEN (*nee* CHACKO) is currently working as a reader at the Central Institute of Indian Languages in Mysore, South India, where she is in charge of the Reading Project. Prior to this, she was the head of the Reading Project at the Department of Curriculum and Textbooks of the National Council of Educational Research and Training in New Delhi and served as a reading specialist with the United States Agency for International Development in Nepal. In both of these places she supervised the preparation and production of reading materials (textbooks, workbooks, manuals, teaching aids, and tests) for elementary schools. She also has a number of professional articles and papers to her credit. She received her Ed.D. in elementary education from the University of California, at Berkeley, under the sponsorship of the late Professor David H. Russell. She worked with Dr. Constance McCullough when she was the adviser to the Government of India.

BERTA PERELSTEIN DE BRASLAVSKY obtained her original qualification in education at the Normal School and at Argentina's National Institute of Secondary Teaching, completed her graduate work at the University of Buenos Aires, and continued her studies of special education in several countries, including France and the USSR. In Argentina she has held a number of important positions in educating the mentally deficient and has contributed to international knowledge of this problem. She has been professor of differential pedagogy at the *Universidad Nacional de la Plata* since 1965. In recent years, she has also been a consultant for UNESCO and has undertaken a number of missions in Costa Rica, El Salvador, Guatemala, Honduras, Nicaragua, and Panama. In 1971, she was a visiting professor at the University of Chile with the support of the World Health Organization. Her participation in educational research has produced numerous articles and several books. Among these have been a number of works on reading, including her best-known book in Latin America, *La Querella de los Métodos en la Enseñanza de la Lectura* (*The Dispute About Methods of Teaching Reading*) published in 1962.

PAUL E. RUTHMAN, a professor of education and associate director of the Reading Center at Southern Connecticut State College, has been an elementary school teacher, principal, and field supervisor. His interest in France and its reading program began during a tour of military duty during World War II. Subsequent trips to France, a French wife, and graduate work in reading have helped to develop his knowledge of reading instruction in France. This background quite naturally led to his doctoral dissertation on the French reading program. His study was done with the permission of the Ministry of Education and included classroom observations in several areas of France as well as research in Paris at the *Institut Pédagogique National* and UNESCO. His degrees were earned at Trinity College (B.A.), Boston University (M.Ed.), and University of Connecticut (Ph.D.—reading and comparative education). His publications include his contribution to *Assessment of Reading Programs,* which is used in Connecticut schools. He has served as chairman of the Connecticut Reading Council and as president of the New Haven chapter of the IRA.

TAKAHIKO SAKAMOTO completed his undergraduate and postgraduate work at the Tokyo University of Education. At present, he works as the director of the Department of the Science of Reading at the Noma Institute of Educational Research, Otowa, Bunkyo-ku, Tokyo. Since 1958, he has been acting as the executive secretary of the Japanese Society for the Science of Reading, which is affiliated with the International Reading Association. Since 1965, he has been one of the members of the Editorial Board of the quarterly journal *Dokusho Kagaku* (*The Science of Reading*), which is published by the Japanese Society for the Science of Reading. In 1967, he spoke on "Beginning reading in Japan" at the 12th Annual Convention of the International Reading Association held in Seattle, Washington. In 1971, he was invited to serve as a member of IRA's International Book Year (IBY) Committee and stimulated the establishment of the various activities of IBY, 1972, in Japan. In December, 1971, his paper

"How Japanese children learn the several writing systems of the Japanese language" was read at the Eighth Inter-American Congress of Psychology held in Panama City. His publications in the field of reading are numerous.

J. LAWRENCE WIBERG, M.D., received his undergraduate education at Wesleyan University, Middletown, Connecticut, and his medical education at Stanford University. He served his psychiatric residency at the University of Colorado Medical Center, where he began research on reading problems in children. He currently is on the clinical faculty of the University of Colorado and is pursuing interests in psychoeducational and psychoanalytic aspects of childhood development.

Part One

Part One

CHAPTER 1

The Rationale and Scope of Comparative Reading

JOHN DOWNING

> The size of this phenomenon of illiteracy and its grave economic, social, and cultural implications explain the growing intensity of the efforts being made throughout the world and the increased research into the application of new methods in order to take a decisive step towards the solution of the problem. In this vast illiteracy field, we see a hundred flowers growing and flourishing, and they must.
>
> MALCOLM S. ADISESHIAH
> Deputy Director General of UNESCO, Teheran, 1970

THIS book represents a new species in comparative reading. As yet it is only like a fresh green shoot, but hopefully it will grow like a strong tree to bear fruit that will help nourish other efforts to increase literacy in the world. Our ambitious hopes are based on the relationship that exists between theory and practice in other areas of human endeavor. In medicine, agriculture, transport, and all fields of technology, theory has proved to be the spur to practical invention. It also has organized thinking about practical problems and has reduced the waste of human and material resources that occurs when haphazard individual efforts repeat the same errors.

The teaching of reading is particularly prone to such waste. Methods of teaching literacy are subject to fashions of educational opinion both within a single country and from one country to another as such fashions spread. What is needed is to anchor the technology of reading more firmly in theory.

This book is based on the hope that the methods of cross-national research and comparative studies, which have proved of such great theoretical and practical value in other fields, will lead to a better understanding also of the fundamental psychological processes of literacy behavior, both in their learning and in their developed functioning.

International Concern for Reading

In recent years there has been an increase in speculative comparisons between learning to read and cultural circumstances. Interest has grown also, although at a much slower pace, in the possibility of conducting objective empirical

3

research on reading by the cross-national method of investigation. Probably the chief forces behind these quickening interests are (1) the continued concern of UNESCO for expanding basic functional literacy in less developed countries around the world, and (2) the rapid expansion of the International Reading Association (IRA).

Literacy is a relative concept. Understandably, UNESCO has tended to emphasize the lower basic levels of the development of the skills of functional literacy. Their chief problem is how to set in motion people's first movement across the baseline from illiteracy into primitive functional literacy. In contrast, the activities of IRA show a much greater interest in the higher levels of reading development. In IRA publications and meetings there is also a concern for the theoretical understanding of the psycholinguistic processes involved in reading and learning to read that is more discernible than in UNESCO publications and activities.

The differences in focus arise quite naturally from the different origins and functions of the two institutions. UNESCO faces the enormous difficulty of helping vast numbers of totally illiterate people make a start in learning to read and write. The massive nature of their task and the severely limited resources available tend to limit attention to what may seem to be the simplest basic and well-tried techniques of literacy training. IRA, on the other hand, began as an organization of reading teachers in the sophisticated school systems of the United States and Canada. Hence, the interests of its members were centered on much more than the initial stage of learning to read, and, even within the area of beginning reading, it was feasible for teachers to consider an infinite range of materials and methods of teaching and the theoretical bases of their differences.

However, although one can understand why UNESCO and IRA have followed different paths, it is clear that any theory of the processes of reading and learning to read must take account of both areas of concern—basic literacy and the more sophisticated teaching and learning of reading. Furthermore, this operates both ways. Theoretical developments will have beneficial repercussions not only in more highly developed school systems but also in basic programs for functional literacy. This underlying continuity in the respective spheres of activity of IRA and UNESCO has long been recognized. For example, William S. Gray,[1] the first president of IRA, conducted the pioneer international survey for UNESCO that led to their classic publication in this field, *The Teaching of Reading and Writing,* in 1956; Gray and other members of IRA have assisted UNESCO from time to time in other studies in this field.

Since about 1964, the board of directors of IRA has made strong efforts to establish IRA councils in many different countries. In 1970, IRA adopted a proposal to establish its first permanent administrative branch office outside North America. It is in Paris—the home also of UNESCO headquarters. It is anticipated that many more countries in Europe will develop IRA councils as a result of this move. Recently, the Executive-Secretary Treasurer of IRA, Dr. Ralph C. Staiger, was invited to update William S. Gray's original UNESCO volume, *The Teaching of Reading and Writing,* for its second edition in 1969.

Currently, IRA is preparing for UNESCO a new handbook for reading. Staiger again is the editor and compiler of the several specialist chapters in what is anticipated will be an important source of practical knowledge in this field.

Another aspect of IRA's increasing interest in international activities is their successful organization of biennial world congresses on reading[2] (Paris, 1966; Copenhagen, 1968; Sydney, 1970; Buenos Aires, 1972). Mention should also be made of the three international symposia[3] on reading organized by the United Kingdom Reading Association, the IRA council in that country.

These international activities of IRA have tended to clarify the mutuality of the aims of IRA and UNESCO in the appropriate fields and, as a result, the potential of international reading research has been recognized, too. A Past-President of IRA, Nila Banton Smith,[4] emphasized these possibilities in her address to the first World Congress on Reading in Paris in 1966: "Eventually we shall have worldwide reading research . . . . This is truly one of the most significant promises which the future of reading holds out to us." Actually, by 1966 some findings from international reading comparisons were already available, but Smith appropriately stressed the future because past efforts had been spasmodic, organized for different purposes, and often lacked scientific rigor. Few comparative studies have aimed at understanding more about the reading process *per se,* and still fewer are scientific. Nevertheless, the student of comparative reading may wish to be conversant with the data from previous studies.

Earlier Investigations

Three types of data are available for comparative purposes from previous studies:

1. From studies that were deliberately designed to make comparisons about reading in different countries.
2. From studies that were designed to describe objectively the reading practices in a particular country.
3. From studies that were limited to a particular country, but that, in addition, made some tentative comparative hypotheses.

The number of previous studies of the first type—that is, direct cross-national investigations—is small. The classic example is William S. Gray's[5] pioneering work for UNESCO. His method relied to an important extent on the review of existing materials from different countries for teaching literacy together with published reports of various kinds. In addition, he obtained special data by sending out questionnaires and making specific enquiries by mail. He also made use of information he obtained in an informal way in private conferences and personal visits to several countries. The only empirical data on reading behavior collected specially for his study were on eye movements in reading for fourteen languages. All this work led Gray to make certain universal generalizations about teaching methods and learning behavior in literacy acquisition.

A more strictly empirical approach has been followed in only very few comparative studies—for example, in the cross-national survey of reading achievements of 13-year-olds in twelve countries made by Foshay[6] *et al.* in 1962. Although such research provides a more reliable basis for comparing achievements across nations, limitations in sampling and the tests used probably preclude the drawing of any conclusions about the nature of the reading process *per se*. Subsequently, this line of investigation of cross-national reading achievements has been pursued further by a team of scholars working together under the title of "International Educational Achievements" (IEA). Alan Brimer is a member of that team, and in Chapter 2 of this book he will describe the progress of the work in connection with his more general consideration of the methodology of cross-national reading research. A detailed review of the study of Foshay *et al.*, and two other paradigms for this type of research constitute the theme of Chapter 3. Gray's international survey was very comprehensive and hence it will be referred to frequently in many of the chapters in both parts of this book.

A few studies have focused on specific problems in the teaching of reading. Several have attempted to relate learning problems to the nature of different languages and the conventional systems used to write them—for example, Lee's[7] investigation of the methods of teaching reading in countries whose languages differ in regularity of grapheme-phoneme relations. These studies are included in the relevant special sections of Part One of this book.

Another special focus of cross-national study in reading behavior was proposed in Klineberg's article, "Life is fun in a smiling, fair-skinned world," published in 1967, which makes comparisons between different reading materials within the United States. He concludes with the proposal that his "analysis made of American readers be supplemented by a comparison with readers of other countries (France, the Soviet Union, Brazil, and Sweden, for example) to determine what can be discovered from their experience."[8] His proposal, in fact, has proven to be very fruitful. Gaston E. Blom and J. Lawrence Wiberg have carried out a cross-cultural comparison of reading materials in respect to their attitudinal content, and they will report their methods and findings in detail in Chapter 5.

Indirect Approaches

The second type of data available from previous studies can be found in descriptions of reading behavior in particular countries.

Two recent articles on reading in *France* provide useful material for comparative purposes. Chiland's[9] article, liberally illustrated with pages from French children's readers, provides a vivid insight into reading in France. She brings out particularly clearly some problems of content, teaching methods, school organization, and teacher training. Lobrot's[10] paper on remedial teaching in France is a useful expansion of the picture of French reading.

The teaching of beginning reading in the *United Kingdom* is clearly and objectively described by Southgate[11] and some of the U.K.'s problems for future development are frankly indicated by Morris.[12] Another recent study of more modest intent is mentioned here as an example of the valuable information that small objective research studies in individual countries can provide when the locale of the investigation is carefully defined and clearly delimited. The study by Abernethy *et al.*[13] of the reading habits and interests of children in Belfast, Northern Ireland is just such a study.

The general conception of reading in the *United States* is well summarized by Austin,[14] and Robinson's[15] survey of provisions in America for children with reading difficulties adds that aspect to the total picture. The history of the teaching of reading, although not well documented in other countries, has been given careful attention in America. Most important is Nila Banton Smith's[16] monumental study, but Staiger's[17] recent short article is an excellent introduction.

Malmquist[18] has provided a characteristically clear and objective statement on provisions for children with reading difficulties in *Sweden*. Gjessing's[19] *Norwegian* report is focused on the concept of reading readiness. His study is one of those that takes us more into the third category of data listed earlier because he does make some tentative comparisons between Norway and other countries. Kyöstiö[20] also makes provisional comparisons in his report of preschool reading in *Finland,* at the same time recognizing some of the methodological problems involved therein.

These individual studies are a useful source of data, particularly at this initial stage in the development of the field of comparative reading studies, but they do have serious limitations that must be taken into account. Most of them tend to be more or less ethnocentric. Although the authors may have an appropriate set to communicate information about reading behavior in their country to experts from other countries, comparative study in this field is so new that everyone is uncertain as to exactly what should be included—that is, which variables are important in comparing one country's reading with another's? This problem is made more difficult because of the very large number of potentially significant variables in reading and in learning to read.

The Aims of This Study

The aims of this book differ from those of previous studies in this field. For example, Gray's classic international survey of reading was "intended specifically for those responsible for organizing and directing literacy programmes with special reference to areas where programmes of fundamental education are operating." Therefore, its scope was limited. Gray stated that it focused "particular attention upon the problems of the underdeveloped areas of the world, owing to the seriousness of the problems being tackled there and the urgent need for help." His aims, similarly, were directed toward the needs of such responsible leaders in those areas:

    1. To provide actual and potential leaders with as clear an outlook as possible on the problem of world literacy in its varied aspects, with special reference to the most effective methods of teaching reading and writing.

2. To provide guidance and concrete suggestions that will enable leaders to develop literacy programmes in harmony with these general facts and principles, and adapted to local needs.

3. To define the nature of the unsolved problems that should be studied in order to promote literacy throughout the world, and to consider means of solving them.[21]

Quite apart from the practical value of comparing reading in different nations demonstrated in Gray's work, the scholar may, of course, be legitimately satisfied in compiling a sort of "natural history" of reading. Making comparisons between reading and learning to read in differing languages and cultures is worthwhile in its own right, simply as an extension of our factual data on reading behavior. *But comparative reading research can have a much more important scientific goal.*

The proposition that is the basis of this book is that by making comparisons between the reading behaviors of people in different cultures and in varying languages we can understand better the fundamental psycholinguistic processes of reading and writing and the way in which these develop. The chief aim of this book is to explore the implications of this proposition for scientific research and theory. Our aim is very different from Gray's, and, therefore, the scope of the work in this book is quite different also. The countries studied in Part Two include highly developed ones as well as those that are undeveloped educationally. Furthermore, although practical applications seem bound to follow, the chief concern of Part One is theory.

The potential theoretical and research value of comparative reading studies may be judged from the wealth of knowledge that has been derived from the use of the comparative method in other sciences, such as psychology, anthropology, and sociology. Witness, for example, how in psychology so much was learned about the development of human personality from the comparisons made between the different child-rearing practices of various cultures.

The potential of such cross-national and cross-cultural research has been very well described with regard to another subject of the curriculum. Husén and Postlethwaite, in discussing comparative mathematics research state:

The school systems of the world represent a series of environments in which human beings learn, and, as a group, are much more varied and contain far greater differences than can be found or created in any one system. Thus educational "laboratory" situations exist in which many of the more profound questions concerning human growth can be studied objectively.[22]

Their remarks apply with even greater force in reading, because it is so much more concerned with *language* itself. Furthermore, the world as a living laboratory of reading behaviors contains a great variety of opportunities for the scientific study of the relationship between differences in *linguistic* variables and behavior in reading and writing and in learning these skills. This is in addition to the other cultural and educational variables noted by Husén and Postlethwaite.

A secondary aim of this book is more limited but may be of greater immediate interest to some of its readers. The reading specialist in any one particular nation can increase his understanding of reading *in his own* language and culture by contrasting it with the reading behavior in the nations and languages described in the chapters that follow. This second aim can be fulfilled for individual readers of this book, but it is hoped that the benefit will be extended to other students of reading. Courses in comparative reading should be established for graduate and undergraduate students of reading. Their value lies not only in the breaking down of students' ethnocentrism in reading, but also in the new insights that such comparisons may bring to children's basic problems in learning to read.

Methods of Research

This investigation attempts to draw on the living laboratory of languages and cultures by sampling countries with contrasting linguistic and educational backgrounds. The resulting book is not a mere collection of "readings" of previously published articles. Nor is it a symposium of isolated contributions. *Comparative Reading* is the outcome of the cooperative work of a team of nineteen writers in a deliberately planned cross-national study of behavior in learning and utilizing the skills of reading and writing. The plan of this cooperative research was as follows.

The fourteen nations included in Part Two of this book were selected deliberately to represent different cultural, educational, and linguistic phenomena. For each nation one or more experts were selected to write a report on reading in that country. A copy of this writer's original paper[23] on comparative reading (presented at the Boston convention of the IRA in 1968) was provided for each of the national chapter authors. This insured that everyone would work toward a common set of aims—although very broadly defined ones. In addition, each author was sent an outline of the probable form of the final report—this book—so that he could see how his part of the project fitted into the total enterprise, and some guidelines for preparing his own report. These pointed out that the future readers of *Comparative Reading* would be concerned to compare one national chapter with another, and that therefore it would be helpful if the author of each chapter would bear this in mind when writing. It was indicated that some of the variables of likely interest in making such comparisons might include

1. The *language*(s) of the country. The *writing system*(s) of the *language*(s).
2. *Political, historical, sociological, and economic* factors.
3. The *schools* of the country, i.e., administration, organization, and conditions as they affect the learning of reading and writing.
4. *Age* of starting school and reading. Nursery school or kindergarten provisions. Parental help. Current opinions on reading readiness.
5. *Methods of teaching* and how they are selected.
6. *Materials of instruction.*
7. School provisions for the learning of reading beyond the beginning reading phase, i.e., development of *intermediate and higher order skills.*

8. The *integration* of the teaching of reading with other aspects of the child's school and everyday life.

9. Provisions for *teacher recruitment and training* as it affects the teaching of reading.

10. *University provisions* for specialist education and research in reading.

11. Provisions for children *who fail in reading*.

12. *Evaluation and testing* methods.

However, the guidelines concluded as follows:

> The above list is only intended as a guide to some of the variables which have been mentioned by people interested in comparing reading in different countries. There may be other more important problems which must be understood in the study of the reading of a particular country.

This last instruction was intended to emphasize the open-endedness of the inquiry, because it was a deliberate aim to leave room for spontaneous responses that would indicate the varying emphases from one country to another.

The analysis of all the resulting data has been a difficult task because there had been no previous inquiry to provide any signposts within this particular field of investigation. However, one of Bereday's principles for comparative education has been remembered throughout the work of analysis, that ". . . never-ceasing watchfulness by the observer to control his own cultural and personal biases." [24] Nonetheless, one must accept that, despite all precautions, this type of analysis cannot help but be influenced by the analyst's theoretical standpoint, and this writer assumes full responsibility for any distortions of the data in the national chapters that may have occurred in the course of their interpretations for the over-all analyses in his chapters in Part One.

However, an important additional precaution has been taken. All the original data from the fourteen countries is published in full so that others may make their own interpretations of them. With the exception of the national chapter on Norway these are all included as Part Two. Owing to lack of space that chapter had to be omitted. It is available, however, in mimeographed form.[25]

The analysis of the data from the individual national reports makes up most of Part One. Following Alan Brimer's contribution on research methodology and the review of previous cross-national surveys of reading achievement in Chapters 2 and 3, respectively, a framework is developed in Chapter 4 for the analysis of all the data from Part Two plus other relevant cross-national or related research. This takes the form of a model of literacy acquisition, for which theoretical grounds are proposed. Evidence in support of this theoretical approach is adduced also in Chapter 4. Consideration of this model led to the divisions represented in the remainder of the chapters in Part One. Chapters 5 and 6 are concerned with motivational and attitudinal factors in the institutionalized ways of teaching children to read. The bulk of material from the national reports of Part Two plus other international material falls into two main categories: (1) the educational environment and (2) the linguistic environment. The first of these is covered in Chapter 7 "The Teacher Variable"; in Chapter 8 the remaining factors are discussed. All the data from these sources on linguistic environments are analyzed in Chapters 9 and 10. The future of work in this field is discussed in Chapter 11.

REFERENCES

1. Gray, William S., *The Teaching of Reading and Writing,* Paris: UNESCO, 1956.
2. Jenkinson, Marion D. (ed.), *Reading Instruction: An International Forum* (First World Congress), Newark, Del.: IRA, 1967. Staiger, Ralph C., and Andresen, Oliver (eds.), *Reading: A Human Right and a Human Problem* (Second World Congress on Reading, 1968), Newark, Del.: IRA, 1969. Malmquist, Eve, and Bracken, Dorothy Kendall (eds.), *Improving Reading Ability Around the World* (Third World Congress), Newark, Del.: IRA, 1971.
3. Downing, John (ed.), *The First International Reading Symposium,* London: Cassell and New York: Day, 1966. Downing, John, and Brown, Amy L. (eds.), *The Second International Reading Symposium,* London: Cassell, 1967. Downing, John, and Brown, Amy L. (eds.), *The Third International Reading Symposium,* London: Cassell, 1968.
4. Smith, Nila B., "The future of reading," in Jenkinson, *op. cit.,* pp. 1–13.
5. Gray, *The Teaching of Reading and Writing, op. cit.* Also *Preliminary Survey on Methods of Teaching Reading and Writing* (Parts I and II), Paris: UNESCO, 1953.
6. Foshay, A. W., *et al., Educational Achievements of Thirteen-Year-Olds in Twelve Countries,* Hamburg: UNESCO Institute for Education, 1962.
7. Lee, W. R., *Spelling Irregularity and Reading Difficulty in English,* London: NFER in England and Wales, 1960.
8. Klineberg, Otto, "Life is fun in a smiling, fair-skinned world," in Frost, Joe L. (ed.), *Issues and Innovations in the Teaching of Reading,* Chicago: Scott, 1967.
9. Chiland, Colette, "The teaching of reading in France," in Downing and Brown (eds.), *The Second International Reading Symposium, op. cit.,* pp. 35–70.
10. Lobrot, Michel G., "Remedial education in France," in Brown, Amy L. (ed.), *Reading: Current Research and Practice,* Edinburgh: Chambers, 1967.
11. Southgate, Vera, "Approaches to beginning reading in Great Britain," in Jenkinson, *op. cit.,* pp. 142–154.
12. Morris, Joyce M., "The scope of reading in the United Kingdom," in Jenkinson, *op. cit.,* pp. 44–52.
13. Abernethy, Dermot, Ferguson, Sheila, McKay, Yvonne and Thompson, Frazer, "Children's in-school reading in Belfast—A suggestive survey," *Reading,* 1 (December 1967), 10–18.
14. Austin, Mary C., "Scope of reading in the United States," in Jenkinson, *op. cit.,* pp. 53–60.
15. Robinson, Helen M., "Provisions made for children in the United States who have difficulties in reading," in Jenkinson, *op. cit.,* pp. 125–133.
16. Smith, Nila B., *American Reading Instruction,* Newark, Del.: IRA, 1965.
17. Staiger, Ralph C., "The geology of reading," in Downing and Brown (eds.), *The Second International Reading Symposium, op. cit.,* pp. 3–7.
18. Malmquist, Eve, "Provisions made for children with reading disabilities in Sweden," in Jenkinson, *op. cit.,* pp. 109–123.

19. Gjessing, Hans-Jorgen, "The concept of reading readiness in Norway," in Jenkinson, *op. cit.*, pp. 70–79.
20. Kyöstiö, O. K., "Reading research at the kindergarten level in Finland," in Downing and Brown (eds.), *The Second International Reading Symposium, op. cit.*, pp. 71–79.
21. Gray, *op. cit.*, pp. 11–12.
22. Husén, Torsten, and Postlethwaite, N., "Intensions and background of the project," in Husén, Torsten (ed.), *International Study of Achievement in Mathematics*, Stockholm: Almquist and Wiksell and New York: Wiley, 1967.
23. Downing, John, "Comparative reading: A method of research and study in reading," in Figurel, J. Allen (ed.), *Reading and Realism*, Newark, Del.: IRA, 1969, pp. 840–846.
24. Bereday, George, Z. F., *Comparative Method in Education*, New York: Holt, 1966.
25. From John Downing, University of Victoria, B.C., Canada.

CHAPTER 2

Methodological Problems of Research

M. ALAN BRIMER

ON first consideration, the idea of making a comparative study of reading on a research basis seems both unprofitable and unnecessary. There is sufficient scope within single countries for research into the multitude of reading problems without multiplying them by the number of countries taking part. Difficulties in reading are so clearly specific to the language and culture in which learning to read takes place that an attempt to generalize them across countries would surely make them less relevant. It might be said that what is most lacking in our knowledge of the acquisition of the reading skill is the specific basis on which to teach the individual child, and that we already have too many broad and general statements that are not easily translated into classroom practice. Why then should anyone entertain the idea of costly, elaborate, and time-consuming coordinated research into reading in different countries?

When one surveys the vast literature on reading research in the manner that Jeanne Chall[1] attempted, it is evident that the great majority of studies comprise surveys of achievement under different practices and conditions, or small-scale studies in which one or two factors are considered experimentally. Until recently, survey studies were suggestive rather than convincing. They examined the way in which a number of independent areas related to each other and to a single dependent variable, the criterion of reading achievement. The object of such studies was to seek to determine the relative importance of each of the variables in its contribution to reading success. Such statistical manipulations of the co-variation of variables made certain important assumptions. They assumed, first, that no important relevant variable had been omitted from measurement and secondly, that the proportionate contribution of variables to the prediction of the criterion, as indicated by their relative weights in a multiple regression equation, estimated their actual importance in learning to read.

Considering just these two assumptions it will be apparent that many studies were based on false premises. The choice of variables to include in a survey is made in the first instance out of a theoretical formulation of the individual differences between children and of the way in which they learn. Because similar fundamental assumptions are made in the design of systems of instruction in a particular country it is likely that some forms of variation will have been eliminated by the organization of the school system and others will not be perceived. Some of the most important and relevant variables will be omitted, in particular those that refer to the different contexts of learning and those that are prevented from variation by legal prescription, such as the age of entry to school. The second assumption is also open to serious question because multiple regression analysis carries no *a priori* implication of causality or even of proportionate contribution to the acquisition of a skill. From a multiple regression equation no more can be derived than a statement of the proportionate contribution to the criterion variance of each of the predicting variables, given the conditions in the particular sample being studied. The outcome of survey work of this kind is that we form the opinion that reading achievement is principally determined by age and intelligence, that methods are less important than good teachers, and that some children have specific reading handicaps that appear at variance with their other skills.

Survey studies require the support of experiment if we are to have any hope of establishing causal relationships between reading success and the host of practices about which we are still in doubt. But experimental research is limited in another way. Normally we do research within school systems where there is a reluctance to change methods or classroom situations and materials merely for the purpose of research. The reluctance increases the longer the term of the study proposed, because it is considered unethical to expose children to a protracted form of trial at the expense of their regular programs. Even when experimental change is permitted by the school system it carries an air of unreality that may improperly benefit or detract from the innovation. It is difficult to introduce the novel without children being aware that something like a "let's pretend" game is going on. The other major disadvantage is the limited number of factors that can be experimentally manipulated simultaneously. An example may help to demonstrate the kinds of problems that arise.

Suppose that the purpose of a study is to discover whether devoting forty rather than thirty minutes a day to the teaching of reading to 7-year-olds will make a difference in their levels of achievement. To test a group of children before and after a period in which reading activities extend ten minutes beyond the normal thirty each day will not enable any change to be attributed to increase in time. The change might have occurred whether or not there had been an increase in time, or it might be attributable to some factor coincidentally related to increase in time. To be sure, it must be compared with an equivalent situation where the time was not extended. It is at this point that the comparison begins to create difficulties. In using another group of children for comparison, any difference may be attributable to the teacher, the children (being individually and collectively less able for example), the situation in which they are taught, or even to the way in which the ten minutes, following the thirty, are spent. It might seem that by using the same group of children and the same teacher, comparing an earlier with a later period, such problems would be overcome, but it would still not be possible to detect whether any difference was attributable to age and previous knowledge. In order to tackle such an apparently simple question a complex design would be required as well as, in all probability, large numbers of children among whom the carefully contrived plans might be found to have gone wrong.

How much easier it would be if it were known that there were already in existence some classes receiving forty minutes and some thirty minutes of instruction—and enough of them so that one could allow for the differences between teachers and groups of children. Unfortunately, within a single country, the normal practices of a school are either laid down by law or are conventionally uniform (like two school sessions per day). Many other circumstances, although not uniform, are so common that the exceptions are few and comparisons are vitiated at the outset.

Ideally one would seek situations already in existence where the conditions are established and institutionalized and that otherwise would have to be set up experimentally. Often the most important questions we would like to resolve could be tackled if we involved other countries where such practices are in existence. Until recently, the difficulty has been that many other factors differ, too, and the linguistic and cultural obstacles have been considered insuperable. Linguistic and cultural problems will be considered in another section but, for the moment, we will concern ourselves with the availability of new techniques and facilities. From work done in operational research has come a set of techniques known as "causal path analyses." The function of these techniques is to allow a number of models of the situation to be accounted for, to be set up, and to be scrutinized for the plausibility of particular causal patterns. The best developed are based on standard multiple regression analysis and maximum likelihood procedures, and there is a whole set of new factor models that have been developed recently. They are capable of handling a very large number of variables simultaneously and dealing with multiple as well as single criteria. They have become practicable with the advent of high-speed computers, which not only permit rapid operations but also the holding of a vast memory store.

These changes have given a new lease of life to comparative education, which has struggled for respectability and survival, because they have increased the range of questions that can be tackled usefully on a between-country, comparative basis. So long as comparative education was doomed to express its questions in terms of the gross differences between countries and could not quantify the similarities between them, it could work only at a crude qualitative level—because even such hard numerical data as the proportion of an age group in school had to be qualified by the conditions under which such a proportion held true and how this proportion was distributed over a country. Instead of asking such inert questions as how like or unlike are two countries' educational systems and processes, or how transferable are the systems and processes of one country in achieving the cultural goals of another, it is now possible to ask how far the multinational experiences can be used to answer general educational questions. Whereas in the earlier phase the greater the difference between countries the fewer the truly comparative questions that could be answered, now diversity increases the range of answerable questions and even challenges the traditional experimental mode of enquiry in the richness of its contribution to knowledge.

Another way of expressing this is to say that, until 1945, the country was the basic unit of analysis in comparative education. Now data can be analyzed by controlling between-country variation and by looking at the residual covariation freed from nationally limited characteristics.

This is the bold new step, represented most directly by the International Educational Achievements (IEA) studies. The second phase of IEA enquiries began in 1966 with the extension of the range of curriculum concern to include the physical sciences, literary studies, second language studies in English and French, social studies, and reading comprehension. Previously IEA had carried out an international study of mathematics (Husén[2]), which represented a landmark in comparative education in that it collated data explicitly gathered for the purpose over a large number of countries in one collaborative survey. The first phase had been distinguished by the close working relationship of eminent scholars and a number of universities in each country. The second phase is still in operation and is even more ambitious. Not only has the number of subject areas been increased and the number of countries, but it has crossed the barrier of language difference that the international character of mathematics had enabled it to evade. The importance of the new venture cannot be overestimated because it has overcome problems of producing equivalent samples across countries and the problems of relating complex background variables to measures of achievement. So far, in its analysis of mathematics data, it has restricted its statistical techniques to conventional multiple regression analysis with the exception that the status of independent variables has been allocated on a basis of logical considerations of priority. In other words, a distinction has been made between variables (1) over which education has no influence, such as socioeconomic status of parents, (2) that are a legalistic or conventional pattern in the country, such as age of admission to school or the structure of the school year, and (3) that are concurrently variable in the child, such as his reading skill.

Although at present plans have not been made to employ causal path analysis, it is likely that these techniques will be used and that the work of Wittrock and Wiley[3] on curriculum evaluation will be taken into account. If the study had been conceived in the first instance as an exploration in causality, it is probable that other factors would have been measured than have so far been considered. Like any other research that is based on a hypothetico-deductive framework, hypotheses of causal relationship must be set up. As the number of variables increases so the problem of forming hypotheses of multiple covariation increases. In other words, there is a limit to the number of relationships that can be entertained in mind by a research worker planning his study. Indeed, there is already room for another technique that will help the research worker to realize the implications of his partial construction of hypotheses to achieve the strategy best fitting his intentions.

Such studies carry with them, despite their optimism, the problems that previously daunted research workers. Perhaps the most serious of these problems, and certainly the most difficult to tease out, is that of language. Behind the overt differences of language lie the conceptual and culturally bound differences that express the manner of making meaning of the world and putting a system of values to it. The development of linguistic theory in the last ten years—and in particular the growth of comparative linguistics—opens the way to further study but currently offers limited practical help to those for whom language is the vehicle for enquiries rather than the focus. The closer that the focus of enquiry moves to that of language and the greater the dependence of data on it the less language differences can be ignored. Reading is necessarily faced with language problems if it operates through the decoding of symbols into inner *speech* and does not operate through ideographs that may or may not be directly linked with spoken language.

Analysis of the Reading Process

Any analysis of the process of reading must recognize first of all what that process is to the accomplished reader before subsequently asking what it is to the learner of reading. An analysis of reading must also recognize the conceptually different modes in which it can be described.

1. It can be said to be the perceptive part of a communication process.
2. It can be said to be a decoding operation.
3. It can be said to be a visual-perceptual act.
4. It can be said to be a stimulus-response process.

As part of a communication process it is an activity through which what was in the mind of a writer is transferred with tolerable error to the mind of another. The transfer is not of substance but of patterned activity. The process of reading initiates in the mind of the reader an activity that is patterned in like manner to that in the mind of the writer. It is, apart from the decoding operation, akin to listening to a tape recording.

As a decoding operation, it presupposes knowledge of the existence of such regularities in the way in which speech sounds make a difference in sensing (phonological competence) that the graphemes of an orthography can be recognized to refer to them. The graphemic symbolic reference may, depending on the language or the orthography, be simple or complex. At a simple level it can imply a unique correspondence between each phoneme and symbol. At a complex level it can imply a conjunction of symbols perhaps modified by their serial position corresponding probabilistically with the phonemes. In English such a difference can be exemplified by the Initial Teaching Alphabet (i.t.a.) and traditional orthography (T.O.) In i.t.a., the phoneme /u/ would be symbolized as ω in whatever context it appeared, whereas the same phoneme in T.O. would be symbolized variously depending on its context. In the decoding mode, ω would always symbolize /u/, whereas T.O. would have a range of possible phonemes linked with any particular spelling associated with /u/. For example, *ough* might be /au/, /u/, /ʌf/, /əf/, /ou/. The probability of *ough* being any one of these would be assessed by the relative frequency of any one of these phonemes or phonemic combinations occurring in a representative sample of English writing. The probability of it being the particular phoneme /u/ is increased when other particular visual symbols, or even the necessity for some unknown symbols, is known. Thus ( ) ( ) ( ) *ough*, in which ( ) represents any necessary but unknown symbol, considerably increases the probability of *ough* being associated with /u/. When the symbols *thr* are substituted for ( ) ( ) ( ), the probability becomes one. This particularly irregular and difficult combination illustrates the mode of probabilistic operation in the abstract. However, in the decoding operation of the reader it is much simpler. The orderly left-to-right vocalizing of phoneme equivalences for symbols means that the reader is confronted with a successive modification of probabilities. *Thr* ( ) ( ) ( ) ( ) in itself markedly increases the probability of ( ) ( ) ( ) ( ) being /u/. *Thro* ( ) ( ) ( ) increases it further and *throu* ( ) ( ) in fact makes the probability one. The *g* and *h* are redundant except as placeholders and perhaps as signals of ambiguity. Thus, decoding operations make use of rules for assembling phonemes as well as symbol-phoneme equivalences; in probabilistic systems they make use of the order of assembly and the spaces occupied to define the phoneme. Above all, however, they make use of the reader's knowledge of the spoken language. It is of interest in this connection that the symbols beginning a word have higher probabilities of particular phoneme association than later symbols. That is to say, it is rare to have to seek beyond two symbols to the right of the initial symbol to determine precisely its phoneme equivalent. Such probabilities are not learned quantitatively and consciously but as action predispositions, intuitively. The learning resembles that by which the range of allophones (intercommunicable variants of the same language) is associated with a given phoneme.

As a visual-perceptual process, reading implies visual discrimination between the characters and between the diacritical marks of the orthography. The characters may differ in shape and pattern, and those having the same shape may differ in spatial orientation—for example, *p, b, d,* and *n, u* in English orthography even within a particular type font. Differences between fonts may permit character equivalence between such diverse shapes as g, g, G, *G*. Thus, the reader must be capable of discriminating characters within the conventions of the particular font presented to him; the sophisticated reader maintains this discrimination over a wide range of fonts. The visual-perceptual act also requires an orderly assembly of the unit characters in a left-right manner within the segregated "word." Whether or not the whole word is perceived as one image, the image accepts a directional order of assembly that allows the word to be reconstituted spatially. Furthermore, the eye movements between focus spans are left-right in order and chunks are perceived having directional, spatial order, which models the temporal speech order.

At a particularly low level of cognitive functioning, reading may be said to be a stimulus-response process. The use of single printed-word presentations with the object of eliciting the desired utterance is an illustration of reading instruction accepting this paradigm. It is doubtful, however, whether any sophisticated reader uses the process despite the speed of response of which he is capable. This view of reading will not be considered further.

Five Important Control Variables

It follows from all these considerations that any comparative research into reading must be prepared to control for variations in the following factors in addition to those normally occurring among speakers of the same language:

1. The efficiency with which the written form of a language is capable of expressing an idea.
2. The degree of command of the spoken forms of the language by the reader.
3. The style conventions of the written forms of the language and the range of registers permitted by them.
4. The efficiency of the orthography, spelling, and spatial organization of the written forms of the language in coding speech for subsequent decoding.
5. The degree of exposure of the reader to situations in which communication through printed symbols is necessary.

Let us examine these five factors in turn.

1. *The efficiency with which the written form of a language is capable of expressing an idea.* Although linguists would probably argue that all languages are capable of expressing an idea that can be expressed in any one of them, it is obvious that some languages are less efficient than others. In order to express the same idea with the same precision, some languages require more words and longer words than others. This becomes particularly evident in the written form of the language, both in the amount of paper covered in expressing the same idea and in the number of circumlocutions that are necessary. The size and currency of the vocabulary are probably its most important features. Without a word that uniquely represents a particular concept, it is necessary to use a large number of words to express the same idea. Similarly, not all languages signal mood in the written form—because the spoken form of the language relies on intonation, which cannot be easily coded in graphemes. Such differences do not always favor the reader of the more efficient language. For example, the reader of the language with a large vocabulary must be capable of comprehending this vocabulary in speech. Thus, given two readers of the same level of reading skill operating in languages that so differ, one would take longer to read while the other would be more likely to meet words he did not understand.

2. *The degree of command of the spoken forms of the language by the reader.* The characteristic of languages that makes it likely that the reader will be familiar with the vocabulary of the passage is to be distinguished from the other source of variation, which relates to the speaker's command of the spoken language. Clearly the circumstances surrounding the reader's acquisition of the spoken form of the language in print will favor his comprehension. In many countries of the world neither the language of instruction nor the language in which most reading takes place is the first language. This may have occurred through the imposition

of a totally foreign language on the school system in former colonial days, or it may have been the result of an attempt to introduce a common language among the educated when the number of indigenous languages was too great to permit books to be printed in all of them. French and English in Africa are examples of the former situation and Hindi in India and Hausa in Nigeria are examples of the latter. It is not the fact of operating through a second language alone that accounts for variability in level of comprehension, but also the way in which the second language is acquired. If it is learned by transfer from the first language, then both comprehension of the first language and the efficiency of transfer learning are involved. It may be, however, that the language is acquired by direct methods, or even in the course of normal public interchange—in which case the status of the first language appears not to be involved. Generally, the more effective comprehension occurs when the language is acquired directly. This is true for many reasons, not the least of them that artificiality in the use of the second language does not occur and there is less confusion of concepts.

More obviously, command of a spoken language will vary with the linguistic maturity of the reader; but, in general, most of the prerequisites of the syntax of the language are acquired by the age of 6 years and most of the phonology much earlier. This appears to hold true across most languages and only in the case of deprivation, either through handicap or disadvantage, is such competence not achieved. Linguistic deprivation occurs in many ways, sometimes through limited speech being used in the home but more often because of the manner in which speech is employed. There is an association between poverty, social class, and restricted use of language. The main characteristic of the restriction is the failure to release linguistic communication from close dependence on environmental context, which results in the failure to employ complex sentence construction. In some societies, child speech is actively discouraged and there is little interchange between parents and children.

3. *The style conventions of the written forms of the language and the range of registers permitted by them.* Not all forms of discourse have written conventions in all languages. Some languages, such as Persian and Hindi, have strong literary conventions that persist into the commercial discourse and carry with them a degree of formality that is not conducive to scientific expression. On the other hand, some of the relatively new written languages of Africa have no literary tradition and lack the conventions that assist the writer in communicating his feelings economically. Under these circumstances, there is no exact parallel for some passages in all languages.

4. *The efficiency of the orthography, spelling, and spatial organization of the written forms of the language in coding speech for subsequent decoding.* Undoubtedly that which lends an air of greatest strangeness to the appearance of the written form of a language occurs when the writing system differs from the characters with which we are familiar. To the user of the Roman alphabet the variations seen in the Greek and Russian alphabets are disturbing and the further remove of Arabic and Hindi characters appears almost as incomprehensible as the various forms of Chinese characters. Variation in the number of characters

is not so important as it might appear at first sight. Until one approaches the number of characters in the Chinese orthographies the difference in difficulty arising from the number of characters alone is very small.

The perceptual distinctiveness of characters is of greater importance, and this relates to their shape and their spatial orientation. The mode of phonemic representation comprises rules of letter order as well as grapheme-phoneme relationships. An alphabet such as that used in English, given the probabilistic determination of phonemes described here, is extremely economical in its use of characters. However, it creates greater difficulty for the learner than, for example, Czech or Spanish, which have relatively unambiguous phonemic reference. But it is important to note that the freedom of individual characters from ambiguity of phonemic reference does not imply a more efficient orthography. Whether or not the more economic orthography yields the more efficient reading is one of the research questions that remains unanswered.

There are many other variables to be taken into account, such as the fact that Arabic omits vowels except for beginning readers and that in the Thai language the placing of the terminal punctuation for a sentence is a matter of personal preference. There are even further differences, such as the right-to-left arrangement of Arabic characters and the top-to-bottom arrangement of Chinese characters.

5. *The degree of exposure of the reader to situations in which communication through printed symbols is necessary.* One final type of difference emerges, and that is the extent of the culture's dependence on effective communication through reading. About half a century ago the characteristic of a sophisticated culture was its dependence on reading. The arrival of radio and television has made the affluent nations far less dependent on reading and in consequence exposes them less to situations that demand it. The importance of reading in a society as evidenced by the amount of time that parents overtly expend on it has a greater impact on children's valuation of the process than is generally recognized. The Western nations may already have reached the point where, so far as children are concerned, reading is an activity that is most in evidence at school and has no great place in the lives of their parents.

The most important need at the moment in cross-national research in reading is to discover ways and means of assigning measurements to the variables outlined here. So far as the assessment of the command of the spoken language is concerned, measures of listening comprehension are likely to provide the answer. Although no such measure will take into account differences in efficiency of spoken languages, the assumption must be made that all languages are capable of expressing all ideas and therefore our interest lies in assessing within each language the degree of mastery of the spoken form. We are in no such happy position in dealing with the written form of the language, and the relative effectiveness of languages with respect to the variables listed here ought to constitute the focus of problems for some of the first comparative studies. The purpose of assigning measures to the variables is to assist in describing them more accurately, rather than to create actual evaluative tools.

Control of Language Performance

The design of international studies of reading achievement and of the factors associated with it is constrained by the need to control those variables listed here that are related to the linguistic functioning on which reading depends. Each of the linguistic functions might be measured separately, but in all probability this would be attempted only if it were designed to make them individually a focus for study. Over-all control of language performance would be better achieved by measuring listening comprehension on some agreed bases. To the extent that individual variation in listening comprehension could be measured across countries and across linguistic boundaries, language performance could be controlled in the assessment of reading skills.

Measures of listening comprehension are less commonly employed in reading research than would be expected from their undoubted usefulness as a control for language variation. Spearritt[4] has carried out a study of listening comprehension in Australia where he has demonstrated that a specific listening comprehension factor exists that can be differentiated from reading comprehension, auditory acuity, and verbal ability. The best known tests (Ammons and Ammons[5] Peabody Picture Vocabulary Test,[6] English Picture Vocabulary Test[7]) are in English and, by and large, they relate only to the vocabulary and hence the semantic aspects of language. To be effective as a control basis for reading research, measures of listening comprehension must involve syntactic as well as semantic aspects of language. By their nature, the syntactic aspects are more difficult to measure, and are usually not separated from the semantic. Thus the Illinois Test of Psycholinguistic Abilities[8] and the Reynell *Developmental Language Scale*[9] employ complete sentences in which a child's task is to indicate comprehension by performing some act that implies that the sentence has been understood. Such tests take rather a long time to administer and are often tedious, particularly for young children. The tests can become extremely formal in their attempts to distinguish comprehension of tense, negation, interrogation, and mood and in their construction of artificially contrived sentences necessary for the elimination of ambiguity that in ordinary speech is controlled by context.

Much more experiment is necessary in the design of listening-comprehension tests before they can be employed in the control manner that has been indicated. The difficulty in their construction lies not merely in avoiding artificiality and tedium, but also in ensuring that the task to be performed operationally coincides with objectives. Because it is undesirable to confuse listening comprehension with reading, no reading skills whatsoever must be assumed. It follows that the response that the child makes to the orally presented situation can either be through an expressive oral response or through some other differentiating signal that does not require language. If an oral response is required, then the difficulty of the task may have more to do with an expressive than with a comprehension function. Benefit undoubtedly lies in requiring a response to actual or pictorially or diagrammatically represented material. If actual material is to be manipulated then measurement must take place in individual settings in which the observer keeps detailed notes on the conformity of the response with preestablished criteria. This leads to subjectivity on the part of the markers and, inevitably, to variation in judgment between them—which normally tends to reduce reliability considerably.

Simple pictorial material on which the child places a mark in accordance with his interpretation of what he hears lends itself more readily both to control of reliability and to clear definition of objectives in an operational form. In order to secure the advantages of this device, the task must be so designed that this difficulty depends minimally on comprehension of the pictures in their own right. Therefore, the pictorial material must be related to the stage of perceptual development of the children being tested and to the cultural variation in pictorial convention and degree of exposure to representational materials. For example, Hudson [10] has demonstrated that African children have considerable difficulty in interpreting spatial relationships in pictures and Kellaghan [11] has shown that concept formation of color is limited among Nigerian children.

Other studies—for example, those of Piaget—have shown that Euclidean geometrical space is a relatively sophisticated conceptual framework that is gradually acquired in childhood but among Asian people is acquired at a much later age. Provided that such distractions from a reliable and valid measurement of listening comprehension can be overcome, a tool of research could be created —which could be employed in group situations and would become a most important measure—not only for reading research but also for individual guidance.

The absence of such a tool and the long process of development that would be required to create it led the International Educational Achievements Committee on Reading Comprehension to select an alternative and admittedly less effective device. The committee developed a type of vocabulary test that, although it depended on reading skill, emphasized the conceptual discrimination of words as more nearly the same or opposite in meaning, in which the words themselves were relatively simple and in which the variation in difficulty lay in the degree of overlap of the conceptual areas semantically covered by each pair of words in juxtaposition. Later in this chapter, when the construction of tests is being discussed, precautions to be exercised in the building of such a test will be mentioned.

Criterion Measures in Reading Research

Whether or not cross-national reading research is concerned with methods, with teaching competence, with initial ability, or with variations in the learning situation, it is likely that the criteria chosen to evaluate them will relate to the effectiveness of reading defined in a particular way. Broadly speaking, reading problems are divisible into three major categories depending on the target populations that are the focus of interest. These areas are beginning reading, silent reading, and reading handicap. The first and third of these often lead to common criterion measures because the handicapped reader is frequently regarded as a reader who is slow to begin. Criterion measures for these groups are usually divided into separate assessments of participatory skills, for example, letter recognition, phonic identification, decoding, word reading, and comprehension. These may be broken down still further into measures of eye movement, articulation, form recognition, phonemic recognition, and the like. In other words, the description of the reading effectiveness of the beginning reader or of the handicapped reader depends on a profile of the types of skill they exhibit rather than on their performance within a single homogeneous domain. By contrast the relatively sophisticated, silent reader exhibits little skill differentiation. Among such groups reading comprehension and reading speed are the most frequently measured variables, although the former far outweighs the latter in importance. Within the vital realm of reading comprehension, very little differentiation of skill is identifiable. A number of factor analyses of reading comprehension have proved disappointing in their attempts to distinguish underlying contributory variables that might help to identify the reasons for individual difference in level of reading comprehension. Although such skills as reading to acquire the gist of a passage, reading for inference, reading for detail, and appreciation of metaphorical and literary use of language have been asserted as separable contributing elements, only the latter has been replicably identified as distinguishable from the others. Level of reading comprehension correlates highly with level of vocabulary, size of vocabulary, and verbal ability. So far as individuals are concerned, there appears to be no good reason for seeking to produce differential measures of reading comprehension skill. It seems that all three of the factorially indistinguishable types of skill quoted here are required and any difference for the individual lies only in the momentary shift of attention. A good reader finds all three easy; a poor reader finds all three difficult.

Interest has also surrounded variation in the content, style, tenor, and degree of formality of the material to be read. Clearly the difficulty of any passage could be varied by making the content more or less eclectic or abstract or interesting. Similarly, the style of a passage may vary from the pellucid to the turgid, from the fanciful to the mundane. The tenor may vary from the poetic to the prosaic, from the lyrical to the narrative, and the formality may vary in degree from the public to the private communication. Each of these ways in which passages may vary is likely to interact with the characteristics of the individual in such a way as to produce a greater or lesser degree of comprehension. Yet, when such dimensions of variation are examined for their differential status in reading comprehension, no coherent grouping is recognizable. It appears that a person who comprehends well is able to apply himself almost equally to material that varies in these ways so long as the task in hand is unambiguously identified.

Such a finding of the homogeneity of the ability to comprehend the printed word among those who can read silently might appear to argue that one test of, for example, reading vocabulary would be quite sufficient. It should be remembered, however, that such findings hold true among the relatively homogeneous educational groups in England and North America where there is an attempt to produce effectiveness over a range of reading material in association with different reading tasks. It could occur that, among other peoples there is a less comprehensive approach to teaching reading, with the result that some materials and some skills might be effectively handled but not others. Moreover, in the interest of preserving the correspondence between the characteristics of reading (which are the objectives of the educational system) and the tasks presented in research studies, an attempt must be made to present a comprehensive coverage.

Reading skills also vary with the type of "set" invoked by the task. A case in point is when one is forewarned that information of a certain kind will appear in what follows and the task is to discover it within the passage. This is to be contrasted with the task of reading a passage and afterward, without prior warning, being asked to recall a piece of information that occurred within it. These two sets toward reading affect the mode and speed of reading and the degree to which there is an attempt to assimilate it. Characteristically, in school children are asked to read and summarize or to read and answer questions or merely to read and understand. Part of the reading task is concerned with the purpose of reading and the degree to which this purpose is made explicit and is understood by the reader.

It will be obvious from this that speed of reading is itself dependent on many of the factors already referred to: the intrinsic difficulty of the passage and the purpose in hand being among the most important. Most people are capable of adjusting their speed of reading both to the difficulty of the material and to the weightiness of the consequence of reading it effectively. However, people differ in the degree to which their silent reading has fully freed itself from vestigial oral dependence and in the degree to which they are prepared to read vigorously rather than comfortably. This is not the appropriate place to discuss eye movements or silent-reading habits, yet we should note that there is a variation in reading speed that is not conditioned by difficulty and purpose of reading only.

Operational Definition of Criterion Measures

The definition of objectives for criterion measures in cross-national studies can only be achieved by operational definition. That is to say, for each objective an exemplary task must be presented that can be replicated at different levels of difficulty and in relation to the characteristics of various passages. This is not an easy procedure and normally it is best done by a small group of people who represent the different cultural and linguistic backgrounds over which the research is to be carried out. It is preferable for them to operate through a single control language, which acts as a mediator for translation of objectives. The IEA studies of reading comprehension employed English as the control language and all operationally defined objectives were presented to participating countries in the English medium. In order to ensure that no ambiguity occurred in translation, a retranslation process was employed: The translated version of the model was translated back into English and the two English versions were compared. Any material difference between the two signaled a discrepancy that might have emerged through the original being ambiguous or through the translation being imperfect. The method is by no means infallible because even a perfect replica of the original may imply no more than consistency in translating into and from an ambiguous mode. Normally, it is safer to have independent translation and back-translation and, if possible, to duplicate the process.

All the usual procedures for test development must be employed to establish the base measures for cross-national study. Thus, comparable samples of children must be used in each country to try out items, among which considerable waste is to be anticipated. It would be more in keeping with the anticipated wastage rate to employ four times the number of items ultimately to be sought. Because items must prove themselves in each linguistic context, after trial, items are analyzed separately for difficulty and efficiency of discrimination for each country. It is to be expected naturally that difficulty of items will be variable across countries, but a necessary condition of the items measuring the same thing in different countries is that the rank order of difficulty should be the same. Similarly, the efficiency of discrimination must satisfy preestablished levels in all countries depending on the level of difficulty of items. In conventional test-construction procedures, items that satisfy the agreed conditions are incorporated with known weights, for each of the participatory objectives, into second trial drafts. The second trial is important because in the first no time limit is imposed and the items are performed in an unstandardized order. In second trial drafts the order of presentation of items is fixed and any serial-order effects of item position can be evaluated. Usually the progression in order is from the easier to the more difficult, which helps to minimize the number of items that are omitted and lends credence to the supposition that the order of total score would be unchanged had a longer time been allocated. Actual time limits are fixed by examining scores at the end of successive intervals and by choosing that time limit that yields the largest variance in the shortest time. Under such conditions, the reliability of the test will be maximized and so too will be the discriminating power of raw score. Although the procedures for administration of the tests and conditions for marking are fully standardized, norms as such are not developed because the actual sample of children used in research will provide a better basis for comparative statements.

Such are the conventional procedures employed in the usual mode of test construction. But, increasingly, there has been a demand for the production of *criterion referenced tests*. The value of such tests lies in the fact that their standards are fixed by reference to some criterion of absolute performance, rather than by comparison with the performance of other children of the same age. Although it is helpful in ordinary classroom studies for a teacher to be able to assess the comparative standards of her own children against a much wider population—with departure from a mean performance being the basis for measurement—in cross-national research and in many other research studies any such comparisons are of doubtful interest. What it is desired to know is whether or not children have reached the standard of achievement that is regarded as intrinsically meaningful. Diagnostic tests of achievement frequently employ such concepts in that they seek to discover whether a child is functionally impaired in some particular skill or not. Relative performance is of no interest in such circumstances, only the fact of being impaired or not being impaired. New methods of fixing scales for the assessment of achievement have been developed (cf. Rasch, *Probabilistic Models for Some Intelligence and Attainment Tests*[12]). The details of such methods are too complex to present here, but it may be noted that their outcome is a set of scales that are independent of the sample on whom they have been tried, provided that the sample includes sufficient range of high and low performance so that the limits of the scale can be fixed.

Sampling

One of the many mistaken assumptions about cross-national research is that its main purpose is to be able to say whether one country is superior to another in some respect. In fact, this is probably one of the few questions that cannot be answered because it makes the assumption that each country is striving toward the same ends under the same conditions with the same investment in education. If the intention were to make such comparisons and to ignore the differences just referred to, then sampling within each country would be in considerable difficulty in defining equivalent target populations. The IEA studies have to some extent fallen into this dilemma of seeking to achieve comparable target populations in each country and have defined the groups of children with whom they are concerned in terms of the length of schooling and in terms of preparation for university admission. The main object in IEA studies has certainly not been to produce a league table of national achievements; the main concern in defining target populations in this way has been to produce educationally homogenous groups across countries. Within broad limits, any reading research must abide by similar constraints. For example, it would be foolish to compare the beginning reading achievement of 5-year-old children across countries where the age of admission to school differed so that some children had received no reading instruction. On the other hand, to leave each country free to decide which children to test would be as damaging to the research as allowing each school in a single country to decide which children it would offer for testing. The samples must be chosen with respect to the problems that are being faced. For instance, if it is of interest to discover the extent to which level of reading comprehension is affected by the introduction of a second language at various ages, samples would be chosen such that variation in age in beginning a second language would be represented in the pooled resource of the contributing nations. Sampling in cross-national reading research thus has far more to do with the representation of degrees of variation in the parameters that are under study than with accurately representing equivalent target populations in different countries.

It must be admitted that the idea of a league table of performance usually lies in the back of the minds of those conducting the research. It is difficult not to seek either to justify the country of one's birth or to castigate it for its inadequate attention to education. Research workers are by no means immune from national prejudice and jealousies, and many who would otherwise be equable in their judgments find themselves becoming prejudiced to a degree in a context where it seems that other national research workers are espousing parochial concerns too closely.

Content of Test Materials

Many factors, attributable to mixed motives, contribute to the prejudicing of measures of achievement. In the preparation for the IEA studies in reading comprehension, appropriate reading material was sought from each contributing country. Both the content and character of the passage for comprehension was frequently surprising. Material from the United States tended to be rather heavily biased toward the North American continent either in terms of historical episodes or geographical reference. Thus, it seemed oddly at variance for one of the most outward-looking nations to offer material that was so insular. Paradoxically, the material offered by other countries in Europe and Asia appeared to have been heavily influenced by exported Americanisms. In certain cases, actual test material originating in the United States was offered by such countries. Some of the less developed countries were surprising in offering highly technical literature, and some of the most developed offered curiously archaic passages. That which a country regards as relevant material for reading comprehension inevitably reflects external influences on its educational system and on its most frequently used tests.

Administration and Organization

Although the organizational problems of planning and preparation are immense, they are probably easier to contend with than the problems that arise in the control of procedures once agreement has been reached. Anyone who has faced the task of survey studies within a single nation is aware of the multitude of practical problems that surround the timing of administration of tests and the accurate recording of personal data. Cross-national research multiplies these problems by more than the number of nations taking part and a highly efficient system of administration must be worked out and given facilities to foresee, to be forewarned of, and to tackle problems as they arise. Some problems can be foreseen in planning and fail-safe procedures devised to deal with them. Assuming that all materials have been constructed, revised, and edited in the various languages well before the study begins, the kinds of problems that can arise are those that surround the availability of children, the safe arrival of materials, and the accurate carrying out of standardized procedures. No one can foresee such things as epidemics, which decimate the school population; or strikes, which close schools; or even revolutions, which disrupt the entire nation. But the most common forms of disturbance of standardized schedules arise through failure to communicate accurately and through the mistakes of ill-prepared research personnel.

Complexity in cross-national research commands the creation of a central international bureau having a permanent director and a substantial staff of applied research workers and technicians, fully equipped in international languages—which means having among the research staff people who can communicate effectively in the four international languages of UNESCO: English, French, Spanish, and Russian. Each member of the central research staff should be capable of face-to-face communication and be literate in at least three of these languages. Such a staff must be internationally mobile, and this means that the funds for cross-national research must be large enough to sustain the budgets of international air travel and living expenses. Moreover, staff of this order are already in great demand by international organizations, and salaries must be at least equal to those currently paid by international organizations. Any attempt to carry out cross-national research on a shoe string budget is likely to be rewarded by confusion and nonevents.

Similarly, in each country national bureaus must be established that are probably best identified with an existing research organization in that country, knowing as it will the problems that are likely to arise and how best to secure the cooperation of teachers and children. The national bureaus are not always as well versed in the techniques of securing rigorous conformity with the procedures laid down, and one of the benefits of international meetings is to communicate the seriousness of failure to conform and suggest those strategies that can be adopted to secure more efficient cooperation. One of the mistakes that is frequently made is to assume that people read all that is sent to them. Research workers are impatient in the face of notices and printed details and they are also very busy people on whom the demands to carry out the intentions of others are already very onerous. It should never be forgotten that face-to-face communication is much more persuasive than written correspondence, and the best way of securing conformity is not to send out reminders but to visit and help.

Accurate procedural control is necessary not merely in the carrying out of field work but also in the reporting of data. It goes without saying that any data that is to be communicated back from national bureaus to the international center must be precoded, but there is room for considerable error both in the coding operation and the conversion of the coded information into punched cards. Briefing and pretraining are necessary if error is not to invade the research at this penultimate stage. The forms of analysis to which the data will be submitted will already have been determined in advance, computer time will have been booked, and programs will have been written and approved. The stage after the arrival of the print-outs from the computer is of equal moment and must be planned for. The increase in the number of people and countries having professional interest in the outcome of the study also increases the jealousies surrounding being first in the field to publish results. The only relevant procedure is to agree on the appearance of one international publication first, followed by, as far as possible, simultaneous publication of the results in each of the participating countries. It may seem both mundane and unnecessary to stress this aspect of cross-national research, but experience has demonstrated that it can be one of the most serious causes of discontent.

As in other fields of human endeavor, research workers are tentatively begin-ning to consider themselves as members of a family of nations rather than as jealous protectors of their national autonomies. Just as comparative education itself has moved through a phase of gross, between-country comparisons, through constructing models of general country similarities to regarding human char-acteristics and human artifacts as continuously variable across countries, so educational research is moving toward integrated multinational studies. The creation of IEA and the reorganization of the International Bureau of Education under the auspices of UNESCO[13] represent the institutional recognition of this change.

It is true to say that methodologies were already being created that would make multinational research possible before the conceptual change took place. With-out them and without the breakthrough in linguistics, progress would have been slow. It must be rapid if it is to take advantage of the current heterogeneity of nations' educational systems and practices. The very existence of the IRA poses, paradoxically, an ultimate threat to the benefits of cross-national research. The greater the communication between nations, the greater the homogeneity will become, as good practices and the findings of research are more widely adopted. There is indeed no time to sit back and wait for the development of better methodologies; mistakes may be made, but despite them the benefits will be immense.[14]

REFERENCES

1. Chall, Jeanne, *Learning to Read: The Great Debate,* New York: McGraw Hill, 1967.
2. Husén, Torsten (ed.), *International Study of Achievement in Mathematics,* Vol. I and II, Stockholm: Almquist and Wiksell and New York: Wiley, 1967.
3. Wittrock, M. C., and Wiley, D. E. (eds.), *The Evaluation of Instruction: Issues and Problems,* New York: Holt, 1970.
4. Spearritt, D., *Listening Comprehension—A Factorial Analysis.* (ACER Research Series No. 76), Hawthorn: Australian Council for Educational Research, 1962.
5. Ammons, R. B., and Ammons, H. S., *Full-Range Picture Vocabulary Test,* Mis-soula: Psychological Test Specialists, 1948.
6. Dunn, Lloyd M., *Peabody Picture Vocabulary Test,* Minneapolis, Minn.: American Guidance Serives, 1959.
7. Brimer, M. A., and Dunn, Lloyd M., *English Picture Vocabulary Test,* Bristol: Educational Evaluation Enterprises (Tests 1 and 2) 1962–1963 (Preschool version), 1969.
8. McCarthy, James J., and Kirk, Samuel A., *Illinois Test of Psycholinguistic Abilities,* Urbana, Ill.: University of Illinois Press, 1961–1963.
9. Reynell, Joan, *Reynell Developmental Language Scales,* Slough: NFER in England and Wales, 1970.
10. Hudson, W., "Pictorial depth perception in sub-cultural groups in Africa," *Journal of Social Psychology,* **52** (1960), 183–208.
11. Kellaghan, T. P., *The Study of Cognition in a Non-Western Culture,* Doctoral thesis, Faculty of Arts, Queen's University, Belfast, 1965.

12. Rasch, G., *Probabilistic Models for Some Intelligence and Attainment Tests,* Copenhagen: Danmarks Paedagogiske Institut, 1960.
13. Previous UNESCO publications in this field are Burnet, Mary, *a.b.c. of Literacy,* Paris: UNESCO, 1965. Gray, William S., *The Teaching of Reading and Writing,* Paris: UNESCO, 1st ed., 1956; 2nd ed. with chapter by Staiger, Ralph C., 1969. Gray, William S., *Preliminary Survey on Methods of Teaching Reading and Writing* (Parts I and II), Paris: UNESCO, 1953. International Bureau of Education, *The Teaching of Reading,* Paris: UNESCO, 1949. Neijs, Karel, *Literacy Primers: Construction, Evaluation and Use,* Paris: UNESCO, 1961. UNESCO, *Simple Reading Material for Adults: Its Preparation and Use,* Paris: UNESCO, 1963. UNESCO, *Literacy and Education for Adults,* Paris: UNESCO, 1964.
14. The phonetic symbols (for example, /u/) used in this chapter and throughout the book are those of the International Phonetic Alphabet, as described in *The Principles of the International Phonetic Association,* London: International Phonetic Association, 1949.

CHAPTER 3

Cross-National Comparisons of Reading Achievement

JOHN DOWNING

ALAN BRIMER's final sentence in the preceding chapter gives us heart to go forward into this area of cross-national comparisons of reading achievement despite the methodological problems he has described. The benefits he predicts from such ventures should be twofold: Despite our mistakes, as Brimer puts it, we shall yet learn much about reading from such comparisons. But also we may learn how to improve our methodology through discovering new variables, for example, as a by-product of our errors in research.

Definitions of "Reading"[1]

One frequently occurring source of error is the ambiguity of the term "reading." For example, in the pioneering cross-national survey of the International Bureau of Education[2] in 1949, ministries of education in forty-five countries responded to sixteen open-ended questions about the teaching of "reading"; but the investigators found the following:

> In examining the replies received to the questions concerning the age at which children are expected to read fluently, it is noticeable that a good deal of latitude has been given to the expression "to read fluently." This no doubt explains the very great range in the different ages at which, according to the information supplied, pupils are expected to attain fluency in reading.

Often teachers and reading experts speak and write about reading without defining or discussing what they mean by it; they seem to assume that everyone shares their concept of what reading is. It is hardly surprising, therefore, that some of the controversies and debates in this field take place on a rather primitive egocentric level. But psychologists, linguists, and others who have attempted to define reading have come up with remarkably different conclusions. For example, Elkonin, in his chapter on the USSR, states that

> reading is a creation of the sound form of the word on the basis of its graphic representation. Therefore, a good reader is one who knows how to create the correct sound form not only of a known word, but also of any unknown word.

Furthermore, he asserts,

> Despite the fact that people often advance the comprehension of a word as a criterion of its correct reading, nevertheless, understanding is not an essential part of the process of reading.

Thus, Elkonin specifically excludes comprehension from his definition of reading, which he states formally as follows:

> Reading is the creation of the sound form of the word according to its graphic model.

And the sound form of the word is defined as "a definite organization of sounds in their timely succession."

In contrast, an American definition by Tinker and McCullough avoids any mention of speech sounds and places an emphasis on comprehension:

> Reading involves the recognition of printed or written symbols which serve as stimuli for the recall of meanings built up through past experience, and the construction of new meanings through manipulation of concepts already possessed by the reader. The resulting meanings are organized into thought processes according to the purposes adopted by the reader. Such an organization leads to modified thought and/or behavior, or else leads to new behavior which takes its place, either in personal or in social development.[3]

This emphasis on meaning has been particularly strong in American definitions of reading since the influential statement of Edward L. Thorndike (1917). His controlled observation of children's oral reading of paragraphs led him to conclude that

> Understanding a paragraph is like solving a problem in mathematics. It consists in selecting the right elements of the situation and putting them together in the right relations, and also with the right amount of weight or influence or force for each. The mind is assailed, as it were, by every word in the paragraph. It must select, repress, soften, emphasize, correlate, and organize, all under the influence of the right mental set or purpose or demand.[4]

In educational publications this led to definitions such as the following one published by America's National Society for the Study of Education in its forty-eighth *Yearbook* regarding elementary school reading:

> Reading is not a simple mechanical skill; nor is it a narrow scholastic tool. Properly cultivated, it is essentially a thoughtful process. It should be developed as a complex organization of patterns of higher mental processes. It can and should embrace all types of thinking, evaluating, judging, imagining, reasoning, and problem solving.[5]

It is this kind of description of reading with the emphasis on meaning and the omission of specific references to the sounds of language that has been popular for the past forty years, especially in the United States.

However, some authorities (Elkonin, for example) have narrowed their definitions and specified the ability to translate graphemes to phonemes and written words to spoken words as being the essence of reading. In recent years this aspect of reading has been given increasing attention as a result of the intervention of the new science of linguistics. Some linguists have tended to single out the learning of grapheme-phoneme correspondences as being the essential basis of reading in alphabetic writing systems. Soffietti states, for example:

> The linguist believes that the printed word acts as the trigger that releases its oral counterpart, which, in turn, releases a meaning we already possess.[6]

Fries, in his book *Linguistics and Reading,* makes the following points:

> Learning to read in one's native language is learning to shift, to transfer, from auditory signs for the language signals, which the child had already learned, to visual or graphic signs for the same signals. Both reading and talking have the same set of language signals for language *reception*. In talking, contrastive bundles of sound features represent these signals; in reading, contrastive patterns of spelling represent these same signals.[7]

Another linguist, Hall, brings out the nexus of the issue in the United States between educators who emphasize the phonic aspects of reading and those who emphasize "reading for meaning."

> any grapheme or sequence of graphemes used in spelling a word always symbolizes ("means") some fact of language, be it a phoneme (as in alphabetic writing) or a morpheme (as in Chinese characters). In any utterance, meaning is conveyed by morphemes and their combinations into phrases and clauses; by the term *meaning,* we here refer to the way in which these linguistic features symbolize the facts of the universe in which we live. Note especially that the SPELLING of any word has no "meaning," i.e., symbolizes nothing, directly, except the linguistic characteristics of the morpheme it represents (in an alphabetic orthography, its phonemic structure); this kind of meaning may be termed *linguistic* meaning, as opposed to *real-life* meaning. This latter is conveyed, not by written (graphemic) shapes, but by spoken morphemes and only by spoken morphemes . . . . Many naive persons tend to think that . . . the relationship between written shape and spoken linguistic form is one of equality and independence, each referring directly in its own way to the real-life situation, and that the same kind of "meaning" is involved in each case . . . . Nothing could be more inaccurate . . . .[8]

Possibly, one reason for this apparent lack of agreement as to what reading is may be the different perspectives of the linguist, psychologist, and educator. However, there exist certain recognizable human behaviors that everyone conceives to be "reading." Thus the British philosopher Dearden writes:

> You could go through a book backwards, from bottom to top and right to left, recognizing all the words there perfectly correctly, but we should hardly call this "reading," and certainly not "reading the book." Nor would it be any adequate reply to the question, "Have you read so-and-so?" to say that you recognized every word in it.[9]

This suggests the conclusion that there is much more to be considered than just the learning of phoneme-grapheme correspondences in an alphabetic language, for instance, if one wants to understand and explain all the variety of behavior that people commonly include when they talk about the everyday life activities of reading. We shall want to include such basic skills as relating graphemes to phonemes as an important part of our study of reading, but it is certainly not the whole of our concern.

Therefore, this writer takes the view that reading is all that variety of behavior that people include in everyday life when they say that someone "is reading." This may bring us into conflict with some more restrictive definitions. For example, Yuen Ren Chao asserts that "visual symbols do not begin to be writing until they have a close correspondence to language. . . . If a sign represents a specific part of language, it is writing, if it represents things directly it is not.'

For example, "the same road sign ' ↗ ' will be read by an English-speaking person as *no left turn*, by a German as *links abbiegen verboten*." [10] However, although " ↗ " may not be "writing" in Chao's definition, it is notable that, in the preceding quotation, he uses the word "read" in describing the English and German behavior in response to the road sign. This *is* reading by our definition.

But it is a special type of reading, and this indicates what needs to be done if we are to avoid the error found in the 1949 International Bureau of Education questionnaire study. Nor does it apply only to that type of investigation. Even when objective empirical tests of reading are applied, the same ambiguity may arise. The reading behavior to be investigated must be defined and specified operationally in either type of research. For example, in research on beginning reading in different countries reading might be defined more narrowly as "the recognition of the auditory and semantic significance of printed or written words," [11] and then one could proceed to specify operationally in detail what are the behavioral criteria for measuring such recognition.

This approach to defining reading is suggested also in Mary Austin's chapter on the United States, Chapter 23. In writing of the first national assessment of reading in that country to be undertaken in the 1970–1971 testing cycle she states

> Objectives for each of the ten areas to be assessed are those which scholars, schools, and lay people consider important for American youth to acquire. In reading for example, the general objectives include comprehend what is read; analyze what is read; reason logically from what is read; make judgments concerning what is read; have a lively interest in reading for pleasure and information.

"Literacy"

Another technical term that has caused error through ambiguities in its definition is literacy. Neijs noted in 1961 that "literacy may vary from slowly deciphering a line of print and laboriously writing one's name to quickly and efficiently scanning a page, rapidly grasping its content, and fluently rendering a message in brief, clear writing. Even for census purposes no universally accepted standards have ever been adopted . . . ."[12] Actually, the conventional definition of literacy at that time was the one proposed by UNESCO's Expert Committee on the Standardization of Educational Statistics in 1951:

A person is literate who can, with understanding, both read and write a short, simple statement on his everyday life.[13]

But already Gray had complained that

For census purposes there is still need for simple, easily administered standards of literacy. Unfortunately, however, no universally accepted standards have ever been adopted. Standards have varied so much and have been attained under such varying conditions that the data are hardly comparable.[14]

UNESCO, in 1962, modified its definition to distinguish between the "literate" and the "functionally literate" individual:

A person is literate when he has acquired the essential knowledge and skills which enable him to engage in all those activities in which literacy is required for effective functioning in his group and community, and whose attainments in reading, writing, and arithmetic make it possible for him to continue to use these skills towards his own and the community's development.

UNESCO also proposed a quantitative standard:

In quantitative terms, the standard of attainment in functional literacy may be equated to the skills of reading, writing, and arithmetic achieved after a set number of years of primary or elementary schooling.

Both proposals were adopted by the International Committee of Experts on Literacy in Paris in 1962, and a later conference at Teheran in 1965 reaffirmed them.

But it is one thing for UNESCO to adopt such definitions and standards and quite a different matter when it comes to actual practice. The Teheran conference recognized this in one way, at least:

Although the concept of literacy work is constantly broadening, there is still no common definition of it for all countries.[15]

The search for a common definition and a universal measuring rod for literacy, or functional literacy, may have led to large errors in statistical reports of literacy levels. At first sight, the proposal of the UNESCO Committee of Experts to measure functional literacy in terms of "a set number of years of primary or elementary schooling" seems attractively simple from the point of view of collecting the data. But the attractiveness of this simplicity of method may have blinded the experts to the dubious validity of such a measure. Schools vary so greatly from country to country that the number of years of schooling or even of grades passed may be grossly misleading. Yet this is the usual measure, as Harman notes

> However, most governments still adhere to the earlier UNESCO standard coupled with a grade completion equivalency (usually fourth or fifth grade) to identify their illiterate or functionally illiterate populations.[16]

Harman demonstrates how this kind of measure combined with extrapolations of the data produced by it cause a very serious distortion of the facts about illiteracy:

> United States government figures placing the rate of illiteracy among the population aged fourteen and above at 2.4% in 1960 grossly understate the extent of the problem. Equally as understated is the 8.3% figure for functional illiterates in the group aged twenty-five and over. In fact over half of that group may be functionally illiterate.
>
> The last collection of data for the individual states was in the 1930 census, all subsequent figures being based on extrapolations from rates and national data. Illiterates were those who, when asked how many years of school they had completed, answered, "None." Functional illiterates were determined on the basis of grade completion data. No tests of any kind were administered. Hence, application of different grade standards results in different assessments of the extent of illiteracy revealed by the 1960 Census data.[17]

This measure's lack of validity is shown clearly by a study cited by Hilliard. In the Woodlawn area of Chicago "although only 6.6% of the group studied reported that they had not gone as far as the sixth grade, 50.7% of the group, when subjected to achievement tests to determine their actual level of functioning, showed up as functional illiterates."[18]

Press reports in United States and Canadian newspapers in September 1970, revealed the findings of a survey conducted by Louis Harris and Associates for the newly established National Reading Council in the United States. Thirteen per cent of the population of the United States over the age of 16 "lacks the reading ability necessary for survival," Harris reported. This might rise to 24 per cent if the number of people who refused to be interviewed were taken into consideration. Harris concluded that even the more conservative estimate "far exceeds the federal estimate"[19]—that is, of 8.3 per cent of adults who are functionally illiterate.

Harman's conclusion is that

> It seems clear that lack of testing, reliance upon grade-completion criteria, and inadequate definitions of functional literacy combine to produce serious official underestimates of the extent of illiteracy in the United States.[20]

This problem is further compounded by national differences in the way each country arrives at its individual estimate of levels of literacy. Thus Harman's conclusion is almost certainly well justified: "Because of the general lack of credible statistics, it is difficult to assess the extent of world illiteracy."[21]

This must be true of the UNESCO estimates and the literacy statistics that will be reported here in some of the chapters in Part Two. For example, in Chapter 16, Biglmaier reports that some German educators relate their country's 1 per cent illiteracy rate to the excellence of their school systems. Similarly, Sakamoto and Makita give a list of five causes of the "very high rate of literacy in Japan" (fewer than 1 per cent are illiterate). As one example they cite "the initial use of phonetic symbols." But, if these explanations have any comparative basis, the very low validity of comparative statistics on literacy rates casts grave doubts on such evidence.

Another weakness of evidence based on literacy rates has been pointed out by Samuels:

> Literacy rates expressed as percentages do not indicate actual performance levels. Two countries may have identical literacy rates, yet the actual level of reading achievement in one of the two countries may far surpass the other.[22]

Thus, for example, although Germany and Japan both have an almost 100 per cent literacy rate, this does not mean that there is no difference in the reading achievements of the two countries. It merely indicates the insensitivity of the measure that is being employed.

The relativity of the concept of illiteracy is dramatically brought out by Mary Austin in Chapter 23, concerning reading in the United States. She cites Chase's concern "with 'higher illiterates'[23] who can absorb and repeat ideas they read but cannot relate them to life around them."

Subjective anecdotal evidence of the comparatively high or low achievements in particular countries is, of course, even weaker than the literacy statistics. For example, although Finnish educators sometimes claim that there are no reading problems in their country, one will feel less confidence in such reports when one discovers, as Samuels did on a recent visit to Finland, that "reading achievement tests specifically designed for the Finnish language and standardized for the Finnish school population had just recently been introduced and a large percentage of children had never been given the reading achievement tests. Since for a large percentage of children neither intelligence test scores nor reading achievement scores were available, it was impossible for anyone to assess with certainty what percentage of children in Finland could be considered to be reading successfully."[24]

World Literacy Rates

The preceding discussion on the problems of defining reading or literacy and the many serious limitations on the evidence available for comparing reading achievement cross-nationally is not presented in any spirit of destructiveness or pessimism. We shall learn to do better research in the future. But in the interim we must make the best judgments we can with the data we have, while exercising the appropriate degree of caution warranted by the limitations of the evidence.

However, there are one or two cross-national investigations that have been more sophisticated in their methodology than the studies discussed thus far. But before reviewing these, it seems appropriate to list the basic data on world literacy available through the UNESCO estimates.

In 1950, it was estimated that approximately 700 million or 44.3 per cent of people of age 15 or older were illiterate. By 1960, the percentage had dropped to 39.3 per cent, but the absolute numbers went up to 740 million people. By 1970, it was estimated by UNESCO, that, if the rate of decrease of the 1950s stayed constant during the next decade, the proportion would go down to 34.8 per cent, but the absolute numbers would have risen again to 810 million people.[25]

There is an important difference between the sexes in literacy rates. Illiteracy has a higher incidence among females than among males. For example, in Saudi Arabia, Somalia, and Yemen the total adult female populations are reported to be illiterate.[26]

Special Cross-National Researches

The chief purpose of the following review is to demonstrate by examples of actual studies the practical problems that face the researcher who undertakes cross-national research in comparative reading. Three paradigms will be examined in detail. They are subjected to intensive criticism to emphasize the methodological problems that must be attended to in planning future investigations.

Pidgeon's Survey of Attainments[27]

Although this comparative study was not planned as such from the beginning, it became the first attempt to make really scientific comparisons between the reading achievements of children in different countries.

The survey was not confined to reading attainments; it included arithmetic also. Comparisons were made on both types of attainment between (1) England and Wales and (2) Queensland, Australia. But only the arithmetic attainments were compared in the case of (3) California, United States. Because reading was not included in the latter country, this will be omitted in the following review.

The design and methods of Pidgeon's research are worth studying as a model of scientific rigor for this kind of comparative study. The sample in England and Wales was restricted to children in the age range from 10 years 9 months to 11 years 8 months. "A random sample of schools was drawn and all children in the age group in each selected school were tested. The selection of schools was made directly from the lists kept at the Ministry of Education of all schools in England and Wales attended by the children concerned. In order to ensure the adequate representation of schools of different types and in urban and rural areas, random sampling was carried out separately in each of these strata. The sampling method was thus systematic but unbiased and was considered effectively random. In all, some 3,180 children attending 91 schools administered by 63 different local education authorities were tested." [28]

In Queensland, Australia, the schools selected were also a stratified random sample. The age group was the same. "The grade system of placement is used in Queensland schools and although approximately two thirds of the children in the defined age group were in Grade V the others were found as low as Grade II (two pupils) and as high as Grade VII (one pupil). In all, 940 children attending 88 schools were tested." [29]

Four tests were used in both countries: (1) a test of nonverbal ability, (2) a reading comprehension test, (3) a mechanical arithmetic test, and (4) a mechanical and problem arithmetic test. These were administered in the same order and with identical instructions in both countries.

The reading comprehension test consisted of sixty incomplete sentences. "The appropriate word necessary to complete the sentence had to be chosen from five alternatives. The items, presented in order of difficulty, ranged from sentences suitable for bright 7-year-olds to those found difficult by children of 14. The test was scored by counting all correct items up to the point at which a gap of seven consecutive wrong answers occurred. Any items correct beyond this point were assumed to be due to chance and ignored. The reliability of the test was 0.958 [by Kuder-Richardson formula 20]." [30]

There was one difference between the testing in the two countries that was found to be unavoidable. In England and Wales the tests were administered by head teachers, psychologists, or trained officials of the school district concerned, whereas in Queensland the testers were teachers. However, in both countries great care was taken in briefing the examiners, and all marking and checking was done by the expert research staffs of the two research organizations—that is, the National Foundation for Educational Research in England and Wales, and the Research and Guidance Branch of the Queensland Department of Public Instruction. [31]

The results are based on the sample of children who completed all four tests. Pidgeon presents these in the form shown in Table 3-1.

TABLE 3-1. Comparison of Mean Standardized Scores for Four Tests Given in Queensland, Australia, and in England and Wales

	Nonverbal test		Reading test		Untimed arithmetic test 1		Timed arithmetic test 2	
	Mean	SD	Mean	SD	Mean	SD	Mean	SD
Queensland,	94.7	12.5	95.3	12.7	100.3	10.6	99.7	10.4
Australia	(0.66)		(0.65) –		(0.54)		(0.57)	
England and Wales	100.48	14.50	100.03	14.51	100.32	14.88	100.39	14.75
	(0.80)		(0.69)		(0.80)		(0.77)	

The tests were standardized by using the data from *all* children who completed each *separate* test in England and Wales. Lawley's[32] method was used for this standardization. "Using the conversion tables prepared, the mean standardized scores of the sample of children taking all tests were thus calculated for both England and Wales and Queensland. Table 3-1 gives these means (standard errors in parentheses), together with the respective standard deviations."[33]

Two interesting facts emerge from Pidgeon's table of results. First, although there are no significant differences between the means of either of the two arithmetic tests, the English and Welsh children had significantly higher mean scores on both the nonverbal and reading comprehension tests. Secondly, the smaller standard deviations in the Queensland results are noteworthy.

Pidgeon made a further analysis of the results that reveals how the lower mean scores of the Queensland children on the nonverbal and reading tests came about. This is shown in Table 3-2, which makes it clear that what was responsible for the lower mean score on the nonverbal and reading tests in Queensland was the smaller proportion of high scorers in that sample as compared with the sample from England and Wales.

TABLE 3-2. Proportions in Queensland and in England and Wales Occurring in Three Groups of Standardized Scores on Four Tests

Range of standardized scores	Expected proportion from normal distribution	Nonverbal test		Reading test		Arithmetic test 1		Arithmetic test 2	
		Q	E	Q	E	Q	E	Q	E
115 & above	15.87	5.73	17.20	5.73	14.89	8.38	17.14	6.04	16.54
85–114	66.52	76.88	68.66	75.40	69.63	85.47	68.47	85.47	68.17
84 & below	17.62	17.40	14.13	18.87	15.48	6.15	14.40	8.48	15.28

Q = Queensland, E = England and Wales.

When one turns to Pidgeon's discussion of these results one is struck immediately by the contrast between, on the one hand, his highly sophisticated research techniques and meticulous treatment and presentation of the data, and, on the other, the vagueness of their relationship to either the theoretical or practical problems of education in general or in reading in particular. We arrive at this point with the answers to the questions posed by the research method, but there seems to be no theoretical or practical reason for having asked them. This is not meant as a criticism of Pidgeon's survey, as such. His is an excellent scientific study, but it suffers from the same defect of numerous studies in comparative education. That is, the aim of the research is nebulous. In other fields, notably psychology, sociology, and anthropology, the comparative method has a more definite purpose—for example, the testing of hypotheses, either *ad hoc* or derived from theory.

In comparative research in education, one too often finds the researcher floundering and sometimes even wallowing in a sea of plausible *ex post facto* explanations for the results of his comparisons.

However, Pidgeon cannot be blamed for that effect in this particular study. The accidental opportunity for trying out a comparative study by scientific methods was too good an opportunity to be missed. Indeed, the most important result of Pidgeon's research is that it gave the lie to all those arm-chair comparative educationists who had declared that such research was not feasible.

Nevertheless, the fact that Pidgeon's report reveals him searching for an *ex post facto* explanation should be a warning for the future. First of all, Pidgeon fields an explanation suggested by his Queensland collaborators: "It was pointed out that this sample of Australian children were completely lacking in test sophistication and that this fact might affect the scores on the nonverbal tests more than those on the other tests."[34] He counters this, however, as follows: "It may well be true that the English sample of children had enjoyed a wider experience of tests in general, although from the information gleaned from the survey reports sent in by many local authorities it is unlikely that many of the children tested had previously been given nonverbal tests or tests of reading similar to the one employed in the survey."[35]

Quite apart from the fact that, at this period in the history of education in England and Wales, children of this age group were enjoying (*sic*) a veritable feast of testing in comparison to the Australian children whose schools were not subject to the "11+" examination, Pidgeon's discussion of this point is supported by no evidence whatsoever. This is in contrast to his care for the scientific method in its technological aspect.

As an alternative explanation he proposes that: "It is possible, however, that the children in England and Wales were more familiar with the type of perceptual material employed in the non-verbal test by reason of the increasing number of puzzle toys now available for children of primary school age."[36] However, he does not explain why there were fewer "puzzle toys" in Australia or provide evidence that this, in fact, was the case.

More generally, and therefore more reasonably, Pidgeon rejects the *assumption* "that the lower scores of Queensland children in any way reflect a lower innate intelligence," because "the different cultural environments of the children in the two countries may well be responsible for the difference in the scores obtained."[37]

The possibility that the words used in the reading test may not have been appropriate for Australian children was considered, but the Australian researcher felt that this was not a serious problem. An item analysis was made on a subsample of the test results from each of the two countries, and only one item showed a serious discrepancy. "This item, answered correctly by approximately 50 per cent of English children and by only 25 per cent of Queensland children, was concerned with the meaning of the word 'conjuror,' which presumably is not so familiar in Australia."[38]

Regarding the larger standard deviations found in the results for England and Wales, Pidgeon suggests that: "this may in part reflect the effects of 'streaming' [that is, homogeneous grouping by ability]. It is sometimes alleged that one of the results of streaming is that the brighter children make more rapid progress than they would otherwise achieve, and also that the duller children, when assigned to a 'C' stream, become more backward, partly as a result of poor morale, and partly because there is a tendency in some schools for the more experienced teachers to be put in charge of the abler streams. It should be noted, however, that, as far as reading is concerned, there were fewer 'poor' readers found in the English and Welsh sample than in the Queensland group."[39]

The root of Pidgeon's difficulty in interpreting his data lies in the fact that his comparative research was not planned to investigate any specific hypothesis. Therefore, if his report of the findings was to be as strictly scientific as his investigatory techniques, he should not have allowed himself to speculate about their causes—at least, not without admitting their *ex post facto* nature and noting their status as tentative hypotheses only.

As was mentioned earlier, the positive value of Pidgeon's study is its demonstration that scientific techniques of measurement, sampling, and the like, can be employed successfully in this comparative field.

The Twelve-Country Study by Foshay et al.

Douglas Pidgeon was one of the authors of the report of the first really large scale attempt to "introduce prominently an empirical approach into the methodology of comparative education."[40] His colleagues in the report were Arthur W. Foshay (USA), Robert L. Thorndike (USA), Fernand Hotyat (Belgium), and D. A. Walker (Scotland). Other colleagues who contributed to the research represented England, Finland, France, Germany, Israel, Poland, Sweden, Switzerland, and Yugoslavia, making up the twelve countries in which the testing took place.

This study was planned from the outset as a cross-national investigation, and Foshay states its aims formally:

1. To see whether some indications of the intellectual functioning behind responses to short-answer tests could be deduced from an examination of the patterning of such responses from many countries.
2. To discover the possibilities and the difficulties attending a large-scale international study.[41]

The 13-year-old was made the target of testing for two reasons, according to Foshay: (1) an earlier age would make comparison difficult "because of differences in curriculum" from country to country; (2) the age of 13 is "near a terminal point" and therefore the test responses would represent "the outcome of the educational system as a whole."[42]

The group of participants in the study met together in June 1959 and agreed on a procedure to be followed in all the twelve countries. The vicissitudes of their proposals indicate the kinds of problems with which this type of research must reckon.

1. Sampling. The original agreement was as follows:

a. The students to be tested would all be aged from 13 years to 13 years 11 months on the first day of the school year whatever might be the school level (grade) at which they were found.
b. The sample population in each country would be between 600 and 1,000 in number.
c. The sample to be tested would be all the children of both sexes residing in a community or communities selected to yield a population of the designated size.
d. The community or communities selected for testing would be as representative as possible of the total population of the country, according to whatever data were available to the participant in the study. If (as was true in some countries) no data were available to aid the participant in his selection, he was to use his own judgment.[43]

Thus the sampling plan was less rigorous than in Pidgeon's own study. But the looser specifications in paragraph (d) here were clearly necessary if any progress were to be made at all with the work. It may contain error of measurement, but we are aware of its possible level and it avoids the worse error of doing no research at all on perfectionist grounds. Furthermore, Foshay clearly specifies the limitations of the sampling as it actually turned out in the event country by country so that the reader of the report can judge the likely representativeness of the samples.[44]

For example, the actual sample sizes ranged from 300 (Switzerland) to 1,732 (Israel), whereas the original plan had been to have 600 to 1,000 children in each country. A more serious problem arises from the different interpretation that each country's researchers placed on paragraph (d) of the original sampling plan. The commonest solution was to sample one or a few communities or areas that were known by previous national research on attainments or sometimes only believed to be representative of the country as a whole. Even if the community in a country is selected on the basis of its attainments being representative of national attainments as measured by tests, this method ought not to be regarded necessarily as the paradigm for future comparative research. Because a particular community or region has scholastic attainments close to the norm statistically for the whole of the country it does not necessarily indicate that its pupils, schools, and homes are representative of national conditions. The sampling procedure should depend rather on the specific problem being investigated cross-nationally.

In some of the countries—Israel and Switzerland, for example—the sample was deliberately limited to a part of the population for practical reasons, but this made the sample clearly unrepresentative of the country as a whole.

Evidence of the irregularity of the sampling procedures is found in one of the tabulations in Thorndike's chapter in the Foshay *et al.* report:

Table 5 shows the percent of cases with fathers at different levels of education or occupation. It is clear from this table that the different national samples were not comparable with respect to distribution of education or occupation of fathers.

What is not clear is the extent to which these sample differences reflect similar differences in the total national population and the extent to which they reflect biases in the specific sample tested in that country. Thus the Scottish sample showed twice as many unskilled and semi-skilled workers as the German sample, two-and-a-half times as many as the Swiss, and five times as many as the sample from Israel. How shall we understand this? Examination of the sampling procedure brings out that the Israeli sample was limited to that segment of the population who were of European origin, that the Swiss sample was limited to Geneva, while several fee-paying schools were excluded from the Scottish sample. Thus, in part at least the differences between nationalities appear to reflect differences in sampling.[45]

In Thorndike's chapter it is recognized that for the sampling "the evidence upon which communities or schools were chosen was rather meagre and impressionistic." And therefore: "Because of these limitations on the representativeness of the national samples, there seems to be little value in comparing the absolute level of achievement in one country with that in other countries. For this reason no country by country tables of mean scores are reported."[46] (However, as we shall see later, the data were used in other ways.)

2. *Tests and measures used.* Background data on the children tested were in respect of date of birth, sex, number of siblings, place in birth order, home language (if different from school language), location of home (that is, size of community), years in school, kindergarten attendance, size of class, father's and mother's education, parental interest, father's and mother's occupation, and score on nonverbal intelligence test.

The tests were of reading comprehension, mathematics, science, and geography. Trial forms of the tests were developed mainly from items from existing tests in England, France, Germany, Israel, and the United States. These trial forms were then pretested in each country before being finally developed. Each test had approximately thirty items in order to have a measure that could be administered in a reasonable amount of time—for example, in under forty-five minutes—but no time limit was to be imposed on the students.

To overcome the problem of national differences in test sophistication, a practice test was constructed and administered prior to the actual testing. "During the practice session students would be encouraged to ask any questions that occurred to them about the practice test and about the project as a whole. Teachers were requested to answer all questions fully, including giving answers to the practice test."[47]

The reading comprehension test consisted of five reading passages, each followed by six or seven test items, for example:

According to the text, considerate driving means
    (a) greeting other people in a friendly way.
    (b) giving help if there has been an accident.
    (c) assisting if there has been a breakdown.
    (d) watching for old and infirm people and children.

In all, there were thirty-three items on the reading test.

The most interesting problem that arises here is that of the translation of the tests into the various different languages of the twelve countries studied. The tests were first prepared in one of three languages: English, French, or German. Then that version had to be translated into the other seven of the eight languages: English, Finnish, French, German, Polish, Hebrew, Serbo-Croatian, and Swedish. The rule of procedure adopted was that, "translation of the test items would be done by each participant in his home language."[48] But this failed to foresee that substantial differences might creep in between items in different languages, thus making the items invalid for comparative purposes. This is the kind of error that has to be expected if we are to learn to improve the methodology of cross-national research.

Foshay frankly described the difficulty they ran into:

> They did not, for example, test the translation by having it translated back into its original language in order to compare the re-translation with the original. This led to occasional differences in items. A striking example of this, as might be expected, was in the translation of a passage in the reading comprehension test, in which the literary quality of the passage in its original French was its main characteristic.
> "*Elle sort d'une touffe d'herbe qui l'avait cachée pendant la chaleur. Elle traverse l'allée de sable a grande ondulations.*"
> "A caterpillar emerges from a tuft of grass where it has been concealing itself during the warm weather. It crosses the gravel path, moving in a series of large ripples."
> "*Quelle belle chenille—grasse, velue, fourée, brune, avec des points d'or et ses yeux noirs!*"
> "What a beautiful caterpillar—fat, hairy, furry and brown, with golden spots and black eyes!"[49]

Foshay assures us that "such difficulties in translation apparently were so small in number and so scattered as to be insignificant. There is no evidence that they seriously influenced the national scores."[50] However, reading specialists will probably feel less confident than Foshay about the comparability of items translated into different languages. Even the double or triple retranslations proposed by Brimer in Chapter 2 may not be fully effective in equating reading test items translated into different languages. Indeed, this would be a valuable research topic for a future cross-national investigation: How does translation affect the reliability and validity of test materials? This kind of basic preliminary research in the cross-national field has not been done, unfortunately.

Thorndike's analysis of item difficulties in eleven of the twelve countries (the Yugoslavia data did not arrive in time—another hazard of cross-national cooperative research) found impressively high correlations between the difficulty of each item from country to country, an average of .87 for the reading test. Thorndike concludes, therefore, that a difficult item is a difficult item "regardless of the school system in which the pupil has been educated or the language in which his schooling has been couched."[51] On the other hand, he found that "passages of French language origin seem to be slightly easier for the French-speaking countries and the passages of either English or German origin for the English- and German-speaking countries."[52]

The reliability of the tests used in this study was shown to be fairly satisfactory. Using Kuder-Richardson Formula No. 20, the estimated reliabilities were .81 for reading, .81 for mathematics, .70 geography, and .62 science.

Some of the background data proved difficult to collect and interpret. Thorndike states that

> An attempt was made to get information on parental education or father's occupation for the children in each country. However, there was very real difficulty in getting comparable data for different countries. Pressures and sensitivities differ from country to country, so that in some it is possible to get information about education and in others it is possible to get information about occupation, but it is rarely possible to get both. Furthermore, the differences in educational structure in different countries make it difficult to establish classifications that will be comparable from country to country.[53]

Another difficulty reported by Thorndike was the ambiguity in the coding of some of the background data:

> Additional tabulations were carried out by size of community in which the pupil resided. Communities were classified into those of under 2,000, those of 2,000 to 20,000, and those of over 20,000 inhabitants. However, there were certain ambiguities in this coding from country to country. It was not entirely clear whether place of residence meant the community in which the school was located, or the immediate community in which the pupil had his home. Thus, in some countries, farm children living in quite rural areas were apparently coded as coming from communities of two to twenty thousand because that is where they attended school.[54]

3. Results. As already noted, Thorndike concluded that the limitations on the representativeness of the national samples precluded comparisons of absolute levels of achievement from one country to another. Therefore, he rejected the presentation of mean score comparisons. Instead, he made "an examination of the magnitude of the differences between countries" and "the differences in patterns of achievement from country to country."

For those purposes, sophisticated statistical analyses were carried out and the results are reported in full by Thorndike.[55] But the logic of his argument, that this treatment of the results is valid whereas the one he rejected is not, is not apparent. If the samples are not representative, it is difficult to see how any statistical treatment can correct this. Either the data obtained do reflect conditions in that country or they do not. The "magnitude of the differences" and "the differences in patterns of achievement" must be influenced by faulty sampling, too. Thorndike does not explain this problem satisfactorily. In this writer's view, this must affect all the detailed comparisons of the study, despite the very impressive technical statistical equipment employed in making them. The display of statistical know-how should not blind us to the fact that validity depends in the first place on the manner in which the data are collected. If the data are of doubtful validity before they go into the statistical mill, the tables of data that emerge must still be polluted by the original error.

By "pattern of achievement," Thorndike means "a country's achievement on the specific tests and sub-tests, relative to its own over-all level of achievement."[56] He evolved a statistical procedure that gave a national profile of its relative strengths and weakness on the various measures. (Note Thorndike's use of the term "a country's" in view of the preceding discussion of the representativeness of the samples.) Relative to its own over-all mean derived from the nonverbal test, as well all four achievement tests, Yugoslavia did especially well in reading comprehension. Scotland, Finland, and England (in that order) also did quite well. These were followed by the United States, Switzerland, Germany, Sweden, France, and Israel, while Belgium and Poland made a poor showing.[57]

These "patterns of achievement" combined the scores for boys and girls. When Thorndike broke down the data to compare boys and girls in each country, in all countries boys were superior to girls generally, except in the United States. However, the girls usually performed better on the reading test than did the boys. This leads Thorndike to conclude that

> This pattern is a universal one, appearing in each one of the 12 countries. We appear to have here a universal and quite stable sex characteristic.[58]

This statement must be contested. First of all, the results of Thorndike's treatment of the data conflict with those of another statistical treatment in this same volume. Hotyat's method of analysis[59] finds girls superior to boys in reading comprehension only in approximately one half of the countries in this study.[60] Furthermore, the reading attainments of girls have not been found to be superior to boys in *national* studies conducted in some of these same countries, some of which were superior in their sampling methods in comparison with the present study.[61] This problem of sex differences in reading ability will be dealt with in greater detail in a later chapter. It is sufficient to note here that the evidence from a number of studies is contrary to Thorndike's conclusion. The fact that his results differ from those obtained in national comparisons between girls and boys tends to increase doubts about the representativeness of the data he is treating statistically. The discrepancy between Hotyat's analysis and Thorndike's analysis of the same data in the same report raises a question about the application of their methods of analysis in this problem. They certainly give different answers to whether girls are superior to boys in reading achievement in all the countries in this particular survey.

Hotyat's analysis includes an interesting comparison between the profiles of the French speaking samples in Belgium, France, and Switzerland and those of the English speaking countries, England, Scotland, and the United States. The latter countries were superior to the former.

In this same report, Pidgeon pursues further a hypothesis derived from his own earlier research comparing Queensland with English and Welsh children (see p. 42). From that study and from several others cited in Pidgeon's chapter in the Foshay *et al.* report he observes that "the general aim of the grade class teacher may tend to result in a relatively smaller dispersion. Perhaps exerting a greater influence, however, is the belief a teacher may have that innate ability is of paramount importance in determining the level of attainment to be expected from a child. Streaming by ability, which is viewed as an administrative device resulting from the acceptance of this belief, will merely tend to enhance its effects. When all these factors act in the same direction the effect will clearly be greatest and this is what happens in England. Here, it is claimed, the aims and, more especially, the beliefs of most teachers and educational administrators lead them to expect wide differences in performance, and this is what is therefore achieved. Where, on the other hand, the grade placement system operates and especially where, within such a system, teachers do not attempt to measure innate ability and therefore do not expect their pupils' attainments to be matched to it, then the dispersion of achievement will be much less."[62]

To investigate this in the present study, Pidgeon expressed the standard deviations on the five tests from the twelve countries in the form of standard scores. He found further support for his hypothesis from the results. "Consistently on every test, England has by far the largest dispersion of test scores."[63] Scotland, which has many similarities to England, came next in this respect. This was true of reading as well as the other subjects tested.

Pidgeon's analysis is notably the most interesting of all the chapters in the Foshay *et al.* report. This is probably because he has a definite question to answer from the data, a hypothesis to test, a problem to solve. The rest of the study suffers from the lack of any clear statement of a theoretical or practical problem of education to be solved by cross-national comparison. This in itself may account for the extreme thinness of the research data, and the superficiality of some of the generalizations made from them.

For example, in discussing the finding that passages in the reading test that originated in one language were slightly easier in that particular language than when translated into another, Thorndike states

> However, even though the differences appear in a fairly consistent pattern, they are generally of very small size. The task difficulty seems to transcend language in considerable measure. Thus, once again, the universality of the reading task is affirmed.[64]

Although this may be true, it is difficult to say how the results given justify such a generalization, especially since it is not explained.

The age level chosen for this investigation is particularly inappropriate for obtaining any really interesting data on the problems of learning to read in different languages and different educational circumstances. Thorndike may be correct in asserting that the language difference is relatively unimportant *at this age level,* but one certainly cannot assume that his generalization would apply to testing younger children. As we shall see in later chapters, the needs and problems of the young novice in learning to read are very different from those of the adult. The reading processes of mature readers may be very similar despite differences of languages and the ways in which they are written, but the learning-to-read process may be quite different at least in some respects in different languages and different writing systems. For similar reasons, Thorndike's assertion that "level of reading ability is the feature with respect to which different educational programs are most nearly uniform"[65] also is not justified by his results. Testing children at age 13 by a single comprehension reading test conceals all the variables in which we are interested. This form of test is almost certain to produce just the homogeneity Thorndike considers to be an important indication of the universality of the reading process. To test such a hypothesis requires the administration of *different* types of reading tests at *differing* age levels beginning at the youngest age at which children in the various countries concerned are first introduced to the tasks of learning to read and write.

Despite these criticisms, the study by Foshay *et al.* represents an important landmark in the development of scientific research in comparative reading. Foshay is justified in stating that

> This is an exploratory study. The participants in this study were working with no extra funds, no extra allotment of time, and without the benefit of a previously developed set of procedures. It will therefore be apparent that both the tests and the sampling procedures do not meet the standards that might otherwise be required. For these shortcomings we are not apologetic; it was necessary to accept them.[66]

His primary conclusion also seems appropriate:

> A large scale project, which depends on similarities in technical and philosophical assumptions in education and in measurement, can be done.[67]

The Peterson Dissertation

A number of American doctoral dissertations have been concerned with reading in other countries, but they have not been truly comparative or empirical. However, in his Ph.D. dissertation, Raymond Peterson[68] attempted to compare the reading and spelling of English and American children at three ages; 7, 11, and 14. Peterson lists five features of English education said to be in contrast with American ways of schooling:

1. English children begin reading at age 5+ and start formal spelling about a year later, whereas in the United States the introduction comes about a year later for both subjects.
2. English children have an additional four weeks in their school year.
3. "The teaching of reading in English schools is characterized by greater emphasis upon phonics than is usually found in American schools." He cites two British basal reading series as examples: Schonell and Sarjeant[69] and O'Donnell and Munro.[70]
4. "The pace of learning to read is faster in English than in American schools." He cites Dixon's[71] comparison of readability of British versus

American basal reading series showing that the rate of introduction of new words is more rapid in the former than in the latter.

5. "The 11-plus assessment in English education has no counterpart in America . . . . The importance of this assessment undoubtedly provides a strong incentive for the pupils to excel in their school work . . . ."[72]

Two other sources of information on these differences are cited by Peterson: Flesch[73] and Rickover.[74] Unfortunately, neither of these authors can be regarded as authorities on either comparative education or the teaching of reading in either British or American education in a scholarly sense.

More specifically, Peterson is not quite correct in some of the five premises listed here. His statement that there is a "greater emphasis upon phonics" in the teaching of reading in England is misleading. It is doubtful if this was true at the time he completed his dissertation, and it is certainly not true today. The most authoritative source on the alternative methods of teaching reading in Britain is the book by Vera Southgate and Geoffrey Roberts, *Reading—Which Approach?* It states that "The majority of basic reading schemes published in Great Britain during the 1950s and 1960s employed a look-and-say method."[75] The Schonell and Sarjeant series (*The Happy Venture Readers*), mentioned as Peterson's first example, has been used by only a small proportion of schools. It is eclectic in method, although it has more phonic material than other similar series published in that period. The second basal series mentioned by Peterson, *Janet and John* by O'Donnell and Munro, is, and has been for many years, the most popular series in England. In the 1960s it was used in approximately 50 per cent of beginning reading classes, although not exclusively of other materials. But Peterson's description of *Janet and John* suggests a phonic bias, and this is certainly not the case. Stott states that the *Janet and John* readers "are planned on a sight method, and this applies even to the so-called phonic series, since it is only the list of words at the back and not the texts which are phonically arranged . . . . The *Janet and John* books . . . do not provide a good introduction to phonics."[76]

Elizabeth Goodacre, in Chapter 17 on reading in Great Britain, notes that: "Since the thirties . . . many teachers . . . reacted quite violently against the idea of teaching phonics and concentrated on global methods as being more meaningful to their young pupils." For example, Dorothy Glynn criticizes the use of phonic methods for beginners on the grounds that "they are not likely to give a child who is just approaching reading the idea of reading for meaning nor will they inspire a sustained and purposeful interest in learning to read."[77]

Typical of the erroneous stereotype of English education that is reflected in some parts of Peterson's dissertation was the mistaken view common in the United States in the early 1960s that the Initial Teaching Alphabet (i.t.a.), introduced in British schools in 1961, is "a phonic method." The truth is that it is, as its name indicates, only an alphabet—an alternative graphic system for printing children's books. For example, one American professor, Vera Ohanian, described i.t.a. as "unmistakeably a phonic approach."[78] Whereas the report of the Schools Council (the official curriculum body for England and Wales) states that "It would be a grave error to assume that i.t.a. had brought about an increase in formal phonic training." [79]

Peterson's third premise is probably only misleading through its brevity. He presents it in relative terms. However, it does tend to convey a greater emphasis on phonics in English schools than actually exists. The single most authoritative publication on the aims of the English primary schools is "The Plowden Report." It states that "the most successful infant teachers have refused to follow the wind of fashion and to commit themselves to any one method. They choose methods and books to fit the age, interest and ability of individual pupils. Children are helped to read by memorising the look of words and phrases, often with the help of pictures, by guessing from a context which is likely to bring them success, and by phonics . . . ." [80] Another authoritative source, which puts the phonics aspect in perspective, is the book by John Blackie, the former chief inspector for primary education in England. It states that "in practice the majority of infants' schools use a combined look-and-say and phonetic method . . . ." [81]

This is in agreement with the evidence of empirical research cited by Elizabeth Goodacre in Chapter 17:

> It is clear that few teachers depend solely upon a single method. None of the researches report any teachers who use only the phonic method, although a number of teachers seem to concentrate on "global methods" (that is, single word or sentence, or a combination of these) and provide no phonic instruction for their pupils. For instance, in the NFER London survey in the late fifties, only 6 per cent did not use phonics, and, ten years later, the proportions were in a Midland city and in Hertfordshire Infant schools 14 per cent and 9 per cent, respectively.

Thus, phonic methods were certainly quite widely used in England, but they were not given the emphasis that a quick reading of Peterson's brief statement might lead one to believe.

Peterson's fourth premise also is misleading—that is, that "The pace of learning to read is faster in English than in American schools." Dixon's readability study is not valid evidence on this matter. The quotation from "The Plowden Report" that has been given here, is relevant again; that is, teachers "choose methods and books to fit the age, interest and ability of individual pupils." The rate of learning cannot be determined from the vocabulary content of basal readers in England, because each child progresses through the series at his own individual rate.

Peterson's first premise also must be questioned. His brief statement that "formal spelling" begins in England at about age 6+ suggests a more deliberate emphasis on spelling instruction than is actually the case. For many years in English infant schools (for children aged 5–7) the emphasis has been taken off the mechanics of written language and placed instead on fostering creative authorship. For example, it is notable that "The Plowden Report" allots four pages to "Children's Writing," which is largely devoted to its creative aspects;

the words "spelling" only occurs once in a passing reference to "inaccuracies . . . which get in the way of communication."[82]

This same deemphasis on spelling is indicated by ex-Chief Inspector Blackie: "It is this insistence on the importance of subject matter, of having something to say that you really want to say, which characterizes the writing of children in a good primary school. It is much better to learn to write correctly as a means of doing this, rather than by doing artificial exercises."[83]

Finally, Peterson is quite right in asserting that the 11+ examination has no counterpart in America, but his evaluation of its educational effects must be questioned. He suggests that it "provides a strong incentive for the pupils to excel." To which pupils is he referring? Presumably the more fortunate ones who do have the ability to excel daily in the classroom. Research in educational psychology shows what is likely to be the fate of other children with less ability in such a system—for example, studies of levels of aspiration. In fact, the educational damage caused by the 11+ exam was one of the chief reasons why it has been largely abandoned since Peterson's dissertation was completed, although in some districts (Leicestershire, for example) it was already on the way out at the time he was writing. Blackie describes the "enormously increased pressure for success in the 11+" examination as a barrier to progress in improving English primary education. He comments that "there was no end to the follies committed"[84] as a result of this pressure. This was the view of England's chief inspector for primary education in reviewing the period that is the setting for Peterson's study.

HYPOTHESIS.   Peterson's dissertation appears to be more scientific and purposeful than the other two paradigms since he does formally state the hypothesis to be tested by cross-national comparison:

> On the premise that learning to read and spell are largely matters of development rather than outcomes of formal instruction, it is hypothesized that any initial advantage obtained by earlier beginning and more formal approach will disappear with the passing of time. To secure evidence for this hypothesis, the design of the study provides for a comparison of the performance of groups of English children on standardized American tests both with the norms for the tests and with the performance of similar groups of American children on the same tests. The comparisons are limited to the approximate ages, 7, 11, and 14.[85]

But in this hypothesis an extension of the premise has crept in: the reference to "formal instruction" in the preceding quotation. Peterson extends this further by asserting that American schools "compared with schools in England . . . are somewhat less formal in their instruction. This being the case, a comparison of differences in achievement of boys and girls in both national samples may provide information relative to the degree of influence of instruction and maturity in achievement in reading and spelling."[86] But it is not the case that English schools are more formal than American schools. In particular, at the youngest age level that is critical for Peterson's hypothesis, the reverse seems true. This is clearly demonstrated by comparing the description of English primary schools in "The Plowden Report" or in John Blackie's *Inside the Primary School* with common practice in the early grades of typical American schools. A number of sources, Rogers,[87] Featherstone,[88] for example, explicitly state that it is the English schools that are more informal.

Thus, Peterson's assumption about English education vitiates his hypothesis and the design of his research at the outset.

POPULATIONS. The city of Leeds was chosen "as being a typical English community"[89]; in the United States the reading data were obtained from Pinellas County, Florida, and the spelling data from Jackson, Michigan. Peterson's case for selecting urban Leeds is that over half of the population of England resides in urban areas. Furthermore, Emmett's earlier study revealed that Leeds children were representative of English children as a whole in respect of verbal intelligence.[90]

Peterson provides very full descriptions of the localities, populations, and social class of the English and American communities in which his investigations were conducted. These permit one to judge their comparability (in these respects) quite well. His description of the educational systems of the three communities is also quite comprehensive, but when he goes beyond description the influence of the erroneous stereotype of English education reveals itself again. For example, he comments that "Perhaps the most distinctive, and to some the most disturbing, feature of American education is the emphasis upon local autonomy."[91] This remark, placed as it is as the introductory sentence to his description of the "United States"—which is in juxtaposition to his commentary on English education—suggests that local autonomy is not a feature of English schools. Actually the reverse is true. Indeed, the English schools are renowned for their individual freedom in determining what shall be taught and how. As Blackie puts it: "In no other country in the world is so much responsibility put on the head teacher, or, of course, so much liberty of decision given to him."[92] This is confirmed by Bereday, an American authority on comparative education: "In England . . . education is almost completely decentralized. Decisions involving the curricula are almost all in the hands of . . . professional teachers . . . . Local authorities receive national funds that help to defray as much or more than one half of their current expenditures; they can also obtain professional advice and educational publications from the ministry's inspectorate. *But in matters of curriculum, methods, and texts, not only headmasters but teachers also are autonomous.*"[93] (Italics added.) Although Peterson may be accurate in his estimation that "uniformity of standards characterizes the English national school system,"[94] this is not because of any uniformity of curriculum imposed by external authority, as his description might suggest. As Bereday points out, "England prefers to rely for its standards on university entrance requirements, teachers' associations, and the compelling cultural traditions. Hence there is no uniform curriculum in England, but only a uniform level of achievement."[95]

Curiously, the nine pages of Peterson's dissertation that are devoted to the ways of teaching reading and writing[96] in the two countries do not support his own generalizations about the differences in the two education systems. For example, he states that in Leeds (1) "more formal methods of teaching spelling are sometimes introduced in the last year of the infant schools"; (2) "Practices in the teaching of spelling in the Leeds schools are determined by the head-teachers without aid of an authorized syllabus"; (3) "The procedure in teaching reading advocated, once the child is ready, is a combination of the sentence, look-and-say, and phonics methods."[97] But in Pinellas County, Florida, for instance, "direction for teaching reading and spelling was derived from several bulletins issued by the Florida Department of Public Instruction and from a more extensive locally formulated guide," and "formal spelling instruction began in the 2nd grade. Weekly plans were provided by *Spelling Goals,* a state adopted series . . . ."[98] Also, in Jackson, Michigan, "The Division of Instruction in the Jackson schools is responsible for guiding the instructional program . . . . Recommendations for weekly schedules of instruction are also provided by the Division of Instruction"; "The introduction of Jackson children to spelling occurs in the latter part of the 1st grade . . . . More formal spelling is introduced in 2nd grade."[99] He mentions phonic instruction as taking place in both Pinellas County and Jackson in the first grade.

It is not clear how Peterson could justify retaining his original generalized premises, which were quoted earlier in this review, in view of his own descriptions of the actual behavior found in these particular schools.

SAMPLING.   Samples were selected to be representative of the populations in intelligence and socioeconomic status. For the three age levels under investigation in Leeds, Peterson selected a sample of 300 children each. He did not use a random sampling procedure, but selected the schools to provide a representative cross-section of Leeds schools in terms of social class and other conventional demographic variables. His 14-year-olds all came from two schools. ". . . a comprehensive school was chosen in order to achieve a sampling of all levels of ability. The proportion of students of higher ability in this school was lower than in the population since many of the more capable students are found in the grammar schools which provide greater opportunity for advanced education and command higher prestige. To avoid prejudicing the sample, testing was conducted in one grammar school and sufficient papers drawn at random to secure the correct proportion of these students."[100] Peterson demonstrates that there is no statistically significant difference between his sample of 14-year-olds thus selected and the proportion of the population that was "in selective secondary places." However, this technique illustrates the hazards of not using some kind of stratified random sampling method—as, for example, in Pidgeon's research, which was described first in this review. There are at least two problems raised by Peterson's sampling procedure: (1) The comprehensive school is intended to be an all-level school in terms of ability. Even though this particular school in Leeds had not reached that goal, it may have had more children of higher ability than the typical secondary modern school in Leeds, in which the pupils who were left over after the 11 + creaming off process had been completed were generally placed. Therefore, Peterson's sample may not be representative of the population in terms of ability. In fact, intelligence tests showed that his sample was significantly above the norm by six IQ points. But so also was his 11-year-old sample (3.5 IQ points).[101] (2) The comprehensive school is the center of the educational trend away from segregation by ability. Its educational climate is likely to be atypical of the rest of the secondary schools in Leeds. As will be seen in later chapters, such variables in the educational environment may be at least as important as the intellectual ability of the pupils.

In Pinellas County all pupils had been tested, and "individual records were drawn to match the Leeds samples according to sex and chronological age. Choices were limited to the same range of intelligence; otherwise the choice was random."[102] However, in a later description of the actual characteristics of the sample, Peterson states that "Pupils in the negro schools, amounting to 14.11% of the total for these grades were not included."[103] The Jackson samples were selected by a similar procedure to that used in Leeds.

Peterson's report on the results of the sampling states that only 138 subjects at the youngest age level in Pinellas County could be found to match the Leeds 7-year-olds. His explanation of this raises another methodological problem:

> It was previously explained that there were insufficient subjects in the Pinellas 2nd grade who were young enough to match all the Leeds subjects from the infant school. Only the older Leeds pupils at this level could be matched.[104]

This is confusing. Were the samples selected by age or by form and grade? Peterson's table of data on this variable has a column headed "Grade," below which is listed "Infant II" for Leeds and "2" for Pinellas. In other places, Peterson uses the term "grade" with reference to the Leeds schools, whereas, in fact, the grade (or "standard") system was abolished in England many years before his study was conducted. Currently, many different kinds of school organization are being tried in English schools, but, probably, at the time of Peterson's study the most common practice was a simple promotion from one age group to the next on the basis of chronological age. In American schools, however, many children are "retained" in the lower grade on the basis of their poor achievements. Thus, Peterson's method has missed the lower-achieving 7-year-olds in Pinellas County as well as the less mature, as far as can be determined from these parts of his report. But intelligence testing indicated that this Pinellas 7-year-old sample was only slightly and not significantly above the norm.[105] However, he attempted to avoid bias in his sampling by using only that part of the Leeds sample that did match the Pinellas sample in terms of age, and he obtained some evidence to show that he was successful in this.[106] This means that both samples are different from what was originally planned.

Peterson recognizes the existence of this difference in school organization in his discussion of the finding that the Jackson 7-year-old and 11-year-old samples were significantly older than the corresponding Leeds samples. "The policy in American schools of retaining children, particularly in the primary grades, could account for the higher ages of the total samples."[107]

TESTING.   Reading was tested in Leeds and in Pinellas on the Stanford Achievement Test batteries for paragraph meaning and word meaning. The former consists in selecting one word from four alternatives to fill a blank in a sentence or short paragraph. It has forty-four to forty-eight items according to level. The word meaning subtest requires the pupil to complete a short definition by selecting the word defined from a choice of four alternatives. It has thirty-eight to forty-eight items according to level.

The Leeds and Jackson children were tested with the Metropolitan Achievement Test's spelling battery. There were twenty-four words at the 7-year-old level and fifty words at the older ages.

Although these are both American tests, Peterson cites evidence from previous studies to show that they are not unfair to English children. Also, "Testers were permitted to give the British spelling of words which differed."[108]

The testers were not strictly comparable in the three communities. In Leeds, the tests were administered by psychologists from the Child Guidance Centre; in Pinellas, classroom teachers conducted the tests; and in Jackson, testing was done by "experienced assistants under the direction of the Office of Pupil Services."[109]

RESULTS.   The Leeds data were compared with (1) the American norms for the test (a) at the same age level (b) at a level one year above (to consider the effect of beginning one year earlier in England); (2) the data on reading obtained from the Pinellas sample; (3) the data on spelling from the Jackson sample. In addition, Peterson made a number of comparisons of the types of spelling errors made by Leeds and Jackson pupils. In Table 3-3 Peterson's results as regards mean scores are summarized.

TABLE 3-3. Leeds Data Compared with Other Data

Test	Age	American norm for same age	American norm for one year older	Mean score in Pinellas	Mean score in Jackson
Paragraph meaning	7	+	−	=	0
	11	=	−	=	0
	14	=	−	−	0
Word meaning	7	+	−	=	0
	11	+	−	+	0
	14	+	=	+	0
Spelling	7	+	+	0	+
	11	+	−	0	+
	14	+	−	0	+

+ indicates Leeds sample significantly superior.
= indicates Leeds and comparison groups equal (that is, no significant difference).
− indicates Leeds sample significantly inferior.
0 indicates comparison group not tested.

The Leeds sample was superior consistently when compared with the American norms except for two measures on which there was no significant difference; paragraph meaning at ages 11 and 14. The result was in a similar direction when the comparisons were made with the American children tested either in Pinellas or in Jackson. The Leeds sample was significantly superior to the American samples on five of the nine measures. On the three measures (paragraph meaning at ages 7 and 11; word meaning at age 7) there were no significant differences. In only one measure on these two types of comparison was the Leeds sample significantly inferior: paragraph meaning at age 14.

On the other comparison—between Leeds children and the norms for American children *one year older*—the Leeds sample was still significantly superior in spelling at age 7, and it was equal in word meaning at age 14; but on the other seven measures the Leeds group was significantly inferior to the older American students.

The misspellings of Leeds children were significantly different from the Jackson samples at ages 11 and 14, the proportion of errors based on phonemic logic being higher in the former.

In his discussion of these results, Peterson cites two previous investigations that produced empirical data showing similar differences between the achievements of American and British children: Scholl[110] (Scotland) and Personke[111] (Burton-upon-Trent, England). He ties these together by citing the research of Vernon *et al.*,[112] which showed that Scottish children were academically superior to English children and that this was particularly so in spelling.

Peterson attributes the Leeds sample's superiority in word meaning to the "presumably greater emphasis on phonics."[113] He states also that "the emphasis on phonics in Leeds produces better spellers."[114] Similarly, he explains the superiority of the Pinellas 14-year-olds in paragraph meaning as follows: "On the other hand, the emphasis on meaning, characterizing the teaching of reading in Pinellas County, seems to encourage development of comprehension skills which increase with maturity."[115]

Although Peterson's argument may seem to neatly fit his data, it must be remembered that his assumption that English schools emphasize phonics at the expense of comprehension has been shown to be inaccurate. However, because of the individual freedom of schools in matters of curriculum and teaching method it is possible that the schools he selected in Leeds were unrepresentative of English education as a whole. It is often stated that phonic methods are favored more in the north of England than in the south. On the other hand, Leeds is adjacent to the county of the West Riding of Yorkshire, noted for its progressive educational approach, in which relevance of written language for the child's own understanding, communication and self-expression is stressed. One would have anticipated that the climate of education in Leeds would have felt some influence from this progressive movement in the neighboring school district.

One of the problems with Peterson's original premises and these discussions of his results in relation to methods of teaching reading is the lack of definition in the field. As we shall see in Chapter 7, terms like "phonics," "look-and-say," and "global methods" are used after the fashion of Humpty Dumpty. Each teacher has his own interpretation of them; therefore, comparisons of teaching methods can be quite misleading if one relies solely on descriptions by these labels. To relate Peterson's empirical achievement test data to teaching methods in Britain and America requires as much objective empirical observation of the latter as he gave to the former.

Another suggested explanation of Peterson's seems more feasible in the light of actual trends in English primary education:

> The superior achievement of the Leeds samples in both word meaning and spelling may be related to their daily composition period, an activity not scheduled in the Jackson schools. Requiring children to write original compositions demands that they know the meanings of words, know how to spell the words, and know how to write the words.[116]

His description makes the activity seem much more formal than is usually the case in practice in English primary schools. For example, children are *not* expected to "know how to spell the words." The emphasis rather is on creativity, expression, and relevance to the child. Spelling is important only to the extent that the child's written communication does in fact communicate. Children are encouraged not to allow themselves to be deterred from expressing what they want to say because of anxieties about formal spelling conventions. This may also explain why the children spelled more phonemically in the Leeds sample. It is a normal practice to encourage children to try to spell a word in such a way that someone else will "get the message." This may not be true of all primary schools in England, by any means, but it is certainly the generally approved policy applied in the majority of schools.

Peterson frankly admits that the data do not fit his original assumptions on one point:

> It might be assumed . . . that the somewhat more formal phonetic approach to reading in Leeds would tend to reduce variability, while the emphasis upon meaning and developmental approach of the Pinellas schools would increase variability. It has been shown, however, that the Leeds samples were significantly more variable in all comparisons at ages 7 and 11.[117]

This may be further evidence that these Leeds schools (like English primary schools in general) were neither as "formal" nor as "phonetic" in their approach as Peterson supposed.

This finding of wider variations among the 7- and 11-year-old Leeds children as compared with the American samples reconfirms the results obtained in both Pidgeon's research and in the investigation of Foshay *et al.* reviewed earlier in this chapter. Such wide variation seems to be a reliable feature of English education in comparison with the schooling provided in other countries. It may best be described as the difference between the individualized teaching aims of the schools of England and Wales and the grade system still in use in many other countries, including the United States.

Peterson's original formal hypothesis gets lost somewhere along the way, but since the Leeds sample remained superior at age 14 in word meaning and in spelling, although not in paragraph meaning, his hypothesis that "any initial advantage obtained by earlier beginning and more formal approach will disappear with the passing of time" is not supported by his data.

Even if there were no differences at age 14, such a result would not necessarily be evidence for Peterson's view that "learning to read and spell are largely matters of development rather than the outcomes of formal instruction." As we shall see in later chapters, there are very many hazards along the child's path through school from age 5 or 6 to age 14. These arise from a multitude of interacting variables that tend to cancel each other out and conceal any advantages for one educational practice over another at the 5- to 7-year-old level.

Future Research

Brimer, in his discussion of methodology (see Chapter 2) in connection with the IEA studies, looks forward to the publication of the next research by this group. Thorndike,[118] one of the IEA team, has indicated that reading achievement will be assessed in thirteen countries, including Belgium, Chile, England, Finland, India, Iran, Italy, Netherlands, Poland, Scotland, Sweden, Thailand, and the United States.

The most interesting difference between this new IEA study and the previous investigation by Foshay *et al.* is the proposed inclusion of a sample of 10-year-olds. However, this still will leave untouched the youngest age groups, which are of such vital concern for understanding the processes involved in the critical stage of the first introduction to the tasks of learning literacy.

Furthermore, the older the age level chosen for such cross-national testing, the more likely it is that variables of real importance in the development of the skills of reading and writing will be concealed. The longer the child is in school, the larger will be the number of uncontrolled variables canceling each other out and giving spuriously uniform results. Such spurious uniformity is further enhanced by the shallowness of the testing in such mass surveys. If we wish to understand better the learning-to-read process then we will need to administer a wide variety of different tests across a range of different age levels in cross-national studies.

Above all we need to inject the important scientific ingredient missing from the first two studies reviewed here—that is, theory and the hypotheses derived therefrom. There should, at least, be *ad hoc* hypotheses. Without them, one tends to get the "league table" attitude about which Brimer has warned us.

The problem of uncontrolled variables canceling each other out and being concealed by shallow testing procedures has just been noted. The three studies of cross-national achievements reviewed in this chapter all show high excellence in their technical design, although some criticisms of them have been suggested.

However, even though they effectively control the variables of well-known importance in psychology and sociology, comparatively little concern is shown for educational or linguistic variables. Because learning to read and write involves language and because this activity is commonly supposed to be learned in schools, one would anticipate more attention being given to variables in these areas. The difficulty is that, hitherto, we have not known what are the similarities and differences in the educational and linguistic environments of the literacy learner. They need cross-national research to be determined. Probably, before comparative reading studies can reveal much of interest regarding the processes of learning to read and reading, it will be necessary to undertake more basic studies to discover these important variables. In this sense, the large-scale achievement surveys such as those being conducted by IEA may be premature, because we do not know what the variables are that ought to be brought under control.

REFERENCES

1. This and the following section incorporate material from a previous article, by Downing, John, "Functional literacy: future needs and current progress," *Symposium* (1969–1970), 9–15.
2. International Bureau of Education, *The Teaching of Reading,* Paris: UNESCO, 1949, p. 13.
3. Tinker, M. A., and McCullough, C. M., *Teaching Elementary Reading,* New York: Appleton, 1962.
4. Thorndike, Edward L., "Reading as reasoning: A study of mistakes in paragraph reading," *Journal of Educational Psychology,* 8 (1917), 323–332.
5. National Society for the Study of Education, *Forty-Eighth Yearbook,* Chicago: U. of Chicago, 1949.
6. Soffietti, J. P., quoted in Staiger, Ralph C., "What is reading?" in Causey, O. S. (ed.), *The Reading Teacher's Reader,* New York: Ronald, 1958.
7. Fries, Charles C., *Linguistics and Reading,* New York: Holt, 1962.
8. Hall, Robert A., Jr., *Sound and Spelling in English,* Philadelphia: Chilton, 1961, pp. 8–10.
9. Dearden, R. F., "Curricular implications of developments in the teaching of reading," in Downing, John, and Brown Amy L. (eds.), *The Second International Reading Symposium,* London: Cassell, 1967.
10. Chao, Yuen Ren, *Language and Symbolic Systems,* London: Cambridge University Press, 1968, p. 101.
11. Downing, John, and Thackray, Derek, *Reading Readiness,* London: University of London Press, 1971, p. 10.
12. Neijs, Karel, *Literacy Primers: Construction, Evaluation, and Use,* Paris: UNESCO, 1961.
13. UNESCO, *Literacy As a Factor in Development,* Paris: UNESCO, 1965.
14. Gray, William S., *The Teaching of Reading and Writing,* Paris: UNESCO, 1956, p. 20.
15. UNESCO, *Literacy As a Factor in Development, op. cit.*
16. Harman, David, "Illiteracy: An overview," *Harvard Educational Review,* 40 (May 1970), 226–244.

17. *Ibid.,* pp. 229–230.
18. Hilliard, Raymond M., "Massive attack on illiteracy," *American Library Association Bulletin* (December 1963), 1038.
19. *The New York Times'* Service (September 14, 1970).
20. Harman, *op. cit.,* p. 230.
21. *Ibid.,* p. 228.
22. Samuels, S. Jay, "Cross-national studies in reading: The relationship between the sound-letter correspondence in language and reading achievement," in Figurel, J. Allen (ed.), *Reading and Realism,* Newark, Del.: IRA, 1969, p. 848.
23. Chase, Francis S., "Demands on the reader in the next decade," in Robinson, Helen M. (ed.), *Controversial Issues in Reading and Promising Solutions,* Supplementary Educational Monographs, No. 91, Chicago: U. of Chicago, 1961, pp. 7–18.
24. Samuels, *op. cit.,* p. 849.
25. UNESCO, *Statistics of Illiteracy,* Paris: UNESCO, 1965.
26. *Ibid.,* pp. 45, 118, and 129.
27. Pidgeon, Douglas A., "A comparative study of basic attainments," *Educational Research,* 1 (1958), 50–68.
28. *Ibid.,* p. 50.
29. *Ibid.,* p. 51.
30. *Ibid.,* p. 52.
31. *Ibid.,* p. 53.
32. Lawley, D. N., "A method of standardising group tests," *British Journal of Psychology* (*Statistical Section*), 3 (June 1950).
33. Pidgeon, *op. cit.,* p. 54.
34. *Ibid.,* p. 54.
35. *Ibid.,* pp. 54–55.
36. *Ibid.,* p. 55.
37. *Ibid.,* p. 55.
38. *Ibid.,* pp. 55–56.
39. *Ibid.,* p. 67.
40. Foshay, Arthur W., Thorndike, Robert L., Hotyat, Fernand, Pidgeon, Douglas A., and Walker, David A., *Educational Achievements of Thirteen-Year-Olds in Twelve Countries,* Hamburg: UNESCO Institute for Education, 1962, p. 7.
41. *Ibid.,* pp. 7–8.
42. *Ibid.,* p. 7.
43. *Ibid.,* p. 9.
44. *Ibid.,* pp. 11–16.
45. *Ibid.,* p. 28.
46. *Ibid.,* p. 21.
47. *Ibid.,* p. 10.
48. *Ibid.,* p. 10.
49. *Ibid.,* p. 19.
50. *Ibid.,* p. 19.
51. *Ibid.,* p. 33.
52. *Ibid.,* p. 39.
53. *Ibid.,* p. 27.
54. *Ibid.,* p. 32.
55. *Ibid.,* pp. 21–41.

56. *Ibid.,* p. 23.
57. *Ibid.,* p. 26, Figure 1.
58. *Ibid.,* p. 27.
59. *Ibid.,* pp. 43–47.
60. *Ibid.,* p. 47.
61. For example: Ministry of Education, *Standards of Reading 1948 to 1956,* Pamphlet No. 32, London: H.M.S.O., 1957; Department of Education and Science, *Progress in Reading 1948 to 1964.* Education Pamphlet No. 50. London: H.M.S.O., 1966; Morris, Joyce M., *Standards and Progress in Reading,* Slough: NFER in England and Wales, 1966.
62. Foshay, *et al., op. cit.,* pp. 61–62.
63. *Ibid.,* p. 59.
64. *Ibid.,* p. 39.
65. *Ibid.,* p. 23.
66. *Ibid.,* p. 9.
67. *Ibid.,* p. 19.
68. Peterson, Raymond P., *A Comparison of the Reading and Spelling Achievements of Groups of English and American Children,* Doctoral dissertation, University of Michigan, Ann Arbor, Mich., 1964.
69. Schonell, Fred J., and Sarjeant, Irene, *The Happy Venture Readers,* London: Oliver and Boyd, 1958.
70. O'Donnell, Mabel, and Munro, Rona, *Janet and John,* Welwyn, Herts.: James Nisbet, 1949.
71. Dixon, W. Robert, *Summary of Selected Measures of Readability for Beginning Reading Series,* Ann Arbor, Mich.: University of Michigan, 1963.
72. Peterson, *op. cit.,* pp. 1–2.
73. Flesch, Rudolf. *Why Johnny Can't Read and What You Can Do About It,* New York: Harper, 1955.
74. Rickover, H. G., *Education for All Children: What We Can Learn from England,* Hearings before the Committee on Appropriations, House of Representatives. Washington, D.C.: U.S. Government Printing Office, 1962.
75. Southgate, Vera, and Roberts, Geoffrey R., *Reading—Which Approach?* London: University of London Press, 1970.
76. Stott, D. H., "Anti-i.t.a.," *The Teacher* (January 22, 1965).
77. Glynn, Dorothy M., *Teach Your Child to Read,* London: Pearson, 1964.
78. Ohanian, Vera, "Control populations in i.t.a. experiments," *Elementary English,* **43** (1966), 373–380.
79. Southgate, Vera, and Warburton, F. W., *i.t.a.: An Independent Evaluation,* London: Murray and Chambers, 1969, p. 53.
80. Central Advisory Council for Education, *Children and Their Primary Schools* (The Plowden Report), London: H.M.S.O., 1967, p. 212.
81. Blackie, John, *Inside the Primary School,* London: H.M.S.O., 1967, p. 56.
82. Central Advisory Council for Education, *op. cit.,* pp. 218–223.
83. Blackie, *op. cit.,* p. 74.
84. *Ibid.,* p. 11.
85. Peterson, *op. cit.,* p. 5.
86. *Ibid.,* p. 7.
87. Rogers, Vincent R., "English and American primary schools," *Phi Delta Kappan,* **51** (October 1969), 71–75.

88. Featherstone, Joseph, *The Primary School Revolution in Britain,* Pamphlet reprinting of three articles in *The New Republic* (August 10, September 2 and 9, 1967), Washington, D.C.: The New Republic, 1967.
89. Peterson, *op. cit.,* p. 9.
90. Emmett, W. G., "The intelligence of urban and rural children," *Population Studies,* 7 (1954), 207–221.
91. Peterson, *op. cit.,* p. 28.
92. Blackie, *op. cit.,* p. 43.
93. Bereday, George Z. F., *Comparative Method in Education,* New York: Holt, 1966, p. 116.
94. Peterson, *op. cit.,* pp. 43–44.
95. Bereday, *op. cit.,* p. 116.
96. Peterson, *op. cit.,* pp. 44–52.
97. *Ibid.,* pp. 44–46.
98. *Ibid.,* pp. 47–49.
99. *Ibid.,* 49–51.
100. *Ibid.,* p. 55.
101. *Ibid.,* p. 77.
102. *Ibid.,* p. 60.
103. *Ibid.,* p. 65.
104. *Ibid.,* p. 67.
105. *Ibid.,* p. 77.
106. *Ibid.,* pp. 88–89, and 91.
107. *Ibid.,* p. 68.
108. *Ibid.,* p. 59.
109. *Ibid.,* pp. 59–62.
110. Scholl, Geraldine T., *The Reading and Spelling Achievement of a Group of English Children As Judged by the Standards of an American Achievement Test,* Doctoral dissertation, University of Michigan, Ann Arbor, Mich., 1960.
111. Personke, Carl Richard, *A Comparison of the Spelling Achievement of Groups of Scottish and American Children,* Doctoral dissertation, University of Michigan, Ann Arbor, Mich., 1963.
112. Vernon, P. E., O'Gorman, M. B., and McLellan, A., "A comparative study of educational attainments in England and Scotland," *British Journal of Educational Psychology,* 25 (1955), 195–203.
113. Peterson, *op. cit.,* p. 152.
114. *Ibid.,* p. 156.
115. *Ibid.,* p. 152.
116. *Ibid.,* pp. 157–158.
117. *Ibid.,* p. 159.
118. Thorndike, cited in Samuels, *op. cit.,* p. 851.

CHAPTER 4

Bases for Comparison

JOHN DOWNING

Sources of Data

THE following brief description of the methods used in the chief studies reviewed in this chapter should enable the reader to judge their worth and limitations:

1. International Bureau of Education,[1] *The Teaching of Reading,* 1949. This publication reported responses from forty-five national ministries of education. Only sixteen questions of an open-ended type were asked—for example, "What is done to help children who meet with special difficulties in learning to read (remedial teaching, individual teaching, psychological investigation, etc.)?" The responses were reported descriptively.

2. William S. Gray, *Preliminary Survey on Methods of Teaching Reading and Writing* (Parts I and II), 1953. Gray states that

> In order to secure a broad view of current methods of teaching reading, a survey was made, first, of the general literature relating to methods and, second, of approximately four hundred different sets of materials used in teaching people to read. Of the latter, more than a hundred sets for children and an equal number for adults were studied personally by the writer with the help of an interpreter when needed. Almost an equal number at each level were studied by reading specialists in the countries for which the materials were prepared. Whereas this survey was by no means inclusive, the materials examined came from all continents and most countries of the world. They are believed, therefore, to be fairly representative of the reading materials and methods used today, with the exception of a few oriental countries.[2]

The results of Gray's surveys were published in two pamphlets. His conclusions are in the form of descriptive generalizations regarding the various ways of teaching children and adults to read and write in different countries and their effectiveness.

3. William S. Gray,[3] *The Teaching of Reading and Writing,* 1956. This book incorporated and expanded the work reported in the two preliminary pamphlets. Gray provides more details of his methods of study. He obtained additional information by sending questionnaires to leaders and field workers. In addition, publishers and authors of primers, readers, and professional books were requested by letter to send certain types of information as well as examples of relevant material. Gray based his reports also on informal discussions with

65

educators from various parts of the world and visited selected centers himself. To review the instructional materials, he prepared a schedule of directions that was used by assistant specialists from twelve different language areas. Gray states that he "reviewed the results of scientific studies made in various countries on the nature of the reading process, factors that affect progress in learning to read, and the relative merits of various teaching methods." All this refers to the work reported in the two preliminary pamphlets. These were submitted to national commissions of UNESCO in member states and to "other recognized leaders in literacy training," with a request for criticisms and suggestions. In the meantime the work continued. According to Gray, "a study was made of the kinds of language used today, the kinds of characters employed in writing them, and the influence of linguistic differences on teaching methods." Also, Gray made a comparison of eye movements in readings for fourteen different languages.

The results of these additional investigations were added to the earlier work, and the latter was modified in accordance with the feedback Gray obtained from his request for criticisms and suggestions. The outcome was a book that is not only a landmark in comparative reading but also the foundation stone for the study of reading within many countries. It has been of great practical significance, too, as the starting point for national programs for improving literacy. Many of the references in this chapter will be to Gray's book.

4. W. R. Lee,[4] *Spelling Irregularity and Reading Difficulty in English,* 1960. One of Lee's studies investigated "whether the way in which a language was spelt had been taken account of in deciding upon methods of instruction or whether it had shaped these methods" and "did children learning to read the more regularly spelt languages make quicker progress?" His method of research was to ask open-ended questions in letters through the mail, followed by further mail correspondence. His original questions were, "What methods are used to teach reading? How is achievement measured? How much time is spent on reading instruction?" He invited his informants "to be as specific as possible." More than thirty countries were included. The format of Lee's reporting is descriptive and nonstatistical. His results were disappointingly inconclusive as regards his own hypotheses, but they constitute valuable information for the purposes of this book.

5. Karel Neijs,[5] *Literacy Primers: Construction, Evaluation and Use,* 1961. This is a practical handbook on how to develop instructional materials for literacy training. It is based on what were the current ideas of linguists and other specialists in the literacy field in 1961.

6. UNESCO,[6] *Simple Reading Material for Adults: Its Preparation and Use,* 1963. Several authors worked on this second practical handbook. Mushtag Ahmed prepared the first draft, and this was revised in accordance with suggestions by Seth Spaulding. Further modifications were made as a result of a workshop, and the final published version was put out as "a guide to writing methods and publishing procedures tried out and proved effective in many countries."

7. UNESCO,[7] *Literacy and Education for Adults,* 1964. This is a report of the responses from sixty-two countries to a questionnaire sent to ministries of education. It concerns itself with "action to promote literacy" and "tuition provided for adults."

8. Mary Burnet,[8] *abc of Literacy,* 1965. This nonprofessional popular description of the "problem of illiteracy and the efforts being made to deal with it" has an interesting basis in UNESCO documentation.

9. Ralph C. Staiger,[9] "Developments in reading and literacy education 1956–1967," 1969. This is an additional chapter appended to Gray's 1956 book, *The Teaching of Reading and Writing,* in its second edition. It is a review of events and publications in the field during the decade following Gray's original work. Although it is very comprehensive in its survey of publications from different countries, it does not attempt to expand Gray's original work in any other way.

10. In Part Two of this book, a number of countries have been selected as representative of varying levels of educational sophistication and contrasting cultural and linguistic environments. An expert on the reading behavior of each of these countries was asked to write a descriptive account of that behavior. This largely open-ended unstructured approach was employed to allow room for each expert to refer *spontaneously* to what struck him as being significant for the country in question. However, in addition, a list of topics was provided to insure that information would be forthcoming on matters that previously have been recognized as important in reading and learning to read. In this and succeeding chapters by this writer any reference to a particular country will be based on its relevant national chapter in Part Two of this book as the source of evidence, unless otherwise stated.

A Model for Cross-National Comparisons

Elkonin's chapter on the USSR makes the point that there is a gulf between the adult's and the child's conceptions of language, and that this arises naturally from their different levels of *experience.* Most adults have forgotten their own early struggles to understand the concepts with which they were bombarded in their childhood. Many other differences between the adult's experiential level and that of the young child get overlooked also, and this tends to make us less sensitive to individual differences in students' backgrounds. Several of the chapters in Part Two will point out the importance of differences in children's environmental experiences even within a single country. For example, in the United States the serious disadvantage of children who come from homes in which there is a severe shortage of books, pictures, magazines, and newspapers will be contrasted with more fortunate children within the same country. A more dramatic discovery of environmental differences was made in India when research on reading readiness revealed that rural children had difficulty recognizing test pictures of a fire engine or a camera—which were quite easy for city students—and that concepts of what had been assumed by the testers to be commonplace occurrences were often not understood by the village children.

The pedagogical implications of these differences in children's experiences from community to community have been pointed out by Goodman:

> Readers can't comprehend materials which are based on experience and concepts outside their background and beyond their present development.[10]

Clearly, then, our map of the different manifestations of the learning-to-read process in the fourteen countries to be studied here must guide us through the wide range of childhood experiences represented in those various cultures. We will need a model of the literacy acquisition situation to take account of the great variations that occur in the linguistic and cultural environments of children. Yet it must be a very simple model if we are to find a common basis for comparing reading across such different languages and cultures.

The diagram in Figure 4-1 is an attempt to provide a simple model of the literacy acquisition process that will be applicable to all cultural and linguistic situations.

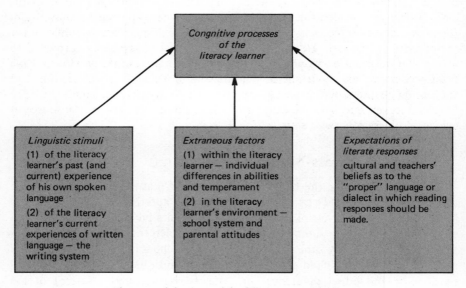

FIGURE 4-1. A model of literacy acquisition.

This book deals with all aspects of this model except one: the extraneous factors *within* the literacy learner. These have been the topic of many excellent books on the psychology of reading, but they are not part of the scope of this project. Their importance is recognized in the model and it is assumed that they will be taken into account in all the discussions that follow.

The model also shows how the literacy learner's understanding and conceptualization of the tasks demanded in literacy acquisition are assailed as it were by three kinds of "voices." First, there is the voice of his own personal experience of language, his comparatively long and still continuing experiential background of receiving and producing speech in his own language or dialect, and his current (and to a lesser extent past) experiences of the written language that now begin to loom so large in his daily life at school. Secondly, from the other side, so to speak, there are the demands of the voice of the school culture, usually represented by the teacher's instruction. These demands may relate to a different culture, language, or dialect than the first voice, and there are other possible conflicts between these first and second voices. The third part of the model is really the cacophony of many voices clamoring to be heard in the literacy learner's efforts to resolve all the various and often conflicting inputs. Although this third part is labeled *extraneous,* the factors it includes are not unimportant. On the contrary, they represent a series of hazards that can impede or even destroy the learner's efforts to acquire literacy. In the chapters that follow on various cross-national differences in the literacy learner's educational environments, we shall see how serious are the hazards sometimes caused by such extraneous factors in the child's surroundings at school, at home, and elsewhere. Other studies have been concerned with the hazards of the child's individual psychological and physiological make-up. Much more needs to be said about the environmental hazards.

Cognition in Literacy Learning

In the model the *cognitive processes* of the literacy learner have been placed at the center. This is deliberately based on two postulates: (1) there are universal psycholinguistic processes in learning to read and write in all languages and under all cultural conditions, and (2) these universals are cognitive rather than perceptual and central rather than peripheral.

William S. Gray's classic cross-national study of reading and writing specifically noted many differences between literacy learning in different languages, but he placed more stress on the similarities. His own cross-language eye-movement studies together with his review of several other investigations of this type led him to conclude that "These studies demonstrate that the general nature of the reading act is essentially the same among all mature readers."[11]

Gray's claim that mature readers of Arabic, Burmese, Chinese, English, French, Hebrew, Hindi, Japanese, Korean, Navaho, Spanish, Thai, Urdu, and Yoruba differed little in their responses measured by his eye-movement camera was not entirely supported by his data. For example, he states that "the number of words per regression reveals striking differences among languages."[12] But he found it impossible to explain these in terms of any of the features of the languages studied. Although he does not provide any precise empirical data, he concluded that "many regressions are due more to such factors as immaturity in reading, type of training received and individual perceptual habits than to the nature of the language."[13]

Furthermore, even if Gray's explanation of the differences he found in words per regression is correct—and therefore eye-movement patterns are essentially the same in all languages—we may still not be entitled to draw the conclusion that the process of literacy acquisition in each is identical.

First of all, a series of studies by Gilbert [14] showed that visual recognition time can be analyzed into peripheral-processing, central-processing, and eye-movement motor-processing time. Holmes and Singer, reviewing Gilbert's work, comment that he has "introduced three new dimensions where one existed before. Speed of reading may now be described in terms of rate of (a) input, (b) central processing, and (c) output as well as in terms of the degree to which (a) sensorimotor skills are involved in stimulus perception, (b) abilities are involved in mediation, and (c) motor skills are involved in response." [15]

Elkonin makes the point in his chapter on the USSR that one needs to look deeper than to the overt perceptual behavior of reading, such as to eye movements, if one is to understand how children acquire the skills of literacy:

> the perception and discrimination of printed characters are only the external side of the process of reading, behind which lies hidden the more essential and basic behavior, which the reader produces with the sounds of language. The speed of eye movement does not define the speed of reading. Nor does the so-called span of apprehension determine the speed of reading (that is, the number of graphic symbols perceived simultaneously). Of considerably greater importance than the speed of eye movements and the span of apprehension is the speed of those underlying more central processes concerned with the behavior of creating the sound form of the word and connected with it, its comprehension.

It may be added that also there is no evidence of isomorphism of eye movements for units of central processing, as seems to be assumed in the perceptual theory of Eleanor Gibson, who asserts for example that "Even first-graders can read 3-letter words exposed for only 40 milliseconds, too short a time for sequential eye movements to occur." [16] But, because a reader takes in several letters in a single fixation it does not necessarily mean that the individual letters are not then processed separately. As Gaspar has pointed out, the reader's scanning of the graphic array is "not necessarily performed by an overt action. . . . It may be sufficient to concentrate his attention on individual letters within his short-term memory." [17]

Moreover, the identity of eye movements in adults does not necessarily imply any identity of central processing in learning to read, as Dina Feitelson notes in her chapter in the UNESCO handbook on reading:

> While for a mature reader the skills related to identifying the written message are essentially similar irrespective of the language in which he reads, this will not be so for beginning readers. For a person who is still laboring at the early stages of trying to identify the symbols set before him, in order to translate them into language units, the relative ease or difficulty of his task will be influenced to a large extent by the features of the symbols he has to deal with, as well as by the nature of their relation to the spoken language. [18]

One cannot assume that the process of the mature reader necessarily parallels that of the novice in reading. They may be quite different.

Similarly, Thorndike's conclusion that "the universality of the reading task is affirmed"[19] may be quite meaningless in view of the fact that it is based on the results of a comprehension test administered to 13-year-olds in the various countries of that particular cross-national survey. The investigation of the specificities and universals of the learning-to-read and reading processes across cultures and languages requires a range of sensitive instruments to measure various aspects of the total skill, and these would need to be applied at much younger age levels for any such conclusion to be valid.

The chief danger in emphasizing the universals of the reading and learning-to-read processes is that it may result in a kind of "black box" theory. That is, one puts language and its written form in at one end of the box and full-blown reading comprehension comes out at the other. Because the latter appears to be "the same" in all languages and all countries (the argument might run) the language input and the central processes that follow in the black box do not really matter. By this line of thinking, we would never make any progress in understanding how people read or how children learn to read.

This black box approach leads also to another type of misconception, one that this book is particularly concerned about combating. Because the end product is "the same" and therefore the processes are too (according to these assumptions) one does not need to consider other people's languages. What is good for our language will be equally suitable for other people's. This ethnocentric or linguacentric view of literacy is all too prevalent already. It leads to an unthinking acceptance of the practices of teaching reading and writing developed in one's own country as being obviously "the best." Curiously, this view actually gets in the way of understanding the reading and learning-to-read processes in one's own language. It is virtually impossible to even begin to understand the psychology of the reading act until one is able to view these processes in the abstract, detached from their concrete and specific manifestations in one's own language. Mountford achieves this in his analysis:

> There are three important differences between articulacy acquisition and literacy acquisition. The first and chief one is that articulacy acquisition is also initial linguacy acquisition; it is the vital once for all move from non-linguacy to linguacy, taking place in the medium of speech. Literacy acquisition is only an extension of linguacy. Secondly, articulacy acquisition is spontaneous, literacy acquisition non-spontaneous .... Thirdly, by definition, articulacy is linguacy exercised in the medium of speech; literacy is linguacy exercised in the medium of writing.[20]

Mountford also points out that, in one respect,

> articulacy and literacy are parallel. Second-language learning is not the same as first-language learning. In learning to speak a second language we are not acquiring articulacy over again but extending our existing articulacy. As literates in our first language of literacy we are not, in learning to read a second language, acquiring literacy over again, but extending our existing literacy .... Literacy is acquired once-for-all, like linguacy itself.[21]

Furthermore, he writes, "One language is as good as another, one writing-system is as good as another, to establish literacy," although he recognizes that, "obviously, some functional kinds of writing-system are more suitable for literacy acquisition than others, but that does not affect the main point."[22]

Lado makes a similar comment:

> Learning to write his first language he has to master the great abstraction involved in representing the sounds of a language by marks on paper. Learning to write a second language, he already knows that marks on paper can represent sounds . . . .[23]

Lado's example provides the immediate key to the locus of the universal processes of literacy acquisition when he states that the student *knows* that marks on paper represent spoken language, that is, cognition. The learning-to-read process is essentially *a cognitive process*. In analyzing the material from the different countries represented here, it becomes clear that the apparent differences in literacy acquisition in the various countries can be related most readily to certain cognitive universals that lie beneath the surface differences of specific languages and writing systems.

Evidence for the Importance of Cognitive Processes in Learning to Read

The task of mastering the skill of reading poses a very complex problem to be solved by the child. The learning-to-read process involves a series of discoveries of solutions to the subproblems that constitute the total complex problem of finding out how to read. In other words, progress in literacy acquisition is made by a series of cognitive restructurings that result from the learner's probes made in the course of his search for solutions. Sometimes the new cognitive structure will be a correct solution, but at other times it will be in error. As the child's attempted solutions approximate more and more closely the reality of each aspect of the reading process, he will achieve more and more cognitive clarity. Therefore, the best measure of a child's progress in solving the learning-to-read problem should be his degree of understanding of the nature of the task. Thus, *cognitive clarity* will be correlated most highly with reading success, while failure in reading will have *cognitive confusion* as its chief symptom.

That cognitive confusion is indeed the most common symptom of reading failure has been clearly demonstrated by Magdalen Vernon. Her thorough and rigorous review of all the research that had been conducted on reading disability led her to conclude that, although this problem has many causes, there was one common symptom that appeared repeatedly in the various descriptions of children who had failed in their attempts to acquire the skills of literacy. Hence, she states that "there may exist different types of reading disability, produced by different factors, and different complexes of factors, in different cases."[24] So much so that "almost the only fact which appears clearly at first sight is the heterogeneity of cases of reading disability—heterogeneous both in the origin and in the nature of the disability. But there does seem to be one fairly universal characteristic of the disability, namely, the child's general state of doubt and confusion as to the relationship between the printed shapes of words, their sounds and their meanings. This confusion resembles that of a young child who is just beginning to read."[25]

Vernon expands the idea further, as follows:

We may conclude that, rather than suffering from some general defect in visual or auditory perception, imagery or memory, the child with reading disability has broken down at some point, and has failed to learn one or more of the essential processes that we have described. He therefore remains fixed at a particular point and is unable to proceed further.[26]

Vernon concludes that

Thus the fundamental and basic characteristic of reading disability appears to be cognitive confusion.[27]

She defines this condition as follows:

The child with real reading disability . . . may indeed have learnt that printed words have some relation to spoken words; and, with a few simple words, he has memorized the spoken word that corresponds to a particular shape. But he does not seem to understand why: it might be quite an arbitrary association. He appears hopelessly uncertain and confused as to why certain successions of printed letters should correspond to certain phonetic sounds in words.[28]

Vernon further found that "to make this association demands a particular type of reasoning process," and that, in reading disability, "the fundamental trouble appears to be a failure in development of this process,"[29] so that the disabled reader remains in a state of confusion over the whole process.

Cognitive clarity represents the opposite face of Vernon's description of the doubts and confusions of disabled readers. Using Vernon's original terminology, if *cognitive confusion* in the particular type of reasoning process involved in learning to read is the most common characteristic of the disabled reader, then, conversely, *cognitive clarity* ought to be the usual feature of the normal reader. The normally developing reader should come to understand why the written and spoken forms of language are related as they are. He should develop a progressively clearer understanding of why certain successions of printed letters should correspond to certain phonetic sounds in words, and Vernon's particular type of reasoning process should be observable in developmental stages, beginning with the *normal* cognitive confusion of the absolute beginner, through a series of problem-solving phases, to a later stage of *normal* cognitive clarity.

Intellectual Abilities in Reading

Indirect evidence for the central importance of cognitive development in learning to read may be adduced from the common finding of the relatively high correlation between intelligence and reading achievement. Success in problem-solving is a measure of intelligence, and, obviously, therefore, intelligence measured by such means is likely to be related to an important degree to the child's success or failure in solving the problems of finding out how to read. Vernon states that "It is clear that these processes are in themselves excessively complicated, and require a considerable degree of intelligence and insight."[30]

Earlier investigators—for example, McLaughlin,[31] Raybold,[32] Deputy,[33] Tinker,[34] and Hayes[35]—claimed that general mental ability is the most important single factor in success in learning to read. Other investigators—for example, Schonell,[36] Monroe,[37] and Stroud[38]—have urged caution in interpreting such results; but, although exceptional cases have been found, nonetheless it is generally agreed that intelligence is a vital factor in success in learning to read. In more recent studies, both Malmquist[39] in Sweden and Vormeland[40] in Norway have reaffirmed the high correlation between general intelligence and reading ability. Malmquist concludes that in his 1969 research "the relation was of such an order of magnitude that it definitely confirms the almost unanimous view expressed by previous investigators that intelligence is an important factor in the development of reading ability."[41]

The finding that correlations between reading achievement and auditory or visual discrimination are higher than between reading achievement and intelligence does not conflict with the evidence adduced here. First of all, the studies that found this—Durrell, Murphy, and Junkins,[42] Harrington and Durrell,[43] Nicholson,[44] and Thackray[45]—indicated only small differences in the correlations. Secondly, visual and auditory discrimination are, to a very important extent, *learned* abilities, that have a substantial cognitive element. It is not the ability to hear different phonemes or see different printed characters that is the difficulty in learning to read. The heart of the problem lies in the cognitive processes that enable the child to conceptualize these linguistic units and understand how the phonological code is related to the written or printed code.

Research into visual and auditory perception, therefore, has proved less fruitful than might have been anticipated according to the commonsense view that reading obviously involves seeing the differences between the characters of the writing system and hearing the different sounds of language they represent. The overemphasis on perception and discrimination has led to a corresponding neglect of cognition and categorization in the learning-to-read process. The importance of categorization in cognitive development has been stressed by Bruner *et al.*: "Virtually all cognitive ability involves and is dependent upon the process of categorizing."[46] Yet, categorizing behavior has seldom featured in research on learning to read. The focus of reading researchers' attention has been on the opposite ability, discrimination. However, at least two studies of visual discrimination have unexpectedly discovered that children who have difficulty in learning to read are *superior* in discrimination abilities to normal readers.

Solomon's research, as reported by Robinson,[47] found that the only predictive result of a Rorschach Test was the undue concern with unimportant details shown by some of her 8-year-old subjects. These children were found to be more likely to fail in reading. This may seem a surprising result according to the commonsense emphasis on discrimination in learning to read, but it would be less unexpected if this finding were related to the less obvious importance of categorizing.

More recently Serafica and Sigel reported that

> The boys with reading disability in this study do not seem lacking in an analytic ability. If the initial phase of learning to read requires differentiation of graphic symbols from one another, the non-readers were better equipped for that task than were the boys who showed no reading problems.[48]

Again, this result is surprising only if perception and discrimination are regarded as the fundamental processes of reading. If cognitive factors such as categorization are accorded their proper significance, we will not find it at all odd that disabled readers are perfectly capable of telling alphabetic letters apart from one another. Their real problem is much more likely to be their inability to categorize them in a logical relationship to the conceptual system they represent.

Their situation is reminiscent of Lado's comment about writing something in a foreign language with a strange alphabet we do not understand:

> It is rather painful to have to copy something written in an unfamiliar alphabet, because we have to copy everything slavishly, not knowing just what features are important. Copying something in our own alphabet, say English, is much easier and faster, because we do not have to imitate every symbol exactly but use the features which we know are important.[49]

The common problem of disabled readers is that they *do not know* which features are important because the underlying categories and concepts have not been developed.

Another apparently strange conflict of research results can be explained by this cognitive clarity theory of reading. A number of researchers have found from correlations between tests administered at the beginning of first grade and at the end of the school year that early letter-name knowledge is the best predictor of reading success—see, for example, Gavel.[50] Yet three different experimenters, each working independently, have found that the deliberate teaching of letter names has no effect whatsoever on other aspects of reading achievement: see Johnson,[51] Samuels,[52] and Ohnmacht.[53]

Piaget[54] and a number of other researchers have shown that the normal relationship between thought and language in concept learning is for understanding to precede verbalization. Thus, the high correlation between earlier letter-name knowledge and subsequent achievement in reading does not mean that the former causes the latter. Knowing the letter names is more likely to be merely a symptom of an underlying development of the corresponding concepts that are related to cognitive clarity in learning to read. Teaching letter names, on the other hand, may be a waste of time and effort since, as Vygotsky has pointed out, one cannot teach concepts in such a direct fashion. In his words, it "accomplishes nothing but empty verbalism." [55]

The problems of literacy learning have not been investigated directly by Piaget, although one of his subjects in *The Language and Thought of the Child* asks "Why are angels always kind to people? Is it because angels don't have to learn to read and do very nasty things?" [56] However, his theory of the development of logic in children is a general one and must be applied to the child's learning of the written form of language also. Therefore, the above-mentioned book by Piaget can provide us with an elementary starting point at least. When children are in the prereading and early reading stage with which we are chiefly concerned in this chapter, their thinking is typically in the relatively primitive stage of development that Piaget indicates as occurring before about age 7 or 8. Thus, young children learning to read may attempt to solve the reasoning problems involved in this task by a very different kind of logic than that applied by adults. Sybil Marshall has expressed her intuitive view of this important difference in colloquial terms:

> children are not solely adults in the making, but creatures in their own right, as tadpoles differ from mature frogs, or caterpillars from butterflies. [57]

As we shall see, this statement is particularly apt for describing the unique way in which young beginners think about the tasks of learning to read and write.

Vygotsky replicated and extended Piaget's original studies on the relationship between thought and language in the child's development. He made a specially important contribution by conducting a pioneer study of children's cognitive growth as it affects learning to read and write. He arrived at precisely two conclusions, both of which provide valuable guidelines for further research on this problem. Vygotsky's two conclusions were

1. It is the abstract quality of written language that is the main stumbling block.
2. The child has little motivation to learn writing when we begin to teach it. He feels no need for it and has only a vague idea of its usefulness. [58]

Vygotsky expands this in terms of his own theory and concludes that the child's "lack of skill in abstract, deliberate activity" fails to match the requirements of written language in these respects.

In summary, one would predict from Piaget's theory that there must be important differences between the young child's view of language and the way it is perceived by adults. Vygotsky's research confirms this. The young beginner does not understand the expressive and communicative purposes of written language. As Piaget showed, the child below the age of 7 or 8—an egocentric stage of development—is not so concerned about communication of any kind. Written language, because it is one step further removed from immediate concrete reality, is of still less interest as a means of communication than speaking. Piaget's theory would lead us to anticipate also that the abstract concepts and principles involved in relating written language to speech would be difficult for

young children to understand because of their limited level of cognitive development. Again, Vygotsky's research confirms this hypothesis. It is this abstract
nature of the literacy task that makes it difficult to learn the written form of
language at this stage.

More Direct Evidence

In Jessie Reid's study of some Scottish children's thoughts about reading, her
aim was "to explore the general level of concept formation with regard to
reading and writing as embodied in the 'technical vocabulary,' to follow the
growth of these concepts and form some idea of the role they may play in
the actual learning of the skills." By "technical vocabulary" she meant "the
language available to them for talking and thinking about the activity of reading
itself."[59]

Reid's method of research was to conduct a "loosely structured" interview
with seven boys and five girls in an Edinburgh school on three occasions; two
months, five months, and nine months after first coming to school. At their first
interview their ages were between 5 years 1 month, and 5 years 5 months.
Reid's purpose was "to get the children to talk and not, in any narrow sense, to
obtain information on specific points."[60] She used a core of standardized
questions, but their order varied as each individual conversation developed, and
additional probing was made as it was found necessary.

The results of Reid's first interviews led to two main conclusions. Her
Edinburgh 5-year-olds showed

1. "A general lack of any specific expectancies of what reading was going to
   be like, of what the activity consisted in, of the purpose and use of it."
2. "A great poverty of linguistic equipment to deal with the new experiences,
   calling letters 'numbers' and words 'names'."[61]

This writer conducted research on this same problem in three phases to
replicate the three interviewing phases in Reid's original study, but also to
provide evidence (1) of the level of cognitive confusion of the absolute beginner,
and (2) of the growth of cognitive clarity as the child progressed during his first
year in school. Three methods of investigation were employed: (1) a replication
of Reid's interview procedure, (2) an extension of the interview in which additional concrete stimuli were presented to the subjects—that is, concrete examples
of literacy situations and artifacts, and (3) two experiments to test the individual's
concepts of "word" and "sound" as segments of spoken language.

Reid provided additional information in a personal communication about her
original subjects and their Edinburgh school, which made it possible to find a
school in England with a similar group of children. As a result, six boys and
seven girls, aged between 4 years 11 months and 5 years 3 months, were interviewed two months after first entering the infant's reception class of a junior and
infants school in England. Care was taken to follow as closely as possible Reid's
original interview procedure.

The replicated interviews produced remarkably similar findings [62] to those Reid had published four years earlier. Some of the questions led to responses that clearly showed that these 5-year-old beginners were indeed in a state of cognitive confusion regarding the purpose and nature of the written language and how or why one should learn to use it in reading.

The use of concrete aids in the extension of the interview procedure provided further evidence of the relevance of Piaget's and Vygotsky's more general conclusions on children's thinking to the particular problem of the development of linguistic concepts in learning to read. The English 5-year-old subjects in this study achieved more in the presence of concrete literacy-related objects than they did in the purely verbal interview situation. The concrete aids facilitated motor and verbal responses that indicated how these young children were groping toward an understanding of the technical concepts of language, although they had been very much less able to use them accurately in the verbal interviews.

The results of the two experiments showed that the categories "word" and "sound" were very poorly understood by these 5-year-old beginners. A word for five of these thirteen children was not a category they could use in discriminating between the auditory stimuli presented. Three children had begun to connect word with human utterance, five more had progressed a little farther to connect it with a meaningful human utterance. But none thought of it as that segment of human speech that adults think of as a word.

The term "sound" was still more poorly understood. About half of these children could make no use of this category. Three children associated it with any human utterance. Only two children had a narrow category for sound. One of these used it to classify noises as not human. The other added phonemes to this category. Not one child thought of a sound as being exclusively the phoneme —as a teacher might in this context of the teaching of reading.

The child's cognitive confusion over these technical terms of language seems likely to be the result of his previous experience of language and of such terms. Human utterance is not segmented neatly into words. In groping for the meaning of the term "word," perhaps the most obvious segment is a chunk of meaning, so "ham and eggs" can just as well be a word as "cheese." The child's experience with the term "sound" is even more likely to cause confusion. In everyday life the term "sound" is used by people for a variety of noises. Indeed, its technical meaning for the teacher of reading is its rarest form in the child's experience. Furthermore, the child's past experience of spoken language does not encourage an awareness of such segments as the word or the phoneme (sound). Pauses within words are sometimes longer than the pauses between words, and the phoneme is rarely heard in isolation.

Growth of Cognitive Clarity

Thus it has been demonstrated that cognitive confusion about the purposes and nature of the tasks of literacy learning and behavior is the normal condition of the young beginner. These subjects were children in a skilled working-class neighborhood, and one would anticipate perhaps higher levels of understanding in children from homes where reading behavior was more frequently practiced by their parents. Nevertheless, even if it occurs somewhat earlier in such children, the child must still pass initially through this stage of cognitive confusion.

The second and third phases of this research showed how cognitive clarity grew in some of these subjects and the individual differences in this development. A minority remained in a state of cognitive confusion even at the end of the year. The others made varying degrees of progress toward cognitive clarity regarding the task of learning to read. These children's responses, as the year moved on, were like the clearing of fog. Gradually, out of their initial confusion, came a clearer and clearer understanding of the nature of the learning and problem-solving tasks they were required to undertake.

Only twelve children were used in this longitudinal analysis because one of the original thirteen subjects moved away from the school soon after phase 1 of the research was completed. Even at the end of the first year at school only one child used the category "a word" in the experiment in any way resembling its technical use by teachers when they talk about language in reading. Three children used the category "a sound" exclusively for the phoneme in the second experiment at phase 2, and by phase 3 four children did so. But other children varied their responses in the "word" and "sound" experiments from phase 1 to phase 2 and from phase 2 to 3 in ways that indicated movement toward a greater understanding of these concepts, or at least the systematic testing of hunches about them.

An analysis of the subjects' individual differences in their response changes from phase to phase in the two experiments suggested their division into three groups according to their rate of development of cognitive clarity:

Group 1: The more rapid developers made fewer random responses. Their categories of word and sound were more sharply limited, and they were closest to being correct in their concepts of these linguistic units. This group consisted of three boys and three girls.

Group 2: The intermediate, slowly developing children made more random responses, but there were some indications of a reduction in this randomness in the later phases. This group included one boy and two girls.

Group 3: The slowest group, showing very little, if any progress. Random responding or lack of discrimination typified their responses at all three phases of the research. Two boys and one girl belong in this group.

These faster, intermediate, and slowest developing groups of children were found to differ in their responses in the interviews and with the various concrete stimuli, too. The more progress they made toward cognitive clarity in regard to the concepts of word and sound according to the experimental data: (1) the better the children understood the communication purpose of the written form of language, (2) the clearer was their conception of the symbolic function of writing, (3) the better they understood the processes of decoding and encoding that relate written to spoken language, (4) the further advanced was their development of linguistic concepts, and (5) the better was their command of the technical terminology for such abstract units of language.[63]

Recently the initial phase 1 research was repeated in two separate studies in Victoria, British Columbia, with substantially the same results as those obtained in England. Also, another large-scale research project was conducted as part of an attempt to construct a group test of conceptual readiness for reading in first-grade children. This test is one of a number of batteries developed for a new Canadian reading-readiness test. One finding seems quite clear: the conceptual readiness test was found to be highly correlated with the test of letter-name knowledge. This is further evidence of the real meaning of the correlation between letter-name knowledge and reading achievement—that is, as a surface indicator of the underlying level of cognitive clarity.[64]

Another independent research report related to these findings was published soon after the study in the English infant school was completed. Meltzer and Herse conducted a series of experiments on the boundaries of written words as seen by American first-graders and some kindergarten children. Their experiments included asking children to use scissors to cut written words off a sentence printed on a card. They also found evidence of confusion in children regarding the meaning of the term "word."

Meltzer and Herse propose the hypothesis that "the incorrect cues to word boundaries used by these children can be considered a logical result of the reading materials to which they were exposed and to their progress in these materials."[65] The children in their study had been using readers in which the words were usually of five letters or less in length and the sentences were very brief, giving many capital letters. Hence, the tendency to divide long words and combine short words and to use "tall" letters as an indication of the boundary.

This fits the explanation given here for children's difficulty in conceptualizing the word as a unit of *spoken* language—it depends on the spoken language to which he has been exposed. The human utterances he customarily hears are not segmented into words. There are no spaces of time between the spoken words. Hence, it is not surprising that children do not understand this concept.

Some of the responses in the phase 3 interviews of both Reid and this writer suggest that the first inkling of the meaning of the term "word" comes only when children have had considerable experience of the written word in reading. "The spaces stop the words from getting stuck together," might be the typical first real insight of the child. At the same time, in analyzing his own speech for the purpose of writing he may learn to isolate the words and separate them in their written representation by larger spaces than those between the letters within words.

The practical implications of these findings have been pointed out in two previous articles.[66] All too often, teachers assume that the purpose of literacy and the meaning of the linguistic concepts they use in talking about reading and writing are just as obvious to their young pupils as they are to them. These things seem so self-evident to the adult that they cannot imagine the child having difficulty understanding them. This leads Elkonin to comment in his chapter on the USSR that:

> The arrangement of a succession of sounds in a word, as well as the discrimination of a single sound in a word, seems an extraordinarily simple act for a normal literate adult. This illusion arises from the fact that, at this higher level of development, the operation occurs by then as abbreviated, generalized, perfected, and automatic mental behavior which requires no effort and causes no problems. But the truth is that this is only the final form of the process of sound analysis of a word.

The child is in a very different situation. He has no conscious notion of such segmentation and ordering of the parts of an utterance, even though his own utterances fit the logic of the analysis that adults make of his speech.

Thus, the evidence from several areas of research—reading disability, correlational studies of abilities related to reading, and intensive studies of the thinking and conceptual development of young beginners—seems to indicate the importance of cognitive factors in literacy acquisition.

Motivation

However, it must be admitted that another set of psychological processes is of such importance also that it vies for pride of place in the model proposed for this comparative study. This is the *motivation* of the literacy learner. Some of the studies cited here could almost equally well have been quoted in support of an argument for making motivation the chief factor in success and failure in learning to read: Vygotsky's and Reid's findings of the child's inability to understand the purpose of the written form of language, and Piaget's conclusion that the child before 7 or 8 years of age is comparatively uninterested in communication with others.

It seems reasonable in the logic of the model to include these motivational influences in its extraneous factors within the individual compartment, although obviously many of the causes of motivation within the individual come from the student's environmental experiences. In the chapters that follow there will be frequent occasions to ponder these motivational factors, for clearly the place of literacy in a culture's priorities in education and the different ways in which these are implemented are bound to exert different motivational pressures on the learner. Therefore, before we begin the major task of relating environmental and linguistic experiences to the literacy learner's cognitive development, it seems appropriate to consider these special influences of cultural differences that may affect the acquisition of literacy skills either directly through cognitive processes or more indirectly in motivation. In the chapter that follows, Gaston Blom and Lawrence Wiberg set out to test whether such cultural differences can be demonstrated empirically through the attitude content of the basal readers of different nations.

REFERENCES

1. International Bureau of Education, *The Teaching of Reading,* Paris: UNESCO, 1949.
2. Gray, William S., *Preliminary Survey on Methods of Teaching Reading and Writing* (Parts I and II), Paris: UNESCO, 1953.
3. Gray, William S., *The Teaching of Reading and Writing,* Paris: UNESCO, 1956.
4. Lee, W. R., *Spelling Irregularity and Reading Difficulty in English,* London: NFER in England and Wales, 1960.
5. Neijs, Karel, *Literacy Primers: Construction, Evaluation and Use,* Paris: UNESCO, 1961.
6. UNESCO, *Simple Reading Material for Adults: Its Preparation and Use,* Paris: UNESCO, 1963.
7. UNESCO, *Literacy and Education for Adults,* Paris: UNESCO, 1964.
8. Burnet, Mary, *abc of Literacy,* Paris: UNESCO, 1965.
9. Staiger, Ralph C., "Developments in reading and literacy education 1956–1967," Chapter XIII of Gray, William S., *The Teaching of Reading and Writing,* 2nd ed., Paris: UNESCO, 1969.
10. Goodman, Kenneth S., "Dialect barriers to reading comprehension," In Baratz, Joan C., and Shuy, Roger W. (eds.), *Teaching Black Children to Read,* Washington, D.C.: Center for Applied Linguistics, 1969, p. 25.
11. Gray, *The Teaching of Reading and Writing, op. cit.,* pp. 59–60.
12. *Ibid.,* p. 58.
13. *Ibid.,* p. 59.
14. Gilbert, Luther C., "Speed of processing visual stimuli and its relation to reading," *Journal of Educational Psychology,* **50** (February 1959), 8–14.
15. Holmes, Jack A., and Singer, Harry, "Theoretical models and trends toward more basic research in reading," *Review of Educational Research,* **34** (April 1964), 127–155.
16. Gibson, E. J., "Learning to read," *Science,* **148** (1965), 1066–1072.
17. Gaspar, R., *The Prediction of Errors in the Reading of English on the Basis of Misleading Analogies in English Spelling,* Master's thesis, University of London, 1964.
18. Feitelson, Dina, "Learning to read," in *UNESCO Handbook for Reading,* Paris: UNESCO, 1972.
19. Thorndike, Robert L., "International comparison of the achievement of 13-year-olds," in Foshay, A. W., *et al., Educational Achievements of Thirteen-Year-Olds in Twelve Countries,* Hamburg: UNESCO Institute for Education, 1962, pp. 21–41.
20. Mountford, John, "Some psycholinguistic components of initial standard literacy," *Journal of Typographic Research,* **4** (Autumn 1970), 295–306.
21. *Ibid.,* pp. 297–298.
22. *Ibid.,* pp. 298–299.
23. Lado, Robert, *Linguistics Across Cultures,* Ann Arbor: University of Michigan Press, 1957, p. 106.
24. Vernon, M. D., *Backwardness in Reading,* London: Cambridge University Press, 1957, p. 186.
25. *Ibid.,* pp. 186–187.
26. *Ibid.,* p. 189.
27. *Ibid.,* p. 71.

28. *Ibid.,* pp. 47–48.
29. *Ibid.,* p. 48.
30. *Ibid.,* p. 188.
31. McLaughlin, K. L., *First Grade Readiness and Retardation,* Los Angeles: The Research Committee of the California Kindergarten-Primary Association, 1928.
32. Raybold, E., "Reading readiness in children entering first grade," *Third Yearbook of the Psychology and Educational Research Division,* School Publications No. 185, Los Angeles: Los Angeles City School District, pp. 98–101.
33. Deputy, E. C., "Predicting first grade reading achievement," *Contributions to Education,* No. 426, New York: Teachers' College, Columbia University, 1930.
34. Tinker, M., "Diagnostic and remedial reading," *Elementary School Journal,* **33** (1932), 307.
35. Hayes, E., "Why pupils fail," *Educational Method,* **13** (1933), 25–28.
36. Schonell, F. J., *Backwardness in the Basic Subjects,* Edinburgh: Oliver and Boyd, 1942.
37. Monroe, M., *Children Who Cannot Read,* Chicago: U. of Chicago, 1932.
38. Stroud, J. B., *Psychology in Education,* New York: Longmans, 1956.
39. Malmquist, E., *Textning och vanlig skrivstil, Experimentella studier,* Research Reports No. 14, Linköping, Sweden: National School for Educational Research, 1969.
40. Vormeland, O., *Begynnerundervisningen i norsk og regning,* cited in Malmquist, E. (See reference 41 here.)
41. Malmquist, E., "A decade of reading research in Europe, 1959–1969: A review," *Journal of Educational Research,* **63** (1970), 309–329.
42. Durrell, D. D., Murphy, H. A., and Junkins, K. M., "Increasing the rate of learning in first grade reading," *Education,* **62** (1941), 37–39.
43. Harrington, Sister M. J., and Durrell, D. D., "Mental maturity versus perception abilities in primary reading," *Journal of Educational Psychology,* **46** (1955), 375–380.
44. Nicholson, A., "Background abilities related to reading success in first grade," *Journal of Education, Boston University,* **140** (1958), 7–24.
45. Thackray, Derek V., *Readiness to Read with i.t.a. and T.O.,* London: Geoffrey Chapman, 1970.
46. Bruner, Jerome S., *et al., A Study of Thinking,* New York: Wiley, 1956.
47. Robinson, Helen M., *Supplementary Educational Monographs* No. 77, Chicago: U. of Chicago, 1953.
48. Serafica, Felicisima C., and Sigel, Irving E., "Styles of categorization and reading disability," *Journal of Reading Behavior,* **2** (Spring 1970), 105–115.
49. Lado, *op. cit.,* p. 95.
50. Gavel, S. R., "June reading achievement of first-grade children," *Journal of Education, Boston University,* **140** (1958), 37–43.
51. Johnson, R. J., *The Effect of Training in Letter-Names on Success in Beginning Reading for Children of Differing Abilities,* paper presented at the AERA convention, Minneapolis, 1970.
52. Samuels, S. J., *Letter-Name Versus Letter-Sound Knowledge As Factors Influencing Learning to Read,* paper presented at the AERA convention, Minneapolis, 1970.
53. Ohnmacht, D. D., *The Effects of Letter-Knowledge on Achievement in Reading in the First Grade,* paper presented at the AERA convention, Los Angeles, 1969.

54. Piaget, Jean, *The Language and Thought of the Child,* rev. ed., London: Routledge and Kegan Paul, 1959.
55. Vygotsky, Lev S., *Thought and Language,* Cambridge, Mass: MIT Press, 1962.
56. Piaget, *op. cit.,* p. 189.
57. Marshall, Sybil, *An Experiment in Education,* London: Cambridge University Press, 1963, p. 106.
58. Vygotsky, *op. cit.,* p. 99.
59. Reid, J. F., "Learning to think about reading," *Educational Research,* 9 (November 1966), 56–62.
60. *Ibid.,* p. 57.
61. *Ibid.,* p. 58.
62. Downing, John, "Children's concepts of language in learning to read," *Educational Research,* 12 (February 1970), 106–112.
63. Downing, John, "Children's developing concepts of spoken and written language," *Journal of Reading Behavior.* (In press.)
64. Evanechko, Peter, Ollila, Lloyd, Downing, John, and Braun, Carl, "Defining reading readiness for better prediction," *Reading Research Quarterly.* (In press.)
65. Meltzer, Nancy S., and Herse, R., "The boundaries of written words as seen by first graders," *Journal of Reading Behavior,* 1 (Summer 1969), 3–14.
66. Downing, John, "The development of linguistic concepts in children's thinking," *Research in the Teaching of English,* 4 (Spring 1970), 5–19. And Downing, John, "Relevance versus ritual in reading," *Reading,* 4 (June 1970), 4–12.

CHAPTER 5

Attitude Contents in Reading Primers[1]

GASTON E. BLOM and J. LAWRENCE WIBERG

THIS study stems from an initial interest in reading disabilities in American school children. The assumption has been made that content is an important contributing factor to the specific problem of reading retardation and disorders and the more general problems of motivation in influencing children to read (Blom et al.[2]; Waite et al.[3]; Zimet et al.[4]). While studying the motivational content of United States primers, these writers were impressed by the presence of certain attitudes and values in the story content. Such attitudes recurred with sufficient frequency and consistency that there seemed to be an established attitude profile characterizing them. "Attitude" was defined as an attribute or characteristic, either personal or impersonal, to which value, such as good–bad, superior–inferior, desirable–undesirable, useful–not useful, wanted–unwanted, important–unimportant, could be affixed. The question was raised if primers from other countries, like the United States, presented attitude profiles characteristic of the given country that would be measurably different in cross-national comparison. Assuming (1) the content of primer reading materials is a way in which cultural, interpersonal, and individual attitudes and values are communicated to children, and (2) national differences do exist between primers of different countries, a clarification of such differences would contribute information about national characteristics in socialization and personality and about psychological and cultural influences on reading instruction in particular and educational systems in general.

Method

An attitude scale and manual for instruction in its use were devised to systematically code and characterize the attitude content of primer stories. A long checklist of attitudes and values and their corresponding synonyms was obtained (Henry[5]). On both *a priori* and empirical bases, the dimensions were reduced and clustered into forty attitudinal sets. These sets were arranged into three groups: *cultural posture, other-directed posture,* and *inner-directed posture:*

Attitudinal Sets

A. *Cultural Posture*
  1. Oldness
    Traditionalism
    Antiquity
    Ancient times

2. Recognition of other countries' nationalities, ethnic groups, and cultures

3. Family togetherness

Attitudinal Sets [cont.]

4. Reference to economic transaction

5. War
   Warfare
   Militarism
   Weaponry

6. Peace
   Pacifism
   Armistice

7. Nationalism
   Patriotism

8. Religiousness
   Devotion to God

9. Education in schools

10. Social regulation and structure
    Social rules and laws

11. Recognition or portrayal of death or realistic danger
    Infirmity
    Illness or injury

12. Presence of food or drink

B. *Other-Directed Posture*

13. Caring
    Helping, aiding, assisting
    Nurturing
    Protecting

14. Uncaring
    Unhelping
    Neglecting, disregarding

15. Selfishness, possessiveness
    Greediness
    Not sharing

16. Conforming, complying
    Compromising, conceding
    Acquiescing, consenting

17. Nonconforming
    Uncompromising, unyielding
    Disagreeing, disputing
    Being obstinate

18. Independence

19. Role Playing
    Learning (not necessarily classroom)
    Imitation (copying others)

20. Working
    Laboring
    Toiling

21. Play
    Sport
    Recreation
    Amusement (as an activity not an affect)

22. Obedience in relation to authority
    Deference in relation to authority

23. Disobedience in relation to authority
    Defiance in relation to authority

24. Interactional physical aggressiveness

25. Interactional passivity

26. Competitiveness
    Rivalry

27. Cruelty
    Meanness, maliciousness
    Tormenting (beyond teasing)
    Ruthlessness

C. *Inner-Directed Posture*

28. Exploring
    Curiosity
    Discovering
    Inquiring

Attitudinal Sets [cont.]

29. Ambition
    Striving, aspiring
    Persistence
    Initiative

30. Lassitude
    Laziness
    Lack of ambition

31. Motor competency
    Motor dexterity
    Agility

32. Motor incompetence
    Motor ineptness
    Clumsiness
    Physical carelessness

33. Intelligence
    Alertness
    Cleverness
    Capableness
    Attentiveness

34. Ignorance
    Inalertness
    Stupidity
    Intellectual incompetence

35. Cleanliness
    Orderliness
    Neatness
    Tidiness

36. Dirtiness
    Disorderliness
    Sloppiness
    Untidiness
    Disorganization

37. Courage, bravery
    Daringness, boldness
    Valor
    Fortitude
    Fearlessness

38. Cowardice
    Unheroic
    Uncourageous
    Faintheartedness

39. Physical strength
    Powerfulness
    Stoutness, brawniness

40. Physical weakness
    Physical impotence
    Lacking in physical power

The cultural posture group contained twelve attitude sets that captured how people live in terms of environmental settings, features of a country, collective symbols, and the like. The other-directed posture group consisted of fifteen attitude sets that identified various interactional behaviors between characters or groups of characters. The inner-directed posture group had thirteen attitude sets describing attitudes that motivated or guided the behavior or characterized behavioral responses of an individual character or a homogeneous set of characters.

Primers used in this study consisted of a complete collection of United States publications and a recently acquired collection of foreign primers currently in use from twelve other countries: France, Great Britain, India, Israel, Italy, Japan, Mexico, Norway, Russia, South Korea, Turkey, and West Germany. An attempt was made to obtain a representative sample of series from each country.

Illustrations and translated word content were used as a basis for attitude ratings. It was recognized that there would be a disadvantage in using translated material and in employing scales based on English word usage and on an

American cultural frame of reference. This has probably introduced an American bias in the findings.

The experimental units of the study were the individual stories in each primer. They were well defined by titles, illustrations, and plots. A total of sixty stories was randomly sampled for each country, except for South Korea for which only forty-six were available. Certain countries, such as the United States, England, and West Germany, had a wide selection of primers available to their children. In some instances, there was a marked disproportion in the amount of material available for analysis from any given country. When a small number of primers was available, all the stories were analyzed. For countries with a large selection of primers, the total population of stories were randomly sampled in a stratified manner so as to include proportional amounts of all publication series.

From the very nature of the attitude scales and the material to which they were applied, difficulty was encountered in achieving high inter-rater reliability between independently rated textbook reading material. *A priori,* overlap and ambiguities in attitudes were eliminated in the coding manual. Two raters were then trained on pilot material.

It was possible to approach the measure of reliability from two directions. If one considered that the raters made an "attitude present" or "attitude absent" decision on each of the forty scales, a reliability of greater than 95 per cent agreement was achieved. If, however, one considered only the agreements once an attitude had been identified by one of the raters as "present," the reliability fell to a minimum of 75 per cent. A measure of true reliability was then between these two extremes (95 and 75 per cent). Disagreements were resolved in a group conference with the authors. The data that were used for the analysis reported in this paper represent consensus data.

Results

The data are empirical and descriptive; they were not intended to be productive of hypothesis support or rejection. However, one general hypothesis was made: attitudes standardized and defined with an English-speaking American bias would differ in frequency of presentation in the content of primer stories in a country by country comparison. The data support this hypothesis. The data are presented in a way to illustrate cross-national differences. The body of the data is somewhat detailed and each facet will not be discussed, rather the reader is invited to compare specific attitude differences between specific countries that might be of particular interest to him.

In Table 5-1 the countries are listed in rank order according to the frequency of presentation of the total number of attitudes in primer content coded by the scales. The number of attitudes are counted from a sample of sixty stories in each country except South Korea, where the results are based on a projected sample of sixty. What is of particular interest is the indication of a certain universality of our English-speaking American-biased scales; the United States ranked eight in number of codable attitudes, an unlikely outcome if the scales were too attuned to an American conception of important attitudes and values.

TABLE 5-1. Frequency Attitudes Rated and Rank Order for Thirteen Countries

Country	Rank	Frequency
South Korea	1	456
India	2	433
England	3	316
Mexico	4	310
Japan	5	295
Norway	6	290
Russia	7	281
United States	8	271
West Germany	9	269
Italy	10	267
Israel	11	251
Turkey	12	251
France	13	248

TABLE 5-2. Partitioned χ^2 Comparison of Countries on Three Attitude Postures ($p < .01$)

Cultural posture

Israel (45%)

India (38%)

S. Korea (36%)
Turkey (33%)

France (31%)
Mexico (30%)
Japan (29%)
Italy (29%)
W. Germany (29%)
Norway (28%)

Russia (21%)
England (19%)

USA (15%)

R (range) = 30% SDD (statistical delineated difference) = 4

Other-directed posture

USA (56%)
_____

        France (55%)
        Mexico (52%)
        England (50%)
        Japan (49%)
        Norway (47%)
        Russia (47%)
        _____

                S. Korea (46%)
                Italy (46%)
                Turkey (45%)
                W. Germany (44%)
                India (42%)
                Israel (40%)
                _____

$R = 16\%$ $SDD = 1$

Inner-directed posture

Russia (32%)
England (31%)
_____

        USA (29%)
        W. Germany (26%)
        Italy (26%)
        Norway (25%)
        _____

                Turkey (22%)
                Japan (22%)
                _____

                        India (20%)
                        S. Korea (18%)
                        Mexico (18%)
                        France (14%)
                        Israel (14%)
                        _____

$R = 18\%$ $SDD = 2$

Table 5-2 gives a breakdown of frequencies of presentation of cultural, other-directed, and inner-directed attitude sets. The per cent value accompanying each country refers to the per cent of the total values rated in the given country that fell in the cultural, other-directed, or inner-directed sets. The partitioned chi square test, described by Castellan[6] with $p < .01$, was applied; the countries are separated along the horizontal axis as represented by the underlines to visually demonstrate where differences between countries exist. When one country is directly aligned with or overlaps another country or group of countries there is no statistically significant difference. Complete separation on the horizontal axis connotes difference.

Table 5-3 presents comparative data on twenty-eight of the forty attitudes that had a meaningfully high frequency of presentation of the attitude in some of the countries and also demonstrated statistically significant differences between various countries as measured by the partitioned chi square test ($p < .01$).

TABLE 5-3. Partitioned χ^2 Comparison of Countries on Twenty-eight Attitudinal Sets ($p < .01$)

Oldness
Traditionalism

S. Korea (42)

    India (34)

        Japan (17)
        Israel (16)
        Italy (15)

            W. Germany (11)
            France (9)
            Norway (7)
            England (6)

                Turkey (3)
                Mexico (3)

                    Russia (2)

                        USA (1)

| *Recognition of* | *War* |
| *cultural differences* | *Weaponry* |

S. Korea (7)   S. Korea (8)
                     Mexico (7)

    Russia (6)
    England (6)
    Mexico (5)   India (4)
    Norway (4)
    Italy (4)   Norway (2)
    Turkey (3)   Italy (2)
    Israel (2)   Russia (2)
    W. Germany (1)   Japan (2)
    Japan (1)   England (1)
                     Israel (1)
        USA (0)   France (1)
        India (0)   Turkey (0)
        France (0)   USA (0)
                    W. Germany (0)

$R = 7$ $SDD = 1$ $R = 8$ $SDD = 1$

Family togetherness

India (17)
S. Korea (17)
<hr>
    W. Germany (13)
    USA (11)
    Israel (9)
    Norway (8)
<hr>
        England (7)
        Turkey (5)
        France (4)
        Mexico (4)
<hr>
            Japan (3)
            Russia (2)
            Italy (2)
<hr>

$R = 15$ $SDD = 2$

Nationalism

S. Korea (19)
India (14)
<hr>
    Mexico (6)
    Turkey (5)
    Israel (5)
    Russia (5)
    W. Germany (2)
    Italy (1)
    Norway (1)
    Japan (1)
    France (0)
    England (0)
    USA (0)
<hr>

$R = 19$ $SDD = 1$

Religiousness

India (27)
Israel (24)
<hr>
    Italy (8)
    W. Germany (8)
    Norway (4)
    Japan (4)
    England (2)
    Mexico (1)
    Russia (0)
    USA (0)
    S. Korea (0)
    France (0)
    Turkey (0)
<hr>

$R = 27$ $SDD = 1$

Reference to economic transaction

India (12)
Mexico (9)
<hr>
    Japan (7)
<hr>
        Turkey (4)
        France (3)
        Norway (2)
        Italy (1)
        W. Germany (1)
        England (1)
        USA (1)
<hr>
            Russia (0)
            S. Korea (0)
            Israel (0)
<hr>

$R = 12$ $SDD = 2$

Education in schools

S. Korea (29)

    Japan (24)

        Turkey (16)
        Israel (15)
        Mexico (14)

            W. Germany (9)
            Italy (7)
            France (7)
            Norway (7)
            India (6)
            USA (4)
            Russia (3)
            England (0)

$R = 29$ $SDD = 2$

Presence of food or drink

India (35)

    Norway (29)
    France (29)

        Turkey (28)
        Israel (27)
        England (26)
        W. Germany (26)
        S. Korea (25)
        Mexico (23)

            Italy (21)
            Japan (19)
            Russia (16)

              USA (15)

$R = 20$ $SDD = 3$

Recognition of death or infirmity

France (22)

        Russia (18)
        Mexico (16)
        Turkey (16)
        Norway (12)
        Israel (12)
        Italy (12)
        S. Korea (12)
        England (11)
        India (11)

            W. Germany (8)
            Japan (6)
            USA (5)

$R = 17$ $SDD = 1$

Selfishness, possessiveness

S. Korea (12)

        USA (7)
        India (6)
        Italy (6)

            W. Germany (4)
            Turkey (3)
            Mexico (3)
            Norway (3)
            England (3)
            Russia (2)
            Israel (2)
            France (1)
            Japan (1)

$R = 11$ $SDD = 1$

Caring, nurturing

USA (45)
India (44)
_____

       Mexico (37)
       S. Korea (35)
       Turkey (33)
       England (32)
       Italy (31)
       Russia (31)

              Israel (30)
              Norway (30)
              Japan (30)
              France (28)

                     W. Germany (22)

$R = 23$ $SDD = 2$

Uncaring, neglecting

England (9)
_____

       Italy (8)

              USA (6)
              India (4)
              Turkey (3)
              W. Germany (3)
              Japan (3)
              Norway (2)

                     Russia (1)
                     Mexico (1)
                     France (1)
                     S. Korea (0)
                     Israel (0)

$R = 9$ $SDD = 2$

Conforming, compromising

S. Korea (22)
_____

       India (18)
_____

           Norway (10)

              Italy (8)
              Russia (6)
              Mexico (6)
              W. Germany (5)
              England (5)
              Turkey (4)
              Japan (3)
              Israel (2)

                   France (1)
                   USA (0)

$R = 22$ $SDD = 3$

Imitation, role playing

S. Korea (26)

      Japan (18)
      Turkey (15)

            Israel (12)
            Mexico (12)
            Italy (10)
            Russia (10)
            England (10)
            USA (9)
            W. Germany (9)
            India (9)
            Norway (8)
            France (7)

$R = 19$ $SDD = 1$

Obedience in relation to authority

India (12)

      USA (7)

            Israel (5)
            Norway (4)
            Japan (4)
            Mexico (4)
            France (3)
            W. Germany (3)
            England (3)
            Italy (1)
            Turkey (1)
            S. Korea (1)
            Russia (1)

$R = 11$ $SDD = 1$

Working

Mexico (35)
India (35)
S. Korea (34)

      France (27)
      Russia (25)
      Japan (25)
      Israel (24)

            Norway (22)
            USA (19)
            Italy (17)
            Turkey (16)
            W. Germany (13)

                 England (11)

$R = 24$ $SDD = 2$

Playing

France (44)

      S. Korea (40)
      England (39)
      Mexico (36)
      India (33)
      W. Germany (32)

            Japan (29)
            Norway (28)
            USA (25)

                 Turkey (20)
                 Russia (17)
                 Italy (16)

                      Israel (13)

$R = 31$ $SDD = 3$

Physical aggression

England (22)

Russia (19)
S. Korea (19)

USA (13)
Japan (13)
W. Germany (12)
Mexico (11)
Norway (9)
France (8)

Turkey (7)
India (7)
Italy (7)
Israel (5)

$R = 17$ $SDD = 2$

Competitiveness

S. Korea (9)

England (6)
Mexico (6)
W. Germany (5)
India (5)
France (4)
USA (4)
Italy (3)
Israel (3)
Japan (3)
Russia (2)

Norway (1)
Turkey (1)

$R = 8$ $SDD = 1$

Exploring, discovering

W. Germany (16)
USA (16)
England (15)
S. Korea (14)

Japan (12)
Russia (10)
Norway (10)
India (8)
Israel (7)
Italy (7)
Mexico (7)
Turkey (6)

France (2)

$R = 14$ $SDD = 1$

Ambition, initiative

England (17)

Russia (15)
W. Germany (13)
Japan (10)
India (9)
Norway (8)

Mexico (7)
USA (7)
Italy (7)
Israel (6)

Turkey (4)
S. Korea (3)
France (2)

$R = 15$ $SDD = 2$

Intelligence, alertness

USA (15)

India (12)

Italy (9)
England (8)
Norway (8)
Russia (7)
W. Germany (5)
Japan (5)
Turkey (4)
Mexico (4)

Israel (2)
France (1)
S. Korea (1)

$R = 14$ $SDD = 2$

Ignorance, incompetence

USA (18)

England (16)

India (15)

W. Germany (7)
Norway (7)

Turkey (5)
Russia (5)
Israel (4)
Japan (3)
Mexico (3)
France (2)
Italy (2)
S. Korea (1)

$R = 17$ $SDD = 3$

Cleanliness, orderliness

S. Korea (49)

Turkey (16)
W. Germany (13)
England (13)
Japan (11)
Mexico (10)
France (9)
India (9)
Israel (9)
Russia (9)
Norway (8)
Italy (7)
USA (6)

$R = 43$ $SDD = 1$

Cowardice

W. Germany (7)

Russia (6)
England (6)
USA (6)
India (4)
Norway (3)
Israel (2)
Mexico (2)
Italy (1)
France (1)

S. Korea (0)
Japan (0)
Turkey (0)

$R = 7$ $SDD = 1$

Physical strength

Russia (17)
_____

      Italy (9)
      _____

            Mexico (6)
            England (5)
            S. Korea (5)
            Turkey (4)
            Japan (4)
            India (4)
            USA (3)
            France (2)
            W. Germany (2)
            Norway (2)
            _____

                  Israel (1)

$R = 16$ $SDD = 2$

Physical weakness

Russia (13)
_____

        India (7)
        Italy (6)
        Norway (6)
        Turkey (6)
        England (6)
        _____

            Japan (5)
            W. Germany (5)
            S. Korea (4)
            USA (2)
            Mexico (2)
            France (2)
            _____

                  Israel (0)

$R = 13$ $SDD = 2$

These results will be considered set by set in terms of posture groups, and a working definition of the particular attitude set will be included. As in Table 5-2, the countries are again separated along the horizontal axis to connote statistical differences between countries or groups of countries. The number in parentheses refers to the frequency (F) of presentation based on sixty stories.

Cultural Posture

Oldness and traditionalism is intended to capture a story's orientation to the past, recognizing the influence of oldness or tradition on the present. It was scored when an old person was present in the story and also when customs or nonhuman items clearly referred to the past or oldness. In Table 5-3 the range

(R) is forty-one frequency points and there are five significantly statistical delineated differences (SDD).

Recognition of cultural differences denotes the recognition in the story of different countries, different nationalities, and the existence of different kinds of people (R = 7, SDD = 1).

Family togetherness defines the presence of a nuclear family unit in a story: father, mother, and child or children (R = 15, SDD = 2).

Reference to economic transaction refers to the depiction of an economic transaction or recognition of economic worth in a material sense (R = 12, SDD = 2).

War and weaponry is applicable to any story in which allusions to war are present. That weaponry is included means that the set applies not only to warfare between countries but also to conflict between police and criminals, hunter with weapon, and the like (R = 8, SDD = 1).

Nationalism is coded in stories that recognize or depict an awareness of the country to which the primer belongs. Flags, national heroes, national holidays, loyalty to country, and so on, are codable content (R = 19, SDD = 1).

Religiousness refers to any mention or illustration of religion. Sometimes this is the entire theme of the story, and at times it is a background clue such as a Buddha, or a church steeple (R = 27, SDD = 1).

Education in schools is coded when any reference to schools or schooling is made. A classroom or school building may be illustrated or children may be carrying schoolbooks (R = 29, SDD = 2).

Recognition of death or infirmity is applicable when there is a general recognition of death or life-threatening situations, including all forms of illness or injury (R = 17, SDD = 1).

Presence of food or drink refers to eating or any illustration or mention of food or drink for animals or humans, but not for plants. By convention, live animals are not considered food (R = 20, SDD = 3).

Other-Directed Posture

Caring and nurturing refers to any character caring and helping another character. It is to be considered an action and distinguished from the effect of care or love (R = 23, SDD = 2).

Uncaring and neglecting applies to a story in which a character in relation to another is being remiss in attending to, voluntarily not caring, or not regarding the needs of others, or withholding aid and attention (R = 9, SDD = 2).

Selfishness and possessiveness refers to interaction when one asserts over another ownership and control of property or power. It refers to being acquisitive in a material sense, to insist on more than one's share, acquiring out of proportion to one's own needs, taking or stealing other than for survival (R = 11, SDD = 1).

Conforming and compromising consists of one's adapting his behavior to facilitate harmonious interaction in a way stronger than to imply mere cooperation. A certain "giving in" is necessary (R = 22, SDD = 3).

Imitation and role playing refers to adult–child, older sibling–younger sibling, or master–pet interactions of imitating, copying, or learning from the more experienced individual. Emulation or role playing on the part of the inferior or inexperienced is emphasized ($R = 19$, $SDD = 1$).

Working is scored when animate characters are involved in roles or activities for remuneration or in reference to an occupation. It is considered present when remuneration is not involved and when the quality of "toiling" is present, such as children doing chores or father chopping wood for a campfire ($R = 24$, $SDD = 2$).

Playing is coded in relation to the activity of amusement, recreation, or sport. It may be solitary or with other ($R = 31$, $SDD = 3$).

Obedience in relation to authority applies to obedient interactional behavior between authority-subject pairs (boy–dog, parent–child, king–subject) and goes beyond mere compliance with authority ($R = 11$, $SDD = 1$).

Physical aggression refers specifically to aggressive physical behavior between characters, and may or may not be hostile ($R = 17$, $SDD = 2$).

Competitiveness applies to activity where one contends in rivalry or strives with another to equal, excel, or be rewarded ($R = 8$, $SDD = 1$).

Inner-Directed Posture

Exploring and discovering is coded when one inquires into, has his interest excited, or displays an eagerness to learn and find out by asking or investigating ($R = 14$, $SDD = 1$).

Ambition and initiative implies a person desiring and acting for advancement, attainment, power, and honor. It varies from a 3-year-old trying to master roller skating to an adult relating to a dream of a better home, job, or country ($R = 15$, $SDD = 2$).

Intelligence and alertness is defined as a keenness in intellectual activity appropriate to the character's age and ability to meet and solve problems, and an ability to comprehend and deal effectively with new situations ($R = 14$, $SDD = 2$).

Ignorance and incompetence is coded when a character displays a lack of knowledge or awareness and not having the appropriate intellectual skills of his age group ($R = 17$, $SDD = 3$).

Cleanliness and orderliness implies being free from dirt, soil, and disorder and applies to such activities as washing, sweeping, putting away, and counting. It means to be clean and free from clutter and the act of doing so ($R = 43$, $SDD = 1$).

Cowardice refers to a character showing a lack of courage, responding with fear or alarm out of proportion to the stimulus, and an unwillingness to take risk ($R = 7$, $SDD = 1$).

Physical strength addresses itself to an emphasis on demonstrated "physiologic" strength and size, being muscular, physically powerful, having physical superiority, and sturdiness (to be distinguished from emotional or psychological strength) ($R = 15$, $SDD = 2$).

Physical weakness refers to a character lacking in strength, being deficient in vigor, being delicate in material or construction, and lacking power ($R = 7$, $SDD = 1$).

A third way to look at the results is to consider the frequency of presentation of each of the twenty-eight attitude sets from Table 5-3 across the entire population of stories. In Table 5-4 the attitudes are listed in rank order according to the number of times the attitudinal set was coded. There is a fairly wide range of frequency with one rather large breakpoint between the first four and the remaining twenty-four sets.

TABLE 5-4. Frequency of Presentation of Attitudinal Sets for All Thirteen Countries in Rank Order

Attitudinal Set	Rank	Frequency
Caring, nurturing	1	428
Playing	2	372
Presence of food or drink	3	318
Working	4	303
Cleanliness, orderliness	5	169
Oldness, traditionalism	6	166
Recognition of death or infirmity	7	161
Imitation, role playing	8	155
Physical aggression	9	152
Education in schools	10	134
Exploring, discovering	11	130
Ambition, initiative	12	108
Family togetherness	13	102
Conforming, compromising	14	90
Ignorance, incompetence	15	88
Intelligence, alertness	16	81
Religiousness	17	78
Physical strength	18	64
Physical weakness	18	64
Nationalism	20	60
Competitiveness	21	52
Selfishness, possessiveness	22	50
Obedience in relation to authority	23	46
Uncaring, neglecting	24	41
Reference to economic transaction	25	39
Recognition of cultural differences	25	39
Cowardice	27	38
War, weaponry	28	28

It is also useful to consider which attitude sets brought out the most differences between countries. In looking at Table 5-3, it is noted that some attitude sets had greater ranges (R) and more statistically delineated differences (SDD). An arbitrarily defined descriptive statistic, FD (factor of differentiality) was devised to combine R and SDD values for each set:

$$FD = R + 20\,(SDD)$$

Using this formula, FD values are listed in rank order in Table 5-5 giving information as to which values maximized cross-national differences such as oldness and traditionalism (rank 1), playing (rank 2), conforming and compromising (rank 3), and so on.

TABLE 5-5. Twenty-eight Attitudinal Sets Rank Ordered on "Factor of Differentiality" $(FD = R + 20\,(SDD))$

Attitudinal Set	Rank	FD
Oldness, traditionalism	1	141
Playing	2	91
Conforming, compromising	3	82
Presence of food or drink	4	80
Ignorance, incompetence	5	77
Education in schools	6	69
Working	7	64
Caring, nurturing	8	63
Cleanliness, orderliness	8	63
Physical aggression	10	57
Physical strength	11	56
Ambition, initiative	12	55
Family togetherness	12	55
Intelligence, alertness	14	54
Reference to economic transaction	15	52
Uncaring, neglecting	16	49
Religiousness	17	47
Imitation, role playing	18	39
Nationalism	18	39
Recognition of death or infirmity	20	37
Exploring, discovering	21	34
Obedience in relation to authority	22	31
Selfishness, possessiveness	22	31
Physical weakness	22	31
Competitiveness	25	28
Cowardice	26	27
Recognition of cultural differences	26	27
War, weaponry	28	25

Discussion

In a previous publication, Wiberg and Blom[7] reported results on a cross-national study of six countries using the same attitude scales and statistical analyses. It can be seen that these procedures were also fruitfully applicable to the data from a large number of thirteen countries in the present study. In the previous study, the findings were related to cross-national findings of other authors using different methods and materials for analysis. The findings on thirteen countries resulted in twenty-eight statistically significant discriminative attitudes, while those of six countries provided seventeen discriminative attitudes. Therefore, it is possible to obtain significant differences in the attitude content of primers from various foreign countries.

Even though the attitude scales were originally constructed from American primers, it is clear that they applied to the large number of countries studied. In fact, seven of the thirteen countries had higher attitude scores than the United States. It would seem that other countries use their primers for socialization of attitudes far more frequently, especially South Korea and India.

From Table 5-2 the data suggest that Israel displays cultural-posture attitudes in high frequency. These consist largely of traditionalism, religiousness, education in schools, presence of food or drink, and recognition of death or infirmity. In contrast, the United States is lowest in the presentation of cultural attitudes. All of the countries are more other-directed than inner-directed, as reflected in the content of their primers. This may be the result of a uniform emphasis being placed on how one gets along with others in social interaction. However, there are considerable differences among the countries as to what other-directed attitudes are stressed.

Table 5-3 presents data on twenty-eight of the forty attitude sets. It is perhaps no surprise that South Korea and India are high on traditionalism while the United States and Russia are strikingly low. India and Israel are high on religiousness while Russia, the United States, South Korea, France, and Turkey have no religiousness. Education in schools is stressed by South Korea and Japan, while this is low in the United States, Russia, and England. Caring and nurturing exists in all the thirteen countries with the United States and India highest and Germany the lowest. When one compares the frequencies of working and playing, both Russia and Israel stress work over play while other countries are either more equal or stress play over work (Germany, Norway, the United States, South Korea, and England).

No doubt the study of an individual society is exceedingly complex and the task is magnified when attempting to make meaningful statements as to differences or similarities between societies concerning stereotypes, moral systems, child rearing, and the like. The systematic study of attitudinal content in reading primers appears to be an important step toward making such statements.

REFERENCES

1. This investigation was supported by a grant from the National Institute of Child Health and Human Development (HDO-03775-01) and in part by the National Institutes of Health Research Facilities (FR-00404-01) from the Division of Research Facilities and Resources. Foreign primers were obtained through the helpful

cooperation of the United States Information Agency. We are indebted to Mrs. Marilyn Hepting for valuable assistance in preparation of the material, to Dr. Donald Stilson for statistical consultation, and to Mrs. Elaine Duchesne and Miss Constance Lunde who did the ratings of primer content.

2. Blom, Gaston E., Waite, R. R., and Zimet, S. G., "Content of first grade reading books," *The Reading Teacher,* **21** (1968), 317–323.

3. Waite, R. R., Blom, Gaston E., Zimet, S. G., and Edge, S., "First grade reading textbooks," *Elementary School Journal,* **67** (1967), 366–374.

4. Zimet, S. G., Blom, Gaston E., and Waite, R. R., *A teacher's guide for selecting stories for children—The content of first grade reading textbooks,* Detroit, Mich.: Wayne State University Press, 1968.

5. Henry, J. A., "A cross-national outline of education," *Current Anthropology,* **1** (1960), 267–305.

6. Castellan, N. J., "On the partitioning of contingency tables," *Psychological Bulletin,* **64** (1965), 330–338.

7. Wiberg, J. Lawrence, and Blom, Gaston E., "A cross-national study of attitude content in reading primers," *International Journal of Psychology,* **5** (1970), 109–122.

CHAPTER 6

Cultural Expectations

JOHN DOWNING

IN the preceding chapter by Blom and Wiberg it is demonstrated that reading materials do differ from one culture to another in respect to attitudinal content. It seems reasonable to infer that such differences may have important repercussions in the experience of literacy learners, both in the cognitive and motivational domains. Cross-cultural studies have shown quite clearly the systematic relationship between the culture pattern of a society and the basic personality and mode of cognitive functioning of the children who are reared according to the institutions in that pattern. However, there exists only limited evidence of the influence of cultural values and expectations on children's learning of literacy.

Goody[1] finds evidence of many social influences on the extent of literacy within cultures. For example, a very common cause of restriction on literacy has been the preservation of secrecy as in religious or magical books. Goody concludes that "such restrictive practices tend to arise wherever people have an interest in maintaining a monopoly of the sources of their power,"[2] for example, the Bārots of Gujarat, a caste of genealogists in north India who are extremely secretive about their books because of their fear that unscrupulous rivals may drive them out of business.[3]

Thus, it cannot be taken for granted that universal literacy is either expected or even desired in all cultures. Reading experts in some countries where the value of universal literacy is regarded as self-evident (in the United States for example), often seem to make this ethnocentric assumption. That it is quite unwarranted is clear from the many contrary examples quoted by Goody. Of particular interest is his discussion of the way in which literacy is restricted by making the written code too difficult for the majority of people to learn easily or effectively:

> The situation of socially restricted literacy is often similar to the technological restrictions imposed by non-phonetic systems of writing, where the sheer difficulties of learning the skill mean that it can be available only to a limited number of people.[4]

Goody regards the Chinese writing system as a particularly apposite illustration of this cultural restriction on literacy. He cites a great deal of evidence from both foreign and Chinese scholars to this effect. For instance, Cheng Ch'iao, the Sung dynasty (A.D. 960–1280) encyclopaedist, recognized that "the world is of the opinion that people who know ideographs are wise and worthy, whereas those who do not know ideographs are simple and stupid."[5]

Goody concludes that China "stands as an extreme example of how, when a virtually non-phonetic system of writing becomes sufficiently developed to express a large number of meanings explicitly, only a small and specially trained professional group in the total society can master it, and partake of the literate culture."[6]

A very frequent problem in literacy is the inertia of written language in comparison with its spoken form and cultural values. Thus, Communist China today does have the national aim of universal literacy, but the Chinese writing system, which previously served well to restrict literacy, is now regarded by many people as a hindrance to cultural aspirations. Mao Tse-tung declared, in 1951, that "The written language must be reformed; it should follow the common direction of phoneticization which has been taken by the world's languages."[7] Chou En-Lai[8] also has spoken in favor of reforming the Chinese writing system. One important benefit he predicts in the universal literacy that this hopefully would facilitate is the unification of the Chinese subcultures through the standard Chinese dialect on which the new alphabetic system would be based.

The belief in equal rights to share in the literary culture of a society has also been related to the writing system of a language. Diringer[9] has called the alphabetic writing system democratic in contrast to other more restrictive systems. Goody[10] points out that "the ease of alphabetic reading and writing was probably an important consideration in the development of political democracy in Greece." However, alphabets vary in their degree of alphabeticism. For example, in Finnish the alphabet is a highly consistent code for the phonemes of that language, whereas English orthography is much less regular in this respect. Furthermore, the complexity of English orthography is due to a large extent to the inertia of written language. When one considers the social history of England and the late development of a national goal of universal literacy there, the hypothesis that twentieth century aims in the English speaking countries are hampered by a writing system more suited to the purpose of restricting literacy cannot be dismissed lightly. The lag between the national goals in literacy and the development of the writing system may be a problem that differs only in degree from one culture to another. When the language and writing systems are shared by several nations the lag may be more serious. For instance, the current "Right to Read" policy of the United States is still operating with a writing system that was developed in England when this "human right" would have been vigorously denied there.

The dramatic contrast between cultures that restrict literacy and those that have the aim of universal literacy serves to alert us to the possibility of other less obvious cultural influences on literacy learning. The data collected in this study do indicate that different cultural priorities have important effects on the teaching of literacy. For example, in Germany reading is "not considered to be a serious problem." In Finland, in 1968, only eighteen full-time special teachers were employed for teaching reading disability cases. Norwegian educators seem curiously detached from reading, almost as if it hardly occurs to anyone to be anxious about it. It is not clear why literacy is not regarded as a serious problem in these countries. It seems to be generally believed that children just do not find it difficult to learn to read in these countries and the chapters on Finland and Germany advance comparative explanations for this. These may reflect the facts, but it remains possible that this lack of a perceived problem may arise from cultural attitudes toward literacy that do not emphasize its importance as much as elsewhere.

Other authors in Part Two make comments about reading in their respective nations that suggest a greater display of national concern, the degree varying from nation to nation. The most extreme positive care for problems of literacy is found in the United States. The vast majority of the world's research, scholarly articles, and theoretical and professional books on reading is sited in the United States. The IRA had its origins in the United States and Canada, and its permanent headquarters are in America. Every aspect of the child's educational environment that is influenced by public educational agencies displays the tangible results of the deepest and most extensive national concern. The following extracts from the chapter on the United States are representative of the public anxiety over this problem in that country:

1. Reading was established as the educational goal of highest priority by former U.S. Commissioner of Education Allen when he launched the "Right to Read" program as a target for the 1970s.

2. Even more recently (1970), a National Reading Council was established to advise the U.S. Office of Education and other government agencies on priorities in the "Right to Read" effort. Headed by a board of trustees drawn from many segments of society, members of the National Reading Council include representatives from business and industry, as well as from diverse professional and lay groups. The council is expected to direct and operate a National Reading Center whose primary purpose is to coordinate all the many activities. . . .

3. Within the past several years, the U.S. Office of Education has allocated nearly $12 million for 257 separate reading research projects. Large additional sums have been invested in support of reading research through the Educational Laboratories and the Research and Development Centers.

Makita[11] has suggested that one cause for the size of the American reading problem may be the difficulties in learning to read in the English language that arise from the complexity and apparent (at least) irregularity of grapheme-phoneme relations in its writing system. Another reality explanation for the American anxiety about reading may be the unusual seriousness of its problems of bilingualism and subcultural dialects. Still another factor that may be pointed out is the economic prosperity that the United States has enjoyed. Americans may have more resources available for investment in literacy. Although it seems impossible to decide what weight should be given to these arguments, one fact remains clear: the United States displays much more concern regarding literacy than does any other country. The American culture seems to value the skills of reading and writing very highly indeed.

Japan also clearly places a high value on reading, but this does not seem to arise from learning problems or failure. For example, there is a sophisticated concern for problems that might pass unnoticed in other countries. Whereas in Britain or America the term "nonreader" implies someone who *cannot* read, in Japan it is used for those who can but *do not* read. TV entertainment is seen as a serious cause of nonreading. Perhaps the most remarkable indication of the Japanese combination of high achievements with serious concern for remaining problems of literacy is their inclusion of "excessive readers" in their classification of children who are "problem readers." This suggests that difficulties in learning how to read are not necessarily the only or even the prime cause of a national emphasis on reading and writing behavior.

In Great Britain, an increasing national concern for the problems of literacy standards has been apparent in recent years. Survey data indicate that teachers believe strongly that not enough is being done, particularly in the training of teachers of reading. This is in a country with a sophisticated school system and comparatively high levels of literacy. In India, which has a very different background, dissatisfaction has been expressed increasingly also by teachers, teacher trainers, and other educators regarding students' poor standards of reading. Very great efforts are being made to improve these standards in the face of numerous serious difficulties of all kinds in India. Perhaps this should be contrasted with the situation in Argentina, which also is faced with great practical difficulties, but where concern and anxiety on a national basis appear to be less in evidence.

France seems to be ambivalent about reading. Official pronouncements give high priority to the teaching of reading for example, "The essential teaching at this age is reading. The first grade is, above all, a course in reading." Yet, official practical provisions seem paradoxically complacent despite research evidence of a very high failure rate. University concern for reading seems to be nonexistent. Reading is neglected in the elementary school teacher's training. Little help is available from manuals or professional books on the subject. Remedial treatment for reading disability is scarce and undeveloped even where it exists. In this case, it seems that the declared high value placed on universal literacy is not paralleled by actions. It is a puzzling situation.

The ways in which literacy is restricted to an elite class have been noted earlier, but sometimes restrictions follow different lines. A high value may be placed on literacy in a culture, but it may be a customary belief that a certain part of the community is less in need of literacy than the rest. The most common form of this discrimination is along sex lines. Historically, in many European countries, girls received less literacy training than boys. Today this same trend still persists in many countries. Furthermore, there seem to be other cultural variations in differential attitudes toward boys and girls that may affect their literacy learning behavior.

Downing and Thackray reviewed the evidence on the causes of sex differences in reading readiness and early reading and concluded that they are "not due to physiological sex differences. It is much more likely to be the effect of the different ways in which boys and girls are brought up and educated."[12]

The American literature on reading is almost unanimously agreed that it is much more difficult to teach boys to read than girls. For example, in the United States 70 to 90 per cent of disability cases are boys. American studies of normal samples of the population show a similar advantage for the girls. Dykstra and Tinney compared 1,659 boys with 1,624 girls from schools in four areas of the United States, and their results clearly justify their conclusion:

> This study yielded further support to the mass of evidence which demonstrates that girls have more advanced visual and auditory discrimination abilities at the readiness stage and are superior in reading ability, spelling ability, conventions of language (usage and punctuation) and arithmetic computation through the second grade.[13]

However, comparisons of the American data with those from other countries make us pause in leaping to the conclusion that these differences in the scholastic achievements of boys and girls are caused by innate constitutional factors related to the physiological differences between the sexes. In some countries, girls are superior to boys, as in the United States, but in others there is no clear difference in their abilities, while in still others the boys are superior.

In France, at centers for reading disability treatment, referrals of boys outnumber those for girls. A Japanese investigation found more boys than girls were disabled readers. But they found little difference in their reading of the Kanji script.

In Britain, the evidence is somewhat conflicting. Some studies confirm the American finding that girls are superior to boys, but the carefully conducted official national surveys and Joyce Morris'[14] important investigation found, if anything, that boys were ahead. However, Morris did report that more boys than girls were placed in special groups for retarded readers.

In several countries boys clearly have the advantage. In Germany, Preston[15] found boys were superior. Statistics on literacy in India show a much higher proportion of males than females achieve literacy, 35 and 13 per cent, respectively. Abiri's[16] large-scale reading experiment in Nigeria found that Yoruba boys achieved superior results to those of the girls.

The cultural causation may be traced as follows. In the chapter on India it is stated that "Social causes are also an important factor in girls dropping out of school—betrothal, and the unwillingness of parents to send grown-up girls to a mixed school." In Nigeria, too, girls have poorer school attendence records than boys. As Downing and Thackray noted, in that country "if some chore needs doing around the homestead, the girl is kept at home to do it, while the boy is allowed to go to school."[17] The fact that the attendance of girls at school in India and Nigeria is less than that of boys would explain the boys' superior achievements in reading in those countries, but the important point to note here is that the girls' poorer attendance is determined by cultural factors.

This encourages us to seek a cultural explanation for the opposite result in countries such as the United States. It has been remarked often that American boys are expected and thereby encouraged to spend more time and energy on muscle activities, whereas sedentary types of behavior are thought to be more proper for girls. Also girls are expected to speak "better" than boys, and this "better" language is more like the formal "good" English found in their school reading primers. If an American father sees his daughter reading a book he is likely to approve, but if his son indulges too much in reading he is more inclined to ask him why he is not out playing a ball game. Furthermore, in the American culture, the teaching of school beginners is thought to be the role of women, and boys may find it less appropriate to model their behavior on their teacher's. All these factors in American culture may readily account for the general superiority of girls in learning to read in the United States. At the very least, it can be concluded that if there are any innate constitutional differences between girls and boys that affect their development of language and reading skills, they can be outweighed by other factors, as they must have been in countries like Germany, Nigeria, and India.

Another cultural dividing line that may exclude a section of the community from the full development of literacy is racial. "Racial" differences in reading achievement also are not necessarily determined by hereditary factors any more than are the differential attainments of girls and boys. The essential basis of the difference between the reading achievement of black as compared with white Americans, for example, is subcultural. Black Americans have gone to schools that were primarily designed for white Americans. Often the black people have quite simply been given inferior educational treatment, because they have been held unworthy of literacy. They didn't "need" to be able to read and write for the low caste role in society for which they were destined. But, even now, when their equal rights are more overtly recognized, the subcultural difference between black and white continues to favor superior literacy in the latter. While "standard" English is "good" black dialect is inferior, substandard, and even "wrong." This attitude is reflected in teacher behavior and instructional materials. The white Anglo's cultural and linguistic experience outside school is closer to the content and language used in teaching him to read. A serious mismatch exists between the black child's experiential background and what he is expected to learn in school. Whereas the white Anglo is expected to learn to read and write his own language, the black child is, in effect, being required to undertake the much more difficult task of gaining his first literacy skills in a second language.

Thus, in these so-called racial differences in reading behavior, one sees again the powerful effect of cultural forces. Clearly, the black child's experience in learning to read must be quite different from that of the white Anglo in the United States. Similar subcultural divisions are likely to be an important influence on literacy in other countries. But, as regards national awareness of this problem, there seem to be great differences from one country to another. The United States during the past decade has shown much concern for "disadvantaged" subcultures. Efforts are being made to improve the teaching of reading in all minority groups. Such a strong concern for subcultural minorities is much less evident in most other countries, although it is clear that the same problem must exist elsewhere, even if it is less serious in degree. Thus, minority-group membership may involve different experiences in learning to read in, say, Great Britain from what it does in the United States.

Sometimes a more overriding aim puts literacy in a position of less importance. In three countries the teaching of reading is put in the perspective of the total *mental health* of the child. In Norway, great importance is attached to the child's "school readiness" (not "reading" readiness). Children who are not ready for school may not begin until 8 years of age. Even the normal starting age is late compared with other countries (in Great Britain 5 is the legal age of entry and there are no school-readiness provisions). Children under 7 in Norway may apply to come to school earlier, but only after a strict medical and psychological examination. Then, if they are found to be sufficiently mature for school work, they may be permitted to start school in the year they reach their sixth birthday. Norwegian educators emphasize also that school must give the child a relaxed and cautious start in reading. Similar attitudes seem to prevail in Denmark. Grade I begins at age 7, and the principle applied at all levels is that the central concern must be the learner that is, the whole person, not some limited segment of his development, such as reading. School readiness is an important feature of Swedish education, too. Seven is the normal starting age, but, if school readiness tests show the child to be too immature for school, entry can be postponed until he is 8. Earlier entry is possible, but only in very unusual cases and only if the child has a tested developmental age of at least 7 years—intellectually, emotionally, and physically. The weight given to the basic motive underlying these practices in Norway, Denmark, and Sweden is indicated by the following comments by the Swedish member of our team:

1. The risk that an "underaged" child will fail in his first contact with schoolwork is otherwise considered to be too great. It is extremely important for the personality development and mental health of the child that the contact with the school be positive from the very beginning.

2. The school must allow them a calm and cautious start in reading. It pays to "waste time" by using a very quiet and slow tempo and a very careful and richly varied method in the early learning stages. Growth in reading cannot be hurried above capacity level without some fatal and far-extending effects. The total personality development of the child may be hurt.

Although it is true that many psychologists and educators in other countries would agree with Malmquist's recommendation, their views more often represent a minority opinion. For example, currently in the United States, there is increasing pressure to introduce *formal* instruction in reading at earlier and earlier ages in kindergarten. The fact that American school systems are ready to hand over responsibility for such activities to outside contractors whose financial profits are determined by children's reading-test scores is clear evidence of the remarkable difference in national educational values that exists between the United States and such countries as Denmark, Norway, and Sweden. Of course, there is danger in such generalizations and the present pressure for early reading achievements in the United States is opposed by many educators there. For example, Goodman writes ironically that

> As long as the ends are spelled out in behavioral goals and the contractor promises to achieve these goals, never mind the bed-wetting, self-esteem, anti-social acts, or effects on other areas of learning.[18]

But, despite such protests, the "accountability" notion and "performance contracting" are spreading relentlessly in American education without showing much concern for the nonperformance mental health outcomes stressed by Goodman.

Nevertheless, in spite of individual differences in the attitudes of people within each nation, the fact remains that pressures on the child to learn literacy skills are much greater in some countries than others. There are clear indications that this is based on cultural values. In the scale of values reading gets a higher priority in some cultures than it does in others. The risk of emotional disturbance due to pressure to learn to read at an early age is considered seriously in some countries but is more or less disregarded in others.

Nor is the comparative priority given to reading in the scale of educational aims the only variation found in these studies. In other cases, the child's experience is affected by the different purposes of literacy that are emphasized in various cultures. Such purposes may differ from time to time in the historical development of education within one country. For example. Staiger[19] has shown how the aims of literacy changed within the United States. In the seventeenth and eighteenth centuries reading instruction was closely related to the Bible and religious materials, and from the end of the eighteenth century until about 1840 there was more concern for patriotic and moral behavior in children's reading. Neither of these purposes is much emphasized today. However, they are related to reading currently in other countries. The purpose of Bible reading in Israel has great significance for reading instruction in Hebrew. The chapter on Japan gives more space to the uses of literacy in moral development and attitude change than do most of the other national chapters. In a special section headed "influence of the content of books," topics such as "soundness of mind," "improving oneself," "social behavior" are used in considering children's reports of books read "in the lower elementary school," for instance. In this connection it seems notable that bibliotherapy appears to have aroused greater interest in Japan than in most other countries. In India, cultural values and ideals are being carefully considered in the new reading materials being developed there currently.

Further evidence of cultural differences in the purposes of literacy learning is the lack of agreement among experts from different countries as to what exactly is meant by such terms as "reading" and "literacy." The purpose of reading and the reader's conception of it have an important influence on learning to read. Therefore, these cultural variations in purpose cannot help but influence the child's experience of reading. They are likely to constitute an important variable in his educational environment.

Time and Facilities Provided for Instruction

Dolores Durkin's well-known article on research on reading readiness in the United States has the title "Children who learned to read at home";[20] it records cases of children who made progress in learning to read prior to any formal teaching. In Finland it is traditionally accepted that parents have a role in beginning literacy training before their children start school. Therefore, it seems legitimate to regard school factors as extraneous to the essential formula; linguistic stimuli—literacy learner's cognitive processes—expected literate responses. Nevertheless, a child's experiences in literacy learning are likely to be importantly affected by the proportion of his childhood that is spent in school and the facilities that his society deems appropriate to provide.

Initiation to School and Reading

The age at which the child has his first experience of school and reading varies greatly from one country to another. The report of the International Bureau of Education published by UNESCO in 1949 provided a list of countries beginning reading at different ages. The range was quite wide, from age 5 in such countries as Lebanon and Uruguay, to age 7 in Afghanistan, Ecuador, and Sweden, for example. However, these differences were not explained.

A lack of precision in the data on this problem should be recognized. The actual age of initiation to some kind of schooling may not coincide with the legal age for compulsory attendance. Often there are kindergartens, and voluntary attendance may be extensive or very limited. Furthermore, the activities in kindergarten may or may not be related to formal learning of the three Rs.

Early starters among the nations included in Part Two are Great Britain, Israel, and Hong Kong. The early age for a compulsory beginning in Britain was chosen almost accidentally in 1870. The reason for Israel's selection of age 5 as the beginning of compulsory education is not stated. Possibly the British custom in this respect had some influence when the British mandatory administration gave way to the new independent state in 1948. Similarly, Hong Kong, where 4- and 5-year-olds are introduced to reading and writing the Chinese characters in kindergarten, is a British colony, and so one may anticipate influence from Britain here also. In Britain itself, the starting age is often even younger than 5.

The opposite extreme is exemplified in the very late start at age 7 in Sweden, Denmark, Finland, and Norway. In Finland it used to be even later. Only in 1921 was it made obligatory to start at age 7. Previously the beginning age had been 9, although more and more communities had introduced the earlier starting age before it became law. Age 7 really is the true age of commencing any formal introduction to reading in school because Finnish kindergartens teach no reading at all. The same is true in Denmark, where "kindergarten is *not* a pre-school institution for *training* children for school." In Norway, the same pattern holds, and a similar attitude, at least, prevails in Sweden.

Traditionally, Finnish parents have had the responsibility for reading instruction before their children entered school, formerly at age 9 and even after this when it was lowered to 7—although one of the reasons quoted for lowering the age from 9 to 7 was that the parents were not very effective teachers. The absence of reading instruction in the Finnish kindergarten is explained by its different function in Finland as compared with some other countries. In Finland, kindergartens come under the Ministry of Social Affairs. Their facilities are considered more as social service than as education, and they are intended mainly for children from poor and broken families. In Norway, too, the central authority responsible for kindergartens is the Ministry of Family and Consumer Affairs.

Earlier in this chapter reference was made to the way in which reading is given a relatively low priority in some of these countries because of the higher value placed on the total development of the child's personality and his general mental health. Finland may have been influenced in a similar way. Certainly, there have been many cultural contacts between Finland and Sweden. Another possibility is that geographical and climatic conditions may have been a factor in determining the late age of beginning school in Finland. The sparse population used to be more scattered across a country where the long period of severe winter weather made travel very difficult over roads that were poor in former times. It was not feasible for very young children to journey far to school. The difficulty of travel in Norway has also influenced the pattern of educational institutions. But these geographical conditions would not seem to apply to the same extent in Denmark. It may be concluded, therefore, that the late start in these countries is due chiefly to different attitudes (1) toward children and (2) toward literacy in their cultures. There is no cultural pressure for precocious literacy behavior, and the educational institutions reflect this lack of motivation quite systematically.

A frequently reported trend in the national chapters of Part Two is the move toward lowering the age of entry to school. This downward trend is particularly marked in the United States. The conventional age when American children start school is 6, and for many years it was contended that a mental age of 6 or $6\frac{1}{2}$ was a prerequisite for learning to read. However, during the 1960s this outlook underwent a revolutionary change. The 1961–1962 survey quoted in the chapter on the United States found that about 25 per cent of the school systems that maintained kindergartens taught reading to some children, whereas the NEA research sampling of 1967–1968 reported that 83.9 per cent provide experiences in reading. The full impact of this expansion on children's experience in kindergarten may be judged by the additional information that 41.1 per cent used more formal structured methods in the 1967–1968 survey. Although not all American children attend kindergarten, this very large swing from informal socialization to formal reading instruction is indicative of a powerful motivating force. There are many other indications, too, that the popular view in America is that children should be given formal instruction in literacy skills at a younger age than was conventional until recently.

Gates,[21] as long ago as 1937, conducted a scientific study of the necessary mental age for beginning reading and showed conclusively that a mental age of 6 or 6½ was not a necessary requirement for reading in some form. Even a mental age of 4 could be sufficient. Curiously, his evidence on this question was almost universally ignored, although Gates' name was then and still is in the forefront of American reading research. Another study by Morphett and Washburne,[22] conducted a few years earlier, had concluded that children should not be taught to read until they had reached a mental age of 6½. Betts[23] evaluated it as being the most widely quoted *and misquoted* study on this subject. The general conclusion drawn from it was quite invalid scientifically and logically because of its limited sampling, that is (1) eight teachers using (2) one particular reading program (3) in English (4) with American children (5) in one particular community. Yet, this severely limited investigation became the champion for the policy of restricting literacy teaching to children older than 6. In the 1960s a number of new studies were reported that questioned this policy and Gates' research of thirty years earlier became better known. This was the period when earlier reading began to be fashionable.

This marked change of fashion in the age of beginning reading in the United States has not been determined by the evidence of research. Therefore, one must seek the explanation elsewhere, and the most likely locus of the cause is in the area of cultural motivation. It may not be just a coincidence that the swing to tough-minded demands for formal instruction in literacy training at an earlier age in American children occurred immediately following the USSR's Sputnik triumph. The aggressive urgency of the increased demands on younger children in the United States is a phenomenon that suggests some traumatic experience on the cultural scale.

However, there is a move toward an earlier start in the schools of other countries too. In Great Britain, where the beginning age conventionally already is very early, there have been proposals for an even earlier start. Germany, Japan, Sweden, Denmark, and Finland also are moving in that direction, but this external similarity to the change in the United States seems to have a different motivational basis, particularly in Sweden and Denmark. In the latter country, for example, politicians, educators, and parents are in agreement that an earlier start in school should be devoted to the kind of creative and imaginative activities currently provided at the kindergarten level, and not to formal instruction. In Britain, too, the demand for an earlier beginning of schooling is not associated with a desire for formal teaching of reading at the younger age. An expansion of *nursery* education is what is being called for. But an interest in earlier reading has been expressed in Finland—that is, earlier than the present age of 7.

In Germany, age 6 has been the conventional time to begin school, although many go to kindergarten earlier. School readiness has been a consideration in Germany, also, and a child's entry to school could be postponed as in the Scandinavian countries. The change in policy is indicated in Biglmaier's chapter in this book as follows:

> Until two or three years ago public opinion did not favor too early a start in school, but the new trend is more flexible. . . . preschool instruction in the three Rs . . . was not given in a kindergarten or school kindergarten until the last few years, following a great public debate on the early intellectual training of children. (Doman's book, *Teach Your Baby to Read,* had been translated.)

This seems to be an example of the modern American influence on educational practices in other countries, which has been found in relation to several other variables. A stronger trend toward earlier instruction in literacy has been noted in Japan too. The Japanese Ministry of Education has stressed the need to include 5-year-olds in the conventional school system. The Japanese members of this comparative reading team do not mention American influence, but it may be noted that the American political influence in Japan bears some resemblance to the German situation. Both Germany and Japan have had American schools on their soil since 1945, and their teachers have received many visits from American reading experts, who probably have not confined themselves entirely to the schools of the dependents of the occupying forces.

Thus, the age of beginning school and the start of formal reading instruction to an important extent have been influenced by noneducational considerations. Sometimes quite accidental circumstances have fixed the age or changed it. Therefore it is concluded that the cultural attitudes toward children and literacy continually exert an influence, not only on deciding the age to begin, but also on the manner in which children shall be first initiated into the literate society.

However, this conclusion must be balanced against the reality-based growth of understanding of how children learn to read. Scientific research is still one of the forces influencing what is done in classrooms, even though it may be *only one* among several and much weaker than some educators may suppose. For example, there is a consensus about the reading-readiness concept that used to be less in evidence.

Gray's aim in his UNESCO survey was to provide guidance to educators. He attempted to distil the best general policy from research findings—that is, *what ought to be done* rather than what was being done in various countries at that time. His conclusion about the age of beginning reading had that basis:

> Many pupils who have not acquired a mental age of 6 can learn to read provided the reading materials are very simple and based on interesting, familiar experiences and the methods used are adapted to the specific needs of the learners.[24]

But this was not the popular view of the time, although Gates' research had established the truth of Gray's contention nearly twenty years earlier. Gates' conclusion from his own research had been that

Statements concerning the necessary mental age at which a pupil can be instructed to learn to read are essentially meaningless. The age for learning to read under one program, or with the methods employed by one teacher, may be entirely different from that required under other circumstances.[25]

As has been noted, for twenty-five years Gates' finding was ignored. Most educators continued to assert that there was some magical moment before which reading was impossible.

Today Gates' concept of the *relativity of reading readiness* is gaining recognition in many countries, as the following quotations from chapters in Part Two clearly demonstrate:

1. *Germany:* "Schools should change to fit the children, not the reverse."
2. *Sweden:* "The concepts of school maturity and reading readiness ought to be looked on as *relative* and not as absolute."
3. *Denmark:* "It is infinitely more important for the school to be ready for the child than *vice versa*."
4. *United States:* "The question underlying readiness studies should be '*What and how is this child ready to learn?*'"

This appears to be one of the universal principles of literacy learning—that is, a child's readiness to undertake a learning task in reading depends on the level of difficulty of that task, and that level can be changed deliberately by the teacher. As Downing and Thackray concluded recently,

In other words, "readiness" implies some kind of gap between the psychological state of the human being and the task he must accomplish. "*Readiness activities,*" *whether in industry or in education are a means of narrowing the gap between the state of the human individual and the conditions of the task to be mastered.* The gap can be narrowed either by changing the individual or by changing the task, or, of course, by doing both these things.[26]

Even if this general principle were accepted universally, it would not and probably should not lead to a universal age for beginning reading. For one thing, individual children within one culture will differ in their readiness. But between cultures, too, there are likely to be differences in environmental factors that would lead to quite a different conclusion as to the average age when reading instruction should begin. For example, it has been alleged that it is more difficult to master the writing system of Chinese than that of English, and that the English system is more difficult than the Finnish, and so on. Thus, the relativity concept of reading readiness might predict an earlier age for beginning in Finland than in England, and the latter country would have an earlier start than Hong Kong, if age of entry were determined by the complexity of the problem solving involved in a country's writing system; but, in fact, almost the reverse is true—Finland begins two years later than either of the other two countries. On the other hand, perhaps the later start in Finland might be due to the relative ease of learning to read in Finnish; that is, less time is needed. Therefore, schooling need not begin so early. But there seems to be no such simple systematic relationship between the nature of the writing system and the age of beginning reading when a wider range of cases is studied. The factors determining the choice of the age to begin are far more complex.

The relativity principle may yet be effective despite these many other influences on over-all policy. Whatever the administrative regulations may be, the teacher exercising this principle may behave quite differently toward his pupil than one who has a more rigid view of readiness. The result is likely to be very different also in terms of the child's experience in his first introduction to the world of literacy.

The Individual's Share of Learning Facilities

The child's initial experience with literacy at school may be influenced too by the number of fellow students who share this experience with him. Experiences beyond the beginning stage also may be affected by the extent to which he shares them with other children.

It is clear from the chapters in Part Two that there is a very wide range of differences in this regard. First of all, the pupil-teacher ratio varies considerably within a country even if there is some general policy that class size should not exceed a particular number of pupils. Rural areas tend to have smaller classes than urban districts, for example. However, if one looks at the average class size for each country, large differences are found at the national level also. In Sweden the class size will not be greater than twenty-five pupils in the first three years of a child's schooling. In Denmark, twenty-eight is usually the maximum. In Norway, the class must not exceed thirty pupils. In the German *Volkschule* thirty-eight is the usual size. In Britain, it is sometimes over forty. In France, in the Paris area, a class may often have fifty pupils.

What are the causes and effects of these differences? Why does one nation have small classes while another has much larger ones? What difference does the size of class make to the learner?

The data available provide little help in regard to the first question. One might predict on common sense grounds that the economic level of a country and the availability of teaching manpower would determine class size, but there appears to be no clear relationship between these factors. Germany, with a very favorable economic position has large classes at the beginning stage of elementary education. Denmark and Norway, which seem less favored economically, have smaller classes. Germany, however, does have a general shortage of manpower. The United States has comparatively small classes, also. Usually American public schools have about twenty-five pupils in their first-grade classrooms. Here economic and manpower conditions would both seem to favor smaller classes. But the pattern is by no means systematic, and it is likely that in respect of this school variable, too, cultural values have their impact. Reducing the size of a class may be more strongly desired by one culture than by another.

However, this does not seem to be true among professional teachers. There seems to be worldwide agreement that classes should be smaller; the reason given is generally that the smaller the class, the larger will be each individual child's share of the teacher's attention and the facilities he provides. This thinking is clearly behind some of the special organizational and administrative arrangements reported from several countries in Part Two. In Sweden, dividing the class in half for a certain number of hourly sessions a week in the first three grades is believed to make an important contribution to individualizing instruction. For instance, one half of the class meets with the teacher for the first two hours of the day. The second half comes to school for the next two hours while the first half undertakes other activities. This permits the teacher to reduce her class size to thirteen students at a time and sometimes to only eight. A similar arrangement is reported in Denmark and the same kind of advantage is claimed. Similar aims are given for the procedure used in some United States schools, where one half of the class begins an hour earlier and goes home an hour earlier than the second half of the class. Each half thereby gets for one hour a day a double ration of the teacher's attention.

However, although the argument for smaller classes seems highly reasonable, the research evidence on the effects of class size on literacy development does not by any means provide clear support for this popular professional belief. Joyce Morris' rigorous investigations in England, for example, led her to conclude that "relatively large classes do not appear to have a deleterious effect on reading attainment." However, she recognized that large classes could be associated with "other circumstances tending to raise scores."[27]

Morris' data are impeccable. Yet they may seem to be in conflict with the findings of a well-known American authority (Holmes) on the psychology of reading, as well as with the popular belief that smaller classes are beneficial to children's learning to read. Holmes was able to demonstrate graphically a systematic relationship between the size of class and the age at which a child was capable of undertaking the task of learning to read. When the ratio has been one teacher to one child, he pointed out, children have been able to accomplish literacy-learning tasks at such a very young age as 3 years. As the number of pupils increases the age prerequisite goes up, too. But Holmes' study was not an integrated empirical survey or experiment. He argued his point from the results of several previously published studies of reading readiness, and the methods and variables of each investigation were extremely different from one investigation to another. Therefore, his conclusion must be regarded as speculative (and provocative):

Other things being equal the earliest age at which a child can be taught to read is a function of the amount of time or help the teacher can give the pupil.[28]

There appears to be no evidence in the cross-national data reviewed here that would help determine the truth of Holmes' contention. Neither the international achievement studies nor the descriptive accounts of the different national chapters show any systematic relationship between size of class and the outcome in literacy behavior. Furthermore, specific investigations of this question have found no necessary connection between class size and achievement. What these cross-national studies do indicate, on the other hand, is an internationally held assumption that smaller classes benefit children's learning by giving them a larger share of the teaching facilities.

What tends to be overlooked, probably, are the other environmental variables indicated by Holmes' reservation, "other things being equal." Indeed, other things may be so *unequal* as to produce the opposite effect in some classrooms. *Teaching time is not the same as learning time.* A class size of fifty may reduce children's effective learning with a good teacher, but a class size of fifty might be a blessing in disguise for pupils with a poor teacher. There may be much less learning in a class of twenty-five taught by whole-class methods than in a class of fifty following the individualized approaches of, for example, the modern British primary school.[29] Before one can assume that increasing the child's share of the classroom environment will bring him automatic benefits one must first ask *what exactly there is to be shared in that particular classroom.* And this must be answered in terms of actual experience for the child.

For these reasons, it does not seem at all odd that no systematic relationship between class size and reading attainments has been found. The variety of experience in the classrooms of different countries is so extremely complex that it would be surprising to find any simple connection of such a kind.

The conclusion reached here is not that class size is of no importance. For the child it probably is important if the school environment to be shared is rich in learning opportunities. For the teacher as a human individual, it is important for additional reasons. The dedicated teacher with a class of forty or fifty pupils striving to give each and every one of them the best learning opportunities he can find is being placed under serious stress. Reducing such large classes, therefore, has its first justification in the mental hygiene of the teaching profession.

Physical Amenities of the School

Gray noted "striking differences between countries in the progress made in establishing schools for children, the conditions under which reading is taught and the nature and scope of the training provided". He classified school provisions into three types:

1. Areas that are just beginning to establish schools.
2. Areas struggling to provide schools for all children.
3. Areas with well organized schools for all.[30]

In the first type he found that "the school buildings, if any, are ill-adapted in space, lighting and equipment to the purposes of primary education." His second category is exemplified by this description: "Whereas excellent schools have been developed in some communities, in large areas of the country no schools of any type are available. The buildings and equipment for the schools that have been established vary all the way from 'extremely limited' to 'very good'." Countries in Gray's third type of area have "unified and well-organized school systems, provide schools for most if not all children, and have reasonably good buildings." Teaching materials and other book provisions varied also in these three categories. In areas of the first type, "the materials used in teaching reading consist largely of a primer based on very formal methods . . . " and "few or no books are available which can be used in applying the skills taught in class." In one area of the second type "at least a score of different primers are in use" but there is a "lack of simple material to supplement the use of the primer" and "many of the books used beyond the first year are largely made up of selections relating to history, geography and nature, most of them too difficult." The third type of area was the most sophisticated in its provision of teaching and other reading materials. Although Gray does not provide any empirical evidence, his conclusion that these variations in physical amenities are important in literacy learning is indirectly indicated by his suggestions for improving such conditions.[31]

The national chapters in Part Two contain examples of areas that seem to fit either the second or third types in Gray's classification, but within each type other dimensions of variation can be discerned. For example, some countries have school provisions that would have qualified them for membership in a particular category long ago; others have attained that same level of sophistication only recently. Japan's "very high rate of literacy" is believed to be due, in part, to the fact that "over a period of 100 years a very strictly organized system of compulsory education has been developed." One might note also the relatively early date of the introduction of compulsory schooling among the German peoples—1619 in Weimar, for instance. On the other hand, Hong Kong can be regarded relatively as an initiate to the higher level of development. The effects of this difference on teacher behavior and literacy learners' experience, however, are not indicated by our data, except that strong motivation to improve education in general seems to accompany this stage of "breakthrough" into the provision of a school place for every child in the community, judging from the Hong Kong chapter.

Argentina and India probably belong to Gray's intermediate category of school provisions, but these two countries differ greatly as one would expect from the many other historical and social differences between them. One particularly interesting dissimilarity seems worthy of note, however, in connection with this topic of cultural motivations. The chapter on India contains many indications of a great national yearning for increased educational opportunities for India's children. Although Chinna Oommen frankly recognizes failures and is ready to criticize many faults in the present school system, her data show the concrete effects of this positive drive: the growth in school population from 1950 to 1960 in classes I through IV by 80 per cent; classes VI through VIII over 100 per cent. In Argentina, although school registration rose steadily to the figure of 90.3 per cent in 1965, national motivation for improved provisions seems to be at a low ebb, as evidenced by the drop in the budget from 24 per cent in 1930 to 9 per cent by 1959. As our Argentinean colleague remarks, "It is easy to see what consequences this unfavorable climate must have on public education." Thus again, the level of national concern and cultural priorities influences the educational environment of the literacy learner.

However, although extreme deprivation with no learning opportunities whatsoever or very scant school provisions obviously must prevent or impede literacy development, there are few data, if any, available on the relative effects of differing levels of provision of specific elements in the physical environment of the schools of different countries. In the chapter on Great Britain a short section on "difficult school conditions" is included in which it is reported that "many classrooms are in old school buildings originally built for 'traditional' rather than 'progressive' teaching purposes." The Argentina chapter mentions that "70 per cent of school buildings are at present dilapidated." These two authors clearly believe that old-fashioned or dilapidated school buildings are related to achievements in literacy learning, although direct evidence is not provided in support of this assumption.

Their belief is supported by the research of Joyce Morris in England. She developed a measure of the "amenities of the school building" on the basis of "a list of the features of school buildings which, from practical experience, were considered to have the most marked effect on school life."[32] Points for a school building were scored in respect of date of building, head teacher's office, staffroom, auditorium and its uses for other school activities (for example, cafeteria), size of classrooms, type of furniture, sinks in classrooms, storage space, type of lighting, sanitation and water supply, cloakroom facilities, playground and field, location as regards noise, and general appearance. She found that good reading attainment was associated with superior buildings: "Efficient teachers and a good supply of attractive materials are not the only components of successful reading development. The present study has shown that good buildings are also associated with a high level of attainment, and it is therefore worthy of note that, in 20 per cent of the schools, lack of space, particularly in infant classrooms, restricted the children's activities and the display of books."

It may be difficult to account for any connection between some of Morris' other school building variables and reading attainment, however. "How can sanitation be related to reading?" might seem an obvious criticism. Yet, the association does not seem so far fetched after extended reflection. Poor sanitation and other unsatisfactory working conditions are bound to influence the teacher's behavior, especially in regard to his choice of a school in which to spend his working days. Thus outdated, ill-constructed, and poorly equipped school buildings are more likely to suffer from teacher shortages than are superior buildings. The latter, in contrast, will be more eagerly sought after as a place of work by teachers. Thus, a kind of "natural selection" process is likely to make poor school buildings the center of attraction for other unfavorable factors in the educational environment.

As regards one particular aspect of the physical amenities of the school environment—*books and other materials for instruction in reading*—the same kind of variation in their provision as was noted earlier by Gray can be seen from the chapters in Part Two. A great variety of available materials in the United States, not only in the form of books, but also involving new technological devices such as computers, TV, and the like is reported. This seems to be a further reflection of the intense concern about the teaching of reading in that country. Other chapters also show evidence of sophistication in the development of a variety of new kinds of materials. Even in countries that are generally less well developed in school provisions, improvements in teaching materials are being attempted, as in India.

However, these references to technical advances within the field of instructional materials may be misleading. Quite apart from the problem of determining their actual effectiveness in children's learning, it is uncertain to what extent these improvements have reached all or even the majority of the populations in the countries in question. For example, although American schools can select materials from a vast array of alternatives put on sale by a host of competitive publishers, what quantity of appropriate books actually gets into each classroom? Comparative quantitative statistics are not available, so this remains a matter of impressionistic observation and speculation.

The core of the reading program in many countries is the *basal reader* series. This continues to be the case in the United States, although this common practice has been challenged from many sides, for example, by proponents of such approaches as "language-experience" methods, "individualized reading," and so-called "linguistic" approaches to reading. Arguments against the use of basal readers center around their failure to suit the *individual's* language, environmental experience, and interests. In spite of this line of criticism, the basal reader series remains popular with teachers probably because its structure and grading of difficulty allows even the less able children to make progress that can be perceived easily by the teacher. For instance British teachers use the basal reader series as a reading curriculum and as a means of evaluating students' progress.

Some critics of basal readers assert that their language content does not relate to anyone's experience at all. "Some primerese is artificial to the point of being non-language,"[33] Goodman complains in the United States. In the chapter on Britain it is remarked that the considerations behind the design of basal readers "resulted in a series of orders issued in a strange, imperative tense totally unlike anything to be found either in children's oral language or in the children's books they enjoyed listening to as stories read aloud: 'Look, Jane, look. See, see the ducks'".

It is curious that this type of accusation is almost identical to the one that used to be made against the materials that were ousted by the basal readers, which are now, in their turn, under heavy fire in the United States and being sniped at in Britain. The old synthetic phonics materials also were criticized for their artificial language. In Britain, the favorite example was "a fat cat sat on a mat." One set of materials in the United States that is said to be new and linguistic provides the following as the child's first experience of sentence reading: "Nan can fan Dan."

When the principle of controlling the vocabulary to provide a reasonable load of new associations to be learned is applied without concern for other learning principles, this "nonlanguage" in the reading materials is likely to be the outcome. If the associations to be graded are phonic, black cats sit on mats while Nans fan Dans. If the associations are in units of whole words, Janes order Dicks to look, look, and look. Neither side in this controversy can afford to raise the question of artificiality of language in its criticism of the other.

Still another argument against American basal readers is that they contain "too few words." This reached its most extreme expression in Trace's book, *What Ivan Knows that Johnny Doesn't*. For example, a typical criticism is his statement that "whereas the fourth-grade reader [in the USSR] has a vocabulary approaching 10,000 words, most American fourth-grade readers have a vocabulary of well under 1,800 words."[34] He also compares American basal readers with Soviet materials at other grade levels with the same result—the American books contain far fewer words.

Harris showed that Trace's estimate of the word count in American basal readers was erroneous. Statistical evidence from an objective survey by Groff[35] indicated that the number of words actually used in American texts was sometimes double that suggested by Trace, and not one series was as sparse in its vocabulary as he claimed. Harris also showed that differences in the structures of the Russian and English languages might lead to different conventions in counting the vocabulary size of books in them: "whether inflected and derived forms are counted separately." Such facts led Harris to conclude that "in all probability, Russian readers do use a somewhat larger vocabulary in each grade than American basal readers do. However, if an accurate vocabulary comparison were to be made, the difference would certainly be far smaller than Dr. Trace wants us to believe. In trying to prove this point he distorted the facts sufficiently to cast doubt upon his conclusions."[36]

It should be added that Trace's comparison of Soviet and American instructional methods is equally misleading. He asserts that in the USSR children begin with synthetic phonics and in only a few weeks are reading sentences and paragraphs, whereas he assumes that all American children learn by the "whole-word" method. This is curiously at variance with the statement by the leading Russian authority on reading in the USSR, who has contributed the chapter on that topic in Part Two of this volume. Contrary to Trace's assertions, Elkonin remarks that "in the USSR, at one time the whole-word method predominated in the schools. When this method was abandoned because of criticism, the change generally caused a deterioration of literacy in elementary school pupils." At the very least, it must be concluded that Trace's description of Soviet methods of teaching reading were as mistaken as his account of the vocabulary in Russian texts.

Nevertheless, despite Trace's serious errors, his assertions that American basal readers contained too few words has been widely accepted not only by laymen but even among members of the teaching profession. In the latter case, the argument has been supported by new evidence. For example, studies of children's spoken vocabulary, such as that by Seashore,[37] are cited to prove that first-graders "know more than 10,000 words" yet their first preprimers "only teach them a handful of words." The logical mistake in this argument lies in the use of the term "word" both for the child's speech and his reading, as if "knowing words" is the same in reading as it is in listening or speaking. The reason for the controlled vocabulary in the basal reader is completely misunderstood in this argument, probably because of the popular misconception that the teaching of reading is in some curious way teaching children to speak. The outcome of this ingenuous view of words in the basal reader has been the production of reading materials with thousands of words and their purchase by many American schools. The result of thus increasing the learning load of *printed words* remains to be investigated, but it seems likely that the additional strain will be intolerable for many young beginners.

This controversy over the materials of instruction, of course, is only a part of the larger issue of the methods of teaching reading. This question affects the literacy learner's experience in two chief ways. First, it influences the teacher's attitudes and hence his behavior in the classroom. Secondly, it determines the books and other materials to which the child is exposed. This problem will be pursued further in the next chapter's discussion of the teacher's attitudes toward alternative instructional methods.

Most countries, at some time or other, go through a period of controversy over the relative efficacy of "global" versus "synthetic" methods of teaching reading, and the materials of instruction naturally reflect this. Whichever approach is used, some kind of core set of instructional materials is usually provided in the classroom. Thus, in Finland a graded series of primers is the usual provision, but they are based almost always on a synthetic phonics approach, whereas in Britain it is more usual for a similar set of basal materials to emphasize the global approach in the "whole-word" or "sentence" methodology. One exception to the general tendency to develop a graded series of instructional books for learning reading is the school system of France, where reading textbooks for different grade levels generally are each written separately by different individual authors, and often there seems to be no attempt to coordinate the writing and skills development program from one level to another. This seems to be a further reflection of the paradoxical lack of technical developments in French reading as compared with the emphasis on the importance of reading in official ministry pronouncements.

It seems obvious that the instructional materials and other reading matter in the classroom must constitute an important part of the literacy learner's school environment, for the set of visual symbols that are the essential stimuli part of our model have their concrete manifestation chiefly in the experiences that students have of these teaching materials and books. However, their selection and the manner in which they are employed often depends on a mediator between text and student. Therefore, the next chapter is devoted to this other important variable in the literacy learner's environment—the teacher.

REFERENCES

1. Goody, Jack (ed.), *Literacy in Traditional Societies,* London: Cambridge University Press, 1968.
2. *Ibid.,* p. 12.
3. Srinivas, M. N., Foreword to Shah, A. M., and Shrof, R. G., "The Vahīvancā Bārots of Gujerat: A caste of genealogists and mythographers," in Singer, M. (ed.), *Traditional India: Structure and Change,* Philadelphia, Pa.: American Folklore Society, 1959.
4. Goody, *op. cit.,* p. 19
5. de Francis, J., *Nationalism and Language Reform in China,* Princeton, N.J.: Princeton University Press, 1950.
6. Goody, *op. cit.,* p. 36.
7. Mills, H. C., "Language reform in China," *Far Eastern Quarterly,* **15** (1955–1956).
8. Chou, En-Lai, Wu, Yu-Chang, and Li, Chin-Hsi, *Reform of the Chinese Written Language,* Peking: Foreign Language Press, 1958.
9. Diringer, David, *The Alphabet: A Key to the History of Mankind,* London and New York: Hutchinson, 1948.
10. Goody, *op. cit.,* p. 55.
11. Makita, K., "The rarity of reading disability in Japanese children," *American Journal of Orthopsychiatry,* **38** (1968), 599–614.
12. Downing, John, and Thackray, Derek, *Reading Readiness,* London: University of London Press, 1971.
13. Dykstra, R., and Tinney R., "Sex differences in reading readiness—first-grade achievement and second-grade achievement," in Figurel, J. A. (ed.), *Reading and Realism,* Newark, Del.: IRA, 1969.
14. Morris, Joyce M., *Standards and Progress in Reading,* Slough, Bucks: NFER in England and Wales, 1966.
15. Preston, Ralph C., "Reading Achievement of German and American children," *School and Society,* **90** (October 20, 1962), 350–354.
16. Abiri, J. O. O., *World Initial Teaching Alphabet versus Traditional Orthography,* Doctoral thesis, University of Ibadan, Nigeria, 1969.
17. Downing and Thackray, *op. cit.,* p. 20.
18. Goodman, Kenneth S., "Promises, promises," *The Reading Teacher,* **24** (January 1971), 365–367.
19. Staiger, Ralph, C., "The geology of reading," in Downing, John, and Brown, Amy L. (eds.), *The Second International Reading Symposium,* London: Cassell, 1967.
20. Durkin, Dolores, "Children who learned to read at home," *Elementary School Journal,* **62** (1961), 14–18.
21. Gates, A. I., "The necessary mental age for beginning reading," *Elementary School Journal,* **37** (1937), 497–508.
22. Morphett, M. V., and Washburne, C., "When should children begin to read?" *Elementary School Journal,* **31** (1931), 496–503.
23. Betts, E. A., *Foundations of Reading Instruction,* New York: American Book Company, 1946.
24. Gray, William S., *The Teaching of Reading and Writing,* Paris: UNESCO, 1956, p. 124.
25. Gates, *op. cit.*

26. Downing and Thackray, *op. cit.,* p. 72.

27. Morris, Joyce M., *Reading in the Primary School,* London: Newnes, 1959.

28. Holmes, Jack A., "When should and could Johnny learn to read," in Figurel, J. A. (ed.), *Challenge and Experiment in Reading,* New York: Scholastic Magazines, 1962.

29. Downing, John, "Language arts in the British primary school revolution," *Proceedings of the NCTE Language Arts Conference, St. Louis, March 5–7, 1970,* Champaign, Ill.: National Council of Teachers of English, 1972.

30. Gray, *op. cit.,* pp. 117–120.

31. *Ibid.,* p. 130.

32. Morris, *Reading in the Primary School, op. cit.,* p. 31 and pp. 139–140.

33. Goodman, Kenneth S., "Dialect barriers to reading comprehension," in Baratz, Joan C., and Shuy, Roger W. (eds.), *Teaching Black Children to Read,* Washington, D.C.: Center for Applied Linguistics, 1969.

34. Trace, Arthur S., Jr., *What Ivan Knows that Johnny Doesn't: A Comparison of Soviet and American School Programs,* New York: Random, 1961.

35. Groff, Patrick J., "The problem of vocabulary load in individualized reading," *The Reading Teacher,* **14** (January 1961), 188–190 and 194.

36. Harris, Albert J., "Ivan and Johnny—A critical review," *The Reading Teacher,* **16** (December 1962), 151–157.

37. Seashore, Robert H., quoted in "A new light on children's vocabularies," *School and Society,* **66** (1947), 163–164.

CHAPTER 7

The Teacher Variable

JOHN DOWNING

GRAY's international survey led him to conclude that

> Without doubt the most important factor in promoting both the general development of children and their progress in reading is the teacher.[1]

Currently in the United States, this belief in the importance of the teacher variable has entered a new wave of popularity following the publication of results of the U.S. Office of Education supported first-grade reading studies and their follow-up investigations. Dykstra states that his results imply that "it is likely that improvement in reading instruction can be brought about more efficiently by improved selection and training of teachers, by improved inservice training programs, and by improved school learning climates than by instituting changes in instructional materials."[2]

Dykstra's conclusion is based chiefly on his finding that there were larger differences in attainment between classrooms using the same methods and materials for reading instruction than there were between the treatment groups experimentally contrasted on the basis of such methods and materials. However, Emans "questions whether Dr. Dykstra has evidence from his research to support this conclusion." Emans' critical analysis is of very great importance in the scientific consideration of this issue:

> The evidence he cited for this conclusion was that there was an extensive range among classrooms within any method. Such evidence is indirect and cannot show a cause-effect relationship. A cause-effect relationship between teacher-learning situation characteristics may exist. Nevertheless, direct evidence is not forthcoming from the research Dr. Dykstra reported.[3]

Furthermore, in this research, as Emans continues, "in which the primary purpose was to investigate methodology and materials and not the teacher-learning situation, the range of the variables of the teacher-learning situation was great. Therefore one can conclude that the influence of methods and materials in this study was probably not as evident as it would have been if the range within the teacher-learning situation had been smaller." In other words, the extensive range of difference between classrooms within any one treatment group was simply a failure to provide adequate scientific controls over these variables, which Dykstra claims, after the event, to be so important.

Lack of a logical design and a consequent inadequate control of the variables in these same American first-grade reading studies has been the criticism leveled by other critics. More specifically, two variables that allegedly were independent variables were, in fact, not isolated and controlled. These were the writing system variable and the instructional materials variable. This led Warburton and Southgate to point out that "To adopt an adequate experimental design is to apply logical principles to a problem,"[4] and they demonstrate clearly that this was not done in these studies.

In spite of these methodological faults, these first-grade reading studies have been very influential. In view of the technical research limitations noted here, the popularity of the findings is remarkable. Possibly, motivational forces of the kind that inflated the significance of the Morphett and Washburne reading readiness study in the 1930s are at work in this case also. Whatever the reason may be, the fact remains that a popular chord has been struck by such generalizations as the following one made by Bond and Dykstra.

> The tremendous range among classrooms within any method points out the importance of elements in the learning situation over and above the methods employed. To improve reading instruction, it is necessary to train better teachers of reading rather than to expect a panacea in the form of materials.[5]

Teacher Training

In the United States there are numerous examples of the importance that is placed on teacher training and the special concern there that such training should include specific attention to the teaching of reading. Although many criticisms of and shortcomings in the current situation have been voiced, it is abundantly clear that much more concern about the training of teachers *to teach reading* is shown in the United States than in other countries if one judges this in terms of actual institutionalized provisions.

The American teacher-training course is not especially remarkable for its length in number of years. Some other educationally sophisticated countries also claim a four-year course. Less well-developed countries have shorter periods of training (one or two years in Hong Kong and India). In the latter country in practice many teachers are untrained and may not even have completed their secondary schooling. Furthermore, in India the realization that the staff of an elementary training college ought to be specialists in elementary education has occurred only recently. Usually trainers of elementary teachers have themselves been trained only for secondary education and they often have no practical experience in teaching in elementary schools. This fact reported from India seems to be one reflection of a more general teachers' pecking order related more or less to the age of pupils they instruct. This is indicated also in the terminology— for example, "*higher* education" for the college and university level. The teacher's pay is often determined by this pecking order with the result that promotion and advancement mean teaching older and older pupils. This leads to the curious situation in India whereby elementary school teachers are trained by people with no qualifications or experience in elementary education, and the pay of elementary teachers is so low that matriculates and graduates are unwilling to join the profession at this level.

This educational status hierarchy phenomenon seems to be widely distributed, although its crudest manifestation can be seen in the chapter on India. Its rationale probably goes something like this, although one rarely finds it explicitly stated: The kindergarten teacher just plays games and reads stories to the children. The elementary school teacher does *teach,* but only very simple things like reading, writing, and reckoning. The secondary school teacher deals with more difficult concepts and specializes in a particular academic subject such as Latin or history. The teacher trainer obviously must be superior because he's in charge of teachers and deals with these specialist subjects at an even higher level. The university professor is at the top of the hierarchy because he teaches these academic subjects at their most complex level. The fact that special professional understandings are needed for each level in the educational system is ignored in this status hierarchy. All that matters is that the learning tasks in kindergarten are easier (from the adult's point of view) than the learning tasks in elementary school, and these are easier than the tasks set by the secondary school, and so on. Also, literacy teaching traditionally is the work of the elementary school teacher, and hence the very words "literacy," "reading," and "writing" may have become tainted by their association with the low status of elementary teaching. The effect of this system in India is simply that the teaching of reading gets no special attention in the training of teachers.

Since the Second World War, many countries have dramatically increased their education budgets. The status hierarchy of educational levels often has resulted in a preponderance of money being spent on expanding university education and on the facilities of the secondary schools as the immediate feeders of the universities. Often the elementary schools have found themselves the "Cinderellas" in this postwar boom. Their poor treatment has not been deliberately planned, but is the accidental outcome of the unconscious derogation of the elementary school. For example, doubtless it was the best of intentions that led Finland in the 1960s to organize special training for upper grades (VII to IX). But special training for teachers of lower grades (I to III) was abolished to make way for the improvement at the upper level. Now grades I to VI are treated together in one training program for elementary school teachers, and, unfortunately, this has led to the further weakening of reading instruction.

In numerous other countries the professional training of teachers in respect to reading instruction is primitive, and the cause may be traceable to the same status hierarchy problem. In Denmark, a four-year course of training includes the goal that it should make every teacher competent to teach reading. But the results are quite variable. The low academic status of reading in Denmark is indicated by its neglect in the Danish universities.

The educational pecking order becomes almost a caste system in the case of France. Elementary schools and normal schools and their teachers have had no direct connection with the other educational institutions, but have formed a separate and sovereign segment of the French school plan. Elementary schools, secondary schools, and the universities each have had distinctive teaching certification requirements. No provision has existed for changes in certification or classification and the title, status, and salary of teachers in the three segments have been quite distinct. The elementary teachers' low caste is indicated by the fact that the French Ministry of Education has been forced to accept untrained teachers to alleviate a shortage of instructors at this level. Even "qualified" elementary teachers usually have not attended secondary schools. Instead they have been educated entirely within the schools of the elementary segment.

It might be thought that such narrow specialization at the elementary level might lead to a clearer perception of the special needs of training teachers for such schools. But Gal emphasizes "how little time is given to training teachers in the teaching of reading,"[6] and Charlier declares that "no courses are given in the teaching of reading or language arts."[7] It is not surprising in all these circumstances, on the other hand, that "higher" education in the French universities has no concern with the chief function of the "lowest" level—that is, the teaching of literacy.

Although less rigidly institutionalized, the same status hierarchy phenomenon has been observed in Great Britain with similar results. Several surveys have shown clearly the neglect of reading in the teacher-training colleges in England. This also, is in a system that generally favors a distinct division between the training of primary and secondary school teachers. Once again, also, the universities until very recently have shown scant interest in reading. No university has a specialized degree in reading. The University of Reading (a city in Berkshire) has the only reading center in the country. It provides a number of short courses of nondegree status. Thus, in Britain too, at the level of "higher education," reading is barely recognized as a subject worthy of academic study.

The curious discrepancy between the existence of specialized training for elementary education on the one hand and a lack of special courses on literacy learning on the other that has been noted in several countries seems likely to be due to the lack of recognition at the university level. A kind of vicious cycle seems to have developed. At the top of the educational hierarchy in the university, reading is rejected as too elementary a subject for its consideration. At the "lower" level in teacher-training establishments, it suffers low status because it is not included in university courses. Psychology, philosophy, and sociology are "good" in this regard. So are subjects that are shared by elementary schools and universities, such as mathematics and history. But reading is a nonuniversity subject, and it suffers in contrast.

In the chapter on the United States a remarkable contrast with the conditions described in the preceding paragraphs is made. For example, programs designed to prepare reading specialists are offered by colleges and universities most frequently at the master's degree (5th year) level either in reading *per se* or in other areas with a major in reading. Several schools give an Ed.D. and/or a Ph.D. in this subject, and there is a serious concern for the university's role in training "researchers in reading." These conditions represent an amazing contrast to the almost total neglect of the subject by the universities of most other countries.

How American reading escaped from the status hierarchy situation is not clear, but one other difference between the United States and other countries is probably related to the acceptance of reading as a worthy concern of universities. The concept of reading as a *developmental* skill arose early in America and it strongly denied that the teaching of reading belonged in the early grades of the elementary school. More and more it has been recognized that reading improvement in a variety of ways can be facilitated all through elementary and secondary schooling and even at the university level and beyond. There are indications that this developmental concept of reading is being taken up more in other countries currently, but not at a rapid rate. Thus, in Great Britain, one of the most serious sources of difficulty in improving reading lies in the traditional view that teaching reading is mainly the task of the infant school (that is, the first two years—ages 5–7). In fact research indicates that children are only just beginning to gain independence in word-attack skills when they transfer to the junior school (ages 7–11), where, because of this conventional misconception, it has been generally believed that the teachers will need no training in the teaching of reading.

The neglect of reading in the training of teachers may have other causes also. For example, in Argentina for almost twenty years teachers have received no training in reading instruction. Here, however, the cause is thought to be the evolution of philosophical ideas and their effects on pedagogy. In Britain, too, one survey showed that the proportion of teachers receiving inadequate preparation in reading has increased steadily over the twenty-year period investigated. This was associated with a concomitant shift from "subject-orientated" to "child-centered" education. There are indications in the chapters on Germany, Denmark, Norway, and Sweden that movement has been in a similar direction in these countries also.

Although countries differ very much in respect to the attention given to reading instruction in teacher training, most of the authors in our team seem to be in agreement that such special training is effective in helping to raise the standards of literacy teaching and learning in the classroom. But it must be frankly admitted that it would be difficult to prove the case for this from any of the data as yet available to us. However, it seems likely that a teacher's behavior in the classroom will differ in relation to the exposure he has had to information regarding the teaching of reading. To take but one example, his choice of methods and materials for instruction is limited by his knowledge of the alternatives that are available. Nevertheless, it must be recognized that very little is known *as to precisely how* the child's actual experience of literacy learning may be affected by differences in the training of teachers.

Nor do our cross-national data contain much information on the *selection* of the teachers who are believed to be such an important factor in the literacy learner's educational environment. There are likely to be differences from one country to another in a number of respects. For example, as the purpose of schooling and the role of the teacher vary in different cultures, so the individuals who volunteer for this occupation will differ, and so also will societies differ in how they screen their future teachers. The ramifications of this aspect of the problem are manifold, and await analysis in some future cross-national study.

Administrative and Organizational Influences

Preservice and inservice teacher training is the most obvious way in which the classroom behavior of teachers can be influenced. But other less overtly manifest or deliberate influences may be equally or, perhaps, even more important. Two such factors are the institutionalized patterns of organization for schooling and the administrative and supervisory procedures for managing the schools.

Within the rather universal conception of preschool, elementary, secondary, and college levels of education, there exists a great variety of different patterns for segmenting schooling. Although the alternatives are sometimes discussed in terms of their educational effects, administrative feasibility and convenience probably more often determine what is done in actual practice. For example, it is very difficult to explain the persistence of the grade system in so many different countries, despite the wealth of research evidence for the importance of individual differences in children's aptitudes and abilities and their lack of relationship with chronological age. Particularly strong evidence of the very serious inefficiency of this grade system is found in three of the chapters in Part II. There can be little doubt that these three examples are merely symptomatic of its ill-effects in other places where the grade system prevails more or less extensively, and where, probably, other more favorable circumstances mitigate the resulting difficulties to some extent.

The most serious damage caused by the rigid adherance to a grade system is what is referred to so graphically in the chapter on India as "stagnation." Students who fail have to repeat the year again and again until they improve. The chief cause of this stagnation appears to be failure in reading. Stagnation in turn causes a serious drop-out problem. For example, in Maharasthra, according to a recent study, of every 1,000 students entering class I, 414 dropped out before completing class IV.

Stagnation is a serious problem in Argentina, also. Grade I repeaters amount to 25 per cent of the total registration there, with a range of 10 per cent in Buenos Aires to almost 40 per cent in Santiago del Estero. In this country, too, the chief cause is failure in learning to read. Similarly, in France, according to statistics published in 1958, 25 per cent of French children were not promoted at the end of the first grade.[8]

The vicious downward spiral of the effects of such stagnation is predictable from research on the psychology of learning: low levels of aspiration, poor self-image, and so on. It is not surprising, therefore, that in the chapter on Argentina one finds that the repetition of grades leads to a general deterioration of the school.

A range of different situations for school organization is found in the United States. But, although "nongraded plans" and "multiaged and multigraded organization" are included, the conclusions in the chapter about the United States show a concern for the limited progress made toward individualization of instruction in American schools.

Several other countries seem to have rejected the rigid grade system more emphatically. Some governments have written their opposition to such procedures into the law. For example, the Swedish education acts of 1962 and 1969 require that the personal resources of the individual child must not only be respected but should be the starting point for the planning of education and teaching. The 1944 education act in England contained a dramatic declaration of the move away from the old system of "standards," or grades. The effective abolition of any official name for "grades" or "standards" and the disappearance of such a concept from teachers' professional discussions is one of the best indications of the reality of individualized education that is to be found in the majority of elementary schools in England today.[9] Thus, it can be stated with confidence in the chapter on Great Britain that there is no problem of "grade repeating" in English schools.

However, segmentation of schooling of another kind has caused difficulties in England, and these are of particular importance in literacy learning. The primary school has been split into two levels: infants (ages 5 to 7) and juniors (ages 7 to 11). Sometimes, it has been only a matter of two departments within the same school all administered by the one head teacher (principal). However, a large proportion of children of the younger age group attend entirely separate infant schools under their own administrative head. This head teacher is nearly always a woman, and such positions have created career opportunities for women in the field of the education of the youngest age group. This probably has been an important factor in the improvement of education at this level. However, it has also caused one serious problem in the teaching of reading and writing to English children. Such teaching conventionally has been regarded as the chief task of infant school teachers. As was mentioned earlier, one effect of this was the development of the notion that junior school teachers did not need to be trained to teach these skills. The seriousness of this misconception was first shown by Joyce Morris'[10] survey, which found that almost 50 per cent of children in the first-year junior classes needed the type of teaching associated with the infant school, whereas most of their teachers were not trained for infant methods and a substantial minority were without any knowledge as to how to teach beginning reading. This problem has been aggravated further by another administrative practice. There are three points in the year when children in England may enter school: September, January, and after Easter. Usually children start school at the beginning of the term in which they achieve their fifth birthday or the one following it. But they are promoted to the junior school or class always in the September following their seventh birthday. Therefore children transferring annually to the junior school or class differ considerably not only in age but also in the length of their infant schooling.

Thus, even where the arbitrary annual grade segments have been abolished, the remaining arbitrary administrative divisions of a child's life according to ideal or average chronological age levels continue to impede the individualization of instruction in reading. This segmentation by administrative arrangements is likely to influence the child's actual experiences in literacy learning via the constraints it places on his teacher's behavior. If getting each child to pass the grade is the official objective, many aspects of the classroom environment are likely to be impoverished from the point of view of the faster learner and to be stressfully overburdening for the slower learner.

It is interesting to reflect that in small rural schools, even though the grade system may be in official use, if the teacher remains in the same position for several years the physical barriers of this arbitrary administrative segmentation are likely to be less noticeable in the child's experience. Some educators have noted that there are psychological advantages in such a situation, and they have advocated its extension deliberately to all primary schools. The most extreme example of this approach is "the classroom teacher tradition" in Denmark, which generally results in the child remaining with the same reading teacher for his first seven years in school. Similarly, in Sweden, the child stays with the same teacher for the first three years.

Experimentation with types of organization that include the child's staying with the same teacher for two or three years is reported in the chapters on Great Britain and the United States. In the latter country, for example, normally a child entering a multiaged primary class as a 6-year-old stays there for three years. Each year the older third of the class leaves and is replaced by a new group of younger children. Significantly, it is noted that this continuity of pupil enrollment helps teachers and pupils to know each other very well. Some similar "vertical-grouping" or "family-grouping" experiments are taking place in Britain, also, and these again result in the child remaining with the same teacher for a longer period than in the conventional pattern of organization.

Besides the greater efficiency of individualization of instruction indicated by the chapters on Denmark, Sweden, and the United States, other facets of the child's experience in literacy learning are likely to be influenced by the longer period of time he spends with the same teacher under these various administrative arrangements. For example, the personal relationship between child and teacher may be different even in the first year because of the teacher's difference in time perspective.

Another psychological effect of the multiaged plan in the United States and the family-grouping organization of some English infant schools is suggested in the chapter on the United States. It is pointed out that when a teacher has children from three age groups he tends to individualize the instructional program more than he would for a single grade. This is because the spread of ages breaks down the popular misconception that all children of a particular one-year chronological age group are for practical purposes identical. The teacher's expectations of his pupils' individual differences increases because he "knows" that their ages differ widely. Thus, the child's individual abilities and style of learning are more likely to be recognized in a multiaged or family-grouped class than in one that maintains a conventional single grade level.

Further evidence of this effect of perceived homogeneity on the teacher's expectations and lack of recognition of individual differences in his pupils may be noted in the results of attempts to organize classes on the basis of ability in addition to or instead of chronological age. Grouping on the basis of homogeneity of ability within an age group is relatively uncommon in the United States. However, some schools use a system of organization whereby children are regrouped across grades for reading-instruction periods on the basis of their levels of attainment in that subject. This is known as the Joplin plan. In Britain this type of organization is rare and goes under a different name—"reading sets." This system has the opposite effect of multiaged classes or family grouping. For example, the Joplin plan has been found to result in teachers treating the class as a whole with little attempt to adjust their teaching to the individual differences in their students.

Although reading sets are rare in Britain, the other form of homogeneous grouping has been very common in junior schools, where it is known as streaming. Pupils are organized within a year group into A, B, and C, classes and so on according to a tested level of attainment or intelligence. The effect of streaming on the teacher's perception of individual differences seems likely to be even more marked than under the Joplin plan. With both age and ability supposedly constant, the child's individuality is still less likely to be expected or recognized. There has been quite a widespread revulsion against streaming in Britain recently, although it is by no means dead. In Denmark, too, the trend is against streaming because of its unsatisfactory effects on children, and, therefore, the division of a class into bright and slow pupils has been discouraged.

Of course, this reaction against streaming clearly is related to other social changes in these countries. For example, in 1969, the German Council of Education recommended *Gesamtschulen* as scientific schools for all because of their better opportunities for the underprivileged and individualized learning. *Gesamtschulen* are also considered to be a possible answer to the challenge of the unified school system (*Einheitsschule*) of East Germany, where a much larger proportion of students of industrial and agricultural workers are studying at universities and colleges than in West Germany.

One other administrative characteristic that varies from country to country is the extent to which the classroom teacher's behavior is subject to control by a higher authority more or less remote from the school in which he works. There is a wide range of differences in the degree to which the teacher's professional judgment regarding curriculum, teaching methods, and instructional materials may be limited by official regulation.

For example, in Japan, the Ministry of Education regulates the number of Kanji characters to be learned in first, second, third, fourth, fifth, and sixth grades. In Israel, too, curricula, achievement levels, and hours allotted to each subject are all determined by the Ministry of Education. However, such centralized control may still provide for flexibility in the choice of methods and materials for teaching reading. Thus, a first-grade teacher in Israel is allowed to choose from a broad range of different psychological and educational approaches. Similarly, in France, the Ministry of Education issues directives that control all curricula, materials, and methods throughout the French public schools. More specifically, with regard to instructional materials, although individual educators are permitted some choice, it must be made from the official list compiled by the Ministry of Education. However, the ministry does not require elementary teachers to use any particular method with these materials.

In Argentina, reading instruction is covered in the "Official Plans and Programs of the Nation and of the Provinces," but teachers are not compelled to use these methods and may elect to use their own. In Hong Kong, the reading curriculum closely follows the "Suggested Syllabus" published by the Government Department of Education. It outlines objectives and general principles but leaves teachers free to formulate their own approaches and to select materials within this broad framework. In Germany, political boundaries and frontiers bring differences in this respect, so that conditions in the different *Länder* of West Germany and in East Germany vary considerably. In Bavaria, only primers with analytic methods are acceptable, while in most of the other *Länder* the teacher may choose among methods and basal readers. But in East Germany only one primer with an analytic-synthetic approach is permitted officially.

In the United States, too, there is considerable variation from one State to another. Some states have official lists of approved materials for teaching reading, and these are more or less wide in the number of choices of alternative materials allowed. Other states have no such lists. However, within each American school system there is likely to be some special school authority influencing the materials and methods used for teaching reading. Often the professional judgment of classroom teachers is exercised in "curriculum committees," which choose the materials to be recommended to the schools. Nevertheless, despite such democratic procedures, one is more likely to find teachers using methods and materials of which they do not wholeheartedly approve in American schools than in the schools of some other countries.

For instance individual school principals and teachers have greater freedom of choice in England. A board of governors protects each individual school's autonomy. This board delegates large responsibilities to the head teacher. The latter always has complete freedom to plan and regulate the organization, curriculum, and discipline of the school. Similarly, head teachers allow their staffs a large measure of personal initiative and their choice of methods. Probably one of the most important differences between the teaching of reading in these two English speaking nations is that in England the locus of control over methods and materials for instruction is clearly and effectively in the individual school, whereas in the United States, although some control obviously is exercised at this level, it is much more likely to be subject to external interference. The English educational policy reflects a high degree of respect for the teacher's professional judgment. In England, the responsibility given to individual teachers assumes that all members of the profession are excellent. In some other education systems the assumption appears to be the opposite. This contempt for the individual teacher is most explicitly stated in the concept of "teacher proof" materials in the United States.

The data do not permit any conclusion to be drawn as to the effects of these variations in external administrative control of the teacher's methods of teaching literacy. However, it seems likely that the teacher's attitude to his work will differ very much according to the degree of responsibility he is given for decisions on methods and materials. But there are likely to be different reactions in different teachers. For example, some teachers will be given greater self-confidence by the faith in them that is implied by freedom of choice of methods. Others may feel uncertain of themselves without more control and regulation by "experts." The length and quality of their professional training clearly must be related to such attitudes, but, if this is reasonably satisfactory, one can hypothesize that the greater freedom of the English schools permits a wider range of teaching behaviors and a wider range of outcomes. The teacher there is free to be a very poor teacher or an extremely good one. In contrast, where the individual teacher is subject more to external control it will be harder for very poor teaching to exist, but, at the same time, exceptional teaching excellence may be prevented too.

Administrative control of the teacher's behavior may be reflected in many obvious ways, such as in the books he may use and the way these are presented to his pupils. But the more subtle effects on teacher's attitudes may be even more important in their influence on the literacy learner's experiences. In particular, the priorities may be less clear and simple for the teacher whose behavior is regulated by external authority. If the teacher is oriented without any reservations to finding the best possible methods and materials for teaching each individual pupil in his class, all known options are open to him. Regulations, on the other hand, may limit the options, and, what is more important, if one eye must be kept on the official regulations, there remains only the other eye for the child's individual needs. Thus, the closeness of match between classroom reading experiences and the child's own particular experiential background seems likely to be determined to an important extent by such external demands for the teacher's attention. In its extreme form, administrative regulation of teaching methods and materials places the teacher in the dilemma of choosing between disobeying the rules and more or less permanently damaging a child's develop-ment of literacy skills or the motivation to use them. In the extreme case, the teacher may decide to break the rules, but more often the dilemma may be less clear. Then the teacher is more likely to feel uncertain of his own judgment of the inappropriateness of the official method for particular pupils and to yield to the hopefully superior knowledge of the "experts." Such considerations sug-gest that the degree of external administrative control of teachers' behavior is probably an important extraneous variable in the literacy learner's educational environment, although the next section shows that classroom teachers have subtle ways of overcoming the decrees of their supervisors.

Teachers' Beliefs and Attitudes

The practical effect of teachers' beliefs and attitudes about reading methods on what is actually done in classrooms is dramatically demonstrated in the chapter on India. It recounts some innovations in methods of teaching that are being attempted, but that have run into the difficulty that often the change of method is *in name only*. A teacher may say she is using "the whole-word method" or "the sentence method" with the textbooks that also are described by these technical terms, but, actually, she may continue to place the conventional emphasis on individual characters and teach their phonic significance by rote learning. Two reasons are given: (1) a lack of training in global methods and (2) the conservative attitude of teachers. Similarly, when the global method was introduced into schools in Argentina, many of the teachers who used it did so alongside the continued use of the analytic-synthetic system because they believed it would forestall failures with the method favored by their supervisors.

Research evidence is actually cited in the chapter on Israel of this effect of teachers' attitudes toward methods. In one study it was found that failure in reading was not evenly distributed over the nine matched classes investigated. Instead a whole class did well or poorly. It was discovered that the classes of those teachers who had not adhered to the precepts of the accepted unstructured method but, in fact, had devoted time to systematic teaching achieved the better results. At the end of the description of the diagnostic reading approach and individualized methods in the chapter on Sweden, it is remarked that it will take time to get the acceptance of all Swedish teachers, in the sense of actual adoption in their classes. Research is cited in the chapter on Britain in which it was found that British teachers are for social and historical reasons "conservative" in many of their attitudes, and that there may be only a small proportion (perhaps 20 per cent) of teachers who are naturally inclined to be "innovators." Dottrens and Margairaz[11] report that two of the four reasons for the persistent use by French teachers of the synthetic method are (1) teachers' rejection of the findings of child psychologists in regard to the reading process and (2) the general passivity of elementary teachers and educational authorities toward innovation.

All these data from Part Two indicate the common observation that the teacher's attitudes and beliefs about methods of instruction determine what is actually done in the classroom. So much so that one must always view with suspicion the labels that are placed on the methodology that is claimed to be in use in a classroom. One must be very cautious also about research on teaching methods that relies on an educator answering a questionnaire that asks, for example, whether he uses "phonic," "sentence," "whole-word," methods. Unfortunately, more objective data are difficult to gather and, consequently, few are available. One study that has investigated this problem more specifically is that of Jeanne Chall and Shirley Feldmann. They compared teachers' responses to a questionnaire about their beliefs and practices in teaching beginning reading with the results of regular observations of the same teachers at work in their own classrooms. They found no correlation between professed methods and actual methods used and concluded that "teachers using one given method vary in their implementation of that method, that these differences in implementation can be observed reliably, and that the observed practices are not related to those the teachers themselves report."[12]

Gray found this same problem in discussing methods of teaching even with authorities in the field of reading.[13] The International Bureau of Education questionnaire survey of 1949 classified teaching methods into three categories:

1. Synthetic Methods. These include the alphabetical method, all the various phonic and phonetic methods, and the methods of direct reading of syllables.

2. Analytic Methods. Among the variants of these methods, also called ideo-visual and sentence (or "global") may be included those which begin with the word, sentence or story.

3. Analytic-Synthetic Methods. These methods are based on the word or sentence, and the most characteristic of them is the so-called common words method.[14]

It expanded these definitions to emphasize their differences. Thus, in the synthetic method "a child first learns the elements of language, i.e., the letters or sounds taken in isolation," and later "puts the elements together" to "decipher" words and sentences. In analytic methods, in contrast, children "begin with words, sentences and passages connected with their activities, needs, interests and everyday concerns." Analysis of linguistic elements comes only after the child has "mastered—'globally'—sufficient associated words and passages." Those who prefer analytic-synthetic methods "seek a middle way with a view to combining the advantages of the other two methods." In them, "children analyze, compare and synthesize more or less simultaneously from the beginning."

Gray abandoned this classification because, for example, there was "disagreement concerning the class to which particular methods belonged." Instead, he used "a historical basis": (1) "Those which were developed early and were originally very specialized"; (2) "Those which are recent and more or less eclectic." However, events in the past fifteen years have not born out Gray's belief that his first category could be relegated to past history. In the 1960s the eclectic basal reader approach came under heavy fire in the United States, and there has been a revival of interest in those methods that Gray described as "developed early" and "very specialized." For example, the alphabetic method that was said by Gray, in 1956, to be "rarely used today"[15] became more widely used again in American schools, at least in some of its aspects, by the end of the 1960s.

Gray divided his first category of "early specialized methods" into two groups: (1) "Those which approach the teaching of reading through initial emphasis on the elements of words and their sounds, as aids to word recognition" and (2) "Those which approach it through the use of words or larger language units, and lay initial emphasis on the meaning of what is read."[16] Although Gray did not name them so, shorthand labels for each of his categories based on his definitions might be "atomistic decoding" methods versus "meaningful chunking" approaches.

In the first of Gray's subdivisions, which has been labeled atomistic decoding methods, he includes all those methods that "are based on the assumption that the teaching of reading should begin with a mastery of the elements of words, namely letters or syllables." He further classifies these "into three main groups: 'alphabetic methods,' in which the names of letters are used in the attempt to recognize and pronounce words; 'phonic methods,' in which the sounds of letters or groups forming phonograms are used; and syllabic methods, in which the sounds of oft-recurring syllables are used." [17] Each of the three groups is described and discussed in detail by Gray.[18] His commentary does not differ substantially from that found in most eclectic textbooks on this subject. But there is general agreement that in these methods the balance is weighted toward an emphasis on *the mechanics of decoding and the units of the code,* hence the proposed label, atomistic decoding. These units may be syllables or individual (or groups of) characters from an alphabet. If the unit of instruction is the character (or group of characters) their *names* may be taught: for example, *h* is learned as "aitch"; *o* as "oh"; and *t* as "tea." Thus, *hoot* is first identified as "aitch, oh, oh, tea." Or the phonemic sounds may be associated with the graphemic characters. Then the grapheme *h* is to be associated with the phoneme that *hoot, him,* and *hen* have in common; the grapheme *oo* is connected with the phoneme common to *moon, too,* and *zoo;* and the grapheme *t* is learned as representing the phoneme found in all three of *pit, cut,* and *hoot.* Alphabetic methods teach the characters' names. Phonic methods teach the grapheme-phoneme associations. There are many varieties of each of these main types of atomistic decoding methods.

Gray's second subdivision of "early specialized methods," which have been called "meaningful chunking" here, is described by him under the heading "Methods which emphasize meaning from the beginning." [19] He states that they are "based on the assumption that meaningful language units (words, phrases, sentences) should be the point of departure. When these units have been recognized as wholes, attention is directed, in turn, to smaller and smaller elements. The extent to which words are analyzed varies widely. This procedure is often referred to as the 'global method.' Since the psychological process by which larger units are broken down into smaller units is known as analysis, methods belonging to this group have often been called 'analytic methods.' It should be added that, as soon as word elements are known, they are used in recognizing new words, so both analysis and synthesis play their part." Again, Gray's description and discussion in detail of these meaningful chunking approaches is quite conventional. He classifies methods within this category according to the size of the unit or chunk of meaning on which each is based—that is, the word method, the phrase method, the sentence method, and the story method—but he concludes from his international survey that "most recent primers for either children or adults do not follow any one of them exclusively. Words, phrases, sentences or longer units are used to introduce reading lessons according to the needs of the occasion." This last comment of Gray's on this category serves to reemphasize the essential educational aim of the meaningful chunking type of teaching method. Although it is true that, as Gray points out, it has been argued in favor of this approach "that children recognize things and ideas as wholes," the fact that the size of the chunk of meaning became unimportant to most advocates of this kind of method indicates that *it is the meaningfulness of the material that is regarded as essential.* It is this characteristic of meaningful chunking methods that Gray noted in reviewing the claims of their advocates that "learning to read thus becomes an interesting, enjoyable and rewarding process."

Gray's other main category, the "recent eclectic" approach, includes both a trend toward eclecticism in teaching techniques and what he calls the learner-centered trend. He concludes that "two distinct trends have arisen: most of the methods now used combine into a single programme techniques which formerly characterized particular methods and they are also based more and more on the immediate interests of the pupil."[20]

These last few pages summarize what Gray presents as a consensus of the realities of professional methods of teaching around the world in 1956. However, the national chapters in Part Two here reveal that this abbreviated consensus conceals a great deal of variation and disagreement. Indeed, one might go further and comment that Gray's perception of the growing acceptance of eclecticism was overoptimistic.

It might be thought that variations in teaching methods would arise quite naturally from differences in the language in which reading is to be taught. Indeed, Gray assumes this in his discussion of divergent methods of word-recognition training. "Of course, the nature of the specific knowledge and skills that should be imparted will vary according to the language,"[21] he writes. He also states explicitly that a "vital factor that influences the choice of methods is the language involved," and that "in selecting methods to use in teaching reading the linguistic characteristics of the language concerned should be studied carefully."[22] Gray mentions a number of linguistic characteristics that should be taken into account in selecting appropriate methods for teaching reading: "the number of meanings which are attached to specific words"; the existence of "tremendously long compound words"; "highly syllabic languages"; "phonetic languages which are not highly syllabic"; and "languages, such as English, which are only partially phonetic."[23]

Some of Gray's terminology appears to be derived from the loose usage that, unfortunately, has characterized discussions of methods of teaching reading. Presumably, he took over this manner of expression in deference to the need to communicate with others for whom such phrases as "phonetic language" did have some meaning. Probably, this particular term originated from the misconception that writing is the primary form of language. Thus, it probably means "phonetic *writing,*" although, of course, this should be "*phonemic* writing"— that is, a writing system that provides a visual code for the phonemes of the primary spoken form of the language. Obviously, English speech is all phonetic and all phonemic. Gray's reference is to the lack of complete regularity of relationships between the graphemes of the English writing system and the phonemes of the primary spoken form of the English language. The alphabet was invented as a written code for phonemes. Therefore, it would seem more appropriate to use the term "alphabetic" to describe writing systems in which the graphemes do more systematically represent phonemes. Thus, Gray is referring to the fact that the English writing system is only partially *alphabetic*. Gray asserts that "in the selection of methods, consideration must be given to special characteristics of the language concerned."[24] He reiterates this principle frequently, including several references to the need to use different methods according to the degree of alphabeticism in the written language to be learned. But in Part II doubts are very quickly raised as to whether, in actual practice, the methods of teaching have been much influenced by the nature of the writing system. For example, although in the chapter on France Bloomfield is cited as indicating that English and French are two of the most irregular languages in degree of grapheme-phoneme correspondence[25]—most French children are taught to read by synthetic phonic methods—several other authors in Part Two suggest that phonic methods are unpopular in English speaking nations because of the irregularity or complexity of the grapheme-phoneme relations in English orthography. Furthermore, even within one and the same language area, one political sub-division may require one teaching method while another recognizes another, as the chapter on Germany indicates.

"Whether the way in which a language was spelt had been taken account of in deciding upon methods of instruction or whether it had shaped these methods"[26] was the subject of direct investigation by Lee. His questionnaire inquiry brought this conclusion:

> Among the most regularly spelt are Finnish and Turkish: Finland favours a synthetic method which Turkey has abandoned. Spanish and the Slavonic languages are also fairly regularly spelt, but while the Slavonic countries have adopted an analytic-synthetic (but mainly synthetic) approach to reading, no unity of method is apparent in the Spanish-speaking world. . . . It is unnecessary to continue. All these languages are more regularly spelt than English, and it is clear that both analysis and synthesis play a part at some stage or other in the methods used to teach the reading of each. Yet a close association between methods and "regularity" does not exist.[27]

Nor have methods changed in the British schools that have adopted the new writing system for English—the initial teaching alphabet (i.t.a.). The i.t.a. system is deliberately designed to regularize the grapheme-phoneme relations in English, but the schools that use it show no signs of changing their beginning methods in the direction of more emphasis on synthetic phonics.[28] On the other hand, in the United States, according to Vera Ohanian, the most usual method of teaching with i.t.a. is unmistakably a formal synthetic phonics approach.[29] Both countries are English speaking. In both countries many schools have adopted the more regular i.t.a. system. Yet British teachers prefer informal meaningful chunking methods of teaching i.t.a., while many American teachers have chosen an atomistic decoding approach to the same i.t.a. writing system.

Lee did not dismiss entirely the hypothesis that regularity of grapheme-phoneme relations in a language's writing system might influence the methods by which it is taught in beginning reading. Although he could find no clear-cut evidence of such a determining factor, he admits that "there seems to be a general tendency, in countries where English is the home language, to abjure analysis and synthesis at the beginning of reading instruction and to postpone it to a later stage. . . . An orthographical influence is perhaps at work, since a breakdown of this kind often cannot easily be made in English." [30] The need for Lee's very cautious and reluctant acceptance of the tenuous evidence for this hypothesis is confirmed in the national chapters in this volume. His stronger impression that variation in teaching method is not much related to the writing system of the language to be read is born out. As Lee found,

No one type of method is in favour in the English-speaking world as a whole, any more than in non-English countries, but whether there is greater controversy about reading instruction methods than in the world at large is doubtful: almost everywhere the merits and demerits of various approaches are keenly discussed. [31]

In summary, none of these investigations has been able to find any necessary connection between the alphabeticism of a language's writing system and the methods by which it is taught. This may appear contrary to what Gray considered to be a self-evident need. It raises the question: *Why have methods of teaching reading apparently ignored this feature of language?*

First, it must be recognized that the limitations of the available data may be distorting or conceal a connection between teaching methods and linguistic characteristics that really exists. It has been noted here that Gray found disagreement among reading authorities in different countries as to the classification of methods. In the chapter on India it is shown how misleading the labels that teachers give to their methods may be, and the research of Chall and Feldmann provides clear evidence that what teachers do may be quite unrelated to what they *say* they do. Lee also remarked that the "names of reading-instruction methods are variously used." [32] This problem cannot be resolved here. The methodological solution is possible, but it will be an expensive one—that is, cross-national observations of actual teacher behavior in reading instruction.

However, although such objective data on how teachers actually do behave in regard to helping their pupils to become literate would be of undoubted value for comparative reading studies, the investment may not be warranted for answering the question of why there seems to be so little connection between methods of teaching and the writing system to be learned. First, the narrow conception of such a connection must be questioned. There are at least three strong reasons for doubting this limited view:

1. The existence of *dialect differences* within one language area may nullify generalizations about grapheme-phoneme relations in its writing system.
2. The alphabetic writing system may not be a code *only for phonemes.*

3. Differences in teaching methods may be based on *educational or psychological considerations* that outweigh concerns about the nature of the writing system.

Goodman points out that

Obviously, phonics programs which attempt to teach a relationship between letters and sounds cannot be universally applicable to all dialects. The basic premise of phonics instruction is that by teaching a child to associate the sounds which he hears in oral language with the letters in written language he will be able to sound out words. But a divergent speaker can't hear the sounds of standard speech in his non-standard dialect because he does not have them or because they occur in different places in his dialect than other dialects. The instruction may be not only inappropriate but confusing. When he reads the lesson he may then be forced to sound out words which are not words in his dialect.[33]

The damage that this teaching behavior causes to the student is serious. As Goodman emphasizes, it "throws a barrier across his progress in assocating sound and print."

Goodman's point throws serious doubt on all generalizations made to the effect that the language of a particular nation must have characteristics that are reflected in the teaching methods in the beginning reading classes of that same nation's schools. If there is any connection between teaching methods and a language's writing system it can only be at the level of dialect, if Goodman's view is correct. There seems to be no direct cross-dialect research evidence on this question, but, because dialect has not been considered seriously in connection with reading instruction until recently, it seems unlikely that any such connection will be found at this level either.

In other words, failure to consider dialect differences within a country has caused this problem to be oversimplified. Goodman's important point is strikingly supported in the chapter on Argentina. The linguistic map of that country is a graphic representation of the fact that one cannot validly generalize about American Spanish, let alone the Spanish language, as in Lee's research. Even in Spanish spoken by educated people in Argentina, there is a one-to-one relationship between phonemes and graphemes in only nine cases. When one considers the exceedingly complex dialectal differences described in the chapter on Argentina, the disparities between the spoken and the written language once and for all prick the bubble of the popular myth of the "perfect regularity" of grapheme-phoneme relations in Spanish.

We must be careful not to reject too much through this debunking. What must be discarded is only the oversimplified comparisons between language and teaching methods. The original hypothesis may still be valid. It is unlikely to be valid for all dialects because of the lack of attention usually given to dialect differences within a country by its schools. However, if one selected a sample of schools where the "standard" dialect of the "educated" subculture was natural to all the teachers and all their pupils, then the original hypothesis could be tested with more reasonable expectations of validity.

A second reason why a simple connection between the alphabeticism of a writing system and the kind of methods used to teach its reading must be questioned is that a writing system may signal other aspects of language besides its phonemes. Lee recognised this weakness in the assumptions underlying the hypothesis he was commissioned to investigate, as the following passage from his report indicates:

> Since it is not only, and perhaps not mainly, the sounds which the reader has to grasp, it would seem a pity to assume, if there is any other sort of guidance which spelling can or does give, that it should guide him to sounds only . . . . Written and printed English is more than a chain of sound-symbols. It possesses other features which help the reader to interpret and understand it; that is to say, to read it.[34]

Furthermore, Lee was well aware that one cannot "assume such [syntactic] features to be absent or unimportant in the regularly spelt languages, i.e., those in which letters are an efficient guide to the sounds. Even if they were absent, we would certainly not be entitled to view this as an advantage."[35]

For these reasons, Lee begins his final conclusions by emphasizing his questioning of the assumption "whether spelling need be looked upon as a guide to sounds alone. Does the written and printed form of the language not give other information too, information of value to the reader, if only he has learnt to interpret the signals, in his efforts to grasp much more than the sounds of words —to grasp phrases of different kinds, utterance types, the relationship of various linguistic units to each other?"[36]

Lefevre's analysis of these other nonphonemic signals gives detailed substance to Lee's argument. Lefevre sums up his description as follows:

> Word-form changes, prefixes, suffixes, and other systematic clues to language structure are generally spelled quite regularly without regard to differences in sound; this regularity corresponding to important structural signals probably compensates for irregular spellings at the phonemic level.[37]

If the alphabetic writing system is not merely a code for phonemes, then the assumption that synthetic phonics is more appropriate for written languages that code phonemes regularly than for those that do this with irregularity is clearly an oversimplification of the problem.

Our third reason for doubting this assumption is that methods of teaching reading are not determined solely by linguistic considerations. Indeed, other educational aims and perceived psychological needs of pupils may be much more important in the teacher's choice of methods. Gray gives some recognition to this when he discusses the "advantages and limitations" of those methods that have been labeled "meaningful chunking" here. He says that "they apply to all languages."[38] It is significant that he considers meaningful chunking approaches to have the same benefits and drawbacks universally across language or writing system differences when one recollects that, as was shown earlier, the essence of these methods is their emphasis on the linguistic *meaningfulness* of the examples of written language presented to literacy learners. The important point for such methods is not so much that the chunk should be larger than, for example, a single letter in writing and a single phoneme in utterance. The size of the chunk as such is not the guiding principle of chief concern. The vital aim in these methods is to ensure that the language represented in the samples of print or writing that are used in teaching literacy will be immediately recognized as meaningful communication by the learner. Therefore, the characteristics of the writing system simply do not matter for the essential purpose of the meaningful chunk methodology of teaching reading. Lee was well aware of this, too, for he writes, "the arguments for a non-synthetic (non-phonic) initial approach to reading seem to apply with as little or as much force to regularly spelt languages as to English."[39]

The national chapters provide several examples of this similarity of educational aims underlying the preference for meaningful chunking methods. In England, more and more attention has been paid to reading for meaning. Many teachers have emphasized global methods as being more meaningful to young beginners. In Denmark, engaging the interest of the pupil and making sure that the reading situation is, from the beginning, a realistic and meaningful one for the child have been given top priority. These two examples happen to come from countries whose languages have notably irregular or complex orthographies. Therefore, the suspicion may still remain that their enthusiasm for nonphonic methods is a rationalization for their avoidance of synthetic approaches inappropriate to their writing systems. However, on the other hand, their emphasis on reading that is realistic and meaningful for the child is not isolated from other aspects of the literacy learner's educational environment. On the contrary, the meaningful chunking methods preferred in these countries articulates well with their over-all educational climate. In the chapter on Great Britain a direct connection is shown between the adoption of this type of method of teaching reading and the general movement toward child-centered education there. Similarly, in Denmark, the over-all development of the child is the objective rather than one isolated aspect such as reading. Therefore, it seems more probable that this preference for a meaningful chunking method of teaching reading is related to general educational aims that attempt to take account of what are perceived to be the psychological needs of young children. This is reflected in the consensus of international opinion that Gray found among the proponents of word, phrase, sentence, or story methods. They generally believed that such methods "promoted habits of thoughtful reading and correspond closely with the child's natural method of learning."[40] These aims can be understood and adopted in any country. Hence, one would not expect to find the incidence of teaching methods based on them to vary systematically with language differences of the kind investigated by Lee.

The opposite aspect of this rationale for meaningful chunking methods is found in the criticism its proponents level against such atomistic decoding approaches as synthetic phonics. Gray gives the international consensus of such objections as follows: "They have been much criticized. If the elements of words are introduced at the start, the child's natural mode of learning is disregarded.

A second weakness is that the teaching of reading is treated as a highly specialized procedure largely dependent on logical considerations. The subject matter is not related directly to child interest," and so on.[41]

Yet there are some extreme differences between languages that seem more likely to influence the teacher's perception of a suitable teaching methodology—for example, the logographs of Chinese and the syllable characters of the Japanese Kana script, as contrasted with phoneme symbols of alphabets. If the written or printed characters do not represent single phonemes it seems hardly likely that a synthetic phonics method could be used to teach reading in a language that employs them. Yet, a careful reading of the chapters on Chinese reading in Hong Kong and literacy learning in Japan reveals that atomistic decoding methods are possible in these languages, too. In Japan, the word method is generally used to teach Kana. Earlier some teachers attempted to use a method similar to the alphabetic method in English, but this has now been abandoned. More to the point as regards our present concern is our Japanese colleagues' report that the "radical analysis method" also is sometimes used. Kanji can be divided into various radicals and several Kanji can contain a common radical. Kanji can be taught, therefore, not as unsystematic symbols but as combinations of different radicals. Furthermore, many radicals have their own meaning. Similarly, the popular view that each Chinese character must be learned as a separate arbitrary symbol for a particular morpheme is challenged in the chapter on Hong Kong, which points out that although the approach to reading is largely "look-and-say," with the whole character as the basic unit, nevertheless the salient features of the radical and phonetic elements of each character are taught. Leong's own detailed analysis of the Chinese writing system in his chapter on Hong Kong makes it quite clear that there are more similarities between learning to read the Chinese and English writing systems, despite their dramatically different immediate external appearances, than most people have imagined.

These data provided in the chapters on Hong Kong and Japan probably will be quite surprising to reading specialists in other countries who have not previously compared their writing systems with the Chinese and Japanese. In particular, they may be surprised to learn that meaningful chunking is not forced on Japanese and Chinese reading teachers simply because their languages are written in large chunks that code directly to meaningful concepts. A kind of atomistic decoding method can be and is used by some teachers in Hong Kong and Japan. Failure to recognize this potentiality is probably the result of the ethnocentricity that pervades the professional literature in the reading field. Because theory and research on reading developed earliest in countries where alphabetic writing systems prevail (particularly in the United States), non-alphabetic systems have been given scant attention. When they are looked at it is usually through ethnocentric alphabetic blinkers. The few cross-national investigations of reading that have been conducted have focused on the regularity of grapheme-phoneme relations, probably because they have been inspired by this obvious feature of alphabetic writing systems. Thus, it is often assumed that the way in which a teacher teaches reading must surely be determined first and foremost by this feature.

What we learn from the Japanese and Hong Kong chapters is that the grapheme-phoneme dimension of difference between alphabetic writing systems is relatively local, and that there is a more universal dimension that does provide a worldwide continuum for classifying differences in methods of instruction in reading. Atomistic decoding and meaningful chunking represent its two extremes. Whether one is dealing with letters that represent phonemes, or a syllabary that signals the relevant sound group, or logographs that signify morphemic units, the same alternatives are available. One can begin by emphasizing the atoms of written language, for instance, either in the separate letters of written words in English or in the radicals of Chinese logographs. Or one can put the emphasis on the larger chunks of written language that convey linguistic meaning. In parallel with this, the alternative emphases are the *mechanics* of the decoding task versus its *communicative function*.

The crux of this difference is located in the stage of initiation to literacy. For example, if the atoms in question are the graphemes of alphabetic writing systems, then the controversy over atomistic decoding versus meaningful chunking is rarely any longer an either-or debate. Thus, in the chapter on France, Chardon is cited as concluding that "the dispute between phonetic and sight methods is somewhat passé."[42] Similarly, in the chapter on reading in Great Britain it is stated that the controversy between synthetic and analytic methods is gradually dying. The center of the storm has shifted. It is more often recognized today that both approaches have a place in reading instruction. But where teachers continue to differ on this issue is usually over the question of which approach should be emphasized *at the initial stage* of learning to read. For example, in the chapter on the United States, it is stated that the difference often lies in the emphasis and timing placed on different aspects of the process. Similarly, many teachers in England recognize that at some time or other children have got to come to grips with the problems of the phoneme-grapheme relationship. However, the majority of teachers believe that phonics is an unsuitable method for young beginners. Scottish teachers generally have a different view from their English colleagues on this question. English pupils tend to be introduced to phonics later than Scottish pupils. Dialect differences between Scotland and England would hardly account for this difference in the teacher's beliefs in these two parts of Great Britain. Indeed, Goodacre's comparison strongly suggests that this difference in teaching methods at the initial stage is related to differences in the over-all educational climates in which they exist.

This focusing of the controversy on to the initial stage of initiation into reading suggests that *orientation* is an important consideration. As Elkonin notes in his chapter on the USSR, methods of teaching reading have their most important influence through transfer effects to other language-learning situations. The method of teaching the beginning stages of learning to read and write must be considered, not only from the point of view of its immediate direct practical results in these particular skills, but also from the longer term view of its further effects in the development of other language skills. This suggests that orientation to the nature and purpose of the reading task is a vital element in the development of cognitive clarity. Until the child *understands why* we have written language, his progress in solving the problems of literacy learning are likely to be impeded by a number of confusions in his concepts of language.

In several of the national chapters evidence is provided that the selection of beginning reading methods is influenced by this problem of orientation. However, our data also give grounds for believing that serious inefficiencies in literacy teaching are often caused through failure to give sufficient priority to orientating the literacy learner to the true functions of reading and writing.

The most noteworthy example of the confusion caused by a narrow and rigid adherence to the atomistic decoding view of beginning reading is reported in the chapter on India. In that country synthetic methods, in which the initial emphasis is on teaching the letters and their sounds, are most prevalent. Then the word, phrase, or sentence is recognized by combining the detailed elements of language. Usually, the teacher writes the character on the board and says its name-phoneme. Then the children repeat it vocally and write its character on their slates. The following day the next character is taught in the same way, and so on, until the whole alphabet has been covered. In these synthetic methods the essential common element is the emphasis on writing the single character at the outset of reading instruction. "Teaching reading" for most teachers in India consists primarily of instruction in the characters of the alphabet.

The outcome of this popular assumption in India is that there are no special provisions for failure in reading because reading disability has not yet been identified as an educational problem. Conventionally it is assumed that reading has been taught adequately if the child has mastered all the characters of the alphabet. Therefore, the possibility that general educational failure may be due to reading disability has hardly been considered seriously.

Three other comments in the chapter on India strengthen the impression that the synthetic methods used there are just one reflection of a more general emphasis on the mechanics of literacy at the expense of orientation to the communicative function of written language:

1. There is a complete lack of concern for silent reading in the primary grades. *Oral* reading is the only "reading" recognized as such. Here, again, more emphasis is placed on the sounds than on meaning.
2. Rote memorization of the content, particularly the recall of specific details, is the main emphasis in teaching the comprehension skills.
3. Silent reading in the later grades means sounding out words rather softly in practice.

Chinna Oommen tells the story of one child who, when asked to read for some visitors, queried "Teacher, with the book or without the book?" This is a graphic illustration of how the teacher's orientation toward the task of instruction becomes the pupil's conception of the meaning and purpose of that activity.

The teacher's definition of reading as it must be taught is adopted by the child as his functional definition of reading. For very many children exposed to the atomistic decoding methods described by Oommen, reading must become an almost meaningless ritual divorced from their past experience of real life and language and only mystically related to their educational aspirations.

It is curious that this need for a functional orientation to literacy at the very beginning stage of learning its skills is stressed much more for adult instruction than in teaching children. For example, Gray's international survey report mentions this need more specifically in those passages dealing with adult literacy than it does in reviewing methods of teaching children. For instance, he reports that "in teaching adults to read wide use is made of the motives which lead them to want to read and the kinds of materials they wish to read. Similarly, instruction in handwriting begins with the motives which stimulate adults to want to learn to write and makes use from the beginning of situations in which it serves useful purposes."[43] In the second edition of the same book, Staiger's[44] additional chapter cites Maguerez's recommendations for giving literacy training to workers in developing countries:

> Training must be constantly linked to environment in order to consolidate learning and to maintain high motivation; training must be global, that is include and relate language study, reading, writing, technical training, arithmetic, manual training, drawing, etc.[45]

Possibly, adults are more certain of their purposes in learning literacy and would more quickly reject any instruction that seemed irrelevant to them. Furthermore, because their classes are more voluntary they would quickly drop out, and the teacher would find himself without pupils. Compulsory education can make children a captive audience of unwilling consumers of the teacher's products.

Gray found more concern for the provision of functional literacy experiences for young beginners in the area of instruction in *handwriting*. For example, he states that the chief aim at the beginning stage should be "to stimulate keen interest among children in learning to write."[46] In the later stages, too, "practice in writing is based on the use of concrete experiences; specific motives for writing are provided which elicit whole-hearted effort."[47] Also, "the motive for much of the practice necessary in learning to write well should spring from a real need for recording or expressing ideas."[48]

These quotations from Gray and from Staiger stress motivation rather than orientation. As was noted earlier, Vygotsky's[49] study of early literacy learning also emphasized the lack of motivation that results from the young beginner's inability to understand the purposes of written language. However, when this question is explored further, the crucial problem turns out to be one of *orientation*, because orientation to the communicative function of reading and writing not only affects motivation, but also the child's development of cognitive clarity in solving the problems of literacy learning. Gray seems to have recognized this to some extent in criticizing atomistic decoding approaches to the teaching of hand-writing: "If synthetic methods are used, attention is focused on the elements of words before pupils recognize their significance either through reading or writing; it develops the attitude that writing consists primarily of copying models rather than expressing ideas."[50]

Although it is not usually deliberately stated, this feeling that atomistic decoding approaches have their chief disadvantage in giving the child an incorrect orientation to the purposes of literacy pervades the criticisms that many reading specialists have leveled against such methods. There are several reflections of this in the national chapters. For instance, in Denmark, changes in teachers' attitudes toward reading have gone hand in hand with more modern views on the teaching of writing. The emphasis has shifted from a concentration on penmanship and orthography to the concern for the development of creative writing. Nor is this type of concern limited to such sophisticated education systems as that of Denmark. Although it is only a limited experiment, one notes a similar concern in the methods being tried in one part of Argentina. Certain teachers in Santa Fe, led by Olga Cossettini, are using a method similar to the language-experience approach as a result of their aim to provide personally relevant motivation for reading.

These examples show that atomistic decoding methods are often rejected and meaningful chunking approaches are equally often preferred for the initial stages of literacy learning because of considerations of motivation and sometimes of orientation, *per se*. These considerations outweigh, in the judgments of such educators, any peculiarities of the language and its writing system. In other words they prefer a meaningful chunking approach to an atomistic decoding one primarily because the former more correctly orientates the child to the communication function of written language and thus gives him stronger motivation to learn how to use it. This is the chief basis for the choice of these educators, and not the mechanical characteristics of the written language.

One must hasten to add that many educators have the opposite preference, but they advance different reasons for their choice. Quite often, they do claim that their method has been chosen because of features of the particular language in which they teach reading.

Dina Feitelson argues this point particularly strongly in her chapter on reading in Hebrew in Israel. She presents a reasoned case supported by research evidence to the effect that, prior to recent changes, the recommended method was one that had been originally developed for English, which has distinctive word shapes but very poor sound-symbol correspondences, whereas Hebrew has no distinctive word shapes but does have a very good grapheme-phoneme correspondence. She cites Schonell[51] and Gagg and Gagg[52] as attaching much importance to the total shape of words introduced in beginning reading. The typical view of these authors, according to Feitelson, is that each word taught in the initial stages should have a distinctive over-all visual pattern. It was such books by British and American reading experts that influenced teachers in Israel prior to the 1960s, she argues. Feitelson proposes that this approach is quite unsuitable for words in printed Hebrew because (1) they lack distinctive visual patterns. (Most common words in Hebrew have either two or three or four consonant graphemes, so that thousands of words are completely identical in terms of over-all word shape.) (2) Hebrew script requires the reader to pay attention to every single detail because one little dot can make an important difference to the meaning. (3) Grapheme-phoneme correspondence in learning to read Hebrew is infinitely easier than in English. For all practical purposes only one phoneme for each grapheme of the Hebrew script has to be learned.

Feitelson's comparison between Hebrew and English in respect of grapheme-phoneme relations must be viewed in the light of what has been said earlier in this chapter. No connection has been found between teaching methods and degree of alphabeticism in languages or even within a language that has two writing systems, one more alphabetic than the other. Of course, it may be argued that there *ought to be* a more logical connection between instructional procedures and the characteristics of the written language to be read, and that the present inconsistencies are due to irrational fashions and unthinking imitation of methods originally developed for quite different languages. However, we must bear in mind the three reasons for doubting whether one should expect to find any simple connection between teaching methods and specific features of the writing system: (1) dialect differences, (2) nonphonemic significances of the code, and (3) educational or psychological considerations of higher priority.

It is interesting to note that it was such psychological factors that accounted for the adoption of the pre-1960s method of teaching reading in Israel. A 1952 article by Jacob Levy[53] placed the child's own interest above all other considerations. Therefore, because a phrase conveys more meaning than single words it is more interesting. Hence, reading should be introduced to the child in phrases. Furthermore, the first-grader is not at all interested in analyzing words into parts, and, therefore, training in word-attack skills should be postponed as long as possible.

Feitelson does not quote Levy as using "word shape" or "visual pattern" in his argument for the pre-1960s methodology. She introduces this matter on the basis of her reexamination of the texts on the teaching of reading in English that were popular among educators in those days. But, actually, although some such texts did attempt to use word-shape and visual-pattern considerations to support their preference for larger chunks of language than individual graphemes, it does not seem to have been, by any means, the core of their methodology. Gray found little concern for this aspect of meaningful chunking. Indeed, his quotation from the same book by Schonell[54] as cited by Feitelson here is that

> One of the great values of the sentence method lies in the help it offers to the pupil from the context and from the continuity of meaning that can be embodied in the material.[55]

Anderson and Dearborn, who are quoted by Gray[56] in his listing of the advantages of the sentence method, actually deny the importance of word shape: "Word-form reading is mainly an adult habit. Among children, only the better readers seem to make use of the word form . . . . What children mainly seem to have an eye for is some detail of the word . . . ."[57]

Thus, the essence of the shift in preference from meaningful chunking to atomistic decoding methods in Israel appears to be *a change in priorities*. In Levy's view, the child's interest and motivation came first, and linguistic considerations were of less importance. Meaningful chunking methods were preferred because they were *meaningful,* not because they were chunks. The recent changes, described by Feitelson, suggest that top priority now is being given to the linguistic features of the material to be taught, and, therefore one can hypothesize that a correspondingly lower priority may be given to the communicative and expressive functions of written language at the earliest stage of learning to read. But this contrast must not be pushed too far. Feitelson's description of the new approach in Israel indicates a conscious striving to incorporate in it meaningfulness as well as structure based on linguistic features.

In the chapter on Argentina, it is mentioned that some educators in that country and in other South American States believe methods should depend on the characteristics of the written language. For example, Lourenço Filho claims that the word method only complicated the reading problem in Brazil because "that system, taken from the North Americans, who have to teach reading almost word by word because of English spelling, has resulted in our overlooking one of the great facilities of our language: its almost completely syllabic nature."[58] Hall also notes that "in English speech, there is no clear boundary between one syllable and the next, as there is in say, Italian or Spanish."[59] However, in the Argentine chapter we are reminded that the grapheme-phoneme relationship there presents greater difficulties than is generally believed. Furthermore, in Spanish, the definition of the syllable boundary is sometimes ambiguous. Gray's earlier conclusion was that the syllabic method "is admirably suited to Spanish and Portuguese, certain vernacular languages of Africa, and other languages of simple syllabic structure. Its basic principles apply also to the teaching of syllabaries, as in Japanese."[60] However, in the chapter on Japan it is stated that the word method is generally used to teach Kana, and the authors quickly move into a discussion of the importance of comprehension in early reading. The chapter on the USSR is particularly interesting on this point. For example, it is noted that Russian children easily divide words into syllables because this segmenting appears clearly as a naturally articulated act. But later Elkonin shows that this ease of segmentation into syllables is a trap in the teaching of reading. He cites Khoklova's[61] experiments showing that the basic difficulty of sound analysis consists in overcoming the natural articulatory segmentation of words into syllables. Another Russian investigation by Zhurova and Elkonin[62] led to the conclusion that a method was needed to destroy the natural syllabic pronunciation of words and free the child from this stereotyped syllabic perception. Thus, teaching methods based on the simple external surface appearance of language characteristics may be a hindrance rather than a help to the literacy learner in discovering how the writing system codes the language. Therefore it seems advisable to view with caution claims made to the effect that a particular instructional method is specially designed or suited to the features of a particular language or its writing system.

As has been noted in the case of Israel, in particular, the controversy over the relative worth of atomistic decoding versus meaningful chunking approaches to reading may reflect a difference in the priorities of educators. Those who prefer the former have as their chief focus of interest the elements and mechanics of the decoding and encoding skills to be taught. Meaningful chunking is chosen by educators whose first priority is to demonstrate to literacy initiates the functional value of these skills. These aims need not necessarily be in opposition, of course, but generally there tends to be more or less of an emphasis in one direction or the other. The size of the chunk of language to be used in beginning is not the real point at issue. This is probably the chief reason why no correlation has been found between teaching methods and the degree of regularity in the grapheme-phoneme relations of alphabetic writing systems, for example.

Logically, this problem can be traced back still farther. We still need to ask what causes one teacher to lean toward teaching the *mechanics* and another to come down more on the side of inducting her pupils into the *uses and purposes* of literacy?

Teacher training, obviously, could be a factor in this problem. For example, in the chapter on England, it is mentioned that during the past four decades child-centered education has been emphasized and reading for meaning has been stressed. But seeking the explanation in teacher trainers rather than in teachers may be only a logical regression.

More interesting is the theory of Southgate and Roberts,[63] which delineates a typology of teachers' beliefs. This is a dichotomy between those who emphasize the mastery of reading skills and those who believe that reading is merely one of children's many interests which should be fostered by incidental learning. This division of teachers' beliefs is between those who believe reading should be *taught* and those who consider that reading is *caught*. Southgate and Roberts recommend that each teacher should decide which of these beliefs comes closest to his own particular opinion. Then he should select his methods and materials accordingly. This theory emphasizes that a teacher teaches best when he is teaching by what he believes to be the best method. Southgate, in an earlier article associated this with her concept of "reading drive"[64]—a sort of perpetual Hawthorne effect providing continuous motivation for reading in the classroom. In Britain, where teachers have long enjoyed the freedom to make such a choice, it is possible that this typology would explain to some extent the variations found in methodology from class to class and school to school, but in many countries the free selection of methods is less easy.

Gray found that it was frequently asserted that it was "impossible to adopt modern methods of teaching because teachers are not adequately trained. In some regions, teachers have had no professional training and are acquainted only with the method by which they learned to read themselves. If asked to use a different method, they express opposition and sometimes resign." In the latter case, the child suffers disruption of his relations with the teacher, and, in the former, according to the theory of Southgate and Roberts, the reluctant teacher will be an ineffective one. Therefore, it is hardly surprising that Gray found that "in many communities it is deemed wiser to continue the use of less effective methods—at least for the time being—than to introduce forcibly new methods before teachers and parents recognize their value." [65]

In the chapter on India it is reported that the same defence against innovation in reading is still being used. The synthetic approach is believed to be easier for untrained or minimally trained teachers to use. The large number of such teachers in India is seen as strongly supporting the continued use of this method. Similarly, the former dominance of the alphabetic method in Finland appears to have been due to the notion that instruction in basic reading was not the proper concern of the schools, but belonged rather to parents or to voluntary infant schools.

In his international survey, Gray concluded that "little or nothing can be gained by a method which arouses hostility, no matter how valid and generally effective it may be. A teacher can usually get best results with a method he knows and understands." [66]

Gray's choice of wording in this quotation is noteworthy—that is, "knows and understands." Thus, referring the question of how teachers come to select a particular method over another back to teacher training is not merely a logical regression. A teacher's choice must depend on his knowledge and understanding of the *alternatives available;* therefore, the extent of institutionalized training in the techniques of teaching reading may be a very important factor in determining the methods by which children are taught reading. What the teacher does not know he cannot choose. Thus, even in a sophisticated school system, such as that of England and Wales, the seriously limited scope of preservice training in the teaching of reading seems bound to severely restrict the range of alternative methods known and understood by teachers. Hence, their freedom of choice of reading methods has been less extensive in actual practice and more illusory than general custom or legislation might suggest.

One further important influence on the choice of teaching methods can be discerned in Part Two—that is, *educational fashions.* Swings of fashion produce changes in methods of teaching that, more often than not, bear little or no relationship to the findings of educational research. There is no real consensus of research conclusions on the comparative advantages of the various alternative methods described earlier in this chapter. Usually, research evidence is selected to support the current fashion when its latest method comes into vogue. Then, a new series of researches tends to develop to "prove" the value of the "new" trend. The reader will find little help from research quoted in support of current methods from one country to another. Thus, in Israel, the swing from whole-word methods to the new phonically oriented sequential and structured reading programs is believed to have brought about a great improvement in reading in which "reading disability" at the end of first grade, as demonstrated by the researchers of the 1950s, has virtually disappeared. This gains some support from the chapter on Finland, in which it is stated that when the analytic method was the subject of research, some investigations found that the results were not better, but, on the contrary, they were often worse. In contrast, Elkonin mentions that when the whole-word method was abandoned in the USSR the change generally caused a deterioration of literacy in elementary school pupils. As was mentioned earlier, Trace believed the opposite was true in Russia, and his book giving this incorrect information is probably partly responsible for the swing-back to phonics in the United States in recent years. Denmark, on the other hand, has seen a swing away from the formal teaching of phonics and spelling of the 1950s to an increasing concern for reading as a process that is functional for the child.

Waves of fashion are noted also in the training of teachers. Thus, in Argentina, the educational literature speaks of "periods of methodism" and "periods of antimethodism," and in the chapter on Britain teaching "fashions" in the English colleges for teachers are recalled.

In the chapter on Argentina there is a section several pages long on the manner of selecting teaching methods that provides a graphic example of the swings of fashion in teaching methods within one country. It concludes that, although some teachers based their choice of method on sincere convictions regarding the underlying principles involved, others reacted more on the basis of a desire to choose the most prestigious method. Even more frequently the main factor was expediency or the espousal of a cause for emotional reasons.

In a field so influenced by fashion it is hardly surprising that controversy is rampant. Some enthusiasts for synthetic phonics and English spelling reform have asserted that this controversy is confined to the English speaking nations where it exists because the irregularity of English orthography frustrates what they believe to be the "best" methods—that is, atomistic decoding approaches. Lee investigated this hypothesis but concluded that "we cannot draw very much evidence from the 'regular spelling' countries to support a view that controversy over reading instruction method is mainly confined to English-speaking countries."[67] On the contrary, he found that "almost everywhere the merits and demerits of various approaches are keenly discussed,"[68] as was noted earlier. Lee's impression is confirmed in Part Two of this book.

The international influence of American views on reading is mentioned in several of the national chapters. This is to be expected in view of the much more sophisticated development of specialist knowledge of reading in the United States. However, several writers question the imitation of American reading practices in other countries on the grounds that the languages and environments may be quite different. In Chapter 2, Brimer mentions that in the development of the test materials for the IEA studies the pervasive international influence of American reading was manifested unexpectedly. Material from the United States tended to be heavily biased in North American content either in historical episodes or geographical reference. Strangely, countries in Europe and Asia proposed test material heavily influenced by exported Americanisms. Sometimes they even put forward actual test material originating in the United States. As Brimer remarks, material that a country regards as relevant for testing comprehension must reflect the influence to which its educational system and most frequently used tests is subject.

Perhaps the University of Chicago has been to reading what Paris has been to women's clothing.

On the other hand, one is frequently struck by the lack of coordination in the reading fashions of the different nations described in Part Two. For example, while "dyslexia" and "word-blindness" as causes of reading disability seem to be growing in popularity in the United States, in Sweden "word-blind classes" have been renamed "remedial reading classes," and in Germany "*Alexie, Dyslexie, Kongenitale Wortblindheit*" are included among the terms that are now outdated. Similarly, in the chapter on Britain the rejection of "payment by results" is noted, while "accountability" is the latest in high educational fashion in the United States.

One of the causes of fashion seems to be a human need for the stimulation of change. Thus, Staiger's updating of Gray's book mentions that "some of the new approaches appear to be derived from a revolt against an established method."[69] Sometimes American school systems have rushed into changes in methods so precipitately that their behavior bears all the marks of change for the sake of change. A previous publication labeled this the "salvation-through-innovation"[70] complex in American reading instruction.

Thus far, this section has focused on the development and functioning of teachers' beliefs and attitudes in selecting between the conventionally recognized alternatives from among the several methods included in our categories of atomistic decoding and meaningful chunking approaches. Earlier it was noted also that cultural attitudes influence the decision as to the appropriate age to begin learning to read. These attitudes seem to be related to teachers' beliefs regarding three other dimensions of child education that affect the literacy learner's classroom experiences and influence the teacher's choice from among the conventional alternative methods. These other dimensions are (1) child-centered versus curriculum-centered thinking; (2) formal versus informal approaches; and (3) individualized versus mass teaching techniques.

Child-Centered Versus Curriculum-Centered Education

The difference in the psychological climate of the child-centered classroom as compared with the curriculum-centered one is very noticeable to the subjective observer, and it seems likely that the literacy learner's experiences will be quite different, too, in these contrasted regimes. This contrast, however, like others being made in this chapter, is a matter of degree of emphasis rather than absolute alternatives. It, too, may be regarded as a question of priorities. Is the teacher's first concern the subject matter to be taught, or is his first priority the individual needs of the learner? The pupil-teacher relationship is likely to be quite different in accordance with the teacher's attitude on this question.

The influence of this difference in attitude on reading instruction has been found in England. A more child-centered type of infant school education, which takes more account of differences in children's learning rates and preschool experiences, has grown out of changes in educational values. If one were to seek a single generalization to compare beginning reading in England with beginning reading in the United States, then, despite many exceptions in both countries, the most valid one would be that the English primary school tends more usually to be child-centered and the typical American elementary school is more curriculum-centered.[71] Some educators may feel that this generalization is unfair, at least historically, to American education. Have not some of the leaders of the child-centered movement been American? Is not the current tough-minded emphasis on "behavioral objectives" and "accountability" a reaction against former tender-minded child-centered schooling? But these protests are of dubious validity. If one looks behind the changes in verbal descriptions of what is done in American classrooms, one finds little evidence of any real nationwide change in teachers attitudes on the child-centered versus curriculum-centered issue. As Featherstone remarks, "in American public schools, with a few notable exceptions, what we call progressive education was never tried. . . . In their famous study of 'Middletown' (Muncie, Indiana) in 1925, the Lynds described the classrooms: 'immoveable seats in orderly rows fix the sphere of activity of each child. For all from the timid six-year-old . . . to the . . . high school senior . . . the general routine is much the same.' When they returned to Middletown 10 years later, in 1935, 'progressive education' had arrived. There was talk of growth, personality development and creative self-expression: '. . . the aim of education should be to enable every child to become a useful citizen to develop his individual powers to the fullest extent of which he is capable, while at the same time engaged in useful lifelike activities.' Along with the new rhetoric, the Lynds noted, went an increased emphasis on administration; there was no basic change in methods of teaching or classroom organization. Their report can stand as a paradigm of what progressive education amounted to in most American schools. Education that treats people as individuals had become a cliché without ever being reality."[72]

Various specific factors in the literacy learner's educational environment are likely to differ importantly according to whether his school is child-centered or curriculum-centered in its outlook. For example, often the curriculum-centered viewpoint results in a rigidly structured school timetable or schedule of lessons, whereas, where child-centered education is the mode, timetables and schedules lose their significance or even may be officially abolished. Thus, in the child-centered education system of England, the primary school timetable has gradually faded into insignificance in the majority of schools, and, in those that are regarded as most advanced, any kind of formal schedule of lessons would be quite impossible. It is in the very flexible integrated-day approach where children sample the available learning activities as their own interests motivate them. In the United States, some schools are experimenting with methods that are breaking down the rigidity of lesson schedules, but they must be regarded as unusual. The child's learning in most American schools is supposed to be divided into arbitrary abstract segments, and he must mentally leap from one to the other at the command of a bell or buzzer.

In the chapter on India, the effects of such segmentation, which is the rule in that country, also, is sensed. The common practice has been to teach each subject in its own separate and isolated compartment. Therefore, very little effort to integrate reading with other aspects of the child's life in or out of school can be discerned. The unfortunate effect of the compartmentalization of subjects in such curriculum-centered schooling is that reading becomes artificially abstracted and separated from the rest of school life as well as the outside environment. "Reading" is then something done only, for instance, between 9 A.M. and 10 A.M. because the principal rings a bell and the teacher says its time to take out the reading books. This may have important repercussions on the literacy learner in our model. The communicative and expressive linguistic functions of literacy are likely to be much harder for the child to discover and understand when reading is so isolated from the rest of real life. In contrast, where reading is from the very beginning used in the service of the child's needs and curiosity whenever a realistic opportunity can be arranged, the child may much sooner discover the true purposes of reading and writing. The principle here is often recognized in the professional literature, but, all too often, the organization of the school works against it. For example, in the chapter on Finland it is noted that the curriculum in the Finnish primary school is organized by subjects from the outset, despite theoretical recommendations that "environmental studies" should be the central focus in the primary grades. Also, the content of Finnish primers does not usually take this total integrated view into account.

Gray discussed this difference but considered it to be a part of the problem of motivation—that is, a search for "less formal and less dull methods of teaching reading."[73] In this connection, he cites Meriam who writes that "The best way to teach reading is not to teach reading but to provide the occasion . . . in which reading functions . . . ." Also, "let pupils read to learn, incidentally they will learn to read."[74] According to our model, the rationale for the approach suggested by Meriam is not merely that it is "less dull," as Gray thought. Much more important is the fact that such methods directly facilitate the child's development of linguistic concepts—particularly those he needs to solve the series of problems in his progress toward cognitive clarity in regard to the reading process.

Formal Versus Informal Approaches

The subheading of the section in which Gray discusses Meriam's article is "Systematic Versus Informal Methods," which is similar to the dimension mentioned here as another focus of differences in teachers' attitudes. This seems often to be related to the matter of child-centered versus curriculum-centered attitudes. Thus, in England both child-centered education and informal methods have flourished together in the last two decades.

It is not clear precisely how this dimension of attitudinal difference may influence the child's experience in learning to read and write. Possibly it cannot be isolated from the other factors mentioned. Lovell has attempted to investigate the effects of informal versus formal methods on children's reading attainments.

In the informal schools "creative work of all kinds is actively encouraged, and considerable use made of the environment in fostering children's interests and in allowing the pupils to follow their own interests as far as possible." In the formal schools "the learning situation was more teacher directed, and the curriculum followed traditional lines." The eleven pairs of schools compared "had remained informal or formal, as the case may be, for some years prior to the testing." Lovell's main conclusions were that "no significant differences have been found between the mean reading scores of children in informal and formal schools, using two age groups in eleven pairs of schools matched for social class." Also, "over all there is no evidence whatever of any deterioration of reading standards in informal junior schools." The way Lovell words this last conclusion suggests that the opposite was being asserted by local critics of informal methods. He adds dryly, "Although there is no evidence that these schools bring superior standards in reading, they may well benefit their pupils in other ways." [75] Lovell might have made the further additional point that since there was no evidence that either formal or informal methods produce superior results on a standardized word-recognition test of reading ability, this leaves the educator free to choose either approach according to his own professional judgment as to which approach will best suit his and his pupils' personal needs. The finding of "no significant difference" is not a sufficient reason for rejecting the innovative method and retaining the conventional approach, or vice versa.

Gray cites an American study by Gates *et al.* that compared experimentally a "modern systematic method" with an "opportunistic method." In the latter method, "to a greater extent, the teacher waited for, and attempted to utilize, the spontaneous urges of the pupils to learn to read, write, spell, etc. To a smaller extent lessons and projects were set which the pupils were encouraged or required to do." Gray considered this to be a test of "informal methods," but some educators would question how "informal" the methods were after reading the preceding description by Gates *et al.* But the formality of the other treatment seems quite clear. According to Gates *et al.,* "the daily lessons were more definitely arranged, periods for study of specific lessons more rigidly prescribed, the accomplishment of particular tasks more strictly required, and the order of the development of topics more fully determined by the nature of the subject matter and more closely adhered to." [76] (The association between formal methods and curriculum-centered thinking seems clear in their description.)

Gray's summary of the test results in the experiment of Gates *et al.* shows several similarities to those found in Lovell's research in England: "On the reading test, there was 'complete failure' in 15 out of 25 subjects taught by the opportunistic method, whereas none failed by the modern systematic method." But five pupils in the opportunistic group "at the end of first grade made scores normally attained only by pupils from 9 to 11 years old," whereas the systematic method "resulted in no exceptionally high achievements." [77] In addition to Lovell's research, two other recent investigations in England are reviewed in the chapter on Britain. Elizabeth Goodacre's conclusions seem to be in conflict with the findings of Gates *et al.* She suggests that during the last twenty years, "traditional" approaches have become associated with methods that produce an elite and a wide range of attainments, whereas "progressive" approaches tend to narrow this range, producing fewer "good" readers but raising standards by improving the attainment level of the less able. As evidence, she cites Lovell's finding that "in one age group . . . there was a tendency for the formal schools to have a higher proportion of both good and poor readers compared with the informal schools."[78] However, she may have overlooked another of Lovell's results, for in the adjacent paragraph he writes that it was in this same age group that "the spread of non-verbal intelligence scores was greater in the formal schools than in the informal schools, although the mean score for the pupils in each type of school was the same."[79]

Her other evidence is that Wiseman[80] found a significant relationship between schools' "progressiveness" and achievement in reading comprehension. He found that aid for the needy was one of the chief features of the "progressive" philosophy. Also, Goodacre cites Gooch[81] as finding that the progressive approach assisted the abilities of the average and duller children at the expense of the more able students. This seems to be the opposite of the results obtained by Gates *et al.* as summarized by Gray in the preceding quotation.

The reason for this conflict of evidence is not surprising. The British and American experiments probably are not comparable. The labels "formal" and "informal" very likely cover a multitude of differences between the teaching methods used in the British studies and in the American experiment of Gates *et al.* Furthermore, many other factors in the research designs must have been different, too. Of particular importance in research on this issue are the criterion tests it employs. Gates *et al.* comment that if reading attainments as measured by objective tests are the only criterion, "the systematic method may lay claim to superiority," but if interest and enthusiasm for reading are considered highly important then their data are inconclusive. Gray adds the wise reminder of a principle too often disregarded in research on education and other social problems: "In trying to find out which of two methods is the better, we must first ask: better for what?"[82]

Proponents of informal methods often seem to exhibit an impatience with testing as such. Possibly they react negatively to the formality that objective testing requires. But, whatever the cause, their neglect in developing valid measures of the outcomes of the aims of informal methods has led to their procedures being tested by inappropriate criteria, as was probably the case in the studies of both Lovell and Gates *et al.* The only serious criticism of the informal methods in the English primary schools made by Rogers is that those who employ them provide no "systematic evaluation of the achievements . . . . Obviously, academic achievement is not the basic goal . . . , but since it is not, what effects do these schools have on children's attitudes toward school, teachers, and peers? How does this experience affect their approach to learning, the problem solving strategies they adopt, their persistence, their curiosity?" He sees this deficiency as unfortunately making it more difficult to persuade other American educators to consider what he "intuitively" recognizes as the benefits of English primary school approaches. What he believes these benefits to be is indicated by the opening paragraph of his article:

> Ideas that American educators have been talking about for a long, long time are being put to practice in a large percentage of English primary schools. Education for life, basing instructional activities on the interests and problems of children, integration of subject matter, emphasis on *learning* rather than *teaching* and on *process* rather than *product,* development of independence and responsibility in children, concern for the creative aspects of learning—all of these are standard phrases in the lexicon of American education. But in England they are more than phrases. They are being brought to life daily in the primary classrooms.[83]

Individualized Versus Mass Teaching Techniques

The other dimension of difference in teachers' attitudes that may affect children's experience in literacy learning is that of individualized versus mass teaching methods. But this is a more complex problem than those already discussed. Rogers notes in his comparison of English and American primary education that "in both countries 'to individualize' is thought of as a good thing," but the implementation of this verbal formula is quite different in the practice of the teachers in England and the United States, respectively. In English primary schools "one individualizes by watching and listening to *children.*" In American schools "individualization of instruction" more often refers to "allowing for differences in speed when moving through some particular 'program'" or telling the child "automatically, if politely, that 'you are wrong, please turn to page 51 for another explanation.'"[84] In the chapter on the United States many variations in American school plans for individualizing instruction are described, but it is interesting to note the way Mary Austin words her conclusion on the future of individualization in the United States: "With the focus of educational reform upon individualized instruction, it is possible that current organizational practices will be replaced by technological devices and learning programs suitable for independent study."

It should be noted also that in the United States a group of reading teachers can be identified as sharing a belief in what they term "the individualized reading program." Indeed they identify *themselves* with this label. Staiger states, "Although there are many variations of the program, some typical common elements are

1. Literature books for children predominate (rather than textbook series) as basic instructional material.
2. Each child makes personal choices with regard to his reading material.
3. Each child reads at his own rate and sets his own pace of accomplishment.
4. Each child confers with his teacher about what he has read and his progress in reading.
5. Each child carries his reading into some form of summarizing activity.

6. Some kind of record is kept by teacher or child or both.

7. Children work in groups for an immediate purpose and leave the group when that purpose has been accomplished.

8. Word recognition and related skills are taught and vocabulary is accumulated in a natural way at the point of the child's need.[85]

Clearly, "individualized reading" as described by Staiger is a well-formulated and specialized approach to literacy learning. A much more general viewpoint found in many countries is the principle that teaching methods and materials should be varied according to individual differences in the abilities of literacy learners. As early as 1925, it was recognized by the National Society for the Study of Education in the United States that schools must be adapted to the differing individuals who attend them. In the years that followed, educators in the United States increasingly reaffirmed the importance of individual performance in contrast to group participation. However, the chapter on the United States shows the wide range of interpretations placed on "individualization" by American educators. Furthermore, although it is concluded that individualization is the most important trend in American education it is added that only a scattering of schools are being affected.

In the chapter on Sweden the efforts being made to individualize instruction there are stressed. Classroom organization and teaching methods are much influenced by the need to tailor reading instruction to individual differences. For example, it is believed that every program of teaching reading should contain both synthetic and analytical methods of instruction in order to allow for a wide range of developmental ages in the same class. Every individual must be given that special assistance specific to his needs. The Swedish concern for individual differences among literacy learners reaches a remarkable level of sophistication in Malmquist's own six-year longitudinal study of a diagnostic reading approach to preventing reading disabilities. Careful early diagnosis and the synthesis of ongoing diagnosis and teaching treatment for students who are expected to have difficulties on the basis of a special reading readiness test battery led to an important decrease in the incidence of cases of reading disability. Even in general practice the Swedish schools emphasize a diagnostic approach and individualized teaching.

The need to take account of individual differences is recognized also in Denmark where individualized methods have been introduced on a wide scale in the elementary grades and in Norway where the recognition that children have many differences in learning styles leads to the aim of teaching with as wide and varied a range of methods as possible. This need is recognized also in countries where resources may sometimes make it difficult to implement the principle of adapting methods and materials to individual differences. Thus, in Hong Kong the needs of slow learners are being catered to by a small number of classes set up under the guidance of the Special Education Section.

Individualization seems more characteristic of the beginning stage than later levels. Thus, in Israel, apart from schools of the kibbutz movements, basal readers are the main tool in developing reading skills. Many class teachers still believe that mass teaching with identical books for all thirty to forty children of the class will meet all the requirements of skill development and motivation. Such factors as these in the literacy learner's educational environment demonstrate that the label "*extraneous* factors" is very appropriate for that part of the model proposed for this comparative study. Rigid mass teaching techniques represent an unnecessary impediment to many literacy learners' progress. Such factors complicate the learning situation to be investigated in reading research.

In summary, the child's experiences in learning to read are likely to be influenced importantly and extensively by the teacher's attitudes toward the issue of individualization versus mass teaching techniques. However, the data available in this study do not permit one to make any reliable generalization as to what the precise effects may be. The one fact that stands out most clearly in the discussion is the heterogeneity of educators' conceptions of the meaning of such terms as "individualization" and "informal approach." If such factors are to be investigated in cross-national research in the future, much preliminary work will be necessary to anchor them securely to observable teacher behaviors. Furthermore, satisfactory criterion tests related to the aims of these approaches have yet to be developed.

Thus, the teacher variable operates as an important extraneous factor in the learner's experiences of relating linguistic stimuli to expected literate responses. Its influence is centered in the teacher's *attitudes*. These may be affected by his professional training, particularly by his knowledge of the available alternative methods, and by prevailing educational values. But many other factors, such as administrative and organizational practices, probably affect the development of teachers' attitudes and beliefs. Attitudes vary in instructional procedures, readiness, child-centered versus curriculum-centered education, formal versus informal approaches, and individualized versus mass teaching methods.

REFERENCES

1. Gray, William S., *The Teaching of Reading and Writing,* Paris: UNESCO, 1956, p. 130.
2. Dykstra, Robert, "Classroom implications of the first-grade studies," in Ketcham, Clay A. (ed.), *Professional Focus on Reading* (Proceedings of the College Reading Association Conference, Vol. 9), 1968, pp. 53–59.
3. Emans, Robert, "*A reaction to* Summary of the second-grade phase of the Co-operative Research Program in Primary Reading Instruction *by Robert Dykstra,*" *Reading Research Quarterly,* 5 (Fall 1969), 120–123.
4. Warburton, Frank, and Southgate, Vera, *i.t.a.: An Independent Evaluation,* London: Chambers and Murray, 1969.
5. Bond, Guy, and Dykstra, Robert, "The cooperative research program in first grade reading," *Reading Research Quarterly,* 2 (Summer 1967), 5–142.
6. Gal, Roger, *Une Enquête sur les Retards Scolaires,* Paris: L'Institut Pedagogique National, 1958.
7. Charlier, Patricia S., *Contemporary Teacher Education in France,* Doctoral dissertation, University of Minnesota, Minneapolis, Minn., 1960.
8. Gal, *op. cit.*

9. Downing, John, "Reading in America as compared with Great Britain," in Clark, Margaret M., and Maxwell, Sheena M. (eds.), *Reading: Influences on Progress,* Stockport, Cheshire: United Kingdom Reading Association; and "Language arts in the British primary school revolution," *Proceedings of the NCTE Language Arts Conference, St. Louis, March 5–7, 1970,* Champaign, Ill.: National Council of Teachers of English, 1972.

10. Morris, Joyce M., *Reading in the Primary School,* London: Newnes, 1959.

11. Dottrens, R., and Margairaz, E., *L'Apprentisage de la Lecture par la Méthode Globale,* Paris: Delachaux et Niestle, 1951.

12. Chall, Jeanne, and Feldmann, Shirley, "First grade reading: An analysis of the interactions of professed methods, teacher implementation and child background," *The Reading Teacher,* **19** (May 1966), 569–575.

13. Gray, *op. cit.,* p. 76.

14. International Bureau of Education, *The Teaching of Reading,* Paris: UNESCO, 1949, pp. 24–25.

15. Gray, *op. cit.,* p. 78.

16. *Ibid.,* p. 76.

17. *Ibid.,* p. 77.

18. *Ibid.,* pp. 77–82.

19. *Ibid.,* pp. 82–87.

20. *Ibid.,* pp. 87–93.

21. *Ibid.,* p. 66.

22. Gray, William S., *Preliminary Survey on Methods of Teaching Reading and Writing,* Paris: UNESCO, 1953, Part I, p. 62.

23. *Ibid.,* pp. 63–64.

24. Gray, *The Teaching of Reading and Writing, op. cit.,* p. 113.

25. Bloomfield, Leonard, "Linguists and reading," *Elementary English Review,* **19** (1942), 125–130.

26. Lee, W. R., *Spelling Irregularity and Reading Difficulty in English,* London: NFER in England and Wales, 1960, p. 7.

27. *Ibid.,* p. 11.

28. Warburton and Southgate, *op. cit.,* p. 53.

29. Ohanian, Vera, "Control populations in i.t.a. experiments," *Elementary English,* **43** (1966), 373–380.

30. Lee, *op. cit.,* p. 14.

31. *Ibid.,* p. 14.

32. *Ibid.,* p. 8.

33. Goodman, Kenneth S., "Dialect barriers to reading comprehension," in Baratz, Joan C., and Shuy, Roger W. (eds.), *Teaching Black Children to Read,* Washington, D.C.: Center for Applied Linguistics, 1969, pp. 21–22.

34. Lee, *op. cit.,* p. 25.

35. *Ibid.,* p. 35, footnote 1.

36. *Ibid.,* p. 70.

37. Lefevre, Carl A., *Linguistics and the Teaching of Reading,* New York: McGraw-Hill, 1964, p. 184.

38. Gray, *The Teaching of Reading and Writing, op. cit.,* p. 83.

39. Lee, *op. cit.,* p. 12, footnote 1.

40. Gray, *Preliminary Survey on Methods of Teaching Reading and Writing, op. cit.,* Part I, p. 9.

41. Gray, *The Teaching of Reading and Writing, op. cit.,* p. 77.
42. Chardon, P., Defond, M., and Durand, P., *Le Cours Préparatoire,* Paris: Editions Bourrelier, 1960.
43. Gray, *The Teaching of Reading and Writing, op. cit.,* p. 257.
44. Staiger, Ralph C., "Developments in reading and literacy education, 1956–1967," chap. XIII of Gray, William S., *The Teaching of Reading and Writing,* 2nd ed., Paris: UNESCO, 1969, p. 283.
45. Maguerez, Charles, *La Promotion Technique du Travailleur Analphabete,* Paris: Editions Eyrolles, 1966.
46. Gray, *The Teaching of Reading and Writing, op. cit.,* p. 211.
47. *Ibid.,* p. 215.
48. *Ibid.,* p. 220.
49. Vygotsky, Lev S., *Thought and Language,* Cambridge, Mass.: MIT Press, 1962.
50. Gray, *The Teaching of Reading and Writing, op. cit.,* p. 214.
51. Schonell, F. J., *The Psychology and Teaching of Reading,* London: Oliver and Boyd, 1946.
52. Gagg, J. C., and Gagg, M. E., *Teaching Children to Read,* London: Newnes, 1955.
53. Levy, J., "The teaching of reading and writing in the first grade," in Levy, J., and Blum, U. (eds.), *Handbook for the First Grade,* Tel Aviv: Urim, 1952. (In Hebrew.)
54. Schonell, *op. cit.,* p. 50.
55. Gray, *The Teaching of Reading and Writing, op. cit.,* pp. 85–86.
56. *Ibid.,* p. 86.
57. Anderson, Irving H., and Dearborn, Walter F., *The Psychology of Teaching Reading,* New York: Ronald, 1952, pp. 214–215.
58. Filho, Lorenço, *A.B.C. Tests* (6th ed.), Buenos Aires: Editorial Kapelusz, 1962, p. 30.
59. Hall, Robert A., *Sound and Spelling in English,* Philadelphia, Pa.: Chilton, 1961, p. 23.
60. Gray, *The Teaching of Reading and Writing, op. cit.,* p. 81.
61. Khoklova, N. A., *The Comparative Psychological Study of the Sound Analysis of Pre-School Children,* diploma dissertation, Faculty of Psychology, Lomonosov, the Moscow State University, 1955.
62. Zhurova, L. E., and Elkonin, D. B., "On the question of the phonematic perception of children of pre-school age," in the symposium, *Education at the Pre-School Age Level,* Moscow: Academy of Psychological Science of the Russian Soviet Federative Socialist Republic, 1963.
63. Southgate, V., and Roberts, G. R., *Reading—Which Approach?* London: University of London Press, 1970.
64. Southgate, V., "Approaching i.t.a. results with caution," *Educational Research,* 7 (1965), 83–96.
65. Gray, *The Teaching of Reading and Writing, op. cit.,* p. 113.
66. *Ibid.,* p. 113.
67. Lee, *op. cit.,* p. 11.
68. *Ibid.,* p. 14.
69. Staiger, *op. cit.,* p. 279.
70. Downing, John, "What's wrong with i.t.a.," *Phi Delta Kappan,* **48** (February 1967), 262–265.
71. Downing, "Reading in America as compared with Great Britain," *op. cit.*

72. Featherstone, Joseph, *The Primary School Revolution in Britain* (Pamphlet reprinting of three articles in *The New Republic*), Washington, D.C.: The New Republic, 1967, pp. 13–14.

73. Gray, *The Teaching of Reading and Writing, op. cit.,* p. 104.

74. Meriam, J. L., "Avoiding difficulties in learning to read," *Educational Methods,* **9** (April 1930), 413–419.

75. Lovell, K., "Informal v. formal education and reading attainments in the junior school," *Educational Research,* **6** (November 1963), 71–76.

76. Gates, Arthur I., assisted by Batchelder, Mildred I., and Betzner, Jean, "A modern systematic versus an opportunistic method of teaching: An experimental study," *Teachers College Record,* **27** (April 1926), 679–700.

77. Gray, *The Teaching of Reading and Writing, op. cit.,* p. 104.

78. Lovell, *op. cit.,* p. 76.

79. *Ibid.,* p. 76.

80. Wiseman, S., *Education and Environment,* Manchester: Manchester University Press, 1964.

81. Gooch, S., "Four years on," *New Society,* **193** (1966), 10–12.

82. Gray, *The Teaching of Reading and Writing, op. cit.,* p. 105.

83. Rogers, Vincent R., "English and American primary schools," *Phi Delta Kappan,* **51** (October 1969), 71–75.

84. *Ibid.,* p. 73.

85. Staiger, "Developments in reading and literacy education 1956–1967," *op. cit.,* p. 280.

CHAPTER 8

Other Extraneous Factors

JOHN DOWNING

Time Available for Literacy Learning

Obviously the amount of practice that the literacy learner gets in developing the skills of reading and writing will determine to an important extent his ultimate attainments in them. The national chapters in Part Two show that this variable is much more complex than might be supposed. It is fairly well known that countries differ in the age at which compulsory education begins (see Chapter 6), and that the length in years of such schooling varies also. But the crudity of matching samples in different countries by age or number of years of schooling quickly becomes apparent in studying these national descriptions.

In some school systems children are required to attend six days a week (Germany and Japan), whereas in many others only five days a week is the rule. In some countries homework is conventional in addition to the school day. (In Hong Kong homework is a compulsory extension of the lesson.) A survey of 100 representative primary schools in Hong Kong found that primary school children *actually* spend from forty-five minutes in the first and second grades up to one and one-half hours in the fifth and sixth grades per school day on homework on Chinese language.

There are also differences in the proportion of the school day that is devoted to literacy learning and related activities. In Hong Kong primary schools, the teaching of the Chinese language takes up about a quarter of the time. In Japan, the proportion of time devoted to language study is $\frac{7}{24}$ in first grade; $\frac{9}{25}$ in second grade; $\frac{8}{27}$ in third; $\frac{8}{29}$ in fourth; and $\frac{7}{31}$ in fifth and sixth. In France, at least 50 per cent of the first-grader's school day is devoted to reading and related language activities. The highly flexible scheduling of school time in England, together with the concerted effort to integrate reading and writing with all other ongoing activities in the English primary schools, makes it quite impossible to obtain any reliable estimate of either the amount of time or the proportion of the school day that English children spend in learning to read and write. Some "progressive" educators might claim that they spend no time whatsoever in teaching reading as such, whereas critical observers might contend that students read all the time. So divergent are these practices that it is impossible to control this variable in research with much hope of reliability.

One dimension of difference does seem worth noting, however. That is the extent to which the learning of a second language cuts into the total amount of time available in the school day. In Finland, foreign languages play a more important role at the secondary level than in some larger countries. Consequently, less time can be devoted there to the mother tongue. At the beginning stage, about one third of the time is spent on Finnish language activities; it decreases gradually so that from the seventh grade on, the share is less than one tenth. Similarly, in Hong Kong, beginning in the third year, children learn English as a second language. The same problem is felt in India where, from the third year, a second language is introduced and in the sixth year a third language is added. (Generally Hindi and English.) Thus, the demands of second language learning put pressure on the amount of time available for literacy learning in the first language.

Although it is very difficult to obtain reliable estimates of the amount of time spent on instruction in reading and writing in different countries, and even more difficult to match them in this respect, nonetheless, there is good evidence to support the view that the amount of time available for literacy practice is a very important variable. A study by Balpuri[1] of literacy teaching in India, according to Staiger, "indicated that the relapse rate into illiteracy was a serious problem. A representative sample of Indians who had received literacy certificates could not comprehend a few paragraphs containing 73 different common words one year later." Staiger indicates the source of this problem, as follows: "An article by Ansari[2] . . . suggested activities to maintain what had been learned."[3]

Mary Burnet puts it more vividly in discussing the fact that literacy must become functional for the individual's needs in his particular environment. "Unless he does this, what 'literacy' he has is likely to rust away from disuse."[4] Gray, too, found that "a surprisingly large proportion of adults who have attended literacy classes and have received certificates based upon 'minimum standards of literacy' sooner or later are unable to engage in even the simplest literacy activities. The most frequent explanation offered is that the training received had been insufficient to enable them to read little, if any, of the material available. Their reading skills disintegrate through disuse. Not infrequently more than 20 per cent of the recruits in countries having very high literacy ratings have been found to be unable to read a very simple passage or write a short letter."[5]

This category of reading failure should be named exliterates, to distinguish them from those who have never been literate at all. Probably, the surprising discrepancy between school statistics and army data in Britain in 1939 can be explained in this way. When large numbers of men were recruited at the outbreak of the Second World War, great consternation was expressed about the very high proportion of "illiterates" among them. The teaching profession indignantly asserted that the statistics "must be false." However, the truth probably is that these soldiers were exliterates who had lost their skills through lack of overlearning (further practice after the first correct response) in school and lack of practice later. Gray's comment, thus, should be applied to literacy in countries with supposedly more sophisticated school systems as well as to the underdeveloped countries to which he was referring when he wrote, "All too frequently there is no follow-up stimulation and guidance to ensure that the abilities acquired play a continuing part in the life of the individual."[6]

One may add also that Gray's words have a broader significance than that given to them in the passage quoted. He made this observation in discussing adult literacy campaigns, but it applies with equal force to the young beginner in the primary school. For the young child reading and writing must, in Gray's same words, similarly "play a continuing part in the life of the individual." The concept of *functional literacy* applies equally strongly to the first-grader as it does to the adult student in a basic literacy campaign. Cognitive clarity regarding the purpose of written language is best learned through experience and confirmation of its true communicative and expressive values.

In Part Two, in the chapter on Japan the interesting "Tohan" and "Mainichi" reports on the reading habits of children and adults in that country are discussed. It is noted that the time spent on reading by children decreased markedly from 1960 to 1965, whereas the availability of television increased inversely from 23 per cent in 1960 to 83 per cent in 1965. Takahiko Sakamoto's observation that television seems to have greatest impact on children of low ability and low motivation, so that they more readily become nonreaders, is repeated.

Thus the amount of time available for the practice of individually meaningful and relevant reading and writing activities clearly is an important factor in the literacy learner's educational environment.

Provisions for the Development of Higher Order Reading Skills

Related to the time factor is the provision of opportunities to develop higher order skills of literacy. Countries differ greatly in this respect. For example, two countries sharing the same language and having sophisticated education systems are Britain and the United States. Yet, the former is still suffering from the misconception that "reading" consists simply of the basic ability to turn written language into speech and meaning, and that this can be taught by the time a child is 7. The consequence is a neglect of reading instruction beyond the infant school level. In contrast, the United States has moved a long way from this naive conception of reading. To many British educators some of the opening remarks in the chapter on the United States may seem amazing, perhaps even ludicrous. It is complained that, in 1967, fewer than 75 per cent of the public high schools in the United States offered one or more reading programs. But it is doubtful if there were any reading programs at all at that level in Britain, except for corrective or remedial classes.

The growth of instruction in developmental reading at the higher levels is of comparatively recent origin in the United States; thus, the real problem there is the failure to reach the goal of universal provision for this kind of learning. Nevertheless, the description of what is being done in American schools will be tantalizing to colleagues in Britain and in many other countries.

There are a few references to an interest in similar developments in some of the other chapters in Part Two. The chapter on Sweden contains more on this topic than others do. In it are listed a number of important higher order subskills. It is officially recommended that teachers continue systematically planned exercises at all levels to stimulate a continuing development of reading. Deficiencies in this respect have been recognized in Sweden, however. It has been found that the speed of reading of many pupils remains fixed at whatever rate was attained by the third or fourth grade, and that this rate is often constant regardless of the purpose of the reading or the nature of the reading material. However, in many other countries there seems to be no awareness that slow and inflexible reading rates may be an important cause of students' difficulties in studying at the secondary school and university levels.

Denmark is another country in which educators seem to have become more aware of the need for continued instruction in reading beyond the early basic stage. Efforts are being made systematically to teach pupils to vary the form and speed of reading according to their needs and the nature of the materials.

Despite these minor exceptions, the most remarkable cross-national difference on this point to be found in Part Two is the wealth of data and the richness of the literature on this topic in the United States, compared with the scant interest shown in it by educators in most other countries. The literacy learner in the United States is very much more likely to be given experiences deliberately designed to develop his reading abilities at these higher levels than a literacy learner in most other countries. Furthermore, the lack of any recognition of the need for such planned experiences in many countries probably results in a quite different attitude by teachers toward the student who is having difficulties in his studies. In an American university he may be accepted as quite normal except for his need for further training in reading. In Britain, for example, it is much more probable that a student who is failing in this way will be regarded as psychologically abnormal—even innately so. Certainly, he will rarely find any official university provision to assist him with his reading difficulties.

Help for Reading Failure

The extent to which cases of reading failure are assisted correctively or remedially also varies greatly from one country to another. Obviously this is related to differences in attitudes and beliefs as to what constitutes "normal" reading ability. "Failure" is always more or less arbitrary as a concept. In the chapter on Denmark Jansen makes this point very strongly:

> Reading failure must be regarded as a *relative condition*. As normal reading instruction is upgraded to meet the new demands for higher and higher standards of literacy, these new targets will represent a further challenge to the weakest readers. Thus, better instruction brings with it the continued requirement for special teaching of the weakest pupils.

The arbitrariness and relativity of the concept of "failure in reading" is well demonstrated by some of the contrasting conditions to be found in different countries. Thus, in India there are no special provisions for reading failure mainly because reading disability has not yet been recognized as an educational problem, whereas in Denmark 7 per cent of public school pupils receive remedial teaching in reading. However, this appears to be related to high standards required in reading. Therefore, many pupils who receive remedial reading instruction in Denmark would probably not be considered in need of it in countries with lower standards.

The type of treatment facilities available also varies from country to country. A statistical survey would be more valuable on this point, but we can note some of the descriptive differences found. "Clinics" are mentioned in the United States, Denmark, Sweden, and Germany. Special classes also are found in these same countries. In the chapter on the United States, in addition, a rich array of different provisions for treatment are described. The vast range of professional literature on reading difficulties and the highly developed technology of American institutions that help students who fail in learning to read are indicated.

In Argentina and France, for example, the orientation of remedial institutions is medical, whereas more commonly it is educational or psychological in the other countries.

In Britain, much research has been concerned with the short-term and long-term effects of removing children from their normal classes for one or two periods per week of remedial instruction. The consensus of this research is that short-term gains of several months of reading age per month of remedial treatment are usually found, but these gains are usually in word recognition rather than comprehension. Follow-up studies for varying periods (up to as long as three years) after treatment have shown little or no difference between students who had received treatment and those who had not. The explanation of these findings may be that large practice effects on tests occur when children are tested repeatedly during remedial treatment. Therefore, the test improvement is illusory, and, when remedial treatment ceases, these children revert to their old poor level of functioning. In spite of this research, these brief moments of remedial instruction, usually, at most, three to five hours per week, continue as the usual pattern of remedial treatment. There is some evidence from research on the use of i.t.a. in remedial reading instruction that, with this writing system, massive doses of treatment for a period of a few weeks or months are more effective than spaced exposures of, for example, a half hour or even an hour per day over a longer time span.[7] This can be contrasted with the typical corrective reading program in France, where children receive only two thirty-minute lessons each week and remain in their regular classrooms for most of that time.

In those countries where reading failure has been recognized as a real educational problem there is a general consensus that it is a very serious handicap for the child's general progress. Furthermore, in all such countries, reading disability is regarded as an intransigent problem. There is little agreement as to its causes and much controversy as to the proper treatment. This seems hardly surprising when one considers the multitude of extraneous factors in the child's educational environment that have already been identified here. So many chance educational hazards may lie along the path of the child's straightforward commerce between the linguistic stimuli of written language and the pattern of responses he is expected eventually to make to them as "reading," that one must anticipate a corresponding variety of educational accidents to produce a bewildering assortment of symptoms.

One of the greatest contributions to our understanding of the problem of reading disability undoubtedly was the important discovery by M. D. Vernon of the "one fairly universal characteristic of the disability," that is, the "general cognitive confusion"[8] that was discussed in Chapter 4 in developing the model proposed for this comparative study. Thus, the many varied educational hazards found in the extraneous factors present in the school environments of the different countries in Part Two may have their chief influence on the literacy learner as *cognitive hazards:* a variety of accidental conditions that create unnecessary "noise" in the stimulus situation; that increase to a more or less intolerable degree the burden of irrelevant attributes to be screened in acquiring linguistic concepts; and that add undue complexity to the problems the learner must solve in developing cognitive clarity in the learning-to-read process.

Test Development

One factor that our colleagues in Part Two were specifically requested to consider was the development and use of reading tests. As might be expected, there appears to be some correlation between sophistication in test development and general sophistication in reading instruction. Thus, tests of reading are long established and highly sophisticated in the United States but are very primitive in their development in India.

Obviously, testing and instruction must influence each other in a number of ways. In the chapter on the United States we are reminded of a wise comment by Ruth Strang: "evaluation helps produce growth as well as appraise it."[9] Similarly, the more tests a country has, the more aware its teachers seem to be of children's difficulties in learning to read. Thus, in India, Rawat's[10] development of a reading readiness test was not only followed by an increased interest in readiness activities, but also revealed problems that hitherto had passed unnoticed. The results of his study raised grave doubts about popular beliefs about the teaching of reading in Hindi. On the other hand, reading disability still is not regarded as an important educational problem in India, probably in part because there has been no standardized testing as yet of the *reading ability* of the "stagnating" students who are seen as a very serious problem in that country's schools. Chinna Oommen frankly faces up to this issue, but other educators seem to be victimized by the notion that if one cannot see a problem it does not exist. In descriptive cross-national research one must constantly be on one's guard against the assertion that a country "has no reading problems." It may just be that there are no instruments for measuring them.

One quite common phenomenon is a negative reaction against testing *per se* in some countries. This is particularly noticeable in the chapters on Great Britain and Denmark. Antitest attitudes, as was pointed out in the previous chapter, seem to be related to a preference for child-centered methods and informal approaches. There is a particular reluctance to use standardized tests as predictors of future status in these countries. For example, the Danish chapter speaks of "This freedom from tests enjoyed in mutual teacher-pupil educational enterprise . . . ." and in England teachers often express the view that "time is better spent teaching than testing."

In the United States, also, in recent years there has been a growing reluctance to use standardized test results to determine the quality of educational programs. However, this change appears to have a different basis from the one in Denmark and England. In American education it appears that tests are being dropped when they are no longer appropriate criteria for measuring the effects of new educational aims and curricula. This gives one hope for innovation and improvement in the teaching of reading. However, American educational research has sometimes been a force for conservatism because it has tested innovations by the criteria of conventional approaches only. One of the most remarkable examples of this mistake was the U.S. Office of Education sponsored first-grade reading studies project, which tested i.t.a. pupils' achievements with conventional tests printed in the T.O. writing system after only seven months, when the majority of the children had not yet transferred to T.O. but were still trying to develop fluency in the i.t.a. writing system!

Home Environment

The home environment, also, can be said to be extraneous. Children without homes do learn to read as do children without schools. But here again "extraneous" must not be regarded as synonymous with "unimportant." The attitudes of parents toward their children's schooling and learning to read and write emerges as a particularly important factor. In some countries, parents give strong support to the teacher's efforts to help their children become literate. In others, the parents seems more neutral, whereas in still others they may even have a negative influence.

Japan is a notable example of the first type. One of the causes of the very high rate of literacy in Japan is believed to be the fact that Japanese parents hold education in great respect and are very eager for their children to learn. Making sacrifices for a child's education is a common part of Japanese parenthood. Judging from the report of the large amount of literacy homework done by Hong Kong children, similar parental attitudes are probably important there, also. An indication of the strength of parental concern for Japanese children's reading is the report that 45 per cent of all parents of the upper-elementary children knew everything their children were reading and 47 per cent said they knew "almost all" in the 1967 Tohan survey. (See Chapter 21.)

Very strong parental concern for their children's reading is also displayed by middle-class "old-timers" in Israel. Not only are they fully aware of their children's daily school activities, but they also take immediate action as soon as they feel that their children are doing less well than they might. Then the parents provide remedial instruction *at home*. Another practical effect of this parental concern has been felt in relation to the poor library facilities in Israeli schools.

In these middle-class homes there are often extensive libraries, and children's books are usually bought regularly, whereas children of the more recent Middle East and North African immigrants are less fortunate in this respect. The religious association with literacy in Israel should be mentioned in this connection also. Reading the Bible in Hebrew is traditionally of great importance in Jewish families.

Within Great Britain a national survey found that Scottish parents displayed greater interest in their children's school progress than did the Welsh or English parents. Also, the Scottish children spent more time in their parents' company. This same survey found that the Scottish children were better readers and concluded that this might be the result of parents reading to their children at home. It was the Scottish fathers who were more likely to read to their children.

Parental interest in education is a factor in Danish reading. There parents' attitudes in this respect are variable. In particular, research has found that parents in rural districts tend to be less interested in education than those in urban areas.

In Finland, the tradition that parents should teach their sons and daughters basic literacy continues to influence the educational provisions for teaching reading.

This factor of parental attitudes may have a negative aspect. One of the chief causes of children dropping out of school in India is the common negative attitude of parents toward the value of schooling. In Argentina, the parents' positive regard for education seems almost unanimous when one notes the nearly optimum level of registration of the child population for grade one. However, the influence of social and subcultural background is indicated by the fact that in the more unfavorable environments the parents soon renounce these initial good intentions. This may be because reading ability is not considered essential for work in such backward environments.

The variable of parental attitudes to reading is likely to be a very important one in cross-national comparisons. The child's initial groping for concepts related to the reading task is importantly affected by the extent to which he has opportunities to share in meaningful reading and writing activities with adults and older children who already know the purpose and nature of these linguistic skills. A number of investigations, for example, have found a positive relationship between children's beginning reading achievements and their preschool experiences of being read to by their parents.

One other factor in the home environment that is thought to be important in several countries is the link between home and school. For example, parental influence in Denmark is believed to be so important as to constitute a specific Danish educational ideology. Nevertheless, parents do not directly influence the content of the curriculum. But the child gains a sense of security through the cooperation of teachers and parents in their educational partnership.

Formal institutions such as Parent-Teacher Associations (PTA) do not necessarily facilitate such cooperation. Often they do work toward that end with some success, but sometimes they become battlegrounds between the opposing beliefs of teachers and parents, and then insecurity is more likely to be felt by many of the children. In the United States, unlike Denmark, PTAs quite often do represent pressure from parents on the curricular content of the school. Many teachers feel such pressure regarding methods of teaching reading. England seems to represent an opposite situation. One English school until only a few years ago had a white line painted on the school yard and a notice board beside it that declared, "PARENTS MUST NOT CROSS THIS LINE." Young's[11] experiments in the East End of London dramatically demonstrated the need for greater cooperation between home and school, and as a result a vigorous movement to improve this situation has begun. However, on the matter of methods and content of teaching, the professional status of the teacher is being strongly maintained, and parents still may not cross the invisible territorial line of professional responsibility.

Sweden also is making increased efforts to relate the child's school environment to that of the home. Swedish teachers previously have been encouraged to make contacts with parents, but recently the Royal Board of Education made it mandatory for the individual teacher to make the first contact with the home. The teacher must communicate with the family of each individual in his class before school starts, or early in the term, and then maintain this contact during the school year. Malmquist avers that a teacher of reading "cannot function effectively unless he knows a great deal about some of the most influential individuals and groups in the student's life."

These psychological influences in the child's home background are not the ones usually studied in investigations of the effects of "home background" on learning to read, but if we are searching for hypotheses for cross-national comparisons, these two factors stand out as important dimensions of difference, (1) the parents' attitudes and related behavior toward their child's reading, and (2) the relationship between the child's teachers and parents.

Book Resources

One variable often considered in studies of the literacy learner's home background is the amount of books and other reading matter to be found there. Similarly, research on school variables often considers the supply of books in that location, too. It seems appropriate to gather all this information together here because it is clear that there is general agreement on the importance of a good supply of books in a wide range of sources. However, the book resources variable is still extraneous, because many children do learn to read with a very limited book environment. Indeed it is possible to learn to read without any commercially published books at all, of course—with self-made books in a language-experience approach.

Denmark is a country in which the value of a rich book environment has been recognized, and good progress seems to have been made toward providing one. The good cooperation between schools and public library services in Denmark is particularly notable. The development of the public libraries themselves is regarded as a powerful factor in the improvement of children's reading. The statistics quoted on reading materials for normal and above-average readers in Denmark are impressive. This is particularly so when one considers the small size of the market for Danish language publishers.

Another explanation for Japan's success in achieving a very high rate of literacy is the many good reading materials available at low prices. There is much indirect evidence to substantiate this in the chapter on Japan.

In contrast is the unfavorable book environment of literacy learners in India. Many schools have no special place for displaying books or for quietly reading them. The number of books provided is very inadequate. In elementary schools, libraries have no real existence and very few books are accessible to children. Nor is the problem confined to the schools. However, educators in India clearly are concerned about the shortage of books and the number of publications for children is increasing steadily. Several government projects for improving the quality of books are in progress also. In many Israeli primary schools, too, libraries are poor in both quantity and quality. Also, public libraries develop slowly and children's sections are often poorly stocked. Israel's Ministry of Education is making efforts to alleviate these shortages, but provisions remain inadequate.

It is not within the scope of this study to gather comparative statistics on the book supply in different countries. The aim here is to show that there is international agreement on the importance of a rich supply of books in the literacy learner's environment at school, at home, and elsewhere. Jansen indicates the process by which this factor influences the literacy learner in Denmark. Where books and reading are a frequent everyday occurrence in the child's life, "when formal education starts in the course of grade I, a natural interest in reading already exists. Teachers in kindergarten classes and in the elementary grades maintain this initial interest by reading stories to the children, by means of the class library, picture books, and the like. At the same time a foundation is being laid for reading."

The essence of this foundation is the orientation provided by natural, everyday life experiences with books and people who read them to themselves and who share them with their children. This kind of initiation to books opens the way to the solution of the first problems to be solved on the way to the successful literacy learner's development of cognitive clarity regarding the tasks of learning to read and write.

Economic Situations

It is also not within the scope of this present study to investigate actual economic factors in the development of literacy. But the need to study such variables is suggested by Samuel's comment that "literacy seems to be affected more by investment in education than by degree of phoneme-grapheme regularity in the language," for example. He shows that, "Finland, with very high literacy, invested 7.6 per cent of its national income in education. The United States, also with high literacy rates but lower than Finland's, invested 6.3 per cent of its income in education. Mexico, with low literacy rates, invested 3.0 per cent of its income in education; and Spain, also with low levels of literacy, invested only 1.5 per cent of its national wealth in education."[12] He makes this point simply as an example of the complexity of the variables in cross-national comparisons of literacy.

One economic factor that crops up in Part II is the question, *"Can the parents afford the cost of schooling?"* This has two aspects: (1) Are fees required and can the family afford them? (2) Can the family afford to forego the economic return that the child's labor would bring if he were not in school? Both these aspects can be seen in the historical development of Japanese public education. By 1900, tuition was free. At that same period, elementary school enrolment increased extremely rapidly. But this growth is also explained in part by the development of modern industry. It led to a higher standard of living and made it feasible for families to manage without earnings from their children's labor.

In India and Argentina these factors still hinder the growth of literacy. In the chapter on India it is noted that the main cause of the school drop-out problem is economic in origin. A child leaves school at about 9 years of age simply to help the family. The close correlation between economic conditions and literacy learning in the different regions of Argentina has been found to resemble Sir Cyril Burt's maps of the direct relationship between retarded learning and poverty in England.

Weakened physical health and malnutrition are other ways in which poverty inhibits learning. Thus, in the chapter on Argentina it is stated that "not the least important contributory cause of school failure is the state of health of the child. In the underprivileged areas . . . a number of related problems can be identified, such as sporadic malnutrition . . . ." The realization that poor nutrition inhibits learning led the British school system to provide inexpensive or free meals of an appropriate dietary standard as part of the reform in *education.*

But this is one of the more obvious ways in which poverty works against literacy learning. During the past decade a tremendous interest has grown in this problem among educators in the United States. The consensus of many different studies is that the "disadvantaged" are not restricted to any one racial or ethnic group. Poverty is the common characteristic of all such people. A great deal of research is being conducted on the mechanisms by which poverty undermines educational efforts to help all American children obtain their full rights to a share in those aspects of the culture that depend on literacy. The complexity of these variables is indicated by Mary Austin's comment in Chapter 23:

> A majority of the learning problems of poor children stem from their backgrounds. Mentioned most frequently in the professional literature as deterrents to success in learning to read are the following: negative self-concept, nonstandard English, deficiency in language skills, restricted background of experiences and concepts, difficulties in seeing relationships, insufficient motivation, and inability to see the value of reading and education.

Such psychological and linguistic effects are hardly touched on by any of the national chapters in Part Two, except the one on the United States. Furthermore, there seems to be no cross-national data on these variables in previous studies.

In conclusion, whether they lie in the school, in the home, or in other aspects of the culture, extraneous environmental factors can importantly affect the simple formula: linguistic stimuli–literacy learner's cognitive processes–expected literate responses. Therefore, the fourth part of our model is essential to understanding the development of literacy behavior, even though it deals with experiences that are "extraneous" to the basic formula. This study of this fourth category of influences has demonstrated the many environmental hazards that complicate the route of the straightforward cognitive development of the literacy learner.

REFERENCES

1. Balpuri, Surenda, "Whither adult education in India?" *Fundamental and Adult Education,* **10** (1958), 171–173.
2. Ansari, Nazir Ahmad, "Follow-up of literacy," *Indian Journal of Adult Education* (New Delhi), **22** (March 1961), 19–20.
3. Staiger, Ralph C., "Developments in reading and literacy education, 1956–1967," Chap. XIII of Gray, William S., *The Teaching of Reading and Writing,* 2nd ed., Paris: UNESCO, 1969, p. 282.
4. Burnet, Mary, *abc of Literacy,* Paris: UNESCO, 1965, p. 14.
5. Gray, William S., *The Teaching of Reading and Writing,* Paris: UNESCO, 1956, p. 27.
6. *Ibid.,* p. 248.
7. Downing, John, *i.t.a.'s Effectiveness in the Prevention and Treatment of Disabilities in Reading and Writing* (paper presented at World Mental Health Assembly, Washington, DC., November 1969), London: i.t.a. Foundation, 1970, p. 27.
8. Vernon, M. D., *Backwardness in Reading,* London: Cambridge University Press, 1957.
9. Strang, Ruth, "Evaluation of development in and through reading," in Farr, Roger (ed.), *Measurement and Evaluation of Reading,* New York: Harcourt, 1970, pp. 35–48.
10. Rawat, D. S., *A Battery of Reading Readiness Tests,* New Delhi: National Council of Educational Research and Training, 1964.
11. Young, Michael, and McGeeney, Patrick, *Learning Begins at Home: A Study of a Junior School & Its Parents,* London: Routledge and Kegan Paul, 1968.
12. Samuels, S. Jay, "Cross-national studies in reading: The relationship between the sound-letter correspondence in language and reading achievement," in Figurel, J. Allen (ed.), *Reading and Realism,* Newark, Del.: IRA, 1969, pp. 846–853.

CHAPTER 9

Linguistic Environments, I

JOHN DOWNING

LINGUISTIC environment refers to the specific setting of the literacy learner's task of relating the visual stimuli of written language to the literate responses expected of him by his community—usually represented by his teacher. This specific language setting varies in three important ways in relation to our model:

1. *The literacy learner's own spoken language,* which he normally has in common with his family and peers. This is "L^1" (the first language).
2. *The writing system* used in the visual stimuli with which he is presented in the early stages of learning how to read and write.
3. *The spoken language that his teacher regards as the proper basis* for the learner's expected literate responses. This is "L^2" (the second language).

"Writing system" has its normally accepted meaning among scientific linguists and psycholinguists; it does not refer to a system for *teaching* writing. Its technical reference is limited strictly to the systematic coding of spoken language by visible marks—usually printed in ink on paper. As Bloomfield emphatically stated, "Writing is not language, but merely a way of recording language by means of visible marks. . . . A language is the same no matter what system of writing may be used to record it, just as a person is the same no matter how you take his picture. The Japanese have three systems of writing and are developing a fourth. When the Turks, in 1928, adopted the Latin alphabet in place of the Arabic, they went on talking in just the same way as before."[1]

In discussions of the problem of the relationship between a spoken language and its writing system, the former is generally assumed to be some "standard" dialect—for example, "standard American English," "the Queen's English," or "received pronunciation." However, it must be emphasized immediately that this standard language can be as elusive as "the average man." Thus, both the L^2 of the teacher and the L^1 of the literacy learner may not coincide precisely with the standard language that is supposed to be coded by a writing system. But L^1 is likely to diverge more often and to a greater degree from the standard than is L^2.

Even if one ignores differences between L^2 and the standard language, there may yet be difficulties in relating the writing system to the spoken language it is designed to represent. For example, the written code may contain ambiguities or complexities to varying extents.

In summary, the literacy learner's linguistic environment may present three important types of difficulty:

1. There may be a *mismatch* between L^1 and L^2.
2. There may be a *mismatch* between the writing system and L^2, even though the latter may closely approximate the standard model on which the former is supposedly based for teaching purposes.
3. There may be a *compound mismatch* of both of the preceding mismatches.

According to our model, the literacy learner's task is to understand how a writing system is related to spoken language. He develops cognitive clarity regarding the nature of this task as he solves the problems of the logical relationships between these two aspects of language. It seems clear that the extent to which these mismatches occur in the child's linguistic environment may affect the degree of cognitive confusion that he is likely to experience in the initial stage of learning to read and write.

Mismatch Between L^1 and L^2

Many children throughout the world face this problem of a discrepancy between the L^1, which has been their chief source of linguistic experience prior to learning literacy, and the L^2, in which they are expected to develop the skills of reading and writing. The reasons for this situation range from educational considerations (the lack of any writing system for L^1) to political reasons (the imposition of an L^2 to emphasize its cultural ascendency over L^1). Because of people's strong emotional attachments to their languages, discussion of the problem of bilingualism tends to be controversial, especially when there are political considerations.

Gray's international survey concluded that "research shows that initial progress in learning to read and write is quickest in the mother tongue."[2] This was based on empirical evidence from studies in three countries: Ghana, Philippines, and New Caledonia.[3] Another UNESCO publication by Neijs echoes this conclusion in respect to adult literacy classes: "In teaching adults to read it is always best for them to begin in the mother tongue. It has also been demonstrated that an individual who is literate in his own language can learn to read and to understand a second language more easily than an illiterate can."[4] Thus, these two authoritative international publications both conclude emphatically that when the language of expected literate responses, L^2, matches the literacy learner's natural first language, L^1, learning to read is quicker and literacy teaching is more effective than when L^1 and L^2 are different. Stated conversely, a mismatch between L^1 and L^2 makes it more difficult to learn literacy.

A more recent review of this problem arrives at similar conclusions to those of Gray's international survey. Stewart notes that:

In many parts of the world, however, learning to read (even with substantial amounts of formal instruction) may be rendered infinitely more difficult by a tradition of writing primarily or exclusively in some language other than the one (or ones) which the population normally learns to speak.[5]

He proposes that in the United States teachers ought "to realize that retardation in the reading of English texts by Mexican-American or Navajo children probably has something to do with the fact that many of these children do not speak English natively."[6]

An interesting example of mismatch between L^1 and L^2 exists in the Irish Republic. English is the L^1 of the large majority of the population, yet initial literacy is taught in an L^2, which is a quite different language—Irish. If it is true that mismatch between L^1 and L^2 increases initial cognitive confusion then it would be predicted that Irish children would be significantly retarded in learning literacy as compared with, say, English children whose L^1 and L^2 coincide as English. Macnamara's careful objective research found that this was indeed the case. His conclusions include the following:

> Native-speakers of English in Ireland who have spent 42 per cent of their school time learning Irish do not achieve the same standard in written English as British children who have not learned a second language (estimated difference in standard, 17 months of English age). Neither do they achieve the same standard in written Irish as native speakers of Irish (estimated difference, 16 months of Irish age).[7]

Nancy Modiano's research in Mexico compared two groups of Indian children. The experimental group began reading in their native Indian tongue and transferred to Spanish reading in the second year. The control group was taught Spanish reading only. The experimental group scored significantly higher *in reading Spanish*. These results led Modiano to conclude that

> The youngsters of linguistic minorities learn to read with greater comprehension in the national language when they first learn to read in their mother tongue than when they receive all their reading instruction in the national language.[8]

Modiano's finding pin-points the stage at which mismatch between L^1 and L^2 is critical. It is most important to avoid increasing cognitive confusion *in the first experiences of problem solving involved* in understanding the nature of the task of learning to read. If the level of cognitive confusion becomes too high for the beginner he receives a setback from which it is very difficult to recover.

At first sight, it might seem strange that learning literacy in two languages is easier than learning literacy in only one. "Surely," it might be argued, "there is more to learn in two languages than in one!" What is overlooked in this argument is the fact that literacy skills can be considered in their own right *quite apart from their application in any specific language*. As was noted in Chapter 4, Mountford has pointed out that, when we have learned to speak our mother tongue, we do not have to learn *how to speak* all over again when we learn a foreign language. We simply transfer our speaking skills to the second language. Similarly, once we are literate in our first language of literacy we do not have to acquire literacy over again when we learn to read a second language. We need only extend our existing literacy. "Literacy is acquired once-for-all, like linguacy itself." [9]

Thus, the literacy learner's task is to acquire *literacy as such*, and not literacy in one specific language. The important question then becomes, "Is it easier to learn *literacy as such* in the mother tongue or in some second language?" and the supposed problem of transfer from one to the other fades to its proper relative insignificance. As we have seen from the evidence, the answer is that literacy is easier to acquire in the mother tongue, and the explanation proposed here for this conclusion is that, when L^1 and L^2 coincide closely in this way, cognitive confusion from this potential source of mismatch is reduced to a minimum.

Some scholars have expressed doubts about this conclusion. For example, Venezky argues that extralinguistic factors may bias experiments comparing learning to read in the mother tongue and a second language. His conclusion is that "the native literacy approach, although possessing obvious cultural advantages over the standard language approach, has yet to be proven scholastically superior." [10] His argument is an important one in relation to the theory proposed in this book, and it must be admitted that the evidence cited here is weakened by it. For example, Spolsky remarks that, "When reading and writing is an alien thing and associated with alien elements of the culture, it is not surprising to find reluctance to associate them with one's most precious possession, language." [11] Thus, Spolsky attributes the success of beginning reading in L^1 rather than in a different L^2 to culturally motivating forces. From the practical point of view this might seem to strengthen the case for initial literacy to be taught in L^1, but from the theoretical standpoint it represents an alternative explanation for the superiority of L^1 instruction.

However, Macnamara's research finding is more difficult to explain on grounds of cultural motivation. In Ireland, L^2 (Irish) has great national and cultural status, whereas L^1 (English) is the language of the rulers who were rejected and overthrown in the rebellion that is still idealized daily in the Irish press. There must, at least, be emotional ambivalence to L^1. Furthermore, strong incentives to learn literacy in L^2 are provided by the education system—matriculation in the Irish language is a prerequisite for entry to the University. Despite these cultural and reality motives in favor of L^2, Macnamara's research shows conclusively that introduction to literacy in it has seriously retarded Irish children's development of *literacy as such*. Therefore, it seems that the cognitive confusion caused by the mismatch between L^1 and L^2 actually smothers any effects that might be derived from cultural motives or reality incentives to learn literacy in L^2.

Thus, cognitive factors are probably of greater importance than motivational ones in this problem, although the latter, of course, can by no means be dismissed as insignificant.

Other arguments against the superiority of beginning the teaching of literacy in the mother tongue over initial instruction in a second language seem super-ficial and irrelevant. For example, the policy of teaching literacy in the mother tongue has been criticized on the grounds that it is vastly expensive. This may be so, but that is a matter for administrators who have to decide if their budgets can afford to produce or purchase materials in L^1. Proponents of the language-experience approach would point out that it costs no more to teach literacy in the mother tongue by language-experience techniques than to teach literacy in a second language by the same techniques. The ingredients of paper and pens are the same. But all this is irrelevant to the basic theoretical issue. The fact remains that a mismatch between L^1 and L^2 is an important cause of difficulty in beginning reading, and this is most likely the result of the substantial increase in cognitive confusion that the literacy learner must clarify to understand the nature of the learning-to-read task.

D^1 and D^2

In the preceding section the mismatch between L^1 and L^2 has been discussed in respect to the most patent examples: where L^1 is English and L^2 is Irish, or where L^1 is an Indian language and L^2 is Spanish. However, this difference is less obvious when L^1 and L^2 are *dialects* of what is commonly taken to be "the same language." If cognitive confusion is caused by mismatch between L^1 and L^2, literacy learners may be more or less confused also if their dialect, D^1, is different from the teacher's dialect, D^2, in which they are expected to make literate responses. For example, Stewart hypothesizes that, in the United States, "the language-learning problems of a Negro-dialect speaker who is trying to acquire standard English are, in many ways, more like those of, say, a Spanish speaker who is trying to acquire English than they are like those of a middle-class English-speaking child." [12]

Österberg makes the same point regarding dialects in Sweden and stresses the *relativity* of L^1 and L^2 differences:

> The study of Scandinavian language conditions, for example, illustrates the relative character of all attempts to draw dividing lines between different languages . . . . Hence it follows from a linguistic point of view that it is the magnitude of the differences between the language variants which is decisive in the question of whether bilingualism obtains or not . . . and it is of secondary importance whether, and in what manner, the combination embraces dialect and language.

Therefore, he states that "it seems justifiable to assert that a bilingual problem exists where two different language variants, on grounds of linguistic differences and/or communication obstacles—partly perhaps of an emotional or social nature—can be described as 'alien' vis-a-vis each other." [13]

Thus, both emotional-motivational and cognitive factors are recognized as operating in mismatches at the dialect level as well as at that of discrete languages.

Although there has been a dramatic increase in concern for this problem of dialect mismatch in the last few years among linguists and psychologists, it has often been ignored and misunderstood by educators. Just as ethnocentric attitudes have frustrated the needs of minority language groups, so also has linguacentrism frustrated the parallel needs of members of minority dialect groups. For example, Spolsky's criticism is that "Teachers and educational systems have often just assumed that everyone speaks the standard dialect. . . . Thus, it has been and still is common for children to come to school and be classified as mentally retarded when they fail intelligence tests given in a language they don't know; to sit for years in a classroom where the teacher ignores that the whole of the class speaks a language he doesn't; to be treated as stupid because their dialect differs from the standard aimed at by the teacher."

The emotional effects of the mismatch between D^1 and D^2 probably arise chiefly from teachers' "erroneous assumption that the 'mother tongue' is the standard language,"[14] as Spolsky puts it. If there were less ignorance of, and therefore less insensitivity toward, such dialect differences there might be a more tolerant climate in which emotional reactions would be less likely to occur. Goodman remarks that "Ironically, well-meaning adults, including teachers who would never intentionally reject a child or any important characteristic of a child, such as the clothes he wears or the color of his skin, will immediately and emphatically reject his language."[15] But all too often teachers regard their D^2 "as the correct and pure version of the language, and treat any variation as corrupt or debased, or careless,"[16] as Spolsky has noted.

The emotional reaction to such rejection is predictable. Language is the holy of holies of culture. Therefore, to attack an individual's language is to commit an act of sacrilege on the innermost cultural sanctum of the personality. The intensely hostile resistance is only to be expected. As Tax puts it, when divergent speakers are required to correct their language:

> They often *cannot* do what the teacher asks, things which seem to them, consciously or unconsciously to denigrate their homes, their people and their culture.[17]

Or, in Goodman's words: "But if the teacher 'corrects' the dialect-based divergent language, this is at cross purposes with the direction of growth of the child. All his past and present language experience contradicts what the teacher tells him. School becomes a place where people talk funny and teachers tell you things about your language that aren't true."[18]

One must recognize that the literacy learner whose D^1 fails to match his teacher's D^2 is discriminated against in many other ways besides denigration of his dialect. Downing and Thackray have shown that "the child's home background and his culture or sub-culture especially are extremely significant determinants of readiness," and that the problem for the member of a divergent subculture is that his whole background of preschool experience as well as his different dialect set him off at school on the wrong foot. "In particular, his teachers and the whole educational system are geared to a different sub-culture from the one which he has naturally accepted as good—good for his parents, good for his brothers and sisters, good for his friends and therefore, good for him."[19]

However, subcultures do not have to be rejected because they are divergent. For example, in Britain, a variety of subcultures and dialects are not only tolerated but their variations in behavior and speech are generally accepted with friendly amusement, although some—the Cockney dialect, for example— are regarded as having low status and are associated with educational problems. Furthermore, the past decade has seen tremendous efforts to break down racial prejudice in the United States. A great deal remains to be done, but already it is clear that prejudice toward minority subcultures is not inevitable. If prejudice toward race and skin color can be relieved, it seems reasonable to assert that prejudice toward dialect can similarly be ameliorated. Thus, in 1965, Loban made the following appeal in the United States:

> In the kindergarten and in the earliest years of school, the emphasis should be upon the child's using *whatever dialect of the language he already speaks* as the means of thinking and exploring and imagining. We need teachers who know that such dialects are essentially respectable and good.[20]

If prejudice and its counterreactions are not an inevitable result of the mismatch between D^1 and D^2, one is still left with the cognitive problems indicated by Österberg's analysis quoted earlier in this chapter.

One must be clear that Österberg is not referring to so-called linguistic deprivation. Some educators have supposed that children's thinking must be defective or deficient because their language is different from the standard dialect. For example, Bernstein has characterized lower-working-class English dialect as a "restricted code" because he proposes that this form of the language is inherently limited and therefore limits the cognitive growth of its users.[21] But Bernstein and others who have followed the original linguistic relativity notion of such theorists as Sapir and Whorf have never succeeded in establishing empirically their hypothesis that language limits thought in any important sense. As Spolsky reminds us, "No experiments have been designed or conducted that show a clear advantage to speakers of one language over speakers of another in the performance of a specific language-aided task."[22]

Others have made more extravagant claims than Bernstein. For example, Bereiter and Englemann have developed instructional programs based on the notion that lower-class children are so linguistically deprived that they do not possess the basic concepts for thinking about school learning problems. As they have no language they must be taught language from scratch.

Goodman states the contrary:

> There is abundant evidence that black children wherever they are and whatever the status of their dialects are not linguistically deprived . . . .

And he flatly denies "the flamboyant, baseless assertions of pseudo authorities such as Carl Bereiter and Siegfried Englemann (1966). The myth of linguistic deprivation which produces cognitive deficits is another example of assuming that children who can't talk like whites have nothing worth talking about."[23]

Although Goodman is referring to the dialects of black and white children in America, his remarks apply with equal force to the notion of the "linguistic incompetence" and "restricted code" of British lower-working-class children.

In another article, Goodman spells out his position as follows: "Every child brings to school, when he comes, five or six years of language and of experience." What is more: "In every respect the process of language development of the divergent speaker is exactly the same as that of the standard speaker. His language when he enters schools is just as systematic, just as grammatical within the norms of his dialect, just as much a part of him as any other child's is."[24]

The cognitive difficulties of the divergent dialect speaker who is trying to learn literacy are not an intrinsic part of his linguistic and mental make-up. He is neither linguistically deprived nor cognitively deficient. The cause of his difficulty lies in the fact that his dialect D^1 does not match the dialect D^2 that is the supposed basis for the literate responses demanded of him. He is hampered and hindered by the fog of ambiguity created by the fact that he is required to develop literacy skills not in relation to the spoken language he knows, but to someone else's speech, which he does not know.

Österberg provides this example: "It is universally asserted, for instance, that the children in the first place should understand what they read. If for example, they say 'mamma' in their daily speech, then the language variant 'mor,' which is not yet linguistically adequate, is unlikely to favour the tempo of reading development."[25] This is at the level of the word unit. If the writing system is alphabetic and its graphemes are to be associated with the phonemes of speech, considerable confusion can be caused if the teacher gives instruction in the relations between the writing system's graphemes and the phonemes of dialect D^2 while the literacy learner is thinking in terms of the *different* phonemic system of his dialect D^1. As Lado, for example, emphasizes, "There is an unbelievably strong force binding the units—the phonemes—of any language in their complex of contrasts. The adult speaker of one language cannot easily pronounce language sounds of another even though he has no speech impediment, and what is even more startling, he cannot easily hear language sounds other than those of his native language even though he suffers no hearing defect."[26] Lado's book is concerned with comparing languages as such, hence his reference to adults in the preceding passage. Children of school age will already have the same "deafness" for phonemes not in their own language or dialect. Hence, Goodman's assertion that "phonics programs which attempt to teach a relationship between letters and sounds cannot be universally applicable to all dialects." What is more significant is his observation that "The instruction may be not only inappropriate but confusing."[27] Lado refers to these difficulties of hearing phonemes that the learner does not possess in his own language as "*perception blind spots*" because the deficiency is not one of auditory *sensation* but of auditory *perception*. Unfortunately, what is well known to foreign language teachers is barely recognized by many reading teachers. As a result, children who speak divergent dialects often are confused by attempts to teach them that certain graphemes represent phonemes that for them simply do not exist. Evidence of this confusion in the reader is regarded by the teacher as just "bad speech," for example, the Cockney who reads *I am hanging my hat on the arm of the chair* as "I ham 'anging my 'at on the harm of my chair." If the Cockney child writes *I ham 'anging me 'at on the harm of me chair* this equally is regarded as some kind of language deficiency. Whereas, in fact, both are signs of the utter confusion caused by insisting that the Cockney must relate grapheme *h* to the phoneme /h/, which the teacher's dialect D^2 does have, but which for the Cockney learner may seem a figment of his teacher's imagination. Or does he suspect his own hearing is defective? What is certain is the considerable confusion caused by teaching children code symbols for sounds that do not exist for them.

Nor is the problem limited to phonemic mismatches, as the Cockney substitution of "me" for *my* indicates in the example. The ramifications of this problem are many, as *Teaching Black Children to Read* has shown in several of its articles. For example, Joan Baratz shows how mismatches in syntactic structures may be as important as discrepancies between the phonemic systems of D^1 and D^2. These mismatches of syntax are a further source of confusion for the literacy learner trying to understand how literacy is related to the language he knows.[28]

Österberg describes vividly how this cognitive confusion over literacy may gradually pollute the total school experience:

> Pupils have difficulty in grasping the links between extramural life and intramural work. Experiences derived in the previous environment are consciously or unconsciously pushed into the background as unfavoured phenomena. What is learned at school obtains no natural anchorage in the children's experiences and spontaneous observations. The school's study content then becomes a separate phenomenon. Progress does not proceed from the concrete, the already known. The matter assimilated becomes associated with theoretical constructions and psychic contents, which in structure and function have no roots in practical life outside the school. What is assimilated becomes the "barely learnt," and as a result processes of forgetting set in more readily. In the same way subjective tiredness, for instance, acquires fairly wide scope and the results of schoolwork suffer generally. The school is constructing a system of study and contributing to a basis of personality development which lacks two fundamental qualities—continuity and personal integration.[29]

Experimental Evidence of the Effects of D^1 Versus D^2 Mismatch

An excellent experiment was devised by Österberg to check objectively on some of these hypothesized effects of the mismatch between D^1 and D^2. It was conducted in the Piteå district of Sweden, which has a "distinctive, archaic and still vital" dialect spoken by some 30,000 people. It has no literature in it, and teachers' attitudes and public opinion generally toward this Piteå dialect are negative. Observations confirmed that Piteå school children and adults suffer from language difficulties. Österberg's hypothesis was that these difficulties "are dialect conditioned and that they spring from the individual's encounter with the standard language" that "begins systematically with school attendance."[30]

To test this hypothesis, Österberg compared an experimental group that was instructed in dialect (D^1) with a control group that was taught as usual in the standard language (D^2). About 350 pupils were allocated randomly to the two groups, and so also were their teachers. Subsequent testing demonstrated that the children in groups D^1 and D^2 were equivalent in school readiness and intelligence, and in other variables also. Training of the teachers and standardization of their methods were equated, too.

Group D^1 began with a ten weeks' period of instruction in the Piteå dialect, while group D^2 received parallel instruction except that it was in standard Swedish. A basal reading series was used that was new to all the teachers in both groups. The content was identical in the D^1 and D^2 readers, except that the text was translated into the Piteå dialect in the former. After ten weeks several tests were administered and a further instructional period of twenty-five weeks began in which *both groups* were instructed in D^2, except that group D^1 was given a gradual transition from D^1 to D^2 in the first four weeks of this second period.

The tests at the end of the initial ten weeks of instruction found the D^1 group to be significantly superior in oral reading, reading rate, and comprehension. The differences were large and Österberg comments that "What first and foremost characterizes D^1 pupils' lead is the mastery of difficult aptitudes in reading technique which we called articulation and the ability to combine and read off both words and word-groups. Thanks to the sureness many of them had already gained in articulation, for instance, they have also to some extent begun to read fluently." [31]

These tests were, of course, administered in D^1 to the D^1 group and in D^2 to the D^2 group. At the end of the second experimental period all tests were given in D^2 to both the D^1 and D^2 groups. Therefore, at this point the D^2 group was being tested in the language in which it had received instruction for thirty-five weeks, whereas the D^1 group had been exposed to D^2 materials for only twenty-five weeks, or somewhat less if one takes into account the four-week transitional period. Yet in reading D^2 material, the D^1 group surpassed the D^2 group.

Österberg's results provide strong evidence that mismatch between D^1 and D^2 is an important handicap in learning literacy. Furthermore, his finding that initial D^1 instruction is superior in transfer to D^2 reading firmly fixes the temporal locus of the trouble. Mismatch has its ill effects in the first initiation phase of learning literacy.

Österberg reports a number of observations made of the children's behavior in the experimental and control groups and relates one comparatively notable feature of the latter. The D^2 pupils become "*generally unsure and their uncertainty affects their performance in lettering, articulation and reading tempo.*" [32] This indicates the manner in which this mismatch produces its harmful results in poorer reading and writing attainments. Österberg's words immediately call to mind Vernon's descriptions of cognitive confusion. Therefore, it seems clear that mismatch between L^1 and L^2 or between D^1 and D^2 creates a higher level of confusion for the beginner. His groping for an understanding of concepts of language and literacy and the problems to be solved in relating them is made all the more a blind trial-and-error process, and thus his progress toward cognitive clarity is hampered and hindered.

From the practical educational point of view, therefore, it is small wonder that Lefevre's *Linguistics and the Teaching of Reading* so strongly emphasizes that "Children should first be taught to read and write the same language that they already speak and understand when they enter school."[33] Lefevre shows that dialect as a "variant of the mother tongue can serve as a basis for language growth and development as nothing else can."[34] The reason he gives is that "Since the child entering school is already experienced at an unconscious level in the basic signals and structures of his language, primary reading and writing instruction should begin with developing his consciousness of them in relation to the graphic system." Furthermore, "If we really want him to learn reading and writing—to become literate—we should not attempt instead to convert him to another dialect, nor to 'purify' his speech."[35]

In Part Two it is revealed that the problem of dialects certainly is widespread, but the causal connection between dialect mismatch and reading failure is not so widely recognized or understood.

Most attention to this problem by public education systems has been shown in recent years in the United States, where many practical efforts are being made currently to cope with both the L^1 versus L^2 and the D^1 versus D^2 mismatches. In the chapter on Argentina keen awareness of the dialect difficulty is shown, but there is less evidence of practical work to overcome it in that country. Numerous regional disparities not only between each other but also between them and the "correct" language taught in schools and textbooks is one important cause of the large proportion of grade I repeaters. This is in spite of the fact that American Spanish enjoys a greater uniformity than that found in Spain.[36]

Many American reading specialists are not aware of the fact that, just as American Spanish is more homogeneous than the Spanish of Spain, so also British English has a much wider range of dialect differences than American English. Yet, although current interest in this problem is quite high in the United States, in Great Britain very little concern has been shown for the problem of dialect as a specific cause of reading difficulties. In the chapter on Britain the L^1 versus L^2 problem of Welsh speaking children is referred to, as well as the same difficulty in teaching, for example, Pakistani, Greek Cypriot, and Italian immigrants in Britain. West Indian immigrants whose trouble is, of course, properly the one of mismatch between dialects of English are also mentioned. But there is little or no concern for the problem of native English dialects. Where action is being taken to assist immigrants in this difficulty it most often seems to take the form of teaching spoken standard English first, after which literacy is taught in relation to the acquired English as a second language. This seems to ignore the consensus of research that literacy is best taught in the first language or first dialect of the child. One intuitive move in this direction is the *Nippers* series of readers, which are thought to have greater appeal to "working-class" children in their story content. However, the linguistic mismatch problem is completely missed in these books because the working-class dialect has been "tidied up" to make the books more acceptable to teachers who objected to the use of "bad grammar." This demonstrates very well the almost total lack of recognition among British educators that dialect represents a reading problem that may be amenable to some practical solution.

In Chapter 19, India's vast linguistic problems—179 languages and 544 dialects—are discussed. China's dialect problem is well known, and in the chapter on Hong Kong one aspect of the difficulty there is mentioned: teachers' preferences for the "common language" (Kuoyu) as the spoken medium of instruction rather than Cantonese, which is the native tongue of most of the pupils.

In the chapter on the USSR, the extension of Elkonin's Russian experiments for teaching children to read in the Armenian and Yakutsk languages is reported, and Gertrude Hildreth describes the usual practice in this respect: "Over fifty different languages are spoken throughout the republics of the Soviet Union. Children first learn to read and write the mother tongue and then proceed to standard Russian if it is not their native speech."[37] Spolsky also refers to this approach in the USSR: "One good example of a 'vernacular first' educational policy is the Soviet Union, where the various Republics provide education in the vernacular as far as it will go, at the same time teaching Russian and ultimately, in most cases, switching to Russian."[38] But none of these sources mentions to what extent this Soviet policy has been extended to dialects of, for example, Russian.

Thus, in varying ways, more or less attention is paid to the principle firmly established by research, stated explicitly by McDavid as follows:

A reading program, in any language, at any stage in a student's career, is likely to be effective in proportion to its use of the language habits that the student has acquired in speaking.[39]

Mismatch Between Spoken and Written Forms of Language

Conventionally, writing systems are classified into three types "according to the units of language that they represent."[40] Thus, Lado lists

1. *Alphabetic* writing systems in which the characters represent phonemes of the language.
2. *Syllabic* writing systems in which the characters stand for syllables rather than phonemes.
3. *Logographic* writing systems in which the characters represent morphemes—that is, units of form and meaning—rather than units of sound such as syllables or phonemes.

All three of these types are represented in the national chapters of Part Two. For example, Great Britain, Israel, and the USSR all have *alphabetic* writing systems, although the actual characters used to represent the phonemes of English, Hebrew, and Russian, respectively, are different. Hong Kong provides a case of a country using a *logographic* system for its Chinese language. Japan uses both *syllabic* and *logographic* systems.

The general belief is that the order of difficulty in learning these alternatives is from alphabetic (the easiest) to logographic (the hardest), with some uncertainty as to the level of difficulty of syllabic writing systems. Thus, Gray accepted the common view of the difficulty of learning literacy in Chinese.[41] As Goody confirms, "Many scholars of China have seen a connection between a low literacy rate and the use of a non-alphabetic script." For example, he quotes one Chinese writer as follows: "The 'Chinese script' of China is certainly too difficult for the masses and only the gentry class can have time enough to learn it, so that politically and culturally it is an enormous impediment."[42]

Number of Characters

What is thought to be the cause of the difficulty in the Chinese logographic writing system? Goody states that "Any system of writing which makes the sign stand directly for the object must be extremely complex." He suggests that this complexity arises in the following manner:

It can extend its vocabulary by . . . making the sign stand either for a more general class of objects of for other referents connected with the original picture by an association of meanings which may be related to one another either in a continuous or in a discontinuous manner. Either process of semantic extension is to some extent arbitrary or esoteric; and as a result the interpretation of these signs is neither easy nor explicit.

Therefore, each new character has to be learned "as a separate sign for a separate word." This means in effect that

a minimum of 3,000 such characters have to be learned before one can be reasonably literate . . . and with a repertoire of some 50,000 characters to be mastered, it normally takes about twenty years to reach full literate proficiency. China, therefore, stands as an extreme example of how, when a virtually non-phonetic system of writing becomes sufficiently developed to express a large number of meanings explicitly, only a small and specially trained professional group in the total society can master it, and partake of the literate culture.[43]

Apart from primitive pictographs, all writing systems use arbitrary signs. Therefore, Goody's criticism of the logographic system essentially is concerned with the very *large number of characters* that the literacy learner must acquire. Halle makes this same point by analogy:

Since the strokes (in Chinese characters) are arbitrary symbols, the writer's or reader's task is equivalent to that of a person trying to remember telephone numbers.

And, since in order to read a newspaper one needs to be able to read several thousand words, the person who wishes to read a Chinese newspaper must have memorized several thousand arbitrary stroke sequences. This task is roughly equivalent to memorizing several thousand telephone numbers . . . . [44]

Both Goody and Halle are external observers of the Chinese language problem. Both are from English speaking nations with the same alphabetic writing system. It is curious that the native authors of the chapters on Hong Kong and Japan, which both use logographic systems, do not seem to view them as being exceptionally complex.

Leong actually quotes the same paragraph from Halle in order to emphasize his disagreement with it: "Although each character has to be learned, the often mentioned reliance on rote memory is overrated. . . . The comparison to memorizing telephone numbers is not quite apt, as chunking and other mnemonic devices can make the task more meaningful and increase one's storage capacity." Leong goes on to present a closely reasoned argument to the effect that there is much greater similarity between learning to read in English and Chinese than is usually supposed. In particular, the Chinese logographs can be analyzed into smaller units that operate systematically, and thus the burden of memorization may be much less than Goody and Halle, for instance, suggest.

In the chapter on Japan it is similarly pointed out that Kanji logographs can be classified according to various radicals. Therefore, students can learn that Kanji are not unsystematic symbols but are constructed from combinations of different radicals.

Hence, the burden of memorizing thousands of characters in Chinese and the somewhat smaller number in the Kanji system of Japanese may have been overestimated. The burden of memorization in the alphabetic writing system has certainly been underestimated in contrast. For example, many parents and reading teachers in Britain and the United States believe that their children have to learn only twenty-six characters in the Roman alphabet, which is the basis for the English writing system. But, in actual fact, English orthography is much more complex. This arises from several sources of additional characters that are often overlooked by adults who have long since forgotten what it was like to be a beginner in literacy learning:

1. Printed characters take alternative forms: capital letters as well as lower case ones, and some variations on the latter. There are also the variations in the cursive form of handwriting. Thus, the word *beg* may have the following alternative graphic forms:

$$BEG, \; Beg, \; Beg, \; beg, \; beg, \; Beg, \; beg$$

2. The units of an alphabetic writing system are not merely the individual characters. The alphabetic system was invented as a code for phonemes— that is, those units of speech sound that make a significant and systematic difference in meaning. English has approximately 40 phonemic units (varying with dialect), which are supposed to be signaled by the graphemic

units of the writing system. Clearly, twenty-six individual letters cannot suffice for the forty phonemes. Also, the variations listed as the first source here do not have any special phonemic function. The English phonemes that do not typically have a single-letter grapheme in the writing system are represented instead by digraphs: *ch, th, sh, ng, oo,* and so on. There would need to be at least forty graphemes to code the forty phonemes if the code were perfectly systematic.

3. There is in addition a great deal of redundancy in the English writing system. Although there are only about forty phonemes, some of them have many alternative graphemes: *ie, y, uy, igh, eye, i, ui,* for the single phoneme common to the words *pie, my, guy, high, eye, rind, guide.*

Ellis, the nineteenth-century linguist, analyzed all the alternative ways of printing and writing the forty or so phonemes of English and found more than 2,000 alternative graphemes.[45]

Other alphabetic writing systems vary in the extent to which their total number of graphemes extends beyond the small number of characters in the basic alphabet. English probably is especially rich in alternative graphemes, but the writing system of Hindi has more than one source of variation—which increases the total number of characters well beyond the fifty-two listed in the basic table of Hindi characters in the chapter on India—for example, the alternative vowel symbols to be employed according to position in the word, and the special symbols for consonant clusters.

Thus, the difference between logographic and alphabetic writing systems may have been exaggerated in respect to their difference in number of characters. Similarly, differences in the length of time needed to learn them may have been overestimated. For example, Goody's claim that "it normally takes about twenty years to reach full literate proficiency" in China, suggests that it takes less time in Britain. But what does "full literate proficiency" mean in these two countries? One could claim that very few people achieve full literate proficiency in the English writing system, if that phrase includes the ability to spell from memory any word according to the conventions of English orthography. Probably, both in China and in England it is more appropriate to recognize that literacy learning is a lifetime process. The existence of an apparently simple and limited alphabet in the latter country may be misleading to educators in judging the time needed for acquiring literacy.

Yet, there do exist some notable contrasts in the number of characters to be learned by literacy learners in different countries. For example, Finnish children have very few to acquire, even when alternatives such as capital and lower-case letters are counted. Japanese children, in contrast, have to cope with several alternative writing systems for the one language: Hiragana, Katakana, and Kanji. But, despite the large number of alternative characters to be memorized, Japanese children achieve remarkably well in literacy.

These considerations lead one to question whether the sheer number of characters to be memorized is *in itself* such a significant cause of difficulty in learning to read and write as has been commonly supposed. Extending one's repertoire of logographic characters in Chinese may not be so very different from extending one's word, phrase, and sentence recognition vocabulary in written English. Both take time and both probably never reach the ultimate ideal level of "full literate proficiency" in any individual.

What is more likely to be of psychological significance in the beginner in literacy learning is the extent to which the features of the array of written characters he meets in his early literacy experiences systematically parallel his past experience of features of spoken language. In other words, how well do the characteristics of the writing system match appropriately the features of language to which he has been and still is continually exposed. If the writing system is a code of one sort or another for units of speech, the child will understand its symbolic and coding function and mode of operation to the extent that the samples of written language he meets actually demonstrate them. In this the number of different characters presented to the beginner could have one important influence.

For example, if the writing system to be associated with the spoken language is an alphabetic one, then the samples of written language provided for the child ought to reflect its alphabetic nature. Only in this way can the learner understand the characteristics of the decoding and encoding processes of reading and writing. One must hasten to emphasize additionally that if the samples also fail to demonstrate realistically the communicative and expressive functions of decoding and encoding, a vital aspect of the written code will be missing. Decoding or encoding are meaningless terms if nothing *relevant* gets coded. However, provided that the material is clearly functional for the learner, it ought to reflect as clearly as possible the way in which the code operates. But, if the writing system has many alternative printed and written characters for the same linguistic units, and the initial learning samples contain a variety of these, it is likely to be more difficult for the beginner to perceive the *system* in the writing system. For example, the English sentence, "I like my pie" quite clearly fits the need to provide beginners with linguistically functional samples, but the basic alphabetic nature of the English writing system is concealed when it is printed in the conventional English orthography:

I like my pie.

All four words contain the same phoneme, which coincides with the whole of the first word "I," but it is represented by four different graphemes: (1) *I*; (2) *i.e*; (3) *y*; and (4) *ie*. Therefore, this sentence provides no experience whatsoever of the essential grapheme-phoneme basis of an alphabetic writing system.

Contrast this with the same sentence printed in i.t.a.:

ie liek mie pie

This initial writing system clarifies the alphabetic coding operation in natural examples of the English language. In a writing system less regular than i.t.a., the same clear correspondence between units of speech and units of writing in an alphabetic system can be obtained by *restricting the vocabulary* used in the samples presented to beginners: *Dan can fan Nan.* However, as this example shows, the vital principle that early decoding and encoding should be functional in communication or expression, which is relevant for the learner, is sacrificed.

Another example of the effects of excessive variety of alternative characters in the initial stages is in the use of capital letters. In one well-known British basal reading series the common and meaningful word "dog" occurs three times in the first little preprimer. But it is printed with different characters each time: *dog, Dog, DOG.* This must make it more difficult for the learner to relate written language to spoken language than is the case in the alternative i.t.a. version of the same book, which has ꝺog, ꝺog, ꝺog, in the same three places in the story.

In the chapter on Finland it is indicated that this problem has been recognized in Finnish reading, too. Beginners learn to read first in capital letters only; lower-case letters are not introduced until *the process* has been mastered in the capital forms of the characters.

Malmquist,[46] in Sweden, was concerned with the problem of when to introduce cursive script in addition to manuscript print for children's writing. There, as in many other countries, children usually begin writing in manuscript print similar to that found in their reading materials. In Sweden it was the convention for children to transfer from manuscript print to cursive script before the end of first grade. Malmquist compared a control group transferring at this usual time with an experimental group that was not required to make the change until the end of the third grade. In all other respects, the backgrounds of the children and their school experiences (including the teacher variable) were matched in the two groups. The experimental group proved significantly superior in the clarity and legibility of their handwriting during the time they continued to use the manuscript print. Furthermore, they were superior in *silent reading comprehension.* At the end of the third grade, the experimental group's cursive writing, which they had been using for only a few weeks, was superior in quality and equal in speed to that of the control group, which had been using it for more than two years. Thus, once again we find evidence that it is the earliest experiences of literacy that are most important. The reduction in the variety of alternative symbols to which the experimental group was exposed during the first two and a half years led to an improvement in reading as well as in writing achievements that was maintained later when the extra alternative cursive characters were added.

In free writing, the emphasis is on developing children's understanding of the communicative and expressive function of writing through their own experience of authorship. The existence of a variety of alternative written symbols either for the same phoneme or for the same morpheme is likely to be an important source of cognitive confusion in this aspect of understanding the logic of the written code for spoken language. For example, in writing the conventional orthography of English, the child must hesitate when writing a word like "cat." He hears /k/ but does not know whether to write *kat* or *cat* because both *c* and *k* are available. Therefore, he hesitates at this choice point. Actually the selection has no simple phonemic basis. But he does not know this, and therefore, it seems probable that the choice is puzzling to him. He hears no difference between the initial phoneme of words he has met in his reading such as *cap* and *kid,* yet they begin with different letters. He may wonder if he has a hearing defect. Hence the noticeable hesitations at such choice points in his written composition.

This is probably a very important source of puzzlement and confusion. It may cause a significant increase in the amount of initial cognitive confusion in the mind of the beginner who is striving to understand how the structure of the written form of language is related to his past experience and developing consciousness of the structure of speech. Writing systems vary greatly in this respect, and one valuable research test of the theory proposed in this book would be a cross-national comparison of hesitations in the writing of beginners in different languages. Even within the same language this could be studied by comparing alternative writing systems for it. Thus, although i.t.a. retains the *c/k* choice point, the traditional English orthography has more: *x, q, ch,* and so on. One would predict more hesitations in the beginner's writing of this phoneme in T.O.

Linguistically, of course, there is no logical mismatch between the units of spoken language and the symbols of written language when the former have two or more alternative symbolizations in the latter. But *experientially* for the literacy learner there may appear to be a mismatch in this situation. Malmquist's experimental data strongly suggest that cognitive clarity was readily developed in his experimental group because the superfluous variety of symbols was reduced. The amount of unnecessary "noise" in the stimulus situation was cut down sufficiently for these students to perceive more rapidly the important structural elements of the code and the way they operate. In contrast, the control group were hindered in their groping for cognitive clarity by the extra superfluous variations in the cursive characters thrust on them before they had mastered the manuscript symbols.

Morphemic Versus Phonological Units

Lado's three-fold classification of writing systems includes one that was based on the visual coding of morphemes (logographic systems) and two in which the units to be coded are *phonological* (syllabic and alphabetic systems). This typology of writing systems seems to be widely accepted. For instance, Gray's international survey used the same three-fold categorization under the labels: "word-concept characters," "syllable-sound characters," and "letter-sound characters," respectively.[47]

However, although these classifications may serve quite well to emphasize the major difference in the kind and size of linguistic units that are the essential elements of each type of code, there are at least two misconceptions that have arisen from the currency of this typology.

The first one is indicated by Gray's description of ideographs: "Each character used in writing represents an idea or concept . . . ." Although Gray adds "more strictly a morpheme," many reading teachers often share the "widespread but false conclusion that Chinese characters stand for 'ideas'"[48] as Robert Hall states. They seem to have jumped to the conclusion that the ideographic code is directly associated with ideas or concepts, which is certainly not the case with normal child beginners. All such children learn the writing system as a code for language, not for concepts. Spoken language is the primary code, written language thus is *a code for a code*. Therefore, all three of Lado's and Gray's types of writing systems have one very important feature in common. They are all linguistic. They all represent units of language.

A second misconception is that each type of writing system codes *only* the unit of language that is singled out as its chief feature in these three categories. This is not true. For example, in Leong's chapter on Hong Kong, specific examples of the phonetic elements in the characters of the Chinese logographic system are provided. Similarly, as was shown in the previous chapter, Lee's research on the relationship between different types of writing systems and alternative teaching methods led him to stress that an alphabetic system is "more than a chain of sound-symbols."[49] It may signal other linguistic features as well as phonemes—for example, syntactic aspects.[50] Hall states that "When there are inconsistencies in the way an alphabetic orthography represents a phonemic system, these inconsistencies can be used in spelling to symbolize differences between morphemes, especially those morphemes which sound alike but have different meanings (homonyms)."[51] Furthermore an alphabetic writing system may contain some ambiguities in its code for phonemes: the *s* in *cats* and *dogs* represents the sounds /s/ and /z/, respectively; yet this is a regular code symbol for this grammatical inflection. Thus, Lefevre comments that "word-form changes, prefixes, suffixes, and other systematic clues to language structure are generally spelled quite regularly without regard to differences in sound" in English.[52]

The chief danger in these misconceptions is that they give rise to over-simplifications about the difficulty of and appropriate teaching methods for instruction in literacy in different types of writing systems. All types of writing are codes for language. Each type may focus its coding process on a charac-teristically different linguistic unit, but other features may be coded in addition to those that are most obvious. Possibly, one may for teaching purposes give higher priority to the most important parts of the mechanism of the code. Thus, Hall recognizes that: "though there are many such instances of mor-phemic differentiation by means of variant spellings in English orthography . . . , this does not mean that the graphic system of English is essentially morphemic, as is that of Chinese. Our English orthography is basically alphabetic (though with a fair number of irregularities); any attempt to teach the reading and writing of English must take this fundamental fact into account from the very start."[53] However, one must add that it is equally important for teachers not to be mesmerized by the writing system's chief coding feature. This eventually must function within the total complex code with all its other coding mechanisms.

Once again this problem revolves around the question of the child's level of cognitive development and his previous linguistic experience *when he first begins the task of learning to read and write*. What aspects of the functions and mechanisms of decoding and encoding can he be brought to understand at that stage?

For example, Laubach's methods may be appropriate for teaching literacy in French *to adults* in a comparatively few lessons, as is stated in the chapter on France. Yet *young French children* have great difficulty in learning to read and write, as is clearly shown in the same chapter. The logic of coding graphemes to grammatical structure may be quite easily grasped by adults, but it may be much more difficult for the child of 6. As Piaget and Inhelder have shown, the logic of children below the age of 7 or 8 is remarkably different from that of adults. In particular, the young child has special problems in handling the abstract operations of adult logic. Progress in the child's development of logic at this age is through the "concrete operations of thought," which "provide a transition between schemes of action and the general logical structures . . . ."[54] Therefore, one may hypothesize that writing systems may differ in their difficulty for the initial literacy learner in accordance with the degree to which the elements of the written code can be made "concrete" for the child. Grammatical units, for example, would seem to be especially difficult for the young child to understand. As has been shown in the research reported in Chapter 4, young beginners have no notion of such concepts as word and sound, which adults use in describing language. Other grammatical abstractions that would explain the coding of inflections, for instance, would be even less concrete for the young child.

Similarly, the phoneme is far from being concrete for the beginner. Many research projects attest to the problems this creates for teaching phonics. In the chapter on the USSR Elkonin's research is especially instructive on this point. For the young beginner, the phoneme simply does not exist. It has no concrete reality. Therefore, the child cannot begin to understand the operations of decoding and encoding the grapheme-phoneme code of an alphabetic writing system *until the phoneme unit has acquired concrete reality through his own actions with it*.

The unit of language that the young child knows when he first comes to school is a much larger one than the phoneme, and it is some kind of meaningful chunk of utterance. At this stage a "word" means for the child simply a hunk of utterance lumped together on the basis of a syncretism of meaning. Furthermore, this aspect of the child's natural development of linguistic concepts clearly favors the introduction of reading and writing in the same kind of perceived units. This seems true of all languages and all writing systems.

Yet it does not necessarily follow that the type of writing system will make no difference to the ease of learning literacy. Although it is true that the child's first initiation to the written form of any language may be most effective through the presentation of sentences, phrases, word phrases, and word sentences, a weaning stage must begin sooner or later. Just as all children have a similar general basis for articulacy in childhood that develops specifically according to the patterns of the language of the particular culture into which they are born, so also all children have a similar cognitive basis for their initial steps in literacy, which then must develop more specifically in accordance with the particular form of the writing system of their language. It is in this weaning process that the differences among the various alternative types of writing system may have varying levels of efficiency for developing the skills of literacy.

In considering this problem it is important to distinguish between the efficiency of a writing system for two quite different purposes: (1) for the ultimate functioning of the more or less fully literate adult (in the reading process, *per se*) and (2) for learning *how* to read and write (the learning-to-read process).

In the chapter on Japan this important difference between the needs of the adult literate in contrast to those of the young literacy learner is illustrated. Takahiko Sakamoto's[55] studies of the eye movements of college students showed that Hiragana sentences required twice as much time to read as the Kanji-Hiragana combination. The reading of Hiragana only was marked by a small span of perception, more frequent fixations, longer fixation pauses, and more regressions. This superiority of the Kanji-Hiragana writing system seems to be due to the fact that the Kanji ideographs stand out boldly as figures against the different background of the Hiragana. These Kanji appropriately represent the main words in the sentence. Furthermore, Japanese words are written with fewer characters in Kanji than in Hiragana. Therefore, the adult reader of Japanese easily skims the shorter Kanji-Hiragana sentence, picking up key ideas that stand out against the background.

But, as these Japanese studies show, what is excellently suited to the *reading process* of the *adult* may not be so appropriate for the *learning-to-read* process of the *child*. Thus, Japanese children do not have to begin with Kanji ideographs. All Japanese sentences can be written in Hiragana only, which seem to be easier *for the beginner*. Each of the forty-eight Hiragana represents the sound of a Japanese syllable. Most children can read some Hiragana when they begin school, or begin to learn them in the first grade. "This period does not last very long, however, because this writing system is so easy to learn," according to our Japanese colleagues. The student makes a gradual transition from all Hiragana to more and more Kanji, as he progresses toward the conventional level of a mixture of Kanji with Hiragana.

In this manner, the young beginner in Japan can quickly learn to use reading and writing at his own level of linguistic functioning. At first, his decoding and encoding activities focus on the Hiragana system, which he can very soon manipulate on the basis of its fewer than fifty characters. Even in the early years of schooling his literacy activities can be relevant and functional and the process clear to him. At the same time the gradual introduction of Kanji works toward their use in a script that will be more effective at the fully developed adult level.

This distinction between the learning-to-read process of the child versus the reading process of the adult is particularly interesting in this Japanese context.

Teachers everywhere, of course, recognize that the child cannot be plunged immediately into the intricacies of the total code as used by adults. For example, in English speaking countries, the number of printed words may be severely restricted (cf. *Look, John, look*) or the vocabulary may be restricted to words in which the grapheme-phoneme relations are regular (cf. *Nan can fan Dan*). The Japanese variation, however, has the advantage that it does not restrict the vocabulary of the literacy learner's early experiences of reading and writing. All words can be written in the simple Hiragana syllabic code.

As Sakamoto and Makita recognize, this same principle is applied in the development of i.t.a. in the English speaking countries. The simpler and more regular code of forty-four characters of i.t.a. allows the full range of English vocabulary to be employed naturally for beginners, while they progress toward the more complex traditional orthography of English. Thus, it may be an advantage for the adult reader of English to have *meet, meat, mete,* while the child beginner is better served by one spelling for all three, as in i.t.a., *meet.*

The use of Hiragana only for Japanese beginners and i.t.a. for English speaking beginners both are intuitively based on the principle of reducing potential sources of cognitive confusion at the stage of initiation to literacy. Whereas *meet, meat, mete* may facilitate the adult's rapid perception of the morphemic differentiation between them, for the young beginner they may be a source of puzzlement and confusion about the nature of decoding *per se.* The use of a simpler writing system to begin with enables the child to grasp the idea of coding language by written symbols and to understand the process more readily.

Another very interesting psychological difference between the morphemic writing system of Kanji and the Kana phonological systems (Hiragana and Katakana) is the evidence that the dyslexic or alexic symptoms of brain-injured patients are different in these two writing systems: Kimura's [56] finding is based on his study of dyslexic disorders in Japanese war-injured patients. Also, S. Sakamoto [57] found that Kanji are retained more easily than Kana when loss of reading capacity is induced by brain injuries. This might be a valuable area for future cross-national reading research. It suggests the hypothesis that different processes are involved in writing systems that code morphemes from those that code phonological units, and that these would be detectable in systematic variations in the dyslexic and alexic symptoms of known brain injury. Alternatively, they may reflect the difference between earlier and later learning.

Thus, linguists and others faced with the task of creating a new orthography for a previously unwritten language, or would-be spelling reformers, face a series of difficult choices. But, as the Japanese experience shows, perhaps the most serious dilemma is the choice between (1) facilitating rapid effective reading in the literate adult and (2) promoting cognitive clarity in the learning-to-read process of beginners. Most English spelling reformers, for example, have concerned themselves with the latter and given little or no thought to the former. In contrast, some academic linguists have rejected reform because of concern for the former, and dismissed rather lightly the psychological needs of the latter. The final practical outcome in literacy development is influenced both by the learning-to-read process and the reading process. The choice depends in the final analysis on cultural values and social priorities.

Complexity of Individual Characters

Dina Feitelson asserts that, for the beginner in literacy learning, the: "relative ease or difficulty of his task will be influenced to a large extent by the features of the symbols he has to deal with . . . . If the graphic symbols the beginning reader has to learn to identify are very complex, with many strokes, curves, and wiggly lines in each of them, his task will be much harder than if they are relatively simple, like for instance, Latin *o* and *v*." However, Feitelson recognizes that this need for simplicity must be balanced against the other need—the characters must be discriminable: "On the other hand, it does seem that whenever there are great similarities among the graphic symbols of a writing system, the beginning reader will find it much harder to learn to identify those symbols easily and constantly. In other words, whenever graphic symbols resemble each other to a marked degree, we will anticipate many more mistakes in identifying them on the part of a beginning reader, than we would for a reader learning to identify graphic symbols which are markedly different from each other . . . ." As an example, she notes that "a great deal has been written about the difficulty beginning readers have in learning to tell *b* and *d* or *p* and *q* apart"[58] in the conventional English writing system.

This at first sight appears to be a rather obvious and straightforward problem, but some doubts about any such simple formula are raised in the chapters on Hong Kong and Japan. In the latter, evidence is cited to show that complex Kanji ideographs are read more easily than simple Kanji characters. Thus, Kawai[59] found that normal adults read more complex Kanji more easily than less complex Kanji, with frequency of usage controlled. To test this feature in the younger learner of Kanji, Kawai conducted an experiment in which subjects had to make verbal associations with nonsense patterns. The general tendency was that the more complex these patterns were, the easier they were to learn.

Nor does the chapter on Hong Kong support the view that characters should be maximally simple for ease of learning or ease of reading. Leong's research investigated the effects of the number of strokes in a Chinese character, which may vary from a single stroke to some fifty-two. Contrary to the simplicity hypothesis, he found that the optimal stroke number is eleven to twelve, plus or minus four and this is probably the threshold for optimal visual cues in the perception of Chinese characters. Leong recognizes that reproduction requires more effort with the larger number of strokes, but he points out that "On the other hand, characters below a threshold stroke number, probably below seven, may reduce the contrastive elements so essential to reading and may make for some cognitive confusion." He cites his own empirical research, which found that Hong Kong children were better able to write complex characters correctly than simple ones.

Thus, the evidence on both Chinese characters and Japanese Kanji ideographs is that their simpler characters are less easy to learn and use than their more complex ones. Therefore, the importance of Feitelson's second factor—the need for discriminability—seems better established than the first one—the need for simplicity. Leong's comment is particularly interesting—that is, that a reduction in the number of strokes in Chinese characters may cause cognitive confusion. Simplification of design may reduce discriminability and raise doubts about the functioning of the code in the child's mind.

Concerning the i.t.a. experiments in Britain, although no specific tests were made, it has often been stated by teachers that the new and more complex characters of i.t.a. are easier to discriminate than the standard letters of the conventional alphabet: i.t.a.'s ꜿh, ʃh, ee, æ, œ, ie, wh, and so on. This seems plausible, but what is more interesting for this present discussion is that these new characters usually, although not always, replace the *digraphs* that would be used in the traditional orthography of English: ꜿh for *ch*; ʈh for *th,* and so on. Why are the i.t.a. characters thought to be easier than the conventional digraphs?

Because the writing system for English is basically alphabetic, one must consider the coding unit that represents the phoneme. For instance, the initial phoneme of *them, this, that* is represented by the digraph *th.* Thus, the first phoneme of all three of these words is represented by a "more complex" grapheme than the remaining two phonemes in each, as regards the physical printed form. Yet, it is generally recognized that digraphs are more difficult to learn than single letters for phonemes. What makes the difference between i.t.a.'s ʈh and the conventional digraph *th?* Both are "complex" graphemes, and indeed they are almost identical.

The essential difference is that *t* and *h* are joined in ʈh but not in *th.* A recent experiment by Oliver, Nelson, and Downing[60] shows how this difference affects the young literacy learner. Four groups of preschool children in Canada were matched for any slight initial knowledge of the letters of the alphabet they might have. All were trained to discriminate graphemes in three phoneme words represented by four letters in conventional English spelling (*chip*). Group 1 used traditional orthography; group 2 used i.t.a. (ꜿhip); group 3 used underlining to indicate the digraph (thus, chip); and group 4 used extra space to mark the grapheme boundaries (thus, ch i p). Group 1 performed the poorest, both on the learning trials and in subsequent transfer tests of the three groups. However, there was no significant difference between groups 2, 3, and 4. In all three cases, what was important was some signal in the code that marked *the grapheme boundary* of the digraph; joining, underlining, or additional space after the second letter of the digraph all helped the children to understand that the two letters were to be treated as a single unit. Group 2 (i.t.a.) had fewer (but not significantly so) errors of combining the wrong letters—For example, *ip*—than did groups 3 and 4.

This experiment demonstrates the effects of reasoning on the child's perception of written language. Cognitive confusion was caused in the traditional orthography group because there was no basis in the code for the logical division of the words into their graphemes. How could the child learn to divide chip into *ch, i, p* rather than *c, hi, p* or *c, h, ip,* when there is no indication of this in the conventional code? The latter provides no experience of the logic he is supposed to acquire. Many English written words contain multigraphs, and the grapheme boundary is never marked (for example, *th, r, ough; l, a, ugh, i, ng*) in the actual print. Only after numerous experiences with such "spelling patterns" as *th, ough,* and the like does the learner begin to recognize them as familiar groupings of individual letters.

Alphabetic writing systems vary among themselves in use of digraphs and multigraphs. It can be predicted that cross-nationally there would be a greater degree of cognitive confusion in identifying grapheme boundaries in writing systems that vary the number of letters in a grapheme without marking the boundary in some special way than would be the case where such variation was not so prevalent. Furthermore, it is likely that the child's development of the *concept* of a grapheme would be hindered where its form is masked by the absence of any marker. Except where there is successful auditory discrimination teaching of the kind described by Elkonin in Chapter 24, one would predict also that this cognitive confusion would pollute the experiential environment that is the basis of the child's development of the phoneme concept. If the phoneme can be signaled in the writing system by a variable number of letters, then the phoneme boundary also is not clearly represented in the code, and it will be correspondingly more difficult for the child to learn to perceive it. He may become puzzled about how many phonemes there are in a word. He may wonder if there are more phonemes in a word than he can hear, and this may lead him to suspect his own "phonematic hearing" as Elkonin calls it. For example, does *thought* have 7, 6, 5, 4, or 3 phonemes in it (cf. i.t.a.'s ʄh au t)?

Thus, the simplicity or complexity of the characters or even the graphemes of a writing system in themselves are probably of much less importance than the extent to which the writing system distinguishes the linguistic code units and their boundaries in samples of the written language. If the child feels insecure as to what precisely is being coded, whether it be in the Japanese Kanji, the Chinese characters, or in the graphemes of English alphabetic writing, cognitive clarity regarding the nature of the coding task to be learnt will be that much more difficult for him to develop. This would seem to be the effect of this example of mismatch between the writing system and the L^2 in which the learner is expected to make his literate responses—that is, when the phoneme boundaries have no reliable parallel marking of grapheme boundaries as is the case in English orthography.

Even when the written code does signal linguistic units systematically it may take a considerable amount of time and experience for the child to develop the corresponding concepts. For example, the studies cited in Chapter 4 show how slowly English speaking children acquire the concept of "a word" despite the fact that English orthography does mark the boundary of the word by extra space. One can hypothesize that this concept develops even more slowly in languages such as Thai, where word boundaries are not signalled in this way. Yet, if we free ourselves of our own national conventions in this respect, we can reflect that the Thai language has less mismatch between L^2 and the writing system; there are no pauses between words in speech, so one does not anticipate spaces between words in print. This may account for the very slow development of the concept of "word" even where this unit has its boundaries marked, as in English. That is, the written unit has no correspondingly clear parallel in the child's experience of speech.

Direction of Reading

Writing systems vary also in the direction in which they are to be read. The written or printed form of English, French, or Spanish is designed to be read from left to right horizontally; Hebrew, for example, although horizontally written, too, must be read from right to left. Chinese and Japanese conventionally are printed in vertical lines to be read from top to bottom. But, whatever the direction and whatever the units (phonemes, syllables, morphemes, or words), all have the common feature of a temporal stream of utterance paralleled by the spatial order in which the speech elements are represented in the written form.

Gray used eye-movement records of reading in fourteen different languages, including all five of those mentioned in the previous paragraph, but he did not find that direction of reading was an important influence. He concluded that "These studies demonstrate that the general nature of the reading act is essentially the same among all mature readers."[61] It is important to emphasize Gray's use of the term "mature readers." The subjects of his eye-movement camera experiments were all adults between the ages of 20 and 50. As has been noted before, the needs of the reading process of mature readers may be quite different from those of the learning-to-read process of beginners.

The problem of the effects of direction of reading is raised most interestingly in the case of Japanese reading. Conventionally, Japanese has always been written vertically, but since the Second World War left to right horizontal writing has become popular. Thus, in Japan today both horizontal and vertical books are commonly available, and children are expected to learn to read in both directions. T. Sakamoto found that vertical reading tends to be superior, but only because of long and intensive experience in vertical reading—the more conventional direction.[62] This is reminiscent of the research of Burt, Cooper, and Martin[63] on the legibility of various type faces for printing English. They found certain type faces were more legible than others. A probable explanation for this difference is that their subjects had been exposed more frequently to these type faces in the past.

Again it must be noted that both these Japanese and these English studies of legibility were conducted with mature readers and not with beginners. Although there seems to be no a priori reason why one direction of reading should be more difficult for the beginner to learn than another, one might anticipate that having to learn two different directions of reading in the same language would be confusing to the child. But in the chapter on Japan no indication is given of the existence of any such confusion. Furthermore, their insistence on the relative rarity of reading disability in Japan suggests that this alternation of direction of reading does not disturb the development of the reading skill.

It would be valuable to obtain direct empirical evidence on this issue, because, if it is indeed the case that the change of direction in Japanese writing does not cause confusion in the literacy learner, then this would have important implications for some of the phenomena of reading disability in other languages.

For example, although Japanese may be printed horizontally (left to right) or vertically (top to bottom), *within either arrangement* the spatial order of linguistic units parallels their temporal order in speech. Thus, so long as one knows which direction is being used on the particular printed page, the reader can rely on the printed order to represent the temporal order correctly. In contrast, some languages ostensibly have only one direction for reading, but the rule is not followed consistently. In English orthography, for instance, the horizontal left to right order of coding is not applied invariably as regards the graphemic representation of phonemes. In such spelling patterns as *a.e, i.e, o.e, u.e* in words like *game, line, bone, tune* the second phoneme must be decoded from letters two and four and the final phoneme is not represented by the final letter but by the last-but-one letter.

Thus, even though there is no mismatch between the temporal order of speech and the spatial order of writing within either of the coding orders of Japanese, there is a mismatch between temporal order and spatial order in English if the learner attempts to follow systematically the general rule of the left to right coding order. It seems notable that one of the commonest symptoms of reading disability in English speaking countries is confusion over the order of reading or writing the letters in a word. Of course, Japanese does not have an alphabetic system, which makes this specific problem impossible in Japan, but mixed order of syllables is not reported as a problem in children's learning of the Kana syllabary script.

It seems a feasible hypothesis that the English writing system's lack of internal consistency in ordering the graphemic symbols for phonemes is a source of cognitive confusion, whereas the consistency of ordering within each of the two alternative directions in Japanese facilitates the development of cognitive clarity in learning how to read. More probable still is the hypothesis that the irregularity of grapheme order in English combines with another source of confusion to produce such errors of reading and writing as reversals: "saw" for *was,* "on" for *no,* and so on. As has been shown elsewhere,[64] Wolfe's [65] study of reversals in disabled readers provides evidence of this combined source of confusion. The three pairs of reversible spellings that produced the greatest number of reversal errors in reading in her experiments with eighteen 9-year-old boys retarded in reading, were *on/no, saw/was,* and *oh/ho.* Other reversible pairs produced very few reversals—for example, *pat/tap, pin/nip, ten/net.* Although Wolfe, herself, did not note this fact, the pairs that produced many reversals in reading all had irregular grapheme-phoneme relations, whereas the relationships were regular in the pairs that tended not to be reversed. For example, in phonetic script *on/no* are/ɔn/, /nou/; *saw/was* are /sɔ:/, /wɔz/; *oh/ho* are /ou/, /hou/, and none would be reversible in that script. Thus, the disabled reader's reversal of such words may be a symptom of his cognitive confusion about the relationship between graphemes and phonemes that manifests itself through his related confusion over the direction of reading. This hypothesis certainly deserves testing in a cross-national study of reversal phenomena in languages that differ in mismatch between L^2 and its writing system.

Letter-Names

Gray's international survey concluded that "the alphabetic method was gradually supplanted by more effective methods and is rarely used today." [66] That was in 1956. Ten years later the trend he noted was reversed, and by the early 1970s a strong revival of teaching letter names had taken place. Let us examine Gray's reason for rejecting the teaching of reading through the names of the letters of the alphabet, and trace the course of the more recent revival of this approach and its current status.

The consensus of expert opinion, according to Gray, was that, "knowing the forms and names of the letters was of little help in recognizing words." In particular, "The chief objection to the alphabetic method is that the sounds of the names of the letters do not always indicate the pronunciation of words." [67] In the chapter on Israel Gray's finding is confirmed. The traditional alphabetic approach to teaching the reading of Hebrew seems incredibly futile and tortuous, although it was not only the inappropriate Hebrew character names that caused difficulties.

The names of the letters in the English alphabet also are sometimes misleading. "Aitch," for instance, is one example of a letter name that does not contain anywhere the phoneme that *h* usually represents, as in *hat, hop, hut*. This aspect of the English writing system has frequently been criticized by would-be reformers. For example, a report of the American Philosophical Society in 1899 attacked "such absurd falsehoods as that of saying 'sea, you pea' spells cup." [68] As long ago as 1551, John Hart proposed changing the names of the English letters as one of a number of reforms he believed would overcome "the vices and faultes of our writing; which cause it to be tedious, and long in learnyng: and learned hard, and evill to read." [69]

However, it might be felt that Gray's condemnation of the teaching of letter names was too sweeping. If it has been thought by people such as John Hart that the English letter names could be reformed to give a better clue to their phonemic significance, may there not exist some languages that already have more appropriate names for the characters or letters of their writing system?

According to two of the chapters in Part Two, this is indeed the case. Kyöstiö, describing the usual synthetic approach to beginning reading in Finland, states that "Usually the teacher says the name of the letter. When it represents a vowel the letter name and the phoneme represented are identical. But in the names of consonants a vowel is always connected with the consonant. For example, 'ko,' 'el,' 'te'. . . ." Chinna Oommen reports in the chapter on

India that: "In Hindi the name of a character and the phoneme it represents are always exactly the same. . . . Thus, in teaching the synthetic approach to reading Hindi, it makes little difference whether the alphabetic or phonic method is used."

Many linguists would object that, despite these remarks by Kyöstiö and by Oommen, the teacher's utterance of a sound for a single consonant character, whether that sound is called name or phoneme, cannot avoid causing a mismatch between the child's experience of the normal pronunciation of that phoneme in the context of continuous speech and the distorted sound produced by attempting to pronounce a consonant in isolation.

But the reasons given by Kyöstiö and Oommen have no bearing whatsoever on the revival of the alphabetic approach in the United States in recent years. This has a quite different basis.

The beginnings of the current return to an alphabetic approach can be traced back to a number of well-known correlational studies. Durrell and Murphy[70] cite Gavel's[71] study of reading-readiness measures related to reading achievement at the end of first grade. She found that the knowledge of letter names among the 1,506 children in her sample on entering first grade correlated higher with reading achievement at the end of the school year than any other measure. This led Durrell and Murphy to conclude that

> Since most letter names contain the sounds of the letter, the ability to name letters should aid in establishing relationships between the phonemes of the spoken word and the printed form of the word. The child who knows letter names has an excellent first step in phonics.[72]

The following year these same authors wrote, "Children who know letter-names learn words more readily . . . ."[73]

These statements are strikingly at variance with Gray's findings. But it is more important to note how far Durrell and Murphy went beyond the research data on which they were commenting. The finding of a correlation between letter-name knowledge and later reading achievement does not entitle one to leap to the conclusion that the former is the cause of the latter. The correlation coefficient shows only that the two measures are connected. Their relationship could be the result of some third factor, for example.

Nevertheless, it must be recognized that several other researchers have found the same high correlation between letter-name knowledge prior to commencing first grade and reading achievement at the end of that grade. Barrett,[74] de Hirsch et al.,[75] Bond and Dykstra,[76] and Dykstra[77] all found letter-name knowledge to be the best single predictor of first-grade reading success. Of this fact there is no question. What must be disputed, however, is the oversimplified logic that led a number of educators to believe that this correlation means that letter-name knowledge *causes* higher attainments in reading and that therefore teachers should give instruction in letter names. For example, Chall concludes that "Knowing the names of the letters helps a child in the beginning stages of learning to read."[78] *Sesame Street,* a popular TV program in the United States, is a children's resource in which money, time, and effort have been invested to emphasize letter names on the basis of this belief.

Barrett, one of the researchers who obtained a correlation (0.59) between early letter-name knowledge and later reading achievement, was careful to point out the danger of jumping to the conclusion that the first was the cause of the second. He recognized that the correlation could be

> a reflection of a rich experience with a variety of written materials which enable children to learn to recognize letters. Thus, it should not be inferred from this study that teaching children to recognize letters by name will necessarily ensure success in beginning reading.[79]

As we have seen already, Barrett's warning has not been heeded, and many American education programs have begun to put a strong emphasis on teaching letter names. They did not wait for the assumed causal relationship to be put to the test in appropriately designed research. Recently a number of independent investigators have conducted carefully controlled experiments on the effectiveness of teaching letter names.

Johnson compared twelve first-grade classrooms in an experimental group with twelve in a control group. Six of the experimental classes used one publisher's letter-name teaching program and the other six used a different publisher's letter-name materials. The control group used materials that did not teach letter names. The results showed that there was no difference between the two alternative approaches to teaching the letter names. Both programs produced significantly superior results in letter-name knowledge in comparison with those obtained in the control group at the end of a three-week training period. But this improved letter-name knowledge had no effect whatsoever on other aspects of reading achievement. Johnson concludes that

> Instruction in letter-names, as provided the two experimental groups during the three week training period did not result in vocabulary or comprehension reading achievement different from that of the control group at the end of the first semester of first grade.[80]

His finding applied to both boys and girls, at all levels of intelligence, and irrespective of the subjects' initial knowledge of letter names or any other of the several readiness measures applied.

Ohnmacht's[81] classroom experiment also found that training in letter names only resulted in reading achievements that were no better than those obtained in a control group with no such training.

Nor did the rigorous laboratory experiments of Samuels find any effect of letter-name instruction on reading behavior. His conclusion was that "The results of the two experiments indicate that letter-name knowledge does not facilitate learning to read words made up of the same letters." Therefore, this "strongly suggests that letter-name knowledge does not help the student learn to read." From these results and a consideration of the place of letter names in the task of learning to read, Samuels concludes that "it seems ill-advised to suggest to teachers that this type of training will promote reading readiness."[82]

A bridge between the conclusions of these experiments and the correlational studies may be provided by a comment of Calfee, Chapman, and Venezky:

> The predictive value of the child's knowledge of the alphabet in kindergarten is well known. Equally apparent is the diagnostic uselessness of this information.[83]

It is useless information because it is only a symptom of some more fundamental factor that has not been identified and measured hitherto. Thus, teaching letter names is like treating the symptom instead of the disease.

As Piaget has pointed out, "Verbal forms evolve more slowly than actual understanding."[84] Hence, letter-name knowledge in kindergarten is probably a symptom of development in an early phase in the growth of cognitive clarity. Conversely, the results of the several experiments of Johnson, Ohnmacht, and Samuels, which show how ineffectual letter-name training is, are quite understandable in the light of Vygotsky's comment on the relationship between thought and language in the child briefly noted earlier:

> Direct teaching of concepts is impossible and fruitless. A teacher who tries to do this usually accomplishes nothing but empty verbalism, a parrotlike repetition of words by the child, simulating a knowledge of the corresponding concepts but actually covering up a vacuum.[85]

More specifically, rote learning of the letter names is a useless activity, if our aim is to develop the fundamental linguistic concepts the child needs for learning how to read and write.

It is possible that formal, direct teaching of letter names may have a result worse than the "vacuum" in the child's mind suggested in the quotation from Vygotsky. For example, learning the name of something one does not understand or even recognize as actually existing in reality may increase the child's insecurity, uncertainty, and confusion about the task of learning how to read and write. This is one possible explanation of Muehl's finding that "the acquisition of letter-names by kindergarten aged children interferes with subsequent performance in learning to associate picture names with nonsense words containing these same letters as the critical stimuli."[86]

A very interesting discussion of the naming of alphabetic characters is to be found in the chapter on the USSR. In Russia, also, the emphasis shifted from teaching letter names to letter sounds, but Elkonin shows how "children are inclined to think that *the sound is the name*." This is "because, in the course of mastering speech, they have learned that every object has its name." He postulates that this natural tendency leads the child into serious difficulty. Unless he is given appropriate experiences he fails to conceptualize the sound as an objective reality. The printed character in contrast is much more likely to be regarded as a concrete object. Then, instead of recognizing that the character is a written symbol for the reality of the sound in the primary spoken form of language, the child reverses the facts and believes the sound to be merely the name of the character.

Elkonin's work in the Soviet Union, reported in Chapter 24, provides many valuable insights into the child's problems in learning literacy, but the preceding quote is of particularly great importance in understanding the causes of cognitive confusion in beginning reading. For example, the teaching of letter names obviously reinforces the child's initial misconception of the relationship between written and spoken language. Formal synthetic phonics programs in which children are taught at the beginning stage that this letter has such and such a sound seem likely to be equally misleading, because, as Elkonin's evidence shows, the child merely regards the sound as the character's name.

Elkonin demonstrates, furthermore, that this tendency to name the characters of the alphabet is related to what teachers in Russia call the "blending difficulty." The same difficulty is frequently referred to by American phonics teachers, too, and therefore Elkonin's explanation should be considered cross-nationally:

> The so-called "blending difficulty" arises when children try to construct the sound form of words not out of the sounds of language but from what they think are the names of the characters. In their "blending" difficulties they demonstrate that their behavior is inappropriately oriented toward the characters they are attempting to name instead of the realities of the sounds of language.

Elkonin's commentary suggests that letter-name teaching and letter-to-sound phonics instruction may actually impede the development of cognitive clarity. His statements apply equally well to languages such as Finnish where letter names are closer to the phonemes represented by the letters. He points out that "This incorrect orientation is facilitated by the fact that often letter names and sounds coincide."

Thus, what Durrell considers to be a good reason for learning letter names is regarded as an environmental hazard in Elkonin's theory. Elkonin attacks the method that "includes the demand for 'clear' pronunciation. This clear pronunciation of a sound is nothing more than giving it a name. Thus this method only serves to provide more distinctive names, and, as a consequence, unfortunately, the best possible conditions are created for the child to substitute name for object. Then the name impedes the perception of the reality of the sound. Indeed, it is impossible to create the sound form of a word from what are viewed as names of either spoken sounds or written characters." Elkonin goes on to provide convincing evidence from the series of experiments he and his colleagues have conducted in the Academy of Pedagogical Sciences of the Russian Soviet Federative Socialist Republic.

Thus, Gray's view that the teaching of the letter names is ineffectual in developing literacy skills seems to have been vindicated by valid research, despite the popular revival of this aspect of the alphabetic method in the United States in recent years.

REFERENCES

1. Bloomfield, Leonard, *Language,* New York: Holt, 1933, p. 21.
2. Gray, William S., *The Teaching of Reading and Writing,* Paris: UNESCO, 1956, p. 12.
3. *Ibid.,* p. 12, footnote.
4. Neijs, Karel, *Literacy Primers: Construction Evaluation and Use,* Paris: UNESCO, 1961, p. 47.
5. Stewart, William A., "On the use of Negro dialect in the teaching of reading," in Baratz, Joan C., and Shuy, Roger W. (eds.), *Teaching Black Children to Read,* Washington, D.C.: Center for Applied Linguistics, 1969, p. 157.
6. *Ibid.,* p. 159.
7. Macnamara, John, *Bilingualism and Primary Education,* Edinburgh: Edinburgh University Press, 1966.
8. Modiano, Nancy, "National or mother language in beginning reading: A comparative study," *Research in the Teaching of English,* 2 (1968), 32–43.
9. Mountford, John, "Some psycholinguistic components of initial standard literacy," *The Journal of Typographic Research,* 4 (November 1970), 295–306.
10. Venezky, Richard L., "Nonstandard language and reading," *Elementary English,* 47 (1970), 334–345.
11. Spolsky, Bernard, *Literacy in the Vernacular: the Navajo Reading Study,* paper presented at the 69th Annual Meeting of the American Anthropological Association, San Diego, Calif., November 19, 1970.
12. Stewart, *op. cit.,* p. 168.
13. Österberg, Tore, *Bilingualism and the First School Language—An Educational Problem Illustrated by Results from a Swedish Dialect Area,* Umeå, Sweden: Västerbottens Tryckeri, AB, 1961, pp. 11–12.
14. Spolsky, Bernard, "Linguistics and the language barrier to education," in Sebeok, Thomas A., *et al.* (eds.), *Current Trends in Linguistics,* Vol. XII. The Hague: Mouton (in press).
15. Goodman, Kenneth S., "Dialect barriers to reading comprehension," in Baratz and Shuy, *op. cit.,* p. 16.
16. Spolsky, "Linguistics and the language barrier to education," *op. cit.*
17. Tax, S., "Group identity and educating the disadvantaged," *Language Programs for the Disadvantaged,* Champaign, Ill.: National Council of Teachers of English, 1965.
18. Goodman, *op. cit.,* p. 18.
19. Downing, John, and Thackray, Derek, *Reading Readiness,* London: University of London Press, 1971.
20. Loban, Walter, "A sustained program of language learning," *Language Programs for the Disadvantaged,* Champaign, Ill.: National Council of Teachers of English, 1965.
21. Bernstein, Basil, "Social class and linguistic development: A theory of social learning," in Halsey, A. H., Floud, J., and Anderson, C. A. (eds.), *Education, Economy and Society,* Glencoe, Ill.: Free Press, 1961.
22. Spolsky, "Linguistics and the language barrier to education," *op. cit.*
23. Goodman, Kenneth S., "Dialect rejection and reading: A response," *Reading Research Quarterly,* 5 (Summer 1970), 600–603.
24. Goodman, "Dialect barriers to reading comrephension," *op. cit.,* pp. 16–17.

25. Österberg, *op. cit.,* p. 66.
26. Lado, Robert, *Linguistics Across Cultures,* Ann Arbor: University of Michigan Press, 1957, p. 11.
27. Goodman, "Dialect barriers to reading comprehension," *op. cit.,* p. 21.
28. Baratz, Joan C., "Teaching reading in an urban Negro school system," in Baratz and Shuy, *op. cit.,* pp. 92–116.
29. Österberg, Tore, *op. cit.,* p. 48.
30. *Ibid.,* p. 133.
31. *Ibid.,* p. 83.
32. *Ibid.,* p. 89.
33. Lefevre, Carl A., *Linguistics and the Teaching of Reading,* New York: McGraw-Hill, 1964, p. 6.
34. *Ibid.,* p. 27.
35. *Ibid.,* pp. 43–44.
36. Rosenblat, Argel, *El Castellaño de España y el Castellaño de América,* Montevideo: Edit. Alfa, 1968, p. 48.
37. Hildreth, Gertrude, "Reading with a rational alphabet: The Russian system," *The Reading Teacher,* **22** (December 1968), 251–261.
38. Spolsky, "Linguistics and the language barrier to education," *op. cit.*
39. McDavid, Raven I., "Dialectology and the teaching of reading," in Baratz and Shuy, *op. cit.,* p. 2.
40. Lado, *op. cit.,* p. 95.
41. Gray, *op. cit.,* p. 36.
42. Goody, Jack, *Literacy in Traditional Societies,* London: Cambridge University Press, 1968, p. 23.
43. *Ibid.,* p. 36.
44. Halle, Morris, "Some thoughts on spelling," in Goodman, Kenneth S., and Fleming, James T. (eds.), *Psycholinguistics and the Teaching of Reading,* Newark, Del.: IRA, 1968.
45. Ellis, A. J., *A Plea for Phonotypy and Phonography,* Bath: Isaac Pitman Phonographic Institution, 1845.
46. Malmquist, Eve, *Overgang from textning till vanlig skrivstil,* Stockholm: Kungl, Skoloverstyrelsen, 1964. (With summary in English)
47. Gray, *op. cit.,* p. 31.
48. Hall, Robert A., *Sound and Spelling in English,* Philadelphia, Pa.: Chilton, 1961.
49. Lee, W. R., *Spelling Irregularity and Reading Difficulty in English,* Slough: NFER in England and Wales, 1960, p. 25.
50. *Ibid.,* p. 34.
51. Hall, *op. cit.,* pp. 7–8.
52. Lefevre, *op. cit.,* p. 184.
53. Hall, *op. cit.,* p. 8.
54. Piaget, Jean, and Inhelder, Bärbel, *The Psychology of the Child,* New York: Basic Books, 1969, p. 100.
55. Sakamoto, Takahiko, *The Affect of Kanji on the Readability of the Japanese Sentences,* unpublished Master's thesis, Tokyo University of Education, 1960.
56. Kimura, K., "Zur Erklärung des der japanischen Schrift eigentümlichen Symptombildes," *Neurologia,* **37** (1934), 437–459.
57. Sakamoto, S., "A contribution to Kanji—Kana problem in dyslexia," *Bulletin of Osaka Medical Association,* **4** (1940), 185–212.

58. Feitelson, Dina, "Learning to read," in *UNESCO Handbook in Reading,* Paris: UNESCO, 1972.

59. Kawai, Yoshifumi, "Physical complexity of the Chinese letter and learning to read it," *Japanese Journal of Educational Psychology,* 14 (1966), 129–138, and 188.

60. Oliver, Peter R., Nelson, Jacquelyn, and Downing, John, "Differentiation of grapheme-phoneme units as a function of orthography," *Journal of Educational Psychology.* (In press.)

61. Gray, *op. cit.,* p. 59.

62. Sakamoto, Takahiko, "On reading skills of vertical versus horizontal sentences," unpublished paper read at the Third Annual Congress of the Japanese Association of Educational Psychology, Nagoya, Japan, 1961.

63. Burt, C., Cooper, W. F., and Martin, J. L., "A psychological study of typography," *British Journal of Statistical Psychology,* 8 (1955), 29–58.

64. Downing, John, *Evaluating the Initial Teaching Alphabet,* London: Cassell, 1967.

65. Wolfe, L. S., "An experimental study of reversals in reading," *American Journal of Psychology,* 52 (1939), 533–561.

66. Gray, *op. cit.,* p. 78.

67. *Ibid.,* p. 78.

68. Downing, *op. cit.,* p. 56.

69. Hart, John, *The Opening of the Unreasonable Writing of Our Inglish Toung,* London, 1551.

70. Durrell, Donald D., and Murphy, Helen A., "Boston University research in elementary school reading," *Boston University Journal of Education,* 146 (December 1963), 3–53.

71. Gavel, Sylvia R., *Patterns of Growth in First Grade Reading,* Ed. D dissertation, Boston University, Boston, Mass., 1957.

72. Durrell and Murphy, *op. cit.,* p. 5.

73. Durrell, Donald D., and Murphy, Helen A., *Speech to Print Phonics: Teachers' Manual,* New York: Harcourt, 1964.

74. Barrett, T., "Predicting reading achievement through readiness tests," in Figurel, J. Allen (ed.), *Reading and Inquiry,* Newark, Del.: IRA, 1965.

75. de Hirsch, K., *et al., Predicting Reading Failure: A Preliminary Study,* New York: Harper, 1966.

76. Bond, G. L., and Dykstra, R., *Final Report of the Co-ordinating Center for First-Grade Instruction* (USOE Project X-001), Minneapolis: University of Minnesota, 1967.

77. Dykstra, R., *Final Report of the Continuation of the Co-ordinating Center for First-Grade Reading Instruction Programs* (USOE Project 6-1651), Minneapolis: University of Minnesota, 1967.

78. Chall, Jeanne, *Learning to Read: The Great Debate,* New York: McGraw-Hill, 1967.

79. Barrett, *op. cit.,* p. 464.

80. Johnson, R. J., *The Effect of Training in Letter-Names on Success in Beginning Reading for Children of Differing Abilities,* paper presented at the American Educational Research Association convention, Minneapolis, 1970.

81. Ohnmacht, D. D., *The Effects of Letter-Knowledge on Achievement in Reading in the First Grade,* paper presented at the American Educational Research Association Convention, Los Angeles, 1969.

82. Samuels, S. J., *Letter-Name Versus Letter-Sound Knowledge As Factors Influencing Learning to Read,* paper presented at the American Educational Research Association convention, Minneapolis, 1970.

83. Calfee, Robert C., Chapman, Robin S., and Venezky, Richard L., *How a Child Needs to Think to Learn to Read* (Technical Report No. 131), Madison: Wisconsin Research and Development Center for Cognitive Learning, University of Wisconsin, 1970.

84. Piaget, Jean, *The Language and Thought of the Child* (rev. ed.), London: Routledge and Kegan Paul, 1959.

85. Vygotsky, Lev S., *Thought and Language,* Cambridge, Mass.: MIT Press, 1962.

86. Muehl, Siegmar, "The effects of letter-name knowledge on learning to read a word list in kindergarten children," *Journal of Educational Psychology,* **53** (1962), 181–186.

CHAPTER 10

Linguistic Environments, II

JOHN DOWNING

Perceived Regularity of the Code

The comparative regularity of grapheme-phoneme relations in alphabetic languages has been analyzed, and it is clear that the standard form of each language does differ objectively from others in this respect. For example, Bloomfield[1] showed that the conventional orthography of written Finnish is an almost perfect code for the phonemes of the standard form of spoken Finnish. He found that Bohemian and Spanish also had comparatively regular grapheme-phoneme associations. Italian, Dutch, and German were less perfect in regard to this feature, but much more consistent than English or French. Many writers have proposed that learning to read should be easier in languages such as Finnish than it is in those such as English, for example; another linguist, Lado, states this as the principle of "regularity of fit.":

> Ideally a writing system should have a one-to-one relation between its symbols and the language units they represent. That is, an alphabetic system should have one letter for each phoneme of the language and no more. And each symbol should always represent the same phoneme. Similarly, in syllabic writing or logographic writing there should be one symbol for each distinct syllable or word, no more and no less. . . . The more regular the fit, the easier it is to learn the writing system once we know the language. English writing is particularly bad as to regularity of fit. Turkish, Spanish, Finnish, and others are better in this respect.[2]

A similar opinion is stated in one of the UNESCO publications. Neijs writes that "In using the Roman alphabet it is of fundamental importance whether the alphabet is used in a phonemic way or not. In a strictly phonemic system of writing, each distinctive sound is represented by one symbol. This in turn means a symbol for each phoneme, a phoneme being defined as a minimum unit of distinctive sound feature. In a language such as English which is highly un-phonemic, the pupil needs much extra guidance in discovering and applying general principles governing the sounds of letters in different types of words—for example, 'hat' and 'hate' and in recognizing exceptions and learning how to deal with them."

> The advantage of phonemic script is that its symbols can be mastered rapidly, whereafter the learner can pronounce words without assistance.[3]

As early as 1906, Clairborne[4] proposed on scientific grounds that the incidence of reading failure must be less among Italian, Spanish, and German speaking people than where English is spoken because of the more consistent grapheme-phoneme relations in those three languages. Maruyama, in a more recent article in the *Bulletin of the Orton Society,* argued as a neurologist that it is harder to learn literacy in English and Danish than in German, Swedish, and Norwegian.[5] Hermann's "medical viewpoint" led him to state that "The greater the divergence between pronunciation and written language . . . the more difficult it will be for the word blind (and for that matter the normal child) to acquire the art of reading and writing.[6]

Actually, the same point of view has been expressed, although on a more intuitive basis, over and over again during, at least, the last four hundred years by various reformers of English orthography.[7] In Part Two of this book several more modern examples of a similar point of view are given. The following quotations are from four national chapters whose authors are of the opinion that learning to read is easier in their countries because of the consistency of their writing systems:

> *Sweden:* The English language, with its great differences between the spoken and the written forms, makes the teaching of reading much more difficult than it is in many other languages, for example, Swedish.
>
> *Israel:* With respect to symbol-sound correspondence, learning to read Hebrew is infinitely easier than learning to read English.
>
> *Japan:* This very high rate of literacy in Japan may be attributed to the . . . initial use of phonetic symbols—Kana, which are easy to learn . . . .
>
> *Finland:* Its writing system is quite regular; that is, each phoneme always has the same letter irrespective of its place in a word. This feature facilitates learning to read enormously.

Kyöstiö's opinion regarding Finnish is confirmed from three other sources. Ranta[8] states that Finland in the 1950s had one of the most literate, if not the most literate, population in the world. An official Finnish source claims that "The fact that Finnish orthography has always been easier than that of many other languages, naturally, also contributed to the spread of literacy."[9] Vikainen[10] has emphasized the comparatively low incidence of reading disability in Finland.

Makita has put forward a similar thesis to explain the difference in the frequency of cases of reading disability in Japan and the United States. A questionnaire sent to Japanese teachers led him to conclude that "the incidence of reading disability in the broader sense is extremely rare in Japan." This led him to question why it was so much rarer than in certain other countries:

> Why, then, is the reported prevalence of dyslexia in Japan some ten times lower than the figure that may be taken as median (10 per cent) for Western countries? It is unthinkable to assume that the Americans and the Europeans have ten times the population with maldevelopment or malformation of cerebral gyri than do the Japanese. It is hardly believable that the prevalence of hemispheral dominance conflict or split laterality is ten times less in the Japanese than in Westerners. It is equally absurd to suggest that children with emotional distress are ten times less frequent in Japan, for the prevalence of behavioral problems and psychosomatic manifestations in Japan is as high as it is in Western countries.

He went on to compare the regularity of the written code for speech in Japanese and in English, which led him to conclude that "the specificity of the used language, the very object of reading behavior, is the most potent contributing factor in the formation of reading disability."[11] In other words, Makita postulates that it is the comparatively inconsistent relations between speech units and written units in English that cause the incidence of reading disability in English speaking countries to be so much higher than in Japan.

Hard research data on this problem is, for practical purposes, almost non-existent. A few studies have provided tangential data. For example, Preston found that, in comparison to the difficulties experienced by American girls and boys, there was a "strikingly high degree of success by German pupils in learning word-recognition." He noted several differences between the German and English languages that may account for the superiority of German children in learning to read, the first of which is that "The German language is more consistent phonetically than the English language." He suggested that, "In learning to read English, some children in the United States, upon discovering that they cannot expect phonetic consistency, develop an insecurity and uncertainty . . . . "[12]

Also, in the chapter on Germany, Biglmaier's research on German children's reading progress is compared with Monroe's[13] study of American pupils. It was found that the learning-to-read process, as regards the ability "to decode and understand written symbols with a low error rate," is completed by German children by the end of second grade, whereas American children do not reach this stage until the end of fourth grade. It is concluded that "This result may be attributed to the more regular grapheme-phoneme relations in the German language." However, Biglmaier also notes that in spite of this common view that German has simpler and more regular grapheme-phoneme relations than English, in Germany there is talk about the possibility of further reducing difficulties by simplifying German orthography. Similarly, Hildreth writes, that "the spelling system in Arabic is strictly phonetic," [14] and that "Armenian children are lucky when it comes to learning to read, write and spell because their language employs a phonetically consistent alphabet which unquestionably eases the learning task." [15] In Greece, she found that "with no spelling inconsistency as in English, there are no phonics problems, no tricky pronunciation rules to learn with their exceptions," so that, "young children catch the alphabetic principle and learn to use it for word recognition and spelling more quickly than with irregular English spelling."[16] Her observations in the USSR led her to state that "Russian compared to English is highly regular in sound-symbol matching. In general, you can trust each letter to have its own sound and no other." Therefore, "Soviet children learn to read their native language rapidly, with ease, during their first year in school . . . ." [17]

These quotations from Hildreth's articles may suggest that she is oversimplifying the facts about grapheme-phoneme relations in these languages and overgeneralizing her observations of reading instruction in the schools of these countries. However, this is certainly the result, in part, to the brevity of the extracts. Furthermore, it must be recognized that Hildreth is writing comparatively rather than in absolute terms. On the other hand, the educators of some of these countries may not perceive their own orthography as being easy to learn. We have already quoted Biglmaier's reaction on this point. Elkonin also is less positive with regard to Russian orthography than is Hildreth, the comparative observer from another country.

Some readers may by now be impatient with the speculative and subjective nature of the data quoted on this issue of the effects of the regularity of the writing system. However, one point is clear: these views are all in the same direction. This cannot be attributed to biased sampling as far as the *educators'* opinions are concerned. The general consensus of people concerned with the practical problem of teaching literacy to young beginners is that the more consistent the relations between the written and spoken forms of a language the easier it is to learn to read and write.

However, some *linguists* other than those quoted so far have expressed doubts about the importance of the difficulty of the irregularity of grapheme-phoneme relations in English. Lefevre, for instance, notes that "Despite the irregular and inconsistent relationships we have noted between phonemes and graphemes, an exhaustive listing would show that there are families and groups of words where the correspondences between sounds and spellings are fairly regular. Moreover, as noted earlier, word-form changes, prefixes, suffixes, and other systematic clues to language structure are generally spelled quite regularly without regard to differences in sound; this regularity corresponding to important structural signals probably compensates for irregular spellings at the phonemic level."[18]

Hall is another linguist who throws doubt on the proposition that the grapheme-phoneme irregularity in English is a serious cause of difficulty in beginning reading. He declares that "In general, English orthography does afford to each phoneme of the language at least one regular, clear and consistent alphabetic representation." Also, "very few words are wholly capricious in their spelling: most irregular spellings are irregular only in the representation of one or two of the phonemes contained in the word . . . ." Furthermore, he claims, "even our irregular spellings are by no means wholly random: they fall, to a large extent, into certain sub-sets which are consistent within themselves." [19] It is interesting linguistically to note the high frequency of conditional structures in Hall's argument.

A number of linguists have sought, like Hall, to demonstrate that English orthography is really quite regular when one knows all the rules for understanding how it operates. However, what the professor of linguistics can understand may be quite incomprehensible to the child of 5 or 6 making his first efforts to comprehend how the writing system relates to his previous experience of language. Unfortunately, a number of linguists who have proffered their advice on the teaching of reading in recent years seem to have had little understanding of child psychology.

The linguist's mapping of the regularities of English orthography may prove far too complex for the young child to grasp. The linguist may be able to provide a description of English orthography that is a perfectly logical proof of its regularity. But the real issue in the psychology of the learning-to-read process is the *perceived* regularity of the code. The linguist's regularity may be far too complex a system for the child to *perceive* as such. As Dina Feitelson points out in the new UNESCO handbook on reading:

> Yet if, in the case of the first language, symbol-sound correspondence was very high, and if, furthermore, symbols appeared in one form only and had no alternative form, the child learning to decode this language would not be called upon to use his powers of logical inference to the extent that a child would in learning a language with a more complicated set of relations between symbol and sound." [20]

In other words, it is a matter of relativity. The linguist's description of the regularity of English orthography is likely to be a highly complex system that taxes the child's intellectual ability to a far greater degree than would a similar description of, say, Finnish orthography.

Commenting on the difficulty of Danish grapheme-phoneme associations, Jansen (Chapter 13 of this book) makes this same point:

> Although there are rules for relating vowel graphemes to vowel phonemes, they are definitely not easily understood by students below the university level, and therefore, no attempt is made to teach these rules to school children.

Research Evidence on the Writing System Variable

Samuels has recognized that "The investigation of the influence of phoneme-grapheme correspondence on reading in a natural setting—i.e., comparing reading achievement among countries in which different languages are spoken—is similar to the studies done in classroom settings in which reading achievement is compared between children reading the traditional English orthography and children reading the modified orthography of the Initial Teaching Alphabet." [21]

The hypothesis one may infer from some of the linguists' remarks quoted here is that if the traditional orthography (T.O.) of English is regular enough for the practical purposes of teaching literacy, then any attempt to make it more regular should make no difference to young learners. As i.t.a. is an attempt to regularize English orthography, a comparison of learning literacy in i.t.a. with learning literacy in T.O. should settle this issue objectively, provided that all other important educational and linguistic variables are held constant. Although certain linguists may still be able to continue to argue that there is no mismatch between the writing system and the L^2 speech basis of literate responses by their logical analyses, the question whether T.O. is more complex than i.t.a. —and, hence, more difficult to learn—can be answered empirically by the appropriate experiment. This issue is of widespread importance, because it is relevant not only to teaching beginners to read and write English, but also to the learning of literacy everywhere. The question to be investigated is *Is the complexity of the writing system's code for spoken language an important causal factor in the learning-to-read process?* The English language, thus, is only an example that provides the material for experiments that have a much wider general interest from both theoretical and practical points of view.

The first experiment comparing i.t.a. with T.O. was begun in Britain in 1961, two years before any American trials began. The original British experiment and the second one—which began in 1963 and was run as a check on the first —were concerned purely with the issue of the writing system variable. The experimental groups learned to read and write with i.t.a., while the control groups used T.O. The research designs attempted to match all other variables as rigorously as possible.

Except for two more recent studies,[22] neither of which have been completed, all the published American i.t.a. researches failed to control certain other important variables. This error arose chiefly through the common misconception that i.t.a. is a teaching method. American researchers thus compared what they thought was i.t.a.—that is, one publisher's set of materials with some other publisher's basal reader approach in T.O. As a result, the American research varied simultaneously not only the writing system, but also the stories, the vocabulary content, and the methods of teaching. Obviously no valid conclusions can be drawn from such experiments because it is impossible to know what effect the writing system has when the experiences of the experimental and control groups are different in other important respects, too. The invalidating effect of the confounding of the variables in most American i.t.a. researches is well documented.[23]

The British i.t.a. research controlled these other linguistic and pedagogical variables in both the major experiments—as is recognized in the independent review commissioned by the Schools Council, the official curriculum body for England and Wales:

> Thus researches in which i.t.a. is tied to one set of materials and T.O. to another cannot be taken as seriously as those of Downing (1967), Downing and Jones (1966), Harrison (1964), in which the materials were the same.[24]

This control was accomplished by selecting the most widely used basal reading series in Britain and having it printed in i.t.a. instead of T.O. Everything else in the materials remained unchanged: that is, stories, vocabulary, illustrations, size of print, teachers' manual of methods, and so on. This research design insured that all the variables in the teaching methods and materials were the same in the experimental and control groups except for the single independent variable, the writing system—i.t.a. in the former and T.O. in the latter.

In addition, all the usual educational, psychological, and sociological variables were matched in these experiments; that is, nonverbal and verbal intelligence, social class, age, sex of children; urban-rural location, type of school organization, size of school, pupil-teacher ratio, and amenities of the building. In order to maintain matching throughout the five years of this longitudinal research it was necessary to rematch on each measure of attainment. Thus, although the numbers fell quite rapidly from 660 in each group in the first experiment, for example, the losses should not be the cause of any bias.[25] The second i.t.a. experiment was a replication of the first, except that an attempt was made to control another variable, the teacher. In pairs of i.t.a. and T.O. classes, the two classroom teachers shared their time equally between the two rooms. This was a smaller experiment and was not continued for as many years as the first study for reasons of finance.

In both experiments the Hawthorne effect was guarded against by providing concrete evidence to the control group teachers of the researcher's equal concern for improving the teaching of literacy in their T.O. classes as well as in the experimental i.t.a. classes.

The i.t.a. writing system provides a higher degree of perceived consistency than does T.O. in four ways:

1. It has fewer alternative graphic symbols for units of speech:
    (a) For a word there is only a single visual pattern, for example, ḍog only instead of *DOG, Dog, dog*. i.t.a. capitals vary only in size not in shape, as in T.O.
    (b) For a phoneme, for example, the vowel phoneme common to each word in the sentence *I like my pie* has four different representations in T.O., but only one in i.t.a., thus ie liek mie pie
2. What may be perceived as gross irregularity of grapheme-phoneme relations in T.O. (or as requiring very complex coding rules) is regularized (or simplified) in i.t.a.: The letter *o* in *on, go, do, oven,* is replaced in i.t.a. thus on, gœ, ḍœ, uven
3. The multiple-character representations of T.O. are generally replaced by a single character in i.t.a. This has the effect of marking grapheme-phoneme boundaries more clearly:

	T.O.				*i.t.a.*		
Phonemes	th	r	ough		ṭh	r	ɷ
	1	2	3		1	2	3

4. The spatial order of graphemes from left to right more closely parallels the temporal order of phonemes in speech:

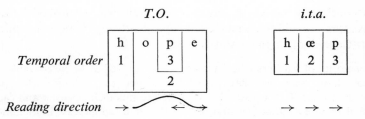

	T.O.				*i.t.a.*		
Temporal order	h	o	p	e	h	œ	p
	1		3		1	2	3
			2				

Reading direction   →

These are the chief features differentiating the i.t.a. and T.O. writing systems. (A full description is available in several sources.)[26]

In order to study the relative effects of the two writing systems, parallel tests of attainments in reading, writing, and spelling were administered at the same times in the experimental i.t.a. and T.O. classes. The measures used were identical except that during the period when the experimental group children were reading and writing in i.t.a. their tests were, quite naturally, printed in the writing system they were learning. There is no other way of measuring the effects of i.t.a. on the learner of literacy *per se*. (Some American researchers tested i.t.a. students in T.O., and thus there is no way of knowing i.t.a.'s effects on literacy learning as such in their investigations. One might as well measure the literacy of a newly immigrated Greek child of second-grade age level by a test printed in English!)

The i.t.a. experimental group was significantly superior on every test administered during the first two years of the research; progress in the basal reader series (after 1 year; 2 years; and $2\frac{1}{3}$ years); Schonell word recognition test (after 1 year; and $1\frac{1}{3}$ years); Neale analysis of reading ability (after $1\frac{1}{2}$ years)—accuracy, rate, and comprehension; length of written composition and breadth of written vocabulary (after 2 years).[27] The second experiment produced similar results.[28]

When the results were analyzed in terms of the incidence of very poor readers in the two groups, the T.O. group was found to have produced significantly more failures than the i.t.a. group. Generally, there were only half as many very poor readers in the i.t.a. group as there were in the T.O. group.[29]

These results led to the following conclusion in the report on the British i.t.a. experiments:

"The traditional orthography of English is a serious cause of difficulty in the early stages of learning to read and write. The evidence from these experiments is quite conclusive that, in comparison with the simplified and regularized system of i.t.a.

    (a) T.O. slowed down children's progress in their series of readers.
    (b) T.O. caused significantly lower scores on all tests of reading, but especially in word recognition and accuracy. The reduction in the learning efficiency of the most able pupils in the T.O. classes was especially remarkable.
    (c) T.O. also produced markedly inferior results in written composition.
    (d) T.O. had a seriously limiting effect on the size of the children's written vocabulary."[30]

This conclusion, based on statistical research, was confirmed by the survey of educators' opinions conducted independently by Vera Southgate for the Schools Council of England and Wales:

The majority of teachers who have used i.t.a., as well as knowledgeable visitors to schools, have concluded that, when i.t.a. is used with infants, better progress is made than when T.O. is used. The observed results include easier and earlier reading skill acquired without frustrations for the child; an increase in the time children choose to spend on reading, in the number of books they read and in their under-standing of the contents of the books, an increase in the quantity and quality of children's free writing; an improvement in children's attitudes and behaviour; and beneficial effects on other school subjects and the general life of the school.[31]

Thus, the evidence from empirical research strongly supports the hypothesis that a simple and obviously regular writing system facilitates literacy develop-ment, whereas a complex and apparently irregular writing system is an im-portant source of difficulty to young children trying to understand how to read.

Even if certain linguists are correct in their assertions that T.O. is not irreg-ular and that therefore there is no mismatch between the T.O. writing system and the L^2 spoken language basis of expected literate responses, nevertheless, the results of these experiments leave no doubts whatsoever on one score: there is a serious mismatch between the child's level of intellectual development and the complexity of the logical operations involved in relating the T.O. graphemic system to the phonemic system of "standard" English as L^2.

The British i.t.a. experiments also provide evidence confirming another find-ing noted several times previously in this book. There appears to be a critical stage when conditions need to be optimally supportive to the literacy learner. This is at the beginning stage when the child is making his first attempts to grope through the many problems that have to be overcome in achieving cognitive clarity regarding the learning-to-read process. Österberg's experiment in teach-ing reading in the Piteå dialect of Swedish also provided objective evidence of this. What mattered was that the mismatch between the dialect and standard Swedish was removed in the child's initial introduction to literacy. Once the child had developed the basic literacy skills they could be transferred to reading in standard Swedish. Similarly in the i.t.a. experiments, once children learned literacy skills in i.t.a., they transferred them to reading and writing in T.O. with no *apparent* trouble. Southgate's report to the Schools Council states that

> Of all the verbal evidence collected in this inquiry, the fact most frequently and most emphatically stated was that children did not experience difficulty in making the transition in reading from i.t.a. to T.O.[32]

Earlier reports on the British experiments with i.t.a. had been less certain on this point. The results of standardized tests administered during the stage when most children were going through the transition from i.t.a. to T.O. showed that *then* i.t.a. students could not read T.O. as well as they could read i.t.a. This suggested a setback to the i.t.a. students' reading caused by the require-ment to transfer to the more complex or less regular T.O. system. Yet, the i.t.a. students, at the early stage in the transfer to T.O., could read T.O. at least as well as the students who had been learning T.O. for nearly two years.[33] Subse-quent follow-up tests of children in their fourth and fifth year at school found that, when the i.t.a. students had adjusted to T.O., their scores on T.O. reading tests were significantly superior to those of students who had been using T.O. from the very beginning.[34]

Perhaps the most surprising result of the British i.t.a. experiments was the superior T.O. spelling achievements of the i.t.a. students once they had passed the transition phase. Southgate's survey reported that "No evidence of a decline in spelling ability was noted in infant classes and there were certain indications of improvements."[35]

The statistical data showed that i.t.a. students were equal in T.O. spelling ability to T.O. students by the middle of the third year (approximately one year after transition in reading on the average). A year later the i.t.a. students' T.O. spelling was superior.[36] At the end of five years they remained still significantly advanced.[37]

Another independent study of i.t.a. and T.O. spelling throws light on the probable cause of the surprisingly favorable effect of i.t.a. experiences on later T.O. spelling attainments. Margaret Peters, of the Cambridge Institute of Education, compared the T. O. spelling errors of i.t.a. students with those made by T.O. pupils. They presented quite different patterns. The i.t.a. students made more errors based on phonemic logic than the T.O. students who made more random unsystematic errors. Peters concluded that "i.t.a.-taught children, with their more systematic and economical attack, present a more receptive base for the teaching of spelling conventions." She suggested that this was caused by their experiences of greater regularity of grapheme-phoneme relations in i.t.a., which left the i.t.a. student, after transition to T.O., with "the sort of non-redundant 'skeletal' structure from which conventional English spellings can be readily developed."[38]

These spelling data provide dramatic evidence of the importance of the writing system variable in the child's first experiences in the stage of initiation into literacy. The writing system, according to Peters' evidence, provides a kind of perceptual training or orientation for the child in his initial groping for cognitive clarity.

An extensive amount of discussion about i.t.a. appears here, and it is important to put it into perspective. It must be reiterated with the strongest possible emphasis that i.t.a. is not a teaching method, or even an educational approach. It certainly is not a set of commercially published materials as some American researchers apparently have believed. i.t.a. is only an alphabet, and furthermore it is merely one example of the special type of alphabet it represents. There are unlimited possibilities for developing other simplified or regularized writing systems (s.r.w.s.) or alphabets for English. Several other s.r.w.s. are already in use. UNIFON is a system that was devised in Chicago in the 1960s (cf. Ratz [39]). Gattegno's [40] *Words in Color* is an example of an attempt to provide an s.r.w.s. in a color code without changing the shapes of the English letters or the spelling of words. A different color system is Jones' [41] *Colour Story Method,* which uses only four colors. By combining color clues with shape clues Jones is able to provide a complete code for English phonemes.

Another way of achieving greater simplicity or regularity of grapheme-phoneme relations is well known to exponents of traditional phonic methods: the inconveniently irregular or difficult words are left out until a later time. An appropriate name for this approach would be "The Language Restriction Method," because the child is not given the full range of language within his listening vocabulary in this method. He is restricted to those words that are "simple" or "regular" in their grapheme-phoneme relations. Thus, his early reading materials are prone to consist of such sentences as *Nan can fan Dan,* or *fat Pat sat flat.*

The language restriction method has never been generally accepted in the English speaking countries. Many teachers have expressed fears that it would foster an unnatural view of language and reading. Nor has it ever been demonstrated as superior to other methods by valid research. From the point of view of this discussion it could be argued that the language restriction method is a case of the cure being worse than the disease. Curing the mismatch between the writing system and the "standard" English of the teacher may result in a treatment that creates a new mismatch between the reading materials and the language of both the teacher and the child. Neither ever speaks or hears in everday life the inane nonlanguage of some language restriction materials that have been published as "phonics" or "linguistic" approaches.

Warburton's review of all the published i.t.a. research reports for the Schools Council of England and Wales led him to the following conclusion:

> There is no evidence whatsoever for the belief that the best way to learn to read in traditional orthography is to learn to read in traditional orthography. It would appear rather that the best way to learn to read in traditional orthography is to learn to read in the initial teaching alphabet.[42]

However, one must not forget that there are two points of view to be taken into account if one accepts the principle that what is suitable for the reading process of mature readers is not necessarily best for the learning-to-read process of children who are just beginning an apprenticeship in literacy. The reverse aspect may be important, also, as has been remarked by Yuen Ren Chao:

> The one-to-one correspondence is of course the easiest to learn. But it is one thing to teach or learn a system and another thing to use it.[43]

The Japanese case may provide an object lesson for other countries who are striving to satisfy the needs of young beginners without disturbing the effectiveness of their writing systems for mature readers. Similarly, the English speaking countries may find it convenient to use simplified writing systems such as i.t.a., UNIFON, Colour Story, Words in Color, or the like for the child's first introduction to literacy while retaining T.O., which seems to be very effective for the purposes of rapid reading at the adult level.

One thing, at any rate, is quite clear from these investigations: the writing system is an important variable in the learning-to-read process. A perceived mismatch between the writing system and the language in which the child is expected to respond is an important cause of difficulty in the early stages of learning to read and write.

Other Aspects of the Writing System

Earlier it was noted that the descriptions that contrast alphabetic with logographic writing systems may be misleading if they cause one to believe that the former is exclusively a code for phonemes and the latter codes nothing but morphemes. A further quotation from Lefevre's account of the English writing system may serve to remind us that it does indeed code aspects of language other than phonemes:

> What makes our spelling system work so well—and it does work surprisingly well—is probably the regular spelling of structural word-form changes, and of prefixes and suffixes, *regardless of differences in their sounds.*[44]

The importance of these and additional aspects of coding in the writing system from the point of view of the young literacy learner groping toward cognitive clarity is well brought out in two recent articles by Jessie Reid. She writes in the first of these that learning to read and write in English involves not only mastering a visual code for speech but also

> learning to do without—or to supply for oneself—many of the clues to meaning that exist in oral communication—not only intonation and stress in the speaker's voice, but gesture and facial expression and the entire situational context in which speech takes place. Some of these are indicated, of course, by punctuation and type and some by illustrations, but in interpreting these an act of imaginative reconstruction must take place.[45]

These other aspects of the writing system—linguistic features that are coded and still others that are not—are well treated by several linguists who have written about the teaching of reading and writing (Lefevre[46] and Hall[47] for example). But, unfortunately, they have been given little consideration by specialists in the teaching of reading and writing.

Compound Mismatches

In addition to the more straightforward types of mismatch (1) between L^1 (the child's language) and L^2 (the teacher's language) or D^1 (the child's dialect) and D^2 (the teacher's dialect) that were described in Chapter 9, and (2) between the writing system and L^2 that have been discussed thus far in this chapter, there is a third situation in which both types of mismatches occur together. That is, the writing system is not easily perceived as matching the L^2 of the literate responses demanded in the teacher's language or dialect; furthermore, the literacy learner's language (L^1) or dialect (D^1) differs from that of the teacher's (L^2 or D^2). Usually, if this is the case, there will very likely be a further mismatch between L^1/D^1 and the writing system. Obviously, if a Spanish speaking child, for instance is being required to relate the English writing system to the English speech of his teacher, that writing system will not be readily related to the child's own linguistic experiences if he has not yet acquired his teacher's spoken English as his second language.

In the case of dialect, this problem is less readily recognized by teachers, but in Chapter 12, Berta de Braslavsky brings out clearly how serious this difficulty is in Argentina. In the previous chapter we referred to the mismatch between the D^1 black American dialect and the D^2 dialect of the teacher's so-called standard English in which the child is usually required to make his literate responses. In such cases there is a compound mismatch because of the complexity of the grapheme-phoneme relations of the traditional orthography whether one is considering D^2 or D^1.

In summary, this compound mismatch can be represented as follows:

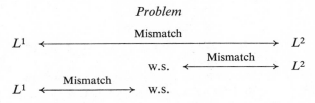

w.s. represents writing system. This can be demonstrated by two typical examples:

1. If the child's language (L^1) is Yoruba and the ultimate goal is literacy in the official language (L^2) English, which has mismatch between its spoken form and its w.s. (T.O.).
2. If the child's language is black American dialect (substitute D^1 for L^1) and the ultimate goal is literacy in one of the acceptable middle-class American English dialects (substitute D^2 for L^2), which again has mismatch with its w.s. (T.O.).

Although our chief concern in these examples is with the phonemic code of the alphabetic writing system, it must be remembered that there are other linguistic differences in addition to the phonological problems to be discussed here. These other important aspects of the problem must be borne in mind constantly in this discussion.

In the previous sections it has been demonstrated quite clearly that either the L^1/D^1 versus L^2/D^2 mismatch or the writing system versus L^2 mismatch is an important cause of difficulty in literacy learning because it raises the level of cognitive confusion, and that this is particularly serious in the earliest stages of instruction when the child is making his first attempts at solving the series of problems in understanding how to read. It seems obvious that, when both mismatches occur together, the confusion will be compounded and the effects are likely to be worse than merely cumulative.

In most countries each of these two simple mismatches on its own is barely recognized. Where one is recognized the other usually is not when both occur together.

There are at least four feasible solutions to this problem of compound mismatch. They can be summarized by showing how the *Problem* diagram would be modified by each of the four solutions:

Solutions

L^2

1 ~~L^1~~ ⟷ c.i.w.s. ⟷ L^2

L^1

2 L^1 ⟷ c.i.w.s. ⟷ ~~L^2~~

L^2 s.r.w.s.

3 ~~L^1~~ ⟷ ~~c.i.w.s.~~ ⟷ L^2

s.r.w.s. L^1

4 L^1 ⟷ ~~c.i.w.s.~~ ⟷ ~~L^2~~

where c.i.w.s. represents complex or irregular writing system and s.r.w.s. represents simplified or regularized writing system. (L is to be changed to D in the dialect case.)

Solutions 1 and 2 are only partial. They deal only with the spoken language mismatch and leave the writing system problem untouched.

Solution 1

In solution 1, L^1 is to be changed to L^2 or D^1 to D^2. In our two typical examples:

1. The Yoruba speaking child would be taught spoken English as his second language prior to being introduced to literacy skills in English, in the simplest case. Actually, in Nigeria, the Yoruba child usually is introduced to literacy in written Yoruba first. At the same time he begins learning spoken English. Then he is introduced to literacy in English. However, in many other cultures there is no written form of the first language. In such a case, English speech is taught first and literacy instruction does not begin until the child has acquired sufficient English. This is a purer example of solution 1.
2. The black American dialect speaking child would be taught the teacher's form of standard English as a second dialect before literacy skills in that form of English are introduced.

This is by now the most popular way of proceeding in second language teaching. But its application in the dialect problem is quite recent. Wolfram notes that there are two dramatically different types of assumption underlying its promotion for overcoming the black dialect difficulty in the United States.[48] First of all there is the Bereiter and Englemann view that black children are *deficient* in language and thought, but, as Goodman has argued, this is an untenable position. The second reason for using solution 1 is based on the assumption that the black child's dialect is *different* but not defective. For example, Venezky states that

> Children whose dialects deviate markedly from standard English should be taught the standard brand before they are taught reading, under the explicit assumption that it is a second dialect and not a more correct dialect that is being taught.[49]

Wolfram notes a number of criticisms of Venezky's proposition. The chief cause for doubting its effectiveness, he shows, is the long history of the resistance of subcultures to learning the standard English dialect. He quotes both Fasold[50] and Abrahams[51] as showing how social forces and peer-group influences maintain the subcultural dialect and reject the standard English imposed by outsiders. Wolfram cites also Kochman's conclusion that this approach is impracticable: "The input in time and effort is prodigious and the results negligible."[52]

Wolfram cites Labov's[53] finding that social perceptions of speech stratification start to match the adult norms at about age 14–15, which is long past the stage at which it is considered educationally desirable to acquire literacy.

Therefore, Wolfram's conclusion regarding what we have termed solution 1 as applied to the black dialect issue in the United States is

> The socio-cultural facts which inhibit the widespread acquisition of standard English even as a second dialect do not suggest this alternative as a reasonable solution.[54]

Wolfram's pessimistic evaluation of solution 1 for this particular dialect problem is in contrast with its popularity in second language teaching. That is, literacy is generally postponed in the second language until its spoken form has been acquired. Also, in the chapter on Germany it is indicated that solution 1 is the traditional method of overcoming the dialect difficulty in that country. It is also reported that "children are taught to speak and pronounce as clearly as possible and not in dialect." This produces "a certain degree of conformity between written and spoken words." Apparently, modifying the child's L^1 to enable him to produce L^2 more effectively narrows down what would otherwise be a greater mismatch between the writing system and spoken German as the child knows it. Possibly, there are specific "sociocultural facts" in the case of the black American dialect that make the problem more intractable than it is in other cultures. In Argentina "remedial Spanish, especially at the pre-school level," is also favored as a means of facilitating the child's initiation in reading.

Solution 2

In this solution to the mismatch the expected literate responses are to be changed. Instead of being in L^2/D^2 they can be in the child's own first language, L^1/D^1. In our two typical cases:

1. The Yoruba speaking child should learn to make literate responses in Yoruba at first and not in English. This is, in fact, the standard practice

in Nigeria—although not with the vernaculars of some other countries. In this case the writing system also is changed because the Yoruba writing system is learned in conjunction with Yoruba speech. Thus, our formula here does not parallel the learning situation in the case of dialect in the second example.

2. The black American dialect speaking child is permitted to make his literate responses in his own dialect instead of in standard English. Again, it is important to note the difference between this case and the previous one. Here the writing system remains unchanged, whereas in the former case it apparently is more obvious that it must be changed to fit the different language, Yoruba.

In the previous chapter it has been noted that it is the general consensus of opinion that solution 2 is best for problems of the first type here. That is, initial literacy learning should be in the vernacular. The research evidence strongly supports this view.

As has been noted, the situation is not quite the same in the case of dialect. Although it is ludicrous to retain the English writing system for Yoruba speakers to make literate responses to in Yoruba, the parallel situation is not so laughable in the case of dialect. At any rate, Goodman proposes that the literate responses part of our formula should be modified without changing the written materials of instruction:

> No special materials need to be constructed but children must be permitted, actually encouraged, to read the way they speak.[55]

In other words, the black dialect speaker is given materials that consist of standard English coded in its code, but he is to decode them, not into standard English, but into the black dialect. It should be remembered that in this book the terms "coding" and "decoding" are used functionally and not in the limited phonic sense as suggested, for example, in the writings of Jeanne Chall. Thus, what is being said here is that the black American dialect speaker is given materials in which a meaningful communication in standard English has been systematically coded in its particular writing system, and this student is required to unscramble or decipher this message into a meaningful communication in his own dialect.

This seems curious at first sight. The author writes his message according to his particular code, and the reader can read the message in his more or less different code.

Wolfram notes that "claims about the comprehension of standard English by lower-class black children vary greatly, but we still lack definitely empirical evidence on this question." He continues, however, "At this point, the most reasonable position seems to be that, for the most part, the dialect speaker has a receptive competence in standard English."[56] He cites Labov and Cohen[57] as indicating that most differences between the black and standard English dialects appear on the surface rather than in the underlying levels of language. Further-more, Baratz[58] found that lower-class black children were able to repeat sentences in their own dialect that they received in standard English in her sentence-repetition test. However, Wolfram and Fasold admit that in the usual mixed dialect communication situation under discussion here "there will be an inevitable information loss."[59]

Wolfram sees only one serious impediment to the implementation of Good-man's solution—that is, the teachers' unfamiliarity with other dialects and the way in which they are related to standard English and its written form:

> Some teachers may inductively arrive at such types of discernment because of the consistency of certain types of pronunciations from dialect speakers, but if the alternative proposed by Goodman and others is to be adopted on an extensive level, it will require the training of teachers in the structural patterns of the dialect.

However, provided this training is forthcoming, Wolfram believes that this solution has "one very practical advantage: it can be established much more immediately than some of the other alternatives."[60]

Solution 3

Our sample cases would each be subject to two changes according to solu-tion 3:

1. The Yoruba child would learn to understand and speak English first as the experiential basis for learning to make literate responses in English. But, in addition, the writing system for English (T.O.) would be modified in some way to reduce the mismatch between the spoken and written forms of English.
2. The black American dialect speaker would learn to use standard English before being introduced to literacy instruction. Then, also, the written form of English would be made to conform more closely with the standard English he had been taught to speak.

In both cases, the complex or irregular writing sytem (c.i.w.s.) of English would give place to a simplified or regularized writing system (s.r.w.s.) if we are considering grapheme-phoneme relations; but, as was noted earlier, the writing system of English, although primarily a phonemic code, does signal other linguistic features, and these must be considered in this solution.

In an experiment conducted by Abiri in Nigeria, the s.r.w.s. used was a special variation of i.t.a., known as WITA (World Initial Teaching Alphabet) or Speech i.t.a. This is the same as the i.t.a. used in English speaking countries except that it attempts to code the patterns of stressed and unstressed syllables in spoken English. Stressed syllables are printed larger and darker, and un-stressed ones are made smaller and lighter. An unstressed syllable containing

/i/ is printed above the line, whereas a syllable with /ə/ remains on the line. Abiri had some six hundred Yoruba speaking children in an experimental Speech i.t.a. group and about five hundred in a control group using T.O. The schools were situated in rural districts near Ibadan and in the urban area of the city of Lagos. The materials and methods were identical in the WITA and control T.O. groups, except for the writing system in which they were printed. Other important pupil and school variables were matched also. He tested all the children periodically over three years.

The experimental group was found to be superior not only during the period when these Yoruba children were learning literacy in Speech i.t.a. but also subsequently when they had made the transition to T.O. Abiri claims that the simplified or regularized system of writing "helped both the more and the less intelligent pupils" and that there were fewer failures in English literacy in the experimental classes.

Some of the pupils in Abiri's experimental classes had been introduced already to written English in T.O. He found that Speech i.t.a. was not effective with these subjects. Abiri states that their "former contact with T.O. probably interfered with their efforts in learning to read WITA later." [61] Another possible explanation for this result is that it is a further reflection of the importance of the *initial* orienting phase of literacy learning. The damage is done by raising the level of cognitive confusion too high when the child is making his *first* trials at understanding the task. If the source of confusion is reduced *at this stage,* the child's problem-solving abilities are primed and the same difficulties can be overcome once the cognitive clarity development has gotten under way.

Turning to the second type of problem—the case of the black American dialect—several successful trials have been made of the use of i.t.a. in schools with children speaking such dialects (in Little Rock, Arkansas and in Pittsburgh, Pennsylvania), but these have not coincided with any attempt to teach standard English first. This means that the mismatch between D^1 and D^2 remains, and probably this causes a mismatch between D^1 and the writing system, which is i.t.a. instead of T.O. in this case.

Goodman has questioned whether i.t.a. can have much value for black dialect speaking children when the language coded by i.t.a. is standard English —and the standard English of Southern England at that:

> The British i.t.a. materials, however, cannot be read literally except with the "received pronunciation" of the BBC. . . . i.t.a. spelling requires pronunciation narrowed to one special class dialect. [62]

Actually, Goodman is not quite correct in his description of i.t.a. Although it is true that i.t.a. probably has a strong basis in the "received pronunciation" of the upper-class English of the south of England, it contains many *deliberate* compromises with other dialects. These are explained by its designer, Sir James Pitman, [63] in his Royal Society of Arts paper.

For example, the i.t.a. grapheme **wh** represents the phoneme heard initially in *whale, when, whistle, Whitsuntide* in Scottish speech. But this phoneme is never heard in the dialect on which Goodman claims i.t.a. is based. Pitman explains that it was included in i.t.a. because of the existence of this phoneme in other speech areas of the English speaking world (for example, Scotland and parts of North America). Several other ingenious compromises are made by i.t.a. to accommodate variations in the phonological aspect of dialect. However, Goodman is quite obviously correct in asserting that no phonemic code such as i.t.a. could possibly serve all English speakers perfectly. Variations in dialect are bound to cause deficiencies from each dialect's point of view. Thus, the teacher in the south of England must cope with the apparently redundant grapheme wh as a concession to his Scottish colleagues.

Goodman claims that "The English orthography has one great virtue in its uniformity across dialects." [64] But the same is even more true of i.t.a. There are no regional spellings of i.t.a. as yet, although some educators believe that the gap between writing and speaking would be made narrower if regional or dialect i.t.a. materials could be produced. In fact, i.t.a. is more universal in its spellings than T.O. because words like *color, rigor, (colour, rigour)* and the like do not vary in American and British i.t.a. materials as they do in T.O. materials.

The essential question regarding the use of i.t.a. (or some other s.r.w.s.) for solution (3) is not whether i.t.a. is a perfect code for the regional variety of standard English as D^2, but whether i.t.a. is a more efficient code than T.O. As we have seen in the earlier section on the mismatch between the writing system and L^2/D^2, the experimental evidence very strongly supports the case for i.t.a. and shows with certainty that T.O. is a serious impediment to literacy learning.

Furthermore, the variations in English speech and dialect are far more numerous in Britain than they are in the United States. The British experiments with i.t.a. were deliberately designed to include a number of contrasting pronunciation areas: Southern England, the West of England, the Midlands, the North, Scotland, the English speaking areas of North Wales, and Northern Ireland. No evidence was found of any difference in the effectiveness of i.t.a. from one area to another in the sense that in every area i.t.a. proved superior to T.O.

The reason for this is probably that i.t.a. can be perceived more readily by the child as a code for language that approximates *some speech he has heard.* Thus, i.t.a.'s *wuns* in *once upon a time* is not quite correct for some speakers of English who would prefer *wons* in their view of the i.t.a. system; but from the same viewpoint it is infinitely better than *once,* which represents no one's pronunciation of that word.

In all its aspects, phonological or other, the writing system is not, and can never be, a perfect transcription of speech. It can only be a partial code—a set of clues to the reconstruction of the spoken message. With regard to the phonemes, i.t.a. is a clearer set of clues, whereas T.O. contains many puzzling complexities. This is true of all the regional variations of English that would be in the position of L^2/D^2 in solution 3.

Solution 4

In solution 4 the literate responses of the learner are no longer required to be in the L^2/D^2 of the teacher, but instead are in the L^1/D^1 of the student. In addition, the writing system is modified to give a closer fit with the learner's L^1/D^1. Let us see how this applies to our two typical examples:

1. The Yoruba child would begin learning literacy in Yoruba. The writing system of Yoruba would be made to match his native tongue—Yoruba, also. In actual practice this is what is done in Nigeria, except that, so far as this writer knows, there are no current experiments in improving the written form of Yoruba. But in other cultures this is not done. If our example were a culture where there was no writing for its language and the conventional educational practice was to require the child to learn literacy in a foreign language (English, for example), then solution (4) would mean developing a simple and regular writing system for the vernacular and teaching literacy in that first. The literate responses would, of course, then be in the vernacular first, too.
2. In the dialect example, the black American child would make literate responses in his dialect at first and not in standard English. Also, the writing system would be modified to match his dialect instead of standard English.

The first case here is quite a common practice, although probably more attention needs to be given to improving the vernacular writing systems. As has been noted more than once already, this general practice of starting literacy in the vernacular is strongly supported by professional opinion and research.

The second case is much more controversial, although a number of authors insist that the mismatch between D^1 and D^2 is not qualitatively different from the one between L^1 and L^2, but only a matter of degree. One would tend to assume therefore that the same general principle would apply to both: that is, the literate responses should be in L^1/D^1 and they should be coded in a writing system that signals L^1/D^1 and not necessarily L^2/D^2. This solution has not been tried out fully as an attack on the black dialect problem in the United States. Only partial attempts have been made.

Shuy has suggested a version of the language restriction method described earlier in this chapter. He proposes that

> In the case of beginning reading materials for nonstandard speakers, the text should help the child by avoiding grammatical forms which are not realized by him in this spoken language.[65]

This is like the phonic and so-called linguistic approaches that engineer the regularity of grapheme-phoneme relations by leaving out the inconveniently irregular words in the language. The difference is that Shuy is referring to grammar rather than phonology, and he is concerned about omitting from the child's first reading materials any grammatical features that are inconveniently different in the dialect from what they are in standard English. But Shuy's language restriction method does not control orthographical difficulties. Hence, it is only a partial solution to the mismatch between the writing system and D^1.

Wolfram has examined the feasibility of this method in some detail and concludes that the feasibility "varies from feature to feature. There are some which can be handled by minor adjustments in current materials; others, however, require the elimination of significant portions of narratives or the cumbersome use of certain circumlocutions if the 'avoidance strategy' which is basic to this alternative is to be carried out rigorously."

Thus, the "avoidance strategy" or language restriction method has the same disadvantage when applied to the problem of dialect grammar as it does when applied to the grapheme-phoneme relations difficulty. If applied consistently it results in an artificial language more or less removed from the child's everyday life experience, which is just the kind of mismatch we are seeking to avoid. This defect probably is sufficient to make this proposed method ineffective. However, mention needs to be made of the advantages for it noted by Wolfram. He points out that

> Material developers would not necessarily have to be as rigorous in their avoidance strategy as we have described above. One might just avoid certain types of grammatical differences while disregarding others.

Also,

> A modification of this method may eliminate some of the most salient features of standard English which might be unfamiliar to the lower-class black child who comes to the schoolroom. Also, it would not incorporate socially stigmatized features of language, eliminating the controversy which inevitably surrounds the codification of nonstandard patterns in reading materials.[66]

The success of Österberg's experiment in Sweden described in Chapter 9 shows that there is no necessity for dialect writing to arouse controversy. It may be, however, that Wolfram's assumption is valid for the specific black subculture problem in the United States.

A second partial use of solution 4 for the black lower-class dialect problem is the proposal to write materials in the vernacular of black American children, except that the orthography used is T.O.—that is, the phonemic code for standard English instead of the vernacular. The following is an example of the changes that would be made in this partial use of solution 4.

Standard English Version

Suzy said, "Look in here, Mother.
David cannot see a girl.
And I can.
Can you see a girl in here?"

Black English Version

Susan, She say, "Momma, look in here.
David don't see no girl, and I do.
You see a girl in there?"

(Wolfram and Fasold[67])

Why is solution 4 only partially carried through? Why is the mismatch between D^1 and the written material corrected in every linguistic aspect except the orthography? Fasold gives two reasons:

1. As we mentioned earlier, the conventional spelling does adequately represent the phonological units of the dialect at a more abstract level, so that, for example, there is formal justification for representing word-final [f] in *toof* as *tooth*.
2. From a sociological standpoint, extra-linguistic matters such as other printed material and official education also make this alternative more reasonable.[68]

Neither of these reasons seems convincing. As regards the first one, in our earlier discussion of the assertions of certain linguists, we saw that what may have "formal justification" in their logic may seem incomprehensibly complex or ambiguous in the child's perception. If Wolfram were correct in his second assertion, no changes in written language would ever have taken place. The same reason was given for not trying the i.t.a. experiment in Britain in 1960, but in the 1970s many bookstores and libraries have i.t.a. books freely available; children's comics have i.t.a. sections; and advertising material appears in i.t.a.

One use of solution 4 has gone a little farther toward total application. Stewart uses an apostrophe instead of writing in full certain unpronounced syllables in his approach to developing black dialect materials: *'cause* for *because; 'round* for *around; 'posed to* for *supposed to*. According to Stewart, this is designed to meet the fact that "Negro-dialect speakers do not always know that a prefix is 'missing' from their version of a particular word."[69]

Thus, the experimental use of solution 4 in its fullest sense remains to be attempted in respect of the black dialect problem.

The Normal Standard English Situation

There is a danger that in the preceding discussion the use of the extreme cases of the foreign language and the black dialect may have given the reader the false impression that mismatch is only a problem of such special groups. This is not so. These extreme examples were used only to make the problem clearer by contrast.

Wolfram and Fasold also make this claim:

When the child who speaks Black English is required to learn to read using Standard English materials, he is given two tasks at once: learning to read and learning a new dialect. The Standard English speaking child, by contrast, is only required to learn to read.[70]

Although these writers quite appropriately stress the greater complexity of the task of the dialect speaking child, their comparison tends to conceal the fact that there are similar mismatches between the child's L^1 and the literate responses' L^2 in the standard English speaking child's task of learning to read, too.

This is a frequent source of mismatch between the child's past experience of language and the literate responses he is required to make. For instance, Jessie Reid believes that the special styles of written language ought not to be introduced in the initial stages of literacy learning:

> sentence forms that belong to story-telling or to written description [for example, *said he* instead of *he said*] should not be introduced prematurely into reading material. It is not enough to ban them from the very earliest books: they should not appear until a child is reading fluently sentences that are as close to his speech as possible.

The same rule must be applied in children's writing, too. Reid asserts that

> it is essential not to let inappropriate notions of "correctness" interfere with the child's crucial discovery of how he can represent, in print, something very close to what he can say. It is also of great importance not to put before children stereotyped models of sentences beginning "This is a . . ." and so on.[71]

Reid's remarks provide a timely reminder to us that mismatch is a universal problem in learning to read, no matter what the language or dialect of the child may be.

Conclusion

It is of crucial importance to take into account the literacy learner's linguistic environment. This is true of all cultural, linguistic, and national groups. The most important universal principle for teaching literacy is that the material to be read and the reading and writing responses the learner is required to make match as closely as possible his past experience of language in the spoken form. The greater the mismatch—or the wider the gap between the child's linguistic experiences and the literacy task to be undertaken—the more difficult it will be for the child to learn these skills.

Such a gap can be closed from two sides. One can provide the child with new experiences of language before teaching literacy or one can change the literacy tasks to meet the child's natural linguistic condition. Both approaches need to be made, but the second approach—according to the consensus of opinion and research—appears to deserve increased attention. Language is an essential part of personality, already well-developed by the age of 5 or 6. Therefore, it is difficult to modify except by extension. The easier way to lead the child into reading and writing is to extend *his* articulacy into *his* literacy. Because it is easier, the channels are open to our teaching of reading and writing and therefore our work will be very much more productive. Later, when he has developed the basic skills of literacy as such, he will be able to apply them in other kinds of language than his own.

The vital stage when mismatch must be avoided is at the first initiation into the written form of language. Cognitive confusion regarding the purpose and nature of written language is at its maximum when the child is first introduced to the task of learning to read and write. The child's attainment of these skills depends on the reduction of this initial cognitive confusion. By solving a series of problems about the nature of written language and the responses he is being asked to make to it, he gradually develops increasing cognitive clarity about how to read. Mismatches between his past experience of language and the features of the written material he is expected to read or the responses he is required to make cause increased cognitive confusion. The result is either delayed development of literacy or even outright failure.

REFERENCES

1. Bloomfield, L., "Linguistics and reading," *Elementary English Review,* **19** (1942), 125–130.
2. Lado, Robert, *Linguistics Across Cultures,* Ann Arbor: University of Michigan Press, 1957, p. 96.
3. Neijs, Karel, *Literacy Primers: Construction, Evaluation and Use,* Paris: UNESCO, 1961, p. 50.
4. Clairborne, J. H., "Types of congenital symbol symblyopia," *Journal of the American Medical Association,* **47** (1906), 1813–1816.
5. Maruyama, M., "Reading disability: A neurological point of view," *Bulletin of the Orton Society,* **8** (1958), 14–17.
6. Hermann, K., *Reading Disability: A Medical Study of Word-Blindness and Related Handicaps,* Springfield, Ill: Thomas, 1959, p. 38.
7. Hodges, Richard, *The English Primrose,* London, 1644; Hart, John, *A Methode or Comfortable Beginning for All Unlearned, Whereby They May be Taught to Read English in a Very Short Time with Pleasure,* London, 1570; Butler, Charles, *English Grammar,* Oxford, 1633.
8. Ranta, T. M., *Method and Materials of Teaching Reading in Finland Under Church and State,* Doctoral dissertation, University of Minnesota, 1964, p. 604.
9. HISC, *Information No. 3,* Helsinki: HISC (July 3, 1963), p. 3.
10. Vikainen, I., *A Diagnosis of Specific Backwardness in Spelling,* Turku, Finland: University of Turku Institute of Education, 1965.
11. Makita, Kiyoshi, "The rarity of reading disability in Japanese children," *American Journal of Orthopsychiatry,* **38** (July 1968), 599–614. Especially 601–602.
12. Preston, R. C., "Comparison of word-recognition skill in German and American children," *Elementary School Journal,* **53** (1952), 443–446.
13. Monroe, Marion, *Children Who Cannot Read,* Chicago: U. of Chicago, 1932.
14. Hildreth, Gertrude, "Lessons in Arabic," *Reading Teacher,* **19** (1965), 202–210.
15. Hildreth, Gertrude, "Armenian children enjoy reading," *Reading Teacher,* **19** (1966), 433–445.
16. Hildreth, Gertrude, "On first looking into a Greek primer," *Reading Teacher,* **21** (February 1968), 453–463.

17. Hildreth, Gertrude, "Reading with a rational alphabet: the Russian system," *Reading Teacher,* **22** (December 1968), 251–261.

18. Lefevre, Carl A., *Linguistics and the Teaching of Reading,* New York: McGraw-Hill, 1964, p. 184.

19. Hall, Robert A., Jr., *Sound and Spelling in English,* Philadelphia: Chilton, 1961, pp. 42–45.

20. Feitelson, Dina, "Learning to read," in *UNESCO Handbook in Reading,* Paris: UNESCO, 1972.

21. Samuels, S. Jay, "Cross-national studies in reading: the relationship between the sound-letter correspondence in language and reading achievement," in Figurel, J. Allen, (ed.) *Reading and Realism,* Newark, Del.: IRA, 1969.

22. Holmes, Jack A., and Rose, Ivan M., "Disadvantaged children and the effectiveness of i.t.a.," *Reading Teacher,* **22** (January 1969), 350–362; Robinson, Helen M., "Effectiveness of i.t.a. as a medium for reading instruction," in Mazurkiewicz, A. J. (ed.), *i.t.a. and the World of English,* Hempstead, N.Y.: i.t.a. Foundation, 1966.

23. Warburton, F. W., and Southgate, Vera, *i.t.a.: An Independent Evaluation,* London: Murray and Chambers, 1969, pp. 256–258; Downing, John, "Current misconceptions about i.t.a.," *Elementary English,* **42** (May 1965), 492–501; Downing, John, "A closer scrutiny of research data on i.t.a.," *Education,* **88** (April-May, 1966), 308–312; Downing, John, "i.t.a.—what next?," in Schick, G. B., and May, M. M. (eds.), *Junior College and Adult Reading Programs—Expanding Fields,* Milwaukee, Wis.: National Reading Conference, 1967. Downing, John, "Cautionary comments on some American i.t.a. reports," *Educational Research,* **13** (November 1970), 70–72; Downing, John, "i.t.a.: American versus British experience," *Phi Delta Kappan,* **52** (March 1971), 416–419.

24. Warburton and Southgate, *op. cit.,* p. 258.

25. Downing, John, *et al., The i.t.a. Symposium,* Slough: NFER in England and Wales, 1967, pp. 128–130 and 148–152.

26. Downing, John, *Evaluating the Initial Teaching Alphabet,* London: Cassell, 1967, pp. 98–120, for example.

27. *Ibid.,* pp. 153–158.

28. *Ibid.,* pp. 268–271.

29. Downing, John, "New experimental evidence of the effectiveness of i.t.a. in preventing disabilities of reading and spelling," *Developmental Medicine and Child Neurology,* **5** (October 1969), 547–555.

30. Downing, *Evaluating the Initial Teaching Alphabet, op. cit.,* pp. 295–296.

31. Warburton and Southgate *op. cit.,* p. 156.

32. *Ibid.,* p. 168.

33. Downing, *Evaluating the Initial Teaching Alphabet, op. cit.,* pp. 236–247 and 293–295.

34. Downing John, and Latham, W., "A follow-up of children in the first i.t.a. experiment," *British Journal of Educational Psychology,* **39** (November 1969), 303–305.

35. Warburton, and Southgate, *op. cit.,* p. 74.

36. Downing, *Evaluating the Initial Teaching Alphabet, op. cit.,* pp. 176–177.

37. Downing and Latham, *op. cit.,* p. 304.

38. Peters, Margaret, "The influence of reading methods on spelling," *British Journal of Educational Psychology,* **37** (February 1967), 47–53.

39. Ratz, M. S., *UNIFON: A Design for Teaching Reading,* Racine, Wis.: Western Publishing Educational Services, 1966.
40. Gattegno, C., *Words in Color: Background and Principles,* Chicago: Learning Materials, 1962.
41. Jones, J. K., *Research Report on Colour Story Reading,* London: Nelson, 1967.
42. Warburton and Southgate, *op. cit.,* pp. 234–235.
43. Chao, Yuen Ren, *Language and Symbolic Systems,* London: Cambridge University Press, 1968, p. 111.
44. Lefevre, *op. cit.,* p. 166
45. Reid, Jessie, "The most important R" (Part I), *Teachers' World,* **3189** (December 25, 1970), 20.
46. Lefevre, *op. cit.,* especially Chaps. 4–7.
47. Hall, *op. cit.,* especially pp. 7, 26–28, and 39.
48. Wolfram, Walt, "Sociolinguistic alternatives in teaching reading to nonstandard speakers," *Reading Research Quarterly,* **6** (Fall 1970), 9–33.
49. Venezky, R. L., "Nonstandard language and reading," *Elementary English,* **47** (1970), 37–40.
50. Fasold, R. W., *Isn't English the First Language?,* paper presented at the annual convention of the National Council of Teachers of English, Milwaukee, Wis., 1968.
51. Abrahams, R. D., *The Advantages of Black English,* paper presented at the Southern Conference of Language Learning, Jacksonville, Fla., 1970.
52. Kochman, T., "Social factors in the consideration of teaching standard English," in Aaorns, A. C., Gordon, Barbara Y., and Stewart, W. A. (eds.), *Linguistic–Cultural Differences and American Education,* special anthology issue of *The Florida FL Reporter* (1969), pp. 116–122 and 156–157.
53. Labov, W., "Stages in the acquisition of standard English," in Shuy, R. W. (ed.), *Social Dialects and Language Learning,* Champaign, Ill.: National Council of Teachers of English, 1964.
54. Wolfram, *op. cit.,* pp. 15–16.
55. Goodman, Kenneth S., "Dialect barriers to reading comprehension," in Baratz, Joan C., and Shuy, Roger W. (eds.), *Teaching Black Children to Read,* Washington, D.C.: Center for Applied Linguistics, 1969, p. 27.
56. Wolfram, *op. cit.,* p. 16.
57. Labov, W., and Cohen, P, "Systematic relations of standard and non-standard rules in the grammar of Negro speakers," *Project Literacy Report No. 8,* Ithaca, N.Y.: Cornell University, 1967.
58. Baratz, Joan C., "Teaching reading in an urban Negro school system," in Baratz and Shuy, *op. cit.,* pp. 92–116.
59. Wolfram, Walt, and Fasold, R. W., "Toward reading materials for speakers of black English: three linguistically appropriate passages," in Baratz and Shuy, *op. cit.,* p. 141.
60. Wolfram, *op. cit.,* pp. 18–19.
61. Abiri, J. O. O., *World Initial Teaching Alphabet Versus Traditional Orthography,* Doctoral thesis, University of Ibadan, Nigeria, 1969.
62. Goodman, "Dialect barriers to reading comprehension," *op. cit.,* pp. 22–23.
63. Pitman, I. J., "Learning to read: an experiment," *Journal of the Royal Society of Arts,* **109** (1961), 149–180.
64. Goodman, "Dialect barriers to reading comprehension," *op. cit.,* p. 20.

65. Shuy, R. W., "A linguistic background for developing beginning reading materials for black children," in Baratz and Shuy, *op. cit.,* p. 125.

66. Wolfram, *op. cit.,* pp. 22–23.

67. Wolfram and Fasold, *op. cit.,* p. 148.

68. Wolfram, *op. cit.,* p. 24.

69. Stewart, *op. cit.,* p. 195.

70. Wolfram, and Fasold, *op. cit.,* p. 143.

71. Reid, Jessie, "The most important R" (Part II), *Teachers' World,* **3190** (January 1, 1971), 18.

CHAPTER 11

The Future of Comparative Reading

JOHN DOWNING

THERE are three main avenues along which comparative reading can be expected to travel: (1) Future research in this new field of enquiry should increase our knowledge and understanding of the basic processes of the acquisition of literacy and its mature functioning. (2) The future provision of courses in comparative reading at the college level should enhance the professional development of educators specializing in reading. (3) The future development of world literacy should be greatly aided by the application of the findings of comparative reading studies.

The Future in Research

Hopefully, we can look forward to progress in cross-national reading research in at least two directions: (1) objective testing surveys of the type being undertaken by the IEA group, and (2) other basic research to determine the important variables in comparative studies.

The future potential of the application of scientific methods of measurement in this area is obviously great, but, thus far, the empirical research that has been conducted has done little more than demonstrate its feasibility and bring out the difficulties to be overcome. The three cross-national achievement studies reviewed in Chapter 3, for example, paved the way for other methodological improvements by their discoveries of unforeseen sources of error.

Specifically, they revealed the following problems: (1) unreliable sampling; (2) insensitivity of tests; (3) inappropriate ages of subjects; and (4) lack of hypotheses derived from theory or practical questions.

The next stage in comparative reading research requires the development of better methodological foundations. For example, we need research on the precise effects of translating reading tests from one language into another. It is not enough to apply the usual statistical procedures that allow us to claim that translation causes "no significant difference," especially when the reading tests used may themselves involve a variety of subskills. Nothing short of deliberately investigating psycholinguistic hypotheses regarding the effects of test translation will tell us what we need to know. Many other problems of this type in cross-national literacy research require similar deliberate methodological investigation.

The measurement and control of *educational* and *linguistic* variables is another area of needed methodological improvement. This applies to reading research in general and even to educational research as a whole—not just to the field of comparative reading. Educational research is in a stage of development rather like that of experimental psychology thirty or forty years ago. There appears to be a self-conscious striving to be recognized as "scientific." Conventional variables that have been found to be important in economics, sociology, and psychology are included in research designs in a rather ritualistic, automatic, un-questioning manner. But, as we have shown in Chapters 5 through 10, there may be other educational and linguistic features of greater significance for literacy acquisition. The number of possibly important variables discovered in those chapters is too great to repeat, but future research should inquire more precisely into their general importance for the design of cross-national reading investiga-tions. We need to know more exactly how these differences in the educational and linguistic environments do actually affect the child's experiences in literacy acquisition and to what extent.

The Future in Teaching

Douglass' article on "Beginning reading in Norway" begins with this intro-duction:

It is sometimes instructive to take a look at the ways of other people as they work with children; not because they warrant being copied, but rather for purposes of contrast so that one may be helped to entertain ideas that could lead to useful modifications in ways of helping children learn.[1]

This is the second area of future expansion for comparative reading, and there is now sufficient scholarly material on the topic for a substantial college course. It would be a valuable course for the student of reading if pursued along the lines suggested in Douglass' article. Many current reading courses and professional textbooks on reading lack this comparative dimension. Ethnocentric presenta-tions of reading miss an enormous amount of useful knowledge that could be shared from one country to another. Also, one does not realize the significance of certain factors in reading in *one's own country* until one notes their absence or different form in others.

This was Whorf's reason for placing such a high value on studying another, preferably remarkably different, language:

in its study we are at long last pushed willy-nilly out of our ruts. Then we find that the exotic language is a mirror held up to our own.[2]

This is the quickest cure for narrow ethnocentrism in the study of reading: experiences, as rich and as wide as possible, of the different ways of teaching reading in other languages and cultures. The student will find that there are many other ways of achieving the goals of reading than are dreamed of in the schools of his own country. Some of these may even be worth trying, but all will, by a series of contrasts and comparisons, bring out in sharp relief the structure of reading at home.

The Future in Literacy Development

Last, but not least, is the importance of comparative reading studies for the development of higher standards of literacy throughout the world. As Dina Feitelson has remarked, "a day should come when the teaching of beginning reading in any language will be regarded as a configuration of a finite number of specific problems which have to be dealt with. Understanding the way any one of these problems was solved in another language may help the educator of the future to benefit from the experience of his peers in other countries."[3]

Recent years have seen a tremendous increase in the efforts of UNESCO and related organizations to expand and improve literacy on a worldwide basis. UNESCO's great concern to attack illiteracy on as many fronts as is feasible is matched by a growing concern among individual nations, too. Malmquist has caught the spirit of this movement:

> The struggle against illiteracy is one of the most important and also one of the most gigantic and demanding tasks of our present generation. This task has two facets. First to eliminate illiteracy. Second to raise the standard of functional literacy.[4]

The past two decades have seen a rapid raising of aspirations in connection with the two facets of literacy development distinguished by Malmquist. A dissatisfaction with the bare minimum of literacy has led to the demand for functional literacy, and in recent years there have been further demands to raise the standard of functional literacy to higher levels.

For instance, Gray, in the intermediate stage of the movement we have just described, believed that "functional literacy" was "that level of ability to read and write which is normally expected of literate people in the area of culture involved."[5] This was in 1955, and his view at the time was that the literacy level that could be expected in the United States would be that achieved usually by students in grade IV.

According to Curry, writing in 1967, a higher level was required for functional literacy in the United States:

> At the present time "functional literacy" is used to refer to a person who has acquired the reading and writing skills which are equivalent to an eighth-grade level of education. . . . The change . . . to an eighth-grade level as a criterion for literacy was brought about because of an awareness that it is becoming increasingly difficult for the individual with less than an eighth-grade level of education to be an effective person in our society—as head of a household, as a citizen, and as a worker.[6]

Curry's remarks bring home the point that functional literacy cannot be related to any fixed level of ability in reading or writing. The level is determined by the changing needs of the individual in his society, and must therefore be flexible. Total illiteracy may have been functional for the serf, but in the modern world higher and higher levels of literacy are demanded.

Jenkinson, in 1967, also called for higher criteria for functional literacy by proposing a new term, "technological literacy," for such a higher level of functioning:

> The period when functional literacy was essential has been superseded by one in which technological literacy is imperative. In terms of level, this range appears to be a minimum of grade VII reading but is rapidly moving upwards to grade IX reading competence.[7]

Nor is this demand for improved national standards of functioning in literacy confined to the United States and Canada. Malmquist, the Swedish authority on literacy research, has called for raising the standard "at least to a 9th grade level. And, very soon, we can reasonably expect the necessity of a further revision of literacy standards, raising the level to a 12th grade reading proficiency.[8]

The term "functional literacy" seems to have developed for the purpose of discussing the minimum level of literacy that must be acquired for an individual to meet the reading and writing demands made on him to function successfully in society. But, in view of the changing needs of the individual in his society, it would seem more useful to define functional literacy generally *as the group of reading and writing abilities that an individual needs for a satisfying and effective life in his society.*

A UNESCO statement that spells this out in more detail deserves quoting again:

> A person is literate when he has acquired the essential knowledge and skills which enable him to engage in all those activities in which literacy is required for effective functioning in his group and community, and whose attainments make it possible for him to use these skills towards his own and his community's development.[9]

The functions of literacy, so defined, make an exhaustive list hardly necessary or useful. However, the following sample of those functions frequently mentioned in the literature may be noted:

1. Individual Welfare: securing information about current events, health, child care, family planning, employment opportunities, techniques in agriculture and industry; meeting civic obligations (selecting a political program and voting); satisfying religious aspirations; pondering critically the accuracy, value, and significance of political communications, advertising, and so on; leisure (access to literary heritage); learning in schools and colleges as well as individually; self-expression through writing.
2. Social Functions: acquiring social identity (see especially Tax[10]); Group progress in health, industry, and so on; international understanding.

On the other hand, illiteracy is commonly recognized as a correlate of ignorance, unproductiveness, backwardness, poverty, disease, crime, superstition, suspicion, and strife.

But today there are three positive functions of literacy that are of outstanding significance for the future progress of man and society:

1. Its communication purpose in education.
2. Its communication purpose in industrial training and work.
3. Its special contribution to critical rational thinking and its reflection in the development of opinions and attitudes.

Functional Literacy in Education

Despite the development of visual and auditory teaching aids—such as film, film-strip, slide and overhead projectors, educational television and radio, and tape recorders—the book with the printed word remains the chief medium of communication to pupils or students. Every secondary school teacher, for example, knows that a boy or a girl who has inadequate reading ability is doomed to failure in most of the subjects he or she is expected to learn at that level. Progress in a pupil's education grinds to a halt without good reading ability. All professional teachers will agree with Sir Cyril Burt's conclusion that, "Reading is by far the most important subject the young child learns at school."[11]

But in the last quarter of a century, although various improvements in the teaching of reading have tended to ease the problem of learning to read in recent years, they do not appear to have kept pace with demands made by other expansions in education.

For instance, the official *Education Pamphlet No. 50, Progress in Reading,*[12] describes the results of the national surveys of reading ability in England and Wales that have been conducted every four years since 1948. These show steadily rising standards from survey to survey. But this progress is deceptive in one important respect when compared to the standards of 1938. *Education Pamphlet No. 18, Reading Ability,*[13] which reported the 1948 survey, suggested that the average reading age of the 11-year-olds was probably twelve months behind that of the same age group in 1938. The 15-year-olds were twenty-one months retarded. This was because the children in the 1948 survey had either been about to learn the basic subskills of reading when the Second World War began or they had spent the whole of their infant and the first part of their junior school careers during the war with all its disruptions of schooling. Therefore, if one accepts the official judgment of the first Ministry of Education survey in 1948, then one must conclude that today's English 11-year-olds and 15-year-olds are probably only about five months and one month (respectively) superior in reading age to their counterparts in 1938. It would be fair to conclude that standards of literacy have improved only slightly, if at all, in the past thirty years in England and Wales.

In contrast, the need for higher standards of literacy for educational purposes has increased tremendously. Secondary education has been improved and expanded in many ways. The legal school-leaving age has been raised and many more children are staying on voluntarily for several years longer at school. Postsecondary education has also expanded enormously. The older universities have expanded their numbers of students and several new universities have been created. Higher education for teachers and technical education have both seen very great expansion as well.

A few perceptive educators foresaw the need to raise literacy standards as a result of this expansion. When he was United States Commissioner of Education in President John F. Kennedy's administration, Francis Keppel, formerly Dean of Harvard's Graduate School of Education declared that

> The better teaching of reading is the foundation of higher standards in our schools and colleges, and other efforts will fail unless this first step is taken.

More recently, Husén, in "Lifelong learning in the 'educative society,'" stated that

> Today's school must put far greater emphasis on the skills or "instruments," that is, subjects which are necessary in order to study other subjects successfully.[14]

Literacy skills clearly are *par excellence* the "instruments" of education.

Taking England and Wales as our case history once again, it must be noted that in the 1960s there was a growing disquiet on a general scale about the serious gap between the rapidly expanding demands for higher levels of reading ability and the lack of any planned systematic effort to improve the teaching of literacy on a developmental basis through not only the primary school, but through the secondary school and beyond. The researches of Pringle *et al.*[15] and of Morris[16] confirmed each other in showing the need to continue the teaching of literacy skills beyond the traditional first three years of primary schooling. Morris showed also that teachers of older classes were poorly prepared in their teacher-training courses as far as the teaching of reading is concerned. Her findings were confirmed in other studies by Gardner[17] and by Goodacre.[18]

These events made it increasingly obvious that a very great effort was urgently needed throughout the school and college systems to raise standards of literacy to the level required by the new educational circumstances. But in the chapter on Great Britain it is indicated that progress in solving this problem continues to be slow. However, one sign of current and, hopefully, future improvement is the growing strength of the United Kingdom Reading Association (UKRA), the British offshoot of the International Reading Association.

The historical development of the increasing concern for functional literacy as the instrument of education has been traced in England and Wales because it is well documented for that country. No doubt parallel events have been occurring in other countries during this period.

Functional Literacy and Manpower

The second positive function of literacy that was noted as being of outstanding significance for future progress was its communication purpose in industrial training and work. As in the field of education, in the manpower area there is in the air a sense of impending crisis. In Britain, manpower experts are beginning to express frustration over the disappointing results of industrial retraining projects that are the result of the inadequate literacy skills of many potential trainees.

Retraining projects in the United States ran into this problem earlier. Jenkinson reports that, "A U.S. government program was organized to train relatively unskilled people for the new world of work." By May 1964, of 107,000 who were approved for such training, only 17,000 actually finished the courses. It is important to recognize that, notwithstanding the small subgroup who completed the courses, the original group was actually "the cream of the unskilled crop. They were by and large the better educated of those who were out of work, and they were neither the very young nor the very old in the work force. . . . While many factors accounted for this large attrition, a major one appears to have been their inability to benefit from instruction in new techniques due to their failure to read efficiently." [19]

Curry has demonstrated that the level of unemployment may actually be determined by standards of functional literacy in the United States. He writes that

Automation, brought about by advanced technology, has reduced the demands in our society for unskilled workers. Today, less than five per cent of all jobs are available to the unskilled worker. . . . A very rapid trend in this direction has been observed during the last two decades. . . . The new technology with its rapid and continuous change is demanding constant on-the-job training for most workers to remain abreast of the changes in most occupations. The current prediction that each individual will have to be re-trained three times during his lifetime points to the need for a literate adult citizenry. . . . The development of the basic communicative skills through Adult Basic Education programs will enable many of the illiterate adults to prepare for another occupation or be trained for the changes in the present occupation or vocation brought about by the new technology. [20]

Patchwork courses for illiterates can only be a temporary expedient. The demands for higher standards of functional literacy are ever increasing. Richard B. Adams of the U.S. Office of Education has shown that by the 1980s, if American education does not meet the greater demands for literacy that will come from the need for training skilled manpower, serious social difficulties may follow. His projection indicates that the shrinking proportion of the population who are employable—and therefore productive—may be impossibly overloaded and squeezed by the expanding proportion of the population who are non-producing consumers either because they are still in full-time education or because their level of functioning in literacy—and hence other skills—is inadequate for the needs of the 1980s.

Thus, a general improvement in standards of functional literacy is a vital key to securing the improved standards of living that are the promise of the new technology. Getting this improved level is clearly a priority job for the schools. Adams states, "The schools of tomorrow will HAVE TO do a better job of teaching and training if our population is to be intellectually equipped to shoulder the burden of the 1980's." [21]

These needs of manpower training reinforce the needs of expanding secondary and higher education. A greatly improved level of functional literacy is imperative for success in both endeavors.

This same problem must be faced in other nations, although United States literacy specialists have been quoted for the case history here.

Functional Literacy and Individual Freedom

The development of mass media, particularly television, has brought many educational and other advantages. However, it also offers opportunities for mass persuasion that could whittle away genuine individual freedom of thought. As television develops, and particularly as means are found to extend its range, the temptation to use it for purposes of mass exploitation will grow. Television is particularly liable to present a biased picture of events. The TV viewer cannot slow down the presentation to mull over the argument, nor can he turn back the TV program to check on an inconsistency in the presentation. Too great a reliance on such mass media could reduce the individual's ability to form really independent views and his capacity to assist in making decisions about the developing life of his community.

The available book in the public library and bookstore allows ample time and opportunity to ponder, to question, and to debate internally with the author. Therefore, there is this further need to increase people's ability to use books and to give them greater comfort and confidence in reading activities. Much more could be done to develop children's abilities in *critical reading*. Then they would naturally search out books to get a full picture of a topic or problem, and would be much more likely to develop into adults who are able to choose logically between alternatives on a basis of knowledge and reason.

Malmquist's two facets of the struggle against illiteracy seem to be interwoven. The first, eliminating illiteracy on a world basis, depends on the success of the second, raising the standards of functional literacy, in the leading nations. But a revolution must come in thinking about functional literacy. The norms of the 1930s proved to be inadequate as early as the 1960s. They will certainly not do for the 1970s and are unthinkable for the 1980s. To raise the level of functional literacy is a tremendous challenge to all teachers and all schools throughout the whole range of our education system.

In view of these extremely important functions of literacy it is not surprising that strenuous efforts are being made nationally and internationally to spread literacy and to raise reading abilities to a higher and higher level.

ADULT LITERACY TRAINING. Much special effort is being put into programs to improve *adult* literacy. Harman cites Julius Nyerere as declaring:

> We must educate our adults. Our children will not have an impact on our economic development for five, ten, or even twenty years. The attitude of our adults, on the other hand, will have an impact now.[22]

This need has long been recognized by UNESCO and its consultants. For example, Gray devoted a substantial part of his study to the problems of teaching reading and writing to adults. The extensive work currently going on in this adult literacy field is indicated by several publications: Harman's article in the *Harvard Educational Review*[23] and issue No. 1 of the *International Journal of Adult and Youth Education.*[24]

The World Conference of Ministers of Education on the Eradication of Illiteracy urged the replacement of traditional literacy campaigns by functional literacy programs closely linked to economic and social priorities and to current and future manpower needs. Many subsequent developments have reflected this policy. Moreover, there has been greater care to avoid the problem of back-sliding into exliteracy. For example, specially designed newspapers for newly literate adults have been produced in some countries. Sometimes the problem of losses to exliteracy has led countries to cut down mass campaigns and to devote their resources to key groups in the population (the Nigerian literacy program for tobacco farmers; the Turkish program for army recruits; and the especially interesting Korean strategy, a program for mothers of school children).

The "functional" aspect of functional literacy is being stressed in a variety of ways. For example, in Algeria, Chile, Ecuador, Ethiopia, Guinea, India, Iran, Madagascar, Mali, Syria, Tanzania, Tunisia, Venezuela, Brazil, Jamaica, Nigeria, Upper Volta, and Sudan, intensive programs, relating functional literacy to occupational training, rural and agricultural sciences, industry, and home economics, are being conducted.[25] Another functional aim stressed is the preservation or revival of native languages and related cultures (literacy instruction in Quiché and Cakchiquel in Guatemala).

A very important development was UNESCO's conception of the Experimental World Literacy Program. This has a similar strategy to the Nigerian, Turkish, and Korean selective literacy programs. Staiger describes this strategy as follows:

> Based on a selective and functional approach, this programme has been applied in a small number of countries, and in sectors where motivations in favour of literacy are strongest. Moreover, the projects within this programme are closely tied to the plans for economic and social development being implemented in each country. Functional literacy projects thus oriented are being carried out over a five-year period (1966–70) in Algeria, Ecuador, Ethiopia, Iran, Mali, Sudan, Tanzania, Venezuela and other countries, in close co-operation with the United Nations, the Food and Agriculture Organization and the International Labour Organization.[26]

Harman makes a special point of UNESCO's inclusion of an *evaluative* component in these experimental programs: "This seems to represent a significant advance, for little meaningful evaluation has been undertaken to date."[27]

Although UNESCO's contribution together with separate state-administered programs represents the largest source of efforts to reduce adult illiteracy, many individuals, volunteer organizations, churches, and missions provide important help. One outstanding individual in this field was the late Dr. Frank Laubach.[28] His *Each One Teach One* approach has brought literacy to adults in many countries around the world. Fortunately his work is being continued by the organization he established during his own lifetime.

The United States and the Soviet Union have made great efforts in the adult literacy field. Harman[29] describes this work in the United States, and Serdyu-chenko[30] is an initial source for information on these efforts in the USSR.

Harman emphasizes the need to tailor functional literacy projects for specific situations and target populations. For example, in the United States "the eighth-grade completion equivalency needs to be supplanted by a clearly defined delineation of adult reading requisites and related functional goals. Income tax forms, driving instructions, job application forms, television guides, and news-papers, among others, could be analyzed to derive a precise definition of adult reading level, which could then become the articulated aim of literacy instruc-tion."

Harman also criticizes "the adoption of grade equivalencies in the transference of actual grade school curricular to adult courses," which often causes adult illiterates to be "equated with children and treated as such." He points out that "Psychological and cultural constraints need to be taken into account in plan-ning literacy efforts. In some cases formalized learning situations such as classes may not be practical and less structured teaching might be more acceptable."

Harman proposes that "Optimally, literacy programs should form the first stage of a continuing 'life-long' adult education. Basic literacy training needs to continue into new materials and subjects. This could be facilitated by the creation of permanent adult learning centers with specially designed curricula. These learning centers could also serve as community centers."

All these proposals are put forward by Harman as an attempt to chart "strategies for future adult basic education." In these, evaluation has the vital role of facilitating and developing programs. His "strategies for the future" also call for "close coordination of efforts" and effective "dissemination of informa-tion among programs." He concludes that

> Finally, if meaningful action is to be taken, professional educators must realize that functional illiteracy is far more wide-spread than has been commonly thought.[31]

However, one very important element is omitted in Harman's proposed strategies. Much greater consideration needs to be given to developing *basic theories and research* for understanding how the processes of literacy acquisition take place psychologically. In all this work, one is struck by the primitive level of its development in comparison with other areas of modern technological advance. In many cases rule-of-thumb procedures are applied with little thought for the potential for improving literacy teaching available in scientific psycholinguistic theory and research.

Future Emphasis—On Children or Adults?

J. C. Cairns, head of the Literacy Division of UNESCO, looks forward to the future:

> The Experimental World Literacy Programme will continue, using flexible approaches and a strengthened emphasis on experimentation, and it is hoped that this will pro-duce increasingly fruitful results. It is likely that more and more countries will include

functional literacy under development financing, with literacy projects as components of development projects. At the same time, the generalization of functional literacy and the adaptation of the concept in a variety of ways within traditional literacy programs may be expected to increase. This, representing as it does a shift in large numbers of national programs toward socioeconomic priorities, is a trend of paramount importance. There are also strong indications that individual segments of the economy, such as trade unions, industries, cooperatives, and so on, are now ready to assume responsibility for literacy training in their spheres of authority. In short, the acceptance and generalization of functional literacy has become apparent, and its effects will be felt in the coming decade.[32]

No one would wish to reduce these efforts for adult literacy development. Obviously, Nyerere is right about the urgency for spreading literacy among adults, and this work will continue. *But one doubt must be expressed strongly.*

In all other fields of human endeavor we have come to recognize that "prevention is better than cure." In medicine we move on as quickly as possible from alleviating the symptoms of disease to searching out and eradicating the root causes of the original sources of infection. Similarly in agriculture we seek to prevent soil destruction rather than try to recover its condition after bad farming methods have done their damage.

The same strategy is lacking generally in the literacy field. If we face the issue frankly, we must recognize that, no matter how urgently needed they may be at this present time, adult literacy programs are stop-gap attempts to make good the lack of facilities for literacy acquisition in the prime learning phase of human development—childhood. We should be more concerned about developing systems of *literacy hygiene* to prevent the illiteracy disease from taking hold on future generations. Future progress in literacy hygiene will depend on work with *children* much more than adults, although such programs as the Korean one for mothers are likely to help in breaking the vicious cycle of illiteracy more rapidly.

The future for literacy hygiene would look brighter if we could see some institutionalized efforts being made toward this goal on an international scale, even if they represented only a small fraction of the total energy being devoted to curing illiteracy in adult populations. If UNESCO, for example, had a center for more basic theoretical studies of children's literacy acquisition in the various languages of the world, one would be encouraged to hope for a more rapid reduction in the incidence of illiteracy at a foreseeable date. The present losses from sheer inefficiency of instructional procedures alone must be phenomenal. Such a center need not be large or expensive. If established in a country strategically placed for cross-language studies, scholars from many nations would be readily attracted by the opportunities thus provided for cross-cultural and cross-language research in literacy acquisition. A reasonable plan of coordination would quickly lead to valuable results that could be disseminated rapidly through UNESCO channels for appropriate practical applications.

Unfortunately, we can discern no institutionalized plan for developing theoretical knowledge of literacy acquisition on such an international scale. What would be regarded as fundamental to progress in international projects in commerce and industry—that is, a basic scientific research unit—has been overlooked in this field.

We hope that it will not appear immodest to dedicate this first study in comparative reading to the aim of international cooperation in literacy hygiene. If our investigation makes some small addition to knowledge and understanding of the psycholinguistic processes of children learning to read in the various languages and cultures of the world, we can feel satisfied that we are making a small contribution to the treatment of illiteracy and to its ultimate prevention.

REFERENCES

1. Douglass, Malcolm P., "Beginning reading in Norway," *Reading Teacher,* **23** (October 1969).
2. Whorf, Benjamin Lee, "The relation of habitual thought and behavior to language," in Spier, Leslie (ed.), *Language, Culture and Personality,* Menasha, Wisconsin: The Sapir Memorial Publication Fund, 1941.
3. Feitelson, Dina, "Learning to read," *UNESCO Handbook for Reading,* Paris: UNESCO, 1972.
4. Malmquist, Eve, "Teaching of reading: A world-wide concern," in Figurel, J. Allen (ed.), *Reading and Enquiry,* Newark, Del.: IRA, 1965.
5. Gray, William S., "Current reading problems: A world view," *Education Digest,* **21** (1955), 28–31.
6. Curry, R. L., "Adult literacy—progress and problems," in Schick, G. B., and Merrill, M. M. (eds.), *Junior College and Adult Reading Programs—Expanding Fields,* Milwaukee, Wis.: National Reading Conference, 1967.
7. Jenkinson, Marion D., "Preparing readers for an automated society," in Figurel, J. Allen (ed.), *Vistas in Reading,* Newark, Del.: IRA, 1967.
8. Malmquist, *op. cit.*
9. UNESCO, "World campaign for universal literacy," in Hayes, A. S. (ed.), *Literacy,* Washington, D.C.: Center for Applied Linguistics, 1963.
10. Tax, S., "Self and society," in Douglass, M. P. (ed.), *Claremont Reading Conference Thirty-second Yearbook,* Claremont, Cal.: Claremont University Center, 1968.
11. Burt, Sir Cyril, "Preface," in Downing, John, tω bєє *or not to be,* London: Cassell, 1962.
12. Department of Education and Science, *Progress in Reading 1948 to 1964, Education Pamphlet No. 50,* London: H.M.S.O., 1966.
13. Ministry of Education, *Reading Ability: Some Suggestions for Helping the Backward, Education Pamphlet No. 18,* London: H.M.S.O., 1950.
14. Husén, Torsten, "Lifelong learning in the 'Educative Society'," *International Review of Applied Psychology,* **17** (1968), 87–99.
15. Pringle, M. L. K., *et al., 11,000 Seven-Year-Olds,* London: Longmans, 1966.
16. Morris, Joyce, "How far can reading backwardness be attributed to school conditions," in Downing, John (ed.), *The First International Reading Symposium,* London: Cassell and New York: Day, 1966.
17. Gardner, Keith, "State of reading," *Crisis in the Classroom,* London: Daily Mirror Paperbacks, 1968.

18. Goodacre, Elizabeth J., "A survey of the teaching of reading," *Abstracts of the 1969 Conference of the British Psychological Society*, pp. 73–74.
19. Jenkinson, *op. cit.*
20. Curry, *op. cit.*
21. Adams, Richard B., "Reading research and the Federal Government," in Schick, G. B. and Merrill, M. M. (eds.), *Junior College and Adult Reading Programs— Expanding Fields*, Milwaukee, Wis.: National Reading Conference, 1967.
22. Harman, David, "Literacy: An overview," *Harvard Educational Review*, **40** (May 1970), 231.
23. *Ibid.*, 226–243.
24. *International Journal of Adult and Youth Education*, **14** (1962), No. 1.
25. UNESCO, *Literacy 1967–1969*, Paris: UNESCO, 1969.
26. Staiger, Ralph C., "Developments in reading and literacy education: 1956–1967," Chap. XIII in Gray, William S., *The Teaching of Reading and Writing*, 2nd ed., Paris: UNESCO, 1969, p. 285.
27. Harman, *op. cit.*, p. 233.
28. Laubach, Frank C., and Laubach, Robert, *Toward World Literacy: The Each One Teach One Way*, Syracuse, N.Y.: University of Syracuse Press, 1960.
29. Harman, *op. cit.*, pp. 234–236.
30. Serdyuchenko, G. P., "The eradication of illiteracy and the creation of new written languages in the U.S.S.R.," *International Journal of Adult and Youth Education*, **14** (1962).
31. Harman, *op. cit.*, pp. 236–237.
32. Cairns, J. C., "The 1960's—A decisive decade for literacy," *Convergence*, **3** (1970), 11–18.

Part Two

Part Two

CHAPTER 12

Argentina

BERTA PERELSTEIN DE BRASLAVSKY

TRANSLATED BY CECIL MILES

The Language of the Country

Argentina's Status Vis-à-Vis American Spanish

Argentina, where the possibility of developing a separate language derived from Spanish was at one time conjectured,[1] where the term "national language" is still heard, and where, it is claimed, "Castilian" rather than "Spanish"[2] is spoken, nonetheless shares in the common heritage of American Spanish, although innumerable local provincialisms are to be found scattered throughout the vast national territory.

Amado Alonso,[3] in his well-known writings on the subject, points out that American Spanish originated from the language that developed out of Vulgar Latin in the kingdom of Castile. It spread throughout the Iberian peninsula, and, at the time of the discovery of the New World, already had acquired a national character. Hence, although the Conquistadors spoke a variety of dialects (depending on their points of origin), Castilian was the common denominator that became the main vehicle of the "remodelling" or "leveling" of the language in its American aspects.

This leveling (again according to Amado Alonso) was the result of the readjustment of the vocabulary to new things and new experiences; a different framework of social relationships that, according to Ana María Barrenechea, resulted in a distortion of certain Spanish criteria (for instance, the use of "learned" or "refined" words on the one hand, or of uncouth or rural expressions on the other, in colloquial contexts which differed from those current in the Peninsula);[4] the predominance of certain demographic, social, and dialectal groups from specific regions of the Peninsula, which generated local characteristics; and the indigenous American contribution—which for obvious reasons varied greatly from one part of such an immense continent to another, and as to the extent and importance of which there is still not general agreement because of differences in methodological approach.

With the gradual decline of the mother country in the seventeenth and eighteenth centuries, the Spanish-American communities tended to consolidate and to accentuate the "Americanized" renewal of the language. Nevertheless, Spanish as spoken throughout the Americas has maintained a basic uniformity both within itself and with that of the Peninsula.

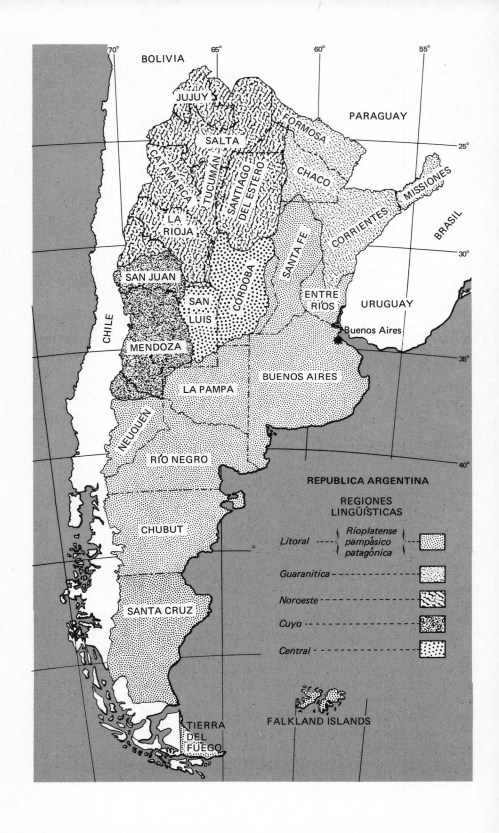

REPUBLICA ARGENTINA

REGIONES
LINGÜÍSTICAS

Litoral -------- { Rioplatense
pampásico
patagónica }

Guaranitica ----------

Noroeste ----------

Cuyo ----------

Central ----------

This uniformity is, according to Ramón Menéndez Pidal,[5] "greater than that enjoyed by the other two main European languages spoken in the American continent" and "greater than that which is found within the Peninsula itself."[6] The same concept is expressed in different words by Angel Rosenblat when he says that "[American Spanish] has, in common with the standard Spanish of Castile, uniformity (but not identity) in its phonemic, morphological, and syntactic systems . . . and even in its basic vocabulary."[7]

The homogeneous nature of the language is, of course, most evident in its cultured and literary forms. There is, on the other hand, considerable diversity in familiar and vulgar speech, which again varies according to the social status of the speaker. As will be stressed later in the section devoted to teaching methods, an understanding of this apparent contradiction is of the utmost importance when considering reading problems at all stages, but more especially at the beginner's level.

Argentine Variations of American Spanish

Berta Elena Vidal de Battini[8] has proposed five linguistic regions in Argentina:

1. The Coastal region.
2. The Guaranitic region.
3. The Northeastern region.
4. The Cuyo region.
5. The Central region.[9]

These geographical variations are considered to have arisen during two important periods: during the Conquest and in the mid-nineteenth century.

As regards the first mentioned period, the early contributions of the indigenous languages cannot be ignored, particularly Guarani and Quechua, which are still in use in some areas as "general languages" of the people alongside the "official language"—Spanish—and also Araucanian. These had considerable influence in regions 2 and 3 and to a smaller degree in 4 and 5. The impact of these languages was, of course, inferior to that of Spanish. Spanish originated in different parts of the Peninsula and arrived by three successive routes of colonization: in the River Plate coastal area, in the Northwestern region from Peru, and in the Cuyo region from Chile.

Because of their comparative remoteness and their relatively late colonization, it was an already Americanized Spanish that penetrated into the last two regions. It gained preponderance over the indigenous languages for a number of historical and cultural reasons: (1) the influence of the Jesuit missions that followed the colonizers; (2) the extermination of the originally sparse indigenous populations; and (3) the interbreeding of the Spaniards with Indian women, especially in the Central, Cuyo, and Northwestern regions.[10]

FIGURE 12-1. Linguistic regions of Argentina. (After Berta Elena Vidal de Battini, *El español en la Argentina,* Buenos Aires: Consejo Nacional de Educación, 1964.)

At the present time, Quechua, Guarani, and Araucanian are spoken as a secondary language only in a few small indigenous pockets. Quechua, for example, is current in the familiar speech of Santiago del Estero, whereas a highly hispanized Guarani survives as the popular language of all social classes in the Northeast. Although the languages themselves are of little importance in the over-all picture, nevertheless individual words derived from them are frequently found in the Northwestern, Northeastern, Andean, and Central zones.

The second point in time mentioned was the product of the wave of immigration that commenced in 1857 as the result of the political slogan "*gobernar es poblar*" (to rule is to populate). New ethnic stock flowed in from all countries in Europe, with a majority of Italians and Spaniards. These newcomers were partly dispersed in all directions, but they also remained in large numbers in the Coastal region (Santa Fe, Entre Ríos, and especially in the federal capital), which thus assumed a highly cosmopolitan structure.

Toward the end of the eighteenth century, considerable French influence was felt both on literature and on politics, but not on the spoken language. Later, in the mid-nineteenth century, notable intellectuals from Germany, France, and Spain sought political exile in Argentina, bringing their own cultural contribution.

At the other end of the scale, the government's policy of encouraging immigration attracted great numbers of working-class men with little formal education, often from dialectal areas of Italy, while from Spain there were Galicians and Basques who had to learn Spanish after their arrival in the country. Mixing with the native lower classes in the cities, the Italians developed a heterogeneous Italo-Argentine language known as *cocoliche,* the existence of which was, however, transitory. It eventually lost much of its Italian content, although there has remained a strong Italian influence on many of the expressions, gestures, and attitudes found in Buenos Aires.[11]

Independently of the preceding influences, a number of rural idioms have arisen in the spoken language of the interior, and these attain a certain dignity of expression in gaucho literature and folklore. The list would be incomplete without mention of the slang terms known as *lunfardo,*[12,13] which were temporarily in vogue during the first decades of the century (especially in view of the popularity of the lyrics of the tango, theatrical comedies, and humor in the press) but which are no longer of any importance.[14]

In the peripheral areas, there is a reciprocal exchange of influence with neighboring countries, and this has been accentuated by the recent immigration of Paraguayan, Chilean, and Bolivian nationals. In frontier zones there are sometimes quite odd idiomatic complexities.[15]

As a result, Spanish as spoken in Argentina is characterized by a number of peculiarities of intonation, syntax, vocabulary, and especially of pronunciation.

Intonation differs somewhat in each of the linguistic regions, in response to the influence of the aboriginal languages, and vocabularies have developed that include numerous Argentinisms.[16] As regards sentence structure, there occur in the Guaranitic area "defective sentence structures, with unconventional use of prepositions,"[17] and in the Northwest, "word order foreign to Spanish syntax is frequent,"[18] probably reflecting the structure of the indigenous languages.

Leaving on one side those morphological and syntactical variations that affect only certain small areas, there is one generalized Argentine usage that deserves special mention. This is the use of the informal second person singular pronoun *vos,* no longer officially a part of the Spanish language, but nevertheless in general use, even among the educated classes, in parts of Central America and to some extent in Uruguay and Paraguay. This phenomenon (which in Spanish goes by the name of *voseo*) is particularly important in any study of Argentine language problems. It has penetrated all the geographical areas and social classes, and has considerable morphosyntactic discrepancies, as contrasted to the norms of the Spanish peninsula (which are, however, recognized as the correct form in the written language). As an additional complication, the use of the pronoun *vos,* while varying somewhat from one area to another, introduces considerable confusion both as regards the pronoun and the verb conjugation; for instance, as a subject, *vos* is always used (*vos lo sabés*), whereas as an unstressed object pronoun it becomes *te* (*a vos te engañaron*). After prepositions there is indecision between *vos* and *te,* although there seems to be some preference for the first (*me hablaron de vos* or *me hablaron de ti; quiere salir con vos* or *quiere salir contigo*). The possessive adjective, however, is always *tuyo.*

As regards the verb forms themselves, those corresponding to *vos* predominate; although etymologically it corresponds to the second person plural (*vos contás, vos sos,* and so on, sometimes with regional variations *vos querés* alternating with *vos querís*), it also retains certain inflexions corresponding to the second person singular (*vos dirás que no es verdad*), and there may be a choice between the two forms (*no quiero que vos lo cuentes* or *no quiero que vos lo contés*).

Hence, the formal-informal relationship is established by means of *usted* and *vos,* respectively; the second person plural *vosotros* (as in the rest of Spanish America) has disappeared, and only *ustedes* remains for both familiar and formal usage.

The interjection *che,* considered by foreigners as a typically Argentine expression, is less extensively used, both geographically and culturally, than *tú,* and it has no morphosyntactic repercussions on the grammatical system.

Changes in the Phonology

In view of their relevance to comparative reading, a few of the numerous mutations that have arisen in the phonic system will be mentioned here, although space will not allow more than a brief and fragmentary summary. It should be noted that most (but not all) of these deviations from the norm are identical or similar to situations found in rural or urban areas of Spain, over wide regions of South and Central America. The complex historical aspects of these changes are beyond the scope of the present work.

Some Vowel Mutations

In general, the vowels are pronounced throughout Argentina with the precision and conciseness that characterize the Spanish language. Vidal de Battini has, however, in her linguistic maps, traced a large number of obvious corruptions in popular, and particularly rural, speech. Although it is possible to cite only a fraction of these here, the following examples will suffice to show how these tendencies can complicate the reading problem.

In the Northwest, in words where the written letters *o* and *e* occur as final, unstressed vowels, these become more closed and approximate *u* and *i*, respectively (*pocu* for *poco, muchu* for *mucho, frenti* for *frente, nochi* for *noche, esti* for *este*). This tendency is associated with Spanish-American areas that have come under the influence of Quechua.

An occurrence that is widely current in both Spain and America is the transformation of two vowels, normally in hiatus, into a diphthong (*pue-ta* for *po-e-ta, pión* for *pe-on*) that actually changes the number of syllables; this may even be accompanied by a change of stress (*páis* for *país, máistro* for *maéstro*). In the eighteenth and nineteenth centuries this phenomenon was accepted usage among educated people, but is today limited to rural areas, although on a wide scale.

The tendency toward diphthongization may result in the fusion of such vowels even between words—for instance, *lu-han vistu andar y li-han dicho qui-andi-alerta* for *lo han visto andar y le han dicho que ande alerta*. It may even result in extreme apocopation, as in *quiesde* for *que es de,* or *quiesti* for either *¿qué es de este?* or *¿quién es este?*

This tendency is somewhat less evident among the popular classes in urban areas, where it only affects the quality of the vowels but never the position of stress. For example, one may hear *tia-tro* for *te-a-tro,* but never *páis* for *pa-ís, máiz* for *ma-íz,* etc. A notable exception to this tendency is found in the Northeastern area where, perhaps due to the influence of Guarani, contiguous vowels retain their identity, sometimes even creating a hiatus where none would normally exist (*mi/hijo, de/oro,* and so on).

Modification of Consonants

Only those phenomena that affect the system significantly, will be mentioned here.

The most important of these are the *seseo* and the *yeísmo*. The well-known *seseo* consists essentially of equalizing the phonemes /s/ and /θ/ as a voiceless sibilant. Although it is universal, almost without exception, in Hispanic America, Vidal de Battini has observed the sporadic use of the opposite, the Spanish *ceceo* (equalization of the phonemes /s/ and /θ/ as /θ/), especially in Entre Ríos.[19]

In *yeísmo,* the typically Spanish distinction between *ll* (/ʎ/) and y (/j/) is found only in the Guaranitic region, in the Andean areas of San Juan and La Rioja, in the northern part of Jujuy, and in the frontier regions adjoining Bolivia. Over the greater part of Argentina these two phonemes become simply /j/ (*cabayo* for *caballo, caye* for *calle*).

The actual pronunciation of this phoneme differs considerably from one region to another, there being three main variations. The first is a fricative, palatal, voiced /j/, which is the most common throughout Spanish America and in parts of Spain. In Argentina, it is found in parts of the Andean and Central regions (Neuquén, Mendoza, San Juan, Catamarca, Jujuy, San Luis, Córdoba). The second is a prepalatal voiced fricative /ʒ/ similar to the French *j* and the Italian *g,* which has acquired the name of "*y rehilada*" (the "burred *y*"). It is found in the city and province of Buenos Aires, in Entre Ríos, Santa Fe, southwestern Córdoba, La Pampa, northern Patagonia, a large part of Tucumán, Salta, and Jujuy. It also occurs in parts of Uruguay and in a few other areas of Spanish America and Spain.

The third pronunciation is a voiceless variant of the foregoing, similar to the French *ch* or the English *sh*. Its frequency (in areas where burring of the *y* is common) varies from place to place.

The Spanish *r*—that is, the initial *r* and the intervocalic *rr*—retains its conventional multiple vibrant sound in Buenos Aires and its zone of influence, but in most other parts of the country it becomes a sibilant fricative, sometimes approaching the *y rehilada* already mentioned.[20] In the rural speech of the Coastal zone and all along the Andes, the *tr* cluster is found as an alveolar fricative, sometimes almost a sibilant.

Another important phenomenon concerning the correlation between the spoken and the written language is the pronunciation of *s* when it is final in a syllable or word. In Argentina, three regional modes are found. There is a retention of the traditional phoneme /s/ in restricted areas such as Santiago del Estero—which also has a very tense and sibilant intervocalic *s* typical of the area, possibly due to the influence of Quechua. An assimilation of a following consonant accompanied by an aspiration of variable intensity occurs over the greater part of the national territory, but a significant difference is observed between the interior and the zone of influence of the capital city, where the final *s* of a word is not aspirated when the following word commences with a vowel. The pronunciation of the rural population is characterized by this aspiration— which is almost identical with the frication of *j* (/h/) (*vamoh a ver*)—whereas the *porteños* or inhabitants of Buenos Aires of the upper and middle classes retain the traditional /s/ (*vamos a ver*). There is also a total loss of the *s* sound at the end of words, which occurs in the lower classes of Buenos Aires and of the Guaranitic region (*vamo a ver*).

In popular and rustic speech, consonant groups are often simplified (*inegable* for *innegable, oservàr* for *observar, dotor* for *doctor*) or even corrupted (*refalar* for *resbalar, dijusto* for *disgusto,* and so on). As in most Spanish speaking countries, the final *d* is mostly lost, as in *salú, felicidá, enfermedá, usté;* and the intervocalic *d* of the past participle (*ado, ido*) is, in rural speech, often weakened, even to the point of disappearance, except in a few regions. The /d/ sound is, however, retained in the speech of city dwellers.

The Writing System

The written language in Spanish is based on twenty-nine letters, or graphemes. It is generally believed that Spanish possesses one of the highest correlations between the spoken sound and the written symbol.[21] While spelling is, in effect, considerably more phonemic than in many other languages (French, for instance and, in particular, English), the inconsistency between the number of written elements (twenty-nine letters) and spoken units (twenty-four phonemes) immediately shows that there cannot be a precise correspondence between phonemes and graphemes.

In a recent study, María Carbonell de Grompone[22] has shown that there is a one-to-one relationship in only nine cases: *a, d, e, f, l, o, p, t,* and *u.* In all other cases a phoneme is represented by more than one grapheme, or vice versa. These discrepancies, as they exist in Spanish spoken by educated people in Argentina, may be partially illustrated by Table 12-1.

TABLE 12-1. Table of Correspondences

Phonemes	Graphemes
/b/	b, v (abajo, avena)
/k/	c, qu, k (casa, queso, kilo)
/č/	ch (choza, cachete)
/g/	g, gu (pagar, pagué)
/i/	i, y (piso, peine, rey)
/h/	j, g (paja, ajeno, general)
/r/	r, rr (rosa, subrayar, arrancar)
/s/	s, c, z, x (seco, cepa, zapato, extraño)
/u/	u, ü (gusano, agua, agüita)
/k/ + /s/	x, cc (examen, lección)
/y/ (In regions that do not make a contrast between the phonemes /ʎ/ and /j/)	y, ll (ayer, callar, yo)
No corresponding phoneme	h (había, deshacer)

The grapheme *h,* although it normally has no corresponding sound, acquires a modifying function when associated with *c* to form *ch,* which is considered as a separate letter of the Spanish alphabet. The letter *u* is also silent after *q,* the combined form being pronounced /k/. Similarly, the *u* has no sound of its own when it is associated with the letter *g* before *e* or *i,* in which case its function is to keep the *g* hard. Without the *u* it would be pronounced the same as *j* (/h/). When it is intended that the *u* and the following *e* or *i* should both retain their intrinsic sounds, this is achieved by means of the dieresis.

The grapheme *x,* when it occurs before another consonant, is usually pronounced in Argentina, as in most of the Spanish speaking world, as /s/, although the influence of orthography may sometimes produce a hypercorrect pronunciation (*extraño* as /ekstraɲo/ rather than /estraɲo/).

In Table 12-1, on the advice of Ana María Barrenechea, we have only included phonemes—that is to say, sounds that have a distinctive character and that may involve a change of meaning. We have not, therefore, included the additional problems presented by the allophones—that is, pronunciations in free variation—

or neutralizations or oppositions, which are obviously not generally covered by writing systems and can never be identical with a particular phonetic alphabet. Spanish orthography includes, exceptionally and unsystematically, nasal sounds in implosive positions, which neutralize their oppositive function and take the articulation of the following consonant. The only case in which this becomes obvious is in the rule requiring *m* to be written before *b* and *p* (although *ñ* is not required before *ll*). Neither has any attempt been made to introduce such graphematical niceties (to cite only one example) as the problems presented by the previously mentioned pronunciations of *s* at the end of a syllable. This would introduce an infinity of permutations that do not lend themselves to analysis.

Other Incompatibilities Between the Written and Spoken Systems

In order to complete the list of difficulties encountered in any attempt to correlate the written and spoken languages, it should be kept in mind that, although in the latter case articulatory analysis can lead to identification of the syllable, visual analysis of the written language only allows us to distinguish words.

Spoken sentences split up naturally into three kinds of sound groups, differentiated on the basis of sound, rhythm, or stress, respectively. They are also subject to subdivision into smaller impulses known as syllables, which are the minimum effective units of speech. Although the unit known as the *word* may appear to be inseparable from the rhythmic spoken continuum that constitutes the sentence, the individual word can, in fact, be separately vocalized—if its meaning is known. On the other hand, rules of syllabication have been devised in which syllables are related to pronunciation. For example, the vowels in true diphthongs and triphthongs (*ue, ie, ai, uai*) are inseparable, but two "strong" vowels must be separated (*a-e, e-o,* and so on). Combinations of the "liquid" consonants *l* and *r* are considered as a single consonant (*bl, cr*). When a consonant occurs between two vowels, it is combined with the second (*a-ve, o-tro, ca-be-za*), although identifiable prefixes may optionally retain their identity (*nos-o-tros* or *no-so-tros, des-am-pa-ro* or *de-sam-pa-ro*). Two consonants—when one is not liquid—must be separated (*dig-no, in-noble*); when a prefix is followed by *s* and another consonant, the *s* must remain with the prefix (*obs-ta-cu-lo, cons-tan-te*), and so on.[23] Even though these rules are clearly part and parcel of the Spanish language, attempts to put them into practice as part of reading education are likely to run into a good deal of interference owing to the various mutations that Spanish has undergone in Argentina as a spoken language. It is clear that the impact of the latter on the methodology of reading, particularly in the case of beginners, is not insignificant.

Political, Historical, Sociological, and Economic Factors

History

The fathers of the revolution for national independence, which began in May 1810, attributed a major part of the "brutalities" of Spanish colonization to the lack of primary education.[24] The first domestic governments, pursuing a policy of cultural and linguistic, as well as political, autonomy, had as one of their aims the teaching of the three Rs, "so that we may cease to be a colony and become a nation."[25] They established projects for the creation of "national schools" (*escuelas de la patria*) to replace the "royal schools" (*escuelas del rey*), but the wars of independence and the subsequent period of political and cultural instability prevented these "ideas (or ideals) of May" from becoming a reality.

After the long, unenlightened period of the tyrant Rosas, who was overthrown in 1853, these ideals were revived and reincarnated in the person of Domingo F. Sarmiento, a vigorous thinker and illustrious writer, who came to be known as the "*maestro de América*" and "*maestro universal de la educación popular.*"[26] He revalidated the currents of self-determination in learning inherited from the generation of 1810 and recast them according to the philosophical tendencies of his time with the changing trends in historicity and romanticism.

Sarmiento was, then, a precursor of "education for development"; he pioneered the evaluation of extrinsic factors, particularly those of a socioeconomic nature, on systematic education. He formulated the hypothesis that "the power, wealth and inner forces of a nation depend on the industrial, moral, and intellectual capacity of its individual citizens, and public education should have as its sole object the maximization of these productive forces";[27] and that "in order to handle the pickaxe and the plough one must first learn to read." Conversely, he argued that "the idiosyncrasies of the underlying organization of our society may shed some light on the state and extent of primary education."[28]

Sarmiento's thoughts were the inspiration behind the law of public education passed in 1884. It was based on a single, free, obligatory, and nonsectarian system, subordinated to the ideal of a democratic education and oriented toward the economic and political aims pursued by his generation. It remained unfulfilled. Its initial success and subsequent inefficacy placed on trial Sarmiento's apparently contradictory teachings on the reciprocal relationship between educational, cultural, and socioeconomic factors.

The censuses of 1869, 1895, 1945, 1947, and 1965 show that school registration rose progressively after the passing of the said law from 20 to 31, 48, 73 and 90.3 per cent, respectively.[29]

Socioeconomic Factors

Figures reflecting the present level of efficiency of the system are not so encouraging, and this can only be explained by the predominance of certain socioeconomic factors in the country in our times.

Argentina can be classified as a developing country. Large areas have been transformed in fairly recent times from a feudal or semifeudal condition into an agroindustrial economy. The country is, however, far from being self-sufficient, because the development of national wealth, and especially of industrial power potential, depends largely on foreign capital.

For reasons inherent in their historical development, some of the twenty-two

Provinces are relatively prosperous (the Pampas, the Central and Coastal regions and part of the Cuyo region), while others remain frankly underdeveloped (provinces of the Northeast, Northwest, and to a lesser extent Patagonia).[30]

The national territory covers an area of 2,776,655 square kilometres and, in 1961, had a population of just over twenty million, which may be assumed to have increased to about twenty-four million. Seventy-eight per cent of the inhabitants are concentrated in the capital city and Coastal region (the federal capital had, in 1960, 14,871 inhabitants per square kilometre and was one of the most densely populated areas of the world. In the province of Tucumán there were 34.1 inhabitants and in the province of Buenos Aires 22 inhabitants per square kilometre).

The provinces of Entre Ríos and Córdoba are of medium density with 10.5 inhabitants per square kilometre; at the other end of the scale are Río Negro with 0.9, Chubut with 0.6, and Santa Cruz with 0.2 persons per square kilometre.

The percentage of potential students registered at the various academic levels are as follows: preprimary 10.4 per cent, primary 90.3 per cent, secondary 26.8 per cent and, college and university 6.7 per cent,[31] showing a progressive falling off with each obstacle within the various cycles.[32] According to official reports, the factors that encourage this erosion at the primary level "are those resulting from: family income level; area of residence—rural, suburban, or urban, with corresponding employment patterns; and demographic factors such as population density, ease of communication, etc."[33] Entry at an early age into the working force in the most backward rural areas and migrations in search of temporary employment, which involve about 25 per cent of the population of the country, account to a great extent for children leaving school prematurely.

Only 48.9 per cent of children registering in grade I manage to complete the seven grades of primary school. The 51.1 per cent who leave before that is an average that breaks down as follows: Pampas region 43.76 per cent; Buenos Aires 49.57 per cent; Cuyo region 55.45 per cent; Patagonia 60.02 per cent; Northwest 72.19 per cent, and Northeast 72.24 per cent.[34] On closer analysis, it is clear that these figures are lower in the more prosperous areas and vice versa, and that there is a precise correlation between literacy[35] and schooling,[36] in inverse proportion to the agricultural population.[37]

A number of conclusions emerge from the statistics, but they will be limited to the following brief summary: (1) About 70 per cent of the children registering in grade I survive to grade III in Buenos Aires and in the Cuyo region and in the Pampas 70 per cent remain until grade IV. In the other three regions the same 70 per cent only complete grade II.[38] (2) Of the total failures, the number of those who repeat (58.83 per cent) is greater than that for dropouts (41.17 per cent), these percentages being heavily influenced by the situation in Buenos Aires (69.81 per cent dropouts, 30.19 per cent repeaters). The percentages of dropouts and repeaters, respectively, in the less-favored regions being Pampa 38.63/61.37; Cuyo 42.92/57.08; Patagonia 35.65/64.35; Northwest 39.92/60.08; and Northeast 39.15/60.85.[39] (3) The percentage of repeaters is extremely high in grade I of primary school: 25 per cent of the total registration in the country, with a range of from 10 per cent in Buenos Aires to almost 40 per cent in Santiago del Estero (the "poor" province of the north).

Just as Sir Cyril Burt demonstrated a direct relationship between retarded learning and poverty in England with maps, similar maps could be drawn for Argentina to show the correlation between schooling, illiteracy, dropouts, and repeaters and economic underdevelopment.

One phenomenon involving the repeaters of grade I, where the main criterion for promotion is success in learning to read, is of special interest. It is known that not the least important contributory cause of school failure is the state of health of the child. In the underprivileged areas mentioned, a number of related problems can be identified: severe sporadic malnutrition (notwithstanding that Argentina statistically has one of the highest nutritional levels in the world), and an unsatisfactory public health situation—121 per thousand infant mortality in Jujuy (Northwest) and insufficiency or absence of doctors and hospital beds in extensive areas of the Northwest, Northeast, and South.[40] Moreover, an environment lacking in cultural opportunities deprives the child of the perceptive, conceptual, and linguistic motivations needed to learn abstract ideas, such as those involved in reading.

If to these are added the regional idiomatic situations involving disparities not only between each other but also between them and the "correct" language taught in schools and used in the textbooks, the reasons for the large proportion of repeaters in grade I and their distribution on the map can be better appreciated.

Another important point is that the repetition of the grades itself encourages a general deterioration of the school; age differences of as much as eight years may be found within the same grade—that is to say a range of perhaps six to fourteen years. The resulting promiscuity must seriously affect social conduct, motivation, and the learning process in general.[41]

To these circumstances must be added the unfavorable educational factors arising partly from insufficient funds and partly from pedagogical stagnation. Seventy per cent of school buildings are at present dilapidated; teachers are in receipt of extremely low salaries (little more than forty dollars a month, or even less in some provinces); institutional conditions are extremely backward as regards personal relationships, disciplinary procedures, and promotion policy; and the supply of teaching material is extremely precarious.

Political Factors

A decline in the school system commenced in 1930 and coincided with a drop in the budget from 24 to 9 per cent by 1959. This situation has given rise to a polarization of political opinions, mostly revolving around Law 1420 on public education, which enjoys general support. One group, including most educators and members of the general public, demands the reconstruction of the public school system on the basis of the democratic principles previously set forth. The other, following the precedent of those who opposed the passing of the law in 1884, consider the law to be a "myth" and are proposing reforms. Since

1967, projects have been put forward in the Ministry of Education that would replace the State's educational responsibilities with a system of monetary grants and establish privileges for private education. These projects were withdrawn because of unfavorable public opinion, but the debate continues, and there is considerable anxiety among educators since the repeal of the Teachers' Law (*Estatuto del Docente*). It had established by means of exemplary (although imperfect) rules such matters as remuneration, tenure, promotions, and pensions. It is easy to see what consequences this unfavorable climate must have on public education.

Schools in Argentina

At the primary level—the function of which is to convey the basic elements of learning, including reading and writing—there exists a system of favorable laws that does not yet apply at other levels. In accordance with the national constitution, Public Education Law No. 1420, which has been in effect since 1884, was later complemented by others. They established (1) subventions to provinces on a sliding scale according to whether they are rich, intermediate, or poor; (2) direct intervention for the establishment of schools in provinces requesting them, with priority for areas of the greatest illiteracy; (3) provision of public medical attention to children of school age; and (4) protection of minors. Moreover, each province has its own constitution and each of these contains articles that have sanctioned the passing of laws that are, in general, more progressive than the federal legislation. All without exception establish free and compulsory education, which in a majority of cases must be secular, and the creation of decentralized, collegiate school boards, sometimes elected by the teachers, parents, and residents. In most provinces, between 20 and 30 per cent of the budget must be set aside for education. As a rule, however, these laws have not been applied, and in any case they are at present officially suspended.

The administration of schools is as complex as the legislation. Besides schools administered by the National Education Council and by the general provincial councils, there exist others managed directly by the Ministry of Education. Private education has expanded rapidly since 1958, with emphasis on the pre-primary and secondary levels. State supervision, as established by law, also has given way as regards this private education to a system of self-determination.

Except in one province, primary education covers a period of seven years, at one grade per year, and promotion from one grade to another depends on a monthly evaluation. A certificate from primary school enables the student to proceed to secondary school. The educational reforms mentioned here, which have been partially put into practice in some regions, propose structural changes that may shorten the period of primary school.

Dispositions specifically covering reading instruction are contained in the "Official Plans and Programs of the Nation and of the Provinces" (see p. 278). There is, however, no compulsion to use these methods, and teachers can elect to use their own.

Age of Commencing Learning to Read

Reading instruction commences in grade I of primary school. Six is the legal age of admission, but there is automatic acceptance at 5 years 8 months, or even earlier under certain conditions.

Generally, nursery schools exist only in factories employing women. Such schools comply with the maternity law that imposes this obligation, but there are also a few private nursery schools.

The educational system provides for kindergarten schools, but these are not compulsory. Registration amounts to about 210,000 for the whole republic, whereas at primary school level there were about three million registrations in 1969.[42] The average annual increase at this level is the highest in the system, but there is a perceptible tendency in favor of urban areas, where families with medium and higher incomes are mostly involved. In this regard, it is interesting to compare the ratio of registration in preprimary and primary schools in the federal capital and in the "rich" province of Buenos Aires (1:5.8 and 1:15.7, respectively) with that occurring in the "poor" provinces of Catamarca and Chaco (1:26.2 and 1:62.7).

Pupils are received in preprimary two years earlier than in primary schools, but they are seldom organized into graduated classes. Staff is not uniformly trained and prereading training programs are not always used.

The degree of cooperation from parents varies with their social and cultural background. The high proportion of registration in grade I, which is near the optimum, indicates almost total unanimity in respect to the parents' positive regard for education, but in the more unfavorable environments the parents soon renounce these good intentions, perhaps because the ability to read is not considered essential for work in the more backward environments. Because they are themselves usually dropouts, they are unable to give their offspring necessary prereading experiences.

The "ABC Test" of Lourenço Filho was translated and put into practice a quarter of a century ago. His theory that the ability to learn to read depends on a certain degree of maturity is shared in Argentina. Filho's view is that, as well as a minimum intelligence level, there must also be a prerequisite level of language skill and a minimum level of maturity in visual and auditory motor coordination for readiness to read. The ideas of Monroe enjoy a somewhat smaller degree of popularity, but research in the matter of dyslexia has given weight to the conviction that there is a set of conditions that must be present before a child is ready to learn to read.

Teaching Methods

Manner of Selection

In the colonial period, the "alphabetic" or "letter" method was applied in the "king's schools." Immediately prior to and after independence, the "national schools," organized on the "monitor" system, issued primers, "alphabet tables," and spelling books. Around the middle of the century, certain mnemo-techniques were adopted, based on the syllabic spelling texts (*silabarios*) of Naharro and incorporating consonant-vowel sequences, the sounds of which were supposed to make collective learning more interesting.

Toward the end of last century, the phonic teaching method appears to have entered the country from Chile, where in turn it had come from Germany, via the United States.[43]

The "word method" arrived precociously in the River Plate area (Montevideo, Uruguay, and the Coastal zone of Argentina, Buenos Aires, and Paraná), probably thanks to the Spaniard José María Torres and the North American teachers engaged for the first Normal School in Paraná. A few notable statesmen, including Pedro José Varela of Uruguay and Domingo Faustino Sarmiento of Argentina, inquired into this method in Europe, and more especially in the United States.

After a good deal of argument, two schools of thought developed. While agreeing that reading instruction should commence at the word level, they were divided on the question as to whether this should be followed by analysis of the word, one alleging that it should not be done, the other developing techniques for putting it into effect. In Montevideo, in about 1874, Romero prepared plac-ards on which words were illustrated with pictures, together with an explanatory booklet. This was severely criticized by Berra, who advocated the system variously known as generating word, basic word, or analytic-synthetic method.

He began with one word (for example, *mano*), separated it into syllables (*ma-no*), then into letters (*m-a-n-o*), subsequently reconstructed the syllables (*ma-no*), and finally printed the word (*mano*). Having done this, he chose further "generating words" containing other letters of the alphabet. When these had been learned by his process, they were incorporated into phrases and sentences, and so on until the whole alphabet had been mastered. It was argued that by this method, commencing with the meaning, proceeding to the symbol, and then incorporating it into more complex significative patterns, visual perception of the written word and auditory perception of the spoken word would march hand in hand with the writing of the word by both teacher and pupil; oral and manual kinesthesia were also said to be developed.

These two opposing positions were embraced in Buenos Aires by Marcos Sastre and Andrés Ferreyra, respectively. They produced two well-known books, *Anagnosia,* which was to "inspire a fondness for reading without alphabet, without spelling, and without primers or spelling books," and *El nene,* a model for the analytic-synthetic method.[44] Later, *Veo y leo* ("I see and I read"), by Ernestina López de Nelson, was the Spanish version of the "look and say" method.[45]

When the "global," "ideovisual," or "natural" method was at its zenith in Europe in the 1930s, one of the most orthodox variations of its "pure" form was elaborated in Argentina. It is contained in *La enseñanza del lenguaje gráfico* (*The Teaching of the Written Language*) by Dezeo and Muñoz. It involves three stages (1) total perception, (2) discrimination, and (3) the blending of these two.

In this system, the breaking up of the word, and even more the concept of individual letters, is forbidden, on the grounds that one is working with "concepts" and not with "words or parts of words."[46] Therefore, when "mental
reading" is performed using placards containing greetings or instructions, these
are to be recognized by their color, shape, the angles involved in the printing, and
so on. Even though the child may erroneously read *mañana es domingo* (tomorrow
is Sunday) as *mañana es lunes* (tomorrow is Monday), or even as *la muñeca es
linda* (the doll is pretty), the teacher is not supposed to try to correct the child
in advance, by imposition, before discrimination and perception occur spontaneously in the child's mind. In this, the authors base themselves on statements
by Bergson in his book *Matière et Memoire*[47] (*Matter and Memory*) that are
supposed to justify this kind of guessing. They also adopted what they called the
conato-cognoscitivo-afectivo principle (roughly, endeavour-recognition-sensa-
tion), and spoke of mental energy, the wish to learn, impulses, and powers or
faculties, which they claim to have taken from the work of McDougall, Spearman, and other disparate psychologists.

There were a number of other partisans of the global method who based
themselves on a more rational interpretation, generally having recourse to the
principles developed by Decroly. Reading books were edited based on more or
less logical interpretations of his doctrine. A few prominent educators adopted
it with enthusiasm and published their experiences, while innumerable anony-
mous teachers improvised on it in their classrooms. Enthusiasts all, many felt
themselves to be devoted apostles of a technique whose major virtues were the
short period supposedly required for proficiency in reading (three months) and
the efficacy claimed for it in the development of written expression as well as in
the improvement of spelling.

Nevertheless, a great many teachers found some difficulty in the application
of a method that relied so much on spontaneity, that preferred or demanded
silent reading from the beginning, and that prohibited the breakdown of words
or any enquiry. There were no legal dispositions to make it compulsory (except
for a transitory decree passed in about 1948 relating to the national schools).
But, because most supervisors favored it, many teachers made use of it, although
in an attempt to forestall failures they interpolated it with others, especially the
analytic-synthetic system. No arguments were forthcoming to question the
well-established principles of the global method.

However, with the passing of time, a number of facts emerged to indicate,
albeit vaguely and without supporting evidence, that this method was anything
but a success. An increasing number of children showed signs of difficulty in
reading, writing, and spelling, both in primary school and, even worse, in alarm-
ing numbers in secondary school.

In 1962, *La querella de los métodos en la enseñanza de la lectura* (*The Dispute
Over Methods in the Teaching of Reading*)[48] appeared. It was a collection of the
systematic criticisms of the global method that had been raised in the 1950s by
those who had studied the difficulties encountered in learning to read, especially
in France. In 1963, the first Latin American seminar on dyslexia took place in

Ciudad de Rivera, Uruguay, which, without condemning the global method,[49] recommended the analytic-synthetic method as more certain of success for the Spanish and Portuguese speaking countries represented.

The subsequent reactions of the European partisans of the global method, which led to a new evaluation of the original attitudes of Decroly, were not discussed, but, as a result of the deliberations that occurred in our countries, a process of equilibration developed that tended to break down the watertight compartments in which these two approaches had existed. This development was experimentally identified by means of surveys in an investigation directed by María Carbonell de Grompone on the results obtained from the application of analytic-synthetic and the global methods.[50] A study of the textbooks published in Argentina in recent years leads us to similar conclusions. It is difficult to find one that complies with the strict norms of the pure global method; a few remain that follow the analytic-synthetic method, but with enough latitude to avoid its monotony. In many cases the word elements are analyzed in other ways, such as color, which often alters the structure inherent in our written language. One also finds a certain erraticism from which it is apparent that there is a lack of familiarity with the conventional methods—without any psychological or pedagogical justification for this omission.

In short, although the choice of method arose in some instances from sincere convictions regarding the underlying principles involved, in others it reflected a desire to choose the most prestigious methods. In still others, perhaps in a majority of cases, the main factor was expediency or the espousal of a cause for emotional reasons.

As already mentioned, these two options were, for the first time we believe, submitted to scientific analysis in the Uruguayan experiment. The conclusions at the end of the first year were in favor of the group (representing a cross section of social and cultural levels) that had been subjected to all the aspects of the analytic-synthetic method. At the end of the second year, however, the two groups had drawn even. But at this point a disastrous effect became apparent. It was observed that a large proportion of the pupils, who had originally been selected on the basis of their psychological normality, had not learned to read (31 per cent of those taught by the global method and 22 per cent of those receiving instruction under the analytic-synthetic method).

The Linguistic Problem

Neither of these two possible teaching methods brings into play those aspects of the language that motivate reading. The partisans of the global method confront the child with any text, whereas the others select their "generating words" at random, guided in each case only by the criterion of interest. Only the official spelling programs take systematically into account the inherent difficulties of the Spanish language. But their teaching is through different channels.

Nevertheless, it was vaguely perceived that the phonetic idiosyncrasies of the language are an important factor in any method of teaching. Sarmiento recognized the superiority of the phonetic method, on the grounds that Spanish is a typically phonetic language, and he emphasized that, because the words are susceptible to syllabic analysis, words can also be reconstructed from syllables readily. When he recommended Naharro's syllabic spelling texts (*silabarios*) he did so because it was a syllabic method. Victor Mercante, the modern specialist and experimenter in psychopedagogy, when discussing the application of the phonetic method in the second decade of this century, called attention to the fact that its difficulties do not arise from the structure of the spoken language, but in every case "from the character of the written language." [51] Lourenço Filho, a Brazilian educator well known in Argentina, has stated that the word method only complicated the reading problem in his country since "that system, taken from the North Americans, who have to teach reading almost word by word because of English spelling, has resulted in our overlooking one of the great facilities of our language: its almost completely syllabic nature." [52]

This writer, in the work previously mentioned, *La querella de los métodos en la enseñanza de la lectura,* cited the most recent contributions of general psychology, genetic psychology, and experimental research in the field of reading. The process was interpreted in the context of modern associationism as a chain of complex functions that, originating from the spoken language, culminates in the difficult moment of its encounter with the written language. Gray's reasons for emphasizing that the method selected must be dependent on the type of language involved were validated for us by (1) the theories of Ananiev [53] on the radical mental change that occurs when the visual center becomes associated in the language sphere; (2) the importance he attributed to the kinesthetic word center as a link between the spoken and written language; and (3) the observations of S. Borel Maisonny and Delaunay [54] on the structural differences between them.

Consequently, it may be possible to recommend three phases in the teaching of reading to beginners: (1) recognition of words and syllables in the continuum of the spoken language through games of auditory and word-motor differentiation (Ananiev); (2) practice in penmanship without signification, but in well-graded sequences culminating in the basic traits of the roman script; and (3) auditory analysis of the vowels of the word as perceived by the ear in order to teach the written uniformity of each one, which is then successively combined with the consonants to progressively construct the written language and then read it. This process should be graded in relation to the difficulties encountered by the child in coordinating his handwriting. These recommendations have been tested by teachers, with satisfactory results, it is believed, although there has as yet been no controlled evaluation.

More recently, experiments have been carried out in the Department of Educational Psychology in the province of Salta, under the direction of Dr. Oñativia, on a method that, it is claimed, adds "a linguistic basis" to the psychological rationale; [55] analytical techniques are introduced based on the structure of the language as an architectural element in the teaching of reading.

These attempts demonstrate the beginnings of a concern for linguistics in the quest for methodology, although some of the hypotheses still have to be tested in the light of the peculiarities of the Spanish language and its Argentine variations.

It was shown at the beginning of the chapter that the grapheme-phoneme relationship in our language presents greater difficulties than is generally believed, but this is not the only problem raised by the need to establish a rapport between the spoken and written language in the act of reading. Although many authors concur that there is, in Spanish, a considerable measure of identity between the spoken and the written syllable, at the same time the definition of the syllable frontier may sometimes be ambiguous, and this may alter the equivalence sought. Taking, for example, the word *oso,* which is often used as the first generative word, it has been observed that a child may pronounce it *os-o.* In the written system his eyes see *o-so* (the correct written form according to the rules of syllabication). This disparity will not facilitate the act of transference.

It is not only that a major degree of inconsistency is introduced by the widespread deviations of the language affecting major areas of the country (such as the *seseo* and *yeísmo*); the problem is exacerbated by the fact that, alongside a uniform written language (if we except folklore and gaucho literature), we find regional mutations of vowels and consonants of the spoken language, which have been partly exemplified in the first section of this chapter. Distortions in the pronunciation of diphthongs and contiguous vowels, the frequent elision of syllables, and the joining up of curtailed words in rural and popular speech, all contribute to disparities between the spoken and the written language and make correlation of the two extremely difficult.

These observations are noted with a view to encouraging emphasis on remedial Spanish, especially at the preschool level, not merely as a compensatory measure in areas of cultural deprivation, but also to homogenize the language. This proposal is not made in any spirit of purism, but solely to facilitate the child's initiation in reading. Other related problems, which will depend largely on the disparity between the written and spoken language, and which are more acute in lower-class and rural surroundings, should be resolved according to the individual requirements of each area.

Teaching Materials

Those who use the global method in its pure form work with materials produced by the teacher and pupils, at least in the beginning stages. For example, in the method of Dezeo and Muñoz the children draw whatever their spontaneous interest suggests, the teacher writes "what it is," and the children copy this as if it were part of the drawing. On the fifth day placards and friezes of determined sizes are introduced, which are like "flags" or "signals" for mental reading. Newspaper cuttings, songs, and stories are also utilized. After the third month, when the children are able to read and express themselves in writing, the third stage begins. Drawing is prohibited and the child commences to make up a "dictionary" of words as he learns them.

The reading textbook is the most important piece of material. In each school the teachers of each grade, with or without the headmaster's agreement, choose a reader from among those previously approved by a special commission of the National Council, and in some cases by the Provincial Councils. These are printed by commercial publishers, and as the most important of these are in the federal capital, the books written in Buenos Aires are the ones that get to be distributed throughout the country. These books, no matter what system they follow, are generally well illustrated in color, sometimes very artistically. This increases the cost of production, which, unfortunately, makes them inaccessible to the school-age population. However, this difficulty is sometimes resolved with the help of school cooperatives.

Sometimes each book comes complete with its corresponding teaching apparatus. Those that followed the analytic-synthetic method used to come with several series of letters and syllables; today both these and the ones that follow the global method come with cards and are printed in such a way as to allow graded activities such as coloring, completing pictures, tracing, copying, and, later, reading. They sometimes recommend the use of friezes and placards as supplementary material.

In the classroom the teachers also use, on their own initiative, modern audiovisual equipment, such as tape recorders and flannel boards. This type of equipment has been standardized in the "integrated method" used in the Salta experiment in order to organize and develop symbolic diagrams. Luis F. Iglesias has, in his book *La escuela rural unitaria,* developed some ingenious materials for the teaching of reading in rural schools where classes are organized into multiple grades (I to VII).

Reading Instruction Beyond the Beginning Stage

The arrangements for reading instruction contained in the Official Plan for studies and programs in primary education are vague, though they contain a number of suggestions for various levels. Reading is included among the miscellaneous instructions for the teaching of "language." For the first two grades these are reading and writing, simultaneously; integrated reading practice; interpretation of punctuation and intonation signs. For the first grade is added: forming and joining capital and smaller letters; reading and recitation of the alphabet. In the third grade the following is added: intensification of silent reading; in the fourth grade: intensification of interpretative reading; in the fifth: commentated reading; in the sixth: intensification of interpretative reading; and in the seventh: intensification of commentated reading. From the third grade onward, in addition to the reading textbook other texts, magazines, pamphlets, and newspapers are to be added with the recommendation that the habit be acquired of extracting the main ideas from a piece of literature, a fable, or a poem. In the fifth grade, management of a classroom library is included.

These guidelines, with notable exceptions exhibit the following deficiencies: (1) they are limited in their application by factors such as bureaucratic impediment; (2) they show the aftereffects of orthodox application of the global

method—which gave emphasis to casual reading instruction, with the elimination of systematic reading after a short while; (3) they are frustrated by the
deterioration of classroom libraries due to increasingly precarious budgets;
and (4) they show disregard of current topics.

All of these factors have contributed to a decrease in the number of good
readers, which is in contrast with the situation that existed twenty or thirty
years ago when reading was encouraged in primary schools through competitions
and prizes.

Integration of Reading Instruction with Other Aspects of the Child's School and Daily Life

From the first grade onward, an introduction to literature adapted to each
grade is included in the language (Spanish) curriculum. Poetry and prose passages
are designated from which the teacher may select at will for recitation and
comment.

There exists an important and qualified trend toward the promotion of a
"good children's literature," integrated by writers such as Frida Schultz de
Mantovani, Dora Pastoriza de Echebarne, and Yolanda Martinez de Elgorreaga. The school system has not responded to any significant degree to this
process, which has sometimes expressed itself as strongly opposed to some of
the commercial aspects of literature intended for children.

Martha Salotti and Ernesto Camilli developed systematic techniques designed
to stimulate oral and written expression that may effectually contribute to the
development of comprehension. A number of recently published books dedicated to the sciences may also serve the same purpose.

Worthy of special mention is the experiment carried out by teachers in Santa
Fe, under the initiative and encouragement of Olga Cossettini, based on "lively,
original material," rather than on didactic devices, including excursions "to the
post office, the blacksmith's shop, the stores, the market place, the river, the
hospital, etc.," with a view to providing personally relevant motivation for
reading.[56]

Recruitment and Training of Reading Teachers

Teacher training took place, until 1969, in the normal school, which represented five years at the secondary level of the Argentine educational system.
This has recently been eliminated and replaced by a school at the tertiary level
that provides two years of specialized training after *bachillerato* (matriculation
from secondary school), but the creation of this new institution has not yet been
implemented.

For almost two decades, teachers have received no training in reading instruction. This incredible fact is explained by the evolution of philosophical ideas
and their effects on pedagogy in our country. At the end of the last century and
the beginning of this one, under the influence of a relatively original positivism,

educational technology, which included reading methods, had a principal place in teacher training. The antipositivist reaction, which condemned the fallacies of European positivism, gave echo in Argentina to all the irrational trends that arose to oppose it and, in the field of pedagogy, substituted for a concern for method other considerations, such as the philosophy of education. As a result of the exaggeration of this tendency, speculation replaced field work, which had often produced promising results. In the educational literature of Argentina, one reads of "periods of methodism" and "periods of antimethodism."

University Provisions for Specialization in Reading

In no university in Argentina is there a chair or an institute specifically dedicated to reading.

In the educational sciences curricula, which exist in the Faculties of Arts (*Humanidades*) in each of the National Universities, the chairs of Primary Level Didactics cover the methodology of reading instruction, but the psychology and theory of reading receive only incidental and cursory attention. The chairs of Educational Psychology usually omit all reference to the psychological processes that underlie learning to read.

According to the information available to us, the only activity worth mentioning in the field of research is the support given by the Faculty of Philosophy and Literature of the National University of Tucumán to the research on the integrated method that was carried out in the province of Salta. For our part, we plan to implement four projects involving research on reading as it affects mentally retarded children, through three grants from the faculty and a fourth from the National Council of Scientific and Technical Investigations, at the Faculty of Letters and Educational Science of the National University of La Plata.

Treatment of Reading Disability

Concern regarding failure to read began to be felt about twenty years ago as an echo of the European investigations, which were limited to the specific inability known as evolutional dyslexia. A few physicians, specialists in neurology and phoniatrics, studied the problem with special reference to anatomic-pathological or genetic etiology, often including all those cases, perhaps a majority, that originated from mesological or even educational causes. This explains why most of the resources for children who fail to read are found in hospitals and in phoniatric, ear-throat-and-nose, or child psychopathology services and are usually run by phonoaudiological reeducators. They can also be found in clinical psychology services, where they are treated essentially on a psychotherapeutic basis that includes some functional exercises.

It has only incidentally been considered a problem that can be dealt with in schools, and even then it has been limited to the study of the impact of teaching methods on preexisting functional disorders. This has, however, resulted in the training of teachers who specialize in the reeducation of dyslexic pupils—who in turn have recourse to phoniatrists, reeducators of motor functions, and psychotherapeutists, depending on the nature of the syndrome—and who concern themselves with the correction of functional disorders while retraining reading abilities. To this end, services have been established in nonhospital situations, such as in private institutions, which train their own personnel.

We know of no preventive or remedial resources in the official school system to deal with the vast field of reading disability—of which the sociopsychological epidemiology is necessarily far-reaching.

Tests and Methods of Evaluation

The ABC test for reading readiness of Lourenço Filho is widely used. It is also employed to create homogeneous groups at the first-year level, preparatory to the application of various methods. In Argentina, María M. Estruch de Morales, Irma Anello de Mendolía, and María A. Lobo de Geoghegan have also developed a reading readiness test.[57]

There are no tests available to facilitate the evaluation of speed, precision, and comprehension at the different stages of learning to read. One can only cite *Pruebas de lectura silenciosa (Tests of Silent Reading)* by Alfredo Ghioldi and Victor Baleani,[58] which is designed to determine the level of comprehension in the different primary school grades.

Our research in La Plata involves the elaboration of reading tests that bring into play the characteristics of our language.

REFERENCES

1. Vidal de Battini, Berta, *El español en la Argentina,* Buenos Aires: Consejo Nacional de Educación, 1964, p. 22.
2. Amado Alonso shows that the terms "*castellano*" and "*español*" are synonymous. *Castellano, español, idioma nacional,* Buenos Aires: Edit. Losada, 1949.
3. Alonso, Amado, *Estudios lingüísticos: Temas hispanoamericanos,* 34th ed., Madrid: Edit. Gredos, 1967.
4. The well-known specialist in linguistics, Dr. Ana María Barrenechea, was consulted when writing this paragraph on "the language of the country." Dr. Barrenechea also provided the information contained in later sections regarding morphological and syntactic variants and the nature of vowels and consonants.
5. Quoted by Tomás Navarro, in *Compendio de ortología española,* Madrid: Librería y Casa Editora Hernando, 1928.
6. Rosenblat, Angel, *El castellano de España y el castellano de América,* Montevideo: Edit. Alfa, 1968, p. 48.
7. *Ibid.,* p. 49.
8. In Vidal de Battini, *op. cit.,* p. 75. As a result of her extensive and intensive travel and exploration, Vidal de Battini produced her extremely detailed "synthetic maps" showing the main linguistic phenomena. Dr. Ana María Barrenechea affirms that it is the first book written in the Spanish language dedicated to teachers showing the dialectal variations and their cultural impact.

9. These regions are Coastal: city and province of Buenos Aires, Santa Fe, most of La Pampa and Patagonia, southern part of Entre Ríos; Guaranitic: Misiones, Corrientes, northern Entre Ríos, Chaco, and most of Formosa; Northwestern: Jujuy, Salta, Tucumán, Catamarca, La Rioja, Santiago del Estero, contiguous zones in San Luis, San Juan, and Córdoba; Cuyo: Andean areas including Mendoza, southern San Juan, northern Neuquén; Central: a zone of transition between regions 1, 3, and 4, consisting of most of San Luis and Córdoba.

10. Only a very few almost pure Indian communities remain: the *Collas* in La Puna (northwest); the *Tobas* in the Chaco (north); and the Araucanians in the southern Andes and La Pampa (center). Various estimates place their number between 50,000 and 150,000.

11. Vidal de Battini, *op. cit.,* pp. 66–70.

12. Gobello, J., *et al., "El idioma de Buenos Aires y el habla de la ciudad," Boletín de la academia porteña del lunfardo,* Vol. I, Nos. 2 and 3, Buenos Aires: Edit. A. Peña Lillo, 1967–1968.

13. Gobello, José, and Payet, Luciano, *Breve diccionario lunfardo,* Buenos Aires: Edit. A. Peña Lillo, 1959, p. 7.

14. The advice of Dr. Ana María Barrenechea in this section is gratefully acknowledged.

15. Capdevila, Arturo, *Consultorio gramatical de urgencia,* Buenos Aires: Edit. Losada, 1967. See "Brazilianisma," pp. 70–104.

16. Garzón, Tobías, *Diccionario argentino,* Barcelona: Borras y Mestres, 1910; and Segovia, Lisandro, *Diccionario de argentinismos,* Buenos Aires: Coni Hermanos, 1911.

17. Vidal de Battini, *op. cit.,* pp. 77–78.

18. *Ibid.,* p. 79.

19. Vidal de Battini, *op. cit.,* p. 105.

20. The burred pronunciation (*pronunciación rehilada*) of *y* and *rr* gives rise to differences in the regional systems in the phonological values of similar sounds. See Guitarte, Guillermo, *"El ensordecimiento del yeísmo porteño"* ("The Development of the Unvoiced 'Yeísmo' in Buenos Aires"), *Revista de filología española,* XXXIX, 1955, pp. 261–283; also Gandolfo, Adriana, "The Spanish *ll, y* and *rr* in Buenos Aires and Corrientes," *Proceedings of the Ninth International Congress of Linguistics,* Cambridge, Mass., 1962, The Hague: Mouton, 1966, pp. 212–215.

21. Gray, William S., *La enseñanza de la lectura y de la escritura,* (*The Teaching of Reading and Writing*), Paris: UNESCO, 1957, p. 64. And Jung, Edmond, "L'orthographe du grec, du latin, de l'italien, de l'espagnol." *Cahiers Pédagogiques,* **44,** 1963, No. 4.

22. Carbonell de Grompone, María A., *"Ortografía y disortografía española," Boletín del Instituto Interamericano del Niño,* **165** (June 1968), 409.

23. Alonso, Amado, and Ureña, Pedro Henriquez, *Gramática Castellana, Primer Curso,* 25th ed., Buenos Aires: Edit. Losada, 1969, p. 213.

24. Belgrano, Manuel, *"Educación," Correo del Comercio,* **3–4** (March 17 and 24, 1810). For some years now numerous authors have condemned these criticisms, arguing that Spain only gave us "what she had."

25. Sarmiento, Domingo Faustino, *Educación popular,* Buenos Aires: Edit. Lautaro, 1948, p. 40.

26. This title was bestowed on him during the World Meeting on Education, Mexico, 1964.

27. Sarmiento, *op. cit.,* p. 26.

28. Sarmiento, Domingo Faustino, "*Educación común. Memoria presentada al Consejo Universitario de Chile sobre estas cuestiones,*" *Obras completas* ("Common education. A memoire presented to the Chilean University Council on these questions," *Complete Works*), Buenos Aires: Edit. Luz del Día, 1952, p. 24.

29. *Analfabetismo en la Argentina* (*Illiteracy in Argentina*), Buenos Aires: *Consejo Federal de Inversiones* (Federal Investment Council), 1963, p. 8.

30. This paragraph refers to the six regions according to the classification of the Federal Investment Board (*Consejo Federal de Inversiones*) based on geographic and economic criteria (per-capita territorial gross product). These regions are The federal capital; The Pampas (provinces of Buenos Aires, Córdoba, Santa Fe, La Pampa); Cuyo (Mendoza, San Juan, San Luis, La Rioja); Northwest (Jujuy, Salta, Tucumán, Santiago del Estero, Catamarca); Northeast (Formosa, Chaco, Misiones, Corrientes, Entre Ríos); Patagonia (Neuquén, Río Negro, Chubut, Santa Cruz, and the "national territory" of Tierra del Fuego). *Educación, recursos humanos y desarrollo social* (*Education, human resources and social development*), Buenos Aires: *Secretaría del Consejo Nacional de Desarrollo,* Series C., No. 73, 1968, Vol. I, p. 316.

31. *Educación, recursos humanos y desarrollo económico-social* (*Education, human resources, and socio-economic development*), Buenos Aires: Secretariat of the National Development Council, Series C., No. 73, 1968, Vol. I, p. 80.

32. *Ibid.*, p. 82.

33. *Ibid.*, p. 224.

34. *Ibid.*, p. 276.

35. Illiteracy, defined as applying to "persons who state that they cannot read or write" represents 12 per cent of the population. A breakdown of this average shows 1.28, 5.99 and 9.48 per cent in the federal capital, the province of Buenos Aires, and province of Santa Fe, respectively, as compared with 26.31, 27.53, and 30.66 per cent in the Chaco, Santiago del Estero, and Corrientes.

36. The national average for school attendance is 85.61 per cent, with extremes of 91.75 per cent in the Pampa and Capital zones, and 72.73 per cent in the Northeast.

37. *Educación, recursos humanos, y desarrollo económico-social, op. cit.*, p. 272.

38. *Ibid.*, pp. 277–278.

39. *Ibid.*, p. 282.

40. Palermo, E. *Tuberculosis, nutrición y condiciones de vida en la Argentina* (*Tuberculosis, nutrition, and living conditions in Argentina*), distribution in Argentina, *Anales Argentinos de Medicina,* 1963.

41. Perelstein de Braslavsky, Berta, *et al., Estudio sobre necesidades de educación especial en Tierra del Fuego* (*A study on the needs of special education in Tierra del Fuego*) by agreement between the National University of La Plata and the government of Tierra del Fuego, unpublished, 1969.

42. *Estadística educativa* (*Statistics of education*), Buenos Aires: Ministry of Culture and Education, 1969.

43. Mercante, Víctor, "*Como se aprende a leer*" ("How one learns to read"), *Archivos de Ciencias de la Educación* (La Plata, 6) (1919), 328.

44. Sastre, Marcos, *Anagnosia*, 3rd ed., Buenos Aires: Gobierno de la Provincia de Buenos Aires, 1852; Ferreyra, Andrés, *El nene,* Buenos Aires: A. Estrada y Cia, undated.

45. López de Nelson, Ernestina, *Veo y leo,* Buenos Aires: Coni Hermanos, undated.

46. Dezeo, Emilia C., and Muñoz, Juan M., *La enseñanza del lenguaje gráfico* (*The Teaching of the Written Language*), Buenos Aires: Edit. Ferrari Hermanos, 1936, p. 279.
47. Bergson, Henri, *Matière et Memoire,* 54th ed., Paris: Presses Universitaires de France, 1953, p. 113.
48. Perelstein de Braslavsky, Berta, *La querella de los métodos en la enseñanza de la lectura* (*The Dispute Over Methods in the Teaching of Reading*), Buenos Aires: Editorial Kapelusz, 1962.
49. Perelstein de Braslavsky, Berta, "*Métodos de enseñanza de lectura y dislexias*" ("Methods in the teaching of reading and dyslexias"), *Fonoaudiolófica,* **3** (1961), publication of the ASALFA.
50. Carbonell de Grompone, María A., *et al., Estudio comparativo de los métodos analíticosintético y global en el aprendizaje de la lectura* (*Comparative study of the analytic-synthetic and global methods in the teaching of reading*), published by the *Sociedad de Dislexia del Uruguay* (Uruguayan Association for Dyslexia), 1967.
51. Mercante, *op. cit.,* p. 326.
52. Filho, Lourenço, *ABC Tests,* 6th ed., Buenos Aires: Editorial Kapelusz, 1962, p. 30.
53. In 1959, we visited the author at the Institute of Pedagogical Investigations in Leningrad, where he explained certain points.
54. Perelstein de Braslavsky, *La querella de los métodos en la enseñanza de la lectura, op. cit.,* Part 4.
55. Oñativia, Oscar V., *Método integral para la enseñanza de la lectoescritura inicial* (*Integrated Method for the Teaching of Reading and Writing to Beginners*), Buenos Aires: Editorial Humanitas, 1967.
56. Cossettini, Olga, *El lenguaje y la escritura en primer grado* (*Language and Writing in the First Grade*), Buenos Aires: Editorial Universitaria de Buenos Aires, 1961.
57. Estruch de Morales, María M. R., Anello de Mendolía, Irma, and Lobo de Geoghegan, María A., *¿Cuándo empezar a enseñar?* (*When To Begin Teaching?*), Buenos Aires: published by authors, 1958.
58. Ghioldi, Alfredo, and Baleani, Víctor, *Pruebas de lectura silenciosa* (*Silent Reading Tests*), Buenos Aires: Editorial Kapelusz, 1962.

CHAPTER 13

Denmark

MOGENS JANSEN

The Languages of Denmark

The national language of Denmark is Danish, which belongs in the same group as the Norwegian, Swedish, Faroese, and Icelandic languages. In the Faroe Islands (a part of the Kingdom of Denmark, with an independent status), with a population of 38,000, the children are taught Danish, and their instruction also is partly in Danish. In Greenland, which is a part of Denmark, the Greenlandic language is spoken by some 35,000 people including about 8,000 children of educational age. These children are taught in both Greenlandic and Danish. In Iceland, Danish is the primary object of second language teaching, and in nearly all fields of further education the textbooks used are in Danish. Danish weeklies are very popular in Iceland.

Outside Denmark, Danish enjoys some further currency among the Danish speaking minority in South Schleswig, North Germany, where 6,500 children attend Danish schools, for example. There the teaching takes place in Danish, but German is also taught. Conversely, it ought to be mentioned that about 1,700 children of Danish parents in the southernmost parts of South Jutland attend German schools where Danish is also included as a curricular subject.

Because of the smallness of its geographic area and by virtue of its historical background, Denmark proper is a linguistically "pure" area. Foreign manpower is a problem of very recent date, and, so far, extremely limited in extent. Complications arising from national problems and language difficulties are few and the great majority of children are unaffected, nor are there any serious problems in connection with dialects.

The Writing System of Danish

The Ministry of Education in Denmark publishes a dictionary[1] that lays down the orthography of Danish. There are no competing orthographic systems at any levels, including the elementary grades. As a matter of curiosity, it should be mentioned that, in 1908, the Danish philologist Otto Jespersen[2] published a small ABC based on a phonetic alphabet of his own invention. No attention, however, was paid to his book by the schools and it had no influence.

The last spelling reforms introduced in Denmark were in 1948, when the initial capital letters derived from the German language were abolished. At the same time it was made a general rule to write the character *å* instead of *aa*. This reform brought Danish closer to the Swedish and Norwegian orthographies.

The Danish orthography is, because of traditions and linguistic developments, "inconsequent." That is, it is not easy to decode the pronunciation of a Danish word from its spelling or vice versa. Of particular significance in this respect is that Danish has a number of silent letters that are vestiges of earlier language forms. These, to a certain extent, impede learning to spell.

The symbols for vowel sounds are also comparatively inconsequent. Although there are rules for relating vowel graphemes to vowel phonemes, they are definitely not easily understood by students below the university level, and therefore, no attempt is made to teach these rules to school children. For example, there is a general trend, observed throughout the history of the spoken language, for vowels that previously were short and close to become open. As regards the graphemic representation of the vowels, however, developments are very slow and lag far behind the changes in pronunciation.

In the area of punctuation, it has become general practice to follow the rules used in Germany. It is permissible to use the less rigid punctuation system adopted elsewhere in Europe, but this is rarely the practice in schools.

Political, Sociological, and Economic Factors

Space here does not permit a treatment of the history of the school system of Denmark. Today Denmark is a "State of Danes" with a population of about 4.8 millions, distributed over an area of 43,000 square kilometers. Previously, Denmark was mainly an agricultural country, but now industries have taken over the leading role. When measured by an international yardstick, differences in cultural level are very small within the borders of Denmark. Nevertheless, in actual practice, the social background in Denmark does create some limiting factors. It cannot be claimed that everybody in the country, within reasonable limits, can obtain the optimum education. A prosperous community is not necessarily a welfare state. In Denmark it is expensive to bring up children, and many of them grow up under conditions that are *not* optimum. In particular, the interest in education varies when urban areas are compared with rural districts. Leaving out of account the upper classes, people in rural districts are much less interested in education than those in urban districts.[3] This situation may first and foremost be attributed to the proportionately few children from the rural districts who attend the gymnasium or other schools at the same level. The phenomenon is attracting ever-increasing public attention, and a number of changes within this area are likely to be made within the next decade or so. One of the contributing factors to this uneven distribution may be the general lack of a tradition for and interest in an academic training among the rural population. It would, however, give a distorted picture if this situation were not also viewed in relation to the well-developed further education system and inservice training facilities provided in most parts of the country. It should be noted also that pupils in the last grade of the public school can apply for financial aid from the Youth Education Fund, although, thus far, this has been without decisive effect. In principle, the cost of all tuition of children and young people, including all educational materials, is met out of public funds. For more details of the current situation as regards economic factors, manpower situation, and so on, reference may be made to the official statistics (*Statistisk årbog*[4] and *Statistik 1968–1969.*[5])

Schools

In its development the Danish school has been under the influence of other European educational systems—first and foremost the German school.

In the twentieth century, however, there has been a pronounced influence exerted by the English, and subsequently also the Swedish and American educational systems. Attention should be called particularly to the structural effect from Sweden and to the philosophic effect from American educators such as John Dewey. The trend away from German influences toward Scandinavian and Anglo-Saxon influences manifested itself strongly following the outbreak of the Second World War.

A Specific Danish Educational Ideology

It is important, though, to emphasize that for more than a hundred years a Danish educational ideology has made itself felt, maintaining that *in principle, the influence exerted by the parents in the home environments must be considered the most important educational factor, and that the parents have the right, as far as possible, to determine the duration and content of their children's school education.*

This ideology can be traced back to the first two great personalities within the folk high school movement in Denmark, Kristen Kold (1816–1870) and N. F. S. Grundtvig (1783–1872), and to the circles that, in the nineteenth century, were the prime movers in the establishment of the Danish folk high school. (See Brickman,[6] Thomsen,[7] Rørdam,[8] and Jansen.[9] Also this writer has related this ideology directly to the reading program in another article.[10])

The folk high school was, and still is, aimed at the further education of young people and adults. Many prominent Danes, including a great number of politicians, have acknowledged their indebtedness to this school—so much so that educational legislation during the past hundred years must have been influenced to some degree.

The right of the parents to make their influence felt in respect of the length of the school attendance period is one of the main principles of the public school in Denmark, although parents have no direct influence on the curricular content.

Compulsory education over a period of only seven years has been maintained in all education acts from 1814 until 1970. In addition to this period, parents are entitled to send their children to school for a further period of from one to six years, within the limits of their children's abilities and interests. Although education is compulsory for a certain period, school attendance is not. The parents are permitted to teach their children at home, but in actual practice this is done very rarely.

The so-called free schools, although few in number, have asserted themselves to a considerable extent from an ideological point of view and have served as a more general source of inspiration. Some decades ago, these schools were established mainly in rural areas, based on the same principles that are fundamental to the folk high school. During the past ten years or so nearly all of the newly established free schools have been in the form of the so-called little schools (from twenty to two hundred pupils), one of the basic principles of which is "free" education. They concentrate to a large extent on the creative development of the pupils. In these schools the parents have a decisive influence, and in most cases the initiative in the establishment of any such school is taken by parents belonging to one of the professions. (A free school receives a refund from the State to cover 85 per cent of total expenses.) Despite the small number of pupils involved (fewer than 1,000 altogether), these schools have exercised a pedagogic influence on educational planning within the public school system.

Parents' committees and school boards have both direct and indirect influence on the public school, although, in many cases, to a limited extent only. At the present time efforts are being made to strengthen this influence.

The Public School System

In 1970, the percentage of school children who were attending school for more than seven years was 97.4, and by 1973 the compulsory period will have been extended to nine years. The public school is owned and administered by the local municipality, which receives a refund of all essential expenses and is supervised by central and regional authorities. The 1958 act governing the primary and lower secondary schools defines the structure of the school and the main content of its curricula. The stated objectives of the public school are "to promote and develop the child's natural gifts and abilities, to strengthen his or her character, and to provide the child with a useful store of knowledge."

Pupils enter grade I when they are about 7 years old (see Figure 13-1). The first lessons in reading start when they are between 7 and 8. Prior to grade I, the school has a "kindergarten class," in which attendance is noncompulsory. At an even earlier stage, there is the conventional kindergarten, which often is a social institution and in which attendance, of course, is also noncompulsory. The kindergarten and the kindergarten class must be treated separately.

The Kindergarten

In the industrial areas in Denmark the kindergarten has become a necessity, and in modern times the establishment of kindergartens must be considered a community problem—and a problem that has not yet been solved. In 1969, the kindergartens could accommodate only some 52,000 children, or about 15 per cent of the children of this age group. Although there is no need for kindergarten facilities to cover all of the remaining 85 per cent, the overall capacity is far from sufficient.

The kindergarten takes children from 3 to 7 years old. During the week it is open from three to ten hours daily. Its aim is to provide the children with security and stimulus, irrespective of their home environment and their parents' occupational level and ability as educators. By virtue of its outer framework, its educational philosophy, and its equipment, the Danish kindergarten is more than a playground for the children. It should be a children's learning workshop where they can develop motor, intellectual, linguistic, and other abilities—but *not* in any *formal* way. It is a place where, gradually, in pace with their personal

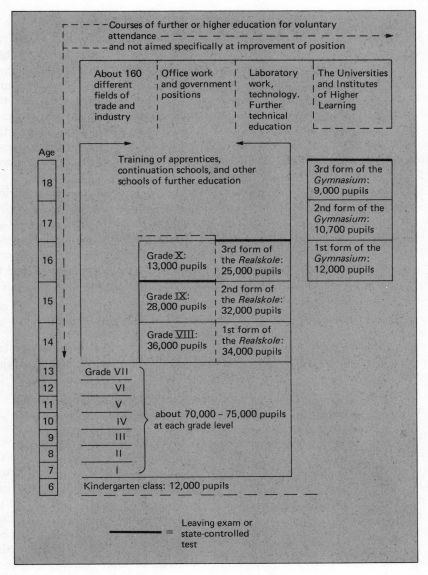

FIGURE 13-1. The Danish school system, 1969–1970.

development, they may gain experience of the normal requirements of the community in which they live: the standards of everyday living, the working life, the social life, the conventions, the mass media, art and creative subjects, and the like. One particular aim of the kindergarten is to provide experiences from which young children can learn to respect other people and to evoke their respect.

A Danish kindergarten is *not* a preschool institution for *training* children for school.

The Kindergarten Class

Many people consider the kindergarten class a natural outgrowth of the kindergarten principles. The kindergarten class is accommodated at the public school. It is open three hours a day, and its purpose is, through play and recreational activities, to promote the motor, social, cognitive, emotional, and creative development of 6- to 7-year-olds. It is often maintained that the kindergarten class is a preparation for school proper. Although kindergarten must be paid for by the parents (or the public authorities), the kindergarten class is free, in line with the free public school. In 1969, the kindergarten classes could accommodate about 12,000 children or somewhat less than 20 per cent of the age group in question.

Entry into grade I in Denmark is, in comparison with some other countries, at rather a late age—that is, 7. Although it is anticipated that parents during the coming years may demand more opportunities for their children to obtain education at an earlier age, there is no indication that they would desire *formal instruction* at an earlier level. On the contrary, politicians, educators, and parents are generally agreed that an earlier start in school should be devoted to the kind of creative and imaginative experiences currently provided in kindergartens or kindergarten classes.

Grade I and Beyond

The system from grade I onward is described in Figure 13-1. Its development will be further described in connection with topics more directly concerned with learning to read.

Age of Commencing Learning to Read

It is a general rule that no formal training whatsoever in the three Rs is given in the kindergarten or in the kindergarten class. Before children can learn to read, it is considered that they must have developed a range of skills within the realm of the primary spoken language. Such skills are thought to be best developed through total real life experiences in a social context and related to natural language, not by the artificially segmented training provided by formal pencil-and-paper tasks. Without such a basis of linguistic development, a reading program would be built on sand. The reading would serve no purpose for the child, and hence he might learn, albeit by accident, that "reading" is nonfunctional.

Parents, too, hesitate to anticipate the formal teaching of reading and writing. In educational circles it is being increasingly recognized that there is plenty of time for children to engage in learning the skills of literacy.

It might be objected that Danish children do *not* have enough time in school to master the skill of reading. As will be described later, a comparatively high percentage of pupils receives remedial instruction. Is this due to the late age of beginning reading and the rather short length of compulsory schooling? Any such conclusion would be based on a grossly oversimplified view of the Danish reading situation. One must also consider that in Denmark (1) the goals in reading are set high even for the weaker students; (2) reading is regarded as a functional necessity for all students; and (3) it is also vital in solving Denmark's future manpower problems.

As a matter of fact, Danish children at the age of 11 generally are well able to manage texts of a parallel level of difficulty both in linguistic complexity and content to those used typically in Western Europe, in Britain, or in America. Possibly, the individualized teaching methods to be described in the next section of this chapter may help to account for the remarkable progress of Danish children that follows their late start in learning to read.

"Reading Readiness"

"Readiness" too often conveys the notion of prognosis for future attainment, and Danish educators have become increasingly hesitant in accepting the validity of such long-term educational prognoses. For this reason, there has been little interest in developing reading or school readiness tests in Denmark. As Lundahl et al.[11] have noted, it is infinitely more important for the school to be ready for the child than vice versa. This principle can be extended to reading. It is far more important for the reading teacher to be ready for the individual pupil than the other way round. Thus, although two tests have been adapted from Swedish and Norwegian instruments, no great interest has been evinced in them, and no attempt has been made to develop a Danish test.

The general view is that each teacher should instruct each child according to his own special individual needs, selecting the methods and materials that best fit those individual needs. In gauging them, the teacher's professional judgment in his observations of the particular child and his professional competence in a free choice of educational materials and teaching aids are what counts.

Teaching Methods

Two organizational factors have an important effect on the methodology of teaching children to read in Denmark: (1) the "classroom teacher" tradition and (2) the more recent development of "division of classes."

The Classroom Teacher Tradition

When a teacher is put in charge of a first grade, he will generally continue to teach Danish to these same children for seven years. In a few cases the teacher may stay with the same class for two or three years only, but it is becoming more and more common for the teacher to continue with the class through grade VII. In rare cases the teacher may even stay with the class or part of the same class through grade X—the final grade of the public school. Thus, the teacher must, from the very beginning, be fully prepared to accept a great responsibility for the entire schooling of the individual child.

Visitors from other countries often ask, "Does the classroom teacher system give sufficient consideration to those children who happen to get a weak teacher?" While it is realized that "weak teachers" exist, it must be pointed out that such teachers function better when working with the same class for a number of years than in a class where they know beforehand that they will stay for only one year. The teachers as well as the children and the parents realize that they must try to get as much as possible out of the instruction because they will be working together for several years.

The comparatively high standard of the four-year training required to qualify as a teacher makes the classroom teacher system possible. Even more important are, however, the inservice training programs and the courses provided at a higher level, both of which are attended by a substantial proportion of teachers.

Division of Classes

During the last decade an important change has been the introduction of division of classes. In grade I all twelve of the weekly lessons in Danish language are no longer taken together by the whole class. For four of the lessons, the class is divided into halves, each taught separately. Because the class contains between 18 and 28 pupils, the divided class is quite a small group.

The chief effect of this division of classes has been to provide a real challenge to the teacher to make his teaching individualized. As a result, individualized methods have been introduced extensively in the elementary grades as the division of classes has spread to grade II, and in some municipalities, especially the larger ones, to grades III and IV. It should be emphasized that in such division of classes pupils have *not* been grouped according to ability or proficiency level. Indeed, direct warnings have been issued against division of a class into bright and slow groups. Experiments with such streaming methods have generally proved unsatisfactory for the children.

Division of classes for a few lessons has proved more satisfactory in its results than previous efforts directed at reducing the size of the whole class—for example, from 32 to 28.

Methodology

The history of the methods of teaching reading in Danish schools has shown a swing away from the concern with a formal teaching of phonics and spelling by drills of the 1950s to an increasing interest in the development of reading as a functional process. Today it is considered of primary importance to engage the interest of the pupil and to make sure that the reading situation is, from the beginning, a realistic and meaningful one for the child. Also, the child's total development is the objective, rather than one isolated aspect, such as reading. Reading, too, is treated within the over-all framework of linguistic development—not as an isolated subject. The impatience with the search for "the correct method" of reading is shown in the title of a recent article, "How long will we go on waiting for 'the great Pumpkin'?"[12] In its place has come a realization that every effort must be made to consider the child's individual linguistic development in the context of all aspects of his growth.

At the same time, the changing world in which our children live and will live requires corresponding changes in education. It is no longer sufficient for children "merely" to learn reading and writing; they must be taught the art of communication. Added emphasis should consequently be placed on development of the first phase of a four-step process: *To comprehend the language → to speak it → to read it → to express oneself in writing.*

This attitude, that reading is no longer looked on as an isolated subject but that reading of Danish is now considered an integral part of the child's general linguistic development and growth, has led to the aim of developing the oral language to a natural and useful level before reading is introduced. Therefore, it has been necessary in the preschool period and during the lower grades to concentrate on creative activities. These activities support the development of conceptual knowledge, oral vocabulary, and so on. In a field investigation by Rasmussen,[13] a number of the periods usually devoted to the Danish language and arithmetic were spent on creative activities and art instead. The general conclusion was that, after grade V, if this change had not increased the proficiency level, at least it had not served to reduce it.

The "head-start" programs of other countries, aimed at making socially and culturally disadvantaged children better equipped to enter a "middle-class school" are unknown in Denmark. Certain variations, which might perhaps best be characterized as differences in readiness between individual pupils, are naturally observed but, on the whole, Denmark is a sufficiently integrated community to permit common long-term goals to be set up for the entire public school, without consideration of subcultures.

There is no methodology in reading bearing an official stamp. The Danish teacher is free to choose his methods. For an authoritative description of modern methods in reading he must look, not to the Ministry of Education, but to individual experts. The only major contribution of this nature, a book that at the same time explains the background for the newer procedure followed in Denmark in teaching Danish and the underlying philosophy, is *Danskmetodik, 1.-7. skoleår (Danish Methodology, Grades I-VII)* written by this author.[14] Two points of general importance are (1) that reading is not emphasized when children first start school, and (2) that there are wide differences from school to school and between individual teachers in the methods employed. However, in spite of this second point, certain general trends can be observed.

The *first six months or so* are mainly devoted to oral language, to prepare the pupils for reading. At the initial stage the teaching methods used in reading are, in most cases, directed at integrated instruction, working with sentences and words. Later on, spelling exercises are introduced and also some practice in phonetics, which provides a good support for many pupils.

In principle, efforts are made to build up a reading program that includes the largest possible number of different supporting techniques. It is characteristic that a teacher of Danish in most cases will describe his teaching efforts at the elementary stage as a "combination of methods."

Generally, an attempt is made *during the following six to twelve months* to teach the children to master the mechanics of word recognition ("rebus reading," cf. Cromer and Wiener[15]) supported by writing and speech-motor activities. At this stage, basal readers are used. These contain a comparatively modest number of words, frequently repeated and accompanied by illustrations throughout. (cf. Jansen,[16] and Jansen and Mylov.[17]) Moreover, the teacher uses flash cards, lets the pupils write experience stories on the blackboard, plays games concerned with the construction of sentences, words, and letters, and encourages various creative activities.

In *grade II* much easy reading filled with illustrations is most frequently concentrated on. Within this field, there has during the last decade been an important development both as regards the volume and quality of the material available. Also, during *the first part of grade III,* the pupils continue to be encouraged to do much easy reading. During these grades the word-recognition method is, as far as most of the pupils are concerned, gradually supplanted by a reading program challenging the interest of the pupils, and more and more varied children's books are made available for this purpose. Instruction is focused on the principle that children *learn to read by reading*.

The textbook system and other materials used in the teaching of Danish are now generally accompanied by teachers' editions that, while trying to explain "how," also provide definite answers to the question "why." These methodological guides in reading, which often are rather detailed, have most likely played a certain part in the change that has been witnessed within the field of language instruction.

Reading Development

Educational psychologists in Denmark tend to proceed rather more by observation and description than through theoretical models. The new reading methodology has been derived, therefore, by observing samples of children in their development of the reading skill. In the course of this development a number of phases have been noted.

"WORD RECOGNITION" OR "REBUS READING" PHASE. During grades I and II usually there is a brief period of processing by recognition of whole words that may be characterized by "guesswork." The pupil directs most of his energy toward recognizing the words and has comparatively little available for achieving comprehension.

The more "clues" that are contained in the text in the form of meaningful content, carefully prepared illustrations, and adaptation of vocabulary, the easier is the transition from "word recognition" to "meaning reading"—a transition that often proceeds rather quickly in the course of grade III.

THE "MEANING READING" PHASE. From the age of 8½ to 9 years, many pupils experience a quick change in reading habits. They are said to enter the meaning reading phase. This term is rather vague and covers at least four different types of reading. One element they have in common, though, is that the pupils are no longer so dependent on details or on guesswork when reading, nor have the pictures any decisive influence on their understanding of an illustrated text. The *four types of reading* at this later stage may be described as follows.

Type 1. In the course of grade IV, if not earlier, reading for meaning starts where the reader *reads and enjoys*. The goal at this stage is manifold and rather vaguely defined, but, at any rate, it can hardly be a question of intentional selective reading. This reading phase is often emotional in character, but two qualities are typical: a special attitude to reading and a specific purpose. The reader remains passive in his approach to the subject matter. All that he wants is to relax and enjoy the experience provided by the reading, but naturally he also understands what he reads. Comprehension, however, is not his primary concern. Reading as such is an achievement—an activity that satisfies a need.

Type 2. Somewhere at the grade IV level, the meaning reading phase will be expanded and the pupil will now *read and understand;* that is, he will afterward be able to answer a number of questions concerning the subject matter, without any prior warning as to whether the questions will deal with the main theme or with details of the text.

This type of reading is very different from that of the word recognition phase, and it probably requires a higher level of maturity than has generally been reached by 8- to 9-year olds. It is a form of reading that one often comes across in connection with homework of a more casual nature, and it is a form of reading that many adults—perhaps the great majority—never outgrow in their reading of nonfiction.

Observations of pupils who either *read and enjoy* or *read and understand* show that these are quite distinct types of meaning reading.

Type 3. A third situation is the *critical approach*. During the reading of a text the content is *reviewed*. The level of maturity required for such reading is so high that, in most cases, one cannot expect pupils to tackle this form of reading until grades VII to VIII, unless they are especially efficient readers or have received specific training. Field observations also seem to indicate that this is a distinct type of reading in which reading effort becomes of minor importance as compared with the specific purpose.

Type 4. A highly skilled reader is also able, at certain intervals, to practice different forms of reading, including skimming and scanning while doing ordinary meaning reading. In this fourth type the reader *varies the speed and form of reading in an active and purposeful manner*. This is the type of reading that places the heaviest demands on the reader and probably combines quite a variety of study techniques.

First, the reader makes a preview. Then he decides what approach to make—that is, he actually defines his purpose. Thereafter, he scrutinizes certain parts of the text, while skimming the rest. He compares some of the material with what he has previously read on the same subject, and during the reading he will be able to "argue" with the author, with himself, and with others who may have written on the same subject—all the time, of course, proceeding with his reading.

In addition, one may note other forms of reading of a more specific nature that are learned at a more advanced level. At the intermediate level, whether within youth or adult education, the teaching of reading takes the form of a whole-person skill training and training of specific skills, a procedure that is being perfected all the time.

Writing

In parallel with changes in teachers' attitudes toward reading have come more modern views on the teaching of writing. There has been a shift in emphasis from the former concentration on fine penmanship by very formal training in handwriting and orthography to the present-day methods combining composition, penmanship, and spelling. Formal instruction in the written language evokes little interest now and much more effort is spent on the development of methods and materials to improve *composition*. Some demands are still made for improvement in spelling, but they are generally related more to the ability and developmental level of the individual pupils.

Influence of Second Language Learning

It must be borne in mind that Danish children are required to attain sufficient proficiency in one or more neighboring languages for their understanding. Also they must learn one or two foreign languages well enough to communicate in them. Modern methods of foreign language instruction have probably had some influence on methods of teaching Danish, too, and these have been more in harmony than in conflict with the educational attitudes described in this section.

Reading Instruction Beyond the Beginning Stage

During the past decade there has been a fairly wide interest in Denmark in further education in reading, aimed not only at the relatively few students entering one of the universities but at *all* pupils.

This form of instruction begins beyond grade VI; it is aimed at developing reading into a tool to be applied in numerous different ways within specific curricular subjects and different spheres of interest.

The problem of improving reading as a tool of education has been approached from two angles: (1) Efforts have been made systematically to teach pupils to read books and publications other than fiction—varying the form and speed of reading according to the nature of the materials and to their own needs. (2) Efforts have been made by publishers to produce materials at a more suitable level of readability for the less efficient readers—without lowering their standards in terms of either content or appearance. In these endeavors, a nationwide testing of the readability of all textbook materials and children's books was instituted in 1970–1971.

In the development of systematic reading programs for the intermediate levels, Swedish educational ideas have had an unusually small influence. American educational views have had more effect—for example, those of Spache. However, the most important factor has been the universal support given by educational organizations, school radio and TV, and professional study groups and seminars. For example, a national eight-week course was transmitted by School TV and watched by about 10,000 school children from grades VII through IX. Subsequently, a corresponding eight-week course for adults—adapted to the age group in question—was telecast to an even larger audience. These courses comprised systematic exercises in speed and comprehension, training in scanning and skimming, and more variation of speed and form in reading. The methodology and results have been described in a previous publication by this writer.[18] Florander[19] also has investigated the effects of teaching reading through Danish TV.

In these TV courses, the emphasis was on *books*—not on reading machines. The public libraries made lists of books and pamphlets available as part of their cooperative effort with the TV courses. (For a description of the development of the public library services in general see Elberling and Bruhns.[20])

These developments in the field of reading in Denmark reflect the growing recognition of the vital importance of reading as a *tool* of learning and discovery. The demand for *reading manpower* is growing even more rapidly. Hence, reading instruction today is aimed at reducing dropouts from the program to a minimum. Toward this goal, it is believed that higher efficiency in reading for the population of Denmark can be achieved best through *individualized* teaching at these higher levels of skill development as well as at the elementary stage. The principle of readiness applies continuously all through these higher stages. So also does the principle that there is no single best teaching method. And the third principle that still applies at all levels is that the learner is to be the center of concern—that is, the whole person, rather than some limited aspect of his development, such as reading.

Integration of Reading with Other Aspects of the Child's School and Daily Life

The official view is that reading not be confined to the periods labeled "Danish"; it is being learned also in courses for other subjects. It is recommended that teachers of social studies and science, for example, cooperate with the teacher of Danish to improve the learning of reading in such areas. However, in actual practice, frequently, this cooperation is on a modest scale.

It is recognized also that reading is to be related to its important role in the child's everyday world outside school. In this connection, books and other reading matter do indeed have an important place in Danish life. Even before the child starts school he has, in most homes, been subjected to the influence of the printed word in newspapers and magazines, and, because of the comparatively well-developed library service, books are an everyday experience. Through these natural experiences of early childhood, to a large proportion of children "learning to read" means "to become a big girl or boy." Thus, by the age of 7 to 8, when formal education starts in the course of grade I, a natural interest in reading already exists in many of them. Teachers in kindergarten class and in the elementary grades maintain this initial interest by reading stories to the children, by means of the class library, picture books, and the like. At the same time, a foundation is being laid for reading.

Reading Materials

In the earlier section on "Teaching Methods" some indication has been given of the types of materials generally used. A major research project recently has been directed at the content of the Danish curriculum. Various aspects of reading are being studied, including analyses of the textbooks in use. In Denmark, textbooks continue to be of central importance because of the prescribed curriculum they are designed to follow systematically. However, at the same time, one must take into account the great freedom officially given to the teacher in the planning of day-to-day activities, and also the fact that tests are very rarely used and are not compulsory.

In this research (cf. Jansen[21]), all readers and other textbook materials used in reading have been analyzed and the results published. Another investigation has been concerned with textbook illustrations (cf. Jansen and Mylov[22]). Uhrskov[23] has reported an investigation of two series of readers in respect to their attitudinal content regarding other nations and peoples.

Textbooks are purchased through the schools' general account for educational materials. The amount that is made available for the purchase of educational materials varies greatly, however, from municipality to municipality, and, as far as the teachers are concerned, it is a common experience that these amounts are nearly always too small. It must be admitted, though, that during the last few decades they have become increasingly liberal. This needs to be taken into account in considering that in many respects the general reading methodology is absolutely dependent on the availability of a large volume of textbook material of a comprehensive nature.

Reading Materials for Retarded (Backward or Disabled) Readers

Increasing importance is being given to books suitable for retarded readers. In 1952, Larsen[24] found only sixty books suitable for teaching retarded readers, and fewer than thirty others that could be regarded as supplementary reading matter for such students. But, in just over fifteen years, the number seems to have increased greatly. Lundahl,[25] in 1969, reported that the latest list of materials recommended (by a committee of reading teachers representing various types of schools) for use in the teaching of retarded readers includes a total of about 475 books and other material. The same author published, in 1968, a supplementary list[26] of 220 books of "easy nonfiction," and, in 1969, a list[27] of 202 "light books for young people and adults." Taking into account overlapping between these lists, the total number of books for retarded readers has grown from fewer than 100 to almost 1,000 in these seventeen years—this for a linguistic area with a population of only 4.8 million people. Furthermore, teachers continue to complain that not enough such books are available.

Reading Materials for Normal and Above-Average Readers

In a linguistic area as small as Denmark it is extremely difficult to maintain a national production of good quality children's books. Only some 30 to 40 per cent are by Danish authors. Of the rest, a little more than 30 per cent are translations from Anglo-American books, and about 25 per cent are from Norwegian and Swedish literature. Within nonfiction for children the percentage of translations, however, is much smaller (cf. Bredsdorff[28]).

Since 1931 all children's libraries have been State-supported, but it was not until 1965 that all municipalities were required by law to set up *public* libraries and children's departments. However, even before 1965 more than 90 per cent of all children in Denmark, had access to a local children's library. Now in each public library a children's department must be developed to comprise four volumes per child (0- to 13-years old) within its service area. If the local school library has no circulation department, the standard fixed for the children's public library is six volumes per child. It is even more if the library has undertaken commitments of a specific nature (with other children's institutions).

During the period 1959 to 1969, although the population of children up to age 13 decreased slightly from 1.09 to 1.08 million, the public library loans of books to children almost doubled. In 1969, for the third year in succession, loans to children went up by two million volumes. In the same year about 50 per cent of all book loans were made to children, and it is expected that in 1970 loans to children will outnumber those for adults.

Jakobsen[29] provides information on the use of *school* libraries in Scandinavia. The school library has become an integral and essential element in the teaching of Danish, furnishing also a collection of material that is being diligently used also in other subjects. Of the total library budget for 1968 to 1969 of some $27,729,636, the allocation to school libraries was $2,199,706. This does *not* include expenditures for premises, personnel, and the like.

Training of Reading Teachers

For admission to the 3½- to 4-year courses offered by the training colleges, the candidate must have passed the *Studentereksamen* (university entrance examination) or have obtained a corresponding diploma. This is a new regulation. Formerly, any person who could substantiate that he was in possession of a sufficient background of knowledge was admitted to a training college, subject to an entrance test.

Currently, a new act on the training of teachers is being implemented, in which greater emphasis is to be given to educational philosophy and psychology. In the past, there has been considerable variation and change in the content of courses for teachers in training. Thus, the teachers in the schools have varied also in their qualifications. The goal set for courses in Danish and in reading at the training colleges is that they should be adequate to make every teacher competent to give instruction in reading. However, the results are quite variable.

The Royal Danish School of Educational Studies has for a number of years provided inservice training courses for about five hundred teachers a year, qualifying them to instruct *retarded readers*. This further study comprises 112 lessons in theory and 24 in teaching practice, and is open only to teachers who have already had some experience. Many teachers have attended these special courses solely, or primarily, with a view to improving their teaching in *normal* elementary classes. At the training colleges now a possibility has been opened whereby prospective teachers can choose a special training course corresponding fairly well with the course just described. In addition, the Royal Danish School of Educational Studies provides various other special inservice courses related to reading (theories of reading, school librarianship, and the like).

But the essential characteristic of the training of reading teachers in Denmark has been the provision of voluntary inservice training in all parts of the country. These courses and seminars have been arranged by local groups of teachers, school psychologists (who in actual practice have done much to interest the teachers in the psychology of reading), provincial departments of the Royal Danish School of Educational Studies, different associations and societies of teachers, and interested school heads. The teachers' comparatively good general training has, to a certain extent, provided them with the necessary background for this continued education in reading instruction, despite some possible inadequacies in their basic training in this particular field. A recent review (cf. Jansen and Leerskov[30]) of articles on methodology published by the educational press in Denmark indicates that teachers have displayed a comparatively strong interest in the teaching of Danish. Publications on the pedagogy of reading have been especially numerous, both in relation to retarded readers and normal pupils. This interest is another reflection of the teachers' enthusiasm for inservice training in this subject, which they undertake on a voluntary basis— not with a view to obtaining credits, but merely to meet the problems encountered in their classrooms.

University Provision for Specialization in Reading

The universities do not provide courses for specialist teachers in reading. Also, in the general study of psychology, the orientation given to theories of reading is extremely limited. This lack of academic provision for advanced study and research in reading is very noticeable. For example, there has been practically no research in this field at the Danish universities.

Reading Tests

Few standardized tests of reading and related skills are available, and these tend to be antiquated in their standardization and in their validity for present-day educational aims.

It is the class teacher's sole responsibility to decide whether a test should be used at all, and, if so, which test should be employed. This is the current situation. Formerly, the schools, especially the larger ones, arranged for annual year-end tests to be given in Danish and arithmetic. In the former subject, however, it was only a question of an oral examination of a purely formal nature, including a few questions in spelling. In most cases it was attended by parents or another teacher. These tests were not usually standardized, not even for the local area. Now that the school is left unstreamed at increasingly higher grade levels, the interest in year-end tests has disappeared, both on the part of the teachers and the authorities. The tests have been maintained in a few large municipalities only.

The trend away from tests in favor of instruction is now so pronounced that, on the whole, no interest is taken in year-end tests until the end of grade VII. In a debate in the Danish Parliament on the subject of basic education, the Minister of Education made the following concluding statement, which passed uncontradicted by all of the seven political parties: "this would lead me to the conclusion that the time has now come where it should be prohibited to arrange tests in connection with the first seven grades. Or worded differently, should it be put on record that the year-end test—as has also become the usual practice at the majority of places—shall not be used during the first seven grades? From what has been said here, this seems to be the conclusion arrived at." [31] This serves better than anything else to show the extremely modest interest in tests evidenced by the authorities.

This freedom from tests enjoyed in mutual teacher-pupil educational enterprise must be the result, at least in part, of the classroom teacher tradition described earlier. When the teacher works with his pupils for a period of several years, he is well able, through his personal knowledge of each individual, to gauge their progress and to diagnose their needs on a more informal basis.

Provisions for Reading Disability

"Dyslexia"

Hermann [32] and a few Danish neurologists have for many years been concerned with the problem of "congenital word-blindness" or "constitutional dyslexia." These views of dyslexia have struck a responsive chord among a group of educators whose work has been specially directed toward helping retarded readers.

A different viewpoint has been expressed by Tordrup. [33] His approach to the problem of seriously retarded readers has a broader perspective based mainly on considerations of the psychology of reading.

At the Danish Institute of Educational Research, efforts have been concentrated on the need to make objective observations[34] of the effectiveness of remedial teaching on children suffering from reading disability (cf. Larsen[35] and Rasborg[36]).

Treatment

Theoretically, help must be provided for all retarded readers whether of high or low intelligence level. In general practice, however, the situation varies greatly from district to district, and in the secondary school (the *real* and *gymnasium* departments) the support given is on a rather small scale.

School psychologists indicate the pupils who are in need of remedial teaching but their decision is not based on any standard tests. The pupil's potentialities are compared with the standard of his own class. This provides a great deal of flexibility, so that while a pupil at one school may receive remedial instruction because he needs it to keep up with the rest of the class, at another school a pupil at the same level may not be recommended for such teaching because he is able to meet the requirements of that school.

Within the public school, 7 per cent of pupils receive remedial teaching in reading. As this remedial program is mainly concentrated on grades III through VI, the number of retarded readers who at some time—whether for a shorter or longer period—have received special instruction will represent from 15 to 18 per cent. If this percentage seems comparatively high, it should be borne in mind that records are kept of practically *all* retarded readers in Denmark. Furthermore, the standards demanded are high in Denmark, because of the stress on books and learning through reading. Thus, many pupils who receive remedial reading instruction in Denmark would probably not be diagnosed as in need of such help in other countries. Indeed, the proportion of students receiving such aid in Denmark might be higher because public school remedial teaching is still being hampered by lack of premises, and in some districts also by a shortage of qualified teachers.

Previously the general trend was mainly to base remedial teaching on corrective spelling methods, but as increasing importance is being attached to reading in the general language program, the situation is changing. Now emphasis is placed on the teaching of reading.

Reading Groups

The most common remedial measure is by instruction of reading groups. Children who are so retarded in reading that they find it very difficult to keep up with the rest of the class are placed in groups of three to five pupils for three to five hours of special instruction weekly. In these courses a specially trained teacher tries to build up a basic foundation to supplement the previous instruction. This instruction is concentrated in grades III through V. It is, however, possible to arrange group teaching throughout the rest of the compulsory educational period, and at many places also in grades VIII through X. About 4 per cent of all public school pupils receive remedial instruction in such reading groups.

Classes of Retarded Readers

In the larger towns, and to some degree also in the rural districts, reading classes are set up that may be attended for one, two, or more years by the pupils who are most seriously handicapped by reading problems. These reading classes are an integral part of the public school, administratively as well as from an educational point of view. They are accommodated in the same building as the normal classes, and, in principle, they also may have the same teacher. (The Danish teacher in the reading classes must, however, be specially trained.)

The goal of the reading classes is to make it possible for the pupils to return to their normal grade or perhaps one grade lower. In view of the fact that the class in all other subjects than Danish follows the normal curriculum, this is often possible. Some pupils, though, remain in a reading class until they leave school. About 0.7 per cent of all public school pupils attend a reading class at some time or other.

Individual Instruction and Other Remedial Measures

Apart from the foregoing, there is a beginning interest in the establishment of *reading clinics* where the children are instructed for a certain number of periods as decided in consultation between the school psychologist, the classroom teacher, and the teacher at the clinic (cf. Rasmussen[37]).

In some cases, however, the possibility also exists of establishing *individual teaching*. This procedure is most common when the difficulties in reading are pronounced and combined with other problems—for instance, of an emotional nature, or where the pupils are retarded to such an extent that attendance in a reading class is prohibited. Individual instruction is also often thought to be more suitable for the older pupils.

Help for Young People and Adults with Reading Problems

At the end of the compulsory school period, young people can still receive free tuition if they are hampered by serious reading or spelling difficulties. Remedial teaching of young retarded readers and spellers in the age group 14 to 18 years may, for instance, be provided at a continuation school, which offers three- to ten-month courses. Of about one hundred schools of this type, two concentrate on retarded readers and spellers, and in a number of the other schools courses are provided for special groups of such pupils. In many situations these courses serve as a good alternative to the public school, as far as individual pupils are concerned.

The civilian education program arranged for the defense forces provides a certain number of weekly lessons in general subjects. Two of these lessons may be used for the remedial teaching of conscripts who have pronounced difficulties in reading and spelling. For many years this instruction has been of importance to many young people. Similarly, the prison administration provides remedial courses for inmates.

Apart from the foregoing, free remedial teaching is being offered every year by other government agencies to about 1,500 young people who have reading and spelling problems. This instruction is provided at reading clinics and special schools with such clinics. The pupils are taught individually or, in some cases, in groups of two or three. The individual pupil may also be given private lessons at home by a remedial teacher. In a few instances the instruction in reading and spelling may also be provided in connection with a rehabilitation or retraining course—for example, in rehabilitating a person who has been injured in a traffic accident. This program is enabled by an act passed in 1954. The act was revised in 1961, in pursuance of a section that decreed that the state is to cover expenses incurred in speech correction furnished outside a government institute provided that the person in question had been recommended for treatment by the relevant institute. This law has also been applied to serious cases of word blindness and retarded reading. For a number of years there has been a marked tendency to interpret the provisions of this act to the best advantage of the individual pupil.

Future Needs for Remedial Treatment

Reading failure must be regarded as *a relative condition*. As normal reading instruction is upgraded to meet the new demands for higher and higher standards of literacy, these new targets will represent a further challenge to the weakest readers. Thus, better instruction brings with it the continued requirement for special teaching of the weakest pupils.

The Spare Time Education Act, 1968

A 1968 act provides for spare time courses for participation on a voluntary basis to be arranged under youth education as well as adult education programs. Provision of any such form of education rests on municipal and private initiative, and there is an extremely wide range of possibilities in respect to the topics and activities that may be taken up. In principle, spare time education is open to everybody, and no person can be debarred from participation in some form of educational activity.

This act may be expected to provide further possibilities for furnishing retarded readers and spellers with needed support. To establish a remedial course, only two applicants are required, and the course must be maintained and continued even if 50 per cent of the participants—one of the two—should drop out. In connection with such special education, no group is expected to comprise more than four pupils. If qualified teachers and adequate material can be made available, legal provisions of this nature may become of great value for young people or adults suffering from reading difficulties.

On the whole, such legislative measures are supported by the different political parties, for one thing because, fundamentally, these provisions contain no new principles. They are aimed at a further development of the adult education program, which traditionally has been based on voluntary participation.

REFERENCES

1. Dansk Sprognævn, Retskrivningsordbog (Dictionary), Copenhagen: Dansk Sprognævn, 1955.
2. Jespersen, O., ABC og første læsebog efter lydskriftmetoden (The ABC and Elementary Reader [the phonetic method]), Copenhagen: Gyldendal, 1908.
3. Hansen, E. J., "De 14–20 åriges uddannelsessituation 1965" ("The educational situation for the 14–20 year age group, 1965"), Vol. I, Social og geografisk rekruttering (Social and Geographical Recruitment), Copenhagen: Social Research Institute, 1968 (with English abstract and English summary), pp. 180–216.
4. Danmarks statistik, Statistisk årbog 1969 (Yearbook of Statistics, 1969), Copenhagen: Danmarks statistik, 1969 (with English index).
5. The Ministry of Education's expert on financial statistics, Statistik 1968–69. Folkeskolen m.v. (1968–69 Statistics on the Public School, etc.), Copenhagen: The Ministry of Education's expert on financial statistics, 1969.
6. Brickman, W., Denmark's Educational System and Problems, Washington D.C.: U.S. Department of Health, Education and Welfare, Office of Education, 1967.
7. Thomsen, O. B., Some Aspects of Education in Denmark, Toronto: The Ontario Institute for Studies in Education, 1967.
8. Rørdam, T., The Danish Folk High Schools, Copenhagen: Det danske Selskab, 1965.
9. Jansen, M., "The scope of reading in Scandinavia," in Jenkinson, M. D. (ed.), Reading Instruction: An International Forum, Newark, Del.: IRA, 1966.
10. Jansen, M., et al., "New cities, educational traditions and the future," in Lauwerys, J. A., and Scanlon, D. (eds.), Education in Cities, London: The World Year Book of Education, 1970.
11. Lundahl, F., et al., "Skolestart" ("Starting school"), Læsepædagogen, 17 (1969), 1–32.
12. Jansen, M., "Hvor længe vil vi blive ved med at vente på den store græskarmand?" Skandinavisk Tidskrift för Läspedagoger, 2 (1968), 6–13. (Available in English under title, "How long will we go on waiting for the great Pumpkin?" and in German, "Wie lange werden wir uns da noch um eine SESAM-Lösung bemühen-?")
13. Rasmussen, G. Kjær, "Østrigsgade-forsøget" ("The field experiment at Østrigsgade"), Læsepædagogen, 14 (1966), 59–79 and 83–84.
14. Jansen, M., Danskmetodik, 1.–7. skoleår 3rd ed. (Methodology of Danish, Grades 1–7), Copenhagen: Gjellerup, 1970.
15. Cromer, W., and Wiener, M., "Reading and reading difficulty: A conceptual analysis," Harvard Educational Review, 37 (1967), 620–643.
16. Jansen, M., Skriftligt arbejde i dansk, 1.–7. skoleår (Written Danish in Grades 1–7), Copenhagen: Danmarks pædagogiske Institut (The Danish Institute for Educational Research), 1966.
17. Jansen, M., and Mylov, P., "Om illustrationer i danske læsebøger, 1.–7. skoleår" ("On illustration of Danish readers for grades 1–7"), Nordisk tidskrift för specialpedagogik, 47 (1969), 3–35.
18. Jansen, M., Om Læsning. Læsetræning med unge og voksne. (On the Subject of Reading. Training Young People and Adults to Read), Copenhagen: Gjellerup, 1969.
19. Florander, J., "Udbyttet af læsetræning" ("The results of a training course in reading"), Læsepædagogen, 18 (1970), 55–83.

20. Elberling, B. V., and Bruhns, I. (eds.), *Læste bøger. Voksnes læsning og biblioteks-benyttelse. (Books that are being read. The reading habits of adults and how they use the libraries. With information on the readers' evaluation of the books in question)*, 2nd rev. ed., Copenhagen: *Danmarks biblioteksskole* (The Royal School of Librarianship in Denmark), 1967.

21. Jansen, M., *Danske Læsebøger, 1.–7. skoleår* (Danish Readers and Textbooks, Grades 1–7), Vol. I, *Registration and analysis*, Vol. II, *Bibliography*, Copenhagen: *Danmarks pædagogiske Institut* (The Danish Institute for Educational Research), 1969.

22. Jansen and Mylov, *op. cit.*, p. 17 and p. 25.

23. Uhrskov, M., *Gennemgang af to læsebogssystemer for danskundervisningen i 3., 4., 5. og 7. skoleår ud fra nogle indholdsmæssige og formelle kriterier (A Review of two systems of readers for the teaching of Danish to grades 3, 4, 5 and 7 based on certain criteria as to content and form)*, Copenhagen: *Danmarks pædagogiske Institut* (The Danish Institute for Educational Research), 1969.

24. Larsen, A., *"Materiale til undervisning af ordblinde og læsesvage"* ("Material for instruction of the wordblind and retarded readers"), *Læsepædagogen,* **1** (1952), 13–15.

25. Lundahl, F., *Læsepædagogens Materiale- og frilæsningsliste (Læsepædagogen's list of educational material and free reading)*, 7th rev. ed., Dragør: *Landsforeningen af læsepædagoger,* 1969.

26. Lundahl, F., *Liste over let faglig læsning og klassehåndbiblioteker (List of easy nonfiction and classroom reference libraries)*, 4th rev. ed., Dragør: *Landsforeningen af læsepædagoger,* 1968.

27. Lundahl, F., *"202 lettere bøger til unge og voksne"* ("202 light books for young people and adults"), *Læsepædagogen,* **17** (1969), 171–172.

28. Bredsdorff, Aa., *Library services for children in Denmark,* 2nd ed., Lund: Lunds Bibliotekstjänst, 1965. Also "The Danish standard for bookstocks and accessions II. Children's departments," *Scandinavian Public Library Quarterly,* **2** (1969), 87–101.

29. Jakobsen, G., "School libraries in the Scandinavian countries," *UNESCO Bulletin Library,* **23** (1969), 310–315.

30. Jansen, M., and Leerskov, A., *Ti års tidsskriftartikler om danskundervisning, børnehaveklasse–7. skoleår (The teaching of Danish* [the mother tongue, "first language"], *as it appears in ten years of educational journals and periodicals)*, Copenhagen: *Danmarks pædagogiske Institut* (The Danish Institute for Educational Research), 1970.

31. Minister of Education, *Forslag til folketingsbeslutning om en reform af de grund-læggende skoleuddannelser (Reform bill of fundamental education systems)*, Copenhagen: Minister of Education, 1969. Introduced in Parliament on January 31st.

32. Hermann, K., *Reading Disability,* Copenhagen: Munksgaard, 1959. Also, *Medfødt ordblindhed (Congenital Word Blindness)*, Copenhagen: Munksgaard, 1967.

33. Tordrup, S. A., *"Stavefejl og fejltyper hos elever fra 5. normalklasse og fra 5. og 6. læseklasse"* ("Spelling errors and types of errors made by pupils from the 5th normal grade and the 5th and 6th reading classes"), *Skolepsykologi,* **2** (1965), 1–69 and 75–91. Also, *"Læseudviklingen hos elever med store læsevanskeligheder"* ("The development of reading among pupils experiencing heavy difficulties in reading"), *Skolepsykologi,* **4** (1967), 1–154 (with English summary).

34. Jansen, M., "A discourse on the formulation of registration form—Danish," in Simon, A., and Boyer, E. G. (eds.) *Mirrors for behavior,* Vol. X, Philadelphia, Pa.: Research for Better Schools, Inc., 1970.

35. Larsen, C. Aa., *Om undervisning af børn med læse- og stave- vanskeligheder i de første skoleår (On the instruction of children encountering difficulties in reading and spelling during the first few grades),* Copenhagen: *Danmarks pædagogiske Institut* (The Danish Institute for Educational Research), 1960.

36. Rasborg, F., "*Om muligheder for at konstatere en behandlingseffekt hos læseretarderede*" ("On the possibilities of ascertaining any effect from the remedial teaching of retarded readers"), in Rasborg, F., and Florander, J. (eds.), *Pædagogiskpsykologiske tekster, bind 2. Forskningsmetodologi (Texts on Educational Psychology,* Vol. 2, *Research Methodology),* Copenhagen: Akademisk Forlag, 1966.

37. Rasmussen, G. Kjær, "*Læseklinik—en rationalisering af læseholdsarbejdet*" ("Reading Clinic—A more effective way of working with groups of retarded readers?"), *Læsepædagogen,* **17** (1969), 127–132.

CHAPTER 14

Finland

O. K. KYÖSTIÖ

Spoken and Written Finnish

The majority (93 per cent) of people (total 4.7 million) in Finland speaks Finnish. The minority's mother tongue is Swedish, but a great number of the latter are bilingual. Finnish belongs to the Finno-Ugric language group, its nearest relative being Estonian and some smaller tribal tongues in Russia; examples of other related languages are Hungarian, Mordvinian, and Cheremis. The present Finnish language comes from a proto-Finnic that was spoken south from the Gulf of Finland at the time of the beginning of our calendar. People who moved from there to Finland during the first centuries A.D. made up, in the course of time, some tribes that spoke their own dialects. Linguists are of the opinion that the Finnish language in its proper sense took on its structure between the eleventh and fifteenth centuries, a time linguistically called the period of early Finnish. This continued until the middle of the sixteenth century when the first Finnish books were printed. The Finnish language received many loan words from Swedish and Russian, as it had done earlier from other Indo-European and Baltic languages. The basic difficulty of the Finnish orthography at that time was the irregularity of its grapheme-phoneme relationships, a feature quite unknown in present-day Finnish.

The nineteenth century was, in many respects, a transitional period that gave a strong impetus to the development of the Finnish language. It was at this time that the orthography arrived at its present regularity of grapheme-phoneme relations in all essential points: the writing of long vowels, geminated consonants, consonantal gradation, and declension and conjugation, for example. The most important tasks of so-called present-Finnish are concentrated on the increasing of special vocabulary, the spelling of loan words, and on the refinement of sentence structure. As a result of this developmental work, the Finnish language, both in spoken and written form, can be considered an entirely satisfactory medium for everyday life, science and culture, and administration and information. Its writing system is quite regular; that is, each phoneme always has the same letter irrespective of its place in a word. This feature enormously facilitates learning to read. (For more about the structure of the Finnish language, see Hakulinen.[1])

School Organization

From the very beginning (sixteenth century), the Lutheran Church of Finland emphasized the importance of the reading skill to everyone and made strong efforts to raise the standard of reading instruction (Vikman[2]). In the eighteenth century, an ordinance imposed this task on parents, and, in cases of their inability, ordered the parishes to establish village schools, or to deal with the matter in some other satisfactory manner. When Finnish primary education was organized according to the act of 1866, the aim was still that all parents should give their children basic instruction in reading before they entered school at age 9. In the course of time, it became more and more obvious that basic instruction in reading and writing organized in this way could not give satisfactory results. Therefore, many communities arranged a lower stage attached to the four-year primary school. This was made obligatory by the act of 1921, which also established a two-year continuation school as a part of primary education. But only the four lowest forms of primary school were an obligatory condition for entrance to the selective secondary "grammar" school. Students not so selected continued for two further grades in the primary school. This system operated until 1968, when a new act providing for a nine-year basic school was approved by Parliament (see Kyöstiö[3]).

According to this, compulsory schooling is from 7 to 16 years, but a voluntary kindergarten and upper secondary school can be attached to the municipal basic school.

The new organization of education is presented in Figure 14-1. Reading is encouraged and developed, especially in the basic school, but it is represented in all school types as an obligatory subject. In such a small country as Finland, foreign languages play a greater role at the secondary level, and therefore as much time cannot be devoted there to the mother tongue. However, those studies support reading instruction in their own way.

The Role of Reading Instruction in Curricula

The Age of Commencing Learning to Read

In kindergartens, reading is not taught at all. This is the result, at least in part, of the way in which the kindergartens are administered. Kindergartens and nurseries work under the Ministry of Social Affairs, which also deals with the preparation of teachers for these institutions. Therefore, the work there is considered more as social help than as education, and it is aimed mainly at children from poor and broken families. The new education act, however, offers possibilities of attaching the kindergarten to the primary school. It may thus provide an opportunity to begin the instruction of reading and writing earlier. Of course, kindergartens in their present form do prepare children for reading by improving their imagination, concepts, perceptive and motor ability, and vocabulary.

Kindergarten, as a part of the primary school, may have great future

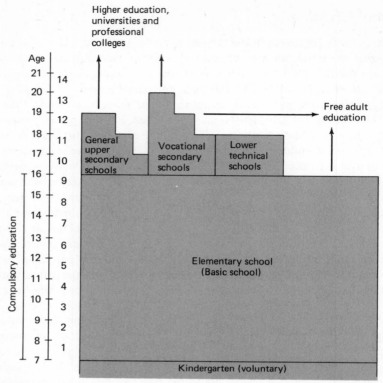

FIGURE 14-1. Organization of education (the new system) in Finland.

importance, because in Finland children enter school at the late age of 7. Some experiments have shown that Finnish children are able to learn reading earlier if the instruction is given according to their abilities and interests (Kyöstiö and Vaherva[4]). Investigations concerning the knowledge of school entrants indicate that a great number of them know letters or can read a little. It is evident that children today get many kinds of useful stimuli for reading in their early years through the mass media. If they are then suitably helped by kindergartens or by parents, this may decisively support their progress. The importance of an early start has been emphasized especially from the point of view of the child's future intellectual development.

Foreign Language Teaching in the Timetable

In the primary school, reading instruction plays a dominant role in the time schedule. Table 14-1 shows how many periods per week are devoted to the mother tongue and to foreign languages in the basic school (forms I to IX) and in the secondary school (forms X to XII), too. The share of the mother tongue is proportionally high at the beginning (more than one third of the time), gradually showing a decreasing trend so that from the seventh grade on, the share is less than one tenth. Clearly, the introduction of a foreign language (at the third and seventh forms) always means a smaller allocation of time for the mother tongue. Compared with the time given to languages in the curricula of other countries, the time devoted to the mother tongue in Finland is less than average.[5] But the time provided for foreign languages is one of the greatest.[6] The reason for this may be that Finnish is easy to learn to read. Also, the greater proportion of time is given to teaching foreign languages because Finnish is not a widely spoken language. Therefore, school authorities are of the opinion that all children should learn at least the elements of a foreign language. Students who continue their studies in a university need still more knowledge of other languages if they are to be able to use foreign reference books. Furthermore, Finland is a bilingual country and the minority's language, Swedish, has been traditionally taught in schools, thus giving still more emphasis to language teaching.

Teaching Methods

As in other countries (see W. S. Gray[7]), the alphabetic method was the first and almost only one used in Finland until the end of the nineteenth century. The reason for its dominance is understandable if one remembers that instruction in basic reading was not considered to be the proper concern of the schools in Finland—it belonged rather to parents or to voluntary infant schools. Gradually, other methods (phonic and various analytic ones) also became known and were introduced into practice. The few investigations into reading methods that exist are too narrow for a thorough presentation of the situation today, but the following general description gives a view of the most common procedure of teaching reading to beginners at primary school.

Teachers usually begin to teach the children in their classes with the assumption that they are illiterate. A primer is distributed from which the children first learn some letters. Often many words beginning with these letter sounds are pronounced and presented in the book. As soon as several letters have been learned, they are combined to make short words. The order of introduction of letters varies from one published reading program to another. The main idea seems to be to find an easy way to build up new words on the basis of the knowledge of earlier learned letters. The Finnish letters are the following: A D E G H I J K L M N O P R S T U V Y Ä Ö, twenty-one letters altogether. B C F Q X Z are used in some loan words. Long vowels sounds are written with two vowel letters, and strong consonants (geminated) with two consonant letters that belong to different syllables. No Finnish word begins or ends with two consonant letters. As mentioned earlier, each phoneme is always indicated by the same grapheme, which facilitates the learning of reading and writing. Reading Finnish letter by letter is therefore quite correct if one knows how to pronounce each individual grapheme (the single exception is the $/ŋ/$ sound).

According to the most commonly used method, the synthetic approach, learning advances from phonemes to syllables. Children do this individually and sometimes also in chorus. "Spelling" is the typical procedure. The letters of the first syllable are spelled out separately, followed by the syllables as a whole.

TABLE 14-1. The Number of Language Periods and Their Proportion in the Timetable

Grade	Basic school											Upper secondary school					Grand total	
	I	II	III	IV	V	VI	VII	VIII	IX	Total	Per cent	X	XI	XII	Total	Per cent	total	Per cent
Mother tongue	9	9	6	6	6	6	3	3	3	51	18-19	3	3	3	9	9	60	16
First foreign language (English or Swedish)			2	2	3	3	3	3	3	19	7	3	3	3	9	9	28	7-8
Second foreign language (Swedish or English)							2	2-5	2-5	6-12	2-4	4	4	3	11	11	17-23	5-6
Third foreign language (French, German, Latin, or Russian)												3-5	3-5	3-5	9-15	9-15	9-15	2-4
Fourth foreign language (French, German, Latin, or Russian)												3	3	3	9	9	9	2
Total Languages	9	9	8	8	9	9	8	8-11	8-11	76-82	27-30	13-18	13-18	12-17	38-53	38-54	114-136	30-37
Total other compulsory subjects	15	15	20	20	22	22	20	17	17	168	61	15-20	15-20	16-21	46-61	48-62	214-229	57-62
Counseling of pupils	1	1	1	1	1	1	1	1	1	9	3						9	2
Selective subjects							4-6	4-9	4-9	12-24	4-9						4-9	1-2
Periods per week	25	25	29	29	32	32	33-35	33-35	33-35	271-277	100	33	33	33	99	100	370-376	100

In addition to these, students may take some optional subjects.

Usually the teacher says the name of the letter. When it represents a vowel, the letter name and the phoneme represented are identical. But in the names of consonants, a vowel is always connected with the consonant: ko, el, te. Sometimes the teacher may *try* to pronounce consonant phonemes without a vowel. The second syllable is learned in the same way. If a word has only two syllables it is pronounced after them. But if a word has more syllables, as many Finnish words do, all the previous syllables are repeated after a new one has been learned; for example:

kou - *lus* - *sa*   (in school)

1.   2.

3.   4.

5.

This makes the reading very jerky and monotonous. Many teachers use a so-called sliding (elastic) movement from one sound to another, thus facilitating the understanding of syllables and words.

A few teachers (3 to 5 per cent) use the analytic method, beginning with separate words or short sentences. Most of them move, however, rather quickly from the analysis of words to the synthetic method. From the point of view of the Finnish language, the analytic method has some basic weaknesses. This method requires that words be, as far as is possible, unchanging in shape, so that children can easily recognize them in a new context. This is, indeed, the case in languages that use prepositions for the inflection of nouns. But in Finnish inflection is produced by several alternative word endings (fourteen cases altogether) that continuously change the shape of words. Also, verbs in Finnish have many conjugational forms (as they do in German). Therefore, if a pure analytic method is used, difficulties occur in finding suitable reading exercises and the procedure becomes easily artificial and uninteresting to children. Some investigations have also shown that the learning results are not better; on the contrary, they are often worse.

Reading instruction is not limited, of course, to formal reading exercises done either in class or as individual reading, with the teacher as a model, or just for enjoyment (cf. Morris[8]). There is, in the lower grades, a great deal of talking, role playing, dialogues, improvization, dramatization, and, at a later stage, essays, reporting, discussions, interviews, reviews, recitations, and speeches.

Instructional Materials

Books play an understandably dominant role in reading instruction. Compared with the older and unpleasant primers, the new ones are interesting and illustrated with colorful pictures from the child's world. Some examples from different years provide a general picture of the development of reading primers in Finland.

In an ABC book from the last century, children had to learn first the different types of characters and to pronounce consonants with all vowels. The method was strictly alphabetic. The content of the booklet was printed in Gothic script and was completely religious. It held the Lord's Prayer, articles of faith, sacraments, God's commandments, and the like. No wonder that force was needed to get children and adults to learn it!

A great advance in teaching reading was made in a reading program by Raitio, a teacher in a normal school. According to his advice, the instruction should begin by analyzing sentences into words, syllables, and sounds. In this way, children will be made aware of the meaning of reading. Raitio calls his method "the combined reading-writing method" because writing goes hand in hand with reading. His primer's first page suggests that it must have been preceded by some formal writing exercises. After reading and writing had been learned through separate words and short sentences and using only small written letters, written capitals were learned by the same method. The next step was to learn Gothic characters. But the old system of using meaningless syllables still prevailed in this phase. Later, usual types (Latin) of printed letters were also taught. Everything was done very systematically. The rest of the book was comprised of small stories with pictures and was printed with different characters. According to the author, the content was related to the child's world, in the spirit of that time. Later (1923) the same author produced a new primer in which reading was taught with small (Latin) letters, but capitals were learned in parallel. Writing was not so closely involved with reading as previously.

A primer by Niemi was in use from the beginning of this century, when infant schools (that is, primary grades I and II) were not yet obligatory in Finland and many country children learned some reading at home or in mobile schools. Children came to school at age 9 and started to learn reading by writing characters. The primer was also used in city infant schools for beginners. The emphasis was placed on learning by writing letters. Niemi advised teachers to talk with children, using the pictures in books to arouse their interest. From writing letters, the instruction moved through cursive letters to the usual printed Latin letters, and gradually from these to Gothic ones. Everything was done using childlike stories.

An interesting transitional period came in the 1920s and 1930s. Infant schools were introduced everywhere and children started reading from the very beginning of grade I at 7. In a reading program by Niemi, Genetz, and Pylkkänen, children learned reading in lower-case print. Capitals were learned at the same time as separate letters. It is interesting that handwritten characters were also taken together with printed ones. Learning to write was also combined from the very beginning with reading. The pictures were in color by this time. Later, Gothic types of letters were also learned because some books, especially religious ones, were still printed in Gothic.

A. Salo, a very distinguished person in the development of Finnish primary education, produced a reading program in 1935. He used only capitals with no separation between syllables. His idea was that separation hampers the understanding of words. But to facilitate spelling, he printed syllables using blue and red colors in turn. The content of reading lessons was predominantly taken from folklore and books by famous Finnish writers. The book was applied to Salo's integrative curriculum.

The latest stage in the development of primers is represented by Kunnas' program of 1968. Basic instruction is again by capitals and separated syllables; small characters are indicated, but reading with them begins after the process has been learned with capitals. The pictures are splendid and express children's everyday life as well as fairyland. The content of the tales is more realistic (actual and city-centered) than in the previous primers.

Typical of Finnish primers is the fact that they are always planned to cover a whole year; thus, each grade has its own reader. Additional books are sometimes used, but, as a rule, the class works as a complete unit.

Besides books, other materials of reading instruction are not so widely used. There are different kinds of flashcards, cards with pictures and letters, loose letters, reading letters, and the like. The blackboard is of course important, especially when reading and writing are combined. Some teachers use flannelgraphs and other audiovisual aids. Teachers who try to take pupils' individual differences into account need many extra materials (pencils, paper, additional booklets, workbooks, and colors) to keep all pupils active and interested.

Integration of Reading Instruction with Other Aspects of the Child's School and Daily Life

Reading is the core subject in the primary school and, proportionally, the most time is devoted to it. According to Salo's global curriculum, the so-called environmental studies should be the center of school life in the primary grades. In practice, however, the work is divided into separate subjects, and the content of the primers does not generally take this total integrated view into account.

At least reading and writing usually go hand in hand. From the very beginning, children write what they have learned to read. Most teachers let children at first copy only print capitals and then, after the first semester, introduce exercises using handwritten letters as well. In the lower grades, the instruction is not so strictly subject-centered and reading has many casual contacts with other subjects too (singing, playing, drawing, and especially environmental studies). One very important aspect is that the content of reading material increasingly is taking into account real life at home and in society.

Reading at Higher Levels of School

A committee has recently planned a new curriculum for the basic school. It reports the aims and content of the different subjects. The goals of teaching the mother tongue are as follows:

1. To guide pupils in their growing linguistic activities, and, at the same time, to encourage them to be judicious listeners, spectators, readers, and keen observers.

2. To guide pupils toward consistently expressing their thoughts in speech and writing, in colloquial language that is good both in structure and style.
3. To teach pupils to read and understand what they read in the way that each reading situation demands.
4. To stimulate pupils' creative activity.
5. To make pupils' modes of expression more accurate and richer.
6. To arouse pupils' interest in their mother tongue and in its linguistic forms.
7. To get pupils interested in language arts.

The instruction should, according to the committee, be focused on the following areas: (1) oral expression and listening, (2) reading, (3) literature, (4) writing, and (5) grammar.

A quotation from the curriculum of the ninth grade in reading and literature (areas 2 and 3) gives an example of the instruction for this level:

> Reading exercises, taking individual abilities into account and emphasizing the learning of good reading technique and habits; silent reading to learn to read quickly and to get a good general but accurate conception of the main points of the material; training to use different kinds of books in the classroom and in libraries.
>
> Examining informational literature and actual articles in journals and newspapers; reading books of different categories: juvenile literature, modern and some classical literature, lyrics and drama from anthologies and monographs; biographies of writers and important tendencies of literature; book reviews in groups and individually.

Teacher Training in Reading

Special training for teachers of the lower grades (I to III) in the primary school does not exist in Finland at present. Formerly, such training was delivered in certain normal schools, but in about 1960 it was stopped when special training for the upper grades (VII to IX) was organized. Since then the training of elementary school teachers covers grades I through VI.

The curriculum in the Finnish primary school is organized according to subjects from the very beginning. Students training to be teachers are assigned to teach certain subjects in different grades. Because of this, the training program introduced in 1960 has meant the general weakening of infant education and that of reading instruction there particularly. Primary school teachers are, of course, trained to teach reading, but this training may be only for reading at a higher level (for reading in grades V and VI). But each teacher must teach in the infant grades (in grades I and II) and they will be allowed to teach reading there as well. Because they have not been trained in the reading instruction of infants they are not provided with a good basis for such work in beginning reading.

A new arrangement introduced in 1968 may channel the situation in a better direction. Because the teacher trainees study for three years on the basis of a high school diploma, they must specialize in three subjects. One of these is the so-called infant education. Reading instruction in grades I to III is an essential part of this training. On the basis of two years' experience with this new arrangement, it seems likely that many women will want to specialize at this level. Teachers of Finnish at the upper level of basic school and in high school are persons who have taken their major (MA) or at least intermediate exam (BA) in Finnish. Their professional training is organized partly in normal high schools and universities. According to some plans, their professional training should later be attached completely to universities. Such plans have also been made concerning kindergarten teachers who are now trained in separate normal schools and have, at present, no concern whatsoever with reading instruction.

In some cities there are clinics for children who have difficulties in reading. In other cities they are helped by special teachers who go from school to school. Altogether, in 1968, only eighteen full-time special teachers were employed for teaching pupils with reading and writing difficulties, and nineteen teachers for children with speech difficulties. These specialist teachers are trained in the Department of Special Education of Jyväskylä University.

University Provisions and Reading Research

Students who study Finnish or literature in universities for their major or lower exam have very little concern—one can almost say none—with the teaching of reading. Their academic subject education and professional training are quite separate. Nor do departments of Finnish or literature have any concern with research in the teaching of reading.

Departments of education also have no concern with teacher training. This has been a matter for teacher-training schools (for primary education) or normal high schools. High school teachers have only taken a small theoretical exam in education in university departments of education. These departments have, however, engaged in research on problems of reading instruction and related factors. In the new organization of teacher training, the role of the departments of education will be more important than it is today. The old normal school will disappear, and research, training, and studies will be combined in the new structure.[9]

Investigations of reading problems are not particularly numerous at present. However, some students have done their Master's or Doctor's theses in this field—for example, the analysis of primers and readers, reading lessons (using Flanders' system and others), vocabulary, pupils' essays, reading interests, reading difficulties, sentence structure, spelling, speech difficulties, and structure of reading ability. Somerkivi's[10] reference book is a good presentation of reading skill and instruction at the infant stage. Vikainen has studied several problems of reading: for example, sentence structure[11] and backwardness in reading.[12] Viitaniemi's thesis[13] is concerned with reading structure. Kyöstiö has investigated reading level among school beginners[14] and 15-year-old students.[15] Reading interests have been analyzed by Lehtovaara.[16] Karvonen et al.[17] have recently (1970) completed the first Finnish vocabulary study on the basis of the essays of children in the third and fourth grades. Also, some achievement and diagnostic tests have been developed to examine oral and silent reading, children's vocabulary, and some psycholinguistic features: the tests of Karvonen, Ruoppila, Tasola, and Viitaniemi. Almost all of these studies are, however, published in Finnish and are not available to English speaking readers; therefore, only a few are referred to here. A new research institute attached to the University of Jyväskylä (Institute for Educational Research) has taken this field into its program. One of its reports has recently been published in English (Karvonen).[18]

REFERENCES

1. Hakulinen, Lauri, *The Structure and Development of the Finnish Language,* Bloomington: Indiana University Publications, 1961.
2. Vikman, K. O., *Suomen kansan lukutaidon synty ja kehitys Ruotsin vallan aikana,* Helsinki: University of Helsinki, 1910.
3. Kyöstiö, O. K., *The Finnish School in Transition,* Oulu: University of Oulu, 1969.
4. Kyöstiö, O. K., and Vaherva, T., "Reading and forgetting among young children," *Scandinavian Journal of Educational Research,* 3 (1969), 129–146.
5. *Preparation and Issuing of the Primary School Curriculum* (Publication No. 268), Geneva: International Bureau of Education, 1958.
6. *Preparation of General Secondary School Curricula* (Publication No. 194), Geneva: International Bureau of Education, 1960.
7. Gray, W. S., *The Teaching of Reading and Writing,* Paris: UNESCO, 1956.
8. Morris, J. M., *Standards and Progress in Reading,* Slough: NFER in England and Wales, 1966.
9. Kyöstiö (1969), *op. cit.*
10. Somerkivi, Urho, *Lukutaito ja sen opettaminen ala-asteilla,* Helsinki: Otava, 1958.
11. Vikainen (Laurinen), Inkeri, *Lausetajun kehityksestä,* Helsinki: University of Helsinki, 1955.
12. Vikainen (Laurinen), Inkeri, *A Diagnosis of Specific Backwardness in Spelling,* Turku: University of Turku, 1965.
13. Viitaniemi, Eero, *Kansakoulun neljäsluokkalaisten lukutaidon rakenteesta ja arvostelusta,* Turku: University of Turku, 1964.
14. Kyöstiö, O. K., "Reading research at the kindergarten level in Finland," in Downing, J. (ed.), *The Second International Reading Symposium,* London: Cassell, 1964.
15. Kyöstiö, O. K., "Reading level among 15-year-old boys and girls," *Kasvatus ja Koulu,* 6 (1962), 289–315.
16. Lehtovaara A., and Saarinen P., *School Age Reading Interests,* Helsinki: Finnish Academy of Science, 1964.
17. Karvonen, J., *et al., Opettajan sanastokirja,* Jyväskylä: University of Jyväskylä, 1970.
18. Karvonen, J., *The Enrichment of Vocabulary and the Basic Skills of Verbal Communication* (Jyväskylä Studies in Education), Jyväskylä: University of Jyväskylä, 1970.

CHAPTER 15

France

PAUL E. RUTHMAN

Historical Factors

Of the European school systems, that of the French has been one of the most influential in Western civilization. Many newly formed nations, including former French colonies, have adopted the French pattern of education. It has been widely emulated by many countries because it quickly produces, under strict government control, a professional elite, and it does not require time-consuming democratic experimentation.

French education, with its cultural heritage, has long been a symbol of learning to Western civilization. A legacy of the Roman conquerors, it was nurtured by the medieval Church until it emerged as Humanism during the Renaissance. Later, it was to become a concern of the people during the upheavals of the Revolution. Since that time the Ministry of Education has evolved a school system that embraces all instruction from the nursery school to the university.

Roger Gal, director of research for the *Institut Pédagogique National,* states that the modern concept of education in France began with the Revolution in 1789.[1] He further states that Locke, Rousseau, and Pestalozzi helped build the new ideal that education was the right of every child. Such an education was to be obtained in vernacular elementary schools, which offered an expanded curriculum of a practical nature. These philosophers apparently influenced the thinking of the Revolutionists in matters of educational reform. An early set of Revolutionary laws, the *cahiers* of 1789, attempted to fulfil many aspirations of the eighteenth century. The desire for vernacular education and public elementary schools was evident in the *cahiers,* which stated that "Education is an affair of the state, also an extension of the culture to the useful sciences for medicine, military affairs, and the arts; and the desire to teach children ethics, belles-lettres, modern languages, science, as well as political and natural law."[2]

From the Revolution in 1789 to the advent of the Third Republic in 1870, France was transformed by many changes in government. However, the gradual establishment of the republican form of government brought with it the development of a stabilized educational system that included instruction at all levels.

School System

A national system of education can be characterized by noting such distinctive features as its control, structure, curricula, and personnel. In France, where the schools have been created and maintained by national decrees, there is total centralization of authority and control. Under a system of rigid structure of school organization, all communities throughout the country must have identical types of schools. This required pattern begins with the kindergarten and terminates with the university. The curriculum at all levels is centrally directed and selection of pupils by national competitive examinations is an inherent feature of the system. Even professional personnel are trained, appointed, and paid by an agency of the government. In brief, no provision for local option or initiative has been made in this national system of education.

The Administrative Structure

The agency of control for this system is the Ministry of Education. This ministry's control is as all-encompassing today as it was in 1876 when Jules Ferry stated, "Let it be well understood that the first duty of a democratic government is to exercise incessant control over public education. We cannot admit that this belongs to any other authority than the state."[3]

The areas of control invested in the ministry are described by Kandel as "the employment of experts, the clear definition of functions, the utilization of expert councilors, and the control of all by the Minister. All branches of education are clearly defined, all schools of the same grade are of similar quality, instruction is based . . . on programs issued by the Ministry, and all examinations for certificates and diplomas are first scrutinized and approved in the Ministry."[4] The dominion of the ministry is, thus, a universal one.

The French education system, as shown in Figure 15-1, is structured on three levels: nationally by the Ministry of Education, regionally by "the academy," and locally by "the department." The Minister of Education, with the aid of his cabinet, formulates policies and regulations for educational activities. His directives, in turn, give guidance to the Bureau of General Inspection, which is responsible for the supervision and control of all types of schools. The work of the bureau is carried on by chief inspectors, each of whom is responsible for a particular aspect of the educational program, such as cooperation with schools of foreign countries; programs in elementary, technical, and secondary schools; adult education; community services; and higher education in the universities and research centers.

In order to administer these national education programs, France is divided into twenty-two regions called *académies,* each of which is further divided into smaller districts called *départements.* Each academy is in the charge of a rector who is also the president of the regional university. In addition to the twenty-two regional universities, which are public and State controlled, there are five private universities in France that are operated by the Catholic Church. The rector fulfills all directives of the ministry with the assistance of several specialized inspectors or supervisors. All educational activities below the university level within a department are directed by an *Inspecteur d'Académie.*

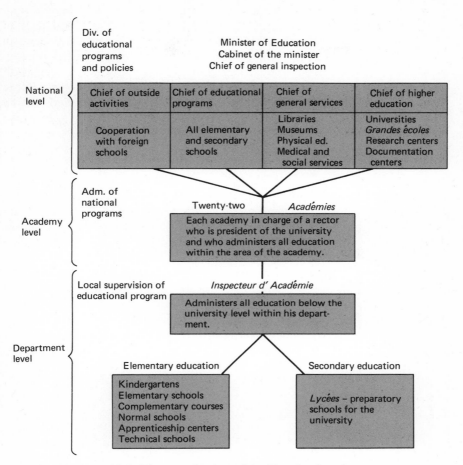

FIGURE 15-1. The organization of the French education system.

The School Organizational Plan

As is shown in Figure 15-2, the French school system provides for learning from age 2 through the university level. The structure, however, is not unitary in nature. The plan contains many variations of schools with widely different purposes, and the levels are not necessarily continuous ones. Elementary schools and normal schools, which are administered by the Director of Primary Education, have no direct relationship with the other educational institutions. These schools and teachers form a distinct segment of the French school plan. *Lycées,* which are college preparatory schools, and vocational schools serve students of the same age level but are not mutually connected in any way. Even in higher education, the *grandes écoles,* which provide training for government service and administration, are separate from the universities. Equivalency among the

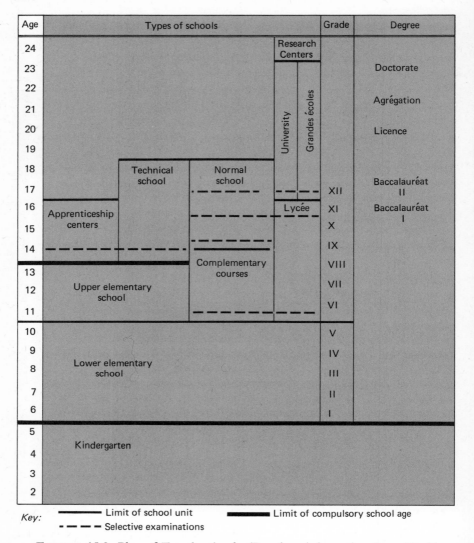

FIGURE 15-2. Plan of French schools. (Based on information from *World Survey of Education,* Vol. III, New York: Columbia University Press, 1961, p. 383.)

many classifications of French education, and even between programs of study within certain schools, is not possible. Thus, in the plan of French schools each segment is terminal in nature and sovereign in purpose. The Langevin-Wallen Reform Bill, passed in 1959, has made certain changes to correct these conditions, some of which are still not operative. Long delays are expected because of the critical shortages, at all levels, of teachers and classrooms.[5]

National directives, which are issued by the Ministry of Education and based on legislation, control all curricula, materials, and methods found in French public schools. Such regulations define courses and subjects to be taught at each level. Furthermore, the official programs stipulate the time allotments for teaching the various subjects and, in some instances, specify the hour at which such instruction shall take place. Additional control of the curriculum is achieved by the selection of instructional materials. Although individual educators may exercise some choice in this respect, all materials must be taken from the official list compiled by the Ministry of Education.

All teaching personnel in France are civil employees and are responsible to the Ministry of Education. Consequently, all aspects of teacher training, appointment, and salaries are developed and regulated on a national scale; regional differences do not exist. A particularly segmented aspect of French education can be seen in the preparation of teachers. Elementary and secondary schools, as well as the university, each have distinctive requirements for teaching certification. Basically, academic preparation places the French teacher in a classification that allows for appointment to one of the three main categories of French schools: (1) the elementary school, (2) the secondary school, and (3) the university. The organization of French education does not provide for changes in certification or classification. Further distinctive differences between groups of teachers are evident in title, status, and salary.

The Place of Reading in the French Elementary School

William S. Gray, in his international survey for UNESCO, *The Teaching of Reading and Writing,* concluded that the success of reading instruction is greatly influenced by the age of children and by the amount of instructional time devoted to the reading program. Teachers' qualifications were also found to be important for a successful reading program in the elementary school.[6] These three fundamental factors are of paramount concern to French educators. They are specifically mentioned by the Ministry of Education in the official instructions for elementary school teachers.

As regards age, the French schools compulsory attendance begins at 6 years. Children who have not attained the age of 5 years and 9 months by the opening of school are not admitted to the first grade. Such children may attend the upper section of the kindergarten, which is reserved for 5- and 6-year-olds. According to the regulations, the age range of the first grade is from 5 years and 9 months to 6 years and 9 months.[7] In actuality, many children are 7 years old before the end of first grade.

Prior to the first grade, most children have spent two or more years in the kindergarten, where they have experienced a six-hour daily schedule that has included some formal learning.[8] Thus, many first-grade children are well above 6 years old, are adjusted to a full school day, and have learned to work with other children, all factors important in readiness for reading.

With regard to the second factor, instructional time, official regulations give explicit directions also on how teaching time is to be used in regulating the national reading program. Exact allotments of time for each subject in the elementary school are specified for all schools, and, because these are official instructions, no deviation from the schedule is permitted. Within this framework of school hours, the Ministry further defines how teaching time must be divided.

The *écoles maternelles,* which combine nursery schools and kindergartens, are supported by the Ministry of Education and have been required by law since 1885.[9] Although classes are provided for children from 2 to 6 years old, attendance is not compulsory. More than 50 per cent of French children, however, do attend kindergarten for two or more years before entering the first grade.[10]

The kindergarten has three programs for the various age levels: (1) the first for children 2 to 4 years old, (2) the middle section for children aged 4 to 5, and (3) the upper section for children aged 5 to 6. All programs follow the same time schedule and are in session five days a week.

The daily program of all sections of the kindergarten includes physical education, music, drawing, language arts (such as dramatics and story-telling), and craft programs. In the upper section, for 5- and 6-year-olds, lessons are given in the initiation to reading, writing, and arithmetic. The official daily schedule for the upper section is presented in Table 15-1.[11] The program of the upper kindergarten section has been described as follows: "Exercises of the middle section are further developed, and new ones appear: so-called exercises in observation, a rich scale of language exercises, freehand drawing, initiation to music, rhythmics, and children's orchestra, and finally initiation to reading, writing, and arithmetic."[12]

TABLE 15-1. Official Instructions for Curriculum of the Upper Section of Kindergarten for 5- and 6-year-olds.*

Time	Subject
8:30–8:45	Group singing
8:45–9:05	Observations (twice weekly). Language (twice weekly). Narration (once weekly)
9:05–9:30	Initiation to reading and writing
9:30–10:00	Drawing
10:00–10:30	Recreation and lavatory period
10:30–10:50	Recitation (twice weekly). Musical initiation and singing (three times a week)
10:50–11:20	Outdoor physical education
11:20–11:30	Putting room in order. Preparation for noon dismissal
	Lunch
1:30–2:00	Varied crafts
2:00–2:30	Initiation to arithmetic
2:30–3:00	Rhythmic exercises and folk dancing
3:00–3:30	Recreation and lavatory period
3:30–4:00	Individual reading games. Elaboration of stories for class book (printing, illustration, and binding)
4:00–4:20	Dramatics, puppets, slides
4:20–4:30	Preparation for afternoon dismissal

* Information taken from *Education in France,* 13, 41–42. (See reference 9.)

Reading-readiness activities are influenced by Decroly's and Montessori's ideals, which include centers of interest and the global or whole-word technique for learning words. Such reading activities are characterized by the experience approach, and efforts are made to provide for individual differences of the several groups within each room. These are based on ability and achievement.

Stress is placed on learning to recognize printed words, which are learned by the whole-word method, and used in experience charts and stories. Considerable attention is given to writing each new word that the child learns to read.[13] Also, children are taught to print their newly acquired words with miniature printing machines. These simple printing devices allow the child to set type for stories he has helped to write and he is taught to bind them in a booklet form. He then has his first book, which he can read without difficulty.[14] Thus, many children learn to read in kindergarten. Those who do not learn to read by the end of kindergarten, however, are still placed in first grade.

Gray,[15] in considering writing and printing aspects of reading programs, describes them as valuable teaching aids to ensure the retention of new sight words as they are learned. This idea of writing all that can be read is imbedded in French elementary education. The official program for the lower elementary school, grades I through V, as shown in Table 15-2 specifies how the thirty-hour school week must be spent.

In the *cours préparatoire,* or first grade, it is obligatory for each teacher to spend ten hours a week in the actual teaching of reading to the whole class.

TABLE 15-2. Official Instructional Program for the Lower Elementary School*

Subjects	Hours		
	Grade I	Grades II and III	Grades IV and V
Citizenship	$1\frac{1}{4}$	1	1
Penmanship	$2\frac{1}{2}$	1	0
Reading	10	$\left.\right\}10\frac{1}{2}$	$\left.\right\}9$
Language	$2\frac{1}{2}$		
History and geography	0	1	$1\frac{1}{2}$
Arithmetic	$3\frac{3}{4}$	$3\frac{1}{2}$	5
Drawing and handwork	$1\frac{1}{2}$	1	1
Singing	$1\frac{1}{4}$	1	1
Written notebook work	0	5	5
Projects and fieldtrips	$2\frac{1}{4}$	1	$1\frac{1}{2}$
Directed physical education	$2\frac{1}{2}$	$2\frac{1}{2}$	$2\frac{1}{4}$
Outdoor recess—free play	$2\frac{1}{2}$	$2\frac{1}{2}$	$2\frac{1}{2}$
Total clock hours per week	30	30	30

* Table based on information from Lebettre, M., and Vernay, L., *Programmes et Instructions.* Paris: Editions Bourrelier, 1961, p. 9.

These ten hours must be divided so that two hours daily are given to reading instruction. The daily reading schedule is further divided into four thirty-minute lessons, two in the morning and two in the afternoon.[16]

To supplement reading instruction, each first-grade teacher is required to spend two and one-half hours each week in the teaching of writing (two fifteen-minute lessons in writing daily). Teachers are instructed to "combine the lesson of reading and writing as these two learnings are considered as one."[17] Furthermore, the child must practice writing all words that are used in reading.

Another extension of the reading program is "language," which must be taught two and one-half hours a week. In the first grade, the language program must include spelling, elocution, recitation, and vocabulary study. Every effort is to be made to correlate these studies with the work in reading; words from the reading book should be used for spelling and vocabulary study. Similar use is made of the stories children have read in elocution and recitation lessons.[18] Thus, the first-grade child in the French elementary school spends fifteen hours of the thirty-hour school week in reading and related language activities. Because there can be no deviation from the time schedule as set forth by the Ministry of Education, it may be assumed safely that at least 50 per cent of the first-grader's school day is devoted to such activities. This is reflected in the official instructions for the first grade: "The essential teaching at this age is reading. The first grade, is, above all, a course in reading."[19]

In the second and third grades, which are known in the French schools as the *cours élémentaire,* the reading program continues to dominate the elementary school day. There is, however, a reduction in the time spent in the language arts to eleven and one-half hours weekly. Of this block of time, nine hours weekly or ninety minutes a day must be reserved for reading instruction, to be given in two daily lessons of forty-five minutes each, preferably the first in the morning and the other in the afternoon.[20] Teachers are instructed to teach writing twice daily for fifteen minutes following each reading lesson.[21] Language lessons continue to be done in conjunction with reading, although no precise time allotment is recommended.[22]

As the child progresses to the fourth and fifth grades, the *cours moyen,* there is a further reduction of instructional time to nine hours a week for the reading and language areas. Writing is not taught as a part of the program on this level.[23] However, more time is still devoted to the reading program than to any other curricular area. Arithmetic, the only other area of concentration, is given five hours a week at this level. Thus, it can be seen that the French elementary school, in accordance with its official instructions, places great emphasis on reading instruction.

Teacher Training in Reading Instruction

The third factor listed earlier was teachers' qualifications. According to Gray,[24] an important factor for a good reading program is the careful preparation of teachers. The French Ministry of Education has provided a nationally controlled teacher education program, which includes preparation and certification, as well as appointment and total financial remuneration. This plan is intended to prepare professional teachers to fulfill the prescribed instructions for the elementary school.

Teachers in the elementary school do not hold degrees and usually have not attended a secondary school for university preparation; rather, they are educated entirely within the scope of the elementary branch of the French school system. As a result, after passing fifth-grade examinations, most future teachers enter the four-year complementary course, now called *collège d'enseignement général,* or school of general education. Although these courses are more advanced than the basic upper elementary school, they are not equivalent to secondary school programs.

As specified by law, graduates of complementary courses between the ages of 15 and 17 are permitted to take competitive examinations for admission to the normal schools that are located in each Department of France.[25]

During the four-year normal school, the first three years are devoted to general education, the final year is spent in professional education. The year of professional education includes three periods of student teaching in laboratory schools operated by the normal schools; each period is of one-month duration.[26] As is shown in Table 15-3, a variety of professional courses is taken. Among these are method and curriculum materials courses in the teaching of science, arithmetic, as well as art, music, and physical education. However, no courses are given in the teaching of reading or language arts.[27]

Such a condition does not coincide with the official emphasis given to these areas of learning in the elementary school. To produce a sound reading program, official regulations for the schools have given attention to proper age and apportionment of instructional time, but they do not appear to have made corresponding provisions for an adequate preparation of teachers who must spend about 50 per cent of the school day in the teaching of reading. This situation is serious because of the limited amount of research materials and professional literature that is available to the teacher.

Professionally, elementary teachers remain quite apart from the professors in the lycée and university. Strict differentiation is somewhat the result of tradition, but is dependent on two inherent factors in the French educational system: (1) elementary teachers are hampered in university work because they lack a classical education, and (2) the universities do not offer courses in elementary education and reading. Thus, the French elementary school teacher can be described as a normal school graduate who has not attended a university and has not earned an academic degree.

In summary, it is apparent that reading instruction has a major emphasis in the French elementary school. The ministry has issued national directives making reading instruction the most important subject to be taught in the elementary school. Yet, paradoxically, professional education for teachers does not include courses in the teaching of reading.

TABLE 15-3. Program of Teacher-Training Studies in the French
Normal School.*

	One-year program	Two-year program	
		1st year	2nd year
Child psychology	3	3	3
Sociology		1	1
General mathematics		1	1
Special methods	6	2	2
Trial lessons		1	1
History of education	1	1	1
School ethics and law	1		1
French	2	2	2
History and local geography	1	1	1
Teaching of arithmetic	1	1	
Science and health	2	1	1
Teaching of sciences		5	6
Rural education	4	5	5
Handwork	2	1½	1½
Drawing and writing	1½	1½	1½
Music	1½	1½	1½
Problems in education		1½	1½
General culture seminar		1½	1½
Physical education	3	3	3
Extracurricular activities	3	3	3
Totals	34	37	37

* Times are expressed in clock hours per week for both programs. Information
taken from Charlier, P. S., *Contemporary Teacher Education in France
and Belgium, p. 104*. (See reference 27.)

The French Language

The description of a language for the purposes of teaching reading is often
oversimplified by the exclusive study of the sound-letter relationship. Such an
approach gives an incomplete picture of the situation according to Samuels.[28]
To gain more insight into how reading is taught in a language, one might well
consider (1) the development and nature of the particular language, (2) its
linguistic characteristics, and (3) how the child is taught to read.

English, with its haphazard development, has assimilated many aspects of
other languages. The difference between the vernacular and the literary language
is often indistinct and somewhat debatable. As a result, English has become a
highly irregular language without order or consistency from the point of view
of vocabulary and letter-sound relationship, as well as spelling.

The French language, however, developed in a more logical manner and has
retained much of its Latin character. After the Revolution serious attention was

given to the instruction of French as it had been codified by the eighteenth-century classicists. Continued guidance by the Academy has produced an organized language with definite standards. Consequently, the idiom of conversation is still quite distinct from the literary forms that people read and write.[29] Two levels of the French language have been referred to as the *normal style* and the *formal style,* the latter being used in formal speech as well as in reading and writing.[30] One can assume, then, that the child learns to read a formal literary language that is organized logically, rather than a variety of the written vernacular.

Another feature of the French language is the nature of its words. Orr compares English and French words as follows:

> The greater autonomy of the English word is paralleled, in the case of words of greater volume and fuller meaning, by the greater individuality of their component elements, their sounds. The French word is far more intellectualized than ours, it is much more of a mere token; its physical make-up counts for less; it is less onomato-poeic.[31]

The word in French is generally submerged in the sentence and its component sounds are less apparent than in English. Furthermore, French words tend to be more oratorical than English words and have a marked preference for abstract modes of expression. Examples of this quality are: *apple tree, pommier; milkman, laitier; ash tray, cendrier; post no bills, défense d'afficher; no smoking allowed, défense de fumer.* The preference for derivation of words as against composition is also noted as a characteristic of French words.

From the point of view of grapheme-phoneme relations, the French language may appear to an English speaking person to be more regular. However, Bloomfield,[32] in reporting the degree of grapheme-phoneme correspondence in various languages, indicates that English and French are two of the most irregular. Thus, it may seem difficult to understand why most French children are taught to read by the phonetic method.

A closer look at the range of sounds in French and English indicates that there are fewer sounds to learn in French.[33] For example, Laubach,[34] an international authority on the teaching of reading in many languages, has developed a series of phonetic lessons for the purpose of teaching people to read in different languages. For reading French he has prepared a set of eighteen phonetic lessons, but he uses thirty phonetic lessons to teach people to read English. Thus, it can be concluded that the phonetic skills are easier to learn in French than in English.

Further simplifications of the French writing system are found in the sound values of the vowel characters. Diacritical "accent" marks indicate to the reader the sound of the various vowels, thus clarifying their pronunciation.

One of the most striking features of the French intonation system is the lack of phonemic stress. In French, all syllables of a word have equal stress, except at the end of a word where there is a heavier, but nonphonemic, stress. Therefore, it is not possible in French to make a phonemic distinction, as it is in English, between the phrases *thĕ Frénch têachër* and *thĕ Frênch téachĕr*. In French it must be done through the syntax as *le professeur de français* and *le professeur français*.

Morphology is another structural component that is unique in French. Rather than determine the number of a noun by listening or looking for its inflectional morpheme, the student simply listens or looks for the form of the definite article that precedes the noun as in *the boy* and *the boys* in English and *le garçon* and *les garçons* in French. The same applies to the possessive.

Although French orthography is far from phonetic, its forms are more organized and regular than in English. Even though the letter-sound correspondence is low, the spelling follows identifiable standards that can be easily mastered. An illustration of this is seen in the irregularity of English verbs and the orderliness of French verbs.

In learning to read French, the pupil is confronted with the task of mastering the rules of an organized language. This language, although not highly phonetic, is systemized, regular, and consistent. The learner is able to identify the characteristics of the language, memorize its exceptions, make use of word derivations, and place more emphasis on the syntax rather than on individual sounds for better reading comprehension.

Teaching Methods

Discussions of reading methods have frequently resulted in a rivalry between advocates of the phonetic and sight techniques. Numerous studies since 1900 have cited the effectiveness of each method, but generally no definite conclusions can be drawn.

Educators in France have conducted limited research on the effectiveness of phonetic and sight methods. However, Chardon, an inspector of elementary education, reports that all French words cannot be learned by sight methods and that it is difficult to begin to read by mastery of the alphabet. He concludes by stating that "the dispute between phonetic and sight methods is somewhat passé; the important issue is that the child comprehends the words he recognizes." [35] Gal,[36] in addition, comments that, in learning to read, the method of instruction is not as important as the application of the teacher in following a sequential program that meets the needs of children. Simon,[37] in discussing the efficiency of various methods of reading instruction in France, states that few comparative studies have been made and the results have been inconclusive.

France, long noted for its intellectual freedom, has carried this spirit to the teacher in the classroom. Although the Ministry of Education carefully sets down the age for instruction, the time to be allotted, and the teaching materials to be used for the teaching of reading, it does not require elementary teachers to use any particular method. The ministry, in its official instructions for the elementary school reading program states, "We do not recommend any method; the best method will be the one that gives the quickest and the most lasting results." [38]

Despite these unrestricted attitudes toward methods of reading instruction, elementary teachers have adhered to traditional techniques. *The Institut Péda-gogique National* states that "the use of new methods has had a disquieting effect on the partisans of traditional methods who hold them responsible for many reading problems."[39] A review of French research in reading indicates that there has been little innovation in teaching methods.

Jean Simon has conducted research in reading methods and assisted Gray in his study for UNESCO.[40] In his summary of French research in the teaching of reading, he reported three methods currently in use in French elementary schools.

1. The *"synthetic* method" (also called literal, traditional, syllabic, or phonetic).
2. The *"analytic* method" (also called global, whole-word, phrase, or sentence method).
3. The *"mixed* method" (also called analytical-synthetic).[41]

Simon concludes, with some reservations, that fewer than 5 per cent of the elementary teachers in France use the global or analytic method, contrasted with 95 per cent who use the synthetic and mixed methods. The synthetic method seems to be used more than the mixed method, the latter having been used to any significant degree only in the past ten years.[42]

Such adherence to the traditional synthetic method has been noted by Simon and reported in detail by Dottrens and Margairaz.[43] According to the latter source, the persistent use of the synthetic method has been attributed to four causes: (1) insufficient knowledge about the analytic and mixed methods, (2) lack of teaching materials needed for effective use of these methods, (3) failure of teachers to accept the findings of child psychologists in regard to the reading process, and (4) the general passivity of elementary teachers and educational authorities toward change.

These conditions appear to be the result of some inherent factors in French elementary education. As was reported previously, teacher-preparation programs do not offer professional courses in reading; nor are graduate work and research facilities available for elementary school teachers. Similar limitations also restrict the acquisition of knowledge about the findings of child psychology.

Another contributing factor is that most instructional reading materials are written for use with the synthetic method. The Ministry of Education[44] has stated that materials used with the analytical method are "made entirely by the teachers themselves." In addition, Simon has reported that "only textbooks published in the last ten years are devoted to the mixed method."[45]

The conservative adherence to the synthetic method seems to receive some support also from the official regulations for the reading program: "the procedures which appear to be successful are those which interest the child in the difficult task of associating sounds and letters which have no realistic connection. . . . For this reason the phonetic method is successful in spite of its oddness."[46] They go on to claim that the child who follows such a method within the prescribed hours of the reading program will "read within three months and will read fluently by the end of first grade."[47] Such influential advice differs widely from what is suggested in an unofficial statement by the proponents of the analytical and mixed methods. Dottrens and Margairaz have cited that "instructional time for learning to read will vary from four to fifteen months for the child who has a mental age of six years and ten months."[48]

The French synthetic program generally has three parts: (1) the study of the characters representing vowel sounds, (2) the study of the symbols for consonant sounds, and (3) the study of syllables, blends, digraphs, and diphthongs. Symbols for the vowel sounds are taught first; as those for the consonant sounds are learned, they are combined. Later, consonant blends and the representations of diphthongs are learned. This synthetic program is taught before the child has a sight vocabulary and, therefore, meaningful reading is delayed until the child has mastered his "phonetic" skills.

Teaching Materials

Reading instruction in the elementary school can be defined as a developmental program that provides for a systematic acquisition of reading skills. According to Gray's[49] international survey of reading instruction, a basal series of readers is the most commonly used type of material for teaching reading. However, the basal reading series, as it is known in the United States, is nonexistent in France. That is, reading books in France have not been produced as a carefully graded series from the standpoint of skills' development and difficulty. Most authors who have written reading textbooks for use in French schools have produced a single volume rather than a series. Also, it has been noted that many publishers have a number of readers for use at the various elementary grade levels, but each of these books has been written by a different author and there is no attempt to coordinate the writing and skills-development program from one level to another.

Gray has stated that, to be effective, the form of a first grade reader should consist of six or more booklets of about fifty pages each.[50] In France, the first-year developmental program in reading stipulates that the number of books to be used should be two. But no indication is given as to the length of these required texts.[51] Educational publishers' descriptions of their books indicate that they vary from seventy-five to one hundred pages in length. The first book is largely an introduction to the method of reading—either the synthetic or mixed method, usually. Advocates of the analytical or whole-word method prefer to use teacher-prepared materials. The second reader in the first-grade program continues with some attention to method but mostly contains short, simple stories. An especially good English source for additional information about the instructional reader in France is Chiland's study.[52] Her illustrative pages are quite representative of the texts found in the *Institut Pédagogique* library at the Ministry of Education in Paris.

Generally, the literature indicates that the content of readers meets the needs for the particular situation in French schools. Representative titles for first-grade readers such as *Between Friends, René and Mary,* and *Fauvette and his Brothers* appear to follow the interests of children.

Similarly, the official reading program in the second and third grades requires two books be used for a year's work. According to various commercial brochures, each of the readers at this level contains about one hundred and fifty pages and has longer stories. Among the titles at this level are *Victor and Nicole* and *Michel and his Animals,* which contain related stories around a central theme. Another book at this level, *Hurray for Reading!,* includes "a variety of lively stories to make children laugh, think, and dream." [53]

Later, in the fourth and fifth grades, all children are expected to possess the mechanics of fluent reading and word analysis. Consequently, the readers are more literary in form. They have been classified by one source [54] as (1) anthologies that include stories by well-known French writers, (2) a short, book-length children's novel, and (3) a series of connected stories by one author. At this level, three books are required for a year's program in reading. It is further recommended that two books be used concurrently—one for silent reading with a written comprehension check, and the other for the oral reading lesson.

Although stories are written to interest the child, other basic aspects of a developmental reading program are not evident in the typical French reading book. One aspect of developmental reading that has apparently been neglected is vocabulary control. Because of the popularity of the synthetic method, such concepts as basic sight vocabulary, controlled vocabulary, and vocabulary burden are not considered in the reading books. Professional books on reading and related literature make no reference to this aspect of reading instruction. Even French advocates of the whole-word and mixed methods have not discussed vocabulary development in regard to reading books.

Thus, the typical reader used in French schools can be defined as an instructional book with a synthetic phonics approach. Although the format and content of such readers were ostensibly considered by the ministry as appropriate for the various grade levels, they were not written as a series and have little relation to each other in regard to vocabulary development.

Textbooks are generally the basis for instruction and have an important place in French education—which is recognized by the Ministry of Education's annual list of reading books for use in the schools throughout France. [55] Yet, despite this official emphasis on the significance of reading materials, the professional literature and French publishers' commercial advertisements make few detailed references to the research used for the preparation of reading materials. [56] Most of the authors of children's instructional reading books in France appear to be practicing educators, such as classroom teachers, principals, supervisors, and instructors in normal schools. There is, however, no evidence that the authors of such books are reading specialists. Some explanation of this situation can be found in a statement by Jules Ferry, "What matters is not the textbook, but the use the teacher makes of it." [57] More recently, Leandri and Boulay have declared, "to have children read well, the reading book should be complemented by the teacher's use of other instructional material." [58]

Gray's international survey also led him to conclude that usually a basal reading series is accompanied by supplementary teaching devices, such as word games, workbooks, tests, and teachers' guidebooks. Durrell,[59] too, indicates the need in the instructional program for library and reference materials as well as visual aids.

The Teachers' Manual or Guide

Gray's view is that a guide for elementary school readers should include "not only the organization of classes and the materials and methods to use, but also the step-by-step treatment of the lessons. . . . This means that the authors of practically every primer should at the same time furnish a manual or guide for the use of teachers." [60] But, in France, one notes that the professional literature for the reading program makes few references to the teacher's manual. Teachers are expected, however, to use books well and to teach beyond the limits of the reader. Although teachers' manuals are sometimes published in France, they are uncommon; therefore, suggestions for such extending activities are not generally available to the classroom teacher. As a result, the only guidance given to the teacher is a one- or two-page preface, sometimes entitled "Use of Method."

In brief, the publishers of a typical reading book consider the preface as a sufficient teachers' guide for proper instructional use. Some exceptions, however, are to be found where manuals are provided for recent editions that advocate the mixed method.

Reading Workbooks

Instructional materials for a modern reading program, according to Burton,[61] usually include three main types: (1) sequential basal books, (2) teaching guides, which suggest a methodology of instruction and explain how to use the readers and workbooks most effectively, and (3) workbooks, which correlate more or less closely with the various readers.

A survey of French professional reading books reveals little in the way of significant information about workbooks that have been correlated with instructional reading materials. In fact, direct information about workbooks has only been found in materials that have been prepared for use with the mixed method of reading instruction.

However, professional books do refer to *cahiers* (notebooks), which are used for many school activities. These notebooks are included in the official list of school supplies and are considered an integral part of the elementary school reading program. In size, the paperbound notebook measures $7 \times 8\frac{1}{2}$ inches, contains a quire of paper, and is ruled in a quadrille manner. Such ruling consists of vertical and horizontal lines that form very small squares, resembling graph paper. This unique style of ruling has been used as a guide for more precise penmanship.

It has been recommended that children in the first three grades be given at least two notebooks each year. Essentially they have been used for reading, language arts, and arithmetic. In the upper grades, the notebooks have been suggested for use in content areas such as history, geography, and science. One notebook must be kept by the school as part of the child's cumulative record, the other is reserved for homework.[62]

Because language activities in the French elementary school are related to reading instruction, the *cahier* might be considered a kind of reading workbook. Such activities as practice in phonetics, vocabulary, spelling, and handwriting are done in these notebooks, and complemented with pictures and illustrations. Mezeix[63] advocates such enrichment of the reading lesson through the child's own illustrations. Nevertheless, the position remains that the typical French reading program has not used workbooks that have been prepared and correlated by the author of the instructional reading book.

Practice Materials in the Reading Program

In writing about practice materials, Durrell remarks that, "no reading book can provide enough materials to assure every child mastery of each phase of reading instruction. . . . Commercial materials and games . . . may be selected and used to reinforce reading instruction."[64]

The Ministry of Education states that "Auxiliary equipment is left entirely to the teacher. The teaching staff finds Montessori and Decroly materials useful as well as other teaching aids worked out by the primary school inspectors. These aids are often made by the teachers themselves, particularly by those who have been trained in the normal schools where they received an excellent grounding in the principles of modern pedagogy."[65] Chardon,[66] a French educator, states that with patience, time, and serious preparation, most teachers can make and develop original games as well as practice materials for the reading skills. A few sources of information in professional books, such as *Méthode de Lecture* and *Précis de Pédagogie,* have given directions for making practice materials. Although these pronouncements encourage teachers to enrich reading instruction by making these games and devices, they are handicapped in putting them into practice by the fact that the minimal professional training neither includes a course in the teaching of reading nor provides research facilities. This problem has been further compounded by the absence of a sequentially developed series of reading books, the lack of correlated reading workbooks, and the inadequacy of teachers' manuals or guidebooks. Consequently, to a great extent, French elementary school teachers must rely on their own ingenuity to provide practice materials for the reading program.

Reading materials thus far described have been used essentially in the first three elementary grades. In the French educational system, it is considered that the mechanics of reading are acquired during the first three years of elementary school.

Library and Reference Material in the Reading Program

The *cours moyen* is composed of the fourth and fifth grades. Its reading program is oriented to the acquisition of more mature reading interests and skills.

Durrell[67] has written that library and reference materials should be related to the instructional reading program at this level. In these grades, the reading program is reduced to nine hours a week and has been officially described as follows: "Without abandoning the basic subjects of the lower grades, emphasis is placed on the study of the content fields."[68] Such a situation implies the need for improved study and locational skills, as well as wide reading in the content areas; but, again, professional literature has made only limited reference to these needs and does not provide explicit directions for instructional purposes.

Although few specific instructions are given to the teacher for reading lessons in books other than the reader, the official regulations allude to reading in recreational and library books. Required equipment for an elementary classroom now includes a bookcase for library books. At least thirty library books must be placed in each classroom.[69] Commercial publishers list many recreational reading books for children, such as *Golden Books,* picture storybooks, adventure stories, and biographies. The ministry periodically publishes lists of books that can be purchased for the classroom library shelf. Thus, recreational reading books are considered to be a part of the reading program, although no specific directions for their use are given.

Data about informational and reference books have been found principally from commercial sources. One professional book, *Le Matériel Educatif,*[70] has reviewed several of these publications. Many are included on the approved list and apparently can be ordered by teachers,[71] but no official directions are given to teachers for the use of these materials.

Dictionaries also are recommended for use in grades IV and V.[72] But they have not been officially required and have not been placed in all schools. In such a situation, it has been suggested that teachers urge parents to purchase dictionaries for school use.

Reading in the content areas, according to Pointud and Tronchere[73] as well as Lebettre and Vernay,[74] is limited to a single text in the areas of history, geography, and science. No materials appear to have been developed for the teaching of such study skills as reading from multiple sources, the use of the index, outlining, or survey techniques. Similarly materials, machines, or audio-visual aids that would be used to improve reading rate and comprehension are not in evidence. The textbook in the content areas is reserved for the oral reading of each selection, preceded by a discussion of illustrations and followed by an oral question-answer period, a written comprehension check, or the writing of a précis.

In summary, the use of library books, reference materials, and content reading serve a minor role in the reading program in the fourth and fifth grades.

Testing in the Reading Program

Reading tests have been considered materials for the instructional program, but Jean Simon reports that all of the tests have had only a limited success in French educational circles.[75] Officially the Ministry has stated that, "As to procedure in the gauging of the children's capacity to read fluently and to understand what they have read, there are various tests. Silent reading tests are used more and more, as well as others advocated by different teachers. The tests which students of the normal schools learn to use are becoming increasingly popular but are in no way compulsory." [76] France, although a pioneer in educational testing, has not utilized this technique extensively in its reading program.

Reading Failure

In France, the extent of reading problems is reflected in the degree of non-promotion. The basic criterion for promotion is fluency in oral reading. Recently there has been a growing awareness among educators that reading problems do exist and that this condition can be corrected. Such concern is recognized by the Ministry of Education, which has published a study of such problems. A report, *The Study of Pupil Non-promotion,* by Gal[77] describes the extent of reading failure in grades I to V in the elementary school (excluding mentally retarded children who are educated in special classes).

This study reports that, in the first section of the elementary school, grades I to V, 32 per cent of all children had repeated at least one or more years. Twenty per cent had repeated one year, whereas the other 12 per cent had repeated as many as five years; 8.1 per cent were not promoted for two years; 2.4 per cent for three years; 1.1 per cent for four years; and 0.4 per cent were not promoted for five years. Gal noted that such figures were national averages and that some sections of France had an even higher rate of nonpromotion—for example, in Eure, which is an agricultural area, there were 43.4 per cent of the children in fifth grade who had repeated one or more grades during the five years of elementary school.

Gal's report further indicated that 25 per cent of the children were not promoted at the end of first grade. This high percentage of failure in first grade was found to be the result of multiple causes, but they all were related to the teaching of reading. Gal emphatically denies any relationship between teaching method and failure in reading. He implies that teachers who consider the abilities of the children and provide them with adequate materials are successful in teaching children to read.

Gal specifies a number of reasons why 25 per cent of French children fail in first-grade reading, the most important being insufficient preparation given to new teachers. He emphasizes how little time is given to training teachers in the teaching of reading and in the psychology of learning. He expresses the hope that this situation will improve when a broader preparation for teaching can be legislated. Educators themselves, according to Gal, are well aware of the need for a more professional approach to reading instruction, but the critical shortage of teachers has forced the ministry to accept instructors who have not attended normal school. (Legislation allows emergency temporary certificates to relieve the teacher shortage.) [78]

The other reasons put forward for these low achievements in reading in the French schools include the change of teachers during the year, and the children's immaturity. It has been recommended that children should not be taught reading until they attain a mental age of 6 years and 6 months; yet reading readiness and sometimes beginning reading are still considered to belong in the kindergarten. The psychological problems of children and poorly prepared reading materials are also blamed for low achievement.

Gal cites two other sources to support his conclusions. Zazzo[79] found that 10 per cent of first-grade children do not learn to read at all, and that 30 per cent of first-grade children do not learn to read fluently. Promotion to second grade is largely based on reading fluency. The same study also found that 50 per cent of children in eighth grade, the final grade of elementary school, have repeated one or more grades. In a study of reading problems in the secondary school, Perrot[80] reported that many students read poorly and have inadequate vocabularies, yet these students are a part of the top 20 per cent of the population selected for secondary school. In general, they were considered intelligent; they understood the lectures by the instructor, but they had low comprehension scores on material read silently.

Treatment of Reading Failure

Because the policy of nonpromotion has neither prevented nor corrected reading problems, remedial teaching has come forward as a possible solution. A significant development has been the establishment of medico-psycho-pedagogical centers in some of the larger cities. Lobrot[81] reports that these centers were originally created by the medical schools and psychology departments in the universities as well as by private groups such as the Binet and Decroly Associations. However, recently, the services of medico-psycho-pedagogical centers have been offered in conjunction with the public schools.

The major function of such treatment centers is to give help to children with learning problems in general, although their work is done principally in the field of reading difficulties. Most centers are staffed by a medical doctor, a psychologist, a social worker, and a clinician who is also trained as an elementary school teacher. Members of the staff work jointly to discover the learning problems of the child.

Children are referred to these centers by the public schools and with parental approval. Applications are accepted for children between the ages of 7 and 12. However, most children who attend are between 8 and 10 years old because they are selected as being more likely to benefit from corrective instruction. Applications for boys outnumber those for girls. The number of applicants has thus far exceeded the available places at such centers.

Each applicant must undergo a complete examination (including a physical examination) and psychological and achievement tests. A case history is compiled by the social worker. If test results indicate that treatment is likely to succeed, the child will be admitted to the center. Atypical children are not accepted by the center because they are cared for in special education classes.

A corrective program is not initiated until the parents and the school principal have been interviewed. In this way the work of the center is explained to them and the cooperation of home and school is enlisted. After that, periodic meetings are held with the parents and principal throughout the school year.

Children in the corrective program receive two lessons a week of thirty minutes each. At all other times they attend school in their regular classroom situations. The individual private lessons are given by the psychologist or the clinician, sometimes by both. If the child is a nonreader, he is given a kinesthetic type of program. Teaching is directed to reeducate the child in spatial relationships and in auditory and visual perception, as well as to provide training in writing. For the child with some reading ability, the mixed method of reading instruction is generally used. This, however, is varied to the pure global or synthetic method whenever it seems expedient. Corrective work is continued until the child reaches grade-level achievement. Most of the reading problems referred to these centers seem to involve emotional maladjustment of the child and problems in the school situation—for example, overcrowding of classrooms. In the Paris area, fifty pupils are often assigned to one room. Under such conditions the teacher must find it difficult to provide for individual differences in his class.

REFERENCES

1. Gal, Roger, *Histoire de L'Education,* Paris: Presses Universitaires de France, 1961, p. 90.
2. *Ibid.,* p. 100.
3. Kandel, I. L., *Essays in Comparative Education,* New York: Bureau of Publications, Teachers College, Columbia University, 1930, p. 98.
4. Kandel, I. L., *French Elementary Schools,* New York: Bureau of Publications, Teachers College, Columbia University, 1926, p. 7.
5. Cultural Service of the French Embassy, *Education in France,* No. 16. New York: French Embassy, January 1962, p. 13.
6. Gray, William S., *The Teaching of Reading and Writing,* Chicago; Scott, 1956, pp. 112–124.
7. Pointud, J., and Tronchere, J., *Précis de Pédagogie: Ecoles Primaires,* Paris: Editions Bourrelier, 1960, p. 78.
8. King, Edmund J., *Other Schools and Ours,* New York: Rinehart, 1958, p. 37.
9. Cultural Service of the French Embassy, *Education in France,* No. 13. New York: French Embassy, March 1961, p. 27.
10. King, *op. cit.,* p. 37.
11. *Education in France,* No. 13, *op. cit.,* p. 37.
12. *Ibid.,* p. 41.
13. Chanson, M., and Olanie, S., *Lecture Globale–Lecture Active,* Paris: Librairie Centrale d'Education Nouvelle, 1949, p. 37.
14. *Ibid.,* pp. 68–72.
15. Gray, *op. cit.,* pp. 114–115.
16. Lebettre, M., and Vernay, L., *Programmes et Instruction Commentés—Enseignement du Premier Degré,* Paris: Editions Bourrelier, 1956, p. 9.
17. *Ibid.,* p. 63.

18. *Ibid.*, pp. 68–71.
19. *Ibid.*, p. 21.
20. *Ibid.*, p. 48.
21. *Ibid.*, p. 62.
22. *Ibid.*, p. 67.
23. *Ibid.*, p. 9.
24. Gray, *op. cit.*, p. 113.
25. Debiesse, Jean, *Compulsory Education in France,* Paris: UNESCO, 1950, pp. 123–125.
26. *Education in France,* No. 13, *op. cit.*, p. 20.
27. Charlier, Patricia S., *Contemporary Teacher Education in France and Belgium,* Doctoral dissertation, University of Minnesota, Minneapolis, Minn., 1960. p. 98.
28. Samuels, S. J., "Cross-national studies in reading: The relationship between the sound-letter correspondence in language and reading," in Figurel, J. Allen (ed.), *Reading and Realism,* Newark, Del.: IRA, 1969, pp. 846–853.
29. Ewert, Alfred, *The French Language,* London: Faber, 1943, pp. 18–19.
30. Valdman, A., *et al.*, *A Drillbook of French Pronunciation,* New York: Harper, 1964, p. viii.
31. Orr, John, *Words and Sound in English and French,* Oxford: Basil Blackwell, 1953, p. 59.
32. Bloomfield, Leonard, "Linguistics and reading," *Elementary English Review,* **19** (1942), 125–130.
33. Mansion, J. E., *Mansion's Shorter French and English Dictionary,* Boston: Heath, 1940, Part 1, p. vi and Part 2, p. iv.
34. Laubach, Frank C., *Teaching the World to Read,* London: United Society for Christian Literature, 1948, p. 21.
35. Chardon, P., Defond, M., and Durand, P., *Le Cours Préparatoire,* Paris: Editions Bourrelier, 1960, p. 36.
36. Gal, Roger, *Une Enquête sur les Retards Scolaires,* Paris: L'Institut Pédagogique National, 1958, p. 14.
37. Simon, Jean, "French research in the teaching of reading and writing," *Journal of Educational Research,* **50** (February 1957), 443–459.
38. Lebettre and Vernay, *op. cit.*, p. 49.
39. Cultural Service of the French Embassy, *Education in France,* No. 7. New York: French Embassy, September 1959, p. 10.
40. Gray, *op. cit.*, Preface.
41. Simon, *op. cit.*, p. 447.
42. *Ibid.*, p. 448.
43. Dottrens, R., and Margairaz, E., *L'Apprentissage de la Lecture par la Méthode Globale,* Paris: Delachaux et Niestle, 1951, p. 2.
44. *International Education Year Book,* Geneva: International Bureau of Education, 1959, p. 88.
45. Simon, *op. cit.*, p. 448.
46. Lebettre, and Vernay, *op. cit.*, p. 50.
47. *Ibid.*, p. 50.
48. Dottrens and Margairaz, *op. cit.*, p. 81.
49. Gray, *op. cit.*, p. 89.
50. *Ibid.*, p. 130.
51. Pointud and Tronchere, *op. cit.*, p. 22.

52. Chiland Colette, "The teaching of reading in France," in Downing, John, and Brown, Amy (eds.), *The Second International Reading Symposium,* London: Cassell, 1967, pp. 35–70.

53. Helier-Malaurie, M., *Vive La Lecture!* Paris: Editions Albin Michel, 1947, p. 5.

54. Pointud and Tronchere, *op. cit.,* p. 191.

55. *Education in France,* No. 7, *op. cit.,* p. 7.

56. Simon, Jean, *Introduction et Rapports Analytique sur des Manuels,* unpublished and undated manuscript at UNESCO Educational Clearing House, pp. 1–12.

57. *Manuals for Primary Education,* Geneva: International Bureau of Education, 1959, p. 114.

58. Leandri, F., and Boulay, L., *Le Matériel Educatif,* Paris: Editions Bourrelier, 1957, p. 121.

59. Durrell, Donald D., *Improving Reading Instruction,* New York: World Book, 1956, pp. 35 and 187.

60. Gray, *op. cit.,* p. 262.

61. Burton, William H., *Reading in Child Development,* New York: Bobbs, 1956, p. 528.

62. Pointud and Tronchere, *op. cit.,* p. 22.

63. Mezeix, P., *et al., Méthodes de Lecture,* Paris: Editions Bourrelier, 1958, p. 42.

64. Durrell, *op. cit.,* p. 29.

65. *The Teaching of Reading,* 12th International Conference on Public Education, convened by UNESCO and the International Bureau of Education, Geneva: International Bureau of Education, 1949, p. 88.

66. Chardon, *et al., op. cit.,* p. 46.

67. Durrell, *op. cit.,* p. 35.

68. Lebettre and Vernay, *op. cit.,* p. 21.

69. *Ibid.,* p. 31.

70. Leandri and Boulay, *op. cit.,* pp. 104–109.

71. Mayer, A., and Guillemoteau, T., *Précis de Législation,* Paris: Editions Bourrelier, 1960, p. 107 ff.

72. Pointud and Tronchere, *op. cit.,* p. 22.

73. *Ibid.,* pp. 113–117.

74. Lebettre and Vernay, *op. cit.,* pp. 161–168.

75. Simon, "French research in the teaching of reading," *op. cit.,* pp. 445–446.

76. *International Education Yearbook, op. cit.,* p. 88.

77. Gal, *Une Enquête sur les Retards Scolaires, op. cit.,* pp. 3–7.

78. *Education in France,* No. 13, *op. cit.,* p. 8.

79. Zazzo, René, "*Conclusion de notre enquête sur l'apprentissage de la lecture,*" *L'Ecole et la Nation,* **60** (July 1959), 7–8.

80. Perrot, Colette, "*Difficultés de lecture en sixième et cinquième,*" *Cahiers Pédagogiques,* **13** (March 1958), 32–33.

81. Lobrot, Michel G., "Remedial education in France," in Brown, Amy L. (ed.), *Reading: Current Research and Practice,* Edinburgh: Chambers, 1967, pp. 112–117.

CHAPTER 16

Germany

FRANZ BIGLMAIER

The German Language

Within the Germanic group the two most frequently spoken languages are English and German. They have several morphological, lexical, and phonological features in common. For instance, they have similar vocabularies, for example:

> *English:* father, mother, son, uncle
> *German: Vater, Mutter, Sohn, Onkel*
> *English:* water, drink, two, six, ten, we, she
> *German: Wasser, trinken, zwei, sechs, zehn, wir, sie*

Grammatical forms may seem more complicated to a foreign student learning German—for example, differences in gender and case—but, on the other hand, spelling in modern German is much less difficult to learn than that skill is in British or American English.

More specifically, in relation to learning to read the language, the grapheme-phoneme relations in German are rather regular in comparison with English. For example, Block[1] found that the number of graphemes used to represent the phonemes of German was smaller than the number of English graphemes employed for writing its phonemes. Meier[2] noted that the number of German graphemes was even fewer if only the most common words were included in the analysis.

Preston, in his study comparing the reading attainments of German and American pupils, concluded that "the German language is more consistent phonetically than the English language," and that this difference "may account for the superiority of German children in learning to read."[3]

However, despite this commonly held view there is some debate in Germany about the possibility of further minimizing difficulties by simplifying German orthography. For example, in German all nouns begin with capital letters, whereas in English capitals are used only for certain names. It is being proposed currently that the capitalization of nouns in German should be reduced. Some teachers and laymen believe that a reform of the German writing system in this *and other ways* would be helpful in reducing the incidence of failure in learning to spell, but others oppose this view.

Political, Historical, Sociological, and Economic Factors

The unity of the German people is one of culture and language, not of race. For example, two thousand years ago in pre-Roman and Roman times German tribes mixed with Celtic ones. Also, many present-day cities of southern and western Germany were founded by the Romans, who brought their culture to the occupied territory.

The Holy Roman Empire of the German Nation was founded in A.D. 961 by Otto I, a Saxon ruler, and lasted, despite the many religious wars of the middle ages, until Napoleon conquered Germany. Renewed unity came from Bismarck's foundation of the Second Reich (1871–1918) and Hitler's short-lived Third Reich (1933–1945).

The defeat of the Third Reich in 1945 led to the division of Germany into four zones occupied by Britain, France, the United States, and the USSR, respectively. Berlin, the former German capital city was treated separately. It was situated within the zone of occupation of the USSR, but the city itself was divided into four sectors; American, British, French, and Russian. Although this situation lasted only about three years in its original design, Germany remains divided by the lines drawn on the map that separated the USSR's military-occupied zone of Germany and the corresponding sector of Berlin from those zones and sectors militarily occupied by the American, British, and French forces. The present division of Germany into what is commonly known as "West Germany" and "East Germany" stems from the creation of the "BRD" in 1948 and the "DDR" in 1949.

The BRD is the *Bundesrepublik Deutschland* (Federal Republic of Germany) in the West plus the former American, British, and French sectors of Berlin. The DDR is the *Deutsche Demokratische Republik* (German Democratic Republic) in the East encompassing also the former Russian sector of Berlin. The BRD is a federation of the states of Baden-Württemberg, Bavaria, Bremen, Hamburg, Hessen, Lower Saxony, North Rhine-Westphalia, Rhineland-Palatinate, Saar, and Schleswig-Holstein. The population and economy of the two territories are quite different. West Germany has fifty-four million inhabitants, East Germany only seventeen million. The population density per square mile is considerably greater in West Germany. The West is also more highly industrialized and urbanized.

Present-day Germany has recovered from two world wars. West Germany "leads the economy of Western Europe and is a strong partner in the Common Market and in NATO, East Germany is emerging as the kingpin of the satellite nations of Eastern Europe. Both use economic strength to work political changes which, in turn, provide a lever for beneficial economic negotiations"[4] as a recent American visitor to both parts of Germany commented.

The School System[5]

In the late middle ages German schools, like schools in other European states, developed out of church institutions. The educated class was small until the seventeenth and eighteenth centuries when the principle of compulsory education was gradually introduced (1619 in Weimar). The supervision of the elementary schools (*Volksschulen*) was generally carried out by church authorities until 1919. After the First World War the subject of general educational reform was widely discussed. A general four-class primary school (*Grundschule*) for all children was introduced. Obligatory school attendance was for at least seven years in the *Volksschule,* plus two or three years part time in a vocational school. Vocational education, which is widely differentiated and has a long tradition (Germany was the first country to make attendance at a vocational school obligatory for all young workers and apprentices in her constitution of 1919), is closely coordinated with general education. The tripartite structure of general education (*Volksschule, Mittelschule, Höhere Schule*) of the nineteenth century was maintained after the First World War and still determines the West German school organization.

Schultze and Führ consider that German education suffered a setback under Hitler's National Socialist regime. They state that

> Under National Socialist rule schools and universities suffered a decline, the consequences of which are still to be felt. Drastic measures were taken with regard to the training of teachers. The *Pädagogische Hochschulen* (Teacher Training Colleges) were dissolved. High school education was shortened by a year; the number of university students sharply reduced. The further development of university education came to a standstill. Many professors from the universities, technical colleges and research institutes were forced to emigrate.[6]

Certainly the last war and its aftermath had chaotic consequences for the schools at that time. When the war ended, in 1945, German public education had come to a complete standstill; schools had been closed or destroyed, and normal instruction had been disrupted. Only a few qualified teachers were available who had not belonged to the now outlawed National Socialist organizations. Lack of classrooms and equipment of every kind hindered the reconstruction of the German school system. Hundreds of thousands of school children had been evacuated from cities to rural areas during the war or had been uprooted with their parents as refugees.

When the German Federal Republic was founded in 1949, the Constitution or Basic Law (*Grundgesetz*) contained only one short article (Art. 7) on education regulating a few fundamental questions: State inspections of schools, religious instruction as a subject of the syllabus in State schools, and the right to private education. The responsibility for schools was placed with the individual eleven *Länder* (states) of the Federal Republic. Each *Land* is autonomous in this respect and has its own constitution and its own Ministry of Education. This favored the development of divergent educational practices and regulations. The constitutional law and the decrees of the respective *Land* determine the aim of education, enforce school attendance, provide for the building and maintenance of schools, the training and inservice training of teachers, school inspection, administration and supervision, and the cooperation of parents in the life and work of the school. In order to overcome the hardships that might arise from differences in standards (especially for children whose families must move from one school district to another) duration of obligatory full-time school attendance, unequal requirements for admission to institutions of higher learning, and so on, the Ministers of Education of the different states of the Republic formed the "Permanent Conference of Ministers of Education for the *Länder*" (*Ständige Konferenz der Kultusminister der Länder*). Through agreements, resolutions, and recommendations at this conference of ministers, a uniform system for German education is sought. The agreements are referred to the separate state authorities or legislatures for adoption or are put into effect by decree, if no legislative action is required. As a rule, the state legislature adopts such suggestions.

The revised version of the agreement of October 1964, among the *Länder* of the Federal Republic, on the standardization of education (the so-called Hamburg Agreement) states that (1) the school year begins for all schools on August 1st; (2) compulsory education begins for all children at the age of 6; (3) compulsory full-time education ends after nine school years, but an extension to a tenth school year is permissible; (4) the duration of school vacations is 75 working days, with summer vacations fixed in the period between July 1 and September 10 (the different *Länder* start at different days to avoid traffic congestion); (5) other holidays occur at Easter and Christmas, and short holiday periods can be fixed at Whitsun and in the autumn; and that (6) all classes are to be numbered consecutively from class I (first year of elementary school) to class XIII (last year at the gymnasium).

The terminology of school types in general education is standardized as follows. The junior division, attended in common by all pupils, is known as "*Grundschule*" (elementary school). The types of school continuing education beyond the *Grundschule* level are known as "*Hauptschule*" (main school, up to class IX), "*Realschule*" (secondary general school, shorter course, up to class X) or "*Gymnasium*" (secondary general school giving access to higher education, up to class XIII). *Grundschule* and *Hauptschule* are also referred to as *Volksschule*. Schools for physically, psychologically, or mentally handicapped children or young people are known as *Sonderschulen* (special schools).

Compulsory education in Germany extends from the age of 6 to the age of 18. *Full-time* compulsory schooling lasts nine years. After this, all pupils who cease full-time attendance in a secondary school must attend a *part-time* vocational school, "*Berufsschule,*" one day a week for three years. The vast majority of young people gets this training simultaneously at their paid employment and in a vocational school. Apprentices must attend the vocational school until the completion of their apprenticeship, irrespective of their age. The emphasis in vocational training is on specialization in the knowledge and skills necessary to carry out the young worker's particular type of work efficiently. The vocational school improves on the skill and knowledge gained on the job in the place of employment and gives insight into fundamental principles. At the same time, instruction in general academic subjects such as the German language and social studies is continued. The final examinations are set and judged by industrial administrative bodies (boards of industry and commerce, boards of handicraft) in collaboration with the vocational school. The leaving certificate is the "*Gesellenbrief*" for trades, the" *Facharbeiterbrief*" for industrial specialists, or the "*Kaufmannsgehilfenbrief*" for business. The "*Berufsaufbauschule*" (promotion type of vocational school) acts as a bridge between general academic education and vocational education. There are also special vocational schools (*Berufsfachschulen*), commercial schools and higher commercial schools, trade technical schools (*gewerbliche Berufsfachschulen*), technical schools (*Fachschulen*), advanced technical schools (*Höhere Fachschulen*), and schools of engineering with entrance to the universities. Through these alternative educational routes (*Zweiter Bildungsweg*) to college and university, going to *Hauptschule* and then on to the vocational schools is not necessarily a blind alley, but can lead to institutions of higher education.

In general, children attend school only in the morning, from Monday till Saturday inclusive. The number of schools with only a five-day week—looked on as an experiment—is still limited, although it is steadily increasing. Newly developing experimental comprehensive schools (*Gesamtschulen*) are full-day schools—from 8 A.M. to 4 P.M., five days a week. The number of lesson periods in the weekly timetable depends on the age of the pupils. School beginners start with about eighteen periods, and this number increases gradually up to thirty-four to thirty-six periods a week. A period lasts usually forty-five minutes. In many schools two periods are merged to form "*Blockstunden*" (double periods) of eighty to ninety minutes. Between lessons, there is always a short interval; once during the morning is the long break (*grosse Pause*). In a morning of five periods, the intervals add up to about forty minutes.

Coeducation is provided by school laws in the three city states of Berlin, Bremen, and Hamburg; it is also usual in most schools in rural districts because of the smaller number of pupils. But in schools with larger numbers—more particularly *Realschulen* and *Gymnasien*—boys and girls are usually taught separately.

The size of classes and the pupil-teacher ratio within the different general schools varies greatly, as the figures for the German Federal Republic show for 1964: *Volksschule* 38 pupils per teacher; *Realschule* 27; *Gymnasium* 20. Since 1950, the size of classes has been steadily decreasing, but there is a large discrepancy between elementary education and secondary education.[7]

There is also a difference in the numbers of hours a teacher is expected to teach in different types of schools. For most of the *Länder* the following figures apply. The percentage of all full-time teachers, allocated to different types of schools and the number and percentage of pupils attending different types of schools in 1964 for West Germany are provided in the following table.[8]

As the table shows, more than half of the school population are attending *Volksschulen* or vocational schools. The numbers of pupils attending *Realschulen* and *Gymnasien* vary from one *Land* to the other and also within one and the same *Land* according to the varying socioeconomic and geographical structures

Schools	Teaching load hours per week	Percent of all full-time teachers	Pupils in 1,000	Per cent
Volksschulen (grades I–IX)	29–30	52.4⎱	8,067	36
Special Schools (III–IX)	27–28	3.2⎰		
Realschulen (V–X)	27–28	12.9	5,470	24.5
Gymnasien (XI–XIII)	24–25	16.4	2,786	12.5
Vocational schools (X–XII part-time and full-time students)	24–28	15.1	5,950	27

of the different areas. Centralized schools are founded in rural areas; the development of comprehensive schools (*Gesamtschulen*) is spreading from cities (such as West Berlin) to rural and industrial areas in North Rhine-Westphalia Hessia and other *Länder*. In 1969, the *Deutsche Bildungsrat* (German Council of Education)[9] recommended *Gesamtschulen* as a scientific school for all, as a school for individualizing learning, for better opportunities for the under-privileged, and as a place for social experiences. *Gesamtschulen* might also be an answer to the challenge of the unified school system (*Einheitsschule*) of East Germany. It is a truth that in the DDR more students of industrial and agricultural workers are studying at universities and colleges (54 per cent) than in West Germany, including West Berlin (only 7 per cent according to an East German source).[10]

In comparison with American schools, for example, the German education system seems to be more specialized at the lower levels. For instance, in the fourth grade, students may already be set on a college-bound course. A much-debated question in Germany today is, "Is this differentiation at such an early age (10 years old) the best way of advancing education?"

Age of Commencing Learning to Read

Preschool education exists on a voluntary basis. Children between the ages of 3 and 6 may attend a kindergarten that is run either by a city or by a church or private organization, but nearly all kindergartens are equipped and financed with public funds. About one third of all children attend kindergarten. In new building areas and rural areas there is a shortage of kindergartens and *kinder-krippen* (nursery schools for children younger than 3 years). So-called school kindergartens have been set up for children of school age who are not considered ready for school.

Preschool instruction in the three Rs (reading, writing, and arithmetic) was not given in a kindergarten or school kindergarten until the last few years, following a great public debate on the early intellectual training of children. (Doman's book *Teach Your Baby to Read* had been translated.) According to the promoters of early preschool learning, the teaching of reading and other language skills should enhance intellectual development. Several experiments on early reading in different parts of Germany were conducted, but the results are inconclusive. From the scientific point of view there is no agreement in these experiments as to what is meant by "reading." Has a youngster mastered the skill of reading when he is able to recognize some dozens of words or identify a car by the first letter of its license plate? Another question that has been raised is whether young children who are trained by eager parents or educators in reading and other skills may be endangered in their emotional development. It is considered that more research and practical work must be done in order to substantially help young children in their intellectual, emotional, and social development.

Until two or three years ago public opinion did not favor too early a start in school, but the new trend is more flexible. Schools that used to admit only children aged 6 years and older are now becoming less rigid in this respect. A combination of kindergarten and first grade is developing in Berlin, Hessia, and some other states. It is called preschool (*Vorschule*). West Berlin has already adopted the first institutionalized preclasses (*Vorklassen*) on a voluntary basis. Most 5-year-olds in West Berlin, for example, now have some kind of preschool education:

Over 20 per cent are in *Vorklassen* (the percentage is likely to increase annually).
About 30 to 40 per cent have *Spielgruppenbetreuung* (play-group activity for twelve weeks in schools prior to grade I).
About 10 per cent attend *Miniklubs* (several hours per week to play with other children).
About 24 per cent attend *Vermittlungsgruppen* (special groups of children in kindergarten preparing for school entrance).[11]

The curriculum of the *Vorklassen* includes, among seven specified learning areas, listening and speaking as language skills in a very detailed manner and as a prerequisite for more complex language skills. Reading and writing are taught in first grade but not in *Vorklassen*.[12]

All children must come to school not later than the age of 6 years. They are examined then to determine if they are ready for school. School readiness tests are administered (there are about ten different school-readiness tests available in German speaking countries); the children are observed in the classroom; and the school doctor examines their physical condition. Children who are considered not ready for school are sent to a school kindergarten or back to their families. The thesis underlying this procedure that one only has to wait until a child is ready for school is no longer generally accepted. The modern view is that waiting without specific training does not necessarily enhance school readiness. Schools should change to fit the children, not the reverse. School-readiness tests should not be an instrument of selection, but should become an aid for diagnosing learning difficulties as the starting point for individualized instruction at the very beginning of school.

Teaching Methods and Materials

In the mid–1960s one could read headlines in German newspapers and magazines such as the following:

Stupid Children or Stupid Methods?
The Downgraded Global Method.
The Thalidomide Case of Education.
Attack Against Global Method.

The public quarrel about methods of teaching reading had—beside unqualified statements and poor propaganda—some good consequences. Public opinion was aroused, laymen and professionals looked on reading as a worthwhile topic for discussion, parents were eager to ask teachers about their methods, and publishing companies were stimulated to improve teaching materials.

In a review of reading primers in German speaking countries (including Austria and Switzerland) L. Reinhard [13] found that, out of seventy-eight primers that were published between 1945 and 1961, more than half used analytic methods. The following table shows the distribution of alternative teaching methods and different written media. "*Sprechspur*" is a kind of shorthand, in which the movements of the writing hand correspond in detail to the inflexions of the voice.

	Methods					
	(A) Analytic		(B) Synthetic		(C) Both methods	
Media	Whole sentence	Whole word	Big letters only	Big and small letters	A and B combined	Total
Print	13	11	20	2	1	47
Script	16	1		12	1	30
Sprechspur	1					1
Total	30	12	20	14	2	78

Some of these primers, by now, have faded into disuse. In 1964, there were about sixty-one primers available, according to Hasler and Schwartz [14]—74 per cent using a global or analytic approach, 10 per cent using a synthetic one, and 16 per cent using mixed forms.

The situation in the different *Länder* of West Germany and in East Germany is very variable. In Bavaria only primers with analytic approaches are recognized, about seven different primers being available; in most of the other *Länder* the teacher may choose among methods and basal readers; and in East Germany there is only one primer with an analytic-synthetic approach permitted officially.

The phonic or synthetic approaches begin with one or two sounds and quite rapidly develop into the reading of whole words. For instance, a new Austrian primer starts with *Mama* and other names and words (*Mimi, Mia, am, im*), which can be made with a few letters (*m, a, i*).[15] Another synthetic primer, *Berliner Fibel,* introduces the first sentence as early as page 7. On the other hand, global methods, which begin with a short story in which the unit of sentence or word is emphasized, nevertheless direct the pupils' attention very early—after some two to eight weeks—to details of words, such as syllables and letters and their sounds. Letters and sounds are analyzed and used to build new words and to form varied or new stories. For example, Reinhard's *Im Wundergarten* is an exponent of global or analytic methods with a clear-cut theory behind it.[16] It distinguishes three main periods or stages:

Stage I: Preanalytic stage or primitive global reading.
Stage II: Analytic stage.
Stage III: Synthetic stage.

During stage I the children learn, for example, a four-line poem:

> *Drei Rosen im Garten*
> *drei Tannen im Wald*
> *im Sommer ists lustig*
> *im Winter ists kalt.*

The child is directed to discriminate the four lines as sentences and the four most important words: *Rosen, Garten, Tannen,* and *Wald.* The text is broken down into sentences and words. The words are learned and used in new sentences ("variation texts"). During this and the next stage, about eighty different words are learned. At the end of this preanalytic stage, children begin to recognize similarities of parts of words and notice the same letters, especially at the beginning of words.

Stage II begins with "optic analysis" (recognizing similarities in words). This will be continued until all the letters of the alphabet except the rarer ones (*x, y, q,* and so on) have been analyzed. In due course, "acoustic analysis" (auditory discrimination) will be introduced so that at the end of this stage children know the common letters and their phonic equivalents. From the very beginning, and in the ensuing grades, children are taught to speak and pronounce as clearly as possible and not in dialect. In this way, a certain degree of conformity between written and spoken words is reached. Many techniques and procedures help to achieve this (rhymes, riddles, jingles, and word families). The learning of the sight words of stage I is still continued, but with less emphasis. A broad variety of words for every letter to be analyzed is needed for this analytic process.

Stage III begins with "tricks" (*Zaubern*). A word is changed to another word by substituting one letter only: for example, *big–bug, Haus–Hans–Hand–Wand–Sand.* Or a word is broken down into its elements, the letters, and built up again.

Rhyming words have more elements in common and, therefore, the common feature is more easily recognized: *H-and, W-and, S-and, L-and*. Also, the coordination of syllables to form new words in a meaningful situation and the coordination of similar words that differ only in one or two letters to meaningful sentences are used. But this stage of "synthesis" within the global method is different from the synthesis within "the synthetic method." The global method always stresses the point of a meaningful situation. There is no drill on isolated letters and letter combinations. Letters are for the child as they really are—meaning-free elements of writing. They know the function of these elements and are now able to use them in new combinations. New words are introduced in the context of mostly well-known words. Later, children read simple texts with more new words in them; finally they are able to read completely new texts with still fewer known sight words. This goal in learning to read can be reached within the first two years, by all normal children, for the German language. In general, it is reached to a certain degree within the first grade.

It should be noted that the three stages of this theoretical approach are not considered as discrete but rather as overlapping, thus:

analytic stage

1. 2. 3. 4. 5. 6. 7. 8. 9. 10.

preanalytic   synthetic stage

A new approach tested by this writer in 1970–1971 and published in 1972 is a "consequent analytic-synthetic approach" that includes programmed materials. Beginning with a story, the sentences, phrases, and words of the story are analyzed. Out of certain basic words, letters and sounds are analyzed and used to form new words. This combination of new words with already-known words forms the basis for varied or new stories. The cycle from story–sentence–phrase–word–syllable–letter sound (analytic part) and back to new words–phrases–sentences–story (synthetic part) is repeated within every unit. A unit may last one to three weeks. Each of the twenty to twenty-five exercises (*Programmierte Übungen*) of a unit is programmed in such a way that the exact objective (*Lernziel*) is stated and directions for the specified task are given. Every single item can be checked by the pupil immediately by a BAS-punch-board (BAS = *Biglmaier-Antwort-Schablone*). At the end of each unit there are tests for the objectives of that particular unit and for that unit together with those of the preceding units. The use of tape-recorders or records is planned as well as—for a later period—typewriters, as additional media to assist in the complex language-learning approach (listening, speaking–reading, writing).

Provisions for Reading Failure

Ranschburg (1916) called the specific difficulty of German children who could not learn reading within the first school years but who, nevertheless, had normal senses "*Legasthenie*" or "weakness in reading."[17] The term *Legasthenie* was redefined, in 1951, by Maria Linder,[18] as the special weakness in learning to read and (indirectly) in spelling found in children of comparatively good intelligence. The term *Legasthenie* as used in Linder's definition is now widely accepted in middle Europe. It is also called *Lese-Rechtschreib-Schwäche* (LRS), as Kirchhoff[19] named it (reading-spelling-difficulties). There are many other terms used by different people, some of them now outdated—for example, *Alexie, Dyslexie, kongenitale Wortblindheit, angeborene Legasthenie, Bradylexie,* and *Schreib-Lese-Schwäche.*

Biglmaier[20] standardized the first German oral reading test and it was published in 1960. It includes three tests: *Leseabschnitte* (oral reading paragraphs, like Gray's), *Worttest* (seventy-five single words), and *Wort-Unterscheidungs-Test* (word-discrimination test). The latter test consists of forty-eight groups of words in which the student must select the right word spoken to him among seven words in each group. Norms for each test up to grade V and for each error (omissions, additions, consonant errors) are given and tabulated on an error profile similar to Marion Monroe's procedures.[21]

Standardized tests of reading comprehension are available for German speaking children in grade II: "*Lesetest für 2. Klassen,* LT2" (Samtleben, Biglmaier, Ingenkamp); in grade III: "*Sinnverstehendes Lesen* SVL 3" (Heinrich Müller); and in grades V to VI and VII to IX: "*Verständiges Lesen* VL 5–6, VL 7–9" (Anger, Bargmann, Voigt). Standardized spelling tests have also been developed during the past decade in Germany for grades II and III: "*Diagnostischer Rechtschreibtest* DRT 2 and DRT 3" (Rudolf Müller); for grade IV and higher: "*Rechtschreibtest* RST 4+" (Hylla, Süllwold, Wicht); and for grade VIII and higher: "*Rechtschreibtest* RST 8+" (Damm, Hylla, Schäfer).[22]

Biglmaier has suggested a classification of types of errors in reading and spelling that could be used also for international comparisons.

1. *Quantity.* Fewer or more phonemes or graphemes than the test word.
2. *Quality.* Additions and omissions of other phonemes or graphemes.
3. *Succession.* Errors in the order of letters, for example, reversals.
4. *Capitalization.* Beginning letter incorrectly large or small.
5. *Word articulation.* Incorrect dividing of a word, contractions.
6. *Sentence articulation.* Punctuation omitted, added, or incorrect.[23]

For a finer analysis, one can look for the location of an error—for example, if it is at the beginning, middle, or end of a word. A differentiation of the main error categories can show what letters or combinations of letters are most confused or what phonetic or spelling rules have been missed.

Lotte Schenk-Danziger has written several articles and a handbook on *Legasthenie*[24] based on her theory that typical legasthenic children show reversals (*Reversionen, Inversionen*) that are symptoms of "*Raumlagelabilität*" (space-positional instability) and are weak in acoustic differentiation. Investigations in error profiles show, however, that reversals are only one category within others that are more important (omissions and consonant errors) according to Tordrup, Biglmaier, Valtin, and others.[25]

The treatment of children having difficulties in reading and spelling is provided usually either in schools by special grouping and special lessons within the class or school (*Förderunterricht*) or for several schools in a special reading class. Special reading classes have been set up in the larger German cities, including Hamburg, Berlin, Stuttgart, Cologne, and Dortmund. Cologne also has a special school for children with reading and spelling disabilities.

Reading clinics have been established by Biglmaier in Munich and Berlin. L. Schmidt[26] had a reading clinic in Aurich for three years; she developed material for dyslexic children. Berlin now has the first reading clinic in Germany with full-time personnel. There, new methods of diagnosing children's difficulties (by individual and group tests) and programmed materials are being developed.

Teachers of elementary and special schools show the greatest interest in reading problems. Only a small group of teachers in secondary schools is aware of the fact that children might fail in school subjects such as foreign languages because of *Legasthenie,* despite their good intellectual capacities. However, generally, in Germany, reading is not considered to be a serious problem. Most of the low-ability children in special schools (*Hilfsschulen*) master this skill. Even in the decades following each of the two World Wars, the rate of illiteracy in Germany remained below 1 per cent of the population. Some would attribute this success to the excellence of the German school system. Spelling is more of a problem and arouses greater interest among teachers and the public.

Reading Research in Germany

As Gray[27] pointed out, today's knowledge of the psychological processes of reading is based on the pioneering studies made in France and in Germany. In the latter country, in the middle of the last century, Helmholtz (1821–1894) constructed an apparatus that enabled research workers to determine experimentally the conditions of visual recognition. Valentine,[28] in his 1844 textbook of physiology, remarked that the individual is able to fixate several letters at the same time. This might be considered the starting point of the as yet controversial issue of whether the reading process is successive or simultaneous in nature. Grashey[29] (1839–1911) maintained, on his authority as a psychiatrist concerned with aphasia, that the letters successively pass the macula lutea, or yellow spot of the eye, and successively provoke relevant sounds. But, at the psychological school of Wundt, in Leipzig, in 1885, Cattell[30] experimentally found, contrary to Grashey's theory, a large difference in the number of letters recognized in a single short exposure between nonsense material (only four to five letters) and meaningful words (twelve to fifteen letters). This result was confirmed by Erdmann and Dodge, in 1898, when they published their *Psychological Studies in Reading Based on Experiments.*[31] It was the first extensive research on eye movements, reading span, reading of meaningful and meaningless letter groups, and recognition, and it led to their theory of "*Gesamtform.*" These findings, according to Anderson and Dearborn,[32] delivered a damaging blow to the alphabetic method and gave support to the movement already under way to revolutionize methods of teaching reading.

At the turn of the century, in 1900, Zeitler[33] found that dominant letters (high and low letters and capitals) are recognized more correctly than others, and that the tachistoscopic span is increased if a consonant group has vowels in it. Messmer,[34] a "pupil" of the famous German professor Meumann, conducted, in 1904, the first research with children as subjects. He differentiated two main types of readers, the "objective" type and the "subjective" type; the latter being predominant among younger age groups. He also concluded from his experiments that, in the recognition of a word, two factors can always be discerned: (1) a visual simultaneous pattern of a whole word and (2) single dominant letters, which are perceived successively. Wiegand,[35] in 1908, used the term "*Gestaltqualität,*" in reporting his experimental study. He employed an interesting technique of tachistoscopic experimentation: the tachistoscope was moved from far distances, where more wisps of grey could be seen, to closer distances to the eye. First high and low letters emerged, then the individual letters at the beginning and end of a word could be recognized; last to be seen were the letters hidden in the middle of the word—the same pattern that has been observed in more recent times in the patterns of oral reading errors of dyslexic children. Kutzner[36] (1916) mainly explored the effects of the quality of the Gestalt on word recognition. He found that misreadings from a considerable distance preserved the approximate length and number of ascenders of the test word; he concluded, therefore, that the word length and the relative position of ascenders and descenders in a word must be the cues by which words are recognized. Korte[37] (1923) experimented with factors of recognition within indirect vision. He found that capital letters are more legible in indirect vision than the small or lower-case letters. Among the lower-case letters *w* was recognized more readily than *c*. Hoffmann[38] (1927) found, in his studies with different reading materials in grades I to VIII, an increase in tachistoscopic span for familiar words with advance in school grades.

Thorner and Heimann (1929) demonstrated that pronounceable combinations of letters could be grasped more readily than nonpronounceable arrangements. Thorner concluded from his experiments on the psychology of reading that "Theoretically the reading process is mainly a process of recognition of Gestalt. Connected with it are processes of auditory-motorial nature, which also tend to create Gestalten. . . . Normally the whole shape or figure is of more importance, but, when more difficult words are to be recognized, dominating letters stand out."[39] Sander,[40] a psychologist from the so-called *Leipziger genetische Ganzheitspsychologie* (besides Krüger, Volkelt, and Wellek), reported the results of several experiments on learning to read from the years 1928–1954. These indicated two different kinds of learning: (1) "*hologen*": from undifferentiated recognition of whole words, toward a stepping out of dominating parts and a confusion of many sounds and their order, and finally toward the recognition of the "*Endgestalt*" with comprehension of the structured word. (2) "*merogen*": starting with a correct recognition of one or some single letters, a nonsurveying of the many letters, toward a "*Vorgestalt*" of comprehension, and finally the *Endgestalt* with complete comprehension ("*Aha-Erlebnis*").

With the frame of reference of *Gestalt- und Ganzheits* psychology in mind, Bosch wrote, in 1937, a prize winning book *Grundlagen des Erstleseunterrichts* (*Foundations of First Reading Instruction*).[41] In former years (1928–1933) he had studied the prerequisites of linguistic objectification within school beginners and found that 6-year-old children, in general, are not able to distinguish between the meaning of words and situations (complexes) and the length of words. Nor are they able to analyze words aurally within sentences or name the first and last phonemes of a spoken word. However, in 1967, Katzenberger and Kluge[42] found, in their critical evaluation of Bosch's studies, that the children in Germany today appear to be better equipped linguistically than those of forty years ago.

In 1941, Hartmann[43] published an experimental study comparing two different initial reading methods: (1) the analytic, *Ganzheits*, or global method and (2) the synthetic method. His results favored the global method. Kern,[44] one of the outstanding promoters of global methods in Germany, in 1956, and also Straub,[45] in 1960, reported striking results in favor of global methods. Since the end of the Second World War, global methods have been introduced in German schools on a broad scale. Most of the published primers are designed for global methods. Among the outstanding authors of these primers are Brückl 1923, Wittmann 1929, Kern 1931, and, after 1945, Reinhard, Walter Müller, and Warwel. Schmalohr[46] criticized the research procedures of the studies made by Hartmann, Kern, and Straub. He tested the often-mentioned hypothesis that global methods produce better results in the long run in analytic abilities and in reading and spelling for both able and mentally retarded children. Schmalohr found in his experimental study no differences between analytic and synthetic reading methods by the end of grades IV and V. Heinrich Müller,[47] in 1964, compared the synthetic, the whole-word, and the global methods and found that at the end of grade II the synthetic method and the whole-word method brought better results than the whole-sentence method. He also found that the mentally retarded achieved superior reading attainments if taught by a synthetic approach. The results of these studies from Schmalohr and Müller are still fiercely discussed from both sides of the controversy.

In this review, which has been confined to experimental studies conducted only in Germany up to the present date (hundreds of German articles and books could be added on the subject of reading, and especially writing or spelling, that are not experimental), it can be seen that reading research started with the fundamental problem of the reading process. Physiologists, psychiatrists, and psychologists debated the issues; new experiments laid the foundations for a more differentiated theory on what the individual identifies and recognizes when he is reading. Gestalt psychology had a great influence on this development—and still has.

Hans Pfaffenberger,[48] in his recent publication, points out that a former monistic model, or the general myth of "*Ganzheitlichkeit,*" has given way to a pluralistic, multifactorial model of recognition in Gestalt psychology. This applies also to younger age groups (2- to 7-year olds). Pfaffenberger describes five types of recognition (mosaic, diffuse-global, reductional, reduplicational, and structural). Kleinhans,[49] in 1966, found four stages within the development of Gestalt recognition in different age groups.

Comparing oral reading rates measured by Messmer (1904) and Bobertag and Kirste (1916) with three hundred German children in 1957 who had been randomly selected from the end of grades I to V, Biglmaier[50] found that children in Germany today read orally significantly faster than in the earlier studies. It might be concluded from other evidence that they read, in general, better than the children of two generations ago. Better teaching procedures, especially those coming from analytic methods, may account for this development.

A second result was surprising: The process of learning to read, in the sense of being able to decode and understand written symbols with a low error rate, is accomplished for German children at the end of grade II. This is in contrast to American children who reach this stage, according to the norms of Monroe (1932), only at the end of grade IV. This result may be attributed to the more regular grapheme-phoneme relations in the German language. However, the development of learning to read within each language seems to follow similar patterns. For both languages, omissions are the main error type after the learning process has been completed; consonant errors are third in importance in all five grades (I to V); and refusals and aided responses are placed last in the pattern of errors in both languages.

In the light of these findings in reading research in Germany the basic question remains, "What is reading? Is reading only a decoding process, is it a thinking process, or is it both?" In agreement with Kainz,[51] it is concluded here that the reading act is a complex process including perceptive, apperceptive, assimilative, associative, and intellectual processes. The different processes penetrate, complement, and assist each other in a way that is different from one individual to another. Research, international as well as national, is called on to define, refine, differentiate, and systemize the facts both for a comprehensive theory and for a sound application in schools, reading centers, and homes.

Dissemination of those research results, practices, ideas, and theories is necessary, on the international as well as the national scale. The more a teacher or a researcher knows about the reading process of good and poor readers—about what research has shown up to now—the more he will be in a position to make better decisions, decisions that might affect a single pupil, a group of students, or thousands of readers using his textbook. Partial information leads to one-sidedness and—if we look to the history of teaching reading—to indoctrination.

REFERENCES

1. Block, Robert, "*Das Kind und die Schule*," in Meier, Helmut, *Deutsche Sprachstatistik*, Hildesheim: Georg Olms Verlagsbuchhandlung, 1967.

2. *Ibid.*

3. Preston, R. C., "Comparison of word-recognition skill in German and American children," *Elementary School Journal, 53* (1952), 443–446.

4. Sochurek, Howard, "Berlin on both sides of the wall," *National Geographic Magazine, 137* (January 1970), 35.

5. For more detailed representation and references see Hylla, Erich I., and Kegel, Friedrich O., *Education in Germany—An Introduction to Foreigners*, Frankfurt, a. M.: *Hochschule für Internationale Pädagogische Forschung*, 1958; and Schultze, Walter, and Führ, Christoph, *Schools in the Federal Republic of Germany*, Weinheim: Verlag Julius Beltz, 1967.

6. Schultze and Führ, *op. cit.*, p. 8.

7. *Ibid.*, pp. 16 and 163.

8. Figures according to Federal Office of Statistics (*Statistisches Bundesamt*), combined from several tables in *Ibid.*, pp. 16, 159 and 171.

9. *Deutscher Bildungsrat, Empfehlungen der Bildungskommission: Einrichtung von Schulversuchen mit Gesamtschulen*, Bonn: Deutscher Bildungsrat, 1969.

10. Günther, Karl Heinz, and Uhlig, Gottfried, *Geschichte der Schule in der Deutschen Demokratischen Republik 1945 bis 1968*, Berlin: Volk and Wissen, Volkseigener Verlag, 1969, p. 141.

11. Schüttler-Janikulla, Klaus, "*Vorklassen in Berlin*," in E. Schwartz (ed.), *Begabung und Lernen im Kindesalter, Bd. 1*, Frankfurt: *Arbeitskreis Grundschule*, 1970. This first volume of the *Grundschulkongress* in 1969, in Frankfurt, also includes several aspects, discussions, and experiments on early reading. (Schmalohr, Kratzmeier, Krüger, Rüdiger, Correll, Biglmaier.)

12. *Senator für Schulwesen Berlin, Vorläufiger Rahmenplan für die Vorklassen*, Berlin: *Senator für Schulwesen*, 1969.

13. Reinhard, Ludwig, "*Fibelfrühling!—Fibelsegen? Eine kritische Sichtung der Leselernbücher für die Zeit 1945–1958*," *Die Scholle, 12* (1958); also, Reinhard, Ludwig, *Grundlagen und Praxis des Erstunterrichts im Lesen und Schreiben*, Munich: Bayerischer Schulbuchverlag, 1962, p. 120.

14. Hasler, Herbert, and Schwartz, Erwin, "*Lehrer und Lesemethoden*," *Westermanns Pädagogische Beiträge, 4* (1966).

15. Lanzelsdorfer, F., and Pacolt, E., *Wiener Kinder lesen*, Vienna: Verlag für Jugend und Volk, 1969.

16. Reinhard, Ludwig, *Im Wundergarten, Fibel in 3 Teilen für Volksschulen*, 1st ed., Munich: Bayerischer Schulbuch-Verlag, 1951; 7th rev. ed., 1967. Reinhard, Ludwig, *Schreiben macht Spass. Eine Schreibfibel für Volksschulen*, Munich: Bayerischer Schulbuch-Verlag, 1965.

17. Ranschburg, P., *Die Leseschwäche (Legasthenie) und Rechenschwäche (Arithmasthenie) der Schulkinder im Lichte des Experiments*, Berlin: Springer, 1916.

18. Linder, Maria, "*Über Legasthenie (spez. Leseschwäche)*," *Zeitschrift für Kinderpsychiatrie, 18* (1951).

19. Kirchhoff, Hans, *Verbale Lese- und Rechtschreibschwäche im Kindesalter*, 3rd ed., Basel: S. Karger, 1964.

20. Biglmaier, Franz, *Lesestörungen—Diagnose und Behandlung,* Munich and Basel: Ernst Reinhard Verlag, 1968.
21. Monroe, Marion, *Children Who Cannot Read,* Chicago: Univ. of Chicago, 1932.
22. All the reading comprehension and spelling tests cited in this paragraph are published at Weinheim by Deutsche Schultests, Verlag Julius Beltz.
23. Biglmaier, Franz, "*Informelle Lehrertests im Rechtschreibunterricht-Fehleranalyse und Fehlerbehandlung,*" *Die Grundschule,* 2 (April 1970).
24. Schenk-Danziger, Lotte, "*Probleme der Legasthenie,*" *Schweizerische Zeitschrift für Psychologie,* 20 (1961) 29–48. Also Schenk-Danziger, L., *Handbuch der Legasthenie im Kindesalter,* Weinheim: Beltz, 1968.
25. Tordrup, S. A., "*Über das Problem primärer Symptome der Legasthenie,*" in Kirchhoff Pietrowicz (ed.), *Neues zur Lese- und Rechtschreibschwäche,* Basel: Karger, 1963; Biglmaier, *Lesestörungen, op. cit.;* Valtin, R., "*Legasthenie: Therapie ohne Grundlagen, Bericht über eine empirische Untersuchung,*" *betrifft: Erziehung,* 10 (1969), 24–27.
26. Schmidt, Lieselotte, "*Bericht über eine dreijährige Tätigkeit in einer nach skandinavischem Muster geführten Leseklinik,*" in Ingenkamp (ed.), *Lese- u. Rechtschreibschwäche bei Schulkindern,* PZ C 2, Weinheim: Beltz, 1967.
27. Gray, W. S., *The Teaching of Reading and Writing: An International Survey,* Paris: UNESCO, 1956.
28. Valentine, G., *Lehrbuch der Physiologie,* 1844, cited in Erdmann, B., and Dodge, R., *Psychologische Untersuchungen über das Lesen auf experimenteller Grundlage,* Halle: Niemeyer, 1898.
29. Grashey, H. v., "*Über Aphasie und ihre Beziehungen zur Wahrnehmung,*" *Arch. f. Psychiatrie u. Nervenkrankheiten,* 12 (1885).
30. Cattell, J. McKeen, "*Über die Zeit der Erkennung und Benennung von Schriftzeichen, Bildern und Farben,*" *Philosophische Studien,* II (1885), 635–650.
31. Erdmann and Dodge, *op. cit.*
32. Anderson, Irving H., and Dearborn, Walter F., *The Psychology of Teaching Reading,* New York: Ronald, 1952.
33. Zeitler, Julius, "*Tachistoskopische Untersuchungen über das Lesen,*" *Philosophische Studien,* 16 (1900), 380–463.
34. Messmer, O., "*Zur Psychologie des Lesens bei Kindern und Erwachsenen,*" *Archiv. für die gesamte Psychologie,* II (1904).
35. Wiegand, C. F., "*Untersuchungen über die Bedeutung der Gestaltqualität für die Erkennung von Wörtern,*" *Zeitschrift für Psychologie,* 1907.
36. Kutzner, O., "*Kritische und experimentelle Beiträge zur Psychologie des Lesens mit besonderer Berücksichtigung des Problems der Gestaltqualität,*" *Archiv. für gesamte Psychologie* (1916).
37. Korte, W., "*Über die Gestaltauffassung im indirekten Sehen,*" *Zeitschrift für Psychologie* (1923).
38. Hoffmann, J., "*Experimentell-psychologische Untersuchungen über Leseleistungen von Schulkindern,*" *Archiv. für die gesamte Psychologie* (1927).
39. Thorner, H., and Heimann, A., "*Experimentelle Untersuchungen zur Psychologie des Lesens,*" *Archiv. für die gesamte Psychologie* (1929).
40. Sander, F., "*Experimentelle Ergebnisse der Gestaltpsychologie,*" "*Über die Sinnerfüllung optischer Komplexe bei Schwachsinnigen,*" *Bericht des 4. Kongresses für Heilpädagogik,* 1929.

41. Bosch, B., *Grundlagen Des Erstleseunterrichts,* 2nd ed., Angermund: 1949.

42. Katzenberger, L. F., *"Schulanfänger und Lesenlernen. Eine kritische Überprüfung der Untersuchungsbefunde von Bosch über die Fähigkeit des Schulneulinges zur Sprachvergegenständlichung und Sprachanalyse,"* Schule und Psychologie, **14** (1967) 11, 345–359.

43. Hartmann, W., *Vergleichende Untersuchungen zum Ganzheitsverfahren vom 1. bis 4. Schuljahr,* Leipzig, 1941.

44. Kern, Artur, and Kern, Erwin, *Lesen und Lesenlernen,* Freiburg: Verlag Herder, 1956.

45. Straub, W., *"Versagt die Ganzheitsmethode? oder lernen ganzheitlich unterrichtete Kinder schlechter lesen als synthetisch unterrichtete Kinder?"* Die Ganzheitsschule, 9 (1960).

46. Schmalohr, E., *Psychologie des Erstlese- und Schreibunterrichts,* Munich: Ernst Reinhardt Verlag, 1961.

47. Müller, H., *Methoden des Erstleseunterrichts und ihre Ergebnisse,* Meisenheim am Glan: Hain, 1964.

48. Pfaffenberger, H., *Untersuchungen über die visuelle Gestaltwahrnehmung vorschulpflichtiger Kinder,* Weinheim: Beltz Verlag, 1960, 1967.

49. Kleinhans, W. H., *Stufen der ganzheitlichen Auffassung bei 2- bis 7jährigen Kindern,* Weinheim: Beltz Verlag, 1966.

50. Biglmaier, *Lesestörungen—Diagnose und Behandlung, op. cit.*

51. Kainz, Friedrich, *Psychologie der Sprache, Vol. IV: Spezielle Sprachpsychologie,* Stuttgart: Ferdinand Enke Verlag, 1956.

CHAPTER 17

Great Britain

ELIZABETH J. GOODACRE

"GREAT BRITAIN" generally refers to England, Wales, Scotland, and Northern Ireland. For the purposes of this chapter, references to Northern Ireland will be omitted. In terms of population, it is the smallest of the four countries, and the teaching of reading there is specific to geographical and economic conditions that are not found in the other three countries.

Indeed, reading research in Great Britain has been so limited that even generalizations about the teaching of reading there as so defined must be based on findings that may well be valid only for the specific region of the countries in which the evidence was obtained. No survey of teaching practices in reading in any of the three countries as a whole has been carried out. Prevailing tendencies are broadly revealed in official publications of the Department of Education and Science and in reports of research carried out by the National Foundation for Educational Research in England and Wales (NFER) and the Scottish Council for Research in Education (SCRE) and officers of local education authorities. Other sources of information include the literature of various national associations of teachers, institutes of education attached to universities, and colleges of education (teacher-training establishments), and the publicity given to new reading materials and media.

School Policy Making

England, Wales, and Scotland are countries with highly individualistic people who possess marked national characteristics. The present educational system in each of these countries is largely the result of an independent growth; it is, therefore, not surprising to find that there are separate services for public education in Great Britain. Modern developments have rendered these services similar in many respects; nevertheless, the three countries each retain a distinctive form and ethos in their individual education services. The Department of Education (DES) administers education in England and Wales, the Scottish Department of Education (SED) in Scotland. Although Wales is legislated for along with England, a principal education act for England and Wales always contains clauses that relate to Wales alone. Indeed, public education in Wales is to some extent separately administered, being under the control of a Welsh department within the DES that is situated in Cardiff, the Welsh capital. Also, it must be remembered that administrative responsibility for education in Britain is not confined to the national government departments. All three British peoples participate in local government and, consequently, there are many local education authorities (LEAs) that administer the education service on the local level and stand in a relationship to the central authority that is unique to Britain. Although the two national services are State-controlled in that they are regulated by acts of Parliament and supervised by government departments, the partnership between the central government, the statutory local authorities, and voluntary effort is such that the central authority can lead and direct but not dominate the relationship. For instance, the central government can shape national policy and define national standards. In 1966, the DES published *Children and their Primary Schools* ("The Plowden Report"),[1] a report of the Central Advisory Council for Education (England), which examined primary education in England in all its aspects and made many recommendations. (Incidentally, only five pages in this five-hundred-page volume dealt specifically with reading.) Two years later a separate report was published for Wales ("The Gittens Report").[2] Scottish education had produced a similar report earlier (in 1965), *Primary Education in Scotland*.[3] Although it was a shorter report than Plowden, it devoted more space to the consideration of the language arts. The Department of Education and Science also, between 1948 and 1964, arranged for five surveys of the reading ability of samples of 11- and 15-year-olds; the results were published in three pamphlets by the Ministry of Education[4] (1950, 1957) and the Department of Education and Science[5] (1966).

Within the broad outline of the national policy, local authorities are encouraged to exercise their right to individual initiative and enterprise, and this right is powerfully supported by the fact that they meet a large proportion of the total expenditure on State education. In practice in the classroom this means, for instance, that teachers will be offered advice on teaching methods and materials not only by Her Majesty's Inspectorate but also by advisers appointed by the LEAs.

In England and Wales an individual school's autonomy is protected by a board of governors whose business it is to watch over the particular interests of their school. The members of these boards are not paid and their service is voluntary. They are usually local people of some authority (rarely, if ever, teachers or parents of children of the school in question), and as "laymen" in educational matters they delegate large responsibilities to the head teacher, to whom they entrust complete freedom to plan and regulate the organization, curriculum, discipline, and extracurricular activities of the school. Similarly, head teachers permit their staffs a large measure of personal initiative in their choice of methods and classroom activities. However, recent research[6] has drawn attention to the way in which staff attitudes toward educational factors differ greatly between schools. They often reflect the favorable or unfavorable attitude of the head teacher to questions of method, type of organization, and curriculum in general.

Language Differences

Although Gaelic is still spoken in remote regions of Scotland, it presents fewer problems in regard to teaching reading than the speaking of Welsh in Wales. In "The Gittens Report" it was estimated that 15 per cent of Welsh children learned Welsh in the home, and, as all Welsh children are encouraged to learn English, these children were usually learning to speak English as a second language at about 6½. They learned to read in English shortly afterward. The phonetic structure of the two languages is different: Welsh is claimed to be more "phonetic" than English in the sense of there being a more consistent phoneme-grapheme correspondence. A comparison between English speaking children and bilingual Welsh speaking children in Wales at 11 years of age made in "The Gittens Report" found that the latter were approximately eighteen months behind the former in reading *in English* and twenty-three months behind the norms for readers of the same age in England. Since these bilingual Welsh speaking children had the problem of mastering two languages and did not begin reading in English—the second language—until about 7, they made good progress. However, the difference between the two groups was still evident at 15 years. There are considerable problems in producing sufficient suitable reading materials in Welsh, and, increasingly, children show more interest in learning to read in English because of the greater range of books. Apparently, they have difficulty in making up for their later start in what is a second language for them.

Although "The Gittens Report" encouraged local authorities to implement bilingual schools and stressed the importance of the survival of the language, it is true that, in many areas of Wales, English is the first language. Indeed, nine tenths of Welsh speakers are concentrated in the underpopulated, mountainous, rural areas of North Wales. It may well be that the bilingual Welsh children also have more problems to cope with generally, coming from older, smaller, country-type schools, and live in many cases in poorer housing.

It must also be remembered that in Great Britain there are immigrant groups speaking languages other than English. The definition of immigrant in the DES population figures is a child born outside England and Wales, or one born in those countries to parents who had not lived there for ten years. The proportion of the total school population who are immigrants is not great, but the distribution of these pupils is very uneven. Figures in 1967 showed that nearly three quarters of those in schools with ten or more were in two regions: 55 per cent in London and more than 17 per cent in the West Midlands. The figure for Wales was less than 0.5 per cent. Most of the remaining immigrants were in four regions: Yorkshire and Humberside, the East Midlands, and the North West and South West outside greater London. The largest group (45 per cent of the total) came from the West Indies and tended to be concentrated in Greater London and the West Midlands. The next most numerous group (20 per cent) was the Indians. Almost equal in size were the groups of Pakistanis, Greek Cypriots, and Italians. Not only do some of the children of these groups not speak English, but the groups themselves differ in their attitudes to their host country. For instance, West Indian families are often shocked at not being accepted by a nation they admire, whereas the Greek Cypriot tends to feel that his own Greek culture is superior. He can live in Britain without any sense of inferiority if he does not become "integrated." In practice, many teachers may have had little experience teaching immigrant children to read in English. Particularly in London and the industrial areas of the English Midlands, some teachers have a large number of immigrant children with a variety of languages and customs with which to deal. They find themselves first teaching English as a second language and then trying to teach these children to read in it.

The London Literacy Survey[7] found that, over all, the reading standards of immigrants were markedly lower than those of nonimmigrants, both with respect to average scores and proportions of poor and good readers, for example, 28.5 per cent of immigrants were poor readers (reading age two years less than chronological age), compared to 14.8 per cent for nonimmigrants. The largest proportion of poor readers was found amongst the Turkish Cypriots, 45.5 per cent; followed by Greek Cypriots, 30.2 per cent; West Indians, 30.1 per cent; Pakistanis, 27.6 per cent; and Indians, 26.8 per cent.

Differences in Attitudes to Education

There are historic and economic differences between England, Scotland, and Wales that result in differences in the value placed on education. A national study[8] of the development of children in the three countries found that on the basis of teachers' judgments, Scottish parents showed more interest in their children's school progress than their Welsh or English counterparts. It was also found that, relatively speaking, Scottish children enjoyed more of their parents' company, both inside and outside the home, and a smaller proportion of Scottish mothers had worked either before their child started school or afterward. In this national comparison, the Scottish children were found to be the best readers, and it was suggested that this might be the result of parents reading to their children at home. It was the Scottish fathers who were more likely to read to their children.

"The Plowden Report," in its survey of English parents, found that the majority of parents liked to read for recreation when they had time, but mostly this was reading magazines and newspapers. In Britain, the State libraries are free, but less than half the sample of English parents belonged to a local library, and, in 29 per cent of the homes, the families possessed fewer than six books apart from children's books. The incidence of book ownership and library usage declined markedly in relation with parent's occupational status.

School Organization

In Britain, the compulsory age for starting school is 5. A primary course is provided for children between the ages of 5 and 11 + (age 12 in Scotland), after which children proceed to different types of secondary schools on the basis of various selection procedures and parental preferences. There are different types of State school organization, but two popular patterns at the primary stage are for infants (aged 5 to 7+) and juniors (aged 7 to 11+) to be organized in separate schools, or a combined type (age range 5 to 11+). The compulsory leaving age is 15, but in many secondary schools pupils stay on beyond this age, and in some secondary schools there are classes of 18- and 19-year-olds.

Starting Age

The choice of 5 as the age for beginning schooling was made almost by chance in 1870. The Consultative Committee, which considered primary school organization in 1933, decided that there were few problems resulting from this practice and made no recommendations about the age of school entry. Thirty years later the Plowden Committee considered the question in more detail. In their report they point out that, with the exception of Israel and a few States whose educational systems derive from the British tradition, Britain was alone in fixing such an early age. But the Plowden Committee seems to have failed to quote in this context any of the evidence that in other countries there are movements to *lower* the school entry age. However, their report does make it clear that the committee was aware of the importance of the early years of learning. The then current demands for the raising of the school *leaving* age, in a time of economic difficulties, may have persuaded the committee that lowering the school entry age was just not feasible at that time.

Length of Infant Schooling

Another important point is that the usual procedure is to admit children to infant schools at intervals of four months—that is, termly intakes. (In many parts of Scotland, however, children are taken on a yearly basis.) In contrast to most countries, which have one school entry point, in England and Wales there generally are three: September, January, and after Easter. However, children are promoted to junior school, or the junior department of a combined department school, only at intervals of twelve months—that is, on a yearly basis. Children must go to school at the beginning of the term after their fifth birthday; they are promoted to the junior school or class in the September following their seventh birthday. This means that the groups of children transferring annually to the junior school or class differ considerably in age and also in length of infant schooling. Also, the number of pupils in the infant school varies greatly from term to term, and this affects learning conditions, particularly for the summer-born children. These children, throughout their schooling, tend to be taught in classes of older children, and more of them are found in remedial classes of backward readers.[9]

This is the situation in regard to legal considerations. In practice, there are social and regional differences in school entry conditions. In areas where there is a long tradition of mothers' working, children are admitted at the beginning of the year in which they turn 5. There is evidence[10] that about 50 per cent of children start their schooling before they are 5. However, more recent estimates suggest that more and more local education authorities are having to exclude these "rising fives," as they are often called. Indeed, in certain areas such as the "new towns," which have high birth rates, there is a lack of places for even the children of statutory age, and some children have part-time schooling or do not start until nearly 6.

Length of infant schooling is particularly important in the British education system, because there is a strong tradition that the task of learning to read is completed in the infant school. The report of the 1931 Consultative Committee stated that "the process of learning to read should be nearly finished by the time the pupil reaches the age of 7. The mechanical difficulties will have been overcome by most of the children." [11] This may have been the expectation forty years ago, but changes in educational philosophy have produced a more child-centered type of infant school education. It takes into consideration the differences between children in regard to learning rate and preschool experiences. Also, educationists have encouraged a higher level of "reading attainment," stressing as they do that reading is not mere word calling, but that children should learn to read with meaning and develop a love of reading that will last them a lifetime. It is gradually being realized that two years may be barely time for some children to *begin* learning to read, let alone to have mastered the mechanics.

A reading survey [12] carried out in Kent, one of the more prosperous LEA's adjacent to London, found that in the late 1950s nearly half the children in the first-year junior classes were in need of the type of teaching associated with the infant school. Most of their teachers, though, were not trained to teach infant methods, and a substantial minority had no knowledge of how to teach beginning reading. This research also showed that being labeled a "poor reader" at 7 affected later chances of success in the educational system.

Research in the 1960s confirmed that many 7-year-olds were in need of systematic teaching of reading, but it is still doubtful whether the training of primary school teachers has adjusted to this more realistic assessment of what the infant school can achieve in two years. The more recent London Literacy Survey found that fewer than half the junior schools (42 per cent) had teachers with specific training in the teaching of reading. The report estimated that only about one in eight of all London junior school teachers had been so trained. Although it must be remembered that London has particular problems, including a proportion of immigrant children (17 per cent of the age group tested), it can be noted that there were twice as many "poor" readers (using a comprehension test standardized on a national sample) and fewer "good" readers in this area.

Class Grouping

In Britain, there is no general policy of "grade repeating." Some schools, however, practice streaming. That is, pupils are organized within a year group into A, B, C (and so on) classes on the basis of level of attainment or intelligence.

It has been found that summer-born children are less likely to be in A classes, and it seems likely that streaming accentuates the disadvantages that accrue from being in the youngest group of a year's intake. These children may be less mature and under greater stress trying to cope with the learning standards expected of them. Shearer[13] examined the effect of date of birth on teachers' assessments of children and concluded that it was the *less able* younger children who suffered most. Even the use of a standardized reading test incorporating age allowances did not, in their case, counterbalance the adverse effect of being the youngest in their age group and of having spent less time in the infant school. Obviously, reading ability is a decisive factor in decisions about children's educational futures. Teachers dealing with large classes in schools with poor systems of record keeping will be influenced by the child's level of reading attainment. Where, however, teachers individualize learning so that their children compete only with their own individual standards, the atmosphere is more likely to be such that children are able in their own time to overcome the initial disadvantages stemming from the form of entry procedure. France and Wiseman[14] reported that the effects of month of birth decreased for older age groups. It would seem that this factor has its most critical effect in regard to beginning reading, particularly for the children who are slower to learn.

"Reading Drive"

Children technically have a two-year period in the infant school, but it must be pointed out that infant schools differ greatly in the time, resources, and importance they attach to learning to read during this period. Southgate[15] focused attention on reading drive, or the importance placed on learning to read in the school setting, when criticizing the control of variables in reading-research design. With Roberts she has more recently outlined two types of approach related to the teacher's basic beliefs about reading. (Described in terms of the importance of mastering reading skills by means of systematic, planned learning or reading considered as only one of children's many interests best mastered by incidental learning.) Southgate and Roberts[16] have suggested that teachers should decide which attitude most nearly approximates their own and then select method, medium, and materials in the light of their choice, thus maximizing their effectiveness. Although such differences in beliefs are observable in some schools, the view of Southgate and Roberts that teachers can rationalize their choice of methods and materials, tends to ignore the importance of teachers' personality characteristics, training and experience, and the limiting factors imposed by school and financial considerations.

Educational Beliefs

The terms "traditional" and "progressive," or "formal" and "informal," appear in research literature to describe the beliefs of teachers that underlie choices in regard to class organization, approach, and educational aims. Lovell,[17] reporting a study in English junior schools (social-class factors controlled), found that there were no significant differences in the children's reading attainments in the formal as compared with the informal schools. However, the *pattern* of scores differed; the formal schools tended to have a higher proportion of both good and poor readers. Wiseman,[18] in his study of Lancashire schools in the north of England, found a significant relationship between a schools' "progressiveness" and the level of reading comprehension achieved. He found that help for the needy was one of the main characteristics of the progressive philosophy, both in education and in other fields of activity. One would expect, therefore, that this basic philosophy would influence teachers' decisions in regard to which pupils to assist most, the amount of time to spend on the skill, and the type of reading to be developed. Also, in this context, teachers' perceptions of their pupils assume importance—that is, whether teachers see *their* pupils as being "needy," "disadvantaged," or "culturally deprived." Expectation, either the child's own, or his teacher's, is known to have considerable influence on the level of attainment.[19]

Concentration on improving the reading attainment of "poor" readers (that is, helping the "underdog") can lead to higher *school* standards if the group mean is considered, which raises the whole question of criterion of reading progress. Should group means be used, or should we be interested in the *range* of scores? For instance, Gooch[20] in a small-scale study of two types of junior school (progressive, or child-centered education with unstreamed classes, flexible timetabling, and project work; and traditional or subject-centered encouraging streaming and competitiveness) found that the progressive approach developed the abilities of the average and duller children at the expense of the more able pupils. It would seem that, during the past two decades, traditional approaches have become associated with practices that produce an elite, and a large range of attainments; progressive approaches have tended to narrow the range of attainments, producing fewer "good" readers, but improving standards by reason of raising the level of the less able. It must be realized that the terms, "traditional" and "progressive" and the like, are likely to change in relation to the practices associated with them. There is evidence to suggest that these changes in educational philosophy take longer to make themselves felt in rural schools, particularly in the remoter areas of Wales and in Scottish schools generally. Also, willingness to adopt more recent educational philosophies appears to be related to the teacher's age.

The i.t.a. Foundation has found that even with the results of a highly organized research program and the enthusiasm of committed teachers, it is difficult to persuade more teachers to change their teaching medium. Research from other sources[21] suggests that the British teaching profession is, for social and historical reasons, conservative in many of its attitudes. There may be only a small proportion (possibly one in five) of teachers who are innovators by inclination.

Difficult School Conditions

Even in schools where the teachers are firm believers in specific educational philosophies or are keen supporters of particular teaching practices, there are often obstacles in carrying out practices. In the primary school a class will sometimes include more than forty students and many classrooms are in old school buildings originally built for traditional rather than progressive teaching purposes. For instance, the National Union of Teachers (NUT) survey of school conditions[22] found that it was possible to have a room that could be used solely for a school library in only 12 per cent of schools. In this survey most teachers were satisfied with the LEA level of spending on books, but there is independent evidence from the educational publishers that individual LEAs differ considerably in the amount of finance they provide for book buying in their schools.

Types of School Organization

The typical English primary school according to the NUT survey is not large in terms of pupils on roll—a third have fewer than one hundred pupils, a fifth more than three hundred. About half are organized as combined department schools (that is, the age range is 5 to 11 years); the rest are either separate infant or separate junior schools. Almost all (97 per cent) are mixed schools taking both boys and girls. There has been some research carried out on the effects of being in a school catering to the age range of 5 to 7 years or 7 to 11, but it has not always been possible to control the effects of other factors associated with particular types of organization. For instance, the separate department schools tend to be larger in size, with more pupils on roll, and to be situated in nonrural areas. Pidgeon[23] concluded that the separate department schools were superior in reading attainment, but this writer,[24] in a study in London, where the association between school size, socioeconomic factors, and type of organization was less marked, found no significant difference between the reading attainment of pupils at 7 in the two types of school. The prospect of transfer at 7 to a different school led to a greater provision of remedial help for poor readers in the infant-only schools; Shields,[25] working in the same city, concluded from her findings that uninterrupted schooling at the age of 7 did not produce better progress than a change of schools. Baird,[26] in a small study, and this writer working in London schools, found evidence suggesting that the combined department schools were more traditional in their approach to teaching reading. Further research in this area would need to distinguish between the effects of differences in material conditions and resources between the two types of school and their distinctive, over-all educational philosophy.

It is among the separate department schools that one discovers more innovators, particularly in regard to experiments in grouping pupils and new types of program organization. The "integrated day" is a type of flexible program used by some schools, but no research has been reported of its effectiveness in relation to teaching reading. "Vertical grouping" is a way of organizing classes so that each class has a range of pupils from the total age group of the school. Mycock[27] made a comparison of vertical and horizontal grouping in infant schools and, as might perhaps have been expected, found no difference in the size of pupils' vocabulary. There was, however, some evidence that slow learners benefited in reading from the vertical grouping, whereas "brighter" pupils progressed better under the more traditional horizontal grouping. The greater demands made on the competence of the teacher by a wide age range in the vertical grouping drew attention to the importance of the quality of the teacher. It would be interesting to examine the effects of length of schooling in an experiment using horizontal and vertical grouping schools.

"The Plowden Report" recommended that the DES should outline a national policy on the structure of nursery and primary education, and that one aspect of this should be a change of the conventional names applied to the stages of education. They suggested a pattern in which the term "First School" would be applied to the 5 to 8 age group and "Middle School" for the 8- to 12-year-olds. A school that served all children from 5 to 12 should be called a "Combined School." In England and Wales, a few local educational authorities have already established this pattern, while other LEAs are considering the practical difficulties in adopting the proposed changes.

Age for Beginning Reading

Nursery School Provision

Plowden reported that about seven in every hundred children in England received some form of education in a nursery school or nursery class before the age of 5. Undoubtedly, the standard of State nursery education has improved over the years, but there has been hardly any increase in the number of children receiving this type of education. The NUT survey reported that three quarters of all nursery places being provided by State funds were in working-class areas. It is very difficult to evaluate the effectiveness of preschool education, as the evidence is weighted by studies of special groups of children. That is, nursery school places are few and the children who gain them tend to be from atypical backgrounds—mothers working long hours, one-parent families, maladjusted parents.

The view of educationists such as Bernstein,[28] that poverty of language is a major cause of poor achievement, has focused attention on the need to provide working-class children from overcrowded noisy homes with nursery education as a means of positive intervention in the circumstances of social deprivation. The expansion of nursery education thus needed seems unlikely. Heavy demands are made on educational finance by other sectors of the service, particularly the tertiary level. However, in the last few years one has seen the establishment of the Preschool Playgroups Association (PPA). A voluntary organization inaugurated in 1961, its aim is to encourage parents to share the responsibility of their children's education prior to compulsory schooling. The Association developed out of the recognition of the current limited physical and social experience of young children in smaller families and mass housing conditions, particularly in the postwar tower blocks of flats or apartments. There is no evidence on the social composition of the Association's membership, although its executives appear to be mostly "professional" women aware of the importance of education, and trained personnel capable of organizing a self-help movement if the State is unable or unlikely to do so.

In the State nursery schools and classes, the emphasis is on language development, and there is little attempt to introduce the systematic teaching of reading. The preschool playgroups follow the same general approach, concentrating on developing adequate spoken vocabulary related to ideas absorbed from experience and the encouragement of motivation to read by listening to stories and joining in with rhymes and finger plays. In the pages of the Association's journal, *Contact,* some mothers have discussed their views on the presentation of reading in these groups, and it is obvious that individual mothers are concerned about the "prereading" stage. Some mothers are teaching their children to read, concentrating mainly on the growth of a "sight" vocabulary. Others in the Association are worried about entering the province of the infant school and do little or nothing to further prereading skills for fear of "doing the wrong thing."

Opinions on Reading Readiness

The NFER research[29,30] suggested that infant teachers in the late 1950s and early 1960s concentrated almost solely on the attitudes and interest toward reading of pupils as the main indications of readiness to read. It was considered that children would show a desire to learn to read when they were "ready," and that teachers should not interfere because of the danger of starting children before they were ready and thus creating a lasting dislike for reading. In the literature of the period it was often suggested that reading was a "natural" process and that each child would reach this stage of development in his own good time. Both Sanderson[31] and Downing[32] criticized this view, and the NFER research indicated the importance of cultural factors in relation to motivation to read. Most teachers, however, considered the assessment of readiness in their pupils as a matter of "instinct," and, in general, few were willing to critically examine their ideas of readiness and analyze them in any detail.

Downing has reiterated Gates' contention that the age of readiness depends on the conditions of learning. If the infant teacher could spend more time helping individual pupils, or if the learning task were made easier, for instance, by using an augmented alphabet and simplifying the complexities of English orthography, would it not be likely that children would not need the same level of maturity? This suggestion carried an important change in the reading literature in Great Britain. It implied that reading was not a once-and-for-all attainment, but rather a process of accomplishments developing one from another.

Methods of Teaching

Knowledge of methods of teaching reading is clearly related to teachers' professional preparation and to the types of reading materials available. The main methods are usually understood to be the alphabetic, sentence, whole-word or look-and-say, and phonic. The alphabetic methods seem to be rarely used in this country, except in English rural schools and in some Welsh schools, where it is usually used in combination with other methods. However, teachers vary in the emphasis and order in which they introduce the different methods. These differences are related to the age of children being taught, the teachers' ideas about readiness, and the teachers' professional preparation and familiarity with the different methods.

It is clear that few teachers depend solely on a single method. None of the researches report any teachers who use only the phonic method, although a number of teachers seem to concentrate on global methods (that is, single word or sentence, or a combination of these) and provide no phonic instruction for their pupils. For instance, in the NFER London survey[33] in the late 1950s, only 6 per cent of the schools did not use phonics. Ten years later, the proportions in a Midland city and in Hertfordshire infant schools were 14 and 9 per cent, respectively.

During the early years of compulsory education in Great Britain, there was a tendency encouraged by what was known as the system of "payment by results" (teachers' salaries were related to their pupils' scholastic attainment). Pupils were to be encouraged to "read," irrespective of their interest or ability to understand what they were reading. The resulting "reading" was often mere word calling. Since the 1930s, the professional training of teachers in the colleges of education has been "child-centered," rather than subject-orientated. Increasingly, in the schools, more attention has been paid to reading for meaning from the very beginning. Remembering the effect of long drill periods spent teaching children their "sounds," many teachers—who had themselves learned to read by these analytic methods—reacted quite violently against the idea of teaching phonics and concentrated on global methods as being more meaningful to their young pupils.

Many of these teachers realized that, at some stage in the learning process, children must come to grips with the problems of the phoneme-grapheme relationship—even though the majority believed that phonics was an unsuitable method for young beginners. However, the NFER researches showed that a proportion of teachers over the years continued with the practice of introducing phonics to children early in their school career, no matter how unpopular the practice might be among teachers generally. In the Kent survey in the mid-1950s, Morris found that some 10 per cent of teachers who taught school beginners (reception class) taught phonics systematically. In the London survey in the late 1950s approximately one in three reception class teachers taught phonics, usually to all pupils. Ten years later in the Hertfordshire schools, the proportion was about the same, but in the Midland city schools—which were all infant schools—the proportion was much less—15 per cent of the sample.

At this point it is interesting to make a comparison with practices in Welsh and Scottish schools. Information from the National Child Development study[34] showed marked differences between the three countries. English pupils were introduced to phonics at a late age. The peak age for the introduction of phonics is from 5 years 6 months to 5 years 11 months, whereas in Wales and Scotland the corresponding age is 5 years to 5 years 5 months. Indeed, in the Scottish schools more than half the 5½-year-olds had been taught phonics, in comparison with 46 per cent of Welsh pupils and 29 per cent of English pupils. These figures were for the mid-1960s; they suggest that a higher proportion of Scottish and Welsh teachers believed in introducing pupils to phonics early in their schooling, in comparison with the "meaning from the beginning" approach of English teachers. Also, this research reported more variability in the English and Welsh samples than in the Scottish. It seems likely that there is more uniformity of practice in Scottish schools.

A recent comparison between Scottish and English schools[35] found that 55 per cent of Scottish teachers provided systematic phonic instruction to their infant pupils in comparison with 22 to 18 per cent of English teachers (Hertfordshire and Midland city). The English teachers preferred to give phonic instruction "incidentally," usually in the form of telling children the sounds of letters and letter combinations while "hearing" them read aloud. With a large class, and remembering the English infant teachers' concern with individual differences, it would seem that one way of systematically covering phonic "rules" would be to follow a programmed phonic scheme of some sort. Separate questions on the use of published schemes showed, however, that such schemes were not popular with English teachers. Only about one in ten were using any change in medium that might draw attention to the "coding" aspect of learning to read (for example, color codes and i.t.a.). Scottish teachers were more likely to depend on a single scheme, and two of the most popular schemes were ones in which phonics was treated in a systematic way from the beginning. These findings suggest that English pupils are introduced to phonics relatively late in their infant school career in an unsystematic fashion. Many of these children would only be beginning to gain independence in word-attack skills at the time of transfer to the junior school. In these circumstances, it would seem necessary for English junior school teachers to be trained in the teaching of reading and to have some knowledge of phonics.

Professional Training

Since 1960, teachers in England and Wales have had a three-year course of training. Prior to this, most teachers were trained for two years; some, immediately after the war, went through an emergency one-year period. Graduates of a university can achieve professional training by completing a one-year postgraduate course. Few of these are to be found teaching reading in a primary school, although some head teachers may be trained graduates.

It is difficult to obtain information about the professional preparation of teachers for teaching reading. In a 1968 survey[36] English teachers were asked for their recollections of their professional training; their answers were analyzed according to the length of time since they had trained. This analysis showed clearly that College of Education courses had changed over a twenty-year period.

Teachers trained in the 1950s had been given a great deal of information about global methods, particularly the sentence method, but few if any received information about phonics, phonetics, or linguistic principles in general. Only one in three believed their college preparation had provided information about all the methods of teaching reading.

However, the most disturbing factor was the number of teachers who answered that their preparation had consisted entirely of a single lecture with an essay assignment and/or reading list. The proportion of teachers receiving this inadequate preparation had risen steadily during the twenty years, and the figure for the group trained in the period 1963–1968 was 40 per cent. Although the training course had been lengthened, more time had not been made available to prepare for the teaching of a skill as basic as reading.

A survey by the young-teacher section of the NUT[37] reported that many recently qualified teachers agreed that their colleges were strong on the creative aspects of learning but not on the basic skills. One of the difficulties in the colleges is who should cover the teaching of reading. If it is included in the work of the English department, it is quite possible for the lecturer responsible for the course to be a graduate whose main subject is linguistics, or Anglo-Saxon, or The Lakeland Poets, but who has never actually had to teach young children to read. On the other hand, if teaching reading is the province of General Methods or the Education department, it is likely that the most experienced (in classroom terms) lecturer will take the course. But he might be an enthusiast for a particular method with little or none of the background knowledge of sociology, educational and experimental psychology, and linguistics that would enable him or her to evaluate the success of particular methods in relation to classroom conditions.

Most of the infant teachers in the 1968 English teachers' survey[38] who had been trained to teach reading reported that their courses had covered the psychological principles of children's development in relation to reading and different methods of teaching, but only half the courses included remedial and diagnostic work. It must be remembered that these teachers were recollecting their training. Many colleges would claim that they did cover these aspects but that students failed to remember what they had in lectures or to relate this knowledge to the practical situation of the classroom. Probably the important point is that many teachers in practice felt ill-equipped to deal with the poor reader. This showed up even more strongly when they were asked about their classroom difficulties. The problem most often mentioned was how to organize reading in large classes, but this was more often mentioned by the teachers who had been teaching longest. It probably reflected the increasing emphasis by educationists on the need to deal with individual differences and their criticism of class teaching methods. Among the more recently trained teachers, the difficulty of dealing with the slow or backward reader and, particularly, the problem of how to detect the poor reader before he becomes a problem were the main causes of concern.

Asked if inservice courses were available, which aspects or problems would they like treated, it was not surprising to find that the majority wanted discussions or courses on the slow reader. Although one in four teachers had been dissatisfied with their training, a third of the group were unable to say what they would find helpful. Among those who did know what they needed, there were requests for information about the higher order skills, the scope and range of reading materials, teaching "disadvantaged" pupils, reading methods (usually phonics and linguistics), and the use of apparatus—including innovations in visual aids and methods of organization. Comparative figures for a Scottish county showed twice as many teachers dissatisfied with their training, and only 19 per cent of the group unable to say what they wanted in inservice courses. Half wanted remedial work and one in ten wanted courses on how to teach phonics. These findings suggest that British teachers are increasingly concerned about their pupils' reading attainment, particularly as it affects their ability to profit from creative learning situations. Children who find reading difficult are at a disadvantage in active situations where they are encouraged to look up information and extend their own interests.

The survey data quoted on teacher preparation suggested that many colleges of education were increasingly relying on their students reading the relevant reading research for themselves. It was, therefore, of interest to know something about the professional reading of teachers. In the 1968 survey,[39] two out of three English infant teachers subscribed to a professional paper. However, most of these took only one regularly, usually a monthly educational magazine taken, according to the teachers themselves, for "its useful classroom pictures." Two out of three claimed to have bought a book on the teaching of reading, although only 43 per cent of the sample could give the book's title. The most often-mentioned reference book was Schonell's *The Psychology and Teaching of Reading,* first published in 1945.

There is some evidence that a relatively high proportion of English teachers in infant schools are what has been termed "first professionals." These are teachers usually of working class origin who are unfamiliar with the idea of continuing their vocational development by studying and reading after working hours or during school holidays. Also, because most of these teachers are women, two thirds of whom are married, it may be difficult to provide inservice courses to attract them. It is obvious, however, that such courses are needed to make up the deficiencies of preparation related to teaching "fashions" in the colleges.

University Provision

It has been suggested[40] that one way in which literacy standards could be improved in Britain would be for universities to establish departments of reading or reading centers in which reading research could be conducted and specialist teachers could be trained to assist with remedial work. The educational status of the teaching of reading would be raised incidentally also by this means.

At the present time, higher degree students can carry out reading research within the faculty departments of English and Social or Educational Psychology of different universities. Two colleges of education provide a one-year and a single-term course on the teaching of reading that can be taken by experienced teachers without a first degree. Teachers' centers and some Institutes provide part-time courses. The only Center for the Teaching of Reading so far to be established is one under the authority of Reading University. This center provides a one-term course for college lecturers as well as two-week "crash" courses for head teachers and advisers sent by local education authorities. The United Kingdom Reading Association (UKRA), which is the national affiliate of the International Reading Association (IRA) organizes an annual conference and study congress.

The NFER has organized a program of reading research and currently is undertaking a national survey of the reading attainment of 11- and 15-year-olds that includes the study of the influence of bilingualism in Wales on the teaching of reading. The National Bureau for Co-operation in Child Care has studied children's reading progress as part of its national child-development project. Some five hundred seriously backward readers were selected from the children in the national project and studied in greater detail. The results of this study are a sizeable contribution. The Schools Council, an influential organization composed of teachers and educationists, has financed research into the language development of young children and the provision of appropriate reading materials. This body also studied the use of the initial teaching alphabet and published an evaluative report [41] of this medium. The DES finances research and gave assistance to J. K. Jones [42] in his experiment into the effectiveness of his Colour Story Reading, a system using a color code intended to simplify the early stages of learning to read.

This brief description of the range and scope of reading research suggests that it is being carried out by researchers in universities, colleges of education, and local and national education bodies, such as the NFER and the DES. However, as there is no central institution with responsibility for coordinating, guiding, and disseminating the results, it is not easy to evaluate the quality of this research. It does appear that research is not cumulative because of poor communication between workers in the field, and, where results are produced, the style of their communication is such as often to be considered "unreadable" by the classroom teacher. The shortage of reading "experts," combined with the paucity of financial resources available for this type of research, results in work that often appears to the classroom teacher to be of little practical worth, and, to the academic, as inadequate because of limitations in scope and lack of scientific rigor.

Materials of Instruction

The NFER research has provided information about the type of reading materials being used in the primary school, particularly in the beginning stages in the infant schools. However, this information does not indicate the extent to which teachers are dependent on published reading materials. But, there is evidence from other aspects of these surveys and the data on professional preparation that teachers place great emphasis on the provision of reading materials and that, for many teachers in the infant school, the published reading scheme or "basal series" acts both as a reading curriculum and a means of assessing pupils' progress.

In the mid-1950s, Morris reported that the most popular published schemes in Kent were *Happy Venture* (Schonell), *Janet and John,* and *Beacon.* These three schemes were "mixed" programs in the sense that they tried to provide alternative approaches eventually leading to fluent reading with facility in word attack. For instance, *Janet and John* (an English version of an American scheme by O'Donnell and Munro) was basically a whole-word approach, but in its "phonic" version the last story in each book was replaced with phonic word lists. *Beacon,* originally published in the 1920s, used alternative introductory books—one based on look-and-say, the other using learned sight-sound associations. From the "book two" stage, the two strands came together, children being encouraged to use context as a guide to word recognition. *Happy Venture,* based on Schonell's concern for motivation and individual differences, made use of progressively more difficult phonic generalizations using short regular words previously introduced in the sight vocabulary. Unlike the earlier *Beacon* scheme, Schonell attached importance to the number of words introduced and the frequency of repetition. This principle of vocabulary control gained increasing importance in the schemes published during the next two decades.

Although *Janet and John* increased its popularity, recent research [43] has shown a gradual change among English teachers from dependency on a single scheme to the use of several schemes, usually similar in approach, based largely on global methods and vocabulary control. English editions of two more American schemes based on the look-and-say approach had been introduced: the *McKee Readers* in 1955, and *Happy Trio* by Gray, Monroe, Artley, and Arbuthnot in 1962. Home grown schemes such as *Queensway, Through the Rainbow,* and *Time for Reading* more often used words drawn from children's vocabulary, although frequently both the characters and interests were predominantly middle class. These schemes were primarily concerned with meaning and evolved out of the readiness climate, which presented reading as something that was "caught" rather than "taught." Many of the creators of these schemes were aware that some visual perception of words was involved, but this was usually to be developed through emphasis on the shape or configuration of words and seeing "bits of words" within whole words. Because this task was difficult, with the limitation set by the neglect of other clues such as letter-sound associations, syntax, and semantic connotations, the number of different words to be learned or recognized at sight was limited and the number of repetitions increased. This convention, particularly in introductory books, of disregarding language structure, resulted in a series of orders issued in a strange, imperative tense totally unlike anything to be found either in children's oral language or in the children's books they enjoyed listening to as stories read aloud: "Look, Jane, look. See, see the ducks."

The notable exception to these developments was the *Royal Road Readers* by Daniels and Diack, originally published in 1954. This series was based on a "phonic word method" that stressed the teaching of letter-sound relationships within words while retaining the importance of reading for meaning. The phonic generalizations were systematically introduced and deduced from words introduced in a meaningful way. Unfortunately, the scheme's illustrations were old-fashioned and the contents were of greater appeal to juniors than infants.

The fact that the pronunciation of certain letters in English is dependent on their position in words does mean that the learning of letter-sound associations can be a difficult task for beginners and the slow or backward. One way to simplify the task is to have reading materials produced in which one letter in color or one written symbol can stand for one sound or phoneme and only that one. Several systems using color have been used in Britain; Gattegno's *Words in Colour*,[44] a somewhat difficult system for teachers to grasp, and apparently most successful with backward older children, and Jones' *Colour Story Reading*.[45] Both systems limit the amount of information to be learned initially, and gradually the color code is dispensed with, as the children read more and more in traditional orthography (T.O.). In i.t.a.[46] children have to learn forty-four symbols, designed to resemble the upper half of letters in T.O. Children using this medium appear to be able to read faster and with greater ease in i.t.a. materials at the beginning stages.

Gradually, the controversy between synthetic and analytic methods is dying out, as it is realized that children use multiple clues in meaningful reading. However, this realization makes heavy demands on the writer of T.O. materials. If color codes or new alphabets are not to be used, the material should ideally be phonically progressive. At the same time it should use familiar words and sentence structures in the child's own language and be based on children's interests. With such material, pupils could practice successful detective work to find clues to the message conveyed by the print, with the confidence that their expectations were likely to be fulfilled.

Most of these expectations derive from children's language experiences. With children from "better" homes, there is a greater possibility of their guesses coinciding with the language in books and for them to make fewer "miscues." Two types of recently produced materials are based on the idea of exploiting children's knowledge of linguistic restraints. The first, a series called *Nippers*,[47] tried to produce materials of greater appeal to "working-class" children. The resulting stories have a realistic content and characters rooted in their environment. However, the characters' reported speech has been "tidied-up," apparently to make the books more acceptable to teachers who objected to the use of "bad grammar." *Breakthrough to Literacy*[48] materials use the stories produced by children as part of the Schools Council's Initial Literacy Program devised by MacKay and Thompson. These reading books are, therefore, based on themes familiar to children in schools. The sentence structure, length, and idiom appear similar to that used by young children in their initial writing in the infant school. However, the books are not phonically progressive—that is, there is no control of sounds within words—and this decoding clue will be absent for children who are linguistically less experienced and who may not always be familiar with the syntax and semantic clues of the language structure used in the classroom.

For nearly a decade there was a dearth of materials suitable for the slow reader, but, gradually during the 1960s, a steady flow of remedial schemes began to appear on the market. Some work has been done with teaching machines, but, generally, in the classroom, few teachers evolve their own planned scheme using published readers, or experiment with technological innovations such as the overhead projector, the continuous film loop, or even the tape recorder. The British Broadcasting Corporation (BBC) has pioneered the use of television for purposes of pupil instruction, starting with programs for backward juniors. More recently the BBC has developed a series on the introduction of phonic generalizations for use with top infant classes.

Methods of Testing and Evaluation

Generally, in England, during the past two decades, interest has centered on the identification of certain standards of literacy, usually at a superficial level, rather than with detailed diagnoses of individual difficulties. Because of the emphasis on the teaching of reading as the task of the infant school, concern for standards has been most apparent in the junior school. The philosophy of the infant school, with its emphasis on children's motivation, led teachers at this level of the educational system to be more interested in the children's desire to learn and in their attitude toward books than in standards of reading attainment. Indeed, this concern often finds expression in the teachers' view that time is better spent teaching than testing. However, the NFER surveys and the more recent work of this writer show that the transfer to junior school affects the attitude of the infant head teacher toward testing. More infant heads seem to be using tests, but the most popular test still appears to be that of word recognition first published fifty years ago. Only about a quarter of the English head teachers in this writer's 1968 survey used both a word-recognition test and a test of continuous prose, a practice recommended by reading "experts." The majority were using a word-recognition test as a means of determining reading standards before the time of transfer, although often the ability being tested was in direct contrast to the aims and relaxed atmosphere of these infant schools.

In this most recent survey, only one in four class teachers used a reading test, usually for purposes of assessing standards and rarely, if ever, for diagnostic purposes. Asked about their record keeping, most of the class teachers answered that they used records (keeping them either in their own record book or on individual pupils' bookmarks) of the pupils' progress through the published reading scheme. Very few teachers did more than record the number of the page read aloud when the teacher "heard" pupils. Also, only a small percentage mentioned any testing of pupils' knowledge of "sounds" or a regular check on pupils' progress. Few diagnostic tests have been published in this country and it would appear that, as most English children learn to read by reading rather than as the result of direct teaching, teachers diagnose children's difficulties by their experience of hearing the type of errors pupils make and associating these with particular reading difficulties, rather than by the use of standardized test procedures. Very little research has been done on these miscues and their relation to different types of difficulty.

Remedial teachers working with groups of slow readers are more likely to use tests other than those of word recognition. However, even among these teachers, there is considerable use of teacher-made, rather than published, diagnostic tests and behavior scales to discover the extent of perceptual difficulties.

In certain cases where children are obviously failing for no apparent reason and are not of low intelligence, or where slow reading progress has led to increased anxiety or behavior problems at school, children will be referred to a child guidance clinic. There is an insufficient number of these clinics and they are unevenly distributed throughout the country. They are usually staffed by a psychiatrist, an educational psychologist, and remedial teachers. Although children may be given both attainment and diagnostic tests, much of the work with individual pupils aims at easing the anxieties associated with failure.

In the 1960s pupils suspected of being "dyslexic" were referred to the Word Blind Centre in London, where they underwent a battery of tests and received remedial teaching over a period of several years. These children were usually referred by medical practitioners or officers of health. Generally, teachers are sceptical about the existence of a distinct syndrome peculiar to the dyslexic child. This center closed down recently.

Provision for slow readers within the normal education service has developed in a spasmodic way and there is insufficient space here to summarize the characteristics of this development. A considerable amount of research has been concerned with the short-term and long-term effects of taking children out of their normal classes for one or two periods per week of remedial teaching. Generally speaking, short-term gains in reading attainment of several months of reading age per month of remedial treatment are frequently found, but these gains are usually recorded on tests of word recognition rather than reading comprehension. Follow-up studies for varying periods (up to as long as three years) after treatment indicate little or no difference between children who have received special attention and those who did not. Large practice effects may be involved when children are repeatedly tested during remedial teaching. The consequent improvement is illusory, and, when remedial treatment ceases, these children resume their ordinary rate of progress. This also raises the question of what happens to such children after they return to their normal classes. Possibly, factors that originally caused problems for these children in learning to read could become less important in the remedial situation but again assume import-ance in the ordinary, often overcrowded classroom, thus affecting reading progress. Cashdan and Pumfrey[49] have questioned the "natural" improvement of the control groups in some of these experiments. It is quite possible that the "untreated" children are in fact receiving help in the form of advice to their teachers from the specialist remedial teacher. The relief of pressure when some of their classmates, often those making greatest demands on the teacher's time and patience, are out of the classroom receiving special attention may also be significant. Indirectly, this highlights again the importance of the *quality* of the teaching pupils receive in the day to day process of their schooling.

REFERENCES

1. Central Advisory Council for Education (England), *Children and their Primary Schools* ("The Plowden Report"), London: H.M.S.O., 1966.
2. Department of Education and Science, *Primary Education in Wales* ("The Gittens Report"), London: H.M.S.O., 1968.
3. Scottish Education Department, *Primary Education in Scotland,* Edinburgh: H.M.S.O., 1965.
4. Ministry of Education, *Reading Ability: Some Suggestions for Helping the Backward,* Pamphlet No. 18, London: H.M.S.O., 1950; also, Ministry of Education, *Standards of Reading 1948 to 1956,* Pamphlet No. 32, London: H.M.S.O., 1957.
5. Department of Education and Science, *Progress in Reading 1948 to 1964,* Education Pamphlet No. 50, London: H.M.S.O., 1966.
6. Morris, J. M., *Standards and Progress in Reading,* Slough: NFER, 1966; Johnson, M. E. B., "Teachers' attitudes to educational research," *Educational Research,* 9 (1966), 74–79; Goodacre, E. J., *Teachers and Their Pupils' Home Background,* Slough: NFER, 1968; Lunn, Joan C. Barker, *Streaming in the Primary School,* Slough: NFER, 1970.
7. Inner London Education Authority, *Literacy Survey: Summary of Interim Results of the Study of Pupils' Reading Standards,* London: Inner London Education Authority, 1969.
8. "Report of National Child Development Study (1958 cohort)," *Times Educational Supplement* (January 9, 1970).
9. Johns, E., "The age factor in reading retardation," *Researches and Studies* (University of Leeds Institute of Education), 24 (1962), 1–7.
10. Pringle, M. L. Kellmer, Butler, N. R., and Davie, R., *11,000 Seven-Year-Olds,* London: Longmans, 1966.
11. Board of Education, *Report of the Consultative Committee on the Primary School,* London: H.M.S.O., 1931.
12. Morris, J. M., *Reading in the Primary School,* London: Newnes, 1959.
13. Shearer, E., "The effect of date of birth on teachers' assessments of children," *Educational Research,* 10 (1967), 51–56.
14. France, N., and Wiseman, S., "An educational guidance programme for the primary school," *British Journal of Educational Psychology,* 36 (1966), 210–226.
15. Southgate, V., "Approaching i.t.a. results with caution," *Educational Research,* 7 (1965), 83–96.
16. Southgate, V., and Roberts, G. R., *Reading—Which Approach?* London: University of London Press, 1970.
17. Lovell, K., "Informal v. formal education and reading attainment in the junior school," *Educational Research,* 6 (1963), 71–76.

18. Wiseman, S., *Education and Environment,* Manchester: Manchester University Press, 1964.
19. Pidgeon, D. A., *Expectation and Pupil Performance.* Slough: NFER, 1970.
20. Gooch, S., "Four years on," *New Society,* **193** (1966), 10–12.
21. Goodacre, E. J., *School and Home,* Slough: NFER, 1970.
22. National Union of Teachers, *The State of Our Schools,* London: NUT, 1964.
23. Pidgeon, D. A., "School type differences in ability and attainment," *Educational Research,* **1** (1959), 62–71.
24. Goodacre, E. J., *Reading in Infant Classes,* Slough: NFER, 1967.
25. Shields, M., "Reading and transition to junior school," *Educational Research,* **11** (1968), 143–147.
26. Baird, C. L., "The role of the teacher of six- and seven-year-old children," *British Journal of Educational Psychology,* **38** (1968), 323–324.
27. Mycock, M., "A comparison of vertical grouping and horizontal grouping in the infant school," *British Journal of Educational Psychology,* **37** (1967), 133–135.
28. Bernstein, B., "Language and social class," *British Journal of Sociology,* **11** (1960), 271–276; also Bernstein, B., and Henderson, D., "Social class differences in the relevance of language to socialization," *Sociology,* **3** (1969), 1–20.
29. Morris, *Reading in the Primary School, op. cit.*
30. Goodacre, *Reading in Infant Classes, op. cit.*
31. Sanderson, A. E., "The idea of reading readiness: A re-examination," *Educational Research,* **6** (1963), 3–9.
32. Downing, J., "Reading readiness re-examined," in Downing, J. (ed.), *The First International Reading Symposium,* London: Cassell, 1966.
33. Goodacre, *Reading in Infant Classes, op. cit.*
34. Pringle, *et al., op. cit.*
35. Clark, M. M., private communication to the writer (June 1970).
36. Goodacre, E. J., "Learning how to teach reading—A research note on the findings of a postal survey," in Peters, M. (ed.), *Conference: Professional Preparation of Students for the Teaching of Reading,* Cambridge: Cambridge Institute of Education, 1969.
37. "Report of survey by National Union of Teachers, Young Teachers' Section," *Times Educational Supplement* (July 4, 1969).
38. Goodacre, "Learning how to teach reading—A research note on the findings of a postal survey," *op. cit.*
39. *Ibid.*
40. Downing, J., Letter in the correspondence column *Times Educational Supplement* (October 13, 1968).
41. Warburton, F. W., and Southgate, V., *i.t.a.: An Independent Evaluation,* London: Chambers and Murray, 1969.
42. Jones, J. K., *Colour Story Reading: A Research Report,* London: Nelson, 1967.
43. Goodacre, E. J., "Published reading schemes," *Educational Research,* **12** (1969), 30–35.
44. Gattegno, C., *Words in Color: Background and Principles,* Chicago: Learning Materials, Inc., 1962.
45. Jones, J. K., "A research report on colour story reading," *Journal of Typographic Research,* **2** (January 1968), 53–58.
46. Downing, J., *Evaluating the Initial Teaching Alphabet,* London: Cassell, 1967.

47. Berg, Leila (ed.), *Nippers* (Five groups of graded books for children aged 6 to 9), Basingstoke, Hants: Macmillan, 1969.
48. *Breakthrough to Literacy* (Materials include Teacher's Manual, Teacher's Sentence Maker, Magnetic Board Kit, Children's Sentence Maker and Word Maker, and 24 reading books), Harlow, Essex: Longman, 1970.
49. Cashdan, A., and Pumfrey, P. D., "Some effects of the remedial teaching of reading," *Educational Research,* **11** (1969), 138–142.

CHAPTER 18

Hong Kong

CHE KAN LEONG*

GRAY[1] distinguishes between three main groups of languages: ideographic languages such as Chinese, syllabaries such as Japanese, and alphabetic systems such as English. Although Chinese differs considerably from English, there are certain parallel features in structure between the two. The following account outlines the salient characteristics of the Chinese language as they relate to reading and attempts to show the isomorphy with English. Practices of teaching reading in Chinese to primary school children in Hong Kong are described as an illustration. A brief discussion of Chinese language reform is given to highlight the effect of the language on reading.

Characteristics of the Chinese Language

Chinese as a system of visual signs with which language is symbolized is a good example of morphemic writing. Each symbol or character represents a morpheme or a minimum meaningful linguistic unit. A character 字 (/dzi/ unaspirated, falling tone) as the smallest functional unit should be distinguished from a word 詞 (/tsi/ aspirated, high-rising tone) as the smallest immediate constituent unit of segmental sentences. Even though a character is mono-syllabic, a word may contain a monosyllabic or polysyllabic morpheme. (The transcription for Cantonese sounds used here is based on the International Phonetic System in S. L. Wong, *A Chinese Syllabary Pronounced According to the Dialect of Canton,* rev. ed., Hong Kong: Chung Hwa Book Co., Ltd., 1968.)

This monosyllabism is a main feature of the Chinese language. Karlgren quotes the German scholar Finck thus:

> the Chinese words consist, not absolutely always but in the majority of cases, of a single syllable; on the other hand, the relation of these monosyllabic words to the whole sentence is not expressed by any marks in the words themselves, but in the first place by a fixed word-order, and secondly—and in a less important degree— by the addition of words the original concrete sense of which is so far faded that they be used for formal purposes somewhat like our so-called auxiliaries.[2]

It is on the erroneous assumption that these auxiliaries form part of the minimum

* Permission is acknowledged to quote from the work of the late Dr. Gustav Herdan. Appreciation is given to Dr. John McLeod of the University of Saskatchewan, Dr. Carl L. Kline of Children's Aid Society of Vancouver, and to this writer's former colleagues in the Education Department, Hong Kong for their helpful suggestions.

morphemic unit that writers such as de Francis[3] and Kennedy[4] raised the "monosyllabic myth." The latter, for example, pointed out that the inclusion of such auxiliaries as 的, 了 would give the language some 5 per cent of disyllabic characters. This disyllabic nature, however, only applies to very rare cases such as the equivalence of "rose(s)" 玫 瑰 and "irritate" 囉 唆.

Chinese is also said to be isolating in contrast to inflexional languages where there is a merging of semantically distinct features either in a single bound form or in closely united bound forms or to agglutinative languages where bound forms follow one another. The character 人 /jên/ means equally "man," "man's," "men," "men's," "the man," "the man's," "the men," "the men's." The use of classifiers overcomes the difficulty.

Chinese is best described as analytical, where each word is a one-syllable morpheme or a compound word or phrase word and where there are few bound forms. This is in contrast to synthetical languages, which use many bound forms, an example being Latin where *canto* means "I sing"; *cantas,* "you sing"; and *cantat,* "he, she, it sings."

In addition to its monosyllabic, isolating, and analytical nature, Chinese has a predominance of vowel sounds and a paucity of consonant sounds. Double consonant blends such as /bl/, /sp/, /nd/, /nt/ are nonexistent. The dominant pattern is for one consonant at the beginning of a vowel, except fricatives (/ts/, /dz/, /ch/, /dj/), which are regarded as single sounds. Furthermore, the final consonants /n/, /ŋ/, /m/, /p/, /t/, /k/ are truncated. Thus, every character must have a vowel sound or a semivowel sound of /n/, /ŋ/, or /m/.

This dominance of vowel over consonant sounds accounts for the relatively small number of different syllables in the spoken form of the language. In the common language (popularly known as Mandarin or Kuoyu) there are 420 different syllables, many of which are quite similar phonetically. This, together with the monosyllabic nature of the language, leads to a great number of homophones. The phoneme /jên/ by itself can be interpreted as 人 "man," 仁 "kind," 引 "lead," 因 "cause," and other symbols; similarly, the syllable /i/ may mean as many as thirty-eight different words including 衣 "clothes," 意 "idea," 一 "one," 依 "depend," 醫 "medicine," 椅 "chair," and 易 "easy."

To resolve this confusion of homophones, a system of musical accents or tones is used. The common language distinguishes between four tones:

1. high level: "mother" 媽, pronounced as /ma/.
2. high rising: "hemp" 蔴, pronounced as /ma/.
3. low rising: "horse" 馬, pronounced as /ma/.
4. low falling: "scold" 罵, pronounced as /ma/.

Southern Chinese, as Cantonese, further adds two tones: namely, the high and low tones for each and an intermediate tone for the low-falling pitch as well, making a total of nine tones. The bases of these tonal differences are (1) duration, or the relative length of time through which the vowel organs are kept in a position, and (2) stress, or intensity or loudness.

The isolating feature of the Chinese language makes for the flexibility of grammatical categories and the possibility of a character in any position. The same character 流 in different combinations can assume functions of different grammatical categories. Thus, in 水 流 "water flows" 流 is a verb; in 流 水 "flowing water" it is an adjective; in 流 行 "popular" the combination is an adjective, and in 河 流 "river" the word is a noun. This fluidity allows for more combinations of characters, enhances the richness of the language, and permits the learner to build up his repertoire.

In the construction of sentences, Chinese shows a clear word order: subject + verb + object. The similarity to English is considerable. One divergence is in the interrogative form, where the same declarative order is used with the addition of the character 嗎 /ma/ to denote interrogation. An example is 他 坐 嗎? /tà tso ma?/ (Does he sit?) where the order subject + verb is preserved. A variant form poses the alternatives "yes" and "no," such as 他 坐 不 坐? /tà tso pu tso?/ (He sits, he sits not.)

These peculiarities—the lack of grapheme-phoneme correspondence; the abundance of homonyms; the differential use of tones as distinguishing features; and the importance of word order—all may seem to add to the difficulties in learning Chinese. However, there are features in the language that help the learning task. To understand this it is necessary to have some idea of the way in which Chinese characters evolved.

Principles of Formation of Chinese Characters

Chinese writing is said to have its origin in the second millennium B.C. Over the years, both the style 字 體 and structure 字 形 have changed considerably. The characters can be grouped into these six categories:

1. *Pictographs* 象 形 字 *are characters based on pictures of objects.* The illustrations here show the change in style, as distinct from structure, over the years; intermediate changes having been omitted for clarity:

moon		to		to	月
to walk, cross-walk		to		to	行
mountain		to		to	山
to hit the target, middle		to		to	中
bow		to		to	弓

2. *Ideographs* 指 事 字 *or diagrammatic characters indicate the idea or ideas they are meant to convey:* 一 "one," 二 "two," 上 "up," 下 "down."

3. *Compound ideographs or suggestive characters* 會 意 字 *are those formed on the basis of associations of ideas suggested by their constituent parts.* Examples

are 明 "bright," from the combination of 日 "sun" and 月 "moon"; 林 "forest," from the doubling of 木 "tree" and 信 "honest," suggested by 人 + 言 "the words of people" (if they can be trusted!).

4. *Loan characters* 假 借 字 *are those adopted for new characters on the basis of identity of sound.* Thus, 來 "come," derived from 來 (originally a picture 來 denoting wheat), assumes the present form because of identity of sound; 萬 (derived from 萬 "scorpion") means "ten thousand."

5. *Phonetic compounds* 形 聲 字 *form by far the largest category, comprising at least 80 per cent of the characters.* Each character in this system consists of two elements, a *signific,* or *radical,* and a *phonetic.* The former determines the meaning and the latter suggests the pronunciation. Thus 河 "river," with 氵 or 水 as the equivalent of the affix "hydro," and 可 as the phonetic, gives the logograph that is both intelligible and pronounceable. Similarly, 銅 "copper" is compounded of 金 "metal" and the phonetic 同.

6. *Chuanchu, or analogous characters,* 轉 注 字 *are mainly new characters patterned after old ones so that they are analogous in meaning but do not share the same sound.* Examples are 爺 "grandfather" with 父 "father" as radical but not the sound of 耶.

It is interesting to estimate the size of the vocabulary of the Chinese language. The oldest style of writing, the Oracle Bone writing 甲 骨 文, dating back to 1766–1122 B.C., consisted of about 2,000 characters. The Small Seal style 小 篆, developed in the Ch'in Dynasty in 221–206 B.C., had 3,300 characters. The authoritative Kanghsi dictionary 康 熙 字 典, compiled in the eighteenth century and one of the standard references in current use, contains about 42,000 to 48,000 characters, depending on the editions referred to. Of these, only about 6,000 to 7,000 are actively used by members of the language community. For children in primary schools, a minimum vocabulary of about 3,500 characters constitutes an adequate corpus for their schooling and practical purposes in their day-to-day work after leaving school. Chuang[5] in a comprehensive study compiled a "fundamental vocabulary" of 5,262 characters—the number almost being the mean between that estimated for primary school children and for adequate everyday use. The list is divided into characters most frequently used with about 2,800 characters; those less frequently used; and those rarely used with about 1,200 characters in each of these latter two categories. Kennedy[6] edited the minimum vocabularies of written Chinese. His list of 1,020 characters includes those used at Yale University, New Haven, Connecticut, for checking purposes. The list of 2,421 characters is the official list for adult education in mainland China. This is further broken down into (1) 1,010 most frequently used characters, forming with another 490 characters a limiting list of 1,500 characters; (2) a supplementary list of 500 characters; and (3) a list of technical terms of 421 characters. Leong,[7] in his experimental work with the active vocabulary of written Chinese with primary third-year children in Hong Kong in 1966–1967, studied 1,851 different characters and the facility with which children at that level could reproduce them. From these studies it would appear that the range of Chinese vocabulary for primary school children of about five hundred to six hundred characters for each of the six years of schooling, with an accumulation of about 3,500 different characters, is well founded.

Written Chinese Symbols As Related to Reading and Isomorphy with English

More than sixty years ago, Huey[8] drew attention to reading as an information-gathering activity. Gates[9] and Strang[10] each pointed out that the "thought-getting" process should be developed as a complex organization of patterns of high cognitive processes. Smith[11] stresses the importance of categorization in reading, which includes detection of difficulties, establishment of relations between categories (for example, grapheme-phoneme correspondence), and the discovery of cues. Similar perceptual learning as described by Gibson[12] is at work in learning Chinese. Although each character has to be learned, the often-mentioned reliance on rote memory is overrated. Halle's comparison of the Chinese writing system to commercial codes used in telegraphic transmission overlooks a number of important characteristics in the language:

> Since the strokes [in Chinese characters] are arbitrary symbols, the writer's or reader's task is equivalent to that of a person trying to remember telephone numbers. And, since in order to read a newspaper one needs to be able to read several thousand words, the person who wishes to read a Chinese newspaper must have memorized several thousand arbitrary stroke sequences. This task is roughly equivalent to memorizing several thousand telephone numbers, something that is far from easy and in the case of writing and reading, also quite unnecessary.[13]

The comparison to memorizing telephone numbers is not quite apt, as chunking and other mnemonic devices can make the task more meaningful and increase one's storage capacity. Similarly, in learning Chinese, the square-shaped characters are composed in such a way that there is what Chao[14] calls elegance in their symmetry and balance. Structurally the characters take on one of these five main forms:

1. Logographs occupying the full square as in 日 "sun," 凸 "convex," 凹 "concave."

2. Logographs balanced vertically as in 門 "door," 休 "rest" (man 人 leaning against tree).

3. Logographs in a tripartite vertical form as in 淋 "to sprinkle" (water on trees).

4. Logographs balanced horizontally as in 早 "early" (sun 日 on top of pole), 牢 "gaol" (cow 牛 in enclosure).

5. Logographs balanced three-ways as in 森 "forest" (multiples of trees 木).

Perceived this way, the characters add much more to meaning. They compare favorably with an alphabetic writing system, such as English, in the information the twenty-six letters can convey. The reference to "arbitrary stroke sequences" of characters loses sight of the degree of orderliness and progression. In general, the strokes fall into these broad groups:

Group:

1.	1. ＼ 2. ／ 3. ⌒ 4. ＼ 5. ＼ 6. ⟩
2.	7. ⅂ 8. ⅃ 9. ⟩
3.	10. ⌡ 11. ⟨ 12. ∪ 13. ∟ 14. ∨ 15. ㇋
4.	16. ㇠ 17. ㇅ 18. ㇆

Group 1 includes beginning strokes running in one direction; groups 2 and 3 those in two directions; and group 4 those in three directions. Thus, the character 河 "river" beginning from ＼ comes under the 1 in the first group; the sequence from the top left quadrant (sometimes from the center-line as in 牢 "gaol") going downward is both logical and easy to follow. Moreover, the fixed number and order of strokes in a character are comparable to the dots and dashes in the Morse code and give the written language its coding character.

Then the number of strokes is often mentioned as overloading the task of memorizing the characters. These can vary from anything with one stroke to about fifty-two strokes and may not be very economical in reproduction. This can be seen by comparing the word "dot" 點, in both English and Chinese, where the latter requires no fewer than seventeen strokes! There is, however, an optimal stroke number analogous to Miller's "magical number seven, plus or minus two."[15] This writer took a count of the stroke number of the 2,830 most commonly used characters in Chuang's[16] list and found the mean number of strokes to be 11.61, with a standard deviation of 4.43. Insofar as Chuang's repertoire can be regarded as *la langue* of the Chinese—it is based on a number of sources such as dictionaries, the Chinese typewriter, and reading materials—the corpus of 1,851 characters of written Chinese derived from the language repertoire of children in Hong Kong in Leong's 1970 study[17] might be regarded as *la parole* of the language. Studies reveal the almost identical results with 11.27 as the mean stroke number of these characters and 4.45 as the standard deviation. The correspondence is all the more remarkable in view of the time span of some thirty years and the different approaches between the two studies. The frequency distribution of the characters by stroke number is shown in Table 18-1.

Although more bits of information can be conveyed with an increase in strokes, more effort is also required in reproduction. On the other hand, characters below a threshold stroke number, probably below seven, may reduce the contrastive elements so essential to reading and may make for some cognitive confusion. There is some evidence for this in Leong's 1968 study of the written vocabulary of Hong Kong children.[18] An apparently simple character 仁 "kind," with only four strokes, was written correctly by 21 per cent of the sample of more than four hundred children. Such a complex form as 健 "strong" was reproduced by 73 per cent of the same sample. Other examples of this differential inverse relationship between ease or difficulty of learning and stroke number

TABLE 18-1. Frequency Distribution of Characters by Number of Strokes in Chuang's List and Leong's List.*

Number of strokes	Chuang's list f	Leong's list f
30	1	
29		
28		
27	4	2
26	2	3
25	14	2
24	16	5
23	11	10
22	19	9
21	32	20
20	42	23
19	53	39
18	72	44
17	105	69
16	119	87
15	191	128
14	207	104
13	220	138
12	263	167
11	268	168
10	254	161
9	224	155
8	217	134
7	171	106
6	110	89
5	91	85
4	74	60
3	34	28
2	15	13
1	1	2
N	2830	1851
M	11.61	11.27
SD	4.43	4.45

*The distribution is interesting and is almost symmetrical. This mean stroke number of 11 to 12 $\pm$ 4 is significant and is probably the limen for optimal visual cues in the perception of Chinese characters.

are found with such characters as 奸 "sly" (six strokes with a facility index of 5 per cent) and 奴 "slave" (five strokes with a facility index of 2 per cent). Although other factors, such as unfamiliarity with concepts, may have been at work, the paucity of strokes may not help in the meaningful differentiation of graphic symbols. In this respect, it should be noted that the Kanji, or Chinese characters component of the Japanese syllabary, all contain symbols of fewer than sixteen strokes.

Even though the regularity of sequence and number of strokes contribute to the configuration, the "whole" of a character needs to be broken down into salient features to distinguish one character from the other. What are the contrastive elements that form the critical unit of written Chinese? A parallel can be found in the feature analytical approach in learning English.

The classic experiment by Woodworth, who noted that "familiar words even as long as 12–20 letters [can be] correctly read from a single exposure of 100 msecs,"[19] is often taken as showing the importance of the "whole" approach to reading. This reliance on template matching by noting the coincidence or congruence with a model provides only a partial answer to conceptual learning (Neisser,[20] Smith[21]). Words and letters can be recognized in new patterns and orientations, in different styles, and with varying blank spaces between them. If one of the templates were DIM, the new stimulus DIN would match it far more closely than D I M does. The experiment by Miller, Bruner, and Postman,[22] with letter-by-letter approximations to English, further demonstrates the inadequacy of the template theory. They succeeded in showing that the amount of information transmitted at any given exposure duration was roughly constant. Although more letters were reported at higher orders of approximation, each letter represented correspondingly fewer "bits" of information because of the greater redundancy. The results of the experiment show that neither a template theory nor reliance on isolated individual letters accounts for the reading process. There must be units "larger" than strings of letters but "smaller" than words that are critical.

This "critical unit of language for the reading process" is defined by Gibson and her associates at Cornell as a "letter-group which has an invariant relationship with a phonemic pattern."[23] Just as Miller[24] has shown that redundant strings of letters, as opposed to random ones, possess a structure that helps in their recall, so Gibson argues that spelling patterns are structured in much the same way. For example, certain clusters of letters, such as QU, always go together at the beginning rather than at the end of a word, the same applies to GL, which is used initially rather than terminally. Gibson mentions three levels of rules: morphological, grammatical, and above all orthographic rules. Extracting the invariance of orthographic structure enables the child to transfer to the learning of new words. This search for invariance is explained by her as "reduction of uncertainty, specifically the discovery of structure that reduces the information processing and increases cognitive economy. This is perceptual learning, not just remembering something."[25]

This spelling-to-sound invariant relationship is inherent in the basic internal structure of Chinese: namely, the radical that gives meaning to the character, and the stem or phonetic that gives the sound. These phonemic-semantic components constitute the critical units in the language. In general, the combination falls into one of these categories:

1. Radical on the left half and phonetic on the right half as in 河 "river" where 氵 or 水 is the equivalent of "hydro."

2. Radical on the left third and phonetic on the right two thirds as in 淋 "sprinkle."

3. Radical between each third of the phonetic as in 辮 "pigtail."

4. Radical on the right half and phonetic on the left as in 動 "movement" where 力 means "force."

5. Radical above and phonetic below as in 牢 "gaol," where 宀 means enclosure, 旱 "drought" with 日 "the sun" perched high up.

6. Radical below and phonetic above as in 盲 "blind," where 目 "sight, eye" is 亡 "lost."

7. Radical outside and phonetic inside as in 閂 "bolt" (to the door 門).

There are, however, variations in the relative positions of the signific and phonetic. From the sample in 7 here one would assume 問 "ask" to have 門 "door" as the radical. However, it is 口 "mouth" that is the signific. This is reasonable if one considers the meaning of the word. In addition, there are characters with an obscure sound component such as 雜 "miscellaneous" with 集 "put together" as the sound component that has been split into 隹 "a bird" and 木 "wood" with 木 under 衣 "clothes" to give the character its symmetrical form. Similarly 染 "dye" has a sound component not far removed from 丸 "pellet" (hence the common misspelling of 染). Morphologically 染 is composed of 氵 "water," 九 "nine" (times), 木 "wood" (a dye stuff in olden days), hence its meaning. Furthermore, there are variant forms of the same character such as 鄰 "neighbor" where a transposition of the radical 阝 to the right is acceptable, thus 鄰, or 朶; 朵 "petal" or 雞 and 鷄 "chicken" where 隹 is the old version of the modern character 鳥 "bird."

As in English, where there is no one-to-one grapheme-phoneme correspondence, one would expect irregularities. What the learner has to look for is the more stable patterns rather than individual elements. Even though the English phonemic system cannot strictly be equated with sounds in Chinese, there is isomorphy between the distinctive functions of phonemes as contrastive linguistic members and the distinctive properties of the 214 radicals. In a number of studies Herdan[26] has elegantly demonstrated the duality of the characters. He makes quantitative linguistic comparisons between the Chinese language and the alphabetic system. He points out that the information processing of 214 radicals in combination with 1,700 phonetics should be viewed in this arrangement: (1) according to the number of strokes of the phonetic; and (2) according to the number of ideograms per subgroup of radicals. By using the first, the variable of the frequency distribution is the stroke number, and the probabilities are the combined lengths of the subgroups for a particular stroke number. By using the second arrangement, the variable is the length of subgroups, and the probabilities are the frequencies of subgroups of a particular length (although not of a particular stroke number). Herdan performs a counting experiment on the characters (numbers and relative frequencies) with regard to the number of strokes in two dictionaries—Mathews' dictionary, with 8,711 characters, and Fenn's dictionary, with 5,798 characters—and finds very similar distributions with peaks at phonetics with stroke numbers three, five, and eight. A further count on Karlgren's dictionary of Chinese and Sino-Japanese, which is arranged according to phonetics, shows remarkably similar distributions. Herdan concludes that the hypothesis is justified: the distribution of ideograms according to the number of strokes in the phonetic is determined by that of phonetics according to the same variable—namely, stroke number. The greater the number of a certain class of phonetics, the greater the number of ideograms using phonetics of that particular class. This relationship is analogous to that between the phoneme distribution of grammatical linguistic form and the total phoneme distribution. From the work of Dewey,[27] Herdan points out that in English more than

> 25% of the total occurrences are accounted for by only 3 letters [e, t, a] or 11.5% of the number of different letters;
> 50% of the total of occurrences are accounted for by 6 letters [e, t, a, o, i, n] or 23% of the number of different letters;
> 75% of the total of occurrences are accounted for by 11 letters [e, t, a, o, i, n, s, r, h, l, d] or 42% of the number of different letters.

From this and from the frequency distribution of German and French alphabets, Herdan emphasizes that the alphabet, although basically combinatorial and probabilistic, is subject to these constraints:

> the choice of the number of elements (letters) in the alphabet, the preference for some letters rather than others, and also the preference for some combinations of letters and the inadmissibility of others. Word length, however—as distinct from word structure in the sense of phoneme arrangement inside the word—is largely determined by combinatorial principles.[28]

This finding is significant. In his analysis of Mathews' dictionary, Herdan[29] finds that these seventeen radical groups (8 per cent of 214 radical groups) account for 50.17 per cent of the 8,711 characters (see Table 18-2). The high frequency of a small number of radicals must necessarily relate to morphological and spelling constraints that are analogous to English. Further evidence is the near isomorphy between the two language systems. Using information theory and the binary coding of letters of the alphabetic system represented by English and Russian and ideographic writing represented by Chinese vocabulary in Mathews' dictionary with groupings under radicals, Herdan offers empirical evidence for their similarity. There exist remarkably similar measures of redundancy in the different codes. In other words, there is a close correspondence in the combinatory property that enables users of the language to use the stability of the relative frequencies for making guesses as to missing parts of the message with a reasonable degree of correctness. From his data, Herdan points out that, for the greater part of the Chinese dictionary (because three quarters of the vocabulary is for radicals with the number of derivatives between 455 and 40) the system of coding by stroke number is largely that of binary coding. Redundancy here is interpreted in this context and does not refer to the quality of the language as a means of communication. It is this linguistic correspondence—the

TABLE 18-2. Relative Frequency of Symbols for the Most Frequently
Occurring Seventeen Radical Groups.*

Radical	Relative frequency of symbols listed under radical (%)	Cumulative frequency
水	5.23	
手	4.87	
口	4.33	
艸	4.10	
木	4.01	
人	3.63	
		26.17
心	3.47	
糸	2.67	
言	2.49	
金	2.45	
虫	2.26	
土	1.94	
肉	1.91	
女	1.84	
火	1.75	
竹	1.70	
酉	1.52	
		50.17

*After Herdan, 1962, Table 30. (See reference 26.)

derivatives or the logical counterpart—Herdan emphasizes, that underlies the isomorphy of the apparently discordant linguistic codes.

Because Herdan's study deals with the dictionary that can be regarded as *la langue* of the Chinese, it may be of interest to study also the frequency distribution of characters by radicals from Leong's 1970 group,[30] which may be considered as *la parole*. This is displayed in Table 18-3.

When allowance is made for the different nature of the two lists of characters, the peaks of both distributions at stroke numbers five and eight are of interest.

What then are the implications to be drawn from Herdan's linguistic studies? If we accept the correspondence between English and Chinese as explained here, then some of the principles and research findings are relevant across linguistic boundaries. As with English, the child learning Chinese should be encouraged and guided to develop reading habits that utilize all the types of constraint

TABLE 18-3. Distribution of Chinese Characters with Regard to the Number of Strokes in the Phonetic*

No. of strokes in the phonetic	Mathews' dictionary		Leong's list	
	f	%	f	%
1	71	0.82	27	1.58
2	241	2.76	84	4.90
3	378	4.34	117	6.83
4	722	8.28	196	11.44
5	*949*	*10.88*	*206*	*12.03*
6	779	8.93	185	10.80
7	763	8.75	166	9.69
8	*985*	*11.29*	*192*	*11.21*
9	833	9.55	160	9.34
10	688	7.89	86	5.02
11	590	6.81	90	5.25
12	534	6.12	75	4.37
13	396	4.54	52	3.04
14	246	2.82	27	1.58
15	149	1.71	17	0.99
16	130	1.49	13	0.76
17	89	1.02	6	0.35
18	60	0.68	6	0.35
19	57	0.65	5	0.29
20	17	0.20		
21	15	0.17	1	0.06
22	14	0.16	2	0.12
Total	8,706		1,713†	

*Modified from Table 3. Herdan, 1964 (See reference 26.)
†138 radicals forming individual characters not included to enable meaningful comparison to be made; hence, the total of 1,713 in the column.

present in the stimulus and to note the contrastive elements in the characters. This ability to recognize and to discriminate graphic shapes before decoding them and to find a phonemic correspondence is a prerequisite in reading. In teaching a character such as 辦 "perform," the teacher should explain the salient feature 力 "to carry out" and highlight this by bringing in minimal pairs such as 辯 "discuss, debate" where 言 "word" is the operative feature; 辮 "pigtail" with 糸 "silk, hair"; and 瓣 "petal" with 瓜 "melon" as the distinctive units. When these linguistically similar characters 辦, 辯, 辮, 瓣 are put together in context, the child is better able to generalize in similar reading environments and to generate his own rule to read new words. Traditional teaching methods using the multisensory approach where the child sees the character, analyzes the structure components, sounds out the character according to the general principles of the phonetic, and traces each stroke in its proper sequence—either with a finger, pencil, or pen—also help to hammer the character in.

In this connection it is interesting to speculate on the connection between ideographic languages and reading disabilities. There is a paucity of literature in the area. One study of reading difficulties of Japanese children is reported by Makita.[31] He finds an incidence of only 0.98 per cent of reading disability in Japanese children and points out that their difficulties tend to occur more with the Kanji component or Chinese character. This rarity of reading disability in Japan must be interpreted with caution because of the different educational philosophies, practices, and provisions in Japan and Western countries. Traditional respect for learning, positive parental attitudes, and keen competition for academic qualifications and jobs may have an effect on reading. Also, Makita's finding that Japanese children have difficulties with Kanji script seems to be at variance with the findings of two other Japanese neuropsychiatrists, Kuromaru and Okada, as reported by Money.[32] Kuromaru and Okada report that their 12-year old dyslexic patient experienced difficulties with the syllabary, Kana, but not with Kanji. This study with $N = 1$ should again be interpreted with caution.

In the case of Chinese, to this writer's knowledge, there has been no systematic study of reading difficulties relating to the language. The work of Kline and Lee[33] in a transcultural study of dyslexia involving 425 Canadianized Chinese simultaneously learning to read and write English and Chinese in Vancouver, Canada, is therefore of some interest. All children in the study with a problem in either language or both were given the WISC, the Draw-a-Person Test, Bender-Gestalt, Monroe Auditory Discrimination Test, Monroe Visual-Auditory Learning Test, and tests for handedness, footedness, and eyedness. On the basis of these results, Kline et al. found a lower incidence of reading disability and postulated possible cultural factors. Although this attempt at transcultural study deserves some attention, certain of its conclusions seem to need more supporting evidence. For example, the lack of specificity of causal factors of language disability is debatable. The suggestion that auditory discrimination is not a significant factor in reading disability may relate only to the study in question. In any case, it is tonal discrimination that is important in Chinese, and further exploration of this is needed. As regards the role of visual perception in reading difficulties raised by Kline, suffice it to quote Money:

> It is quite conceivable that the dyslexic is a person who has difficulty not only in establishing the necessary lexical concepts, visual and auditory, . . . and in relating the visual and phonic image, but who is in some manner a nonvisile cognitional type. He is perhaps a person weak in visual imagery and visual memory of all types, the opposite of the person with eidetic imagery and photographic memory.[34]

Little is known as yet about how the necessary lexical concepts are established in learning to read in Chinese. It would be worthwhile to replicate Kline's work with more rigorous experimental design and statistical treatment. If the linguistic correspondence between English and Chinese can be empirically demonstrated, it will certainly be of academic and practical interest to make a cross-linguistic study with equivalent groups of "normal" and dyslexic Chinese children learning Chinese and groups of English children learning English with a view to unearthing auditory, visual, and kinaesthetic processes in the reading task that are common to learning different language systems.

In the foregoing, an attempt is made to explain the learning of Chinese as a linguistic code and the possibility of using lexical and structural constraints in the learning task. It is this writer's belief that a knowledge of the nature of the Chinese language and an understanding of the reading task—its discriminatory and decoding aspects—are central to good pedagogy. In the barren field of the investigation of reading in Chinese, a great deal remains to be done in the way of research and development of classroom practices for more efficient learning and teaching in that language.

Reading Practices in Hong Kong

Hong Kong, situated to the south of China, is a tiny British Crown Colony. Since the end of the Second World War, its population has increased steadily with natural birth and the influx of refugees from the mainland. The figure now exceeds the four-million mark. Of this number, 98 per cent are Chinese. This huge population has brought with it problems in education, housing, and medical and other social services that have been tackled and gradually overcome in an efficient manner. Since the early 1950s the government has pursued an ambitious program to build schools and educate teachers. It is still being pursued with vigor. Thanks to the untiring efforts of both government and voluntary agencies the target of providing a free government or subsidized primary school place for every child who wants it was achieved in 1971. Considering the shortage of land, the resources available, and other competing claims, this is no mean achievement. By the end of March 1970, enrollment at the various levels of education was: kindergartens, 135,000; primary schools, 746,000; secondary schools, 255,000; and the two universities, more than 5,000. (See the Hong Kong Education Department Annual Summary, 1969–1970[35] and the Hong Kong

Government Annual Report, 1970.[36]) The staggering enrollment of more than one million students out of a total population of four million plus explains the difficulties encountered in educational provisions. Although quantity is catered for, quality is not lost sight of, as evidenced by the establishment in the past decade within the Education Department of such special units as the Special Education Section and the Research, Testing, and Guidance Section—the latest being the Educational Television Unit which became operational in 1971. All these are tangible efforts to help teachers and pupils and to improve the quality of education.

In the primary school the teaching of the Chinese language occupies about a quarter of the time. From the third year onward, children are also taught English as a second language—although this starts from the primary or junior I level in some schools. In the field of teaching reading in the language, the curriculum follows closely that of the suggested syllabuses published by the government's Department of Education. The objectives and general principles are outlined in this guide and teachers are left free to formulate their own approaches and select materials within a broad framework. Although this leaves the teacher freedom to plan and conduct his teaching, it has been suggested that a more structured guide—with definite suggestions for procedures and materials—geared to the less imaginative teacher might be worthwhile. Moreover, with technological changes coming to Hong Kong, which has been transformed from an entrepôt to a city-state with a number of diversified light industries, a curriculum more in keeping with the needs of pupils and with an empirical base should be developed. This is of importance not only at the secondary level but also at the primary level, as many youngsters do not proceed beyond the sixth year of primary schooling plus one or two extra years at junior technical schools.

This need for more structured guidance for teachers is related to the need for more scientifically designed textbooks and supplementary readers for reading in Chinese. Even though some improvements have been shown in these over the years, a great deal is still left to be desired in the way of vocabulary control, interest level for children, and technical aspects such as illustration, format, type fount, and the like. In an unpublished vocabulary count undertaken by this writer in 1962 of three "popular" series of primary readers, the divergence in vocabulary size was considerable. Although all three series keep to the 3,500 characters spread out over the six years, the gradation from year to year and the lack of correspondence in the actual characters used are quite marked. This is shown by the differing number of characters introduced in the first-year primers of the three series: 473, 541, and 717. A Working Party, in which this writer was research consultant, appointed by the Director of Education to study the teaching of Chinese frankly acknowledges this in its report.[37] Some of the unsatisfactory aspects of the reading materials are pointed out: their inadequate regard for readability, their lack of correspondence with the experiential background of children, and their lack of stimulation in the teaching of reading for comprehension. The report urges immediate action to overcome the deficiencies.

Both the reading materials and curriculum guide need to be investigated on an objective and ongoing basis.

Even though materials are important in the teaching and learning of reading, teachers are of greater importance. Of the primary school teachers who had only one year of training, only a handful remain. The majority have had the now normal two-year training. All teachers in secondary schools are university graduates. There is a need, as in many other places, for more intensive training in the psychology and pedagogy of reading. By and large, many primary school teachers rely heavily on the curriculum guide and the series of readers in use. The approach to reading is largely "look-and-say," with the whole character as the basic unit. The new character is pronounced and explained at the beginning of a lesson and the salient features of the radical and phonetic are pointed out. These characters are then related to their context. The children are trained to read silently from the lower grades onward. After reading the passage the children are asked comprehension questions and are helped to revise the new characters through repetition by both the teacher and the taught. Then the children are required to write these new characters as homework and, in the higher grades, to do exercises relating to the passage read. One common feature in the teaching of reading in almost all schools is the requirement of homework as a compulsory extension of the lesson. The Working Party finds in its survey of one hundred representative primary schools that primary school children *actually* spend from forty-five minutes in the first and second grades to one hour and one and a half hours in the fifth and sixth grades per school day on Chinese language homework. This demand must seem unreasonable to their Western counterparts. To some extent, this is the downward result of a severely competitive secondary entrance examination at the end of the primary schooling. Although homework should not be excessive and should be of a certain quality and quantity, the exercises in spelling and in answering questions must help to fix the graphic patterns of the characters and the teaching of the rules of the lexical and syntactical aspects of the language. Moreover, the readiness program in a number of kindergartens and preschools calls for closer examination. More often than not, children of 4 and 5 are introduced to the formal work of learning to read and write characters without adequate sensory-motor and preconceptual training. There is a definite need for an imaginative approach to teaching methods together with an awareness and active use of appropriate audiovisual media. The Working Party found in its survey that some teachers are "far too formalistic, sticking rigidly to the Herbartian method of presentation" and that "a definite attempt must be made to impart to the pupils the functional use of the language." This criticism of teaching methods and the emphasis on the quality of teachers are not peculiar to Hong Kong or to the teaching of Chinese. Morris,[38] in her monumental work on reading, emphasizes these aspects in her findings. They may well have a universal application.

Children are assessed regularly on standards and progress in reading, through informal tests and examinations. There is a public examination at the end of the sixth year of primary schooling. The formation of the Research, Testing, and

Guidance Unit in 1963 has done much to assist children and teachers. Through its annual testing program, involving standardized attainment tests in the basic subjects created by the unit, an increasingly large number of primary schools are enabled to use the accumulated results for the guidance of their pupils. Action researches on languages and elementary mathematics are yielding results. To cater to the needs of slow learners a small number of classes have been set up under the guidance of the Special Education Section.

Although much has been done, much more remains to be done. There are large unexplored areas in the teaching of reading in Chinese. One relates to the use of the common language (Kuoyu) as the spoken medium of instruction rather than Cantonese, which is the native tongue of the indigenous Hong Kong and Southern Chinese population. The other is the study of the language pattern and reading processes of disadvantaged Hong Kong children who live in over-crowded conditions in tenements and who form a large segment of the primary population. Related to this is the problem of reading difficulties in the language and the differential effect that deprivation and disadvantage have on dull and bright children. If brightness is more susceptible to debilitating environmental forces, as found in Wiseman's[39] study, preventive and compensatory teaching strategies are necessary to ensure a larger "pool" of abilities. This has practical implications in a city-state such as Hong Kong. It depends for its growth and prosperity on human resources.

Chinese Language Standardization

The Chinese movement for standardization is associated with reforms of the writing system. This dates back to the end of the sixteenth century with the Jesuit, Matteo Ricci; it was followed by such efforts as those of Sir Thomas Wade and Herbert A. Giles in the nineteenth century. The first official attempt at reform came in 1918 when the National Phonetic Alphabet was published. This was followed in 1928 by the Gwoyeu Romatzyh (G.R.) 國 語 羅 馬 字 adopted by the Chinese Ministry of Education. Letters of the Latin alphabet are used for transcribing segmental phonemes and tones. This G.R. (National Romanization) found a competitor in the latinization movement, but neither scheme made much headway because of interruption during the Sino-Japanese War and the Second World War.

Since 1949, the government in mainland China has embarked on language reforms in an organized manner. Very briefly, the movement centers around:

1. The adoption of the common language as the standard national spoken language.
2. The simplification of characters by reducing the stroke numbers for characters; for example, 麗 "elegant, graceful" with nineteen strokes becomes 丽 with four strokes.
3. The introduction of a latinized phonetic alphabet coexisting with the written character to reduce illiteracy.

   As the Chinese language has not undergone any substantial structural changes, it is difficult to estimate the impact that the current reform will have. It is also difficult to conjecture what may happen if the morphemic script is replaced by a phonemic writing system and the effect that might have on reading. Such a transformation, if it does come about at all, will be an extremely slow process as there are linguistic, cultural, and social factors militating against it. As an example of the violation of the linguistic principle of character formation, the simplified character for 國 "country" written as 口 neglects the importance of the stem, which is 或 rather than 囗. Similarly 種 "to cultivate (grain)" when written as 种 with 禾 "grain" in 中 "middle" overlooks the root 重. Thus, any Chinese language reform in the direction of simplifications must follow definite linguistic rules and forms. An arbitrary simplification may succeed in reducing the number of strokes, but it may lose the important dual combinatory property of the signific and phonetic that is so important in the decoding of the graphic symbol. This, however, is not to say modification or reform is not desirable. The adoption of the common language as the universal spoken language is calculated to bridge the gap in communication between people from different parts of the country and to make for some ease in reading. The simplification of strokes in characters, if carried out with regard to the principles of efficient coding, may have some effect on children and adults learning to read. On the latinization of the language, Chao, himself an ardent pioneer advocating such a move, thinks there is little danger of the characters being abolished too soon and that these will remain in use for many years, if not indefinitely, as a parallel form of writing. He further puts forward "visionary proposals" that a universal system of symbols will involve about two hundred monosyllabic symbols as an ideal system of visual and auditory codes. Such universality might be approached via human or mechanical "translations" and will have to be left to "future dreams and schemes."[40] Until such a time comes, reading in Chinese may continue to utilize the inherent structural characteristics of the existing code for maximum information processing.

REFERENCES

1. Gray, W. S., *The Teaching of Reading and Writing: An International Survey* (Monograph in Fundamental Education X), Paris: UNESCO, 1956.
2. Karlgren, Bernhard, *Sound and Symbol in Chinese,* rev. ed., Hong Kong: Hong Kong University Press and London: Oxford University Press, 1962.
3. de Francis, John, *Nationalism and Language Reform in China,* Princeton, N.J.: Princeton University Press, 1950.
4. Kennedy, George, A., "Monosyllabic myth," *Journal of the American Oriental Society,* **71**, 3 (1951).
5. Chuang, Chai-hsuan, *A Fundamental Vocabulary of Chinese Characters,* China: China Press, 1938 (in Chinese).
6. Kennedy, George A., *The Minimum Vocabularies of Written Chinese,* New Haven, Conn.: Yale University Press, 1954.
7. Leong, C. K., *An Experimental Study of the Vocabulary of Written Chinese Among*

Primary III Children in Hong Kong, paper presented at the Fifteenth Annual Convention, IRA, Anaheim, Calif., 1970. See also *Vocabulary of Written Chinese: Contemporary Usage Among Junior III Children in Hong Kong,* Hong Kong: Government Printer, 1968.

8. Huey, E. B., *The Psychology and Pedagogy of Reading,* New York: Macmillan, 1908. Reprinted at Cambridge, Mass.: MIT Press, 1968.

9. Gates, Arthur I., "The nature of the reading process," in *Reading in the Elementary School,* Part II of the 48th Yearbook of the NSSE, Chicago: U. of Chicago, 1949.

10. Strang, Ruth, "The nature of reading," in Strang, Ruth, McCullough, Constance M., and Traxler, Arthur, E. (eds.), *Problems in the Improvement of Reading,* 2nd ed., New York: McGraw-Hill, 1955.

11. Smith, Frank, *Understanding Reading,* New York: Holt, 1971.

12. Gibson, Eleanor, J., *Principles of Perceptual Learning and Development,* New York: Appleton, 1969.

13. Halle, Morris, "Some thoughts on spelling," in Goodman, Kenneth, S., and Fleming, James T. (eds.), *Psycholinguistics and the Teaching of Reading,* Newark, Del.: IRA, 1968, p. 18.

14. Chao, Y. R., *Language and Symbolic Systems,* London and New York: Cambridge University Press, 1968.

15. Miller, G. A., "The magical number seven, plus or minus two: Some limits of our capacity for processing information," *Psychological Review,* **63** (1956), 81–97.

16. Chuang, *op. cit.*

17. Leong, *An Experimental Study of the Vocabulary of Written Chinese Among Primary III Children in Hong Kong, op. cit.*

18. *Ibid.*

19. Woodworth, R. S., *Experimental Psychology,* New York: Holt, 1938, p. 739.

20. Neisser, Ulric, *Cognitive Psychology,* New York: Appleton, 1967.

21. Smith, *op. cit.*

22. Miller, G. A., Bruner, J. S., and Postman, L., "Familiarity of letter sequences and tachistoscopic identification," *Journal of Genetic Psychology,* **50** (1954), 129–139.

23. Gibson, Eleanor J., Pick, Anne, Osser, Harry, and Hammond, Marcia, "The role of grapheme-phoneme correspondence in the perception of words," *American Journal of Psychology,* **75** (1962), 554–570. Also, Gibson, E. J., Osser, H., and Pick, A. D., "A study in the development of grapheme-phoneme correspondence," *Journal of Verbal Learning and Verbal Behaviour,* **2** (1963), 142–146. Also Gibson, Eleanor J., "Experimental psychology of learning to read," in Money, John (ed.), *The Disabled Child: Education of the Dyslexic Child,* Baltimore, Md.: Johns Hopkins Press, 1966.

24. Miller, G. A., "Free recall of redundant strings of letters," *Journal of Experimental Psychology,* **56** (1958), 484–491.

25. Gibson, Eleanor J., "The ontogeny of reading," *American Psychologist,* **25** (1970), 136–143.

26. Herdan, Gustav, *Language As Choice and Chance,* Groningen, Holland: P. Noorhoff, 1956; *The Calculus of Linguistic Observations,* The Hague: Mouton 1962; *The Structuralistic Approach to Chinese Grammar and Vocabulary,* The Hague: Mouton, 1964.

27. Dewey, G., *Relative Frequency of English Speech Sounds,* Cambridge, Mass.: Harvard U.P., 1923.

28. Herdan, *Language As Choice and Chance, op. cit.,* p. 136.

29. Herdan, *The Calculus of Linguistic Observations, op. cit.,* p. 136.
30. Leong, *An Experimental Study of the Vocabulary of Written Chinese Among Primary III Children in Hong Kong, op. cit.*
31. Makita, Kiyoshi, "The rarity of reading disability in Japanese children," *American Journal of Orthopsychiatry,* **38** (1968), 599–614.
32. Money, John, "Dyslexia, a post conference review," in Money, John (ed.), *Reading Disability: Progress and Research Needs in Dyslexia,* Baltimore, Md.: Johns Hopkins Press, 1962.
33. Kline, Carl L., and Lee, Norma, "A transcultural study of dyslexia: Analysis of reading disabilities in 425 Chinese children simultaneously learning to read and write in English and in Chinese," *Bulletin of the Orton Society,* **19** (1969), 67–81. Also, Kline, Carl L., and Lee, Norma, "A transcultural study of dyslexia: Analysis of language disabilities in 277 Chinese children simultaneously learning to read and write in English and in Chinese," mimeographed, personal communication, February 1970.
34. Money, *op. cit.,* p. 27.
35. *Hong Kong Education Department Annual Summary, 1969–70,* Hong Kong: Government Printer, 1971.
36. *Hong Kong Government Annual Report, 1970,* Hong Kong: Government Printer, 1971.
37. *Report of Working Party on the Teaching of Chinese,* Hong Kong: Government Printer, 1968.
38. Morris, Joyce, *Standards and Progress in Reading,* Slough: NFER in England and Wales, 1966.
39. Wiseman, Stephen, *Education and Environment,* Manchester: Manchester University Press, 1964.
40. Chao, *op. cit.,* p. 226.

CHAPTER 19

*India**

CHINNA OOMMEN (nee Chacko)

Languages of the Area

THE subcontinent of India is a very large area, measuring about 2,000 miles from south to north and about 1,850 miles from east to west.

It contains 179 languages and 544 dialects, according to the linguistic survey of Grierson.[1] (But this is probably a serious underestimate.) These have been classified into four distinct family groups: Indo-Aryan, Dravidian, Austro-Asiatic, and Tibeto-Chinese.

Indo-Aryan Languages

The Indo-Aryan languages are descended from the ancient speech of the Indo-European invaders who came to India from the Eurasian plains. The oldest form of Aryan speech is to be found in the *Vedas,* believed to have been completed in the tenth century B.C. The middle Indo-Aryan dialects are supposed to have developed from Vedic Sanskrit and to have spread gradually over northern India during the period of Aryan expansion between 600 B.C. and A.D. 100. The early Buddhist literature is enshrined in Pali, which is one of the earlier Indo-Aryan dialects. By the tenth century, the middle Indo-Aryan dialects had gradually developed into modern Indo-Aryan languages, the most important of these being Sanskrit, Hindi, Gujarati, Bengali, Assamese, and Oriya. The Aryan family is numerically and culturally of the greatest significance here. In the undivided India, 70 per cent of the people belonged to this group; the Dravidian family comes next with 25 per cent; the Austric language with only 1 per cent; and the Tibeto-Chinese language with still less.

Dravidian Languages

The Dravidian languages were indigenous to and prevalent in peninsular India. Some of the important languages among them are Tamil, Telegu, Kannada, Malayalam, Todda, Kota, Khand, Oraon, and Rajmahal. Tamil, the oldest member of this group, preserves a good deal of the general character and vocabulary of the ancient Dravidian speech.

Austro-Asiatic Languages

Primitive tribes represented in the hills and jungles of central and northern India speak Austric languages. These languages are believed to have come to

* The Editor wishes to acknowledge gratefully the assistance of Mrs. S. Sandhu of Victoria, B.C., in preparing the Hindi and Malayalam characters for this chapter.

India with the invaders from the northeast, long before the Aryans. The Kol or Munda group, which includes Santhali, Mundari, Khasi in Assam, and Nicobarese in the Nicobar Islands, are some of the Austro-Asiatic languages.

Tibeto-Chinese Languages

Small tribes along the southern slopes of the Himalayas, in north Bengal, and in Assam speak Tibeto-Chinese languages. Such tongues belong mostly to the Mongolian race. Maithili and Manipuri, for example, belong to this group.

Although it is true that there are very many languages in India, the preceding statistics must be viewed with caution. More than one hundred of the languages referred to are merely tribal dialects belonging to the Tibeto-Chinese speech family and are found only on the northern or northeastern fringes of India. Many are used only orally now and not as separate literary languages. The speakers of these languages have come to regard Hindi as their language of literary expression (for example, Marwari, Rajasthani, Central Pahari, and Kosali).

Of these various tongues, the government of India officially recognizes fifteen major languages used by large, advanced, and organized groups (except for Sanskrit) with a current literary practice and traditions. They are Assamese, Bengali, Gujarati, Hindi, Kannada, Kashmiri, Malayalam, Marathi, Oriya,

TABLE 19-1. Population Speaking the Sixteen Major Languages of India

Language	No. of people in 100,000s	Per cent
Hindi, Urdu, Hindustani, Punjabi	1,499	46
Telegu	330	10
Marathi	270	8
Tamil	265	8
Bengali	251	8
Gujarati	163	5
Kannada	145	4
Malayalam	135	4
Oriya	132	4
Assamese	50	2
Kashmiri	19	1
Sanskrit	1	
Sindi	13	

Punjabi, Sanskrit, Tamil, Telegu, Urdu, and Sindhi. The population speaking each of these languages is shown in Table 19-1.[2]

Although Sanskrit is spoken by a very small number of people, it is included because most of the other languages have borrowed heavily from it and, in that sense, it has been a basic language. All these languages draw from a common literary tradition in Sanskrit and a common background of thought and experience. Their scripts and alphabets reflect a common Indian phonetic system, with the exception of Urdu. Sanskrit words in the languages of India, Aryan, and Dravidian are a visible symbol of the underlying unity of India.

There are also important similarities within certain language groups. For example, Oriya, Assamese, and Bengali are closely related although they have their separate literatures. Assamese, Urdu, and Hindi have a common structure, grammar, and syntax. The main difference between them is in the content of their vocabularies. Hindi draws heavily from Sanskrit; Urdu depends on Persian and Arabic. Within what is known as the Hindi speaking area, various dialects are spoken. Among these the written form of *Khari-boli* (standing speech) has emerged as the standard form of Hindi writing over all of India. So also, there are many common elements in Malayalam and Tamil and in Gujarati and Marathi. These patterns of similarities among Indian languages reflect geographical factors as well as historical association among the different linguistic groups.

Territorially, these languages are spoken in fairly well-defined regions, but, within them, there are large sections with mother tongues other than the regional language. This situation is particularly notable in the larger cities. Furthermore, bilingualism is probably quite common, although at present there is no authentic data on this.

Official Languages

Limitations of space make it impossible to deal with all the languages of the geographical subcontinent of India. Therefore, this chapter will concentrate on the political entity—India. For example, Pakistan will not be discussed. For the same reason, only Hindi will be treated in detail. Article 343 of the constitution provided that the official language of the Union would be Hindi in the Devnagari script and the form of numerals for official purposes would be the international form of Indian numerals. English would, however, continue to be the official language for a period of fifteen years from the commencement of the constitution. An amendment of the official languages bill specified that, after 1965, when Hindi was to become the principal official language of the Union, English would continue as the subsidiary official language for as long as might be necessary.

One should remember in this connection the unique position of the English language and its influence on India and Indian languages. Not only have all the Indian languages borrowed freely many words and idioms (such as "pulling the leg" टाँगा खींचना), but also most Indo-Aryan and Dravidian languages have borrowed the punctuation system of the English language.

The Nature of Hindi

According to Grierson, the word "Hindi" is Persian, not Indian, and properly signifies a native of India as distinguished from a Hindu or non-Muslim Indian. The word "Hindi" or "Hindustani," in a rather loose way now, includes all the speeches and dialects current in India to the east of Punjab, east of Sind, north of Gujarat and Maharasthra, west of Orissa and Bengal, and south of Nepal. These speeches and dialects are linguistically within the orbit of Hindi and are called the western Hindi dialect. They include Kanuji, Bundeli, Braj-bhasa, Vernacular Hindustani, and Hindustani, the speech of Delhi.[3]

Hindi can be confined to the form of Hindustani in which Sanskrit words abound—and that, hence, can be written in the Devnagari character—as opposed to Urdu, which is a special form of Hindustani in which Persian words are of frequent occurrence and that can only be written in the Persian character. The earliest specimens of Hindustani are in Urdu, for they were poetical works. The great difference between the poetry of Urdu and that of western Hindi lies in the system of prosody. The vocabulary of Hindi is of four types: (1) pure Hindustani words, (2) words borrowed from Sanskrit, (3) words borrowed from Persian, including Arabic, and (4) words borrowed from other sources.

Hindi, like every Aryan language of India, is based on the modified Sanskrit of A.D. 1000. It has only two genders. Gender is often dependent on the termination rather than sense. Usually, the "ee" endings are considered to be feminine. But there are exceptions to this rule. Thus, Hindustani *pothi* (a small book) coming from the Middle Indo-Aryan *pothia* and from Sanskrit *pustika* is feminine—an inheritance in the matter of gender from the *prakrit*. As an equivalent of this word, the Perso-Arabic word *kitab* is feminine. The word *grantha* (book) of Sanskrit, however, retains its masculine gender in its Hindi form, *granth*.

In Hindi, the verb in the past tense behaves like an adjective. In fact, in its origin it is a past participle adjective. When it is intransitive, it qualifies the subject and undergoes change according to the gender and number of the subject. Thus, for example, *main aya* is "I (masculine) came," feminine *main ayi*, plural masculine, *ham aye*, plural feminine, *ham ayin. Mainne ek raja dekha* is "I saw one king"; literally, "by me one king he was seen"; *Mainne ek rani dekhi* is "I saw one queen"; literally, "by me one queen she was seen." So, *Main-ne tin raniyan dekhin* is "I saw three queens"; literally, "by me three queens they were seen." This makes Hindi a little complicated. The mass of the people outside the western Hindi area, however, have simplified matters by ignoring constructions of the preceding types. In the bazaar Hindi, people use only one construction: *Ham raja(ko) dekha; ham aya–main rani(ko) dekha* ("We saw a king; we came, I saw a queen"). The grammatical complications of standard Hindi have, in this way, been smoothed in the colloquial Hindustani of the masses; however, standard literary Hindi and the Hindustani of the people in western Uttar Pradesh and Eastern Punjab ignore it. Thus, the grammar is simplified according to local habits, and, on the whole, the pronunciation does not present any complications to people outside the western Hindi area. These adaptations have helped the easy acceptance of Hindi as a great palaver speech.

In Hindi prose, which follows the almost universal rule of Indo-Aryan dialects, the order of words is fixed and can only be altered for the sake of emphasis. Except when it is deliberately changed to lay stress on a particular word, this order is invariably followed: (1) the introductory words of the sentence, such as conjunctions and the like; (2) the subject; (3) the indirect object with its appurtenances; (4) the direct object with its appurtenances; and, finally (5) the verb. Adjectives and genitives precede the word they qualify. For instance, the sentence which in English would run, "I gave John's good book to you" would be in Hindi prose, "I you–to– John's good book gave."[4] In Hindi there are no prepositions. Instead it has post positions, placed after the word.

Another feature of Hindi is its use of a noun with an equivalent of the verb meaning "to do" or "to make," to form the verb from the noun—for example, *viswas karna*, "to believe." The literal translation will be "to do faith." Similarly, *agya karna* is "to make command." By doing this, Hindi does away with the ambiguity that can result from using the noun itself as a verb.

There are three levels of speaking the Hindi language: (1) to younger persons and people below one's status; (2) to people of equal status, and (3) to people above one's status and to people who are older than the speaker.

In Hindi speech, phonemes generally retain their full value and are not elided or changed in combinations. Where minor changes occur in vowel sounds the modification follows a simple consistent pattern.

The Writing System

Space here allows a detailed description of the writing system only of Hindi, although it has features that are comparable with many other Indian languages. For example, all Indian languages, with the exception of Urdu, are written like Hindi in direction—that is, from left to right. The Hindi characters are:

Vowels

अ आ इ ई उ ऊ ऋ ऋ ए ऐ ओ

औ अं अ:

Consonants

क ख ग घ ङ च छ ज झ ञ

ट ठ ड ढ ण त थ द ध न

प फ ब भ म य र ल व श

ष स ह त्र क्ष ज्ञ ड़ ज़ ड़

These include the three consonant characters borrowed from Urdu to write words that have been adopted from that language. One of these, ज़ is showing signs of becoming obsolete because most people pronounce the corresponding phoneme as they would the Hindi grapheme ज. The secondary alternative symbols used for all the Hindi vowels except two are more complex. These are listed here. The primary character is presented first in each example, followed by its alternative symbol:

1. आ ा   7. ए ॅ

2. इ ि   8. ऐ ॅ

3. ई ी   9. ओ ो

4. ऋ ॄ   10. औ ौ

5. उ ॖ   11. अं ं

6. ऊ ॗ   12. अः :

The choice between the two alternative characters for the same vowel depends on the position of that vowel relevant to the consonants in the word.

In Hindi, like Sanskrit, each character in a word is joined together by a "headline," which consists, for each symbol, of a horizontal line at the top of the character; thus, अ क. The symbol is not complete without it. The effect for distinguishing a word as a unit may be seen in an example, thus कमला.

Another feature of the Hindi writing system is the special treatment of the clustering of two or more consonant characters. In contrast to English—in which, for example, in a cluster such as *sk* the single letters *s* and *k* retain their original form and position unchanged—in Hindi (and in other Indian languages) the form of the single characters may change when they are combined in a cluster. For example, स + क becomes स्क. Part of the first character is omitted and the second letter is written in full. If one of the secondary vowel symbols is to be written on the top or the bottom of the character, it is written on the top or bottom of the second character, for example, स्के or स्कू (not स्के or स्कु). Although this may be interpreted as adding still more symbols to the total number to be learned in the Hindi writing system, it should be borne in mind that this modification of characters combined in a cluster may signal more clearly the presence of the cluster as such.

Clustering is further complicated by the different ways of modifying the members of a cluster according to the characters to be clustered. For example, one consideration is whether or not the characters to be combined are the same or different, as in the following two examples:

1. Same characters combined: स + स = स्स.

2. Different characters combined: स + प = स्प.

But there are a few exceptions to this rule. For example, त + त becomes त्त, and not त्त. Also, when the characters to be clustered are rounded, half of the character is written below the other, as in the following two examples:

1. Same rounded characters combined: ट + ट = ट्ट.

2. Different rounded characters combined: ह + व = ह्व.

A cluster with र is written in different ways, depending on the position in which it appears. If it precedes, it is written in one way, if it follows it is written in another way. In the latter case, again there are two ways, depending on the form of the other character, as in the following examples:

1. र + म = र्म.

2. म + र = म्र.

3. ड + र = ड्र.

There are three-letter clusters also:

$$ष + ट + र = ष्ट्र.$$

The comparative degree of complexity of the Hindi writing system vis-à-vis that of other languages discussed in this book can be judged from what has been described thus far. However, two further conventions should be mentioned. First, the use of the "Halant" sign, \, indicates less than the full phonetic value. However, this sign is not written at the end of a word because the reduction in phonetic value always occurs anyway when a word ends in a consonant. Secondly, there is a special sign for nazalization. It is known as "Chandra-bindu," and is written thus, ँ , for example, in हँसना.

The punctuation system is generally the same as for English, except that the sign for full stop or period is a long line । instead of the dot. In poems, two lines are used for full stop and one line for a comma, as in Sanskrit.

Schools in India

The responsibility for education lies chiefly with the State governments. The constitution requires them to provide free compulsory education until pupils reach age 14. The Union government is responsible for the maintenance of the central universities and other institutions of national importance; the promotion and coordination of research; the determination of standards in higher educa-tion; the promotion of cultural relations with other nations of the world, as well as within the nation; and the promotion of the Hindi language along with other Indian languages. It is also responsible for education in the Union territories and for the central schools, which are instituted for the children of the central government employees who hold transferable posts.

The Union government's Ministry of Education deals directly with some of these programs, whereas others are administered by agencies of the ministry, such as the University Grants Commission, the Council of Scientific and Industrial Research, and the National Council of Educational Research and Training (NCERT).

Primary education is now free throughout the country. Middle school is also free in a number of States. In a few States, Madras, Kerala, Kashmir and Punjab, education up to (but not including) the college level is free.

Although education is primarily a State responsibility, the central government and the State governments work together in the formulation, implementation, and evaluation of the various programs. The State governments also receive a grant-in-aid from the central agency responsible for this work.

At the State level, the Minister of Education heads the Department of Education. His policies and programs are implemented and discharged by the Director of Public Instruction who is a permanent government official. Political changes in the ministry do not affect his position, thus maintaining continuity of administration. He is assisted by a number of district educational officers, inspectors, and textbook and evaluation officers.

The local government, the city corporation, municipal council, and the village *Panchayat* are responsible for providing primary education in their respective areas. The accepted pattern is eight years of primary education: primary school (ages 6 to 11) and middle grades (ages 11 to 14).

In recent years there has been a phenomenal growth in the school population. For example, in classes I through IV the population in 1960–1961 increased by 80 per cent of the figure for 1950–1951. In classes VI through VIII the population more than doubled in the same period. In classes IX through XI the growth rate was even greater. The decade to 1970–1971 will probably show a rate of increase at least as great.

However, this increase must not be seen as automatically producing a parallel rate of improvement in literacy standards in India. A very serious dropout problem must also be reckoned with. According to a recent study made in Maharasthra of every 1,000 students entering class I, 414 dropped out before completing class IV (183 had dropped out already in class I, 118 in class II, 88 in class III, and 25 in class IV). There is no all-India study of this problem yet, but these Maharasthra figures are probably fairly typical. On the other hand, it should be noted here that this 41 per cent rate of dropouts is much lower than the 82 per cent rate in 1922–1923 and the 59.6 per cent of 1955–1956. Furthermore, between 1911 and 1961, not only had elementary education expanded very considerably in numbers of pupils, but also elementary schools were established in remote rural areas, where formerly there had been little or no provision. These circumstances might be expected to have increased the dropout rate.

The main cause of this dropping out of school is economic. A child is removed from school when he is about 9 years old to help in the family. Social causes are also an important factor in girls dropping out of school—betrothal, and the unwillingness of parents to send grown-up girls to a mixed school.

Educational causes of wastage lie in the existence of incomplete schools, the prevalence of stagnation (that is, grade repeating), the dull character of most schools, the absence of ancillary services such as school meals and school health, and the average parent's or child's negative attitude toward the value of schooling.

The curriculum for primary school consists of the three Rs, a craft, physical education, nature study, and creative arts (dance, music, and art). In the third year, a second language is introduced, and in the sixth year a third language is added. (Generally Hindi and English.) Where Hindi is the mother tongue one of the southern Indian languages is taught. Thus, the study of languages forms an important part of school education. The three-language formula has now been generally accepted. In primary schools, each grade teacher is responsible for the teaching of all subjects. Subject specialists are found only in secondary schools.

The accepted pattern is to offer three years of secondary education—after eight years of elementary education—with diversified courses to give a vocational bias and make it a terminal point for entry into a trade or profession. This is followed by two years of predegree courses at the university and three years of study leading to the first degree. The latest Education Commission recommendation is to put the two-year predegree course in the high school.

The central government has initiated certain improvements, such as the establishment of the State Bureau of Education and Vocational Guidance, State Evaluation Units, and the State Institute of Science. Selected multipurpose schools have been strengthened generally, and science education has been improved in secondary schools.

A centrally sponsored crash program was formulated in September 1964, with the object of strengthening school science laboratories, school libraries, and science teaching in secondary schools. The central government will have given 100 per cent assistance when this scheme is completed.

Age for Beginning Reading

The age for compulsory education is 6, but many states start at 5 and 5+. The child must be 5 years of age before the school year starts if he is to be admitted to class I, where reading and writing instruction begins the very first day. There is usually no provision for a reading-readiness program in the elementary school.

Although there has been some increase in the number of nursery schools since 1951, the proportion of students who have had nursery school experience prior to joining elementary school remains negligible. For instance, there were 51,500,000 students in elementary school in 1965–1966, but the number of students in the nursery school was only 178,958. The plan for the provision of nursery schools differs from state to state. Most of the nursery schools are privately run by interested individuals or institutions. The fees vary between 2 and 50 rupees (that is, from about 30 cents up to 7 dollars), according to the nature and locality of the school. As the compulsory education act does not include preprimary education, there are no financial provisions, and this accounts for the slow progress in its development. A shortage of trained nursery school teachers is another major factor. Only a few states have training schools for nursery teachers. The child development departments of various universities shoulder the major responsibility for their training.

Another reason for the slow development of nursery schools is the attitude revealed by such parental comments as "in elementary school where children *learn* they don't have to pay fees. While in nursery school (the baby class) where they only *play,* we are asked to pay." Nevertheless, private nursery schools continue to increase in all cities and towns.

Prior to 1962, no study of reading readiness had been conducted in India. However, since then, there has been an awakening interest in the subject. Child development departments of different Home Science colleges have taken an interest in the different factors involved in readiness and in finding methods for promoting and developing it. A few studies of children's vocabulary have been conducted, the most extensive work in the pre-school area being that of the South Indian Teachers' Union of Educational Research.

The date that marks this increased interest is 1963. In that year the important investigation of the problem of reading readiness by the *Reading Project* of the *National Council of Educational Research and Training* (NCERT) was begun. A series of five tests was devised by Rawat[5] to check the readiness of students when they begin school: (1) word meaning, (2) sentence meaning, (3) copying, (4) visual perception, and (5) auditory discrimination (beginning and ending sounds). Following preliminary studies to establish their validity and reliability, the final tests were administered to a representative sample of 3,500 school beginners in Delhi schools, and this provided the basis for their standardization.

Among the most important findings was that 40 per cent of these beginners could not discriminate aurally the various sounds in Hindi. Discriminating ending sounds was found to be more difficult than discriminating beginning sounds. There were a few sounds that only about 28 per cent of the students could discriminate.

It was also revealed that children from villages had difficulty in recognizing pictures—such as of a fire engine or a camera—that were easily identified by the students from towns and cities. Furthermore, children's concepts of what the testers assumed to be commonplace occurrences were often not clear.

The copying test revealed the serious handicap of directional confusion in many pupils. Also, motor control and finer muscle development in many children were not adequately developed for writing the intricate Hindi characters.

The results of this study threw serious doubts on some commonly held educational beliefs about the teaching of reading in Hindi. Previously, it had been assumed that pupils have no problem in discriminating sounds. The fact that 40 per cent could not discriminate between phonemes, and that there were some sounds that as many as 70 per cent of the children could not recognize, clearly showed the need to change the common practice of giving almost no pre-reading training in auditory discrimination.

One outcome of this study was the development of a reading-readiness kit consisting of a series of charts, flash cards, and flannel graphs, with a teacher's manual by the NCERT Reading Project.[6] This was distributed free to all Delhi schools, which now provide a readiness program of four to six weeks. It aims to develop the requirements for reading readiness: concept development, auditory and visual discrimination, hand-eye coordination, writing abilities, and higher mental skills (such as sequential thinking, classification, generalization, language development, enriching vocabulary, and orientation to school and classroom procedures).

This new trend in Delhi has led to a more general awareness of the need for readiness. For example, seminars on readiness are being conducted at various child development departments and teacher-training colleges. The *Indian Educational Review* devoted an entire chapter to reading readiness in 1966. Elementary teachers are showing a clearer understanding of the lack of readiness in many school beginners. Unfortunately the institutions that train primary teachers still take little initiative in teaching student trainees how to develop readiness. The nursery-teacher-training institutions, in contrast, have given a great deal of attention to this matter in their courses. However, only a very small percentage of teachers are trained by such nursery-training institutions.

Teaching Methods

The most prevalent methods are synthetic methods, in which the initial emphasis is on teaching the letters and their sounds. The word, phrase, or sentence is then recognized by combining the detailed elements of language. Both alphabetic and phonic methods are used. The vowels are taught first, because they are conventionally ordered first in our alphabets, and then in the following order: consonants, combinations of consonants with vowels or *matras,* clusters (combinations of two consonants), and, finally, words.

In Hindi, the name of a character and the phoneme it represents are always the same. Each consonant character is usually pronounced with the *schwa* sound, but at the end of a syllable or a word it is pronounced fully without the *schwa* sound. (Cf. in English, /n/ in *chin* but /nə/ in *China.* If English letters were named in the same way, *n* would be named "nə" not "en.") Thus, in teaching the synthetic approach to reading Hindi, it makes little difference whether the alphabetic or phonic method is used. Typically, the teacher writes the character on the board, she says its name/phoneme, the children repeat the name/phoneme, and they write its character on their slates. The following day the next character is taught in the same way, and so on, until the whole alphabet has been thus treated.

Ease of writing may also determine the order of teaching the characters of the alphabet. The child is taught to write the easiest symbol first. For example, in Malayalam, the first character usually taught is ഩ, then ഩ, then ഩ, then ന, ഺ, ഽ, and so on. After several characters are learned, the combinations are taught.

ഩഩ ഺഩ ഺഩ ഽഩ

As there are many symbols to be learned, the school year is devoted to teaching all the characters and related words. At the end of the primer there will be three to four stories, each of about six to seven sentences.

In these synthetic methods the first essential common factor is the emphasis on writing the single character at the outset of reading instruction. A second common element is, of course, the presentation of the reading process as one in which single sounds and characters are the starting point for constructing whole words for ultimate recognition. Most teachers in India have a narrow concept of "teaching reading," which is essentially instruction in the characters of the alphabet. Once the child has mastered the alphabet it is assumed that the basic task has been accomplished and that he will be able to read any word by sounding out its characters.

If these synthetic methods are discussed in comparison with alternatives such as the word or sentence methods used in other countries, it is usually asserted that the synthetic approach has several advantages for schools in India. The most common claim made for it is that it is the best method for achieving good spelling ability. But, also in connection with India's practical problems of the present time, it is claimed that the synthetic approach is easier for untrained or minimally trained teachers to use. The fact that there is still a large number of such teachers in India is seen as an especially strong point in favor of the continued use of the synthetic approach.

In the past decade there has been some change in the initial approach. Methods such as the word method and the sentence method, in which the initial emphasis is on the meaning of what is read, have been introduced in certain parts of India. Also, primers and readers for class I have been written based on these approaches.

But often the change of method is *in name only*. A teacher may say she is using "the whole-word method" or "the sentence method" and she may be using textbooks that are also described by these technical terms, but, in actual fact, she is still placing the conventional emphasis on teaching children to write individual characters and to rote learn their phonic significance. This continuation of the synthetic approach under the cloak of a different methodological label occurs for two reasons: (1) a lack of training in the global methods and (2) the conservative attitude of teachers, which places a high value on time-honored methods. Thus, drilling pupils in writing and sounding the alphabetic characters continues to be the most popular method even in classrooms that allegedly use word or sentence methods.

In the later grades, the lesson is sounded out word by word. The meanings of difficult words are explained and the synonyms are given. In most cases, the teachers read from the book, sentence by sentence, and the children are asked to repeat the material. It is believed that this method will help children develop proper pronunciation and enunciation.

Silent reading is nonexistent in the primary grades. "Reading" means *oral* reading. Here again, more emphasis is placed on the sounds than on meaning. Repeating the lesson by heart is taken to be the mark of good reading. As one youngster queried, when asked "to read" for some visitors, "Teacher, with the book or without the book?"

The word-study skills—namely, word meaning, word recognition, and word analysis—taught at the primary level are very elementary. Instruction in word meaning generally is concerned with synonyms, antonyms, and gender. In word recognition, only sounding out is taught, and writing the clusters in the words in the first three grades is treated as a word-analysis skill. Later, instruction is given in the rules for combining words.

Recall of the content, particularly the recall of specific details, is the main emphasis in teaching the comprehension skills. Instruction in the higher mental skills—such as generalization, classification, comparison, reasoning, drawing conclusions and inferences, and getting the main idea—is very seldom given, even in the later grades. Summarizing is taught in the later grades mainly in connection with poems. Silent reading is also introduced in these grades. But in practice this means sounding out softly.

Despite the claims made by the adherents of the older alphabetic and phonic methods of effectiveness in teaching spelling, in actual practice the number of errors in spelling committed by high school and college students in writing their mother tongue is generally admitted to be appalling. Dissatisfaction has been expressed increasingly by teachers, teacher trainers, and other educators. An informal pilot study in spelling conducted in the Delhi primary schools revealed that there is a great deal of confusion when it comes to writing characters that are similar in sound and form, or both. There are many such characters in the languages of India.

In Hindi:

1. Similar in both sound and visual form.

अ आ

ओ औ

ए ऐ

2. Similar in sound (aspirated or unaspirated).

क ख

ग घ

प फ

3. Similar in visual form.

म भ

स म ह ड

य थ ढ ड़

In Malayalam:

1. Similar in visual form.

ഭ ട്ട ന ന്ന നു നൗ ന ഩ

2. Similar in sound and visual form.

ഇ   ഈ   ഉ   ഊ   അ   ആ

3. Similar in sound.

ഭ   ബ   പ   ഫ   ക   ഖ

Furthermore, there has been an increasing awareness of students' poor standards of reading. Except for their ability to reproduce the precise contents of the text, the ability of Indian students to obtain information by reading is recognized as being far from satisfactory.

These deficiencies in spelling and reading attainments have aroused educators to seek a new approach to teaching literacy skills. This demand led to the launching of the NCERT Reading Project. Under the guidance of the American reading specialist Constance McCullough, of the Teachers' College, Columbia University team, the Reading Project has evolved a new teaching methodology with special new materials, including a series of textbooks, workbooks, teachers' handbooks, and teaching aids. This method, first practiced in 1964, in Delhi schools, has now been taken up by all central schools and adopted throughout two Hindi speaking States. The materials were prepared for teaching reading in Hindi, the mother tongue. The method's success has led other States to seek guidance from the Reading Project in introducing this method in their States along with appropriate new textbooks. No comprehensive evaluation of the approach has been made as yet but this is currently under way. The Department of Education has administered questionnaires to more than two thousand teachers who are teaching by this method.

In the new approach, instead of using one method exclusively, a combination of techniques is used. The rationale for this eclecticism is that each of the several alternative teaching methods has its strong and weak points. If a combination of methods is used, the deficiencies of one approach should be offset by the strengths of another, as Gray[7] pointed out in his international survey of the teaching of reading and writing.

For example, a story approach is used to motivate the children to read for meaning immediately, even at the beginning stage; but if a word approach and a phrase approach are added simultaneously, children learn to read smoothly in phrases rather than jerkily in a word-by-word manner. A character-form and sound approach are used, too, so that children can decode new words. However, the structural analysis of words is also taught to enable children to learn to recognize parts of words immediately (verb ending, for example) instead of relying on sounding each character separately.

Accordingly, the primer and the reader start with short interesting stories with full-page pictures. Each page contains only a few words and sentences and these words are repeated more than fifteen times in the same story to aid recognition by sight. The pictures give clues to the child regarding the words and sentences contained in the story. The teacher, with leading questions, guides the reading of the students when they do the first reading. In this approach, the first reading is done silently, so that the students can give attention to meaning and word form from the beginning. This helps their oral reading, also, because they already know what is written and its meaning. Thus, they can read with proper enunciation and expression.

At the end of every lesson a few characters are introduced. These are selected on the basis of the general utility of the character and its frequency of occurrence in the present or next lesson. Care is taken to avoid visual or auditory confusion by ensuring that no two characters that are alike in form or sound, or both, are taught in the same lesson.

Two pictures of words from the childrens' vocabulary—which start with the sound to be taught—are given in the book, with the names of the pictures written beside them. The teacher helps the student to identify the pictures. The class and the teacher repeat the words several times. Then the teacher asks, "Can you hear a sound that is the same in these two? What are they? Listen 'Kup' 'Kamal.'" The students discover the sound, /k/, instead of the teacher telling it to them. Then the teacher directs the children to look at the written words against each picture again and reminds them that these represent spoken words, which are the names of the pictures. Then the teacher asks them to identify the written character that is the same in each written word and to identify its sound. Each child identifies it with his finger in his book. The teacher writes the character on the board and lets the children identify its sound. Each time she makes the children say it aloud. Finally, she teaches them to write the character according to the proper sequence, as set out in the book.

In this way the child's learning employs many alternative channels: hearing, speaking, seeing, and writing. When enough characters have been learned, words can be made for practice. Here also rote learning gives way to discovery because the child is led to discover the letter for himself. If it were merely told, he would remember it with less assurance. Furthermore, in this approach the child learns how to learn for himself as well as to learn the particular fact. It is said by teachers using the new approach that, after a few lessons, children turn to skill pages and identify the symbols by themselves. For example, if a child forgets the sound represented by a character, he needs only to think of two words that contain it in order to generalize. The children are also encouraged to analyze wholes into parts. In this method, meaning, name, and form are given attention even in the beginning stage, and this is continued throughout.

Apart from teaching characters, skills in word recognition—such as recognizing the word in a sentence through context clues—are taught at the end of each lesson. Comprehension skills also are taught after each lesson: for example, identifying the main idea, sequential thinking, comparison and contrast, predicting outcomes, and reasoning are taught even in the first grade. As the students proceed through the grades increasingly complex skills are taught.

The teaching methods used in the new approach developed by the NCERT Reading Project will be referred to again subsequently.

Returning now to the conditions that prevail generally in the schools of India, a brief description of the teaching of intermediate and higher order skills seems relevant. The prescribed syllabus usually specifies instruction in intermediate and higher order skills. In the middle and secondary grades most attention is given to formal grammar—that is to the construction of different types of sentences; parts of speech; gender; tense; prefix and suffix; root words; analysis of sentences; and rules regarding structure of words, known as *Santhi* and *Samas*.

In the secondary grades, the teaching of these skills is continued. Meter, prosody, figures of speech, and etymology based mainly on Sanskrit grammar are taught at this stage. In both middle and secondary grades, the emphasis is more on formal than functional grammar. Much time is devoted to the teaching of Sanskritized terminology, and writing ability is developed. Essay writing, letter summarization, question and answer forms, and description are taught.

Evaluating, critical reading, creative reading, detecting propaganda devices, arriving at generalizations, and reading for the main ideas of a passage are still not generally taught, nor are they prescribed in the official syllabus. However, the new curriculum for language, prepared by the NCERT Reading Project, includes these skills and many others, such as noticing cause-and-effect relationship, reading to make comparisons, following directions, anticipating outcomes, following a sequence of ideas or events, the structure of paragraphs, the design of writing, as well as grammar and creative writing. The textbooks have been prepared, on the basis of this curriculum, with passages and selections that lend themselves to the development of these skills. Exercise pages for developing the skills are included in the textbook. In addition, the teacher's manual recommends a number of activities to reinforce these skills. Provisions for study skills are also made in the new curriculum. The NCERT textbooks contain various types of literature: prose, poetry, autobiography, stories, plays, and essays.

In general, the prescribed textbook plus one or two supplementary texts constitute the main source of literature to be read in the course. Students are not usually required to undertake much extra reading. However, most high schools have extracurricula activities, such as literary clubs, that provide a variety of ways for extending the students' interests in literature.

Teachers' Manuals

Every school has a copy of the State prescribed syllabus on the basis of which the teacher prepares the monthly plan of instruction. But in many States very few teachers' manuals or handbooks are available at present. This lack is particularly unfortunate because so many teachers are untrained. Now, however, that NCERT is providing comprehensive teachers' manuals with definite directions for the use of each book in the new reading program. These manuals include plans for developing readiness, specific lesson plans interleaved with pages from the children's texts, and guidance for evaluation. The manuals are provided free to the teacher.

In each vernacular language, there are one or two books on language teaching in general, but there are very few professional textbooks providing information on the teaching of reading. *Teaching Reading: A Challenge*[8] is the only professional book devoted exclusively to this topic.

Materials for Instruction

At present, in the absence of adequate facilities, proper equipment, and other instructional aids, the textbook occupies a central position in teaching at all stages and probably will continue to do so for many more years to come. It is the main tool both for the teacher and the student. Moreover, because it is easily available and fairly inexpensive, it is within the reach of most children. Textbooks must be bought by the pupils, but there are special provisions for issuing free books to the needy. A reader is prescribed for each class, and in the higher grades, one or two supplementary readers are added.

India has no uniform policy regarding the production of textbooks. In some States manuscripts are submitted by private authors in open competition. These are reviewed by experts in the field, whose evaluation is the basis of selection for publication. In some States, books are prepared by a special textbook committee in the State Department of Education. This trend is gaining ground rapidly as nationalized books are considered to be less expensive and better.

Although it is a great achievement to have these specially designed textbooks—which are a substantial improvement over the previous ones—there is still much to be desired in the quality and standards (design, layout, type size) of reading books currently produced in India. Furthermore, the language used in them is usually highly formal, their content is not well organized, and too much information is likely to be crammed into one lesson. Lack of technical knowledge of textbook production, lack of funds, and poor printing facilities are responsible for these generally low standards.

NCERT has provided a lead in bringing out better quality textbooks at moderate prices in a variety of subject areas as well as in reading. In the reading materials, the NCERT team has taken account of a wide spectrum of important factors, as well as the more usual ones of teaching methodology and learning theories. For example, children's interests and attitudes, reasoning skills to be developed, and cultural values have been considered.

Workbooks are not compulsory. However, although the pupils are not obliged to buy them, the use of workbooks is becoming an increasingly common practice in the schools. Teachers seem to find workbooks particularly helpful under prevailing conditions of overcrowded classrooms and in one-teacher schools where the spread of age, aptitude, and ability is broad. The NCERT program includes a series of supplementary workbooks.

Supplementary Materials

Until ten years ago, most books were very poor translations of foreign books and equally poor reproductions of classic tales. But, recently, the number of publications for children has increased considerably. The government has initiated several projects for improving the quality of books and encouraged improvement by other means. For example, the Ministry of Education gives awards each year for the best books produced for children in all the regional languages. Also the National Book Trust of India was established to further the improvement of books.

The Children's Book Trust of India, a private organization, is devoted exclusively to the publication of good but low-priced children's books. These books compare well with good books produced anywhere in the world. Also, the Southern Languages Book Trust, Writers' Guilds, *Sahitya* Academies (Literature Societies), and numerous private publishers are bringing out supplementary reading materials for school-age children. Most of these are for the 10-to-16 age groups, so that children under the age of 10 remain poorly supplied. Some major newspaper concerns bring out children's magazines, but these are few in number and a real scarcity of such materials prevails.

Very few reference materials such as encyclopedias, picture dictionaries, or dictionaries are available at the elementary level. Even in high school libraries these are not always provided.

Children's Libraries

Very many schools have no special place where books can be displayed or where children can read quietly. In these circumstances it is not surprising that the number and variety of books provided are inadequate. In the elementary schools a library usually exists in name only, and very few books are available. Even these books are not accessible to children.

At present there are only a few libraries in India that are exclusively for children. A survey of public libraries in South India shows that only three exist that are exclusively for children, although in almost all libraries there is a children's section.

Three institutions have made a particularly important contribution in making books more readily available to children. First, *Bal Bhavan,* an organ of the Ministry of Education, has made excellent provisions for children's libraries in three cities. Efforts are under way to establish *Bal Bhavans* all over the country. The Nehru Memorial Fund will meet 60 per cent of the cost of these and the rest will be borne by the state.

The second institution is the Indian Institute of World Culture in Bangalore and its children's library with a collection of 9,000 books. This library is a delightful place where a variety of reading materials are attractively displayed. Third is the Children's Book Trust, which has one of the best children's libraries in India, with a wealth of books, magazines, and journals from all parts of the world.

The Integration of Reading Instruction with Other Aspects of the Child's School and Everyday Life

In schools in India the common practice has been to teach each subject of the curriculum in its own separate and isolated compartment. Language teaching and reading are not exceptions to this general rule. Hence, one can discern very little effort to integrate reading with other aspects of the child's life in or out of school.

However, in the NCERT Reading Project, more concern for creating links with other aspects of the child's life has been shown. For example, not only are selections from the great classics and epics of India included in the readers, but also there is a deliberate attempt to include material related to present-day life and themes within the experience of children who live in modern India. Cultural values and ideals are carefully considered in these materials also. Besides providing material in harmony with the children's own culture, there is a conscious effort to develop values in accord with India's international outlook. Furthermore, a definite attempt is made in these materials to correlate the teaching of reading with the learning of other subjects of the curriculum, by teaching important concepts and attitudes required in these other areas of study. For example, reading selections are provided that are typical of reading matter found in certain subject areas.

Perhaps it should be mentioned particularly that material related to important festivals and religions are included in order to develop a greater understanding of the various religions of India consonant with the secular nature of the country.

Teacher Training

Every State has a number of teacher-training schools both for primary and secondary levels, but these training facilities are very inadequate, except in two or three States.

A student must matriculate to enroll in any elementary training institution. Graduates are also admitted to this program, but the poor salary and low status attached to primary school teaching tend to deter the best students from working at this level.

The present duration of the training period for elementary teachers in most States is two years for matriculates and one year for graduates. But there is still no all-India policy on this. For example, in some states it is only one year for nongraduates.

There is no provision at present for graduates to obtain higher specialized training in elementary education. The faculty members in the elementary training schools usually are themselves trained for secondary education and they often have had no actual experience teaching in elementary schools. Only recently has the realization begun to develop that the staff of an elementary training college should be specialists in elementary education.

The present syllabuses of elementary teacher-training schools are far from satisfactory as far as professional courses are concerned. In some states, the majority of the time is devoted to the teaching of general subjects, language, mathematics, science, and social studies, and little time is available for instruction in methods of teaching, school organization, educational psychology, and other professional subjects. The total time devoted for practice teaching is not consistent either, varying from one State to another.

The government of India recommends that the minimum general education of elementary teachers should be the satisfactory completion of their secondary school work. However, as a result of a shortage of teachers, there has been some relaxation of this rule. For the middle school it is recommended that teachers should be trained college graduates. It is suggested that the headmaster of every primary school with more than two hundred children should be a trained graduate also.

However, there are some problems in implementing these programs. First of all, the pay of an elementary teacher is so low that matriculates and graduates are not willing to join the profession at this level. Secondly, they are unwilling to work in remote and inaccessible areas. Although, in recent years, a special allowance has been paid for work in such places, the response has not been very encouraging. Besides, as has been said earlier, there is a great shortage of matriculates and graduates. But future prospects seem better, because the rate of expansion of secondary and university education in India is so great now that the difficulty in obtaining an adequate number of matriculates or graduates to staff the elementary schools should be eased in the near future.

Only graduates are admitted to secondary training colleges, where the training period is one year for B.Ed. and two years for M.Ed. The curriculum includes both general and specific education courses. The general courses are philosophy and sociology of education, advanced psychology of education, and advanced philosophy of education. Methods of research and educational statistics are included at the M.Ed. level. The specific education courses are teacher education, curriculum planning and development, experimental psychology, guidance and counseling, educational administration, preschool education, adult education, and elementary education. At the M.Ed. level the student is required to write a dissertation. Practice teaching is an integral part of the secondary training program but, as in the elementary colleges, the time allotted to school practice varies from state to state.

As may be inferred from this description, the teaching of language arts and reading in particular does not get any special attention in the training of teachers at either level. However, the training program is currently under revision and more emphasis is likely to be placed on the teaching of the language arts in future.

Inservice teacher-training programs are conducted at State level as well as at the central level every year to acquaint teacher trainers and teachers with the newer trends in various fields at different levels. In the NCERT Reading Project an initial group of teachers was trained to use the new materials with the appropriate teaching methodology. These teachers, in their turn, conducted workshops for other teachers in their districts, and this was continued until all the five thousand elementary teachers involved were oriented to this new approach in reading in India.

With a view to improving the quality of education at various levels, particularly at the primary and middle levels, centrally sponsored State institutes of education were started during 1963–1964, in all States except Nagaland. These institutes are to train school teachers, headmasters, inspecting officers, and the staff of training institutions; to conduct research studies and investigations in the field of elementary education; and to produce suitable literature for the benefit of teachers.

Reading Research

All major universities have provisions for specialist studies in the field of education, but this is not necessarily in the teaching of reading. According to a survey conducted by NCERT,[9] the Indian universities between 1930 and 1961 produced research on the following topics related to the learning of reading:

1. Children's vocabulary.
2. Children's reading interests.
3. Language development.
4. Analysis of language texts.
5. Analysis of children's literature.
6. Methods of teaching reading.
7. Studies of comprehension.
8. Test development.
9. Remedial reading.
10. Reading readiness.

Most such studies were made as part of the dissertation requirement for the M.Ed. degree. But, in addition, now the State institutes of education and various departments of education at the State level are conducting research in education. NCERT has made an especially significant contribution in educational research throughout India. However, in reading it has published only one study so far (of reading readiness). Another investigation (of reading tests) has been completed recently.

Of the studies listed here, the NCERT investigation of reading readiness has been described in detail earlier in this chapter. Most of the other topics have been only slightly researched, but the first two items—children's vocabulary and children's reading interests—have received more attention from educational researchers in India.

The most notable of the vocabulary studies conducted in the training departments of Indian universities are those by Lakdawala,[10] Rawal,[11] and Vakil[12] of the recognition and reproduction vocabulary of Gujarati children at ages 11, 12, and 13. The vocabulary of younger children in Hindi, Gujarati, and Marathi has been investigated in a number of M.Ed. dissertations.

More than thirty studies of reading interests have been conducted by students in the different training colleges of the country during the past few years to fulfill in part their M.Ed. degree requirements.

They have attempted to explore the reading interests of boys and girls in the different languages—Hindi, Bengali, Marathi, Kannada, Gujarati, and Punjabi. Generally, researchers have investigated the reading interests of high school pupils rather than those of younger pupils at the elementary level. Most of these studies have methodological limitations that create some uncertainty as to the representativeness of their samples and the reliability and validity of the questionnaires employed.

Reading Disability

There are no special provisions for children who fail in reading mainly because reading disability has not yet been identified as an educational problem. Neither is there any objective tool to measure reading ability or reading disability. The students who fail are made to repeat the year again and again until they show a general improvement. This procedure causes many children to "stagnate," as they are retained in a lower grade. This stagnation has been shown[13] to be a very serious problem in India. It seems probable that a great number of these stagnating students are failing because of poor reading abilities, but only recently have the teaching of reading and its significance arrested the attention of educators. It has been assumed conventionally that reading has been taught adequately if the child has mastered all the characters of the alphabet. Therefore, the possibility that general educational failure may be the result of reading disability has hardly been considered seriously. However, judged even by minimal standards, the proportion of the population of India that is illiterate would not be a cause for complacency. The 1961 census[14] found that only 24 per cent of the population of India is literate: 34.5 per cent of males and 13.0 per cent of females. The lower proportion of females who are literate is probably chiefly the effect of various sociocultural factors. There are also very large differences in the rate of literacy from one State or territory of India to another: for example, only 11.0 per cent in Jamu and Kashmir and 15.2 per cent in Rajasthan, but 46.8 per cent in Kerala and 52.7 per cent in Delhi. The causes of these large differences would be a significant topic for comparative reading research.

REFERENCES

1. Grierson, G. A., *Linguistic Survey of India,* Vols. I–XI, Calcutta: Government Press, 1918.
2. Government of India, *Report of the Official Language Commission,* New Delhi: Government of India Press, 1957.
3. Chatterjee, S. K., "Languages of India," *Gazetteer of India,* New Delhi: Ministry of Information and Broadcasting, 1965.
4. Grierson, *op. cit.,* Vol. IX, p. 43.
5. Rawat, D. S., *A Battery of Reading Readiness Tests,* New Delhi: NCERT, 1964.
6. Reading Project, *Reading Readiness Kit,* New Delhi: NCERT, 1966. This was developed by this writer (when a Senior Research Officer of NCERT) with the assistance of other staff under the guidance of Dr. Constance McCullough.
7. Gray, W. S., *The Teaching of Reading and Writing: An International Survey,* Paris: UNESCO, 1956.
8. Reading Project, *Teaching Reading: A Challenge,* New Delhi: NCERT, 1966.

9. Reading Project, *A Classified Bibliography of Research Studies on Reading Conducted at Indian Universities,* New Delhi: NCERT, 1963.
10. Lakdawala, U. T., *The Basic Vocabulary of Gujarati Children at the Age of 13 Plus,* Bombay: University of Bombay, 1960. Also *Gujarati Vocabulary of Children Between 6 and 10 Years,* Bombay: University of Bombay, 1951.
11. Rawal, R. T., *The Basic Vocabulary of Gujarati Children at the Age of 12 Plus,* Bombay: University of Bombay, 1959.
12. Vakil, K. S., *The Basic Vocabulary of Gujarati Children at the Age of 11 Plus,* Bombay: University of Bombay, 1955.
13. Prakash, Ved, "Stagnation and wastage," *Indian Yearbook of Education,* New Delhi: NCERT, 1965.
14. Government of India, *1961 Census,* New Delhi: Ministry of Information and Broadcasting, 1968.

CHAPTER 20

Israel

DINA FEITELSON*

Israel and its Peoples: Past and Present[1]

ISRAEL has existed as a State only since 1948, yet its beginnings reach back to a much earlier time. In order to understand the place of reading in Israel today it is necessary to have some knowledge of past events.

Even after the destruction of the Second Temple by the Romans in A. D. 70, Jews continued to live in the area known today as Israel, and to flock there from the lands of their dispersion. Several ancient communities have persisted without interruption to the present time. In addition, the second half of the nineteenth century saw the emergence of new and much larger waves of immigration, which embraced mainly East European Jewry, and brought ever-increasing numbers back to their ancient homeland. At that time, and until the First World War, the area that is now Israel was part of the vast Ottoman Empire. With the dissolution of the Ottoman Empire after the First World War, the administration of the area was entrusted to Great Britain.

During British mandatory administration, immigration continued, so that when the State of Israel was proclaimed in May 1948, there were already 650,000 Jews in that part of Palestine that henceforth would be Israel. The predominant factor in the first years of statehood was the tremendous increase in population. Within three years the population doubled, and it doubled once again within the next fifteen years. Although these statistics are the result in part of natural increase, they are mainly the result of immigration. The astounding feature of mass immigration after the State was established in 1948 was that, contrary to earlier times when most of the immigrants came from Europe, the majority now came from the Arab countries of the Middle East and North Africa.

In 1968, the population of Israel numbered 2,841,100 of which 11.8 per cent were non-Jews.[2] The other 88.2 per cent, the Jewish population, was comprised of the following groups:

44.0 per cent Israeli-born.
28.8 per cent born in Europe, the Americas, or Oceania.
27.2 per cent born in Africa or Asia.

* The author wishes to thank Mrs. Eleanor Rosenberger and Mr. Ira Krakow of the Center for Cognitive Studies, Harvard University, for their help in the preparation of this manuscript.

Among the Israeli-born group, again more than half were the children or second-generation descendants of fathers born in Asia or Africa.[3]

Thus, the problem of the tremendous increase in population was compounded by the fact that a predominantly European-American society changed, within twenty years, to one in which the majority had its origins in the Middle East and North Africa. The implications of these drastic changes will become evident later in our discussion.

When the earlier European settlers who arrived in this remote part of the crumbling Ottoman Empire found no indigenous educational institutions to satisfy their needs, they founded their own modern schools. In time, these developed into an autonomous Jewish educational system that continued on its independent course throughout the period of British mandatory administration.

All levels of education, from preschools to institutes of higher learning, were represented in this system of education, and, as time progressed, Hebrew became the sole medium of instruction in all of them.

Consequently, when the State of Israel came into being in 1948, the nucleus of a fully developed educational system already existed, and the transition to a full-fledged national system administered by the newly created Ministry of Education and Culture was relatively smooth.

The Educational Setting

One of the first laws passed by the newly elected parliament of the young State was the Compulsory Education Law, which made nine years of free schooling, from ages 5 through 14, available and compulsory to all. At the time of this writing, a second law—which adds two more years of free and compulsory education—is in the process of being implemented.

Since statehood, schools catering to the diverse non-Jewish minority groups have been administered by the Ministry of Education. Naturally, the Compulsory Education Law also applies to these groups.

Schools for the minorities operate in their own languages and according to their own cultural traditions. They have their own teacher-training institutions, curricula, and supervisors. In view of the fact that reading in these schools is taught in different languages—none of them Hebrew—they will be omitted from this discussion.

Given the constant flux and the extremely complicated circumstances of the Israeli educational setting, its description in a concise, brief statement is impossible. To try to do so would be to court the risk of gross oversimplifications and inaccuracies. However, in order to serve the reader who does not have the time or inclination to get more deeply involved in its intricacies, an attempt must be made to make *some* generalizations.[4]

The engineers of the Israeli educational system came in the main from the European continent; thus, the European continental tradition is evident in many of its aspects. In essence, it displays the influence of centralized planning and a centralized administration, with all the great benefits, but also the accompanying disadvantages, of such a system. For example, although it may be argued that such centralization makes for rigidity and lack of adaptation in the face of changing needs, it also readily permits radical and far-sweeping changes, once such changes are decided on. As we shall see, both these elements of a centralized system have played important roles in regard to reading as it exists in Israel today. Administrative and educational policy, curricula, levels of achievement, and even the number of hours allotted to a subject in any one type of school are all decided on and implemented by the Ministry of Education.

The basic structure of the educational system that was in effect until recently is presented in Table 20-1.

TABLE 20-1. Structure of the Educational System in Israel

Age	Type of institution	Duration in years	Fees
5–6	Kindergarten	1	Free
6–14	Elementary	8	Free
14–18	Academic secondary	4	Depend
	Vocational	2–4	on parent's
	Agricultural	3–4	income

In this system, the kindergarten was a one-year institution from which the child proceeded to a neighborhood eight-year elementary school. Most schools had two classes at each grade level and a total population of about five hundred to seven hundred pupils. In eighth grade, all pupils took a countrywide test, the results of which determined to a large extent what type of secondary schools they would attend—and especially their eligibility for academic secondary schools. Although fewer than half of the children used to pass this test, in fact, about 80 per cent of the graduates of elementary schools did continue to some kind of secondary education.

The extension of compulsory education by two more years has triggered a gradual transition to a 6 + 3 + 3 system in which it is hoped that pupils will find their way by a more gradual and thorough selective process. One of the aspects of the new plan is that kindergartens will probably become part of the neighborhood elementary schools, thus freeing teachers from much of the administrative work of a separate institution.

For the special purpose of studying reading in Israel, one more pertinent fact should be added. From the early days of the Hebrew school system to the present time, the study of the Bible has been and continues to be one of the main subjects throughout all grades, from second grade on. For this to be effective, therefore, one of the cornerstones of the system is that a satisfactory level of independent reading must be attained by the end of first grade. The importance of this basic assumption will come up time and again in our further discussion.

Learning to Read—The Traditional Way

Hebrew, as it is spoken in Israel today, is an ancient language that was revived for daily use by the settlers who arrived around the turn of the century. Until then, for generation upon generation, learning to read Hebrew meant learning to decipher a dead language that the student did not comprehend.[5]

The traditional way of learning to read Hebrew has many elements in common with the so-called alphabetic method[6] of learning to read. Irrespective of language, the main characteristics of this approach for the student are (1) to first learn the *names* of the letters rather than the letter *sounds*, and (2) to learn the names of *all* written symbols and sometimes also a number of rules *before* he proceeds to the deciphering of words.

One may consider now what this method used to entail in fact for the young child learning to read Hebrew. In those days learning to read began early, in many communities as young as age 4. The first step was to memorize each of the thirty-six symbols used in Hebrew writing.[7] Because many of the Hebrew letters resemble each other closely, learning to recognize and name them was no mean feat, and there are numerous tales about the mnemonic devices invented by teachers in order to facilitate this arduous task.[8]

After mastering this step, the child reached the second stage, in which he learned to combine each consonant with each vowel; however, he still referred to them by name.[9] Once the more than two-hundred possible combinations had been thoroughly mastered, the child proceeded to the next step, which in fact required that he unlearn much of what had just become so firmly established.

Now, at last, he acquired a skill that would be of direct use in decoding: he learned to *sound* phonemes while looking at the graphemes. In order to do so, he had to learn to inhibit the immediate association (that is, letter *names*), which by now came naturally when he looked at a specific graphemic consonant-vowel combination, and to say aloud only the last part of that chain of associations.

Once all the combinations had been remastered in this new way, the child proceeded to the last stage in which abstract rules about reading were memorized. Only then was he confronted with *words* to decode. At this early stage of decoding, no attention whatsoever was paid to the meaning of the words the child was made to decipher in a tongue foreign to him. In some places, it was even an accepted practice to make the child decipher the last word in a line first, proceed from there to the one before it, and so on, until he finally reached the first word of that line.

Considering the young age at which children started on this devious process, most authorities seem to agree that, despite personal reminiscences to the contrary, learning to decode required two to three years.[10]

Once this was accomplished, the child went on to study the Holy Book. In fact, this meant many more years of monotonous drill in which a text in a foreign language was acquired laboriously by way of word-for-word translation. Were it not for the fact that these past teaching practices provide a frame of reference without which it would be difficult to understand later developments in the teaching of reading in Israel, they would not be discussed here. Moreover, it is assumed that in other countries the teaching of reading has gone through roughly parallel stages, and that at times social forces have been more influential than specific research findings in shaping the way reading was taught.

The Modern Way—Learning to Read Before the 1960s

It will be remembered that the educational system in what is now Israel was initially established by pioneers who left their homes in Eastern Europe in order to set up a new way of life in a new country. A basic part of their creed was their deeply ingrained commitment to change, to the forging of new patterns freed from and unhampered by the traditions of the old. Among those traditions was the schooling they themselves had received. One can easily imagine the loathing and abhorrence with which these young radicals looked back on long hours of confinement in crowded schoolrooms mechanically repeating a meaningless drill. This was not the way in which they envisaged education in the new society they were setting out to create!

Their quest for new ways brought them into contact with centers of educational thought in the West, and especially in the United States, just at a time when new trends had gained ascendence in many of them. This was the time of the progressive education movement, when the influence of Dewey and Thorndike was at its peak, and Gestalt psychology in Europe and behaviorism in America were widely acclaimed.

All these theories appealed to the imagination and reasoning of the Hebrew educational reformers and provided further confirmation of their basic beliefs. Small wonder that they tended to accept these theories of education avidly and indiscriminately, and to incorporate them in educational theory and practice as respectable and absolute truths in no need of further confirmation. Beginning reading seemed especially suitable for the implementation of these theories. The child and his own interests became the focal point for all teaching. Consequently, any rigid division into subjects was dropped in favor of a so-called center-of-interest approach.

As time went by, the new educational practices became more firmly established and institutionalized. Hebrew textbooks proliferated and, in their wake, educational texts for the teacher. By the 1940s, a clearly defined center-of-interest way of teaching reading had become widely accepted and was officially recognized as the only permissible approach. All primers in use incorporated this method, and it was also the only one taught at teacher-training colleges. Books and articles that dealt with the teaching of beginning reading showed a great deal of consensus on the pertinent details of this method.

In describing it, reference will be made chiefly to the writings of Jacob Levy, one of the leading language-arts specialists of the day. His 1952 article, "The teaching of reading and writing in the first grade," in *Handbook for the First Grade,* the first in a series of handbooks covering all grades of elementary school, is probably the most authoritative statement on the subject.[11] Further-more, actual classroom practice of that time adhered very closely to the method as he prescribed it.

As seen by Levy and his contemporaries, the child's own interest is para-mount to all other considerations in constructing a program. As long as the child is motivated and reading activities are part of his over-all program, all else will follow. Consequently, Levy states explicitly that he does not recognize any innate structure of subject matter in learning to read. According to him there is no "easy or hard," no "before and after." The only distinction Levy recognizes are "words which *interest* the child and those that do not."[12]

Reading, for Levy, is mainly a *visual* skill, and as adults grasp whole phrases—and because a phrase also essentially conveys more sense than single words (and is therefore more interesting)—reading matter is to be introduced to the child most often *in phrases*. In time, children will be able to pick out single words from the phrases learned and rearrange them into new ones.

Reading activities are mainly via "class charts," on which the teacher writes the phrases or songs to be learned, together with appropriate illustrations. Furthermore, she is required to equip each child with small duplicates of all the words learned, so that he can use these in structuring new phrase com-binations. Levy assumes that first-graders are not at all interested in analyzing words into their component parts. He, therefore, advises teachers to postpone training in word-attack skills for as long as possible. Moreover, he argues that, left to themselves, children will eventually discover similarities between parts of different words. They will infer, on their own, the relationship between written symbols and speech sounds and even be able to create new combinations. Levy prefers this "natural" way of acquiring reading to all others, even though it might in some cases prove to be a very lengthy process.

However, for those teachers who might become impatient with the length of the process, he does outline a strategy for *helping* some of the children to infer relationships between visual symbols and the sounds of spoken language. He feels that a teacher should resort to such a strategy only as a last resort, when very many words have already been introduced, and when at least some of the children are already reading independently. Levy would confine these efforts exclusively to pointing out that words sometimes have similar endings, beginnings, or syllables.

He warns that analyzing words into single letters, or even putting words together from single letters, might quickly deteriorate into formal drill, instead of following the guiding principle that reading activities should arise exclusively, and at all times, from the general activities in the class. "Therefore, I do not think that it is advisable to introduce games with single consonants or vowels. One can trust that, in the course of time, our children will learn by themselves to analyze words also into their basic properties—consonants and vowels—by reading many and varied texts, texts which delight them and are connected with their work and interests."[13]

Until the 1950s, this way of teaching reading was widely used and, in general, considered very satisfactory. Most first-graders did acquire reading without undue difficulty and, by April or May of their first year in school, children used to receive their first reader at a special ceremony attended by their proud parents.

In the book-centered culture of the early settlers, this ceremony was in fact invested with some of the significance of a *rite de passage*—henceforth the child was considered "a reader." Another important point to note is that only on thus becoming a reader did the child in fact receive his first primer. In the preceding stage, while he was in the process of acquiring reading, it was the teacher who had to supply all that he was going to read, mainly by writing texts on the blackboard or on charts.

With the advent of mass immigration from the Arab countries in the early 1950s dramatic changes occurred in this happy state of affairs. With the great increase in school population and the resulting shortage of well-trained and experienced teachers, failure to acquire reading in the first grade rose alarmingly.[14]

Some schools accepted a failure rate of 50 per cent at the end of the first grade with equanimity, blaming it mainly on the extremely deprived conditions in which immigrant children lived at that time and on the lack of motivation and interest on the part of their parents—many of whom had received very little education themselves.

A study sponsored at about that time by a private research organization was designed to gain a better understanding of the causes for the widespread failure in the first grade. Ten first-grade classes, nine of them from schools in which failure was rampant, were studied intensively throughout the academic year. Children were tested three times during the year, observed in the classroom situation, and visited in their homes. Teaching practices were recorded and analyzed, and teachers were interviewed at great length.[15]

Although the study came up with a number of startling findings and recommendations, the one of interest in this framework concerns reading. Contrary to expectations, failure to acquire reading was not evenly dispersed among the nine matched classes. Quite the contrary, the pattern was one of *the whole class* doing well or poorly. When these findings were related to the teaching styles that had been recorded in the classroom observations, it turned out that the classes of those teachers who had not adhered to the precepts of the accepted method—but who, in fact, had devoted time to reading activities *per se* and even to systematic drill—achieved much better results than those in which reading activities arose mainly in the context of the center of interest on which the class was working.

During the next few years, the incidence of failure in learning to read grew to such proportions that it became a serious threat to the structure of the curriculum in which, as was stated earlier, the study of the Bible was the core subject.

Finally, accepting the contention that improvement might be achieved by way of a change in teaching procedures, the Ministry of Education set up six independent exploratory teams. Within two years, this work resulted in four sets of structured materials for teaching beginning reading. Since 1960, when these materials were first made widely available, many more authors and publishers have issued sets of materials.[16] At present, a first-grade teacher can make her choice from a very broad offering of different psychological and educational approaches. However, because three of the four initial experimental approaches resemble each other closely in many aspects, and because several of their common elements have also been retained in materials that were published at later dates, these common characteristics can be explored here. However, it should be clearly understood that they do not represent a complete consensus of opinion.

The Hebrew Writing System: Implications for Teaching Reading

A concise statement about the Hebrew writing system would probably run somewhat like this: Hebrew writing is alphabetic with symbols for twenty-two consonants (five of which change form at the end of a word) and nine vowels. The direction of reading is generally in zig-zag fashion from top to bottom and from right to left, as demonstrated in Figure 20-1. However, this statement does not give a full picture of some of the subtle intricacies of Hebrew writing, nor does it mention two more qualities that are of importance in beginning reading—namely, visual features of the script and grapheme-phoneme correspondence.[17] These two will be focused on now.

The method of teaching reading described by Levy originally reached the Hebrew school system from English speaking countries. Therefore, it might be useful to examine some of the basic assumptions of that method in the light of their applicability to the Hebrew writing system.

On reexamining texts on the teaching of reading in English that used to serve

FIGURE 20-1. Example of direction of reading in Hebrew writing.

as guidelines for the educators of the day,[18] one is impressed by the importance attached to the over-all *shape of words* introduced in the early stages of learning. It was repeatedly stressed that only words with distinctive visual patterns—ascenders, descenders, or both—should be learned at this stage. Children, it was argued, would have difficulty recognizing printed words that lacked a distinctive over-all shape, such as *in, on, or,* and *one.*

Moreover, each word should possess a pattern of its own, different from that of other words. The presentation of several written words all with similar visual patterns—as, for example, in *cat, mat, sat*—should therefore be avoided. Children who are being trained to react only to over-all word shapes would have no way to avoid confusing them because they would all have the same

pattern—namely, ▟▌ In fact, words for primers and preprimers were to be

chosen mainly on criteria of visual distinctiveness.[19]

As has been shown elsewhere in greater detail,[20] these precepts seem singularly inapplicable to Hebrew print, which can boast only one ascender and one descender (four of the final consonant graphemes are also descenders, but as they are without exception the last character of a word they do not contribute much to variability of word patterns either). Thus, words in written Hebrew lack distinctive visual patterns and differ from each other mainly in length. However, as most common words in Hebrew have either two or three or four consonant graphemes, virtually thousands of written words will be identical in terms of over-all word shape as defined by the English language reading specialists referred to earlier.

In addition, many Hebrew consonant graphemes resemble each other closely, so that telling them apart requires paying attention to minute details of character shapes. Furthermore, Hebrew vowel symbols are much smaller than those for consonants and are most commonly written below the latter. For the beginning reader this means, in fact, that the vowel graphemes—which in the early stages of reading are very important clues for successful decoding—tend often to be overlooked because they are so tiny and because they are, as it were, hidden away. Actually, in Hebrew, one single dot can assume several different vocal meanings, depending on its location in relation to the other graphic symbols that form a given word.

Given the fact that Hebrew script lacks distinctive word patterns but requires that the beginning reader pay attention to every single detail, be it even one little dot, a method of teaching that trained him to rely mainly on over-all word shapes clearly would not be effective.

On the other hand, Hebrew boasts of a nearly perfect one-to-one symbol-sound relationship. Actually, only two consonant graphemes can assume two sound values each. What is more, one simple rule applies in both cases. Thus, with respect to symbol-sound correspondence, learning to read Hebrew is infinitely easier than learning to read English. For all practical purposes, it entails only learning one phoneme for each grapheme of the Hebrew script.

In retrospect, it seems that for many years children in the Hebrew school system learned to read their language—which has no distinctive word shapes but which boasts of an extremely good symbol-sound correspondence—in spite of the fact that their teachers were recommended to use a method originally developed for a language with distinctive word shapes but very poor symbol-sound correspondences. What is thought provoking is not why this way of teaching eventually resulted in widespread failure, but rather *how it could have been successful for so long*.

Visits to the pupils' homes made in the 1952 study cited earlier provided some tentative answers to this enigma—answers that have since been substantiated by countless parent interviews, although never put to the test in a controlled setting. Of the ten first-grade classes that were followed in that study, nine were drawn from schools in which failure was rampant, whereas the control group was from a school in a well-established middle-class neighborhood. In the visits to the homes of the control group, what stood out most prominently was the extent to which parents were aware of and involved in even the smallest details of their children's lives in school. Even though these middle-class homes were visited relatively late in the school year, parents commented on the fact that their children had been tested in the first weeks of school by the research worker who visited them. Moreover, in many cases they remembered actual items of the initial test that their child had been unable to answer. In the course of the interview it also became evident that they had taken steps to fill in these gaps in their child's knowledge. The mother of one child told how, upon learning from her child that he had not known "what melts," she had immediately put water on to boil for tea and melted sugar in it so that, as she concluded, "you can be quite sure he now knows what 'melt' means."[21]

Such parents are thus not only fully aware of what is learned in class day by day, but they also tend to take immediate action whenever *they* feel that their children are not doing as well as they might. What is more, they have at their command adequate techniques for dealing with such supposed lags. The following two statements are typical of those that recurred numerous times in parent interviews over the years: "We thought our son read very well and we were delighted with his progress. But when he fell ill in the middle of the term we suddenly discovered that all he did was guess. So I [the father] explained the principle of the thing to him and by the time he returned to school a few days later he could really read." And, "With my first daughter I still believed the parents should not interfere. Poor her, she still had difficulties in the third grade. With the other two I didn't wait. I taught them right from the beginning. They had no problems and read well before the end of the year!"

In short, what seems to have happened is that a method of teaching that was singularly unsuited to the special features of the Hebrew writing system appeared successful as long as work done at school was supplemented by a great deal of individual help at home from parents. When such help was unavailable, large numbers of children did not acquire reading.

The common denominators in most of the new reading programs are that they are sequential and structured. Visual symbols are introduced gradually and are related immediately to their sound value. At each stage, reading is confined only to those graphemes that have been learned already. Materials for class use cover stages of learning, starting from the very first day. In many schemes these materials are distributed according to pages, so that the child assembles his "reader" as he goes along and is not exposed to written symbols he has not yet learned. It should be clearly understood that although graphemes are introduced one by one, sequences are usually structured in such a way that, from the very beginning, the child deals exclusively with meaningful words and phrases.[22]

A 1966 Ministry of Education survey, in which a test that had been used in a 1949 survey was readministered, documents the great improvement in beginning reading. Not only had "reading disability" at the end of first grade, as documented by the researchers of the 1950s, "virtually disappeared," but improvement was so great that, by 1966, achievements in schools in immigrant areas were better than the 1949 scores of schools in the comparatively well-established areas (that is those serving the "old-timers").[23]

Reading Beyond the Beginning Phase

The dramatic and highly successful changes at the beginning reading stage have so far not been accompanied by corresponding developments at later levels. Except for schools in the kibbutz movements, basal readers are widely used as the main tool in developing reading skills. Many class teachers still naïvely believe that lessons in which an identical text from identical books is read at a uniform rate by all thirty to forty children in the class will not only foster a myriad of reading skills but will also accustom them to read for fun.

The misconceptions in regard to this last aspect are especially criticial when one realizes that a new school system such as the Israeli one, with severely limited funds, is apt to be hampered by inadequate library facilities. In many Israeli primary schools, libraries are poor quantitatively as well as qualitatively. Often they are administered by teachers on a voluntary basis and thus are open infrequently. In fact, in many schools a child will have access to no more than one book per week, and this only while school is in session.[24] Also, public libraries develop slowly and in many of them children's sections are still poorly stocked.[25]

Another differentiating factor between children of old-timers and children of new immigrants thus emerges. In the homes of the former there are often extensive libraries, and children's books will usually be bought regularly. In homes of this kind children will be compensated for the inadequate school and public libraries, a factor not operant for children in homes lacking an adequate supply of books.

In line with the Ministry of Education's basic policy of providing better than average services to schools in which there is a concentration of children from homes that lack intellectual stimulation, extra funds for school libraries have been made available to schools in immigrant areas. Although help of this kind has alleviated acute shortages, many school libraries and facilities are still inadequate as the sole source for satisfactory leisure-time reading habits.

On many counts the post-initial-reading program in the Israeli school system seems to leave a lot to be desired, but it is important to realize that, although communal work from a class reader is at best a very uncertain way to develop many of the post-initial skills, it does foster one type of ability: namely, reading comprehension. Work on any one passage, directed by the teacher and shared by all the children, will elicit both obvious and hidden meanings, deal with the author's interests and tools, view the passage or work in relation to wider issues, and, finally, dwell at great length on the language aspects of the text.

An expert from abroad might well feel that such a procedure, although perhaps useful if carried out at different levels of reading matter, can hardly be considered to contribute to every child in the class. However, such a reaction does not take into account one of the basic underlying facts about basal readers in Israel: namely, that at present they are ungraded. Moreover, the reading matter in these basal readers, although often pedantic and boring, is nearly always at a level of difficulty that will tax even the most advanced children in class. Working in common as a whole class, then, does not mean, as it would in the context of graded basal readers, that some of the children are working far below their level of ability.

Furthermore, the type of activity described here is not confined to work in language *per se*. The fact that, from second grade on, at least four periods a week and sometimes many more, are devoted to Bible study has already been mentioned. Once again, this means that all children, actively directed by the teacher, will be working on the same text—in this case, a classical one with an extremely compelling story line expressed in beautiful and concise language. What is more, Bible study in this context means not only reading a text to the point of becoming familiar with it, but, in effect, studying it so that it is actively mastered. Children are expected to know and comprehend every word of the text and to be able to use them in relating a given passage. Also, in this case, the text that is thus studied and internalized provides a challenge even for the most able children.

In the higher grades of elementary school, children are introduced to Rabbinic literature, thus becoming aware that one can reach beyond obvious meanings to ever-deeper levels of understanding. With time, this process is expanded and, by adolescence, children will have become aware that in this seeking for hidden meanings there is no final point, and that they as well as their teachers can only participate in the process.

It would seem, therefore, that the great amount of time devoted to this one type of reading activity would certainly prove beneficial in terms of the acquisition of certain attitudes and aptitudes.

However, the question of precisely what skills are developed by this approach to learning—and, furthermore, whether these skills are transferred to other more mundane reading activities—needs to be investigated. In the absence of such research it is hypothesized that, while a great amount of time and energy on the postbeginning level is devoted to one type of reading activity, other important areas are neglected. The outcome of both the concentrated work in one area and the apparent neglect of others has yet to be assessed.

REFERENCES

1. For a comprehensive analysis of Israeli society, see Eisenstadt, S. N., *Israeli Society,* London: Weidenfeld and Nicholson, 1967.
2. All statistics in this chapter exclude the Administered Territories in which, at the time of this writing, schools continue to be run along Jordanian or Egyptian lines.
3. Central Bureau of Statistics, *Statistical Abstract of Israel,* Vol. 19, Jerusalem: Central Bureau of Statistics, 1968.
4. For a detailed description and analysis of the various aspects of education in Israel, see Kleinberger, A. F., *Society, Schools, and Progress in Israel,* Oxford: Pergamon, 1969. Also Bentwich, J. S., *Education in Israel,* London: Routledge, 1965.
5. The fact that Hebrew was revived only relatively recently has another important side-effect: namely, many parents speak Hebrew less well than their children and thus cannot help them effectively in their schoolwork.
6. As described, for instance, by Huey, E. B., *The Psychology and Pedagogy of Reading,* New York: Macmillan, 1908. Reissued at Cambridge, Mass.: MIT Press, pp. 240–255.
7. In the Hebrew writing system there are twenty-two consonant graphemes, five final consonant graphemes, and nine vowel graphemes.
8. Scharfstein, Z., *Ha-Heder b'Hayye Amenu (The Cheder in the Life of the Jewish People),* Tel-Aviv: Newman, 1951 (in Hebrew), p. 98.
9. *Ibid.,* p. 100.
10. *Ibid.,* p. 102.
11. Levy, J., and Blum, U. (eds.), *Handbook for the First Grade,* Tel-Aviv: Urim, 1952 (in Hebrew).
12. *Ibid.,* p. 100.
13. *Ibid.,* p. 106.
14. A number of pioneering studies by M. Brill, R. Baki, A. M. Dushkin, H. Enoch, and Gina Ortar had in fact documented school failure before mass immigration got under way. According to them this kind of failure was especially severe in first grade and occurred nearly exclusively in a few poor neighborhoods settled by non-European Jews.
15. Feitelson, Dina, "Causes of scholastic failure among first graders," *Megamot (Behavioral Sciences Quarterly),* 4 (1952–1953), 1–84 (in Hebrew).
16. This tends to bear out Chall's contention about the spread and influence of "fashions" in reading. Chall, J., *Learning to Read: The Great Debate,* New York: McGraw-Hill, 1967.
17. For a more thorough discussion, see Feitelson, D., "The relationship between systems of writing and the teaching of reading," in Jenkinson, M. (ed.), *Reading Instruction: An International Forum,* Newark, Del.: IRA, 1967, pp. 44–50.
18. For example, Schonell, F. J., *The Psychology and Teaching of Reading,* London: Oliver and Boyd, 1946. Also, Gagg, J. C., and Gagg, M. E., *Teaching Children to Read,* London: Newnes, 1955.

19. Gagg and Gagg, *Ibid.*
20. Feitelson, Dina, "On the teaching of reading in non-European languages," *English Language Teaching,* **16** (1961), 39–43. Also, "The alphabetic principle in Hebrew and German contrasted to the alphabetic principle in English," *Highlights of the IRA 1965 Pre-Convention Institute, Linguistics and Reading,* Newark, Del.: IRA, 1966, pp. 44–50.
21. The only item that her child had failed out of a total of forty!
22. For more detailed descriptions of a few of these schemes see Bloom, S., "Israeli reading methods for their culturally disadvantaged," *Elementary School Journal,* **66** (1966), 304–310. Also "Changing the teaching of reading in Israel," in Adiel, S., *et al.* (eds.), *Ten Years of Compensatory Education,* Jerusalem: Ministry of Education (in Hebrew), 1970. Also Braverman, S., "A phonetic method for teaching reading," *Urim,* **25** (1968), 115–120 (in Hebrew). Also Feitelson, Dina, "Structuring the teaching of reading according to major features of the language and its script," *Elementary English,* **42** (1965), 870–877.
23. Adiel, S., "Reading ability of culturally deprived first graders," *Megamot (Behavioral Sciences Quarterly),* **15** (1968), 345–356 (in Hebrew).
24. Meir, M., "The use of the school library," *Second Annual Collection of Essays,* Jerusalem: Israel Reading Association, 1969, pp. 51–57 (in Hebrew).
25. Ben-Shach, L., "In the municipal library," *Second Annual Collection of Essays,* Jerusalem: Israel Reading Association, 1969, pp. 58–61 (in Hebrew).

CHAPTER 21

Japan

TAKAHIKO SAKAMOTO and KIYOSHI MAKITA

Writing Systems

IN Japan four separate writing systems are used. There are two kinds of *Kana* (namely, *Hiragana* and *Katakana*), *Kanji,* and *Roma-ji.* Hiragana and Katakana are phonetic symbols, each being monosyllabic without meaning by itself. With few exceptions, each character has only one phonetic pronunciation. Because the relationship between written symbols and spoken syllables is so very regular, these two systems are easy to learn, and in this respect they seem similar to the i.t.a., which has been designed to ease reading difficulties in English. Almost all children can read Hiragana before they are of school age. The number of symbols in Hiragana and Katakana is forty-eight each, but two of these are not used at the present time. In Figure 21-1 some examples of Hiragana are shown. The symbols of both series are simple, but Hiragana is more cursive in shape than Katakana.

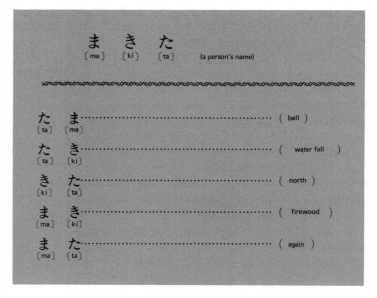

FIGURE 21-1. Examples of spelling with Hiragana.

440

With the forty-six symbols of either system, plus other marks that give additional phonetic values, one can write any word in the language. When a child has learned three Hiragana symbols (for example, for the three syllables in the name of one of these writers, *Ma-ki-ta*), he can write five more words by combining these same symbols in other permutations of the same syllables they represent, as shown in Figure 21-1.

Kanji characters are ideographs that originally came from China. They are, therefore, often called Chinese characters, from the literal translation of the term into English. Kanji, however, are not completely Chinese but today are very typically Japanese. They are read differently and the significance of some characters is entirely different from that of the Chinese.

Because they are ideographs, each Kanji has its own meaning. They are quite numerous but now are "officially" limited to 1,850 characters for daily use. These characters are combined to make up the majority of the Japanese vocabulary. Kanji are more complicated and square in shape than Kana. In Figure 21-2 some examples of Kanji are offered. Unlike Kana, each Kanji usually has several alternative readings that range from monosyllabic to quadrisyllabic sounds. Kanji, therefore, are more difficult to read.

Roma-ji is merely the application of the Roman alphabet to Japanese. When European missionaries first arrived in Japan, they taught the Roman alphabet, but it did not spread widely until it was included in the curriculum of elementary school education after the Second World War. Today it is used all over the country, mainly to show the reading of the names of places, towns, stations, and persons for the convenience of people from foreign countries. In this chapter, therefore, the reading of Roma-ji will not be considered.

As mentioned earlier, Kanji came from China (via Korea) and were used to write Japanese. Later, some of the characters were simplified into Katakana and Hiragana. From that time on, several combinations of the three writing systems have been used:

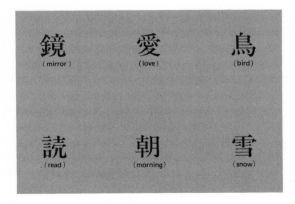

FIGURE 21-2. Examples of Kanji.

1. Kanji only.
2. Hiragana only.
3. Katakana only.
4. Kanji with Katakana.
5. Kanji with Hiragana.

The usage of Kanji with Hiragana has spread more widely than the others and is the standard writing system today. Katakana is used mainly to write the names of foreign peoples, cities, countries, and foreign words that have entered the Japanese language.

In Figure 21-3 examples of Kanji-Hiragana combinations are shown. Each of the five lines in this figure is a sentence that means "I like to read books." The reading of each sentence is identical. The first line (line 0) is written in Hiragana only. This written sentence is acceptable but would not be produced by adults. Children learn the Kanji for "books" in the first grade so that they can read the second line (line 1), in which the two Hiragana for "books" are replaced by the single Kanji for "books." When they have learned the Kanji for "read" in the second grade, they can read the third line (line 2), in which that Kanji takes the place of the corresponding Hiragana. In the same way, sixth-graders can read the fourth line (line 6) and junior high school students can read the fifth line (line 7), in which the maximum number of Kanji are used.

The transference from an all-Hiragana sentence to that of a Kanji-Hiragana combination is, therefore, the replacement of some Hiragana by the corresponding Kanji with the same phonetic reading. This is quite different from the transference in English from i.t.a. to T.O., which frequently requires the learn-

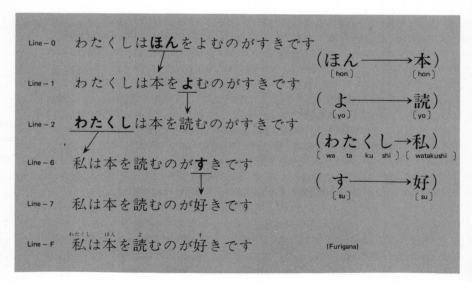

FIGURE 21-3. Graded examples of Kana-Kanji combinations.

ing of different arrangements of the same characters learned first in i.t.a. in another order (for example, dien becomes *dine*).

Moreover, to ease the transition from Hiragana to Kanji, a method called Furigana is sometimes employed. This is illustrated in the last line (line F) of Figure 21–3. The phonetic reading of each Kanji is indicated by the attached Hiragana. Even when a child does not know a Kanji, he can read it with the help of Furigana. Books and magazines for children are printed in the combined Kanji-Hiragana style together with Furigana.

The question may be raised as to why the Japanese use the Kanji-Hiragana combination in spite of the fact that they could communicate with Hiragana only—it is a simpler writing system. The answer is that this combination can be read more quickly and more accurately. Takahiko Sakamoto[1] photographed the eye movements of college students when they were reading short sentences of identical meaning but written in one condition all in Hiragana only and in the other condition in the Kanji-Hiragana combination. The reading of the all-Hiragana sentences required twice as much time as the other. Also, in the case of the all-Hiragana sentences, a shorter perception span, more frequent fixations, longer fixation pauses, and more regressions were recorded in comparison with the Kanji-Hiragana combination. There are several reasons why the Kanji-Hiragana combination is superior to the other writing system:

1. Each Kanji has its own meaning so that nouns, roots of verbs, adjectives, and adverbs can be written in Kanji. In other words, key ideas or key words in each sentence are expressed in ideographs. Line 7 in Figure 21-3 includes four Kanji. The first Kanji means "I," the fourth one, "like," the third one, "read," and the second one, "books." The reader sees each of the four important elements in Kanji.
2. In an average sentence, from 25 to 35 per cent of the total number of characters are written in Kanji; for example, in the sample sentence, 33 per cent of the total characters are written in Kanji. It must be emphasized here again that the visual images of Kanji and Hiragana are quite different: Kanji are more complicated and squarer in shape than Hiragana. Kanji stand out, therefore, from the main background of Hiragana and can be recognized easily.
3. It takes fewer characters to make up words using Kanji than it does using only Hiragana, as we saw in Figure 21-3. It takes sixteen characters in line 0 while only twelve in line 7.

Thus, the reader can easily skim this shorter Kanji-Hiragana sentence, picking up key ideas that stand out against the background.

Reading Standards in Japan Today

Literacy

It might be hypothesized that the rate of literacy in Japan could not be very high because the Japanese must learn four different writing systems and, furthermore, a minimum of 1,850 Kanji characters. However, in spite of these supposed difficulties, more than 99 per cent of the people in Japan are literate, the major exception being the mentally retarded.

According to the results of comparative research reported in 1964 by UNESCO,[2] the Ministry of Education of Japan reported that the problem of illiteracy has been completely solved. By definition, an illiterate person in Japan is one who cannot read or write Kanji, Hiragana, and Katakana at all. Accordingly, 2.1 per cent of the entire population was judged illiterate in 1948. Another survey reported, in 1955, that the rate of illiteracy was less than 0.8 per cent.

This very high rate of literacy in Japan can be attributed to the following causes:

1. The initial use of phonetic symbols—Kana—which are easy to learn.
2. The compulsory education program from the first through the ninth grade. Over a period of one hundred years a very strictly organized system of compulsory education has been developed.
3. Japanese parents have great respect for education and are very eager for their children to learn. Making sacrifices for a child's education is a common part of Japanese parenthood.
4. Publishing companies have made available many good reading materials at low prices.
5. Movements to stimulate reading have been very successful: National Reading Week, the reading movement for mothers, the mother-child 20-minute reading program, reading groups, and book report contests.

Reading Habits of Children and Adolescents

According to the statistics of "The Tohan Report,"[3] which investigated 799 upper-elementary and 894 junior high level children in Tokyo, in 1967, girls on the upper-elementary level read 3.0 books a month whereas boys read 2.6 books, on the average. In junior high school, girls read 2.2 books a month and boys read 1.8 books.

Literature was the most popular subject, followed by history, geography, and science. Literature was read by girls more than boys, and history, geography, and science were chosen by more boys than girls. Activities at home frequently chosen by the upper-elementary level children were (1) watching TV, (2) playing with friends, (3) reading, (4) studying, (5) sports, and (6) picnics. In junior high, they were (1) TV, (2) studying, (3) reading, (4) playing with friends, (5) helping the family, and (6) sports.

The parents' concern for their children's reading was high. To the question "Do you know what book(s) your children are reading now?" 45 per cent of all parents of the upper-elementary children answered, "I know everything they are reading," and 47 per cent said, "almost all." There was no response of "I don't know at all." On the junior high level, the parents' concern was a little lower than those of the upper-elementary level. But still, 89 per cent of all parents stated "everything" or "almost all."

It might be concluded from the results of "The Tohan Report" that the average Japanese child reads many books of good content in spite of the negative influence of television. Parental concern seems to be a factor in this. However, educators have noticed an increase in nonreaders among school children as a result of the influence of television. If we define "readers" as those who read one or more books during a certain month of investigation, and those who do not as "nonreaders," "The Mainichi Report"[4] found that only 1 per cent of all elementary school children were nonreaders in 1963. Since then, the number of nonreaders has increased rapidly and, by 1965, it reached 10 per cent. Also, 27.4 per cent of junior high and 29.4 per cent of all senior high school students were nonreaders in 1965.

The major causes of such nonreading were (1) play (boys, 36.2 per cent; girls, 26.4 per cent), (2) watching television (boys, 26.4 per cent, girls 24.5 per cent), and (3) reluctance (boys, 29.9 per cent, girls, 22.7 per cent). Other reported reasons for nonreading were insignificant.

The time spent for reading per day has also decreased. Citing "The Tohan Report" and "The Mainichi Report," T. Sakamoto[5] pointed out that the time for reading had decreased remarkably from 1960 to 1965. Only 13 per cent of all the investigated elementary school children read books for thirty to sixty minutes a day in 1965, whereas 40 per cent did so in 1960. On the other hand, those who spent fewer than thirty minutes a day had significantly increased during the same period. In 1960, the rate of television circulation to the entire population was only 23 per cent, but it reached 83 per cent by 1965. Sakamoto concluded that although the development of television has adversely affected the reading activities of children, it has not succeeded in eliminating their reading entirely. Television seems to have affected most those children of low ability and those who lack motivation; they more readily became nonreaders.

Reading Habits of Adults

Of Japanese adults, 71.3 per cent read books and magazines in 1964. Surveying 5,047 people over 16 years of age, "The Mainichi Report" showed that the younger generation read more than older people and that this was more marked in the case of women. The average reading time was thirty-two minutes a day. But television seems to have negatively affected adult reading too. In 1961, the average reading time per day was forty-three minutes. The time spent watching TV per day was seventy-six minutes; it went up to 138 minutes in 1965.

Teachers are good readers. The Asahi Press reported, in 1964, that 83 per cent of 1,769 teachers (elementary to senior high) read one or more books a month. Sex or age made no difference in the number of books read, but older teachers read technical books more than younger teachers did. Those with senior positions (principals and head teachers) read more than other teachers.

Housewives have proven to be the worst readers. Interviewing 799 housewives in Tokyo, the Asahi Press reported, in 1962, that only about 20 per cent read one or more books in the month preceding the interview. Of the nonreaders, 75 per cent answered that they did not read because they were too busy with housekeeping. (Yet, 45 per cent of all the housewives watched TV more than three hours a day!)

School Provisions

Many specialists in Japan agree with the Ministry of Education that the success of the compulsory education system is one of the main reasons why Japan has overcome the problem of illiteracy. The increase in the enrollment of pupils in elementary schools can be considered an aspect of this success. The first nationwide "compulsory" elementary school system began in 1872, when The Government Order of Education was promulgated. The enrollment of pupils was not large in the beginning, primarily because education was not entirely free of charge and also because many children had to go out to work to help support the family. By the year 1900, however, tuition was totally paid for with government funds and, at that time, there was a sudden corresponding jump in elementary school enrollment. This increase is also explained by the development of modern industry, which gave the nation a higher standard of living and enabled more families to manage without their children taking up employment. Kaigo[6] has indicated the interrelationship between the development of the economy and the rise in school enrollment. He states that, in the first year of Meiji (1868), more than 70 per cent of the children did not attend school and were illiterate. The progress from this condition to that of almost no illiteracy today has required repeated efforts over half a century to reform and administer the elementary school system. From 1900 on, attendance increased gradually, coming closer and closer to the goal of "no family without primary education." For these reasons, and also owing much to the efforts of the Ministry of Education, the level of enrollment reached 99 per cent by the year 1920.

At the present time Japan has a nine-year compulsory education system— six years in elementary school and three years in junior high school. There are 22,578 elementary schools and 11,249 junior high schools all over the country. Enrollment is 99.9 per cent in both. About 80 per cent of those who finish junior high school attend senior high school. About one fourth of Japanese youth attend colleges or universities.

Age of Commencing Learning to Read

The less complex Hiragana system is used in the beginning reading program in Japan. All books and other materials for young children are now printed in this medium. Many children learn Hiragana at home before school age, although it is not taught until the first grade (at age 6) in the elementary school curriculum.

The National Language Research Institute reported, in 1954, that children in Tokyo read an average of 30.0 out of 46 Hiragana on entering elementary school. In addition, they read 5.8 Katakana, 5.4 Kanji, and 7.9 Arabic numerals. Even children in rural areas were able to read 23.8 Hiragana, 3.6 Katakana, 4.4 Kanji, and 6.5 numerals. This evidence shows that most children are ready to read before school age. Through the standardization of *The Sakamoto Reading Readiness Test,*[7] it was found that reading readiness in Japan is attained at about 4½ years of age.

It is the general practice that no letters or characters are taught in the curriculum of nursery schools and kindergartens, but children learn Hiragana in their daily lives through books, toys, TV programs, and other means with the help of their family. It is quite evident that family concern for the reading of children greatly affects their reading ability at this stage.

In a study of 348 first-grade children, Nakano[8] found that parental concern for the reading ability of their children was a very important factor in readiness. Although he found a high correlation between reading ability and IQ, Nakano could distinguish clearly two particular groups of children: (1) those with poor reading ability but high IQ, and (2) those with high reading ability but low IQ. According to Nakano, special efforts had been made at home to teach Hiragana for the latter group.

Mothers usually have the most influence on children. Recently, mothers' concern for their children has increased greatly. The main reasons might be that (1) the automation of home life has given them the leisure to pay more attention to their children, and (2) the importance of mental development in the preschool age group has been recognized. These factors seem to have raised the reading ability of preschool children. One report says that 31 per cent of 3-year-old children in Tokyo, 58 per cent of 4-year-olds, and 83 per cent of 5-year-olds can read all the Hiragana symbols. Such children have more of a desire to read and parents are eager to buy illustrated books to encourage them. They are enthusiastic to know which picture books are good for children and what factors attract their interest.

A questionnaire about kindergarten picture books was answered by 464 parents from all over Japan. According to Ichiro Sakamoto et al.,[9] parents buy two or three picture books a month. Of these books, 49 per cent are bought at bookstores and 39 per cent at kindergartens and at other places. It is noteworthy that many picture books are available through kindergartens. Books are selected on the following basis:

1. Parents' opinion, 47 per cent.
2. Children's request, 30 per cent.
3. Teachers' recommendation, 14 per cent.
4. Approved book list, 6 per cent.

Ichiro Sakamoto et al. point out that parents today have a tendency to buy beautifully illustrated picture books, whereas their selections in former days depended more on the efficacy of instruction. The picture books most liked by children are those dealing with animals, daily life scenes, fantasies, vehicles, and science, in that order. There is little enthusiasm for the theme of war.

The results of an experiment are also reported in the same article. Sixty children from 3 to 5 years of age were asked to select from alternative illustrations of the same events in a story. It was found that they preferred (in order of importance) those with (1) puppets representing characters, (2) no blank space, (3) clear colors, (4) no heavy outlines, (5) background scenes, (6) cartoon-like pictures, (7) personification, (8) multicolored scenes, (9) perspective, and (10) facial expressiveness.

The traditional principle that children not be taught Hiragana in kindergarten is now outdated. The Educational Research Institute of Shiga Prefecture reported in 1969 that all surveyed kindergarten teachers taught the reading of Hiragana when it was requested by the children. When they noticed mistakes in reading and writing 57 per cent of them corrected the errors. All teachers wrote Hiragana on the blackboard to indicate the date, the day of the week, and the names of absentees.

The present state of early reading, as described here, has brought up for public discussion the question of whether or not Japan should change her compulsory education program. The necessity to include 5-year-old children in the school system has been stressed by the Ministry of Education and by many other specialists. The possibility will be carefully examined in the near future.

Currently, all children begin to learn Hiragana in the first grade. This period does not last very long, however, because this writing system is so easy to learn. The Ministry of Education has required 46 Kanji characters to be learned in the first grade, followed by 105 in the second grade, 187 in the third, 205 in the fourth, 194 in the fifth, and 144 in the sixth. The total number of required Kanji has been 881 in elementary school. (Increased to 996 in 1971.) Repeating the explanation given in the first part of this chapter, forty-six meaningful words in Hiragana, taken from the latter half of the textbook for first-graders, are replaced by their corresponding Kanji. Children learn the meaning as well as the phonetic reading of each. The teaching of Katakana begins in the latter half of the first grade and is completed by the end of the second grade.

It might be hypothesized that learning to read Kanji is very difficult because it is complicated in form. This complexity, however, does not necessarily affect learning adversely. Fukuzawa[10] singled out three factors that influence reading: (1) complexity of the character, (2) frequency of appearance, and (3) the idiomatic meaning of each character. As a result of an investigation in which 396 children (third through seventh grades) were tested, he reported that the most important factor was the familiarity of the character. The frequency of each Kanji in books was another factor, whereas the complexity of characters had no significant effect on learning. Kawai[11] supplemented this with further information on the complexity of characters. He conducted an experiment of paired-associate learning between nonsense patterns and meaningful words. The subjects were asked to recall twelve two-syllable words in association with twelve patterns. The twelve patterns were divided into six different complexity levels as well as into one level of irregularity and one level of regularity. Contrary to some expectations, the irregularity or regularity of patterns had no relationship to the paired-associate learning, but the complexity level did. The least complex group of patterns (level 1) was the easiest to learn. But with this exception only, the general tendency was that the more complex the patterns were, the easier they were to learn. In order to confirm this result, Kawai tested the reading of 160 less complex Kanji and 160 more complex Kanji on normal adults and college students. A significant difference indicated that the more complex Kanji were read more easily than the less complex Kanji, when the frequency of usage was controlled. The higher the frequency of usage was, the easier they were to read correctly. Kawai concluded that this might be the result of the more complex characters having more information or cues for discrimination learning.

To some degree, however, learning Kanji is difficult because each Kanji has usually two or more alternative readings, and Japanese has a very large number of Kanji. In order to overcome these difficulties, the subject of the Japanese language is greatly emphasized throughout the elementary school curriculum, although this covers, as well, arithmetic, social studies, science, drawing, crafts, music, home economics, and physical education. In the first grade, seven hours a week are devoted to language study out of a total of twenty-four hours, followed by nine hours out of twenty-five in the second grade; eight out of twenty-seven in the third; eight out of twenty-nine in the fourth; and seven out of thirty-one in the fifth and sixth grades. In junior high school, children must learn 969 additional Kanji within the three-year period in order to master all 1,850 Kanji for daily use. It should be noted that Japanese children attend school on Saturday as well as Monday through Friday.

Methods of Teaching

The "word method" is generally used to teach Kana. In former days, some teachers attempted to use a method similar to the alphabetic method in English, but this has now entirely disappeared. Another is the "writing method," which is similar to the VAK or VAKT procedure of G. Fernald. A child writes each Kana repeatedly with his finger on the table or in the air, pronouncing it over and over again at the same time. After that he is asked to write the Kana several times, tracing dotted lines. Through this practice, he learns reading by the combination of pronunciation, visual perception, and motor activity.

The "radical analysis method" is also used sometimes. Kanji can be divided into various radicals, and there are several Kanji that contain the same radical. One can teach, therefore, that Kanji are constructed by using combinations of different radicals and are not unsystematic symbols. In addition, many radicals have their own meanings. The left side of each Kanji in Figure 21-4 is a radical that means water, and every Kanji in the Figure is related to water in one way or another. Children are able to learn these Kanji rather easily by the radical analysis method.

To a certain degree, some Kanji are pictographic, so that teaching the derivation of Kanji is another popular method used to stimulate children. For instance, the Kanji for moon was derived from the shape of the crescent moon, and that for tree was derived from the shape of branches and roots. This kind of pictorial explanation is effective only in the case of simple and basic Kanji. The radical analysis method and the "derivation method" may motivate children only in the beginning stage of learning. Japanese teachers realize that the only way to teach such a great number of Kanji is to arrange for children to encounter them as often as possible.

Reading comprehension and reading guidance are emphasized a great deal. The main purpose of Japanese reading education is not only to make children literate but also to enforce the understanding of the morals of stories and to promote sound personality development.

One of the traditional and most widely used methods of teaching reading is called *Sandoku-hō* (the "three-step method"). After a brief introduction, the lesson proceeds as follows: (1) reading through, (2) reading in detail, and (3) appreciation. In the first step, the pupils are asked to read the story aloud from beginning to end and are encouraged to give a brief summary. Reading errors or pronunciation mistakes are corrected in this step. After the first reading, the teacher asks them to discuss their own experiences related to the story they have read. At the same time, they are required to read rather quickly and to grasp the rough outline of the story. The second step is the most important. The pupils are asked to think over the entire story for detailed comprehension by means of character (Kanji) analysis and phrase and sentence relationships. The final step is to lead the pupils to understand what the writer wanted to tell them; in other words, the moral of the story.

Kurasawa[12] pointed out that the "5W 1H method" is applied to the first two steps of the three-step method. According to his explanation, *who, what, when, where,* and *how* are the important factors in the first step. The proper way to grasp what is written is to look at who appears; what sort of person he is; when, where and how he behaves; or what happens where and how. *Why* is important in the second step. By thinking out why a certain fact developed in such a way, or why a hero said such and such a thing, children not only clarify

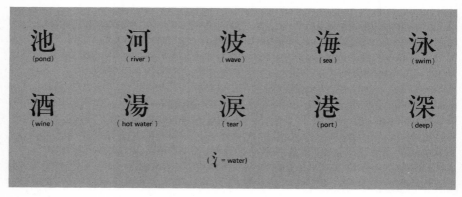

FIGURE 21-4. The "water" radical.

the details, but also form the habit of reading between the lines, or of skipping over a few lines—a useful practice for making themselves imaginative or creative readers. In addition, *why* plays an important role in making clear the writer's intention, thought, and standpoint, Kurasawa added. He also emphasized that group thinking should be encouraged through the following sequence of class activities:

1. A problem or a question is brought out.
2. The pupils understand the problem by talking about it.
3. Small groups (or individual pupils) read, discuss, and take notes.
4. They report the results of the discussions to each other.
5. Finally, they write their conclusions on the blackboard.

Another method is called *Ichidoku-sōgō Hō* (the "one-step synthesis method"). It has also been termed the "single reading synthesism" by I. Sakamoto.[13] It is in opposition to the older three-step method. Based on the dialectic of the psychology of thinking in the USSR, this method emphasizes synthesis and rejects analysis. Children are taught to understand the moral of a story through a one-time reading only. Throughout the reading, they are instructed to pause at any point that is particularly important or where there is something they do not understand. During this pause, they may write down anything they have in their minds concerning the story—questions, opinions, predictions, comments, or summaries. The children's thoughts are then presented and discussed in the class. Through group participation, each child's understanding becomes deeper. The children then continue to read until they come to the next pause, and repeat the same procedure again and again. Finally, when they come to the end, they understand the moral of the story, having synthesized what they learned at every pause.

Textbooks

For a period of forty years, up until 1947, all elementary school textbooks were prepared by the Ministry of Education and all schools throughout the country used the same texts. This was discontinued after the 1947 education reform and a policy of examining privately compiled textbooks was initiated. From that time on, textbooks compiled and published by private companies have been used. These texts, however, must still be approved by the Ministry of Education. In the earlier stage of this 1947 education reform, the Ministry of Education published a model for textbooks, and private companies followed this model in order to gain approval. Also, private textbooks are regulated by the ministry's official pamphlets, *The Course of Study* and *Textbook Standards*. Although several series of textbooks are published at the present time, not one has a unique feature in content. Textbooks are usually selected by a committee from each local board of education. No research has been done to determine a superior series of textbooks so far.

Teacher Preparation and Training

A teacher must teach all subjects to the same children in elementary school. There are no special reading teachers or remedial teachers in Japan. In junior and senior high schools, there are special teachers for each subject. A teacher's license is given to a person who has a bachelor's degree and has finished certain required courses over a period of four years. About 10,000 elementary school teachers are graduated each year. Every local board of education, as well as the Ministry of Education, prepares training programs for teachers. In almost all prefectures, and in big cities, there are local government educational institutions that also give teacher training. Universities also provide some postgraduate training programs for schoolteachers. The Japanese Society for the Science of Reading (JSSR), which is affiliated with the IRA, holds an open session every month and an annual convention every summer. Other associations also hold summer sessions for teachers of the Japanese language, so that meetings are held at some place almost every day throughout the vacation season.

Recent Research in Reading

I. Sakamoto,[14] in his lecture at the First World Congress on Reading held at UNESCO House, Paris, touched on several recent major research activities in Japan: studies of personality formation through reading, standards of reading, bibliotherapy, diagnosis and remedy of reading disability, readability, and methods of teaching reading.

Readability

Anzako[15] singled out two factors that affect the difficulty of Japanese sentences: (1) the length of each sentence and (2) the number of Kanji per sentence. He examined reading textbooks from the first to the sixth grade and determined the average sentence length and the average number of Kanji per sentence for each grade. According to those statistics, Anzako made up a scale for the readability measurement of children's books. His formula is

$$LD = T_{SL} + T_{NK}$$

where LD stands for the level of difficulty, T_{SL} stands for the T-score of the sentence length, and T_{NK} stands for the T-score of the number of Kanji.

Horikawa[16] emphasized that factors affecting the readability of the sentence might depend on what kind of a sentence it is. He discusses two types of sentences: (1) "explanatory sentences," such as those describing a statistical table or giving information on a traffic accident, as seen in the newspapers, and (2) "literary sentences," such as those used in the translation of foreign novels. With the exception of very extreme cases, Horikawa concluded that, in the case of explanatory sentences, the more Kanji they include, the more readable the sentences are, and that the complexity of sentences does not affect the readability. In the instance of literary sentences, however, the less Kanji they include and the shorter they are, the more readable they are.

Morioka[17] developed a scale of readability for adults. During his long period of study, he analyzed many sentences from every kind of magazine and also from textbooks of the Japanese language, of social studies, and of science for grades III, VI, IX and XII. Morioka found that two factors are important for the readability of Japanese: (1) average sentence length in terms of number of characters per sentence and (2) the percentage of Kanji in relation to the entire sentence.

Despite these efforts, vocabulary was not taken into account until I. Sakamoto[18] published a basic word list. His list includes 22,500 words, which are required learning for children by the end of the ninth grade and that cover 98 per cent of all words appearing in books for students below the ninth grade. The most basic 5,000 words, which are required learning by the end of the third grade, are classified as category A. The next group of 7,500 words, which are required by the end of sixth grade, are listed as category B. The last 10,000 words, needed by the end of ninth grade, are designated category C.

Each level (A, B, and C) is divided into two to four 2,500-word groups in accordance with the difficulty of each word. On the basis of this list, I. Sakamoto[19] adopted the concept of "vocabulary weight" in measuring readability. His formula is

$$VW = P_B + 2P_C + 3P_E$$

where VW stands for vocabulary weight, P_B stands for the percentage of B-class words, P_C stands for the percentage of C-class words, and P_E stands for the percentage of words not listed.

The length of sentences was analyzed in I. Sakamoto's[20] subsequent study of readability in terms of "the weight of sentence length." Taking two factors into account—vocabulary weight and sentence (length) weight—his research is currently in progress to establish one complete formula for readability.

Contrary to the element-counting methods of readability measurement, Shiba[21] tested the validity of applying the cloze procedure, introduced by W. L. Taylor,[22] to the Japanese language, and supported Taylor's belief that the cloze procedure can be applied to any language in any culture.

Legibility

Japan has a rather long history of research in legibility because of the complexity of the Japanese writing system. One of the problems is that of horizontal versus vertical writing, because Japanese can be written either way. The sentences in Figure 21-4 are printed horizontally from left to right, but they are quite acceptable when printed vertically (from right to left). Although it has long been the Japanese custom to write vertically, left to right writing has become popular since the Second World War. With the exception of arithmetic, the textbooks of all subjects for elementary school children, for instance, were printed vertically until the end of the war. At the present time, however, only those of the Japanese language and social studies are printed vertically. But, even there, some pages are done horizontally. The general publishing world, on the other hand, is reluctant to adopt wholesale horizontal printing for fear of a negative reaction on the part of those adults who have not been exposed to it previously.

Studies of legibility have never proven the superiority of horizontal writing to vertical writing. T. Sakamoto[23] reported that when subjects responded to lines of meaningless patterns, the efficiency of horizontal eye movement was superior to that of vertical movement. But when they read meaningful sentences, eye movement along vertical lines was more efficient than that of the other. He concluded that although the eyes may move naturally from left to right more smoothly than from top to bottom, long and intensive experience in vertical reading has made them accustomed to move vertically.

For the most part, newspapers, books, and magazines use vertical printing today. Horizontal printing is employed in technical books, scientific journals, and in the fields of business and government. But horizontal writing seems likely to become more popular in the future, when the people who have been less exposed to vertical printing—the postwar generation—constitute a majority of the Japanese population.

Several studies have contributed to improving the legibility of horizontal printing. T. Sakamoto, Muraishi, and Kaga,[24] in a series of studies using the speed-of-reading method, the short-exposure method, and measurement of eye movement, found the optimum space between letters and between lines as well as the optimum type face for a newly designed teletypewriter. T. Sakamoto[25] conducted a multifactor experiment by the speed-of-reading method, in which the following factors were compared: (1) type size, 8-point versus 9-point, (2) line length, 7.0 cm. versus 4.5 cm., and (3) space between lines, 4-point versus 5-point. He concluded that the most legible lateral printing of Kanji-Hiragana was that employing 8-point type size, 7.0 cm. line length, and 5-point spacing between lines.

Obonai and Sato[26] investigated the relative legibility of Kana by the distance method. They reported that, as far as distance is concerned, (1) less complex Kana were more legible, (2) straight lines enhanced the legibility of each letter, while curved lines hindered it, and (3) a dominance of vertical, or a dominance of horizontal, lines made the letter more legible.

Matsubara and Kobayashi[27] also investigated the relative legibility of individual Hiragana and Katakana and classified their legibility. However, the reliability of this study must be questioned because of the method of measurement. Three arbitrary Kana were printed at the top of the test paper, followed by five lines in which a mixture of Kana appeared at random. The subjects were asked to cross out the three arbitrary letters in the five lines. All forty-six Kana were tested using the same procedure. The number of letters crossed out, those omitted, and those incorrectly crossed out were the measurements of each Kana. In this procedure, if one of the three letters were quite illegible, it must have adversely affected the measurement of the other two letters. In other words, the three letters must have mutually affected each other, so that it was impossible to determine the relative legibility of all forty-six Kana. The relative legibility of each Kana needs to be investigated, therefore, in a different way.

Influence of the Content of Books

I. Sakamoto et al.[28] analyzed about 3,000 book reports written by students from primary grades through senior high school to investigate what factors had "inspired" them in their reading. These were classified into categories of personal, social, and cultural problems. Generally speaking, those impressed by topics dealing with personal problems were most frequently found among primary school children. Social problems impressed junior high school students, and cultural problems impressed the senior high school students.

Children in the lower elementary level were inspired by such themes as "soundness of mind" and "improving oneself"; "improving oneself" and "social behavior" impressed the upper elementary level children; among the junior high school students, "attitudes toward others" and "forming one's view of life" were the most impressive features; while senior high school students found "forming one's view of life" the most interesting factor.

In book reports of nonfiction works, "scientific attitudes" and "social contributions" were the outstanding themes, whereas "affection" and "soundness of mind" frequently appeared in those of fiction. "Scientific attitudes" and "attitudes toward others" appealed more to boys, whereas "forming one's view of life" and "affection" appealed to girls.

An experiment by Rai[29] investigated the influence of reading on children's attitudes and opinions. Two books were prepared, each of which had an opposite conclusion ("idealistic" and "realistic") about the same theme—the problem of vocation. The subjects were eighth-grade children. Before and after reading, their attitudes toward vocation were tested by a questionnaire. The opinions of the children leaned toward the viewpoint of whichever material they had read, but the changes in their attitudes caused by the idealistic book were greater than those caused by the realistic one. There were no changes of opinion among those who had no interest in the problem dealt with in the materials. Those whose opinions did change seemed to have been influenced by their insight into the situation during the reading. The changes were mostly dependent on the ability of the students to understand the content of the material and their prereading attitudes toward vocation. Personality traits such as aggressiveness, depression, or feelings of inferiority, inferred from personality tests, were shown to have some relation to the changes of opinion.

I. Sakamoto et al.[30] studied children's attitudes toward the characters in the stories they read. Two stories were prepared, one had to do with everyday activities in school life, and the other was about a murder committed by a boy in an unusual situation. The length of each story was about 1,600 words, involving six critical scenes. Seventy-seven fifth-graders and seventy-five seventh-graders were asked to read both stories and to respond to a questionnaire that was designed to identify the reader's attitude toward the protagonist in every critical scene. Their attitudes were classified into the following types:

1. Alignment (a reader who sides with the person in the story).
2. Criticism (a reader who opposes the person).
3. Insight (a reader who points out a better solution).

Of all pupils in this experiment, the insight type was found to be more prevalent when the story of school life was read; more of the criticism type showed up when the murder case was read. It was shown that the type of story determined different responses in about 70 per cent of the pupils. Boys leaned more toward criticism and girls toward the insight type. Age made no significant difference.

Bibliotherapy

Bibliotherapy, according to Schubert's[31] definition, is the selective use of books for their therapeutic effect on children who are mentally or emotionally disturbed. A group of members of JSSR interested in bibliotherapy compiled a list of readings useful in psychotherapeutic approaches, and this was published in the journal of JSSR (*The Science of Reading*), in 1963. Since that time, several case studies have been published with brief English summaries, among which Okami's reports on bibliotherapy for juvenile delinquency have been outstanding.

Okami[32] treated a 16-year-old boy who had left home, wandered about for eight days, and had been arrested for stealing. Through a series of interviews Okami found that the main cause of the problem was the lack of affection in the boy's home as a result of his father's egotism. The boy was found to have an inferiority complex also, because he was often made a fool of by his elders, who were more intelligent. Okami assigned several story books for him to read, the contents of which were expected to be helpful in releasing his hostility toward his father and also in readjusting himself to his family. In a series of twelve interviews, the boy was encouraged to tell how the stories affected him. Okami asked him what lessons he found in the stories and whether he could put them into practice. These counseling procedures seemed to be effective in helping the boy gain insight into his socioadaptive behavior. Within five months, he not only became a good member of his family but a diligent student in school. The effects were confirmed by the Rorschach Test, which was applied three times during the period. Okami concluded that the essential factor involved in the maladaptive behavior was the breakdown in communications attributable to the lack of affection and mutual understanding in the family, and that bibliotherapy had been demonstrated as an effective method of treating this type of maladjustment.

Subsequently, Okami[33] has reported three cases of teenage boys arrested for rape, in which bibliotherapy was used to treat the personality disorders diagnosed as the basic cause of their delinquency.

A younger patient was the subject of another of Okami's case histories.[34] This was a third-grade boy with an IQ 109 who was enuretic, uncooperative, aggressive, told lies, and often stole. Okami attributed the boy's enuresis and other behavior problems to emotional difficulties. His parents were divorced and he had been placed in a protective institution. After he read *Thumbelina* and *The Ugly Duckling,* he was able to explain the meaning of not being accepted by others. He saw the reflection of his own problem and behavior in the stories.

When he read *The Little Match Girl,* he expressed his criticism against the father in the story. After reading *The Picturebook Without Pictures,* he realized why the heroine was isolated. When he read *The Story of Babe Ruth,* he was impressed by the way the man had pulled himself out of delinquency. The counseling was carried on for four months and his behavior problem decreased gradually until he was accepted by others. His bed-wetting decreased also to one fourth of the frequency of the pretherapy period. Group therapy would have been more effective, Okami noted, for a young child like this.

I. Sakamoto *et al.*[35] have pointed out that the effects of bibliotherapy do not always appear immediately after treatment. From the results of their own research, in which six sixth-graders with emotional instability and behavior problems were treated, they reported that (1) in all six cases bibliotherapy was proved to be effective, and the effects appeared in the following three ways: (a) immediately after the treatment; (b) gradually, after a period of temporary resistance; and (c) gradually, after a period of nonreaction. (2) The personality maladjustments of each child had been corrected through the treatment. (3) It might be necessary to motivate children when their reading abilities are poor, and also to deepen their understanding through discussion following the reading sessions. (4) Stories of high quality were very effective as aids in bibliotherapy. (5) Three principles of bibliotherapy mentioned by Shrodes[36]—insight, identification, and catharsis—were also observed in these cases.

Reading Tests

Nine different reading-ability tests, one reading-readiness test, and one reading-interest scale have been standardized (nationwide) in Japan. Of those, the ones written by I. Sakamoto are the most widely used. Diagnosis is an important feature of most of these tests.

Treatment of Reading Disability

Specificities of Reading Disorders in Japan

Before discussing the provisions for children who fail to read, it is necessary to discuss some characteristic aspects of reading difficulties in the Japanese language. Studies concerned with the impairment of reading capacity have been conducted in two ways, as is the practice elsewhere. One approach is to elucidate the function and mechanism of acquired reading impairment through the clinical observation of organic brain lesions caused by head traumas, brain hemorrhages, neoplasms, and other damages. The other is to study the developmental reading difficulties, in which there are no apparent causes, centered around what one might call congenital word blindness in developmental sequences. It cannot be denied that researchers of the latter approach often try to explain the mechanism of developmental reading difficulties by finding analogies with the knowledge obtained through the former approach. Although the opinions of the foremost neuropsychiatrists in Japan have not been in disagreement with localization theory (Kleist[37]) in the broader sense of being pertinent to the mechanism of acquired alexia or dyslexia, some practical differences have been noted because of the nature of the Japanese writing system—that is, the two decoding systems of Kanji and Kana. As mentioned in the first part of this article, the Japanese mainly employ the combination of these two systems.

While Kana represent phonetic decoding symbols more or less comparable to the Roman alphabet, Kanji are ideographs that directly carry the meanings the symbols represent. The clinical manifestation of acquired alexic-dyslexic disorders presents a unique difference between these two decoding systems. Kimura[38] suggested this difference in his article on dyslexic disorders of the Japanese. Based on his experience treating war-injured patients, S. Sakamoto[39] pointed out that Kanji are retained more easily than Kana when loss of reading capacity is induced by brain injuries, and even more so in the case of compound characters. Subsequent reports by Imura[40] and many other clinicians served to endorse Sakamoto's finding, and it has now become generally recognized.

Severe cases of congenital word blindness are rare in Japan as elsewhere. A few reports by Obi,[41] Kuromaru et al.,[42] and Anzai et al.[43] agree that there is greater difficulty reading Kana than Kanji. It might be added that, if we assume that the writing system is a distinct feature of Japanese alexic-dyslexic disorders, more difficulties should be found in the reading of Kana than of Kanji, regardless of whether the disorder is acquired or inborn.

Although we do not have sufficient statistical data, the incidence of severe word blindness among children is considered to be very rare, as in other countries. It is the opinion of these writers that dyslexic cases of varying degrees are centrifugally clustered around a nuclear condition of severe word blindness and labeled with tags of alexia, dyslexia, reading disability, reading difficulty, reading retardation, or whatever other term may be preferred, finally fusing into the so-called poor reader. In fact, it is well known that children with such poor reading capacities make up a formidable portion of the practices of child psychiatrists and educational consultation services in Western countries; hence, it seems reasonable to expect that such children with more or less poor reading capacities ought to exist also among Japanese children.

Incidence of Reading Disability Among Japanese Schoolchildren

However, Japanese child psychiatrists have never encountered a child with this circumscribed difficulty in the reading area. Educational consultation services have never experienced such a case, at least to the knowledge of these writers, if children with general intellectual retardation are excluded. This fact that the incidence of children with poor reading capacity differs so much between Western countries and Japan, but that manifestations of other child psychiatric casualties do not differ so much, aroused the curiosity of Makita,[44] and led him, in 1966, to conduct a survey to discover the incidence of poor readers among school-age children. Prepared questionnaires were sent to schoolteachers asking them to report children to whom teaching reading was difficult in any way. The result, obtained from 247 schoolteachers covering 9,195 pupils through random samplings, indicated the incidence of such poor readers was but 0.98 per cent of the surveyed children. Although instructions were given to exclude those with general intellectual retardation or visual impairments, a small portion of this figure might have included such children. Consequently, the percentage of children with some reading disability in Japan was suggested to be less than 1.0 per cent, which is much lower (ten to twenty times) than that of certain other countries.

What could cause such a marked difference? There have been various theories on the etiology of reading disability. Some researchers have wanted to attribute it to anatomical malformation or faulty development of the brain (Critchley,[45] Geschwind,[46] Hinshelwood[47]). Some have tried to explain it from a neurophysiological point of view, mainly focusing on the problems of laterality or hemispheral dominance (Mountcastle,[48] Orton[49]). Genetic inheritance has been taken into consideration (Hallgren[50]); emotional conflict is emphasized as playing a dominant role (Blanchard,[51] Gann,[52] Missildine,[53] Tulchin[54]); and there are also views that consider it a mere developmental retardation, as far as milder difficulties are concerned (Eisenberg,[55] Rabinovitch et al.[56]). None of these theories has been sufficient to make clear-cut explanations for the pathogenesis of reading disability. Moreover, there is no reason to believe that Japanese children are ten to twenty times better equipped with morphological brain structures, neurophysiological functions, or favorable genetic influences, or that they are emotionally under less stressful situations, or that they have any other more favorable conditions compared with Western children.

On the other hand, it is noteworthy that no such studies in Western cultures ever dwell on *the nature of the language* to be read, the very object of the reading function. Perhaps it is because all these theorists have taken the Roman alphabet for granted as a fixed and immutable variable and have not been exposed to other languages represented by decoding systems other than this. One reason for such a marked difference in the incidence of poor readers may be the philological nature of the Japanese language and the mode of its perception—that a perceived figure leads to the understanding of its sound and its meaning.

In reading Kanji, ideographic as it is, a visually perceived figure of a symbol is transmitted more directly to the loci controlling the comprehension of meaning, and the phonation of how it is read becomes a secondary procedure dependent on the meaning or on the way in which the compound is used. Kana, on the other hand, are phonetic signs that usually consist of a consonant and a vowel, represented in a single letter and carrying no meaning *per se*. Kana, then, are more comparable to the Roman alphabet. The difference, however, lies in Kana being representations of syllable sounds that are consistently read in the same way. The Roman alphabet represents unitary phonemes, and the ways they are read in a language such as English vary according to their combinations. In other words, whereas each syllable sound is represented by a specific corresponding Kana in Japanese, as is each phoneme in the i.t.a. medium for English, this is not the case in the traditional use of the Roman alphabet in English. Thus either stable or unstable script-phonetic relationships are caused. Although there is no difference between Kana and the conventional use of the Roman alphabet in English, inasmuch as the comprehension of a spelled word is not to be expected unless the reading of each individual letter is completed, the multiple variability of the reading of an alphabetical letter in languages such as English is more confusing and misleading.

The aforementioned characteristic of Japanese dyslexics in cases of acquired brain damage, where Kanji is more easily retained than Kana, could be ascribed to the difference between the modes of perception of the two systems. According to the survey of these writers, it might be of some interest to add that, although the number of poor readers of Kana gradually decreased and became non-existent beyond the fourth grade, this was not so with Kanji, especially from the third grade on. It is the opinion of these writers that the difficulty of reading more complex or uncommon Kanji in higher grades has something to do with a relatively lower intellectual capacity. It may not be going too far to assume that the nature of poor readers of Kanji is probably quite different from that of poor readers of Kana or of the Roman alphabet.

Provisions for Children with Reading Disorders

Specific provision for children who fail in reading is almost nonexistent in Japan. The rarity of cases with reading difficulties does not necessitate remedial facilities. Makita's[57] study also utilized another series of questionnaires. These were sent to a limited number of child guidance clinics, educational counseling services, and other child study institutions asking about their experience with reading difficulties. All responses were negative except for a single case of congenital word blindness. The negative responses reinforced the conclusion that we have hardly any cases that call for clinical attention.

Nor have educational authorities ever considered the need for any specific provisions. Schoolteachers have been successful on the whole in coping with children who have reading retardation problems, and, excluding general mental retardation, they hardly seem to be faced with cases beyond their reach. Without any specialist reading teacher, without any auxiliary device such as i.t.a., and without any systematized remedial measures, mildly disabled children in reading seem eventually to catch up with their classmates, primarily as a result of the efforts of their teachers.

Clinical Evaluation

First of all, visual impairment and general mental retardation have to be excluded from this discussion. Again, because of its rarity, the evaluation of children who read poorly is not an integral part of child psychiatry in Japan. Weakness in reading may occasionally be inferred from vocabulary subtests of ordinary intelligence tests, fully recognizing that the degree of reading skill cannot always be parallel with intellectual endowment. Monroe's[58] reading index is commonly used in child psychiatric practice in English speaking countries, but although similar testing methods have been devised and standardized, they are rarely used by clinicians in Japan. Such testing methods are almost totally limited to the field of education for discriminating between good or poor readers among ordinary children.

Problem Children in Reading

"Problem children in reading" is the expression used in Japan to describe otherwise ordinary children whose reading abilities are poor, or whose reading activities are abnormal. T. Sakamoto[59] classified such children into seven types, based on I. Sakamoto's original terminology. There are two general categories: (1) problem children in reading *ability* and (2) problem children in reading *behavior*. The former refers to how well they *can* read, whereas the latter is related to how they *do* read. Problem children in reading ability are subdivided into (1) "retarded readers" and (2) "disabled readers." The definition of these two terms is the generally accepted one, cf. Schubert.[60] Problem children in reading behavior are divided into: (3) "deflective readers," (4) "fickle readers," (5) "premature readers," (6) "excessive readers," and (7) "schizoid readers."

Deflective readers are those whose reading interests are circumscribed—who read, for example, only comics or only science fiction. Fickle readers are children who start to read many books but rarely finish them. Premature readers are those who want to read books for older children or for adults. Excessive readers read so much that they are diverted excessively from all other activity. Schizoid readers are those who have an abnormal interest in reading and, finally, confuse the world in the story with the real world. In addition to these seven types, "reluctant readers" can be considered another type of problem children in reading behavior.

Disabled readers have been studied under the definition of children whose achievement in reading is significantly below expectancy for their mental ability. From this definition, several operational methods to determine disabled readers have been developed. For example, a child is designated as a disabled reader if his reading age is two years or more below his mental age and if his reading achievement value is less than -10 (or -5), where the reading achievement value is the intelligence test T-score subtracted from the reading test T-score. Recently, the latter method has become the most commonly used in Japan. T. Sakamoto and Takagi,[61] however, questioned the accuracy of subtracting the intelligence test T-score from the reading test T-score for these reasons: (1) The higher a child's measured intelligence is, the greater is the probability of his being designated a disabled reader. It has been proven that the reading-achievement value has a negative correlation with the intelligence test T-score. (2) This method is based on the hypothesis of a $Y = X$ relationship between the reading test T-score, Y, and the intelligence test T-score, X, even though this relationship had not been proven.

Consequently, Sakamoto and Takagi calculated regression formulas for grades IV, V, and VI, depending on the coefficients of the correlation between the T-scores on the two tests. For each of 664 pupils, a new expectancy score was determined and the differences between these scores and the reading

T-scores were calculated. Sakamoto and Takagi thus succeeded in justifying an adequate measurement procedure. By this new method children were classified as able or disabled readers. The latter included more boys than girls. They were less efficient in the speed of reading and sentence comprehension subtests. Little difference appeared in these two groups in the subtest reading of Kanji. Differences in profiles on the intelligence test revealed that the disabled readers scored lower on "logical thinking" and "sentence arrangement" and higher than the able readers on the "understanding principles" and "completion of progression" subtests. It was further found that more of the able readers had their own desks at home and read more than thirty minutes per day than did the disabled readers.

REFERENCES

NOTE: Journals and books published in Japan are printed in the Japanese language. These references followed by (BES) have a brief English summary. Those followed by (BGS) have a brief summary in German.

1. Sakamoto, Takahiko, *The Affect of Kanji on the Readability of the Japanese Sentences,* unpublished Master's thesis, Tokyo University of Education, 1960.
2. UNESCO, *Literacy and Education for Adults,* Paris: UNESCO, 1964.
3. Shuppan Kagaku Kenkyu-sho, *Children and Reading,* Tokyo: Shuppan Kagaku Kenkyu-sho, 1968.
4. Mainichi Shimbun-sha, *Report of 1965 Reading Survey,* Tokyo: Mainichi Shimbun-sha, 1966.
5. Sakamoto, Takahiko, "Reading and reading guidance," in Katsura, Hirosuke, *et al.* (eds.), *Social Life and Mass-communication,* Tokyo: Kaneko Shobo 1969, pp. 207–236.
6. Kaigo, Tokiomi, *Japanese Education—Its Past and Present,* Tokyo: Kokusai Bunka Shinkokai, 1968.
7. Sakamoto, Ichiro, *The Sakamoto Reading Readiness Test,* Tokyo: Maki Shoten, 1953 (in English).
8. Nakano, Sukezo, "A study on children's achievement in reading 'Kana' letters," *The Bulletin of the Faculty of Education* (Tokyo University of Education), 3 (1957), 111–122. (BES)
9. Sakamoto, Ichiro, Fujii, Masumi, Tsutsumi, Yoshiko, and Arai, Yoshiko, "Picturebooks with infants," *The Science of Reading,* 12 (1969), No. 2, 23–29. (BES)
10. Fukuzawa, Shusuke, "Developmental study on the factors of the difficulty in reading 'Kanji' (ideographs in Japan) (1)," *The Science of Reading,* 11 (1968), No. 3, 16–21. (BES)
11. Kawai, Yoshifumi, "Physical complexity of the Chinese letter and learning to read it," *Japanese Journal of Educational Psychology,* 14 (1966) 129–138, and 188. (BES)
12. Kurasawa, Eikichi, "Reading instruction in Japan," *The Reading Teacher,* 16 (1962), 13–17.
13. Sakamoto, Ichiro, "The scope of reading in Japan," in Jenkinson, M. D. (ed.), *Reading Instruction: An International Forum,* Newark, Del.: IRA, 1967, pp. 33–43.

14. *Ibid.*
15. Anzako, Iwao, "On the criterion of book selection from the viewpoint of difficulty of sentence," *The Science of Reading,* 1 (1956), No. 1. 29–33.
16. Horikawa, Naoyoshi, *A study of readability in Japanese sentences* (Report of the Research Institute of the Asahi), Tokyo: Asahi Shimbun-sha, 1957.
17. Morioka, Kenji, "Readability and listenability," in Endo, Yoshimoto *et al.* (eds.), *The Esthetics of Language,* Tokyo: Nakayama Shoten, 1958, pp. 209–248.
18. Sakamoto, Ichiro, *Basic Vocabularies for Education,* Tokyo: Maki Shoten, 1958.
19. Sakamoto, Ichiro, "Assessing the vocabulary weight of sentences—An attempt to approach readability," *The Science of Reading,* 6 (1962), Nos. 1-2, 37–44.
20. Sakamoto, Ichiro, "Assessing the weight of sentence length—An attempt to approach readability," *The Science of Reading,* 8 (1964), No. 1, 1–6.
21. Shiba, Sukeyori, "A study of readability measurement—Application of cloze procedure to Japanese language," *Japanese Journal of Psychology,* 28 (1957), 67–73, 135. (BES)
22. Taylor, W. L., "Cloze procedure: A new tool for measuring readability," *Journalism Quarterly,* 30 (1953), 415–433.
23. Sakamoto, Takahiko, "On reading skills of vertical versus horizontal sentences," unpublished paper read at the Third Annual Congress of The Japanese Association of Educational Psychology, Nagoya, 1961.
24. Sakamoto, Takahiko, Muraishi, Shozo, and Kaga, Hideo, "A study of legibility of Kana," *Proceedings of the 28th Annual Congress of the Japanese Association of Applied Psychology,* 1961. Also, Muraishi, Shozo, Kaga, Hideo, and Sakamoto, Takahiko, "A study of legibility of Kana letters," *Proceedings of the 27th Annual Congress of the Japanese Association of Applied Psychology,* 1961. Also, Muraishi, Shozo, Sakamoto, Takahiko, and Kaga, Hideo, "On the criteria for optimum type face," *The Science of Reading,* 5 (1960), No. 2, 19–24. Also Muraishi, Shozo, Sakamoto, Takahiko, and Kaga, Hideo, "A study of letter (Katakana)—Discrimination," *The Science of Reading,* 6 (1962), Nos. 1-2, 23–27. Also, Muraishi, Shozo, Sakamoto, Takahiko, and Kaga, Hideo, "A study of legibility of Katakana," *Proceedings of the 30th Annual Congress of the Japanese Association of Applied Psychology,* 1963.
25. Sakamoto, Takahiko, "Space between letters and lines, and words per line in lateral writing," *Scientific Asahi,* 25 (1965), No. 2, 91–95. Also, "Legibility of print in lateral writing," *Scientific Asahi,* 26 (1966), No. 3, 39–46.
26. Obonai, Torao, and Sato, Yasumasa, "Two studies on readability," *The Bulletin of the Faculty of Education* (Tokyo University of Education), 2 (1956), 40–51. (BES)
27. Matsubara, Tatsuya, and Kobayashi, Yoshiro, "A study on legibility of Kana-letters," *Japanese Journal of Psychology,* 37 (1967), 359–363. Also, "Study of legibility of Kana-letters," *Perceptual and Motor Skills,* 25 (1967), 36.
28. Sakamoto, Ichiro, Hayashi, Kumiko, and Kamei, Michiko, "A developmental study on the points of inspiration in reading," *The Science of Reading,* 10 (1967), No. 3, 1–9. (BES)
29. Rai, Akiko, "An experimental study on the change of opinion caused by reading," *The Science of Reading,* 10 (1967), No. 1, 26–35. (BES)
30. Sakamoto, Ichiro, Ishii, Masako, and Kuratani, Michiko, "An attempt to diagnose children's attitudes in reading stories," *The Science of Reading,* 12 (1969), No. 3, 17–27. (BES)

31. Schubert, Delwyne G., *A Dictionary of Terms and Concepts in Reading,* Springfield, Ill.: Thomas, 1964.

32. Okami, Sadao, "A study of bibliotherapy on the delinquent (4th report)—A case of a boy who left home," *The Science of Reading,* **10** (1967), No. 1, 1–7. (BES)

33. Okami, Sadao, "A study of bibliotherapy on the delinquent (5th report)—A case of a sex offender," *The Science of Reading,* **10** (1967), No. 2, 9–15. (BES). Also, "A study of bibliotherapy on the delinquent (6th report)—A case of severe delinquency," *The Science of Reading,* **10** (1967), No. 3, 18–24. (BES). Also, "A study of bibliotherapy on the delinquent (9th report)," *The Science of Reading,* **11** (1968), No. 3, 22–28. (BES)

34. Okami, Sadao, "A study of bibliotherapy (8th report)—A case of enuresis nocturna," *The Science of Reading,* **11** (1968), Nos. 1-2, 48–51. (BES)

35. Sakamoto, Ichiro, Matsumoto, Ritsuko, Nakamura, Yoshiko, and Shimada, Sanae, "Case studies on bibliotherapy applied to emotionally unstable pupils," *The Science of Reading,* **11** (1968), Nos. 1-2, 52–65. (BES)

36. Shrodes, Caroline, "Bibliotherapy," *The Reading Teacher,* **9** (1955), 24–29.

37. Kleist, K., "Introduction: contemporary schools of psychiatry: Wernicke and cerebral localizers," in Mayer-Gross W., Slater, E., and Roth, M. (eds.), *Clinical Psychiatry,* 3rd ed., London: Baillière, Tendall and Cassell, 1969.

38. Kimura, K., "*Zur Erklärung des der japanischen Schrift eigentümlichen Symptombildes,*" *Neurologia,* **37** (1934), 437–459. (BGS)

39. Sakamoto, S., "A contribution to Kanji-Kana problem in dyslexia," *Bulletin of Osaka Medical Association,* **4** (1940), 185–212.

40. Imura, T., "Aphasia, its specificity in Japanese language," *Psychiatria et Neurologia Japonica,* **47** (1943), 196–212.

41. Obi, I., "*Über die angeborene Lese- und Schreibschwäche,*" *Psychiatria et Neurologia Japonica,* **59** (1957), 852–867. (BGS)

42. Kuromaru, S., Okada, Y., *et al.,* "On developmental alexia and agraphia," *Journal of Pediatrics,* **25** (1962), 853–858.

43. Anzai, E., *et. al.,* "*Lese- und Schreibstörungen bei einem 6 jährigen Knaben,*" *Psychiatria et Neurologia Japonica,* **68** (1966), 629–640. (BGS)

44. Makita, K., "The rarity of reading disability in Japanese children," *American Journal of Orthopsychiatry,* **38** (1968), 599–614.

45. Critchley, M., "The evolution of man's capacity for language," in Tax, S. (ed.), *Evolution of Man,* Vol. II, Chicago: U. of Chicago, 1960. Also, *Developmental Dyslexia,* London: Heineman, 1964.

46. Geschwind, N. "Disconnection syndromes in animal and man," *Brain,* **88** (1956), 585–644.

47. Hinshelwood, J., *Congenital Word Blindness,* London: Lewis, 1917.

48. Mountcastle, V., *Interhemispheric Relation and Cerebral Dominance,* Baltimore: Johns Hopkins Press, 1962.

49. Orton, S., "Word blindness in school children," *Archives in Neurology and Psychiatry,* **14** (1925), 581–615.

50. Hallgren, B., *Specific Dyslexia: A Clinical and Genetic Study,* Copenhagen: Munksgaard, 1950.

51. Blanchard, P., "Reading disabilities in relation to maladjustment," *Mental Hygiene,* **12** (1928), 772–788. Also, "Attitudes and education in disabilities," *Mental Hygiene,* **13** (1929), 550–563. Also, "Psychogenic factors in some cases of reading disability," *American Journal of Orthopsychiatry,* **5** (1935), 361–374.

52. Gann, E., *Reading Difficulty and Personality Organization,* New York: King's Crown Press, 1945.

53. Missildine, W., "The emotional background of thirty children with reading disability," *Nervous Child,* **5** (1946), 263–272.

54. Tulchin, S., "Emotional factors in reading disabilities in school children," *Journal of Educational Psychology,* **26** (1935), 443–454.

55. Eisenberg, L., "Reading retardation: I. psychiatric and sociologic aspects," *Pediatrics,* **37** (1966), 352–365.

56. Rabinovitch, R., *et al.,* "A research approach to reading retardation," *Research Publications of the Association for Research in Nervous and Mental Disease,* **34** (1954), 363–396.

57. Makita, *op. cit.*

58. Monroe, M., *Children Who Cannot Read,* Chicago: U. of Chicago, 1932.

59. Sakamoto, Takahiko, "Problem children in reading," *The Bulletin of the Noma Institute of Educational Research,* **26** (1969), 1–22.

60. Schubert, *op. cit.*

61. Sakamoto, Takahiko, and Takagi, Kazuko, "A study of disabled readers," *The Science of Reading,* **11** (1968), Nos. 1-2, 1–15. (BES)

CHAPTER 22

Sweden

EVE MALMQUIST

Beginning Age and Reading Readiness

THE age at which the majority of children are introduced to the teaching of reading varies from country to country. Although it is as young as age 5 in Britain and 6 in the United States, the Scandinavian countries—Denmark, Finland, Norway, and Sweden—and also the Soviet Union do not introduce reading until the age of 7, and sometimes even later, depending on the maturation level of the individual child. In Sweden it is felt that there is satisfactory support from psychological research and from pedagogical experience for the view that it is of great advantage to children to start school as late as 7. Swedish educators are aware that the chronological age of the child is not always equated with the developmental age of 7 years, which in psychological circles in Sweden is claimed to be necessary for school readiness. Some children are so slow in developing important reading readiness factors that they are not considered mature enough to start school until they are 8 or 9 years of age.

If children, according to special school-readiness tests, are considered immature for school, it is possible to postpone their schooling until they are 8. But such pupils who are not quite ready for ordinary schools are put in special school-maturity classes that have a very small number of pupils (not more than fifteen, but often fewer). Here the teacher is supposed to be able better to stimulate the child's development toward reading readiness.

On the other hand, there are children who are very advanced in their development and who might profit from the teaching in the first grade even if they have not yet reached the normal age. If children, according to the results of medical examination and the results of psychological tests, are considered sufficiently mature for schoolwork they may be permitted to start school the year they pass their sixth birthday—if this occurs during the first six months of the year. Such permission is, however, given only in very exceptional cases, and each child must have attained (according to conventionally used tests) a developmental age of at least 7 years—intellectually, emotionally, and physically. The risk that an "underaged" child will fail in his first contact with schoolwork is otherwise considered to be too great. It is extremely important for the personality development and mental health of the child that the contact with the school be positive from the very beginning.

During his first days in school, the child should not have cause for anxiety and ill-feeling owing to tasks that are above his ability. On the contrary, he ought to be given confidence that he has the resources to benefit from what the school can offer. Every child ought to be given the opportunity to feel the great satisfaction and motivation for continued work that is connected with success.

For this reason, schooling in Sweden is started very cautiously and with the aim of making the child's transfer of activities from home to school easy and endurable. The teacher does her best to create positive attitudes in the children toward school and the working life there. The teacher has also to try to fulfil in the beginning situation as well as later on in school life her difficult but essential task of establishing proper relationships between capacities and tasks, with due consideration to individual differences between her students.

Maturity and Readiness—Relative Concepts

Many Swedish psychologists and teachers are of the opinion that the late beginning age is one important contributing cause of the relatively low number of cases of reading disabilities at the elementary school level in Sweden.

This writer is of the opinion that it is quite possible to teach some children to read and write at a considerably earlier age than 7, probably in some cases at 4 or 5. But for successful teaching at that age it is necessary to change the usual methods and to use other types of textbooks and materials than are common in Swedish first grades at present.

In other words, the concepts of school maturity and reading readiness ought to be looked on as *relative* and not as absolute. Concepts of this kind should be considered in terms of the learning and adaptation that the first-year curriculum demands of beginners. The age at which children start school is of great importance when determining the requirements for maturity for school. The age requirement is also related to the number of pupils in a class. Furthermore, the requirement will depend, for example, on the competence of the teachers, the nature of the instructional material, and on the methods used in teaching.

Stimulating Reading Readiness

Swedish reading specialists are very anxious that both parents and teachers be aware that even if the majority of the children are ready to be taught reading when they start school, there are always some who, for different reasons, even at 7 or 8 years of age, have not reached the desired readiness level.

We cannot expect that these children will, without further attention, make normal progress in reading. Whatever the reasons are for their lack of reading readiness, the school must allow them a calm and cautious start in reading. It pays to "waste time" by using a very quiet and slow tempo and a very careful and richly varied method in the early learning stages. Growth in reading cannot be hurried above capacity level without some fatal and far-extending effects. The total personality development of the child may be hurt.

It has been found to be very important to try to *stimulate* the child's development toward reading readiness and not only—which is still very common—*wait* for the readiness to appear at a certain chronological age. For the teacher to bring about such a stimulation of the child's development efficiently, she must first of all try to get as good an understanding and knowledge as possible of each individual child's stage of maturity and background of experiences.

In addition to conventional school-readiness tests, therefore, an extended series of observations and measurements are now made by teachers, school psychologists, and doctors at the beginner's first meeting with the school. This is in order to get information that is as complete and reliable as possible concerning every individual's level of development in different respects. A good knowledge of the resources of the particular pupils in different areas is one of the fundamentals of planning the teaching in an appropriate and effective way, and the primary teacher in Sweden today is well aware of this fact. In order to supplement the test results the teacher, therefore, takes her time during the first weeks and tries, by conversation with the children, and by games and other amusing exercises of a fairly spontaneous and free character, to observe their maturity and capacity:

1. Which children, for example, are strikingly small and weak physically, or remarkably fumbling in their movements?
2. Which children seem to be shy and afraid and find it difficult to adapt themselves to their comrades?
3. Which children seem to be independent and confident?
4. What degree of listening ability do the children have and how do they express their thoughts verbally?

Contacts with the children's parents are naturally considered to be of invaluable importance for the teacher as an aid in getting this essential information concerning the unique personalities of the children.

Some decades ago, both parents and teachers in Sweden had the notion that all children should be taught reading as soon as they started first grade. Regular reading exercises, often of a technical character, were started, therefore, from the very first week of school. This is no longer done. Many children need preparatory teaching of various kinds before the real teaching of reading starts. Teachers at the primary stage in Sweden, as a rule, spend much time during the first weeks in the first grade in conversational exercises and listening exercises.

Development of Speaking and Listening Ability

The ability to listen in an active and concentrated way is considered very important for the development of reading ability and is therefore stressed by special practices. Far from all children possess this ability when they start school.

The children are given opportunities to tell stories spontaneously on the basis of their own experiences and observations. But they are also taught how to study and evaluate pictures from different areas: from different homes, from the forest, from the beach, from the toyshop, and from the station. Country views and town views alternate. It is likely that a good many children from the study of these pictures will become acquainted with some common objects and concepts that they had not known earlier. In that way the development of their vocabulary will also be stimulated. During these introductory exercises the children learn the general concepts and expressions that they will need to understand during their reading training later on. Such expressions as the following, for example, are explained and used: to the left, to the right: beneath and in front of; up and down; at the beginning of the line; and at the end of the line.

Language Development in the Early Years of Life

There is enough research evidence to give reason to state that a child's progress in learning to read depends, to a considerable extent, on his experiences with the use of the spoken word in his preschool years.

Learning to read is, for most children, the very first encounter with a type of learning involving abstract symbols intended to be associated with previous experiences.

If the child has not been given opportunities to acquire such a background of meaningful concepts: if the words presented in print are not a part of his speaking vocabulary and are not used with real adequate understanding, he will most likely be greatly handicapped in his reading efforts from the very beginning.

The development of language and speech evidently play important parts in the formation of the reading and writing readiness of beginners. It is, therefore, from this writer's point of view, a complete waste of time to try to teach a child to read until he can articulate clearly and without difficulty and before he really has something to say. The child must first be able to express his thoughts, to tell stories, or to ask questions in a comprehensible manner. Children who are late in their speech development or who show signs of serious speech defects must first be helped to cultivate appropriate speaking habits before the actual reading instruction begins.

Development of Visual and Auditory Perception

If the beginner is to succeed in his attempts to acquire elementary reading functions, a certain degree of maturity in visual perception is demanded. The ability to recognize even small visual similarities and dissimilarities is an essential factor of so-called reading readiness.

When they start school, most Swedish children have attained a desirable degree of development in this respect. But many need special training. Simple series of pictures of objects well known to children are used in exercises in visual discrimination. The passing from "searching games" among pictures and patterns to different kinds of regular and more formal reading exercises will be made easy in this way.

The modern teacher at the primary stage uses fundamental exercises concerned with the direction of eye movements during reading. During the first weeks of the first grade, teachers also try to develop the auditory perception of their children. Rhymes provide excellent preexercises for the coming work for the ear, with the evaluation and the differentiation of different sounds in connection with phonic training.

Today there is no sharp demarcation line between the period of the first grade, when preparatory exercises for stimulating reading readiness take the majority of the lesson time, and the period when the teaching of reading as it is usually understood starts.

Exercises in speech, listening, visual perception, auditory perception, games with puzzles, dominoes, patches, picture games, hand-manipulative exercises, and song games are used together with simple introductory lessons in reading, but to a decreasing extent in favor of more regular exercises in reading techniques.

Exercises for Stimulating Reading Readiness

A person who is reading must be able to associate printed symbols with their linguistic meaning. He does not grasp the meaning of the printed or handwritten text unless he also understands the linguistic units that are represented by the written symbols in their descriptions of subjects, actions, ideas, thoughts, and so on. A satisfactory ability to listen, see, and speak is fundamental to learning how to read and write.

A fully articulated reading- and writing-readiness program can contribute substantially to *preventing* the occurrence of many cases of special reading and writing disabilities.

As has previously been emphasized, a child must have reached a certain level of maturity in different areas before he is ready to acquire complex reading and writing abilities without too many difficulties. The elementary reading and writing program is based on such prerequisites as these:

1. The child's ability to *listen* attentively to sounds and linguistic signals must be sufficiently developed.
2. He must be able to imitate and *understand* these signals.
3. He must speak reasonably well.
4. His vocabulary must be sufficiently large.
5. He must have a capacity to distinguish and discriminate *visually*.
6. His *motor capacity* must have reached a satisfactory level of development.

Teaching Methods in Beginning Reading

In Sweden the teaching of primary reading is still, to a great extent, based on synthetic methods.

Swedish teachers are aware, however, that a pure phonic method would not be very well suited to languages with a more complicated spelling. Swedish spelling is relatively phonetic, at least much more so than English spelling. This writer is of the opinion that the English language, with its great differences between spoken and written forms, makes the teaching of reading much more difficult than it is in many other languages, for example, Swedish.

The particular letters—the symbols for the sounds—are in Sweden generally taught in connection with exploring specially composed pictures in the textbooks. The children have to tell a little story about what they can observe in a picture. Those words, which are mentioned by the children, will become the starting point for sound analysis. The first attack is consequently made from the basis of sentences and words that are understandable and form whole units from the child's viewpoint. After that the various elements in the words—the sounds and the letters—are analyzed.

The children have to tell how a letter sounds in the beginning of the word or in the end of the word. In that way the actual sound is identified. They get practice in imitating this sound both individually and in chorus. The teacher shows them the printed letter for the sound, and they draw it in the air. They have exercises in writing the letter in manuscript; and they cut it out of papers and magazines. The teacher lets them suggest words in which the letter is an element. They play and sing and work in different ways with the letter in order to support the retention of learning.

The most difficult part of the learning procedure for most children is the association between the visual shape of the letter and the sound to be produced by the child at the sight of it. To recognize certain letters and combine them with certain sounds is an extremely abstract process and, therefore, very difficult for many children to learn. The experienced teacher knows this and, consequently, is very careful not to advance too quickly.

Limitations and Weaknesses of the Phonic Method

The phonic method is considered to be of great value in the teaching of reading at the primary level. It provides pupils with a safe technique to blend sounds into syllables and words. They can even successfully attack and understand words that they meet for the first time. And that is not the case when the word method —often called the look-and-guess method in Sweden—is used as the basic procedure.

The phonic method has certain limitations, however, that are recognized by Swedish teachers. When using this method the teacher starts with elements of words—sounds and letters. These elements are very abstract for the child. They might, therefore, very easily be uninteresting and difficult to learn. Children who are weak in auditory perception will sometimes experience great difficulties when trying to blend the sounds to make words.

The learning procedures will often be very formal. Meaningless elements are repeated again and again. If the method is the only one used in the teaching of reading, the child may experience difficulties in understanding the content of the text, and the oral "reading tone" may be dull and unnatural. But, today, most Swedish teachers use *several methods* to teach reading. From the very beginning they direct attention to the *meaning* of what is read.

With reference to the wide range of developmental ages in the classroom, it is held that every program of teaching reading should contain both synthetic and analytical methods of instruction. Otherwise there would be no provision for the aim that every individual should receive just that special assistance he needs.

When using combined methods the teacher attempts to select and to use those features of a variety of approaches that seem to him to best fit the actual teaching situation: that is, a situation made up of the capacity and needs of individual children, the learning materials available, and his own skill and personality.

Teaching Materials

Vocabulary in Basic Readers

In the first reading exercises in modern Swedish readers the children will come upon words with only very simple and clear structures.

In the beginning, the words consist of two or three letters only. It is considered favorable to start with concrete nouns. Other parts of speech are then successively introduced, beginning with adjectives and verbs. What is still more essential, the exercises begin with words the children are expected to know very well and that they use in their speech. According to the results of reading research, it is especially important that children in their first reading lessons find words that have something to tell them: words they understand. When they have read a word sound by sound and, after that, discovered that they have got something out of the reading that they can recognize from their own experience and can understand, then they have gained the fundamental idea of the art of reading.

This first step is considered to be extremely important in creating a desire in the child to read and in creating that joy in reading that is fundamental to all real progress in learning to read.

Mere endless repetitions of meaningless elements of words are not approved of any more by Swedish teachers. Contrary to the point of view in former days, comprehension is now considered to be the heart of reading even at the beginning stages in the first grade. Meaningful material, therefore, is used even in more technical exercises.

In accordance with results gained in recent research studies, Swedish educators try to avoid introducing words that are visually similar to beginners in reading. It has been noted that children find it very difficult to keep apart words that are similar in configuration. Therefore, words that look very much alike are introduced on different occasions instead, to avoid children confusing their close resemblance.

It has also been found that it is appropriate to insert a few five- or six-letter words in texts that contain many short words of two or three letters. By contrasting a few words in this manner and by emphasizing the typographical differences, the text becomes, as a whole, easier for the child to read. In this manner, the eyes get some focal points and the many words with similar configuration are not so easily confused.

If students can, in one fixation, recognize and understand a whole word, they will know how it should be pronounced even before they have begun to read it. Thus, it becomes easier for them to produce a more natural intonation, which will correspond to the spoken language, than would be the case if an extreme phonic technique had been employed. But there is also the danger that some children will start guessing when reading, without paying attention to those details that constitute the basic sounds of each individual word. In such instances, the teacher usually lets them resume a sound-to-letter-oriented type of reading.

It is considered extremely important for the development of the child's reading ability that the first instruction be offered in a slow tempo with slowly increasing levels of difficulty. The child's learning to read must not be forced, particularly not on the primary grade level. Rather, it should be geared to his level of development and learning rate. Every learning step should be covered thoroughly and with care. Methodological procedures should be considered carefully. The foundations need to be secure and sound.

Exercises should be repeated many times so that the students become absolutely certain of each part before going on to something new. In order to avoid exercises becoming dull, they should be varied. Different kinds of supplementary exercises and work assignments should be added to the program. This is particularly important for children who work at a slower rate than others. Frequently, it becomes necessary to individualize instruction and to divide the class into different reading groups in order to satisfy individual interests and needs. It is not possible just to limit one's efforts to any "middle group" of the average class. The requirements for carefully contemplated attention to individual students become, naturally, even more accentuated in instances of special remedial instruction.

In modern textbooks in reading for beginners, the vocabulary is carefully controlled; it is relatively limited; and it is selected with consideration given to the level of difficulty of the words and their frequency in the Swedish language. Unusual words are avoided. Such vocabulary items are better learned later.

By systematically repeating all words that have already been presented in the text and clearly indicating all *new* words being introduced at each page of a book in some specific manner, it becomes easier for the students and for the teacher to follow the gradual progress of the individual pupil in the reading program. It thus becomes possible for them to focus their mutual efforts on such points in the reading program where help is most needed.

Because those words that have been introduced in the book are frequently repeated in different contexts, the students soon learn to recognize total word pictures, thereby stimulating the development of expressive reading. As an example, the frequency of each word included in one basic reader series *Jag kan läsa* (*I Can Read*) is indicated by this writer.[1] The teacher is equipped with manuals in which the new words introduced on each page of the various books are listed. Such an arrangement is considered to be of great value for the teacher's preparation of word study within reading lessons.

This basic reader series consists of five books for grades I through III, besides workbooks, supplementary readers, word and picture games, and diagnostic reading test batteries. In books one and two, which the majority of the children are able to cover during the first grade, there are introduced 846 different words in a running text of 13,639 words. Through books three and four, in a comparable way during the second grade, another 1,116 words in a running text of 27,601 words are introduced. In book five of the series, which is supposed to serve as the basis for the teaching of reading in grade III, another 2,680 words are introduced. There are, then, 4,642 different words introduced in this series in a running text of 86,570 words within the framework of five basic books for the first three elementary grades in Sweden.

Individual Differences and a Diagnostic Approach

One of the main regulations of the Swedish education acts of 1962 and 1969 is that the personal resources of the individual child must not only be respected but should be the starting point for the planning of education and teaching. According to the objectives stated in the school law, the school has to stimulate each child's personal growth toward his development as a free self-active, self-confident, and harmonious human being. The school must give individual education.[2]

In a school where the greatest possible consideration has to be given to the interests and capacities of the individual pupil, the needs and performances of the students within a class must vary. Children of the same chronological age differ widely in their capacity to learn, their intelligence, their background experiences, and in all kinds of personality traits. Research workers all over the world are in agreement on this point. The need of organizing instruction to provide for these differences is therefore evident and urgent.

This writer's own investigations of first-grade children in Sweden uncovered a range from 4 years and 11 months to 11 years and 8 months in mental age, while differences between the children's chronological ages were very small.[3]

A great range of ability in other variables at school entrance was also noted in another experimental study in Sweden.[4] There were several children in the population studied ($N = 386$) who had very little knowledge of the letters in their own names. Of these children 2 to 3 per cent knew all the small letters; 80 per cent could not read a single word in an easy prose test standardized for the end of the spring term; and 1 to 2 per cent reached a standard equivalent to that of the beginning of a third-grade reading level.

Under such circumstances, one cannot justify teaching all children on the assumption that all need the same kind of teaching. Most teachers recognize these great differences *between* children and *within* children as to various capacities, background experiences, and personality traits. But, nevertheless, they often—at least in Sweden—seem to strive intensively to get all the pupils in the class up to established norms. This main goal of the teachers is necessarily of little satisfaction and stimulation for the bright pupils and too frustrating and unrealistic for the very slow ones in the class. More and more teachers, therefore, try to find a solution by letting children on about the same reading level form separate working groups during a minor or greater part of the time assigned to reading exercises.

The need for organizing instruction to provide, in an adequate way, for individual differences is more and more found to be evident and urgent, although much still remains to be done in practical application.

In order to be able to choose good procedures for teaching, a teacher must have a clear conception of the objectives of her reading instruction. Only if the teacher has realized the broad purposes of the reading program as a whole, can she successfully develop more detailed goals and make plans for separate lessons to achieve those subgoals necessary to meet the needs of individual children.

An awareness and knowledge of the goals are considered prerequisites for an appropriate selection of methodological and organizational procedures as well as reading materials to fit the program.

Therefore, to a greater extent now than previously, a diagnostic approach and individualization in teaching are stressed. Steps to further this have, *inter alia,* included the following:

1. The class size has been reduced to a maximum of twenty-five in the first three years and to thirty in the remaining six years of compulsory schooling. (At the present time the mean size, for the country as a whole, lies between seventeen and eighteen children per class.)

2. The practice of having the child start school at the age of 7 has continued, but a certain flexibility as to beginning age is allowed.

3. Better opportunities than before for individual tutoring, small-group teaching, teaching in clinics, and the provision of special classes of various kinds.

4. Into the teaching load of every teacher of the first three grades there is now written a weekly two-hour block of time for tutoring any individual in his class, who, in his judgment needs such help.

5. Another procedure that has contributed significantly to the individualization of teaching is to divide the class in half for a certain number of hourly sessions a week for teaching reading, writing, and mathematics in the first three grades and biology, chemistry, physics, and English and other languages, including Swedish, in the higher grades. In the first grade, for instance, one half of the class meets with the teacher the first two hours of the day. The second half comes to school for the next two-hour period, during which the first half is free to play or engage in other activities. By this means, the teacher has no more than thirteen students at a time, often no more than eight to ten—ten hours out of the child's weekly schedule of twenty hours.

6. Success must be assured. Growth in reading, as in other learning, cannot be hurried without some undesirable, and even damaging, effects on some children. Therefore, the transition from home to school is made as easy as possible by having the children go to school for only two hours a day the first two or three weeks of school and in groups of no more than twelve or thirteen children. With these beginning 7-year-olds the accepted opinion is that it pays to "waste time", to start very easily, by introducing a variety of reading-readiness experiences and using materials on a difficulty level far below the capacity level of many children. This "make haste slowly" policy permeates the teaching of reading, with the emphasis on interest and easily won achievement. It is believed that this skill is central to much of the child's subsequent learning.

Early diagnosis is the keynote. Even before the child enters school his over-all readiness is tested. With the new smaller class size and the additional time available for individual tutoring since 1962, the teacher has better opportunities than before for using a diagnostic approach and to provide learning steps, methods, and procedures suited to the individual learner.

The tendency is to emphasize the kinds of material the individual child enjoys, to stimulate his interest in reading so that he, with interest and amusement, may reach out to, and enjoy, books of his choice, often somewhat below his capacity level. Then, when it is time to begin instruction in the various reading skills, the teacher is urged to use materials systematized as to sequence, so that the child is steadily challenged to raise his level of performance. The guidelines from the Royal Board of Education stress that the step from one phase to another must not be too big and that there must be a great deal of repetition of every skill. Here, too, the teacher must watch with a careful diagnostic eye for traces of boredom. When the teacher succeeds in choosing the correct time to introduce correct reading materials, the optimum of constructive influence on the development of the child is reached.

Previously, teachers asked, "How many pages, or how many books, should I have my students read before the end of the term?" Teachers are now urged to ask, "Where are my various pupils as to reading ability just now? That is where I am going to start with each one, right now." Such a diagnostic approach also requires the teacher to have a clear picture of the particular interests of each individual, discovered through a close observation of his likes and preferred activities, through interviews with parents.

7. In this connection, we might point out that, although previously teachers were encouraged to make contacts with the parents of the children, the Royal Board of Education has now made it mandatory by specifically stipulating that the individual teacher has the responsibility of making the first contact with the home. Thus, in order to get a picture of the student's out-of-school activities and pattern of living, the teacher has to communicate with the family of each individual in the class before school starts, or early in the term, and then at frequent intervals during the school year.

When the teacher has been given adequate training to handle these contacts with the home in a skillful and tactful manner, this kind of intercommunication is likely to give him valuable help in his job. It is generally assumed that a teacher of reading, or a teacher of any other subject, cannot function effectively unless he knows a great deal about some of the most influential individuals and groups in the student's life.

8. To obtain the most from this intimate knowledge of the student, as well as to achieve a satisfactory follow-up, it has long been a practice in Sweden to have the first-grade teacher continue with his class through the third grade. The fourth-grade teacher, similarly, stays with his class for three consecutive years for the essential part of the school day. However, teachers in specialized areas such as athletics, art, handicrafts, and music extend the classroom resources by their contributions.

In short, to prevent reading disabilities, both a diagnostic approach and individualization of teaching are stressed. Furthermore, the concept of reading readiness is applied not only to the beginning stages of reading, but—in accordance with the new curriculum—to all reading levels in all subjects. The teacher is expected to ask himself at all points whether the individual is ready (is adequately mature) to grasp the reading, to utilize it, and to incorporate it. In other words, to ask whether the pupil is able to gain both an understanding from the reading and the ability to put this understanding to use. This approach is also applied, in many ways, to the teacher's guidance of the student's development and to his interests and tastes in recreational reading in or out of school.

These ideas are accepted by nearly everyone. They may even sound trite and so obvious that they are not worth restating. To put them into practice, however, is another matter. It will take time to get all Swedish teachers to accept these views completely, in the sense of applying them in their classes.

Special Arrangements for Children with Reading Disabilities

Since 1938, Sweden has had special classes within the compulsory school system for the treatment of children with reading disabilities. Classes of this kind were in the beginning called "word-blind classes" but are now known as "remedial reading classes." Children with special reading and writing disabilities but normal or above normal intelligence may be sent to these classes to receive special teaching and treatment. Remedial reading classes of this type have subsequently been introduced in many communities all around the country, especially in the cities and in densely populated areas. The way in which rural areas care for children with special reading disabilities will be mentioned later.

In Sweden by now it has been clearly recognized that the sphere of reading disabilities comprises problems of essential importance and of extremely wide range with regard to both the community and the individual. Interest in and understanding of problems connected with reading disabilities of various kinds among children and adults have gradually increased among teachers and administrators. In 1947, there were twenty-two remedial reading classes in Stockholm and no reading clinics; in 1972, there were 159 remedial reading classes and seventy-two reading clinics within grades I to IX of the elementary school, where less serious cases receive individual teaching several hours a week. A similar development has taken place in school districts all over the country.

A remedial reading class has relatively few pupils. In grades I and II there are about ten children per class; in grades III and higher, somewhat more, but rarely more than fifteen.

In the reading clinics the pupils are ordinarily taught individually or in groups of not more than three or four pupils. An intimate cooperation between the class teacher and the reading clinic teacher is considered a necessary prerequisite for good results in this type of remedial treatment. Special procedures for cooperative activities between teachers, psychologists, medical doctors, and parents are recommended by the school authorities.

Scheduled Hours for Individual Teaching

Since 1964, primary teachers have been able to use *two of their scheduled hours per week to individually teach* children with reading difficulties. This reform is very important. Every teacher in grades I through III has at his disposal two paid hours per week, when the rest of the class is free, to work with one, two, or three of the pupils having special difficulties. In this way, the occurrence of some cases of severe reading disabilities can be prevented by early diagnosis and immediate treatment.

If the child's difficulties are very severe, special help is arranged. In any rural or urban community throughout the country, a specialist working individually two hours per week with a child can be hired and paid for by the national school authorities. If such special remedial teaching is arranged, the child stays in his own class. He still belongs to his class and only gets extracurricular assistance. Even the teaching at a reading clinic can be said to be done within the framework of ordinary class teaching in Sweden. The child belongs to his usual class at the same time that the treatment and teaching at the reading clinic are going on.

The reading clinic is a very successful teaching and treatment institution for providing quick and efficient help in many cases of reading disabilities. But if the student has little help and support from his home in overcoming his difficulties, if he has deeply rooted emotional disturbances, if he displays personality maladjustment symptoms in association with the reading difficulties, and if he has evident difficulties also in subjects other than reading, he will benefit most by being placed in a remedial reading class, according to the opinion of Swedish reading experts. In such a class the child with reading disabilities can be given the necessary therapy in a more permanently protected milieu.

Methods of Remedial Teaching

Remedial teaching in reading in Sweden—individually or in smaller groups, in reading clinics, or in remedial reading classes—does not differ in a real sense from ordinary good and efficient teaching in reading in a normal class. The supporting special teaching, possibly, is arranged according to a more carefully elaborated plan, more systematic and intensive than the teaching in a normal class. But there are no basic differences in the principles of methods used between these various forms of organization of the teaching of reading. It is only a question of *differences in degree*. In special teaching, the aim is to take into consideration individual differences among and within the students regarding resources and the special lacks and difficulties within different areas.

A treatment program based on a careful diagnostic investigation is made up for each pupil. The aim is to provide the best supporting measures where they are most needed and in such a well-adjusted sequence that the development toward the goal will not be unnecessarily impeded by different kinds of learning barriers.

The ordinary teacher works according to the same aims. The special teacher, however, is assumed to have individualized methods, materials specially arranged to suit the various pupils, special apparatus, and special experts to a considerably greater extent than the ordinary teacher to meet individual student needs.

The procedure, on principle, for the efficient special teaching and treatment of a child with reading disabilities will include the following:

1. Diagnostic measuring steps.
2. Teaching and treatment based on the results of the tests used.
3. Renewed diagnostic testing.
4. Continued testing and treatment from time to time, modified according to the test results.

The diagnosis is not to be considered finished as soon as it has been carried out in the beginning of a teaching period. It is supposed to continue all the time the teaching is going on—day by day and week by week.

Prevention of Reading Disabilities

This writer has reported a 6-year longitudinal study,[5] showing that it is possible to decrease, markedly, the frequency of reading disability cases through a careful diagnosis and a subsequent teaching situation synthesizing ongoing diagnosis and treatment for those who could be expected to experience difficulties judged from the results of a special reading-readiness test battery.

The pilot study comprised twenty classes with a total of 386 pupils, and the field experiments of seventy-two classes with a total of 1,653 pupils from twelve cities. To test the hypothesis that it is possible to reduce considerably the number of cases of special reading disabilities during the first three years at school, an experimental control-group method was applied.

The differences between the groups were studied by, among other methods, analysis of covariance. A series of multiple regression and correlation analyses was made in order to study the predictive power of various predictors of reading and writing ability in grades I to III. The reading-readiness variable consistently had the highest predictive power, between 58 and 86 per cent of the combined predictive power of the three predictors, regardless of the criterion variable concerned. Significant group mean differences in five cases out of six supported the hypothesis, as did the occurrence of a region of significance demonstrated by a method of matched regression estimates. Starting from an operational definition of specific reading disability, it was found that more than four fifths of the cases identified as potential cases of reading disability were prevented from occurring.

In a subpopulation comprising pupils from the two groups who had initially scored low on certain tests during the first term of grade I, a number of criterion variables were subjected to analysis of variance, using different multifactorial designs. The results of these analyses were also interpreted as support for the main hypothesis that remedial instruction in reading clinics has a positive effect on the development of both reading and spelling ability. The frequency of pupils with both reading *and* spelling difficulties was found to be consistently lower in the experimental groups than in the control groups, in the experimental groups less than 1 per cent as against the expected 5 per cent. The reading-clinic teaching also reduced the variance among pupils in the experimental groups in relation to the variances of samples used in reading and spelling test standardization. An analysis of the reliability of the selection of pupils for reading-clinic instruction, based on predictions from test data only, showed that the risk of a pupil needing clinic instruction not being assigned to such a clinic can be kept at a low level (1) if the selection for reading clinics is checked and corrected regularly during grades I to III by using the prediction instruments tested here, and (2) if available places in clinics are distributed so that a certain "surplus selection" is made in the first year, particularly during the first term.

Development of Functional and Creative Reading Ability

From the first day at school, the child should be helped to view his studies, his experiences, from a kind of research point of view. The intention is to aid him to explore, to investigate, to find out for himself and to promote his individual work through a variety of sources, and then to help him interpret and evaluate. Even at that early age, he can readily find and compare similarities and dissimilarities and assess what seems true, false, reliable, predictable, and the like. The child should be encouraged to bring his reactions, his thoughts, and his feelings to the surface; to make his own evaluations on the basis of his findings; and to compare them with the evaluations of others.

As he proceeds through school, it is expected that he will learn to interpret and evaluate more and more critically, developing his capacities to identify propaganda, to evaluate advertisements, to discern the values of literature, and to discriminate between good and inferior literature. It is hoped furthermore, that in his social and personal life he will learn to evaluate his behavior and goals and create a philosophy of life according to his own standard of values.

It is assumed that learners today need a much broader range of reading skills than before, because, in our rapidly changing world, they may not be able to rely for long on the facts they have learned in school. This represents a shift from an earlier philosophy in which stress was put on teaching as many facts as possible, submitting the learners to rigorous tests, and then grading the results of these tests.

The climate in which the skills are now taught has also undergone a change. Formal examinations are avoided. Tests are used as a means, within the total educational process, of assessing growth in achievement and the personality development of the individual child. Monthly grading, as used in many countries, does not exist in Sweden, and there are no formal examinations at the end of the nine-year compulsory period of schooling.

In the primary grades, the reading program is generally centered around readers that are being used in class. At that stage supplementary materials consist, to a great extent, of stories that are used to satisfy the needs of students for imaginary excursions and for stimulating their interest and desire in reading.

At the end of the third year, students have generally learned to read fluently and to understand the meaning of what they are reading. They can follow a sequence of events in a story and react to it.

Reading of Pure Nonfiction Prose May Cause Problems

Not seldom, it has been found that many students read extremely well all narrative texts in their readers and also books with stories of adventures that correspond to their level of maturity. When, however, they are confronted with pure nonfiction prose—that is, in the fourth grade—they demonstrate evident signs of reading difficulties. At this point in their education, they encounter assignments in history, social science, geography, and mathematics, for example, that constitute experiences of a kind for which they are not sufficiently prepared. Furthermore, they frequently meet with compact text materials that include many new and difficult terms and expressions on virtually every page.

In appropriate contemporary reading programs, arranged according to the recommendations of the Royal Board of Education, introductory exercises in study techniques are already included at the primary level to make the transition to reading more functional in the upper grades—that is, easier, faster, and more effective. Every school subject has been found to require special exercises and study techniques, depending on its particular content matter, terminology, and character. Swedish teachers are, therefore, recommended to give their students in respective subjects special help and training in the art of relating picture and text; reading maps, tables, formulas, and graphical representations of various kinds; and reading indexes, word lists, and dictionaries. Swedish teachers have realized more and more that none of these study skills is ever completely assimilated at any grade level. It is, therefore, recommended that they continue to offer systematically planned exercises at all grade levels and in all subjects in order to be able to stimulate the continued development of their students.

Different Motives for Reading—Different Reading Procedures

Research as well as practical experience point to the teacher's pedagogical procedures and systematically arranged approach to the different subordinate skills that constitute reading comprehension as playing a dominant role in the development of a student's reading ability throughout the school grades.

It is important to realize that there is no single all-inclusive kind of comprehension in reading applying to all types of reading. Students must learn to read in *one* manner when a general survey of the reading material is assigned, and a totally *different* approach must be used when a careful analysis of the details in a piece of writing is called for.

Similarly, students should be made aware that the approach to reading can be extremely different, such as when reading an exciting novel for pleasure, and reading instructions for procedures for how to do something (that is, how to prepare pictures for different letters, how to answer questions, how to build a model airplane, how to sew a dress, or how to use a camera).

Many Swedish children read all the materials they encounter in one and the same manner and at the same speed, no matter what the purpose of the reading is. Reading difficulties of this type are extremely common and quite serious.

When we train children who suffer from reading disabilities in reading comprehension to find the answers to specific questions, we find that it is very common for these students to require special assistance in selecting what is relevant and what is not in order to carry out their assignments.

Students also need to learn the techniques of skimming in order to be able to find quick answers about various details in the reading text and also to get a general impression of the content of the text.

Students Who Devote Too Much Attention to Details

Even children who are good readers tend, at times, to devote more attention to details than is desirable. The teacher should, therefore, try whenever possible, and on all levels of development, to stimulate the ability in his students to judge what kind of details may be required to achieve complete comprehension of the text in a given reading assignment. It is obvious that one has to be more watchful about specific details if he is trying to understand a recipe for how to bake a cake than he would be if the activity were to get some general idea about the content of a story.

As teachers, we should, under all circumstances, regard it a primary duty to convey to our students a notion that a student who reads, understands, and remembers most details is not, for those reasons, necessarily a more effective and better reader. Rather, a good reader is someone who understands the purpose of a certain kind of reading, and who can successfully *vary his modes of reading to fit the level of difficulty of each text as well as the purpose of the reading assignment.*

The Purpose of Reading Determining the Approach

The teacher should, therefore, already on the elementary level of reading instruction, condition her students to reflect on what they want to gain from each particular reading venture and to select the most appropriate approach for their purpose. Under all circumstances, the student should know *why* he is supposed to read a certain thing. Only under such conditions can his reading become truly effective.

Students Who Read Without Motive

Formerly, learning was regarded as a process, the primary purpose of which was to permit students to acquire particular knowledge and to remember specific data. Therefore, students were frequently allowed to read in a mechanical fashion without any motive or, at best, with some very insignificant motivation for reading. Whether students had been successful or not in their reading attempts was measured mainly by having them retell what was written in the book.

The modern reading teacher, however, looks on learning as a process that offers her students the possibility of learning how to adjust to new situations and to solve problems that they may have an interest in and a motivation for trying to solve. If students are given clear motives for their reading efforts that they can completely accept and then read with these motives in mind, there is good reason to believe that their reading will become effective.

The Purpose of Reading Deciding Reading Speed

Research in the psychology of reading has demonstrated that *the purpose of reading* is one of the most important factors in determining reading speed, along with the extent of details and the depth that are required for a student to arrive at an understanding of the content. It is, therefore, extremely important that students make clear to themselves *why* they are reading in order to select the appropriate reading approach. They should be induced to think very carefully about what it is that compels them to read; that is, whether it is to find answers to certain questions, to prepare them to read the text aloud for others later, to learn the text by heart, to derive an opinion regarding two opposing viewpoints regarding a question, or to check the spelling of a word. The purpose of reading—the motive—must be identified and accepted by the reader. Only then does reading become really effective.

Broadly speaking, reading skills range in steps from (1) comprehension and understanding, to (2) reactions and critical reading, to (3) evaluation, retention, and application of findings, to (4) creative reading. The first three steps deal with the reader's responses to the material. If this can be called reacting, then creative reading can be described as "acting" or "acting creatively," the highest goal of reading. It is expected that the child will be helped by being engaged to a degree in all four of these steps from his very first lessons in formal reading. Even before learning to read, from the first day in school, the child should be helped to develop his ability to draw inferences, to make generalizations, and to anticipate coming events.

Reading in the Content Fields

Students must also be helped to become successful, inquiring readers in specific subject fields such as arithmetic, in which a difficulty with reading—an inability to get at the meaning of the problem—will cause additional problems. The student needs to be taught the meanings of certain key words, how to read directions and explanations, and various means of presenting quantitative facts and relationships so that he can understand the problem to be solved. Similarly, in history, a student often needs help in perceiving the meaning of events, dates, and places, as well as in following the writer's reasons for reaching particular conclusions. Various subjects, in a variety of content fields, present different problems in reading comprehension. The special type of reading required in a given field should be taught within that field according to the recommendations by the Royal Board of Education (1969): "Every teacher at any grade level and teaching whatever subject should be a teacher of Swedish."

Flexibility in Reading Speed

Investigations made in Sweden into the rate of reading in the elementary and upper grades have come up with some disquieting results. It was found that for a great number of pupils reading speed remains fixed at whatever rate was attained by the third or fourth grade. Furthermore, this rate does not change regardless of the purpose of the reading or the nature of the reading material. Swedish students, especially in the higher grades of the compulsory school and the gymnasia, evidently need more help to modify their pace of reading from very slow reading with high concentration up to rapid scanning. With each passing year this adaptability in reading is becoming more urgently required of students, no matter what their content field. In Sweden, programs of teacher preparation have just recently started to emphasize this concept of flexibility in reading instruction.

Identifying and Accepting the Goals of Reading

As has been shown earlier, the motive for reading must be identified, acknowledged, and accepted in advance, in order that the reader may cope most efficiently with the materials to be explored. A teacher who accepts this view does not restrict questions about the reading as if the answers were some kind of secret to be revealed *after* the reading has been completed. Instead, he clarifies the goals of the reading *before* the students begin to read. The learner, accepting the goals, and having been given clues for how best to achieve them, then chooses the reading attack that seems the most promising to him.

Involving Reluctant Readers

If the learner, upon graduation, throws his books in the corner and promises himself never to touch those detested things again, one can scarcely say that his teachers have succeeded in their task, regardless of the amount of knowledge he may have obtained. Instead, the teachers' goal should be to create in the student a love for books, an enduring joy in reading, and pleasure in learning as revealed in the desire to explore, to analyze, and to evaluate writings of both an educative and an entertaining nature.

The reluctant readers in our classes have often eluded our attention. They can read, but they do not. In order to prevent reading disabilities from developing among these students, it has been urged that special attention be given to them until they reach the place where they can experience the fun and excitement that reading can give and can see its great usefulness in their own world.

Here a diagnostic approach is recommended, including an exploration into the individual's out-of-school life. Possibly, his parents or peers do not hold reading in high regard, and he may have accepted their assessment rather than his teacher's enthusiasm. (This is especially likely to happen in cases where the teacher's enthusiasm is less for the value and purpose of the content of books than it is for the mechanical aspects of reading. It may also happen where the reading materials have encompassed too limited a range of interest.) On the basis of this general information the teacher can diagnose the difficulty and introduce the student to reading and to group projects that are more relevant to his interests. Furthermore, it is hoped that the teacher can help the learner move toward a clarification and acceptance of his own capabilities and special interests and thus toward a greater degree of self-realization, which may well include a degree of self-liberation from any overidentification with the ideals and points of view of other individuals in his particular world. It is in this pursuit of self-realization that a close cooperation between the classroom teacher and the school librarian, as well as the neighborhood librarian, is urgently advised. Children need help in learning how to choose books of interest and of a suitable degree of difficulty.

The Fourth Dimension in the Reading Process—"Creative Reading"

Some reading specialists have broken down the process of learning to read into three stages:

1. The mastery of word recognition, the identification of words, letters, sounds, and syllables.
2. The ability to use language functionally.
3. The capacity to engage in critical and reflective thinking, and to answer questions relative to what has been read.

This writer sees these three steps as the *raison d'être* for *a fourth step,* a dimension so important that it should be introduced to whatever extent possible from the first day of reading. The three preceding steps should be dealt with similarly from the beginning in a dynamic interaction. In that way, the ultimate goal, this fourth dimension, can be more fully realized. This step can be referred to as "creative reading": the capacity to reach beyond what the writer has been able to transfer to the printed page and to go beyond criticism and evaluation.

We are referring to the capacity to see, detect, and envisage *new* problems. *New* means looking forward, searching, and asking questions, coming up with *new* discoveries in thought and feeling. In other words, to be able to answer questions cannot be considered adequate. We need, as teachers, to foster the ability of our pupils to put forward new questions and new problems. We already have at hand machines that can be set up to provide rapid-fire answers. It still remains for man to formulate questions that are relevant and fruitful, to develop values and attitudes, and to assume the responsibility of his social and emotional fulfillment.

In short, previous reading goals can serve as a springboard, a mere point of departure, for the vehicle from which the creative forces of an individual can soar. Creative reading liberates the reader, profoundly influences his innermost life and his ability to realize himself, and helps him to solve problems he may need to confront. As this writer sees it, the beginning reader today, more than at any time in the past, will need and want to achieve this level of reading.

If we want to encourage constructive, vibrant, creative, divergent thinking in our pupils, we must have the teaching of reading guided by the interests and motives of our pupils. No matter what the degree of technological development between now and the end of the century, children will still experience important human needs that we, as teachers, will need to recognize. Children will still want to experience achievement, mastery, and success, rather than failure and inadequacy. They will still need to be recognized, wanted, approved, admired, and loved, rather than ignored, turned down, or excluded. They will continue to need to feel relaxed and secure, rather than anxious or filled with fear and uncertainty.

We would like our Swedish teachers of reading to understand these vital human emotional needs and the psychological drives in our pupils and to provide for their fulfillment.

The Role of Reading in the Next Few Decades

We can anticipate that for those whose professional lives will span the years of 1980 to 2040, there will be two to three changes in the occupation. A person's reading ability, his study skills, how he can gather data, digest it, and modify his behavior, based on a clear comprehension of the information at hand, will have a great bearing on his ability to keep up to date.

By the use of computers we can, today, gather, organize, check, and report information in a way and in quantities that were undreamed of only a few decades ago. But there are limitations on the amount of knowledge we human beings can acquire and effectively utilize during our lifetime. The heavy flow of extensive data and information from computers will create reading problems of great significance for people in tomorrow's world. Without proper training in making intelligent decisions as to the exact kind of information we need, and in the ability to do rapid selective reading, we will drown in the informational deluge.

Since the educational reforms of the 1960s in Sweden have been increasingly put into practice, constant remodeling, both of goals and of procedures has had to be expected. At the time of the adoption of the great reform of 1962, the Minister of Education expressed a view that this would be the last great school reform. But Swedish educators can anticipate constant reevaluation and revision in the future, with reforms introduced as needed, creating, as the years go by, a kind of "a rolling school reform," derived from the joint work done with students, teachers, and researchers in education throughout the land.

Concluding Statement

Central to all these changes is the ability to learn to read effectively, not only for survival in the labor market but, far more significantly, for self-fulfillment and a balanced view of life. The requirements for reading have entered a dimension referred to earlier as creative reading. It demands the capacity to reach beyond the printed page to see, detect, and envisage new problems and to make new discoveries in thought and feeling. Modern technology has created answer-giving machines. As humans we are par excellence the question makers. More than ever man must be released to formulate relevant and fruitful questions, so that he can develop those values and attitudes that will lead him to assume the responsibility of his own social and emotional fulfillment.

The ability to read creatively will become, in the years ahead, one of the most important tools for self-liberation and self-realization. It will provide a life line to pull the individual through the oceanful of challenges and wonders, such as we can but vaguely visualize, that are in store for those who will live their productive lives in the twenty-first century, the students we teach today.

REFERENCES

1. Malmquist, Eve, *Jag kan läsa,* Stockholm: Natur och kultur, 1967–1969 (Books 1–5).
2. The Royal Board of Education, *Läroplan för grundskolan,* Stockholm: Utbildnings-förlaget, 1969. Other relevant publications by the same authority are *Läroplan för grundskolan,* Stockholm: Utbildningsförlaget, 1962, and *Läroplan för gymnasiet,* Stockholm: Utbildningsförlaget, 1967.
3. Malmquist, Eve, *Läs- och skrivsvårigheter hos barn. Analys och behandlingsmetodik,* Lund: Gleerups Bokförlag, 1971.
4. Malmquist, Eve, *Barnens kunskaper och färdigheter vid skolgångens början* (Research report No. 1 from the National School for Educational Research), Stockholm: Kungl. Skolöverstyrelsen, 1961.
5. Malmquist, Eve, *Lässvårigheter pa grundskolans lågstadium. Experimentella studier* (Research report No. 13 from the National School for Educational Research), Stockholm: Kungl. Skolöverstyrelsen, 1969.

CHAPTER 23

United States

MARY AUSTIN

ESTABLISHED as an area of early concern, reading gained priority status in the New World when the Massachusetts Bay Colony decreed, in 1642, only twelve years after its settlement, that parents and guardians should see that all children were taught to read and to understand the laws and religious principles of the Colony. Five years later, in 1647, the Massachusetts legislature passed the first act relating to schools, requiring every town of fifty or more families to appoint a schoolmaster to teach children to read and write, and every town of a hundred households to provide a grammar school to prepare youths for the university. Other Colonies soon gave priority to the teaching of reading, whether their schools were the function of the State as in New England, the arm of the Church as in the Middle Colonies, or the responsibility of the home as in the south.[1]

The importance of reading continued to increase in the next three centuries, although the emphasis on it in the young nation shifted somewhat from period to period. Fortunately, these changing emphases, along with the methods and materials of the time, have been carefully detailed by Nila Banton Smith[2] and Mitford Mathews,[3] who reveal the fascinating story of reading instruction in the United States. Staiger[4] and Dodds[5] present shorter views in more recent articles. These sources serve as excellent introductory material for comparative studies.

Staiger[6] presents the "geology of reading" (Figure 23-1). He depicts the influences on American reading instruction from approximately 1607 to 1962. On the left side of the diagram, Staiger uses Smith's[7] designated historical periods, adding dates for convenience. Typical characteristics of instruction appear in four columns at the right of the "Grand Canyon of reading." The clarity of the diagram outweighs its possible oversimplification and may lead serious historians to expand on it with descriptions of the various periods.

In surveying trends in American reading instruction, one notes more activity in this significant area of the curriculum since the mid-twentieth century than during any single period prior to 1950. To what cause or causes can this burst of activity be attributed? Undoubtedly, the answer will be found in the series of dramatic changes experienced by American society during the years following 1950. All of these changes—the population explosion, the technological revolution, the exponential increase in knowledge, the criticisms of education, the student and faculty rebellions—have direct implications for education and

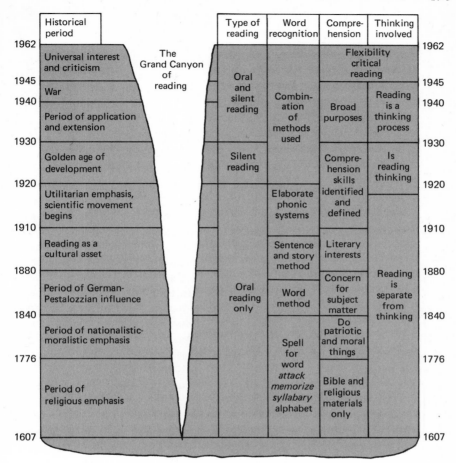

FIGURE 23-1. American reading instruction: a historical cross-section. (After Ralph Staiger, "The Geology of Reading," in John Downing and A. L. Brown, Eds., *The Second International Reading Symposium,* London: Cassell, 1967.)

for the teaching of reading. Major attention will be devoted in this chapter to recent developments in reading, while brief reference will be made to earlier events to lend perspective to the current scene.

Education in the United States

Because there is no system of national education in the United States, schools and colleges come under the jurisdiction of state governments. The states in turn delegate the prime responsibility for schools to local boards of education whose members are elected. Thus, fifty state systems of public education are functioning independently throughout the country. In addition, hundreds of nonpublic schools enroll thousands of pupils. Federal interest in and support of education, however, have resulted in a marked increase of important legislation, particularly during the last twenty-five years.

The Office of Education is the central educational agency of the Federal Government. It was established as a unit of the Department of Health, Education, and Welfare in 1953. Its chief officer, the U.S. Commissioner of Education, is a Presidential appointee. The Office of Education administers federally sponsored programs related to education, handling appropriations that have multiplied rapidly since 1960. A number of these programs affect reading, either directly or indirectly: the National Defense Education Act (1963) provided institutes for the inservice training of teachers; the Elementary and Secondary Education Act (1965) and its amendments authorized grants for (1) elementary and secondary school programs for children of low-income families, (2) school library resources and instructional materials, (3) supplementary educational centers and services, (4) strengthening state departments of education, and (5) educational research and research training; the Education Professions Development Act (1967) is intended to improve the quality of teaching and help meet critical shortages; the Education Resources Information Center/Clearing House on Retrieval of Information and Evaluation on Reading (ERIC/CRIER) at Indiana University makes much of the voluminous literature in reading available; and support of bilingual programs enables many schools to offer the teaching of English as a second language. These special provisions are expanding the quality and quantity of education from preschool to adult education.

Perhaps the most striking testimonial to American public education is the fact that at the beginning of the twentieth century only about 4 per cent of the eligible age group graduated from high school, whereas today almost 40 per cent of our youth enters college. Thus, mass education has become a highly successful enterprise and a relatively unique reality among major nations.

Languages of the Country

The United States has been described as the "melting pot" of the world. People come to its shores bringing their many different languages, customs, and cultures. That America has been enriched by diverse groups is unquestionable. Many newcomers learn English, take responsible positions in business and the professions, and become citizens of the United States. Their children acquire English through the schools, learn to read according to the prevailing system or systems, graduate, and make contributions to society. Nevertheless, speakers of English as a second language experience problems that are of concern to school people.

Several geographical areas throughout the country have large concentrations of nonnative speakers of English (NNSE) in the public schools. Great numbers of Spanish speaking people live in the Southwest, including California, in addition to a large American Indian population. Since 1961–1962, Cuban refugees have arrived by the thousands in Dade County, Florida. In New York City, where there has always been a large number of nonnative speakers of English, the majority since 1945 has been Puerto Rican.

Over and beyond whole linguistic communities of NNSE, the population of the United States speaks a variety of dialects. Learning to read a dialect that is not his own may be difficult for a child, for as Goodman (1969) writes, "The more divergence there is between the dialect of the learner and the dialect of learning, the more difficult will be the task of learning to read."[8] Divergent dialects have been studied as special problems, but the focus of this section will be on teaching English as a second language.

Presently, there are coordinated efforts to collect and disperse information on teaching English as a second language (ESL), largely through the work of the National Council of Teachers of English, the Modern Language Association, the National Association for Foreign Student Affairs, the Speech Association of America, and the Center for Applied Linguistics. Conferences on Teaching English to Speakers of Other Languages (TESOL) sponsored by these groups led to the formation of the national organization and the publication of its journal, the *TESOL Quarterly*.

Problems of Teaching English As a Second Language

Although research on teaching nonnative speakers of English is comparatively recent, many problems have been identified. In the first place, mathematics and reading achievement are weak areas for these students. Reports consistently indicate language retardations of two to five years. Understandably, the school dropout rate is twice the national average.

Morris,[9] in writing about the reading achievement of American Indians in the Southwest, notes a second problem: children can succeed in reading in the lower grades when decoding is emphasized, but they lack success at advanced levels in learning activities that require abstract conceptual manipulations. Nance[10] points to similar problems among Spanish speaking children in California, saying that often they are word callers because they are products of "instant reading" programs. He refers to "language loyalty" and the rejection of culture as barriers to language competence. Nance also cites as problems the training of teachers and the location of proper materials.

Rosen and Ortego[11] identify additional problems in their discussion of Spanish speaking children in the Southwest placed in regular sequences of instruction with other children. The authors state that this procedure may appear to offer equal educational opportunity for all, but, in actuality, the reverse is true. Hispanic-Americans, who lack the verbal skills and cultural background of Anglo children, start their school experiences far behind their Anglo counterparts. Moreover, the problems of these children are compounded by teachers who do not communicate with them in the only language they know. Failure can be expected when these children are promoted year by year with no assessment of their readiness for more complex reading and learning tasks.

Concern for the social and cultural adjustment of Cuban pupils in Florida led to a number of early studies. The reports of "cultural shock" that resulted from the sudden separation of students from their communities, friends, and in some cases, parents, led to the recommendation of bilingual education rather than education in English only. The rationale for this proposal recognized that the Cuban students needed continued linkage with their heritage.[12]

Clearly, the mastery of English as a second language is much more than an impersonal acquisition of linguistic skills. It can involve the learner's total experience, past and present. If it should happen that his first culture group and the target culture are unaccepting of one another, the learner may be faced with even greater obstacles.

Programs for NNSE

Finocchiaro[13] deals with a variety of ESL teaching situations, including factors that should be taken into consideration in devising appropriate programs. Among them, she mentions that if the language of the community is the language the students are learning, the teacher can count on practice outside the classroom and increased motivation on the part of students. The pupil's age, background, and degree of competency in a first language are other important considerations. The socioeconomic structure of the community is a factor also in that students from disadvantaged areas may possess added handicaps to learning English. The attitudes of parents toward the learning of a second language are critical. Programs should give students status by helping them develop and retain pride in their native culture. Attempts to effect a mutually accepting attitude between NNSE and established members of the community should be undertaken.

Reports of educational programs in New York City and Miami, Florida describe general practices in teaching NNSE. These cities test students to determine their levels of competence and provide instruction on the basis of the results. Miami (Dade County) has established bilingual schools where one half of the students and teachers are native English speakers and the other half are Spanish speakers. For one half of the school day, lessons are in English; for the remainder of the day, lessons are in Spanish. By the end of sixth grade, it is hoped that students will be fluent in both languages and accepting of both cultures.

New materials such as the *Miami Linguistic Readers* have been published for use with ESL students. According to the program, teachers rely heavily on building oral language skills as pupils learn to read, making certain that they master the sounds and basic structures of language and that they acquire a functional vocabulary that can be used in daily communication.

Teachers should also remember, as Morris indicates,[14] that the teaching of oral English and the teaching of reading are not identical processes. Obviously, lack of verbal facility in English handicaps pupils in reading, but oral fluency and general English language ability do not insure growth and success in reading. Morris indicates further that teachers of NNSE must concentrate more on building children's experiential backgrounds and on facilitating concept formation.

Rosen and Ortego (1969) name three types of reading programs that appear to help Hispanic Americans. Of particular value are (1) a linguistic approach, similar to the one used in Miami, (2) an experiential approach, and (3) a bilingual approach. In the latter, students learn first to read in their own language. There is some evidence that the bilingual approach may lead to more success than other methods.[15] Rosen and Ortego, however, caution educators that as helpful as programs, materials, and methods are, they do not deal with the essentials of the problem; they only deal with the symptoms. They, with others, believe that the essence of the problem lies in the "preverbal conceptual domain."

At present, the nation's largest bilingual program, developed by the Southwest Education Development Laboratory (Austin, Texas), is being field tested in twelve school districts in major cities across the country in preschool through grade VI. The program teaches science and mathematics in the Spanish speaking child's own language while he is learning to read English as a second language. First reports indicate that almost all pupils are achieving at or above grade level on the Iowa Test of Basic Skills at the end of third grade.

The results of early childhood education programs are also significant. The goal of these programs is to help children develop enough skill in oral language to perform successfully in a regular public school first grade.

Looking Ahead

In view of the world-centered nature of communication, the teaching of reading to nonnative speakers of English will continue to gain significance during the coming years. The problems are extremely complex in this area, primarily because theories, methods, and materials that have been developed for native speakers appear to be applicable only in a limited way to nonnative speakers.

The teaching of English as a second language extends beyond these aspects. Further clarification and knowledge of the relationship between language and thought are needed now. Can concepts be formed without language to mediate, manipulate, and store thought? What are the variables that determine one NNSE's success in reading achievement and another's failure?

Undoubtedly, further research will be helpful in determining whether specific methods will be effective—that is, the advisability of translation, of learning to read first in the native language, and the effect of secondary language acquisition on concept development.[16]

If, as it now seems likely, language learning is motivated by the desire to be like valued people in the environment, what steps can be taken to activate these desires, to accelerate the process of acculturation? Gardener[17] found that students of a second language experience feelings of anomie, that is, they feel lost between two cultures, belonging to neither. How can such feelings be dissipated to the advantage of the learner? Gardener noted also that during specific stages of their development, young people are subjected to extreme pressure from peers and the linguistic community to use the native language and to conform to the first culture. How can such pressures be reduced, if not entirely eliminated? These are a few of the many questions remaining to be answered before the effective teaching of English to nonnative speakers will become a reality.

School Organization

School organization relates directly to any discussion of American reading instruction because of its general impact on classroom behavior and learning climate. Most educators agree that school organization facilitates learning insofar as the plan or structure assists the instructional staff and learners in attaining their goals; it is what the teacher does to encourage or foster learning within a given organizational pattern that is important.

Instruction may be organized both *vertically* and *horizontally*. Vertical arrangement shows how pupils move from year to year along a continuum of curricular experiences in a *graded, nongraded,* or *multigraded* progression. Horizontal organization concerns the placement of pupils with teachers and in instructional groups, as in *self-contained classrooms* and *departmentalized plans, heterogeneous* and *homogeneous* classes, *team-teaching* situations, and others. Research evidence for each plan continues to grow, as it should if schools are to find better ways of differentiating instruction. For a fairly comprehensive review of grouping practices and research in various countries, the reader should turn to Yates.[18] Anderson and Ritsher[19] and Sartain[20] review factors that influence pupil progress, including innovations in school organization.

Vertical Organization

GRADED SCHOOLS. For more than a century, grade-level classes have prevailed in elementary and secondary schools. Introduced in America by Horace Mann, in the 1830s, following his European visit to educational institutions, Prussia's graded plan spread throughout the United States in response to the demand for schooling by a rapidly increasing population. At first, graded organization appeared to be a more efficient means than previous patterns because it permitted better use of teacher time in working with a narrowed range of pupil differences. In time, however, it became clear that this type of organization differentiated neither curriculum, methods, nor materials in accordance with individual learning rates.

Almost without exception, school districts maintain twelve years of schooling. Many have added kindergarten for 5-year-olds and some are now offering two years beyond grade XII in public community or junior colleges.

In many states children enter first grade at 6 years of age. They proceed to junior high (grades VII to IX) at about age 12, and to senior high (grades X to XII) at about age 15. However, there is great variability among school systems. One system may have divisions such as those just described, while another will offer an elementary school of grades I to VI and a secondary school of grades VII to XII. Another pattern may be an elementary school of kindergarten to grade VIII and a secondary school of grades IX to XII. In general, the 6–3–3 and 8–4 year plans are about equally prevalent, although slightly fewer in number than the 6–6 plan. Together these three account for almost two thirds of the school organizational structures in the United States.

Acknowledging the weaknesses of conventionally arranged junior high schools, many systems are beginning to adopt "middle schools," which attempt to provide an educational program designed for the special needs and interests of pre- and early adolescent pupils. Among the noteworthy features of middle schools are (1) a span of at least three grades, including grades VI and VII with no grades below V or above VIII, allowing for the gradual transition from self-contained elementary classrooms to the departmentalized secondary schools; (2) such flexible approaches to instruction as individualized instruction, team teaching, flexible scheduling, independent study, and tutorial programs, all with the goal of stimulating students to learn how to learn; (3) faculty with both elementary and secondary school certification, or some teachers with each type; (4) special guidance programs; and (5) departmentalized courses in some areas, such as industrial arts and home economics.[21]

NONGRADED PLANS. Rollins[22] indicated that the trend away from traditional graded schools reflects the philosophy that the individual child with his different abilities, disabilities, interests, and personality is the most important element in the educational program. Nongrading eliminates class grouping and promotion by arbitrary grade-level designations. Found most often in the lower elementary school, nongrading disappears rapidly after the third grade. Schools having a nongraded program usually include all early elementary grades in a primary unit (K through III or I to III), although some are continuing into grades IV through VI (intermediate unit). Children who would normally be in these classes are placed in the nongraded sequence, grouped by reading levels of which there may be from ten to fifteen in a three-year unit. A number of secondary schools have initiated a nongraded sequence, and nongrading may be found in secondary subjects such as English, foreign languages, and social studies. Descriptions of both elementary[23] and secondary[24] programs are available.

Those who favor a nongraded organization for elementary schools cite the following advantages: (1) It offers a solution to the promotion dilemma without the trauma of failure and retention for the nonachieving pupil. At the beginning of each year the pupil engages in learning activities for which he is ready, according to this continuous progress plan. (2) Because children are not expected to accomplish the same amount of work in a year, each child can progress at his own pace—a majority completing a unit in three years. More able pupils can complete the work in two years, whereas slower pupils may take four. (3) Nongrading removes the pressure to compete with other pupils and results in fewer emotional problems and less disruptive behavior. (4) Pupils have time to master each area of the curriculum, rather than repeat or skip what is misunderstood.[25]

Many schools are trying new approaches to nongrading. In some instances, grades I, II, and III have been abolished in favor of "educational family units," composed of 100 to 120 pupils, four teachers, four teacher aides, several student teachers, various specialists, and a learning director.[26] Each unit is subdivided into four "home base instructional groups." Each home base has one teacher who is responsible for the learning that takes place there. Specialists in curriculum assist the home base units in diagnosing and prescribing programs for each child. The learning director oversees the entire unit and assesses individual pupil progress.

Drawbacks of nongrading appear to result from misunderstandings of the arrangement. Parents and school personnel sometimes find it difficult to become accustomed to changes from grade expectations in pupil evaluation. Another drawback may be the extensive record keeping that is necessary. Because a pupil's progress is measured neither by artificial standards nor comparisons with other pupils, but by his own academic growth, teachers need complete records for reporting to parents and for the child's future teachers.

MULTIAGED AND MULTIGRADED ORGANIZATION. The *multiaged plan* distributes equal numbers of 6-, 7-, and 8-year-old children in each primary class within a school and equal numbers of 9-, 10-, and 11-year-olds in each intermediate class. Usually an attempt is made to have classes contain a representative sample of the abilities and achievements of the entire school population of those particular ages.

Both multiaged and nongraded classes increase the probability of learning success for children who might otherwise experience difficulty when they are grouped by age and/or grade. Proponents of nongraded and multiaged organizations, however, view the curriculum in different lights. The former group permits children to move through a graded curriculum at their own paces; the latter encourages teachers to help pupils find their own personal sequences rather than to accept existing sequences as being appropriate for all children.

Basic to the concept of multiaged classes is the belief that *the wider the range of individual differences, the richer the learning environment*—children learn more from each other when they are placed with children of diverse ages, interests, and abilities. Educators also comment that children in multiage classes mature more quickly than those in regular classes because the older pupils assume more responsibility and the younger ones follow their examples.

Another distinctive feature of this plan is the *continuity of pupil enrollment*. Normally a child who enters a multiaged primary class as a 6-year-old will be a member of that class for three years. Each year the older third of the children will leave and be replaced by a younger group. Educators believe that the experience that every child has of seeing his position change in physical size and intellectual maturity over the three-year-period is very beneficial to the child. The continuity of pupil enrollment also enables teachers and pupils to know each other very well, because the teachers remain with their classes in most situations.

A third feature of multiage grouping is the possibility of *more individualization of instruction*. Those who have studied the plan since its beginnings in 1955 credit its success in large measure to the fact that when a teacher works with children from three age groups he individualizes the instructional program more than for a single grade, for which he often assumes that pupil achievements are similar. In nearly all multiaged classes, then, the reading program is individualized. Much of the teacher's time with young children focuses on background-building discussions, making individual experience stories, and composing group experience charts. For children who have developed some reading independence, individualization consists of self-selected trade books with needed reading skills being taught from the books selected. Reading instruction in multiaged classes does not vary significantly from the individualized program in many self-contained classrooms.

Horizontal Organization

The most frequent form of organization in the elementary school is the *self-contained classroom,* in which one teacher works with one grade-level class. Each classroom teacher usually teaches reading on the elementary level; the English teacher or a special reading teacher offers reading instruction at the secondary level when it is included in the curriculum. Classes may be homogeneous or heterogeneous, but within each class the conventional practice is to form subgroups by reading level, although individualized reading has grown in popularity since the 1960s.

Claimed as unique features of the self-contained elementary classroom are the teacher's ability to meet the personal-social needs of pupils through child-centered teaching and to provide unity in the child's instructional program by correlating several curriculum areas. Both features can be advantageous for the development of skills and habits in reading. On the other hand, those who oppose the one-teacher plan maintain that no one person can be knowledgeable in all instructional areas. They also charge that individual differences among learners of a given age tend to be ignored by a grade-level curriculum and the grouping practices found within these rooms. Obviously, in schools where the latter is true, pupils are handicapped when methods and pacing of reading instruction are largely the same for all.

A trend toward increased use of *departmentalization* in elementary schools, particularly in the upper grades, can be noted from 1955 to the present. This plan of organization, with its emphasis on specialist teaching, has been customary for many years in secondary schools. However, it represents a departure from the self-contained rooms of elementary schools that traditionally have not employed subject-matter specialists in major curriculum areas.

Studies of the effectiveness of departmentalization in elementary schools have led to inconsistent findings, perhaps because so few teachers assigned as specialists have had content and methods courses beyond those offered to the elementary generalist.

Classroom placement of students may be *homogeneous* or *heterogeneous,* the latter being most common in the United States. Homogeneous (ability) grouping is a method of reducing the range of individual differences in learning within a classroom by placing together pupils of about the same age whose reading achievement and/or intelligence is similar. Heterogeneous classes contain children of approximately the same age but whose range of ability may be wide;

their achievement and needs in reading often are quite dissimilar. In either situation, teachers usually regroup children for reading instruction by reading levels or needed subskills development, unless individualization is provided.

Cross-class or interclass grouping for reading (referred to as redeployment or a modified Joplin plan) is practiced in some schools. For a designated period, children move to the classrooms of other teachers for group instruction in reading at a particular level. Groupings occur across grades (as in fourth, fifth, and sixth grades), or when there are several classes at the same grade level. In the latter instance, pupils are deployed to rooms where they receive instruction with others of similar abilities.

The Joplin, Missouri, plan became popular several years ago through its claims of success in encouraging wider reading of recreational materials and higher teacher enthusiasm for reading instruction.[27] However, several disadvantages of the plan were evident: for example, the practice of treating the class as a whole with little effort to adjust instructional techniques to accommodate individual differences, and the tendency to isolate reading from the other areas of the curriculum.[28]

Although theoretically it is possible to distinguish between homogeneous and heterogeneous groups in reading, any subgroup in a classroom organized homogeneously by reading ability will remain heterogeneous to a large extent. Research indicates that ability grouping does not, in actuality, place children together who are of equal ability for a given period of time. Rather, the range of ability continues to increase as children mature.

Literature about grouping may be found in Harold Shane's[29] brief historical review of organizational practices and a summary of research in the 1950s, William S. Gray's historical review of patterns of instruction in reading,[30] and the University of Chicago's Reading Conference papers, edited by Helen M. Robinson.[31]

Team teaching takes place when two or more teachers cooperatively plan and conduct instruction for the same group of students, regardless of academic level—elementary, secondary, or college. Sometimes called *cooperative teaching,* the plan includes a variety of organizational patterns in which teams differ in number from two or three who may share instructional responsibility for forty or more students to teams of eight for more than two hundred students. Some teams may be organized by one grade level, whereas others will include two or three levels. Ideally, team members will have had training in, as well as sufficient time for, the cooperative planning desired to ensure proper coordination of learning activities. Among the literature about team teaching, a book edited by Shaplin and Olds[32] gives detailed discussions of the theory and practice underlying the plan.

Several different features are combined in team teaching: flexible grouping, utilization of staff specializations, flexible scheduling, use of teacher aides, and team planning. Flexibility appears to be an essential component of successful team-teaching situations. Depending on the learning activity of pupils, groups may vary in size from large to small. Such curriculum areas as social studies, science, and literature often lend themselves to large-group teaching. When all team members are not involved in large-group sessions, some will be free to work with small groups or individuals, perhaps in developing skills in reading or mathematics. Tewksbury[33] points out that staff in certain schools believe team teaching can provide a way for teachers to conduct multilevel instruction. Children can be regrouped from time to time during the day and week according to performance levels.

INDIVIDUALIZED INSTRUCTION.   In 1925, the National Society for the Study of Education recognized the need to individualize instruction in schools:

> It has become palpably absurd to expect to achieve uniform results from uniform assignments made to a class of widely differing individuals. Throughout the educational world there has therefore awakened a desire to find some way of adapting schools to the differing individuals who attend them.[34]

Increasingly during the following years, educators in the United States reaffirmed the importance of individual performance in contrast to group participation. Individualized instruction in reading today goes beyond the earlier plan of permitting each child to progress at his own rate. Nor is it limited to reading achievement alone; it is concerned also with pupil "interest in reading, his attitude toward reading and his personal self-esteem and satisfaction in being able to read."[35] At its best, an individualized reading program enables teachers to assess reading as a functioning component of a child's development —physically, mentally, socially, emotionally, linguistically, and experientially. At its worst, it develops scanty skills, supplies insufficient materials, fails to diagnose pupil difficulties, and provides too little time for pupil conferences.

Lazar defines individualized reading as

> a way of thinking about reading—an attitude toward the place of reading in the total curriculum, toward the materials and methods used, and toward the child's developmental needs. It is not a single method or technique but a broader way of thinking about reading which involves newer concepts concerned with class organization, materials, and the approach to the individual child.[36]

Individualized reading uses Olson's foundational principles of seeking, self-selection, and pacing.[37] Philosophically, the program is based on the concept that children can read better, more widely, and with greater interest when they are encouraged to choose their own reading materials.

The *individual conference,* rather than group instruction, is the unique feature of this approach. During the conference the pupil usually reads aloud a passage he has selected. The teacher notes the child's reading errors, checks his understanding of word meanings and story content, discusses the book with him, and makes provision for skills development either in a small group or through independent worksheet assignments. Conferences take place from two to four times each week for two- to ten-minute periods.

Obviously, a high level of teacher effectiveness is a prerequisite for a successful individualized reading program. Equally obvious is the need for students to assume large parts of the responsibility for their own skills development. In addition, the informal nature of the individualized classroom makes careful *record keeping* essential.[38]

The brevity of this description should lead interested readers to books and articles by leading proponents: Veatch,[39] Hunt,[40] Barbe,[41] Brogan and Fox,[42] Darrow and Howes[43] and the Conference Proceedings at the University of Delaware devoted to individualization.[44]

Toward Increased Individualization

The variety of school organizational arrangements is almost unlimited. Not all patterns, however, are actual variations in classroom organization. Individualized reading and team teaching, for example, are not often unique to any one organizational procedure but are adjuncts to those already in effect.

Increasingly, the science of group dynamics will be explored during the next decade. The analysis of group interaction, leadership, characteristics and behavior of groups in different teacher-created classroom climates, and the like may contribute immeasurably to an understanding of the values of various organizational patterns. The resulting school situation will be more dynamic and flexible than in the past, with an emphasis on learning rather than teaching.

The facilitation of learning is not entirely dependent on organizational structure, teaching skills, scholarly knowledge, curricular planning, use of audiovisual aids, or even an abundance of books. "The facilitation of significant learning rests upon certain attitudinal qualities which exist in the personal relationship between the facilitator and the learner."[45] Its emphasis is on recognizing, respecting, and encouraging each individual. Only in this manner can an individual develop to his fullest potential as a self-actualizing, fully functioning member of society.

With the focus of educational reform on individualized instruction, it is possible that current organizational practices will be replaced by technological devices and learning programs suitable for independent study.

Age for Beginning Reading

Traditionally, American children entered first grade at the age of 6, and, for many, admission to school was tantamount to beginning to learn to read. In the early 1900s, a few psychologists and educators raised their voices against the routine initiation of reading instruction for all first-graders, but the concept of "reading readiness" did not become widespread until the 1920s. During that decade, three events focused attention on readiness: (1) A study of "Pupils' Readiness for Reading Instruction Upon Entrance to First Grade," cosponsored by the International Kindergarten Union and the U.S. Bureau of Education (1926). (2) The use of the term "reading readiness" in articles in *Childhood Education* (January 1927). (3) Reports of three studies of reading readiness summarized by William S. Gray in 1928.

During the same period, a new interest in measuring pupil achievement led to the discovery that large numbers of children were failing to complete a prescribed first-grade curriculum, usually because of limited success in reading. Shortly thereafter, concern for these failures brought a pronouncement that reading problems were caused by premature instruction. Subsequently, the recommendation proposed for the prevention of reading difficulties was the postponement of instruction until readiness had been established. Although this solution appears irrational in view of the present theory, which emphasizes multiple causation of reading problems, it was consistent with existing psychological tenets founded on the importance of heredity and the law of recapitulation. As Durkin points out in her discussion of prevailing psychological beliefs of that period, the marked influence of G. Stanley Hall and Arnold Gesell, developmental psychologists, resulted in a concept of man that stressed "a predetermined nature which unfolds in stages."[46] Accordingly, many psychologists and educators associated the child's ability to learn to read with a specific stage of development, and if he encountered difficulty they assumed that he had not yet reached the appropriate stage of maturity. Similarly, they assumed that passing time would produce "the flowering of readiness" that would ensure success. Environmental factors such as ethnic background were given little place in the determination of readiness. Relatively ignored, too, were those who advocated that readiness can be cultivated by appropriate activities.

The mental-age concept of readiness attracted educators during the 1920s. A growing interest in objective measurement brought many group intelligence tests, some of which were administered to first-graders, into the schools. In referring to data from these tests, writers were quick to point out that children with mental ages of less than 6 made up the bulk of failures. Others maintained that children should possess a certain mental age before starting reading instruction. Among them was Grace Arthur (1925), who stated that a mental age of 6 to 6.5 was necessary for "standard first grade achievement."[47] But it was the research report of Morphett and Washburne (1931), much publicized and quoted, that gained solid acceptance of a mental age of 6.5 as prerequisite for beginning reading.[48]

Reading-readiness tests were another product of the 1920s. Theoretically, these tests were designed to assess abilities, such as visual and auditory discrimination, whose relationship to success in reading was obvious. In applying the results of these tests, however, school people preferred to make use of composite scores for dividing children into groups of "ready" and "unready" candidates for instruction. Thus, they tended to ignore the potential diagnostic values of subtest scores.

The implementation of reading-readiness programs in the 1920s followed closely after the introduction of readiness tests in the schools. Educators usually gave allegiance to one of two types: Proponents of the *unfolding behavior* doctrine looked on the program as a vehicle for presenting worthwhile activities to a child until he matured further; those who defended the point of view that *environment* also affects readiness regarded the program as preparation for beginning reading experiences. The latter group tried, at least in theory, to introduce content according to the specific deficits of individual children—deficits identified by an analysis of reading-readiness subtest scores and by teacher observation. Undoubtedly, some innovative programs were imaginative, but in many schools all first-grade pupils, ready or not, were expected to participate in workbook-oriented activities. Regardless of philosophical differences among educators at that time, formal reading instruction for all children began by the second semester of first grade.

Adherence to the maturational concept of readiness extended well into the 1950s. Educators were maintaining that normally intelligent children cannot learn to read before age 6.5 and that levels of maturation are reached with the passing of time and cannot be achieved by teaching (environment).

On the other hand, not all educators supported a maturational concept of readiness in the 1930s; in the vanguard was Arthur Gates. Worthy of special note is his report (1937) describing four different methods of teaching reading to first-graders:

> Reading is begun by very different materials, methods, and general procedures, some of which a pupil can master at the mental age of five with reasonable ease, others of which would give him difficulty at the mental age of seven.[49]

From another study, Gates and his associates concluded that the best time to begin reading instruction is not dependent completely on the child himself, "but it is in a large measure determined by the nature of the reading program."[50]

Thus, even in that decade, significance was being attached to the kind and quality of reading instruction a child received; it was recognized by a dissenting minority that changes in instruction could affect a child's readiness, perhaps to a greater extent than mental age and maturation. These findings were largely ignored until two events occurred, one was Sputnik (1957), and the other was a conference on new educational methods at Woods Hole, Massachusetts, chaired by Jerome Bruner (1959), whose well-known statement, "any subject can be taught effectively in some intellectually honest form to any child at any stage of development,"[51] ushered in a new era in education.

In the 1960s, some new concepts of readiness emerged, highlighted by the writings of James McVicker Hunt[52] and Benjamin Bloom.[53] They emphasized the importance of early stimulation for learning. Bloom, for example, stated that the first five years of life comprise the most crucial period for the development of many characteristics, including intelligence. He particularly stressed the major role of early environmental factors.

In addition to the invigorating psychological climate of the 1960s, a critical examination of readiness programs was spurred by the revival of the Montessori method of education, the work of O. K. Moore and his computerized typewriters, the Durkin reports of early readers in California and New York,[54] and the experiment with early reading in the Denver School system.[55] As a result, some interesting contrasts can be seen between earlier reports and more recent ones with regard to reading instruction in the kindergarten. A national study in 1961–1962 reported that slightly more than a quarter of the school systems that maintained kindergartens taught reading to some children.[56] A research sampling in 1967–1968, done by the National Education Association (NEA), found that more than four fifths (83.9 per cent) provide experiences in reading. Specifically, the latter study indicated that 41.1 per cent used largely *structured* methods—instruction through *formalized* classroom procedures; 36.5 per cent used *unstructured* methods by *exposure* to experiences; 6.5 per cent used *both* structured and unstructured approaches; and 14.4 per cent reported no experience offered. Clearly, the role of the kindergarten is changing, judging not only from the numbers of systems having specific curriculum experiences in reading in their kindergarten programs but also from the ways in which these experiences are presented.[57]

Future Emphases

The question now is, "How does an educator in the 1970s view reading readiness?" First, he must understand that the concept is too complex for simplistic generalizations. Readiness to read is a product of the interaction in varying combinations of both maturation and environmental factors. To this interaction, another dimension must be added that takes into account the relationships among a child's abilities, the kinds of learning opportunities available, and the demands of a specific reading-learning task.

In contrast to past practices, future endeavors will more than likely concentrate on the following: (1) a more flexible position about the optimum time to begin reading instruction, with provisions for children who can already read upon school entrance, or who are nearly ready, and for those who will not be ready until later; (2) an assessment of readiness to learn as well as readiness for beginning reading in kindergarten or in first grade in school systems that do not offer kindergarten; (3) an imaginative prescription based on the results of early assessments, learning styles, and interests of individual children; and (4) pre-reading programs to develop certain skills and merge unobtrusively into the beginning reading program.[58]

Previous research has been influenced too often by the question: "Is the child ready to begin to learn to read?"[59] Some of these studies have added to the knowledge of characteristics that help in predicting success in learning to read. First-grade reading level, for example, appears to be predicted more readily by the visual discrimination of letters and words than by visual discrimination of forms and pictures.[60] There is still the need, however, to search further for basic types of predictive tasks. Measures of auditory-visual integration, visual-motor coordination, and others of recent interest may be possibilities for exploration. Hopefully, future investigations that attempt to identify optimum combinations of visual discrimination tasks and predictive combinations of readiness factors in general will result in a clearer understanding of the importance of independent predictors and the interaction of various predictors. Conceivably, highly reliable individual subtests will be located for diagnostic purposes. Such findings will make a significant contribution only to the extent that teachers can relate them to teaching methods and materials. In other words, the question underlying readiness studies should be, "*What and how is this child ready to learn?*"[61]

From cross-sectional and longitudinal studies, psychologists and educators will continue to accumulate a body of evidence about cognitive styles and cognitive structures. Readiness probably depends on these factors and on an even less explored relationship between readiness and affect.[62] Details about these relationships are far from complete at this time.

It may be entirely possible also, as former U.S. Commissioner of Education Allen has said, that schools of the future may be able to write "educational prescriptions" for every pupil. He advocated (1970) that every local school district should have a central diagnostic center with a computer that would carry a complete history of each child—his family background, his cultural and language deficiencies, his health status and needs, and his general potential. Using these data, trained personnel could prescribe a school program for each child and, if essential, for his family.[63]

Teaching Methods and Materials

Currently, in the United States, there are more programs and systems available for reading instruction than for any other area of the curriculum. The past decade brought the i.t.a., the language experience approach, Words in Color, various linguistics programs, individually prescribed instruction, more than thirty phonics innovations, O. K. Moore's responsive environment, a new focus on individualized reading, a revival of the Montessori movement, programed learning, and several new basal reading series. Some of these programs accent aspects of the reading-learning process and neglect others. Two reasons may account for this phenomenon: (1) reading theory and practice have been undergoing experimentation and change for a number of years; and (2) the definition of a process determines how that process will be implemented in the reading program. Clearly, no definition of the reading process emerged during the 1960s that was acceptable to all educators, psychologists, linguists, or the general public.[64]

Various approaches to beginning reading were evaluated in the ambitious Cooperative Research Program in First Grade Reading Instruction supported by the U.S. Office of Education. The relative effectiveness of these programs was tested by comparing pupil achievement in them with the achievement of pupils who learned to read by means of basal readers. The findings have been reported in volumes by Bond and Dykstra[65] and Dykstra.[66] In addition, *The Reading Teacher* published articles by individual investigators who participated in the first-, second-, and third-year projects. The conclusions of the large-scale studies indicated that there is no consistent advantage for any of the methods when pupils were followed through three years of schooling. Furthermore, the evidence showed that qualities of the teacher, the school system, the specific school, and the pupils outweighed differences in methodology in their influences on reading achievement. None of the methods examined eliminated reading failures. Dykstra (1968) states that "it is likely that improvement in reading instruction can be brought about more efficiently by improved selection and training of teachers, by improved inservice training programs, and by improved school learning climates than by instituting changes in instructional materials."[67]

Bases on which school systems make decisions about the adoption of particular methods and materials for the teaching of reading will be discussed in the remainder of this section. Descriptions of current methodology can be found in other sources.[68]

Selection of Reading Programs

The task of selecting a reading program or programs often assumes Gargantuan proportions in urban areas. Curriculum committees may work for months before choosing materials that appear to meet their criteria. Perhaps the "communication ambiguity" contributes as much as, if not more than, any other single factor to the difficulty encountered in comparing various reading systems. Stated objectives of reading programs may be couched in such glowing terms that educators cannot help but agree with them. Comprehensive statements of goals also add to the assessment problem of determining the merits of strategies whose aims are nebulous.

A well-structured program gives evidence of a close relationship between objectives, strategies, and evaluation measures. To assist in making final decisions, committees may use checklists or models for evaluating instructional materials. Together or individually they serve as standards for comparing the strengths and weaknesses of several programs. Frequently, if a model is used, the model will contain goals that have been organized into a hierarchy of skills ranging from basic word recognition to those underlying critical reading ability. The language in which reading aims are stated may be derived from the *Taxonomy of Educational Objectives, Handbooks I* and *II.*[69] The objectives themselves may be drawn from the cognitive and affective domains, because both need to be clearly stated as goals, implemented in the methodology of the program, and evaluated as aims worthy of attainment. The following format depicts one way to gather data about programs.

	Stated		Provided for in strategy		Included in evaluation	
	Yes	No	Yes	No	Yes	No
Objectives						

Although considerations such as cost, classroom organization, type of pupils, and competencies of teachers necessarily are included in the choice of reading programs, consensus on definition of the reading process is crucial. Consequently, as new materials appear on the market, many school people reexamine their theories and practices in the teaching of reading in their attempts to move forward in curriculum improvement. Usually they agree at the outset that reading is part of the total communication skills process, including listening, reading, speaking, and writing. They often concur that learning styles of students should receive priority in deciding on teaching methodology and materials. Although some schools abide by a limited view of reading, most systems are guided by a broad conception of the reading-learning process in their decision-making tasks.

In the United States, few educators will disagree that reading is the meaningful interpretation of written and printed symbols. The difference often lies in the timing and emphasis placed on different aspects of the process. One group may view initial reading efforts as being primarily decoding, a view that holds that the child's major task is to convert writing into language. Techniques and materials used to achieve decoding skill may consist of instruction in regular word patterns (man, can, fan, pan) or letter-by-letter sound relationships. If the child is a native speaker of English, he is presumed to possess meanings for the symbols he can decode. Understanding, interpretation, and application receive emphasis later in the program, usually as part of the subject-area study.

A second group may hold that word recognition *and* comprehension are essential components of beginning instructional programs. Thus, the reader must learn to respond to printed symbols with the same proficiency that he would if the author's message were spoken rather than written. Materials based on this view go beyond decoding to include practice in understanding the author's meanings. The reader's experience and knowledge of word meanings and sentence structure enable him to engage in meaningful communication with the writer.

A third point of view emphasizes that it is not enough for children to "grasp" the author's meanings; they must also evaluate them critically. Do the writer's ideas confirm the readers' experiences? Is the content consistent with other materials that students have read about the same topic? Does the author's background allow him to write with authority on his chosen subject? Often this level of comprehension is called reading between and beyond the lines.

A fourth group says that the reading process may not be complete until another component is present: application of ideas gained through reading, whenever such application is appropriate. In other words, until printed material that passes the readers' critical examination becomes part of their thoughts and actions, the reading task may be incomplete.

Once school systems have examined diverse points of view about the reading process, they should adopt a definition that best suits their student population and the expectations of their communities. Committees entrusted with the responsibility of making recommendations for the purchase of reading materials will then be able to employ that definition throughout their work.

With the flurry over new approaches to reading instruction, a truism may be necessary. Dozens of new programs may evolve, but unless they are teachable, they are chaff and not wheat, regardless of the label on their packages. To be valuable, programs must be effective instruments in the hands of confident and competent teachers. Therefore, they must have basically sound content— linguistically and psychologically—clear procedures for students, and supplementary material that leads to the achievement of goals inherent in the philosophy, psychology, and methodology of the programs.

Following analyses of the programs under consideration, many schools proceed to evaluate their appropriateness by introducing them in pilot or trial classrooms. Not until evidence has accumulated from such studies do these systems make their final decisions about new programs and materials. Unfortunately, such care is not universally exercised in the United States. With the availability of huge sums many systems failed to heed the "Buyer Be Wary" resolution of the IRA[70] and to observe proper precautions in evaluating innovations according to predetermined professional standards. In schools where there were no established guidelines, wasteful purchases became a major course of action. To reverse this process will require a determined and informed strategy.

No matter which program or programs are adopted, there is unanimous agreement that teachers must be instructed in the appropriate use of instructional tools. They benefit from demonstrations and supervised practice periods until they gain skill in handling new equipment and materials.

Future Directions

Inevitably, the increasing influence of private industry on educational technology and methodology has resulted in an avalanche of both software and hardware for classroom use. To aid educators in selecting from among alternative products related to education, Project EPIE (Educational Products Information Exchange) was developed recently. As an initial screening agency, such services may prove helpful. Many school systems, however, have adopted procedures of their own for keeping on top of the rising tide of educational materials and programs. They are establishing curriculum materials centers where new products can be studied by professional teams, tried in classrooms, and evaluated for their usefulness in specific situations. Where such practices are in effect, wise decisions can be reached and public monies can be expended to the advantage of both pupils and teachers.

The 1960s witnessed the advent of computers that use programed reading materials for self-instructional purposes at all levels from the beginning years through college and adult levels. Undoubtedly, computers and other devices will incorporate instant feedback systems for developmental programs in reading as well as for informational ones in other areas. Educational television reached a new peak of public interest with the "Sesame Street" program for young children. By 1980, it is safe to predict, the use of TV as a medium of teaching reading in schools and homes will be widespread. There is already the possibility of full-sized TV screens that can operate from capsules, instamatic fashion, and be heard by children through individual receivers according to their needs. These, and a host of other autoinstructional devices, will call for different techniques for evaluating their effectiveness with individual learners.

Having utilized new approaches to reading, schools will promote, even more vigorously than in the past, the platform that pupils must read extensively on their own. Independent reading will become a major objective, because it is the ultimate goal of reading instruction.

Of special significance for the 1970s is the need for definitive information on the reading process itself. Much remains to be learned about what reading is and how children actually learn to read. Basic and applied research should be devoted to how the reading process functions.

Development of Intermediate and Higher Order Skills

For many years, reading instruction in the upper grades (grades IV through XII) of American schools remained much the same as it had been during the earlier part of the twentieth century. Many systems did not offer reading classes beyond the sixth grade, and, in those that did provide them, the basal series and their accompanying practice materials served as the chief instructional tools through grade VIII. These series emphasized the sequential development of word-recognition skills, word meanings, various levels and rates of comprehension, study skills, oral reading, and independent recreational reading. In addition, the balanced reading program in the elementary and secondary years usually provided for the acquisition and application of reading skills to other curriculum areas, special help for students with reading difficulties, and ongoing appraisals of pupil progress.

Present Status of Reading in Upper Grades

Despite the fact that important studies present overwhelming evidence for establishing reading programs in the later school years (see Penty,[71] Bledsoe,[72] Nachman,[73] and Whitmore and Chapman[74]), Lietwiler,[75] in 1967, reported that fewer than three quarters of the public high schools in the United States offer one or more reading programs (designated as developmental, corrective, and remedial in her study), while only one third offer both developmental and remedial reading. Several explanations suggest why secondary school reading programs have increased slowly: the majority of principals lack sufficient expertise to organize and direct a reading program; few schools employ reading specialists; many reading teachers lack training; and space, funds, and facilities are limited.

Studies also have directed attention to the need for distributing responsibility among *all* staff members for various aspects of reading instruction. DeBoer and Whipple (1961) summarized the implications of studies dealing with the teaching of reading in the content subjects:

> Thus, reading is not a generalized skill that, once developed in an English class, can be applied in a special field. Rather, reading involves the ability to interpret

this or that particular area of experience. Basic instruction, no matter how excellent, is not enough. Reading abilities must be developed in the areas where they are to be used.[76]

Moore's statement (1969) reflects these findings:

If the reading problems facing the schools today are to be resolved, it is necessary for teachers and administrators to acquaint themselves with (1) techniques for developing efficient reading and study habits, and (2) ways of developing mature, creative reading habits which will continue to serve students long after school years. *All* teachers can, to some extent, be involved in the teaching of reading; *some* must be involved to a very high degree.[77]

Detailed information about reading in the upper grades and high school is available in Huus,[78] Artley,[79] McCullough,[80] Moore,[81] Karlin,[82] Herber,[83] Bamman, Hogan, and Greene,[84] Strang, McCullough, and Traxler,[85] Marksheffel,[86] Dawson,[87] Hafner,[88] and Sheldon.[89]

Unfortunately, at the time of writing this chapter, it is not possible to say that content area teachers have been convinced sufficiently that they have crucial roles in providing reading guidance, but progress continues to be made in that direction.

Developing Higher Level Skills

In the past, the cognitive aspects of reading were often either neglected or minimized in favor of teaching the basic skills. More recently, however, teachers have begun to attempt to help students acquire higher levels of thought through the development of more advanced language study and comprehension skills.

McCullough (1969) presents an excellent review of the literature about newer developments in word recognition, sentence structure, word meaning, sentence meaning, and sentence function. If teachers heed her strong plea for emphasizing the "relativity that pervades all language and language-related activities"[90] in their teaching, the foregoing elements of the reading process do not need to be expanded here.

Russell[91] and others have called for reading with greater depth of meaning. Davis[92] has indicated that comprehension among mature readers is not a unitary mental skill or operation, whereas Cleland's[93] construct of the intellectual processes of comprehension and Barrett's[94] "Taxonomy of the Cognitive and Affective Dimensions of Reading Comprehension" dispel once and for all any possible misconceptions of educators about the singular nature of comprehension.

Barrett divides reading comprehension into five major categories: (1) literal comprehension (2) reorganization (3) inferential comprehension (4) evaluation and (5) appreciation. Within each category, he provides examples of specific types of tasks that teachers can use as bases for developing purposes and questions for reading guidance. The taxonomy suggests the complexity of skills needed by mature readers and the intelligent planning that must take place in arranging systematic learning experiences of appropriate difficulty for each pupil.

Teaching students to read critically (Barrett's "evaluation") is one of the most commonly expressed aims of instruction. Educators generally have felt an increasing sense of urgency in finding better ways to teach this skill, particularly in the upper grades. Although critical reading is introduced in the primary grades, its placement at a high level in the taxonomy leads to a logical concentration of attention in the later school years.

Critical reading, as defined by Robinson, is the "judgment of the veracity, validity, or worth of what is read, based on sound criteria or standards developed through previous experiences."[95] Mueller[96] prefers "evaluation" to "judgment," because "judgment" is frequently used to describe decisions based on values and may connote a less objective approach to making decisions.

Robinson's definition receives support from well-known authorities, many of whom have compiled lists of skills appropriate for critical reading. One of the most comprehensive, yet concise, is that given by Huelsman (1951):

1. To define and delimit a problem.
2. To formulate hypotheses.
3. To locate information bearing on specific problems.
4. To determine that a statement is important for a given purpose.
5. To distinguish the difference between facts and opinions.
6. To evaluate the dependability of data.
7. To recognize the limitations of given data even when the items are assured to be dependable.
8. To see elements common to several items of data.
9. To make comparisons.
10. To organize evidence that suggests relationships.
11. To recognize prevailing tendencies or trends in the data.
12. To judge the competency of a given author to make a valid statement on a given topic.
13. To criticize data on the basis of its completeness and accuracy.
14. To criticize a presentation on the basis of the completeness and logic of its reasoning.
15. To suspend judgment until all evidence is assembled and evaluated.[97]

Although experts disagree as to the specific skills embodied by critical reading, most concur "that whatever the skills are, they add up to a predisposition on the part of the reader to evaluate the ideas presented by the author."[98] If it is realized that critical reading does not exist in a vacuum by itself, it can be thought of best as closely related to critical thinking. From Russell's definition of critical thinking as "a process of evaluation or categorization in terms of some previously accepted standards," it can be agreed that critical reading is in reality critical thinking applied to written symbols.[99]

In the upper grades, the teaching of reading involves teachers in the content areas. Within the content areas, the social studies probably make the greatest demand on reading skills and time. This is especially true of critical reading abilities, because the social studies deal with human relationships and, therefore, with controversial issues.[100]

The development of critical reading in the social studies as in other content areas can best be accomplished through systematically planned experiences in a curricular design that encourages problem solving, inductive reasoning, and frequent verbal expression among pupils.[101]

Furthermore, the social studies teacher must serve as an "intellectual agitator" to fulfill his responsibility in stimulating readers to react thoughtfully to printed matter. He must employ the art of questioning to assist students in noting similarities and differences, making generalizations and evaluations, analyzing sequences and structures, and seeking verification of information.[102]

Several studies have indicated a relationship between teachers' questions and the quality of pupils' thinking. Taba,[103] for example, found an almost perfect correspondence between these two variables. That teachers can be trained to improve their questioning patterns was revealed by Schreiber,[104] who found that prior to training teachers usually asked factual recall questions; after training there was an increase in the variety of questions and in the frequency of questions that encouraged inquiry, hypothesizing, problem solving, and generalizing. Other research workers obtained similar results. To aid teachers in developing higher level thought processes via questioning, Sanders[105] translated Bloom's taxonomy[106] into pertinent questions. Guszak[107] also offers valuable help to those who wish to alter their verbal-solicitation-response interaction with students.

Not only do teachers need to ask better questions, but students also need direct instruction in phrasing probing questions. Based on the findings of Glaser[108] that instruction in logical analysis improves critical thinking ability, some use of logic in judging printed materials will have value for teaching students to read critically. Two elements of logic—validity and reliability—are contained in the following queries, which students should learn to pose: What are the chief arguments used? Are these arguments supported by fact and reason? What assumptions appear openly or lurk implicitly behind statements? What means of evaluation are used for the facts, reasons, arguments, and conclusions? Does the author evaluate his own data, and does he recognize and evaluate his assumptions? What errors or fallacies appear? Has the author supported his conclusions so that they are appropriate and invite justifiable acceptance?

Many social studies classes use the inquiry-conceptual approach in which students discover concepts rather than memorize a multitude of facts and generalizations, as in the past. The teacher provides diversified materials to accommodate all ability levels. He introduces discrepant information, questions, or conclusions to stimulate the reorganization of students' thinking. The wide variety of sources encourages students to analyze and compare different points of view, to reach decisions as to which are acceptable, to recognize that value differences cannot be reconciled easily, and to suspend judgment until they have consulted and evaluated many sources. In this program students are freed from "covering" material and are given time to question, investigate, compare, and formulate ideas. These steps should lead to growing independence on the part of learners with less reliance on teacher direction. According to Flanders,[109] pupils show an increase in spontaneity, initiative, and problem-solving behavior in a classroom climate that results from a teacher's integrative, as opposed to dominative, behavior. Integrative behavior includes accepting and supporting the ideas of pupils, stimulating pupil participation in decision making, and praising student efforts. Such a classroom climate results in increased pupil learning potential.

Despite the importance of critical reading, too little has been done to promote this ability. There continues to be an overreliance on single texts, an acceptance of the halo effect of printed words, an avoidance in dealing with controversial subjects, an emphasis on conformity in learning, an acceptance and use of stereotypes, and an apparent indifference to the need for reading critically. Obviously, these barriers must be removed.[110]

Fortunately, these circumstances and attitudes are changing. More meaningful, thought-provoking material is becoming available. Research is developing practical techniques for promoting critical reading and critical thinking.[111] Methods are being devised for measuring achievement in nonmechanical reading skills.[112] A more balanced view of the reading program is emerging that recognizes the full import of critical reading.

Students today are being taught that many problems cannot be answered with certainty, that recognized experts often express opposing points of view, and that tentative conclusions are acceptable.[113]

There is, then, consensus concerning the importance of critical reading. Chase states the need cogently in his concern with "higher illiterates" who can absorb and repeat ideas they read but cannot relate them to life around them. He regards them as a threat to civilization. He says, "I hold that the values which thoughtful men cherish are more endangered by illiteracy than by the atomic bomb and its offspring."[114]

Other Skills in Upper Grades

The ability to read rapidly has received much attention in the last decade, particularly at the secondary, college, and adult levels. Presently, more school systems are devoting time to the development of speed of comprehension in the elementary grades.

Recognizing that speed of comprehension is an asset, some school systems have invested extensively in mechanical pacing devices and rely heavily on their use. Such reliance appears unwarranted, however, because speed of reading can be increased by students who are strongly motivated to practice reading faster without pacing equipment. Furthermore, *flexibility of reading* rather than speed *per se* is the appropriate skill to be emphasized.

Students in many developmental reading programs are learning to adapt and to readjust their reading speeds according to specific reading tasks, taking into consideration their purposes for reading the materials, the style of the author's writing, and their knowledge and background in the particular area about which they are reading. Practice in reading a variety of materials and for various purposes can lead to improvement. Group discussions of factors that influence speed and instruction suited to individual needs also prove helpful.

Smith's (1964) findings substantiate the need for flexible reading rates and purposes. In her examination of textbooks used in grades VII through XII, she found distinct patterns of writing fundamental to specific disciplines. The content area teacher is in the best position to help students understand the common patterns used in his field of specialization and to assist them in setting purposes for reading these patterns.[115]

The development of meaningful concepts continues to be a major instructional goal in the later school years. Because an accurate understanding of the meanings of words is directly related to comprehension and reasoning, most content area teachers willingly take responsibility for the specialized vocabulary of their fields. They often aid students also in acquiring broader general vocabularies through direct teaching and the use of context methods.

Vocabulary growth has been the subject of numerous studies over the years. Dale and Razik[116] provide a valuable source for older studies of vocabulary development, including those related to the frequency and difficulty of words and their meanings.

Future Programs in Upper Grades

Reading as an instructional activity in the later school years needs to be greatly extended. The next decade will provide more developmental, as well as corrective and remedial, programs for students in grades VI through XII. Content area teachers will gain increasing expertise in developing the specialized skills of their particular fields. Ideally, these provisions will result in upgraded basic skills, higher level reading and thinking abilities, and flexible reading rates and approaches—while reading interests and tastes continue to mature.

Provisions for Poor Readers

Reading was established as the educational goal of highest priority by former U.S. Commissioner of Education Allen when he launched the "Right to Read" program as a target for the 1970s. Educators generally agree that the right to read should be a reality for all—that no one should leave school without the skill and the desire to read to the limits of his capability. Allen felt that failure to create a *desire* to read is as much a failure in assuring every individual the *right* to read as not teaching him the necessary skills.[117]

There are several reasons for concern about the teaching of reading in the United States. Despite the best efforts of classroom teachers, a surprisingly large number of boys and girls is more or less seriously handicapped in activities that involve reading. Estimates of the extent of reading deficiencies throughout the country vary from 8 to 40 per cent of those in school attendance. Although it is granted that reports reflect differences in research designs, statistical treatments, and investigator interpretations, as well as differences in definitions of what actually constitutes reading disability, nevertheless, "a sizable minority of students are unable to profit from reading instruction which seems adequate for the majority."[118] Indeed, several studies, including a Health, Education, and Welfare report, indicate that about 15 per cent of the children in school have problems in learning to read. The percentage is known to be higher among disadvantaged youth. For reasons that remain obscure, boys comprise from 70 to 90 per cent of reading disability cases.

Major developments have occurred within the past twenty-five years in the study of reading difficulties. Particularly significant are those in the areas of prevention, assessment, prescription, and organized instructional programs. These developments are reflected in such recent trends as earlier identification of potential learning problems, better methods of selecting students who need help in reading, growth in understanding the variety of factors that contribute to deficiency in reading, improved diagnostic tools, greater concern for choosing appropriate instructional strategies for differences in learning styles and experiences of disabled readers, programs for greater numbers of students in need of special reading instruction, and increased interprofessional cooperation among those engaged in the diagnosis and treatment of reading deficiencies.

Space does not permit discussion of each of these developments, but the trend toward early identification of potential reading failures is especially notable. Early assessment and intervention would in many instances obviate the need for subsequent remediation. The prediction of success or failure, therefore, became the subject of several studies during the last decade. Some investigators took single variables such as visual-motor competence, auditory discrimination, and self-concept or anxiety level as measured in kindergarten or first grade to predict reading achievement a year or so later. A few constructed batteries of predictive tests. De Hirsch, Jansky, and Langford,[119] for example, developed a battery of tests of a child's perceptuo-motor and linguistic organization that attempted to predict spelling and writing in addition to reading achievement. Perfect prediction was not achieved, and most of the tests necessitated individual administration. Hopefully, the next decade will bring accurate group screening tests or batteries of tests for the use of classroom teachers.

Efforts have been initiated also to untangle the web of confused terminology used to describe individuals whose reading is unsatisfactory. Harris[120] and Gunderson[121] offer definitions of such terms as "reading retardation," "reading deficiency," "reading disability," "dyslexia," "primary and secondary retardation," "specific language disability," and others—all of which have been applied to cases of reading disability. Throughout this section, *reading deficiency* and *reading disability* will refer to those individuals whose reading ages are below 90 per cent of expectation, with respect to intelligence and educational opportunity as measured by currently available valid tests.[122]

Causes of Reading Disability

A survey of the literature on causes of reading difficulty indicates considerable disagreement among authorities. A number of neurologists and psychiatrists write about primary reading disability, or dyslexia, and secondary reading disability. Rabinovitch,[123] for example, emphasizes the distinction between the two, stating that primary cases arise from the child's biopsychological or constitutional make-up (internal factors) and the secondary from environmental and educational experiences (external factors). Some whom Rabinovitch would label as primary cases may have brain lesions from injuries or diseases, but most do not show clear neurological defects. For those with unquestionable neurological involvement, Rabinovitch uses a third category, "brain injury with neurological defects." Because some symptoms commonly associated with primary disabilities may be found among those included under secondary disability, differential diagnosis is not easily accomplished.[124]

Currently, many people are interchanging the term "minimal brain damage" for severe reading disability. Harris[125] prefers the terms "delayed and irregular neurological development" as being not only more appropriate but also less threatening to all concerned about the child's lack of progress.

Regardless of fads that appear and disappear, most educators recognize the multifactorial nature of reading disabilities. Knowing that reading is a highly complex process, they examine a number of possible contributing factors as they study each child's specific problems. Chief among them are those related to the psychological, social, educational, and physical development of the pupil. Although the research and professional literature pertaining to these factors cannot be reviewed in this chapter, reference can be made to sources by Robinson (1961),[126] Harris (1968),[127] and Harris (1969).[128] Moreover, there are literally hundreds of excellent professional books and articles about this specialized area, for example, Harris (1970)[129] and Strang (1969).[130]

Diagnosis and Remediation

Several new theories of diagnosis and treatment have resulted from studies of etiological factors in the 1960s. Perhaps the most widely discussed among them are the Delacato theory of neurological integration, Kephart's theory of motor and perceptual training, and Frostig's theory of specific perceptual training. Because they are of relatively recent origin and interest, brief descriptions will be included here, although none has produced sufficiently supportive evidence to warrant its adoption with large numbers of disabled readers.

Delacato's major tenets and therapeutic procedures are contained in three books.[131] Central to his theory is the belief that if a child's neurological development does not proceed through a certain sequence, the child will display difficulties in reading, speech, and mobility. Delacato maintains that difficulties based on poor neurological organization can be corrected by training the child from the stage at which impaired growth occurred through succeedingly higher levels until total neurological integration is reached. He uses a number of procedures to achieve the desired neural integration: proper patterns of creeping, crawling, and walking; sleeping in prescribed positions; eliminating music; forcing the child to establish one-sided dominance by occluding the eye opposite from the dominant hand, and others.

Glass and Robbins (1967) analyzed some fifteen studies presented by Delacato as evidence of the effectiveness of the theory of neurological integration. Their analyses raise serious doubts about the validity of all of the experiments.[132] This is not to say that Delacato's therapy for improving reading performance will not be useful with certain children; rather, future experimentation with these approaches must observe the methodology and techniques of empirical research before conclusions drawn from them are acceptable.

Kephart[133] advocates a program that places heavy reliance on readiness for learning and the hierarchy of generalizations required by the child to manipulate his environment more effectively. He views learning difficulties as the result of disturbances in this developmental sequence.[134] Consequently, his program includes procedures for assessing mastery of basic motor and perceptual skills, followed by training exercises for the improvement of motor control and flexibility, the development of hand-eye coordination, directionality, and form perception. Chalkboard activities play a prominent role in establishing directionality. Several reports are available on the use of Kephart-type approaches with kindergarten children and with groups of reading disability children, but research data from controlled studies are conspicuously absent.

Frostig[135] emphasizes specific perceptual skills in her five-part "Developmental Tests of Visual Perception." She has devised picture and pattern workbooks for first-graders, special kits for kindergarten and prekindergarten youngsters, and a set of more than three hundred worksheets in ditto-master form as the basis of her exercises for improving the five areas measured by her test: position in space, eye-hand coordination, form constancy, figure-ground perception, and spatial relationships. Many schools are using the Frostig test and its accompanying training program to promote readiness in young disadvantaged children. Present research does not support the claim that the total score or the part scores are substantial predictors of reading disabilities.[136] Needed now perhaps are a revision of this test or new ones to accurately diagnose perceptual skills.

The last decade brought increased interest in the possibilities of drug therapy for problem readers. Smith and Carrigan[137] hypothesize that an excess or deficiency in two chemicals, acetylocholine and cholinesterase, could cause a physiological difficulty in the transmission of nerve impulses to the brain that would lead to reading disability. Medication was prescribed to pupils with reported success to effect the change assumed necessary in their brain chemistry. Today, new drugs may prove valuable in treating reading disabilities to the extent that they reduce restlessness, increase attention span, improve concentration, and make poor readers more accessible for remedial work.

A number of approaches for teaching reading in developmental programs has been tried in remedial sessions; included are modified alphabets, color systems, phonic and linguistic approaches, and programed instruction. Undoubtedly, more evaluation studies than are presently available will be helpful in determining their effectiveness in remedial teaching.

Programs for Disabled Readers

Schools commonly provide *remedial* and *corrective* instruction for the reading handicapped. Often the distinction made between them is on the basis of the degree rather than the nature of student difficulty, although there is no consensus of definition. A brief glimpse of the past may clarify how these terms came to be used.

Smith,[138] who reviews the history of remedial work in reading in the United States, points out that between 1880 and 1910 specialized work with children was undertaken by the medical profession and by psychologists. In the following decade, when reading tests were introduced, the results disclosed that thousands of school children were not reading according to expectation. Justifiably concerned school personnel initiated remedial reading classes to alleviate the situation.

Gradually, the term "remedial reading" appeared more frequently in the literature from 1916 to 1940 to designate instruction provided for groups of reading retardates. In contrast, today, remedial reading usually refers to the teaching of severely disabled readers who are likely to be working two years or more below their capacities and to require specialized diagnosis and intensive long-term treatment. Instruction may take place individually or in small groups outside the regular classroom with a special teacher of reading. Remedial reading for these students often occurs concurrently with therapy from other professionals, particularly when deep-seated problems coexist.

"Corrective reading," a term of recent vintage, describes the type of work for students whose reading deficiencies are less severe—perhaps not more than one year or so below their potential—and who possess no major barriers to achievement when appropriate group instruction is given within the regular classroom or by a corrective reading teacher who adjusts the program to their particular needs and abilities.[139]

Children, of course, do not fit into neat categories, and the severity of their reading difficulties extends along a continuum from mild to severe. Their placement in corrective or remedial instructional programs may depend more on the services available in the district than on the severity or nature of the problem.

Although specific activities vary from one locale to another, or from school to school, the major goal of remedial and corrective reading programs is the improvement of reading skills among students whose reading achievements fall below expectation. In working toward this goal, school systems usually employ one of three organizational structures: reading clinics, remedial classes, or corrective classes.[140]

The *reading clinic* serves as a specialized facility for the diagnosis and treatment of severe reading problems, often by an interdisciplinary team composed of psychologists, reading specialists, speech therapists, social workers, medical personnel, and others. Usually in a central location, the school clinic is easily accessible for testing appointments and intensive remedial instruction on a one-to-one basis. In some instances, instruction takes place in groups of two or three with highly individualized procedures.

Reading centers located in universities and colleges also offer clinical diagnostic and remedial services as an important component of their training programs for reading specialists.

Remedial classes are found in well-equipped rooms for the diagnosis and instruction of moderately severe reading disabilities. Subsequent to individually administered tests and a carefully planned teaching program, instruction is carried out in groups of two to five or on an individual basis by special reading personnel whose background of preparation generally includes advanced courses and reading clinic practicum experience.[141]

Corrective classes may take any one of several forms. In addition to the efforts of classroom teachers to differentiate instruction within self-contained rooms, and other patterns of organization referred to in a previous section, some school systems employ corrective reading teachers to provide group instruction for children whose reading difficulties are less pronounced than those in the two former categories. Students leave their classrooms to meet with the special reading teacher a half-hour to an hour a day, three to five days a week. Like the classroom teacher, the corrective teacher emphasizes the sequential development of word-attack skills and comprehension at each child's instructional level. Unlike the classroom teacher, the corrective teacher uses special materials and techniques to remedy particular deficiencies until pupils achieve sufficient mastery of the skills to enable them to function successfully in a classroom reading program.[142]

Another type of corrective program transports pupils to the nearest school reading center for special help. Pupils may travel there two or three times a week for forty-five to sixty minutes of individual or group teaching at their proper instructional levels, continuing at the center until they can work independently in their home classrooms.

In a third type of corrective program, pupils may be transferred from their local schools to one in which a reading center is located. There they are placed in classrooms where they receive instruction in all areas other than reading. Scheduled according to the results of group diagnostic tests or informal reading inventories, boys and girls receive help in classes of six to twelve from teachers who have had advanced reading courses but not necessarily clinical experience.

Throughout the United States a number of private organizations offer either full-time or part-time remedial help to children and adults. Some of these centers appear well-qualified for the work they have undertaken, but, unfortunately, many are not. The IRA's statement of minimum standards for staff qualifications and professional ethics should serve as an initial screening of private centers and their work.

Regardless of the program in which special reading instruction has taken place, one of the greatest problems following remedial work is preparing the pupil to return to the classroom and to remain there successfully. Having gained some degree of confidence, the returnee should be prepared for the adjustment to the learning pace, for independent work, and the intermittent reinforcement of a classroom.

From a long-range point of view, the prevention of reading difficulties is as important, if not more so, than their correction. Typically, in the past, pupils with reading disabilities received little attention before the upper elementary and secondary school years. Recently, however, the trend toward an earlier identification of potential reading problems has involved kindergarten and primary grade teachers in assessment programs to detect reading failures as soon as possible. Together with group reading-readiness testing and individual study, well-trained and experienced teachers are in the best position to discover all, or almost all, children with learning problems. When early identification leads to a developmental program of early intervention, success in overcoming reading difficulties can happen during the child's first year in school.

For those children who appear to need help beyond the kindergarten year, many school districts have adopted a form of grouping between kindergarten and first grade, called interim, connecting, or developmental classes. In most instances, interim-class children will be able to return to the regular program at the end of the year. Special classes are provided in some schools for those children whose difficulties may be severe enough to extend beyond the second grade, always with the expectation, however, that they will reenter regular classroom situations as soon as possible.

Aspirations for the Future

Every child who fails to learn to read or experiences difficulty in reading should be the recipient of intensive and appropriate reading instruction in an optimal learning milieu. Educators voice their commitment to this ideal, realizing that to deny such help to the pupil with a reading disability denies him fruitful learning experiences, limits his sources of information, and affects his self-concept and his contributions to society ultimately. Hopefully, accelerated interest in the improvement of reading instruction for all children through the "Right to Read" program will lead to a marked reduction of reading failures in the public schools.

To help local schools improve student reading ability, the U.S. Office of Education (1969) developed a chain of reading centers across the country. These centers are located in the libraries of colleges that prepare teachers and specialists in reading and offer graduate training and research programs.

Even more recently (1970), a National Reading Council was established to advise the U.S. Office of Education and other governmental agencies on priorities in the "Right to Read" effort. Headed by a board of trustees drawn from many segments of society, members of the National Reading Council include representatives from business and industry, as well as from diverse professional and lay groups. The council is expected to direct and operate a National Reading Center, whose primary purpose is to coordinate all the many activities related to (1) the development of public support for the project, (2) the training of citizen volunteers, and (3) the assistance provided to states that undertake similar programs.

Many people have called for the improvement of reading research. Chall

(1967) points out that too much of it has been undertaken "to prove that one ill-defined method was better than another ill-defined method."[143] Presently, in the area of reading diagnosis and remediation, much research is either unsupportive of current theory or inadequate in itself. Controlled experiments should be conducted to examine the crucial conditions of learning and the characteristics of various types of disabled readers. In addition, Clymer (1967) identifies the need for practical studies to answer such questions as: "Does a summer corrective program produce results? Can greater growth in reading skills be expected from having the reading specialist work with classroom teachers in improving their instructional techniques for the slow reader, or should the reading specialist work directly with the children?" He also suggests the "I wonder what would happen if . . . ?" type of study, perhaps with no specific controls, tests, or experimental designs. The results of these imaginative attacks on problems may generate hypotheses that are amenable to scientific investigation.[144]

Sociological and Cultural Factors

Since the early 1960s the United States has been engaged in a massive effort to upgrade the achievement of disadvantaged children. Because education is believed to be the key that can break the interlocking cycle of poverty and ignorance, the inability of the disadvantaged to read and their subsequent failure in school present major challenges to contemporary educators. As a result, federally supported projects have been developed to aid poor children, experiments and studies have been conducted, and a voluminous literature now describes the characteristics and needs of the disadvantaged and gives some recommendations for alleviating their problems. Generally speaking, progress in determining who the disadvantaged are far out-distances investigations to determine how they are best educated. At present the nation still needs a long-range program to provide maximum impact on the millions of children who desperately require compensatory education.

Who Are the Disadvantaged?

Poor children have been given many descriptive labels: culturally deprived (actually they are not deprived of a culture, it is that their culture is not the culture of the majority); culturally disadvantaged; socially handicapped; inmigrant; economically restricted; disaffected; of a low socioeconomic group; educationally deprived; underprivileged; slum children; and others. Undoubtedly, these terms refer to children whose homes and families reveal similar cycles of poverty, dependency, learning difficulties, delinquency, vocational and career problems, and social relationship problems. Briefly, when these people are compared with the upper or middle socioeconomic groups, they are found to be lacking economically, socially, and, of greater importance, educationally.

The disadvantaged do not come from one racial or ethnic group, but they do tend to be from such minority groups in the United States as the Blacks, Puerto Rican, Mexican, mountain white, and American Indian. They are most evident in the slums of industrial cities to which they moved in search of better opportunities; they are found also in rural areas, for example, in Appalachia. As a group, their common problem is poverty.[145]

No assumption should be made that all disadvantaged children are characterized by the same traits. Nevertheless, Webster (1966) indicates that the following characteristics tend to produce negative effects on learning for these children:

> *Concern for the Here and Now.* Individuals living in impoverished environments find that the demands of the present are pressing: little time or energy is expended in speculation about the future nor is value attached to this. Adults in such settings exhibit this "here and now" orientation in their attitudes and behaviors, and the children for whom they serve as models adopt a similar outlook on life.
> *Concrete and Functional Versus the Abstract.* Research indicates that individuals from socially disadvantaged environments tend to possess cognitive styles which require extensive use of concrete examples in perception and in learning. This phenomenon is of importance when one considers the great emphasis that is placed upon the abstract in the curriculum of the school and in the teaching act.
> *Difficulties in Seeing Relationships.* The child socialized in an impoverished environment does not have experiences which require classifying, relating, and integrating knowledge. Such learners, then, display gross inadequacies in their abilities to engage in these kinds of intellectual activities.
> *Active Learning Versus Contemplative Learning.* As a child advances through school, the learning process becomes increasingly more contemplative in nature. This factor possibly explains, in part, the growing alienation of the disadvantaged student from the school and its content. Research indicates that socially disadvantaged persons tend to be more physical and expressive in their personal styles; learning can best be accomplished when the process is involving and of an active nature.[146]

A majority of the learning problems of poor children stem from their backgrounds. Mentioned most frequently in the professional literature as deterrents to success in learning to read are the following: negative self-concept, nonstandard English, deficiency in language skills, restricted background of experiences and concepts, difficulties in seeing relationships, insufficient motivation, and inability to see the value of reading and education.

Another handicap suffered by poor children is the dearth of books, pictures, magazines, and newspapers in their homes. The printed page is rarely encountered by youngsters from deprived backgrounds; yet, print is the mainstay of schools, teachers, and the educative process. Pupils who have limited contact with these media in their early years possess a serious disadvantage when they enter learning situations that depend on oral and written language.

This disadvantage is further compounded in the classroom by the fact that teachers frequently take for granted a middle-class value system that is unfamiliar to their pupils. In reality, these children are caught between two value systems, usually distinctly different—that of poverty-stricken people to whom sheer physical survival becomes the chief goal and that of the well-fed, comfortable middle class.[147] Middle-class values, such as thrift in the use of material objects, are foreign to the poor. Inhibition of fighting, practice in social amenities, aggression through words rather than acts, and an ability to forego immediate for later rewards are other middle-class values that the educational system often tries to impose on disadvantaged children.

Disadvantaged youth frequently reject the goals of the school. It is not difficult to understand why this happens, if one considers that rewards for success in school involve delays of weeks, or even years, in some instances. Because the disadvantaged have such need for immediate satisfactions, many schools have adopted the procedure of "operant conditioning," rewarding specific desired behavior for both individuals and groups. Tokens that can be exchanged for something else or for certain privileges seem to have a motivating effect on these students; they become more receptive to learning.

It must be an uneasy feeling for young learners to move into a situation where they are subjected to spoken and written communication, an unfamiliar value system, and subtly defined behavioral limits. Small wonder they are unable to master effectively the school-imposed information and skills. The sight of some of their more advantaged peers achieving with ease must disturb them even more. Fortunately, more educators are employing strategies that help disadvantaged learners to become comfortable with the unfamiliar. Teachers are recognizing that these pupils need help in understanding the totally foreign setting and in exploring, with a sense of security, the data and skills being offered them.[148]

Moreover, as Hurley (1969) points out, the general failure of poor children to learn often results from a "self-fulfilling prophecy" held by school personnel. Hurley believes that when teachers and administrators have fixed ideas about poor children's inability to succeed, the children will respond by failing. In other words, the lack of self-esteem fostered in many disadvantaged homes is too often reinforced by school experiences.[149]

Reading Achievement and the Disadvantaged

The disadvantaged child has many things lacking in his intellectual development by the time he enters school. His learning deficits related to prereading skills are associated with auditory discrimination, concept formation, and language development.[150] All of these deficits pose problems when he is faced with the task of learning to read, and, consequently, his readiness falls short of his more advantaged peer who may be reading words or phrases at home. A study by Hanson and Robinson[151] on the reading readiness of average, advantaged, and disadvantaged and their later achievement in the primary grades showed that the disadvantaged were less ready to learn to read and that the difference increases through the grades.

It was the discovery of such discrepancies that led to the implementation of programs to help these children "catch up" with the norms of their peers. Educators advocated reaching children earlier in life with preschool programs.

Today, many of these preschool programs concentrate on academic learning, as opposed to the enrichment activities and social learning provided in earlier years. To ensure success in school that is dependent on reading performance, these programs are dealing with cognitive areas that may have been hampered by development in limited environments.[152]

The place to start obviously is not at learning how to read, but rather by learning how to learn.[153] Whereas middle-class children come to school already equipped with many learning skills, such as listening, verbalizing and conceptualizing, lower-class children are more dependent on the school itself for acquiring these skills and using them to learn to read and write.[154] Most disadvantaged children lack the parental guidance, attention, and variety of experiences that would help initiate and sustain their progress in school. Thus, teaching methods based on the assumption that children already have acquired "readiness" will have little effect on lower-class children.

Perhaps the most vital aspect of learning readiness and also of successful reading is still that of experience. For this reason the standard picture clues in reading materials, which serve to trigger the middle-class child's memory, make no connection for the poor child. His limited experiences may block him from identifying with or conceptualizing from a picture. But perception and cognition are *learned* behaviors[155] and a school that is truly oriented toward the poor child can use a more dynamic methodology and purposely teach them.

In constructing a meaningful classroom environment, a teacher must take into account children's specific modes of learning. These modes may be quite different from those of middle-class children. For example, many disadvantaged children find it difficult to learn "orally." They are physically oriented and they react to visual and kinesthetic stimuli.[156] They can respond more readily to emotion and drama than to introspective, abstract presentations.

The trend toward placement of emphasis on early childhood and prekindergarten programs in recent years is exemplified in New York City. Schools in that city have conducted an extensive program for 130,000 children in Early Childhood classes in 267 schools in poverty areas since 1967. Smaller classes, more books, parent involvement, and paraprofessionals from the immediate neighborhoods have been of great value.

Harris and his associates,[157] who conducted research in twelve predominantly Negro schools in New York City, provide a notable example of studies during the 1960s. The entire report and its nine recommendations deserve attention in establishing a reading program for the disadvantaged. The results showed without question that disadvantaged first-grade Negro children can make substantial progress in reading. Furthermore, they learn to read by the same methods that succeed with middle-class white children. It was also abundantly clear that the teacher proved to be a far more important influence than the particular method used.[158]

Lloyd (1969) underscores five essential areas for concentrated efforts to effect improvement in reading:

1. Establish more prekindergarten classes with carefully planned programs of instruction.

2. Plan with the staff a sequential, developmental reading program, prekindergarten through adult classes, with special emphasis on effective beginning reading programs and on the use of corrective clinical services for pupils at all grade levels.

3. Reduce class size and initiate more creative organizations for teaching reading.

4. Design and implement new and imaginative programs for preservice and inservice work in reading.

5. Involve the parents and community people in helping their own children to read better.[159]

Lloyd states that although these practices will not be the "open sesame" to improved reading achievement for the disadvantaged, the united efforts of all who work with these children will enable them to learn to read.

Tutoring

Educators have found numerous resources for teaching and learning situations today. Among them, the concept of "youth tutoring youth" is still fairly new. For this reason, the professional literature on the subject of tutoring is not voluminous, but it is increasing. Notable is a scarcity of empirical studies that may be termed "scientific," in contrast to the number of descriptions of tutorial projects and the proliferation of opinions about the advantages such projects possess. All of these have accelerated the introduction of tutorial programs in many schools and communities.

Stauffer (1967) states that the tutorial approach as a medium of instruction in elementary schools is sound. He adds that able children usually make good tutors. He believes, however, that the less able should also be given a chance to perform in this role.[160]

That such a technique as tutoring has potential for both the tutor and the tutee has been demonstrated in reported achievement and behavioral gains. Lippitt and a University of Michigan team found that the behavior of student tutors improved when they were placed, perhaps for the first time in their lives, in positions of responsibility. In learning to teach, the student tutors often learned how to learn. Cloward's study (1966), using potential dropouts as tutors for fifth- and sixth-graders supported the hypothesis that tutoring is an effective means of increasing reading achievement for elementary level underachievers with beneficial "side-effects" to the psyche of the tutor. Cloward also found that "assigning Negro pupils to teenage Negro tutors of the same sex tended to maximize the achievement of pupils."[161]

Very little is reported about using older elementary school children as tutors for younger ones, but this strategy is worthy of investigation also.

What Does the Future Hold?

Emphasis on compensatory education continues to be placed at the preschool level. A lesson learned from the nation's first efforts to accelerate the achievement of the disadvantaged is that compensatory education is most effective when it involves children at the early ages of 2 and 3 and then provides follow-through programs once they are enrolled in school.

There is no magic that will teach the disadvantaged child to read. Riessman pointed out that

> Teaching deprived children does not consist of gimmicks or tricks. Much more decisive are certain basic attitudes. Effective teachers use different techniques. . . . There is not just one right approach, although there are many wrong approaches.162

If, as it appears, there is no one best educational model for the disadvantaged, compensatory education should be integrated with the best of traditional practices.163

Regardless of what procedure or what reading materials are used, teachers and administrators must take an attitude of "positive expectancy" toward these pupils. Instead of their faults, the focus must be on their assets. Especially with disadvantaged children, diagnostic teaching and individualized instruction should be used. Each pupil must see the purpose of instruction and must feel rewarded by some sort of objective evidence or positive reinforcement.

Findings of nutritionists studying the effects of malnutrition on children may eventually make major contributions to work with the disadvantaged. It has been suggested that malnutrition can cause irreversible brain damage, lessened intellectual capacity, and impaired psychomotor functioning. The earlier this long-term cumulative effect of poverty is identified in individual children, the sooner measures can be taken to counteract these possible deterrents to learning.

Evaluating Progress in Reading

Educators generally agree that continuous, functional assessment of school programs and pupil achievement are essential. For the most part, they also recognize that evaluation should encompass a broad spectrum of formal and informal procedures. What school people may fail to realize, however, is that educational evaluation varies in quality, depending on precisely stated objectives, carefully selected appraisal techniques, and the skill of those individuals who undertake the evaluation acts of description and judgment.

Fortunately, contemporary educators can turn to several helpful sources. Englehart's *Improving Classroom Testing* (1964)164 provides an overview of the principles of test construction. *Measurement and Evaluation in Reading,* edited by Farr (1970);165 *The Evaluation of Children's Reading Achievement,* compiled and edited by Barrett (1967);166 and *Reading Evaluation,* by Austin, Bush, and Huebner (1961)167 describe procedures for appraising school or classroom programs and the reading performance of individual students. Strang's *Diagnostic Teaching of Reading* (1969)168 includes suggestions for formal and informal evaluation strategies. Harris' *How to Increase Reading Ability* (1970)169 offers a variety of techniques, including several for studying student reading interests and attitudes, whereas Johnson and Kress' *Informal Reading Inventories* (1965)170 gives practical help in using oral reading as a diagnostic tool. *Educa-*

tional Evaluation: New Roles, New Means, edited by Tyler (1969),[171] and *Evaluation of Reading,* edited by Robinson (1958),[172] are excellent sources of theoretical and practical material.

Buros[173] has contributed immeasurably to knowledge about tests through the *Mental Measurements Yearbooks,* which he has edited. Professional reviews of most tests in common use can be found in these volumes. With the publication of *Reading Tests and Reviews* (1968), Buros made available the wealth of material to be found in the reading sections of the first six *Mental Measurements Yearbooks.*

For many years, testing and evaluation were virtually synonymous. Indeed, achievement testing has had a long, if not always glorious, history in the United States. Horace Mann recognized the need for comparative data as early as 1845, but it was J. M. Rice who became the "father" of modern educational testing with the publication of his famous study of achievement in spelling in 1897. It initiated a movement of profound importance in American education. The following years saw the development of standardized tests in many subject matter and skills areas. Significant advances in testing resulted from insights gained during several large-scale studies, including the Eight-Year Study of the Progressive Education Association (1942), which used objective measures to evaluate a broad range of educational objectives rather than solely factual information.

Traditionally, school people have attempted to improve instruction by examining the results of achievement testing programs. Intermediate goals for using test scores in reading can be differentiated as (1) *placement* of pupils in classes or groups according to their knowledge or skill in reading; (2) *diagnosis* of pupil weaknesses for the purpose of focusing remediation; (3) *assessment* of change in pupil progress after a period of instruction; (4) *prediction* of pupil achievement or chances for success; and (5) *evaluation* of the school reading program to learn how effective it is. Over the years, testing has served many useful purposes.

Obviously, testing and/or measurement and evaluation are related. There are, however, important distinctions between them. A major distinction pertains to educational objectives: evaluation is related to the full range of objectives about which a school or teacher is concerned, whereas testing is limited to specific purposes, such as the measurement of skill in word recognition. In addition, tests, by nature of their standardization on groups of children, provide information about group progress or about individuals in comparison with norming populations. As Ammons notes, "Evaluation . . . is the description of the progress of an individual toward certain objectives about which standardized information may not be available."[174]

Changing Practices

Undoubtedly, one of the major changes during recent years has centered around the concept of evaluation as involving more than the collection and analysis of information. Generally speaking, evaluation is a four-step process:

(1) stating purposes according to the needs of an educational community; (2) obtaining evidence as to how well these purposes are being realized; (3) interpreting the collected information; and (4) redefining goals, establishing new purposes, and planning appropriate programs to achieve the modified purposes. Only through this complete process can useful information be provided for judging decision alternatives; for, as Strang points out, "evaluation helps produce growth as well as appraise it."[175]

In the last decade, school people grew noticeably reluctant to use standardized test results as the chief determinants of the quality of educational programs. They realized increasingly that evaluation must examine behavior in its broadest sense with emphasis on the interrelated aspects of thinking, feeling, and overt actions. They moved toward a broader concept of evaluation for a number of reasons: (1) an emphasis on individualization and the decline of ability grouping made group scores less valuable; (2) dramatic curriculum changes invalidated tests deemed appropriate as measures of previous course content; and (3) a growing concern for the misuses of tests, such as placing too much confidence in their results and misinterpreting test scores, caused many to turn to other evaluative procedures. Furthermore, school people became interested primarily in assessing the impact of instruction on the acquisition of skills and understandings rather than on fact-finding abilities.

A widely accepted use of informal, or teacher-constructed, evaluative procedures for instructional purposes has become evident in recent years. These informal devices, which supplement more formal measures, may include such items as checklists, questionnaires, records of books read, reading inventories, learner self-appraisals, teachers' anecdotal reports, descriptions of teacher-learner conferences, and direct observations of the learner at work. The teacher's continuing appraisal of the learner, based on the methods and materials of instruction, provides excellent information about his progress, which then becomes an integral part of the learner's instructional program.

Many schools are presently reformulating the objectives of their reading programs, often stating them in behavioral terms.[176] Whether objectives are determined logically according to analyses of learning processes and content (taxonomies), the structure of discipline (Bruner), or behavior (Mager), or they are based on the theoretical approaches of Guilford (intellect) or Gagné (learning), they must be defined clearly. Vopni (1968–1969) uses a series of questions to test for clarity:

> Who is to exhibit the behavior? What action is the learner expected to perform? What is the situation that stimulates the learner's performance? What object is being acted upon or interacted with? What constitutes the set of acceptable responses? What special constraints or restrictions or limitations, such as time and materials available, are imposed?[177]

When reading skills are translated into specifically stated objectives, teachers are able, as perhaps never before, to place children in the skills continuum where they can perform successfully.

Glaser (1963) introduced the concept of criterion-referenced measures.[178] According to this concept, the teacher is able to determine student achievement by using a criterion that shows a student's degree of competence, independent of the performance of others. In this way, the teacher becomes more knowledgeable about the reading skills a pupil can, or cannot, apply, and the pupil's actual performance provides the information essential for appropriate prescriptions.

The evolution of American society plays a prominent role in changing evaluation techniques by creating new conditions for education that make possible different approaches in working with children. Such changes are inevitable because new educational practices require different evaluative procedures. The widespread interest in programed instruction, for example, generated a yearbook of the National Society for the Study of Education (1967) in which Dale[179] describes certain characteristics of former innovations that have been combined in programed instruction: activity analysis and specification of behavioral objectives; criterion tests of terminal behavior; and feedback on the results of learning efforts and instructional designs.

No one can debate the fact that marked changes in collecting and utilizing data occurred during the 1960s. Giant electronic computers followed by newer minisized ones collated and analyzed information at incredible speeds. But technology, notwithstanding, school people still must make decisions about what data to collect and how to use them. Finally, these data must be placed in proper perspective through relevant interpretation by the groups concerned.

National Assessment

During the 1960s, national assessment of education became a highly controversial, much-discussed, and often misunderstood issue in the United States. By 1969, it was a reality: the first cross section of schoolchildren (ages 9, 13, and 17) and young adults (ages 26 through 35) was examined in science, citizenship, and writing. Progress in reading was part of the next testing cycle in 1970–1971.

This project represents the first comprehensive evaluation ever undertaken of the status of American education. When reports were released to the public they contained samples of items, along with percentages of examinees at various age levels who performed the exercises easily or with average or great difficulty. Educational policy makers expect to use the results in formulating decisions about school curriculum.

The objectives for each of the ten areas to be assessed are those that scholars, schools, and lay people consider important for American youth to acquire. In reading, for example, the general objectives include: comprehending what is read; analyzing what is read; using what is read; reasoning logically from what is read; making judgments about what is read; and having a lively interest in reading for pleasure and information.

An interesting distinction between standardized achievement testing and national assessment has been made. In national assessment the test item itself serves as the unit of interpretation, as in polling studies. Moreover, forthcoming generalizations will be related to the achievement of broad subclasses of population rather than to specific students, schools, or school systems. Stated in another way, assessment is concerned with how well a group of people can answer a question instead of how well an individual can answer a group of questions. The latter difference made the project more acceptable to educators who wished to forestall the inevitable comparisons between and among school systems. Results will be reported also by region, type of community, size of community, race, sex, and parents' educational attainment.

Francis Keppel, who conceived the idea for this type of educational census when he was U.S. Commissioner of Education, indicates that the value of national assessment will be apparent in a decade or so when future results can be compared with accumulated "bench marks."

Accountability

Today's critical new concept in evaluation is accountability. As adopted by the U.S. Office of Education's Bureau of Educational Personnel Development, accountability links student performance with teacher performance and shifts the primary responsibility for learning from the student to the school. If, as has been predicted, accountability becomes widespread in the 1970s, the accountability auditor will be an important addition to many school systems.

Performance contracting is a natural accompaniment of accountability. Recently, several independent firms, as well as educational textbook publishers, have underwritten, with a money-back guarantee, the total investment a school district makes in their materials. Pupil achievement will be measured by standardized reading tests selected by the schools. School systems will then be reimbursed at the end of the year in proportion to any failure of their classes to read according to or beyond a given level. An interesting modification of performance contracting is that teachers will be allowed to compete with contractors by receiving grants for developing contract projects.

Many of the newer tools for evaluation, such as criterion-referenced tests, task analysis, taxonomies of objectives, and analytical schemes for describing teaching, are associated with a concern for accountability. They are instruments for assessing the results of teaching procedures on learner behavior, educational innovations, and instructional methodology and materials.[180]

Teacher Education

Classroom Teachers

Enormously expanded enrollments in elementary and secondary schools during the period that followed the Second World War brought literally thousands of students into American colleges and universities. Moreover, increased numbers of pupils created a growing demand for college graduates to teach them and a great need for college personnel to teach the teachers—akin to a problem of geometric progression.

When collegiate institutions paused to recover their breath from the rocketing pace, many began to reexamine their offerings to prospective teachers with renewed vision and vigor. As a result, interest in the quality of teacher preparation gained unprecedented momentum during the last decade. This direction in higher education was somewhat overdue, for studies relating to teacher competence in the early 1960s rarely advocated the continuance of traditional preservice curricula. According to the Conant report[181] and the Harvard-Carnegie reading studies[182] such programs were no longer adequate; they prepared teachers neither for their present not future roles. Generally speaking, the reports of the 1960s encouraged the development of different strategies and experiences for those who would guide classroom activities during the latter part of the twentieth century.

That educators should look at the teacher and his training to improve pupil achievement in reading (rather than a specific method, material, or plan of organization), received substantial support from the findings of the well-known Cooperative Research Program in First Grade Reading Instruction (1967). From their analysis of data at the Coordinating Center, Bond and Dykstra proposed that

> Future research might well center on teacher and learning situation characteristics. ... The tremendous range among classrooms within any method points out the importance of elements in the learning situation over and above the methods employed. To improve reading instruction, it is necessary to train better teachers of reading rather than to expect a panacea in the form of materials.[183]

Similar findings by Harris and Morrison (1969) strengthened the superiority of the teacher's position. They stated that

> Costly procedures such as smaller classes and provision of auxiliary personnel may continue to give disappointing results if teaching skills are not improved. It is recommended, therefore, that inservice workshops and expert consultive help be provided for all teachers and especially for those with minimal experience.[184]

New models of teacher education are being designed in several locations. Not only will these models attempt to eliminate former deficiencies at the preservice and inservice levels, they also will be the result of recent developments in education and related fields.

With regard to weaknesses, the first Harvard-Carnegie study (1961)[185] made it clear that while college reading instructors had every reason to believe they would mold the future teaching practices of their students, such was not the case. School personnel agreed that cooperating teachers exerted unchallenged influence on the instructional behavior of beginning teachers. When college instructors were invited to enumerate reasons for this predicament, they suggested (1) insufficient time for needed course content; (2) absence of opportunities for student observations of skilled teaching of reading; (3) ill-timed placement of the "reading methods" course in the curriculum; and (4) apprenticeships that proved to be less than effectual in developing professional competence. Interviews revealed further that instructors seldom obtained feedback about how well their students performed during student-teaching periods to assist them in evaluating their course content. In addition, studies of inservice needs and deficiencies have been made to identify remediable areas.[186]

Obviously, one cannot learn to teach solely from textbooks or theoretical discussions. Such learning comes from involvement in at least three areas: the arts and sciences, the professional studies, and the schools. A notable trend toward greater flexibility in requirements occurred in many institutions of higher learning during the 1960s. The arts and sciences offer breadth in such multidisciplinary subjects as psychology, sociology, history, economics, literature, and linguistics. Proponents of newer approaches to teacher education, however, rarely assume the doctrinaire position that educators in the 1970s be enrolled in a curriculum that is completely oriented toward the liberal arts. On the contrary, most agree that students who are planning to teach should be exposed to a rich melange of courses while they are acquiring information in depth about the child, the school, and the learning process. Hence, many colleges are moving toward a distribution of study in the arts and sciences over the total training period, rather than adhering to the usual concentration of academic courses during the first two or three years.

In professional education, psychology of learning and educational philosophy are taking on new dimensions. Sound concepts of growth and development are vital components of the former, with emphasis on developmental imbalances as well as normalcies. Cognitive and affective factors are receiving more consideration, as are the learning styles of individual pupils. Increased attention is being given also to the theories of Piaget and Bruner, accompanied by suggested practices in classroom management arising from these theories. Ideally, too, prospective teachers of reading are gaining information about communication disorders and are becoming better acquainted with the work of vision, hearing, speech, and neurological specialists. Foundation courses (Introduction to Education) are being enriched by contributions from anthropology, political science, economics, sociology, history, and philosophy—often on a team-teaching basis. Sociology, in particular, is assuming greater importance because it holds the promise of clarifying the effect of social determinants on psychological processes. Furthermore, by the year 2000, it is anticipated that 60 per cent of the American population will be found in three major urban centers. Prospective teachers must acquire expertise in dealing with problems of low-income groups, especially in developing the language and reading skills of the economically deprived.

New programs are beginning to contain more study of evaluative procedures than in the past; included are the formulation of behavioral objectives, formal and informal tools of assessment, test construction theory and practice, formative and summative techniques, and curriculum revision.

The need for strengthening present courses in reading methodology has been well documented.[187] A number of colleges and universities now require at least two courses in reading for those who are preparing for elementary school certification, one in developmental and one in diagnostic and corrective techniques. Secondary teachers, to whom only limited offerings in the teaching of reading have been available in the past, have more opportunities to study developmental and remedial strategies, with attention being directed to the application of reading and study skills in the content areas.[188] A few institutions have expanded their roster at the undergraduate level to enable education majors who wish to specialize in the communication skills to take elective courses and/or independent study in this area.

Severe critics of contemporary teacher preparation contend that the hiatus between what the public expects of teachers and the kind of baccalaureate curriculum provided to meet these expectations is widening rather than closing. Although this may be true in some institutions, newer programs contain elements that ultimately will eliminate the distance between theory and practice. Earlier experiences with children in a variety of activities appear to be the real breakthrough to better teaching performance. Planned exposure and direct participation from the freshman year on should produce better results. According to this premise, many colleges are offering opportunities for students to serve as tutors, teacher-aides, and group workers at settlement houses and to observe in classrooms and reading centers. Close supervision by master teachers hired by colleges, sometimes on a two-year rotation basis, provides students with resource people for planning and follow-up discussions of their work with children. Without such resources, prospective teachers often find their initial efforts both frustrating and haphazard. During a third year, theory and practice are being combined again as teaching candidates observe and participate in regular classrooms and in university and school reading centers. They may also study two or three children to learn as much as possible about them physically, socially, and psychologically. Exploratory teaching in the junior year followed by student teaching in the senior year—both under the supervision of master teachers—is doing much to reduce the gap between campus theory and classroom practice in those institutions that retain a four-year program of teacher preparation. More schools are moving toward an intensive experience in one classroom and extensive participation in several classes for their students. This helps one to acquire a personal teaching style rather than become a carbon copy of one master teacher.[189]

Within recent years, several universities have extended teacher preparation from four to five years, recognizing that maturity and competency require additional time and training. The fifth year of preservice can be devoted to a paid internship in a classroom supervised by an able teacher and to further professional course work. Because the focus throughout the fifth year is often on learning by means of examined experiences, there may be opportunities for community study in which interns can observe and participate in activities in the community. Involvement is also possible through neighborhood committees and school and community organizations. Throughout teacher preparation, whether undertaken for four or five years, greater emphasis is being placed on relevant experiences, activities, and accomplishments.[190]

Future

Without doubt, a number of the innovations that will be made in education during the next decade will continue to be technological.[191] Much conventional course content can be mastered through electronic devices. Use of these instructional aids will free professors to devote time to achieving goals related to higher competencies, values, and social skills. College teachers are learning to use a variety of techniques to make reading practicum experiences valuable. Microteaching, for example, serves in many programs as an advantageous intermediate step between methods courses and actual classroom work. As preparation for student teaching, microteaching facilitates the examination of segments of the teaching-learning act, usually for the purpose of concentrating on the development of specific competencies. After viewing his teaching efforts, the student can reteach the same concept to a new group and reanalyze his teaching skills. Although they are not new, simulation techniques are fairly recent additions to many teacher-preparation programs. Many common problem situations, such as specific teaching strategies, conferences with pupils and/or parents, and evaluation of learning, can be simulated for discussion purposes.

But a focus on teaching procedures and the dissemination of information makes sense only in an unchanging environment. Because dramatic changes are taking place, much greater emphasis must be placed in teacher-education programs on conditions that facilitate learning—on helping teachers understand *how, why, and when the child learns,* and how learning feels to the child from the inside. An important condition, obviously, is the quality of interpersonal relations between facilitator and learner. Increasingly, then, teacher education is attempting to expose and sensitize candidates to the subtleties of personality structure. Group dynamics, counseling techniques, and sensitivity training have become more prominent in the curricula.

Hamachek,[192] in reviewing research on teacher effectiveness, indicated the importance of instructional procedures and interaction styles as determinants of superior teaching. In both areas, Flanders[193] has contributed to the growing fund of knowledge, and his findings are being included in many undergraduate preparation programs. Effective procedures for working with groups and individuals are being developed through involvement in and examination of techniques employed in interaction analysis.

Research during the next decade should bring educators closer to an understanding of the specific forms of teacher behavior that affect the child's learning ability in reading. Questions such as, "Can teacher effectiveness be measured? Can degrees of competence in teaching be distinguished? What forms of motivations or class management may produce superior results? What forms of cognitive teacher behavior are related to good achievement?" are a few of the unanswered questions posed by Harris[194] and Artley.[195] As Artley points out

we should be able to indicate that a teacher who possesses certain characteristics, who uses certain techniques and certain types of instructional media, and who provides in certain ways for the differentiated needs of children, will stand greater chances of having learners who are higher on a scale of reading maturity than teachers who do not have these characteristics and understandings, and who do not perform these instructional acts.[196]

In the past, teachers reflected the strengths and shortcomings of the colleges that prepared them initially, the master teachers with whom they did their student teaching, and the school systems that employed them and provided in-service education for their continued professional growth. By the mid-1970s, several changes in teacher preparation may be in effect. School systems antici-pate dramatically different preschool and elementary school teachers by then, as products of a research program sponsored by the United States Office of Education's (USOE) National Center for Educational Research and Develop-ment. Most of the new teachers will be specialists in a particular area of elemen-tary education with broad knowledge in others.

New training programs call for *performance objectives, individualized instruc-tion,* and much *classroom experience with pupils.* For example, one performance objective in the teaching of reading might be that "the teacher should be able to select approaches for helping individual pupils acquire literal comprehension skills." The performance criterion might then be that "given three children who have not satisfied evaluative criteria for literal comprehension, the teacher will select (any given number) of approaches or materials—one or more of which will enable the children to pass the criterion test within three lessons."

Faced with an actual teaching-learning problem, the prospective teaching candidate seeks a solution by engaging in one or more alternative activities— the reading of professional books and journal articles on related topics, partici-pation in a microteaching clinic, attendance at a lecture, surveying and selecting materials at a curriculum center, or working with children. From these options, he should discover effective strategies for each of his three pupils. Even though the teaching strategies chosen by different candidates will vary, the final test remains constant: *does it work?* Subsequently, the prospective teacher will demonstrate his ability in a classroom setting to a team of trained observers before proceeding to the next performance objective.

Clearly, new teacher-education-program designs will recognize the need for more effective cooperative arrangements between schools and colleges. Both will share in the responsibility of preservice teacher training and in the continuing education of teachers on the job.

Reading Specialists

During the 1960s the shortage of qualified reading specialists became em-barrassingly apparent for several reasons. The burgeoning school population required not only more classroom teachers, many of whom lacked adequate preparation, but also greater numbers of specialists to meet the diverse needs of teachers and pupils. Furthermore, in some systems, positions in reading were created hastily to enable local projects to secure funding of compensatory education for disadvantaged children. Many colleges and universities contributed to the shortage by directing their attention to the preparation of specialized personnel in reading only recently. The limited number of trained specialists led to the placement of able classroom teachers in positions for which they were singularly unequipped. Later, these teachers attempted to develop competency through inservice work, participation in government-financed reading institutes and fellowship programs, and university courses in reading and related areas. As a result, there are more well-qualified persons in the reading profession today than at any time in the past, although the demand still exceeds the supply.

Just as there are differences in availability of reading personnel, there are differences in job titles and functions, largely because of the shifting emphasis in the roles of certain specialists. For example, in moving from a traditional supervisory concept of teacher observation, conferences, and information giving to a program in which the staff cooperatively gathers and exchanges professional knowledge, the reading consultant must often be a coordinator, a facilitator, and a person who creates a climate for the personal growth of each staff member through group processes.[197] Although some disagreement about roles exists among writers, Robinson's (1969)[198] delineation will be helpful in classifying responsibilities of specialists bearing such titles as *remedial reading teacher, reading clinician, reading consultant, reading coordinator, college teachers of reading,* and *researchers in reading.*

Similarly, differences exist among programs designed to prepare reading specialists. Colleges and universities offering preparation do so most frequently at the master's degree (fifth year) level either in reading *per se* or in other areas with a major in reading. A small number of institutions enroll students in sixth-year-certificate (advanced study) programs in reading, and several give an Ed.D. and/or a Ph.D. Post-Doctoral training in reading is virtually non-existent at this time.

Almost without exception, college reading programs meet and surpass state certification requirements where they exist and the recommended minimum standards of the IRA (1968). The latter's recommendations pertain to the training of two categories of reading personnel: those who work directly with children either as reading teachers or reading clinicians and those who work directly with teachers as consultants or supervisors with prime responsibility for staff and program. Intended for these specialists, the minimum standards demand three years of successful classroom experience as a prerequisite to admission to a planned graduate training program in which the prospective reading specialist should take a minimum of twelve semester hours in graduate-level reading courses. These courses include (1) foundation or survey of reading; (2) diagnosis and correction of reading disabilities; and (3) clinical or laboratory practicum in reading, which provides supervised practice in diagnosis and remedial instruction. To complete the Master's degree program, the special reading teacher may select from among courses in measurement and/or evaluation, psychology, literature for children and/or adolescents, and related areas. A sixth year of graduate study is recommended for those who wish to become reading clinicians, reading consultants, or reading supervisors.

Two sources of information about college curricula for preparing reading specialists will be useful. Both Robinson (1969) and Austin (1968) present common and unique elements of the programs offered for each specialty.[199]

For the reading specialist, particularly, there should be continuous access to further formal education and other forms of professional stimulation. He must become a "self-teacher" who seeks personal ways of "self-renewal." Only through this combination can the quality of leaders be assured for the improvement of reading instruction in the United States.

Researchers in Reading

Ideally, the activities of the professor of reading should reflect an appropriate balance between teaching and research, both in preparation for and fulfillment of his role in a college or university setting. Until recently, however, his training has led to research production that has been less impressive than his success in the instructional realm. Now, more than in the past, the professor's research efforts and skills appear to be receiving higher priority as a result of supportive funds from foundations and governmental agencies. Hopefully, better training and a higher regard for undertaking worthwhile studies will result in quality output.

The program for training researchers in reading probably will continue to include a block of formal study in research design and methodology. Statistical and computer analysis techniques will be developed, as well as measurement and evaluation procedures. Over and beyond these basic courses, increased attention is given in many programs to the importance of an internship, perhaps by means of a special residency in local schools where the trainee will have ample opportunity to gain guided firsthand knowledge and experience through participation in evaluative and experimental studies.

Throughout his advanced work in reading, the Doctoral candidate should receive training in research procedures by involvement in departmental projects or in studies conducted by his major professor. Several research or studies centers throughout the country offer appropriate facilities and personnel for basic research on problems and processes of reading education. Participation in these projects from the formulation and proposal-writing stages through the funding, implementation, analysis, and evaluation phases should expose the prospective researcher-teacher to problems during a period of careful supervision before he undertakes independent studies. A group project often has the further advantage of permitting the student to assume responsibility for special portions of the total project, thus offering practical experience in conducting and reporting his assigned areas. Through such experiences, too, the faculty become colleagues with students in the learning enterprise.

Moreover, Doctoral students should have opportunities to affiliate with a research and development center for additional on-the-job training when such facilities are available. Such centers usually focus on significant areas in education and encourage interdisciplinary approaches to studies of cognitive behavior, learning theories, sociology of educational innovations, and others.

Flexibility in the training of the researcher-teacher can be obtained through independent study and research seminars. Because Doctoral candidates have ability, enthusiasm, and energy, they must find value and relevance in their professional studies. The researcher-teacher will be in the enviable position of being able to dispell the false dichotomy of long-standing: the educator who overemphasizes techniques to the neglect of the art and science of teaching, while the academic ignores the realities of schools and the needs of children.

In this age of human unrest and technological marvels, teaching is a challenging profession at all levels. It is especially challenging for the researcher-teacher in higher education. His direct influence on those who serve in the nation's schools, when combined with the indirect influence that he exerts over the thousands of pupils in the classrooms of teachers whom he has trained in reading, places an awesome responsibility on his shoulders. To succeed in this role, the researcher-teacher must be a highly creative, provocative person—one who is as exciting in his college classroom or seminar as he is in his area of research speciality.

Concluding Statement

In the United States, the broad aims of education remain relatively unchanged, but the means of obtaining them have altered notably. The general goals are well expressed by Piaget (1964) who wrote,

> The principal goal of education is to create men who are capable of doing new things, not simply of repeating what other generations have done—men who are creative, inventive, and discoverers. The second goal of education is to form minds which can be critical, can verify, and not accept everything they are offered. The great danger today is of slogans, collective opinions, ready-made trends of thought. We have to be able to resist individually, to criticize, to distinguish between what is proven and what is not. So we need pupils who are active, who learn early to find out for themselves, partly through their own spontaneous activity and partly through materials we set up for them.[200]

It is the need for individuals who are creative and critical thinkers that provides the impetus for improved reading instruction and, in particular, for increased individualization of instruction.

Clearly the predominant characteristic of American education in the present decade will be one of change. Pressures from both inside and outside the schools have led to organizational and curricular revisions. In contrast to the last decade, however—which may be described as a period of change for the sake of change, a time when the pendulum tended to swing from one extreme to its opposite—the 1970s may prove more rational. Researchers and practitioners realize more fully that desired changes in the learner are the true goals of education, and that instructional methods and materials are but the "means" to produce these changes.[201]

Undoubtedly, the most important trend of the last few years has been toward the individualization of instruction—away from rigid patterns of classroom and school organization to informal, independent learning opportunities in which progress is evaluated according to the learner's own pace.

Impressive as the change appears, the extent is limited to a scattering of schools. Within them, the quality varies from outstanding to good, and elementary schools exceed secondary in innovative practices. The large measure of autonomy enjoyed by administrators and teachers within decentralized school systems encourages experimentation with new approaches, especially in systems where professional leadership for innovation is exceptional.

Although the tempo for experimentation in reading continues to accelerate, there remains a mountain of unanswered questions. In all probability, greater efforts toward the definition of the essential features of effective learner-centered reading programs will be made in the 1970s. The Cooperative First Grade Studies[202] indicate the need to concentrate research on the entire learning situation; that is, the interaction of pupil, materials, classroom environment, and teacher behavior. Chall[203] also points to the need for precision in defining reading and its component parts. Another line of investigation might be to determine the nature and causes of reading pathology. Studies of motivation could supply a better understanding of the effects of extrinsic and intrinsic "rewards." These are only a few of several possibilities.

Much of the research in reading has been criticized for its fragmentary nature. Perhaps this phenomenon results when investigators undertake studies that appear to arise *ex nihilo:* each new group is left to "reinvent the wheel," as it were, through its inability to see the field in perspective. Chall states the necessity for "synthesizers and theorists—people who pull together the evidence from the hundreds and thousands of small studies and try to build theories."[204] Research workers could select from among the best-related studies or theories, cast them into meaningful models, and test those that emerge for their effectiveness in classroom settings. This task is, in and of itself, monumental, but the replication of the best studies in a variety of locales and with pupils of different capabilities and backgrounds would in time produce an impressive data bank from which new programs might be conceived.

Today, reading as a field of study attracts a wider range of professionals. Psychologists, social scientists, instructional technologists, measurement specialists, philosophers, sociologists, medical personnel, linguists, and educators are attempting to eliminate reading failures by improving reading practices. Spache[205] and Jenkinson[206] discuss the interaction between and among the disciplines, describing past and potential contributions of research in allied fields to the knowledge essential for teaching reading. Although many participants view their efforts as disparate contributions, several interprofessional groups are actively engaged in the prevention and correction of reading problems.

It is encouraging to note also that interest in cross-national studies of reading has grown since Gray's[207] international survey of the teaching of reading and writing. Some comparative studies in reading have been conducted by Preston[208] of word-recognition skills of German and American children, and by Hildreth,[209] who reports on reading in the Arabic, Armenian, and Greek languages. Myriad factors make cross-national investigations a fertile field for research. Studies in mathematics by Husén[210] may provide a model for future cooperative reading research.

With the establishment of the new Targeted Research and Development Program on Reading by the U.S. Office of Education, it now appears that every child will move closer to becoming a competent adult reader. With this goal as a beacon, three projects have been initiated: (1) the development of a criterion test for 10-year-olds that will predict adult reading ability; (2) an examination of the professional literature to determine what is already known and what remains to be learned in order to produce models of the reading process, of the beginning reading process, and of language development; and (3) the construction of a profile of reading achievement in the nation by age, sex, ethnic background, and other factors. The over-all nature of the Targeted Research and Development Program on Reading is detailed by Penney and Hjelm[211] and Gephart.[212]

Within the last several years, the U.S. Office of Education has allocated nearly $12 million for 257 separate reading research projects. Large additional sums have been invested in support of reading research through the Educational Laboratories and the Research and Development Centers. Moreover, the U.S. Office of Education continues to demonstrate strong commitment to research in this critical area of the curriculum.[213]

Following a study of recent research findings in reading in order to identify major research needs, Penney and Hjelm (1970) concluded that a new program of research in reading is essential. They have outlined some of its desirable features:

> its initial focus should be upon basic research and theory-building rather than upon instructional approaches; it should encourage active collaboration among many scientific disciplines; its component projects should be clearly and logically related to each other so that they could have cumulative impact.[214]

Hopefully, the possibility of this important shift in policy in the U.S. Office of Education's support of reading research will add further insight into the reading related processes that will enable American educators to provide dramatically improved instruction in reading for the 1980s.

REFERENCES

1. Dodds, William J., "Highlights from the history of reading instruction," *The Reading Teacher,* **21** (December 1967), 274–280.
2. Smith, Nila Banton, *American Reading Instruction,* New York: Silver Burdett, 1934, 2nd rev. ed., Newark, Del.: IRA, 1965.
3. Mathews, Mitford M., *Teaching to Read: Historically Considered,* Chicago: U. of Chicago, 1966.

4. Staiger, Ralph C., "The geology of reading," in Downing, John, and Brown, Amy L. (eds.), *The Second International Reading Symposium,* London: Cassell, 1967.

5. Dodds, *op. cit.*

6. Staiger, *op. cit.,* p. 4.

7. Smith, *op. cit.*

8. Goodman, Kenneth S., "Dialect barriers to reading comprehension," in Baratz, Joan C., and Shuy, Roger W. (eds.), *Teaching Black Children to Read,* Washington, D.C.: Center for Applied Linguistics, 1969, pp. 14–28.

9. Morris, Joyce, "Barriers to successful reading for second-language students at the secondary level," *TESOL Quarterly,* 2 (September 1968), 158–162.

10. Nance, A. D., "Teaching English to speakers of other languages: Problems in California," *On Teaching English to Speakers of Other Languages,* Champaign, Ill.: NCTE, 1965. pp. 33–37.

11. Rosen, C. L., and Ortego, P. D., "Language and reading problems of Spanish speaking children in the Southwest," *Journal of Reading Behavior,* 1 (Winter 1969), 51–70.

12. Bond, Burtis, "Some aspects of educating the Cuban refugee student," *Clearing House,* 38 (October 1963), 77–79.

13. Finocchiaro, Mary, *English As a Second Language: From Theory to Practice,* New York: Regents Publishing Company, 1964. Also, *Teaching English As a Second Language,* New York: Harper, 1958.

14. Morris, *op. cit.*

15. Rosen and Ortego, *op. cit.*

16. Modiano, Nancy, "National or mother language in beginning reading: A comparative study," *Research in the Teaching of English,* 2 (Spring 1968), 32–43.

17. Gardener, R. C., "Attitudes and motivation: Their role in second language acquisition," *TESOL Quarterly,* 2 (September 1968), 141–150.

18. Yates, Alfred (ed.), *Grouping in Education,* New York: Wiley, 1966.

19. Anderson, Robert H., and Ritsher, Cynthia, "Pupil progress," in Ebel, Robert L. (ed.), *Encyclopedia of Educational Research,* 4th ed., New York: Macmillan, 1969, pp. 1050–1062.

20. Sartain, Harry W., "Organizational patterns of schools and classrooms for reading instruction," in Robinson, Helen M. (ed.), *Innovation and Change in Reading Instruction,* 67th Yearbook of the NSSE, Part 2, Chicago: U. of Chicago, 1968, pp. 195–236.

21. "Middle schools in theory and fact," *National Education Association, Research Bulletin,* 47 (May 1969), 49–52.

22. Rollins, Sidney P., *Developing Nongraded Schools,* Itasca, Ill.: F. E. Peacock, 1968, p. 19.

23. Goodlad, John I., and Anderson, Robert H., *The Nongraded Elementary School,* rev. ed., New York: Harcourt, 1963.

24. Brown, B. Frank, *The Nongraded High School,* Englewood Cliffs, N.J.: Prentice-Hall, 1963.

25. "Nongraded school organization," *National Education Association, Research Bulletin,* 43 (October 1965), 93–95.

26. "Educational family units," *Newsreport,* 4 (February 1970), 17.

27. Powell, William R., "The Joplin plan: An evaluation," *Elementary School Journal,* 64 (April 1964), 387–393.

28. Austin, Mary C., and Morrison, Coleman, *The First R: The Harvard Report on Reading in Elementary Schools,* New York: Macmillan, 1963, pp. 73–74.
29. Shane, Harold G., "Grouping in the elementary school," *Phi Delta Kappan,* **41** (April 1960), 313–318.
30. Gray, William S., "The evolution of patterns of instructional organization," in Robinson, Helen M. (ed.), *Reading Instruction in Various Patterns of Grouping, Supplementary Educational Monographs, No. 89,* Chicago: U. of Chicago, December 1959, pp. 14–19.
31. Robinson, Helen M. (ed.), *Evaluation of Reading, Supplementary Educational Monographs, No. 88,* Chicago: U. of Chicago, 1958. Also, *Reading Instruction in Various Patterns of Grouping, Supplementary Educational Monographs, No. 89,* Chicago: U. of Chicago, 1959.
32. Shaplin, Judson T., and Olds, Henry F., Jr. (eds.), *Team Teaching,* New York: Harper, 1964.
33. Tewksbury, John L., *Nongrading in the Elementary School,* Columbus, Ohio: Merrill, 1967.
34. Washburne, Carleton W. (ed.), *Adapting the Schools to Individual Differences,* 24th Yearbook of the NSSE, Part 2, Chicago: U. of Chicago, 1925.
35. Smith, *op. cit.,* p. 378.
36. Lazar, May (ed.), *A Practical Guide to Individualized Reading,* Board of Education Publication No. 40, New York: Bureau of Educational Research, 1960, p. 76.
37. Olson, Willard C., "Seeking, self-selection and pacing in the use of books by children," *The Packet,* **7** (Spring 1952), 3–10.
38. Spache, George D., and Spache, Evelyn B., *Reading in the Elementary School,* Boston: Allyn, 1969, p. 128. Also, Spache, George D., *Classroom Organization for Reading Instruction: An Annotated Bibliography,* Newark, Del.: IRA, 1965.
39. Veatch, Jeanette, *Individualizing Your Reading Program,* New York: Putnam, 1959. Also, *Reading in the Elementary School,* New York: Ronald, 1966.
40. Hunt, Lyman C., Jr. (ed.), *The Individualized Reading Program,* Proceedings of the Annual Convention, No. 11, Vol. 2, Part 3, Newark, Del.: IRA, 1967.
41. Barbe, Walter B., *Educator's Guide to Personalized Reading Instruction,* Englewood Cliffs, N.J.: Prentice-Hall, 1961.
42. Brogan, Peggy, and Fox, Lorene K., *Helping Children Read,* New York: Holt, 1961.
43. Darrow, Helen Fisher, and Howes, Virgil M., *Approaches to Individualized Reading,* New York: Appleton, 1960.
44. Stauffer, Russell G. (ed.), *Individualizing Reading Instruction,* Proceedings of the 39th Annual Conference, Vol. 6, Newark, Del.: Reading-Study Center, University of Delaware, 1957.
45. Stoff, S., and Schwartzberg, H., *The Human Encounter: Readings in Education,* New York: Harper, 1964, p. 420.
46. Durkin, Dolores, *Teaching Them to Read,* Boston: Allyn, 1970, p. 21.
47. Arthur, Grace, "A quantitative study of the results of grouping first grade children according to mental age," *Journal of Educational Research,* **12** (October 1925), 173–185.
48. Morphett, M. V., and Washburne, C., "When should children begin to read?" *Elementary School Journal,* **31** (March 1931), 496–503.
49. Gates, Arthur I., "The necessary mental age for beginning reading," *Elementary School Journal,* **37** (March 1937), 497–508.

50. Gates, Arthur I., and Bond, Guy, "Reading readiness: A study of factors determining success and failure in beginning reading," *Teachers College Record,* **37** (May 1936), 679–685.
51. Bruner, Jerome S., *The Process of Education,* Cambridge: Harvard U.P., 1960, p. 33.
52. Hunt, James McVicker, *Intelligence and Experience,* New York: Ronald, 1961.
53. Bloom, Benjamin S., *Stability and Change in Human Characteristics,* New York: Wiley, 1964.
54. Durkin, Dolores, "A fifth-year report on the achievement of early readers," *Elementary School Journal,* **65** (November 1964), 76–80. Also, "Children who read before grade I: A second study," *Elementary School Journal,* **64** (December 1963), 143–148.
55. Brzeinski, Joseph E., "Beginning reading in Denver," *The Reading Teacher,* **18** (October 1964), 16–21. Also Brzeinski, Joseph E., Harrison, M. Lucile, and McKee, Paul, "Should Johnny read in the kindergarten?" *The Education Digest,* **33** (October 1967), 44–46.
56. "Kindergarten education, 1967–68," *National Education Association, Research Bulletin,* **47** (March 1969), 10–13.
57. Durkin, Dolores, "When should children begin to read?" in Robinson, Helen M. (ed.), *Innovation and Change in Reading Instruction,* 67th Yearbook of the NSSE, Part 2, Chicago: U. of Chicago, 1968, pp. 30–71.
58. King, Ethel M., "Beginning reading: When and how," *The Reading Teacher,* **22** (March 1969), 550–553. Also, Durkin, "When should children begin to read?" *op. cit.*
59. MacGinitie, Walter H., "Evaluating readiness for learning to read: A critical review and evaluation of research," *Reading Research Quarterly,* **4** (Spring 1969), 396–410.
60. Barrett, Thomas C., "The relationship between measures of pre-reading visual discrimination and first-grade reading achievement: A review of the literature," *Reading Research Quarterly,* **1** (Fall 1965), 51–76.
61. MacGinitie, *op. cit.,* p. 410.
62. Grimes, Jesse W., and Allinsmith, Wesley, "Compulsivity, anxiety, and school achievement," *Merrill-Palmer Quarterly,* **7** (October 1961), 247–271.
63. *Education USA, Washington Monitor,* Washington, D.C.: National School Public Relations Association, April 20, 1970, pp. 187–192.
64. Clymer, Theodore, "What is 'reading'?: Some current concepts," in Robinson, Helen, M. (ed.), *Innovation and Change in Reading Instruction,* 67th Yearbook of the NSSE, Part 2, Chicago: U. of Chicago, 1968, pp. 7–29.
65. Bond, Guy, and Dykstra, Robert, *Coordinating Center for the First Grade Reading Instruction Programs,* Final Report of USOE Project 5–0341, ERIC Document No. ED 013714, Minneapolis, Minn.: University of Minnesota, 1967. Also "The cooperative research program in first grade reading," *Reading Research Quarterly,* **2** (Summer 1967), 5–142.
66. Dykstra, Robert, "Classroom implications of the first-grade studies," in Ketcham, Clay A. (ed.), *Professional Focus on Reading,* Proceedings of the College Reading Association Conference, Vol. 9, 1968, pp. 53–59.
67. *Ibid.,* pp. 58–59.
68. Bush, Clifford L., and Huebner, Mildred H., *Strategies for Reading in the Elementary School,* New York: Macmillan, 1970; Chall, Jeanne, *Learning To Read:*

The Great Debate, New York: McGraw-Hill, 1967; Dechant, Emerald V., *Improving the Teaching of Reading,* 2nd ed., Englewood Cliffs, N.J.: Prentice-Hall, 1970; Durkin, *Teaching Them to Read, op. cit.;* Smith, Nila B., *Reading Instruction for Today's Children,* N.J.: Prentice-Hall, 1965; Spache and Spache, *op. cit.;* Tinker, Miles A., and McCullough, Constance M., *Teaching Elementary Reading,* 3rd ed., New York: Appleton, 1968; Wittick, Mildred Letton, "Innovations in reading instruction: For beginners," in Robinson, Helen M., (ed.), *Innovations and Change in Reading Instruction,* 67th Yearbook of the NSSE, Part 2, Chicago: U. of Chicago, 1968, pp. 72–125.

69. Bloom, Benjamin S., *et al., Taxonomy of Educational Objectives, Handbook I, Cognitive Domain,* New York: McKay, 1956, p. 119. Also, Krathwohl, David R., Bloom, B. S., and Masia, B. B., *Taxonomy of Educational Objectives: Handbook II: Affective Domain,* New York: McKay, 1964.

70. "'Buyer be wary' cautions IRA," *The Reading Teacher,* **20** (April 1967), 599.

71. Penty, Ruth, *Reading Ability and High School Dropouts,* New York: Bureau of Publications, Teachers College, Columbia University, 1956.

72. Bledsoe, Joseph, "An investigation of six correlates of student withdrawal from high school," *Journal of Educational Research,* **53** (September 1959), 3–6.

73. Nachman, Leonard, Getson, Russell, and Odgers, John, *Pilot Study of Ohio High School Dropouts, 1961–62,* Columbus: State Department of Education, 1963.

74. Whitmore, P., and Chapman, P., *Dropout Incidence and Significance at Modesto High Schools, 1961–64,* Modesto, Calif.: Modesto Public Schools, 1965.

75. Lietwiler, Helena Keehne, "A descriptive study of reading programs and practices in public high schools in the United States," *Dissertation Abstracts,* No. 10, 3895–A, Washington, D.C.: George Washington University, 1967.

76. DeBoer, John, and Whipple, Gertrude, "Reading development in other curriculum areas," in Witty, Paul A. (chairman), *Development In and Through Reading,* 60th Yearbook of the NSSE, Part I, Chicago: U. of Chicago, 1961, pp. 54–74.

77. Moore, Walter J., "What does research in reading reveal—About reading in the content fields?" *English Journal,* **58** (May 1969), 707–718.

78. Huus, Helen, "Innovations in reading instruction: At later levels," in Robinson, Helen M. (ed.), *Innovation and Change in Reading Instruction,* 67th Yearbook of the NSSE, Part 2, Chicago: U. of Chicago, 1968, pp. 126–158.

79. Artley, A. Sterl, *Trends and Practices in Secondary School Reading,* Newark, Del.: IRA, 1968.

80. McCullough, Constance M., "What does research in reading reveal—About practices in teaching reading?" *English Journal,* **58** (May 1969), 688–706.

81. Moore, *op. cit.*

82. Karlin, Robert, "What does research in reading reveal—About reading and the high school student?" *English Journal,* **58** (March 1969), 386–395.

83. Herber, Harold L. (compiler and ed.), *Developing Study Skills in Secondary Schools, Perspectives in Reading, No. 4,* Newark, Del.: IRA, 1965.

84. Bamman, Henry A., Hogan, Ursula, and Greene, Charles B., *Reading Instruction in the Secondary Schools,* New York: McKay, 1961.

85. Strang, Ruth, McCullough, Constance, and Traxler, Arthur, *The Improvement of Reading,* 4th ed., New York: McGraw-Hill, 1967.

86. Marksheffel, Ned D., *Better Reading in the Secondary School,* New York: Ronald, 1966.

87. Dawson, Mildred A. (compiler), *Developing High School Reading Programs,* Newark, Del.: IRA, 1967.

88. Hafner, Lawrence E., *Improving Reading in Secondary Schools,* New York: Macmillan, 1967.

89. Sheldon, William D., "Reading instruction in junior high school," in Witty, Paul A. (ed.), *Development In and Through Reading,* 60th Yearbook of the NSSE, Part I, Chicago: U. of Chicago, 1961, pp. 305–319.

90. McCullough, *op. cit.,* p. 689.

91. Russell, David H., *Children's Thinking,* Boston: Ginn, 1956. Also, "The prerequisite: Knowing how to read critically," *Elementary English,* **40** (October 1963), 579–582.

92. Davis, Frederick B., *Identification and Measurement of Reading Skills of High School Students,* Philadelphia: University of Pa., 1967.

93. Cleland, Donald L., "A construct of comprehension," in Figurel, J. Allen (ed.), *Reading and Inquiry,* Proceedings of the Annual Convention. No. 10, Newark, Del.: IRA, 1965. pp. 59–64.

94. Barrett, Thomas C., "Goals of the reading program: The basis for evaluation," in Barrett, Thomas C. (compiler and ed.), *The Evaluation of Children's Reading Achievement, Perspectives in Reading, No. 8,* Newark, Del.: IRA, 1967, pp. 13–26.

95. Robinson, Helen M., "Developing critical readers," in Stauffer, Russell (ed.), *Dimensions of Critical Reading,* Newark, Del.: University of Delaware, 1964, pp. 1–12.

96. Mueller, Ruth G., *Personality Attributes and Teacher Training As They Relate to Pupil Cognitive Skill Development of Critical Reading Ability,* unpublished Ph.D. dissertation, Cleveland, Ohio: Department of Education, Case Western Reserve University, 1970, pp. 2–3.

97. Huelsman, Charles B., Jr., "Promoting growth in ability to interpret when reading critically: In grades seven to ten," in Gray, William S. (ed.), *Promoting Growth Toward Maturity in Interpreting What Is Read, Supplementary Educational Monographs, No. 74.* Chicago: U. of Chicago, 1951, pp. 149–153.

98. Livingston, Howard, "An investigation of the effect of instruction in general semantics on critical reading ability," *California Journal of Educational Research,* **16** (March 1965), 93–96.

99. Russell, "The prerequisite: Knowing how to read critically," *op. cit.,* p. 579.

100. Burton, W. H., Kimball, R. B., and Wing, R. L., *Education for Effective Thinking,* New York: Appleton, 1960.

101. Harvison, Alan R., "Critical reading for elementary pupils," *The Reading Teacher,* **21** (December 1967), 244–247.

102. Lorge, Irving, "The teacher's task in the development of thinking," *The Reading Teacher,* **13** (February 1960), 170–175.

103. Taba, Hilda, *Teaching Strategies and Cognitive Functioning in Elementary School Children,* Cooperative Research USOE Project No. 2404, San Francisco, Calif.: San Francisco State College, 1966.

104. Schreiber, Joan E., "Teachers' question-asking techniques in social studies," *Dissertation Abstracts,* No. 28: 523–A., Iowa City: University of Iowa, 1967.

105. Sanders, Norris M., *Classroom Questions,* New York: Harper, 1966.

106. Bloom, *et al., op. cit.*

107. Guszak, Frank J., "Teachers' questions and levels of reading comprehension," in Barrett, Thomas C. (compiler and ed.), *The Measurement of Children's Reading*

Achievement, Perspectives in Reading, No. 8, Newark, Del.: IRA, 1967, pp. 97–109.

108. Glaser, E. M., *An Experiment in the Development of Critical Thinking, Contributions to Education, No. 843,* New York: Bureau of Publications, Teachers College, Columbia University, 1941.

109. Flanders, Ned, "Teacher influence in the classroom," in Amidon, Edmund J., and Hough, John (eds.), *Interaction Analysis: Theory, Research, and Application,* Reading, Mass.: Addison-Wesley, 1967.

110. Marksheffel, *op. cit.,* p. 257.

111. Wolf, Willavene, "The logical dimension of critical reading," in Figurel, J. Allen (ed.), *Reading and Inquiry,* Proceedings of the Annual Convention, No. 10, Newark, Del.: IRA, 1965, pp. 121–124. Also, Wolf, Willavene, Huck, Charlotte S., and King, Martha L., *Critical Reading Ability of Elementary School Children,* USOE Cooperative Research Project No. 5–1040, Columbus: Research Foundation, Ohio State University, 1967. Also, Saadeh, Ibraham Q., "The teacher and the development of critical thinking," *Journal of Research and Development in Education,* 3 (Fall 1969), 87–99.

112. Wolf, Willavene, "A factor analytic study of the Ohio State University critical reading tests," *Journal of Research and Development in Education,* 3 (Fall 1969), 100–109.

113. Marksheffel, *op. cit.,* p. 253.

114. Chase, Francis S., "Demands on the reader in the next decade," in Robinson, Helen M. (ed.), *Controversial Issues in Reading and Promising Solutions, Supplementary Educational Monographs, No. 91,* Chicago: U. of Chicago, 1961, pp. 7–18.

115. Smith, Nila Banton, "Patterns of writing in different subject areas—Part I," *Journal of Reading,* 8 (October 1964), 31–37. Also, "Patterns of writing in different subject areas—Part II," *Journal of Reading,* 8 (November 1964), 97–102.

116. Dale, Edgar, and Razik, Taher, *Bibliography of Vocabulary Studies,* 2nd ed., Columbus: Bureau of Educational Research, Ohio State University, 1963.

117. Allen, James E., Jr., "Target for the 70's," *American Education,* 5 (December 1969), 2–4.

118. National Advisory Committee on Dyslexia and Related Reading Disorders, *Reading Disorders in the United States,* Washington, D.C.: Department of Health, Education, and Welfare, August 1969, p. 8.

119. de Hirsch, Katrina, Jansky, Jeanette J., and Langford, William S., *Predicting Reading Failure: A Preliminary Study,* New York: Harper, 1966.

120. Harris, Albert J., "Diagnosis and remedial instruction in reading," in Robinson, Helen M. (ed.), *Innovation and Change in Reading Instruction,* 67th Yearbook of the NSSE, Part 2, Chicago: U. of Chicago, 1968, pp. 159–194.

121. Gunderson, Doris V., "Reading problems: Glossary of terminology," *Reading Research Quarterly,* 4 (Summer 1969), 535–547.

122. *Ibid.*

123. Rabinovitch, Ralph D., "Dyslexia: Psychiatric considerations," in Money, John (ed.), *Reading Disability: Progress and Research Needs in Dyslexia,* Baltimore, Md.: Johns Hopkins Press, 1962, pp. 73–79.

124. Harris, *op. cit.,* pp. 169–170.

125. *Ibid.*

126. Robinson, Helen M., "Corrective and remedial instruction," chap. XX in *Development in and Through Reading,* 60th Yearbook of the NSSE, Part 1, Chicago: U. of Chicago, 1961, pp. 362–366.

127. Harris, *op. cit.,* pp. 167–178.

128. Harris, Theodore L., "Reading," in Ebel, Robert L. (ed.), *Encyclopedia of Educational Research,* 4th ed., New York: Macmillan, 1969, pp. 1069–1104.

129. Harris, Albert J., *How to Increase Reading Ability,* 5th ed., New York: McKay, 1970.

130. Strang, Ruth, *Diagnostic Teaching of Reading,* New York: McGraw-Hill, 1969.

131. Delacato, C. H., *Neurological Organization and Reading,* Springfield, Ill.: Thomas, 1966; *The Diagnosis and Treatment of Speech and Reading Problems,* Springfield, Ill.: Thomas, 1963; and *The Treatment and Prevention of Reading Problems,* Springfield, Ill.: Thomas, 1959.

132. Glass, Gene V., and Robbins, Melvyn P., "A critique of experiments on the role of neurological organization in reading performance," *Reading Research Quarterly,* 3 (Fall 1967), 5–52. Also, Robbins, Melvyn P., "The Delacato interpretation of neurological organization," *Reading Research Quarterly,* 1 (Spring 1966), 57–78.

133. Kephart, Newell, C., *The Slow Learner in the Classroom,* 2nd ed., Columbus, Ohio: Merrill, 1971.

134. Dunsing, Jack D., and Kephart, N. C., "Motor generalizations in space and time," in Hellmuth, Jerome (ed.), *Learning Disorders, I,* Seattle, Wash.: Special Child Publications, 1965, pp. 77–121.

135. Frostig, Marianne, and Horne, David, *The Frostig Program for the Developmental Test of Perception,* Palo Alto, Calif.: Consulting Psychologists Press, 1964.

136. Olson, Arthur V., "Relation of achievement of test scores and specific reading abilities to the Frostig Developmental Tests of Visual Perception," *Perceptual and Motor Skills,* 22 (February 1966), 179–184. Also "School achievement, reading ability, and specific visual perception skills in the third grade," *The Reading Teacher,* 19 (April 1966), 490–492.

137. Smith, D. E. P., and Carrigan, Patricia, *The Nature of Reading Disability,* New York: Harcourt, 1959.

138. Smith, *American Reading Instruction, op. cit.,* pp. 155–156.

139. Smith, Nila Banton, "Questions administrators ask about reading in secondary schools," in Robinson, H. Alan, and Rauch, Sidney J. (eds. and compilers), *Corrective Reading in the High School Classroom, Perspectives in Reading, No. 6,* Newark, Del.: IRA, 1966, pp. 114–129.

140. Austin, Mary C., and Smith, Carl B., *Survey of Title I Reading Programs in the Fiscal Year of 1966,* U.S. Office of Education Contract 3–7–000168, Final Report, Cleveland, Ohio: Case Western Reserve University, 1967.

141. *Ibid.*

142. *Ibid.*

143. Chall, *op. cit.,* p. 314.

144. Clymer, Theodore, "Research in corrective reading: Findings, problems, and observations," in Johnson, M. S., and Kress, R. A. (compilers and eds.), *Corrective Reading in the Elementary Classroom, Perspectives in Reading, No. 7,* Newark, Del.: IRA, 1967, pp. 1–10.

145. Passow, A. Harry, and Elliott, David L., "The nature and needs of the disadvantaged, Part 2—The disadvantaged in depressed areas," in Witty, Paul A.

(ed.), *The Educationally Retarded and Disadvantaged*, 66th Yearbook of the NSSE, Part 1, Chicago: U. of Chicago, 1967, pp. 20–39.

146. Webster, Staten W. (ed.), *The Disadvantaged Learner: Knowing, Understanding, Educating*, San Francisco, Calif.: Chandler, 1966, p. 477.

147. Crosby, Muriel, "Reading and literacy in the education of the disadvantaged," *The Reading Teacher*, **19** (October 1965), 18–22. Also, Deutsch, Martin, "The role of social class in language development and cognition," *American Journal of Orthopsychiatry*, **35** (January 1965), 78–88.

148. Fagan, Edward R. (ed.), *English and the Disadvantaged*, Scranton, Pa.: International Textbook Company, 1967, pp. 49–50.

149. Hurley, Rodger, *Poverty and Mental Retardation: A Causal Relationship*, New York: Random, 1969.

150. Mills, Queenie B., "The preschool-disadvantaged child," in Newman, Harold (ed.), *Reading Disabilities: Selections on Identification and Treatment*, New York: Odyssey, 1969, pp. 437–443.

151. Hanson, Earl, and Robinson, H. Alan, "Reading readiness and achievement of primary grade children of different socio-economic strata," *The Reading Teacher*, **21** (October 1967), 52–6 and 79.

152. Bereiter, Carl, and Englemann, Siegfried, *Teaching Disadvantaged Children in the Preschool*, Englewood Cliffs, N.J.: Prentice-Hall, 1966.

153. Mills, *op. cit.*, p. 443.

154. Cohen, S. Alan, *Teach Them All to Read: Theory, Methods, and Materials for Teaching the Disadvantaged*, New York: Random, 1969, p. 8.

155. *Ibid.*

156. Metfessel, Newton S., and Seng, Mark W., "Correlates with the school success and failure of economically disadvantaged children," in Horn, Thomas D. (ed.), *Reading for the Disadvantaged: Problems of Linguistically Different Learners*, New York: Harcourt, 1970, pp. 75–96.

157. Harris, Albert J., and Serwer, Blanche L., *Comparisons of Reading Approaches in First Grade Teaching with Disadvantaged Children*, USOE Cooperative Research Project N.2677, New York: Office of Research and evaluation, Division of Teacher Evaluation, City University of New York, 1966.

158. Harris, Albert J., Serwer, Blanche J., and Gold, Lawrence, "Comparing reading approaches in first grade teaching with disadvantaged children—Extended into second grade," *The Reading Teacher*, **20** (May 1967), 698–703.

159. Lloyd, Helene M., "Reading instruction for the disadvantaged: Is it adequate?" in Smith, Nila B. (ed.), *Current Issues in Reading*, Newark, Del.: IRA, 1969, pp. 134–147.

160. Stauffer, R. G., "Should you use pupil tutors?" *Instructor*, **77** (August–September 1967), 35. Also, Horst, H. M., "Student tutors reduce high school failures," *American School Board Journal*, **101** (July 1940), 51–52.

161. Cloward, Robert D., *Studies in Tutoring*, New York: Research Center, School of Social Work, Columbia University, 1966, p. 41.

162. Riessman, Frank, *The Culturally Deprived Child*, New York: Harper, 1962, p. 81.

163. Edwards, Thomas J., "Language-experience attack on cultural deprivation," in Shell, Leo M., and Burns, Paul C. (eds.), *Remedial Reading: An Anthology of Sources*, Boston: Allyn, 1968, pp. 279–285. Also Wynn, Sammye J., "A beginning reading program for the deprived child," *The Reading Teacher*, **21** (October 1967), 40–47.

164. Englehart, Max D., "Improving classroom testing," in *What Does Research Say to the Teacher?* Washington, D.C.: NEA, 1964.

165. Farr, Roger (ed.), *Measurement and Evaluation of Reading,* New York: Harcourt, 1970.

166. Barrett, *op. cit.*

167. Austin, M. C., Bush, C. L., and Huebner, M. H., *Reading Evaluation: Appraisal Techniques for School and Classroom,* New York: Ronald, 1961.

168. Strang, *Diagnostic Teaching of Reading, op. cit.*

169. Harris, *How to Increase Reading Ability, op. cit.*

170. Johnson, Marjorie S., and Kress, Roy A., *Informal Reading Inventories,* Newark, Del.: IRA, 1965.

171. Tyler, Ralph W. (ed.), *Educational Evaluation: New Roles, New Means,* 68th Yearbook of the NSSE, Part 2, Chicago: U. of Chicago, 1969.

172. Robinson, *Evaluation of Reading, op. cit.*

173. Buros, Oscar (ed.), *Reading Tests and Reviews,* Highland Park, N.J.: Gryphon Press, 1968.

174. Ammons, Margaret, "Evaluation: What is it? Who does it? When should it be done?" in Barrett, Thomas C. (compiler and ed.), *The Evaluation of Children's Reading Achievement, Perspectives in Reading, No. 8,* Newark, Del.: IRA, 1967, pp. 1–12.

175. Strang, Ruth, "Evaluation of development in and through reading," in Farr, Roger (ed.), *Measurement and Evaluation of Reading,* New York: Harcourt, 1970, pp. 35–48.

176. Smith, Carl B., "Evaluating Title I and innovative reading programs: Problems and procedures," in Farr, Roger (ed.), *Measurement and Evaluation of Reading,* New York: Harcourt, 1970, pp. 60–79. Also Barrett, "Goals of the reading program: The basis for evaluation," *op. cit.*

177. Vopni, Sylvia, "What is evaluation?" *Educational Horizons,* **47** (Winter 1968–1969), 75–81.

178. Glaser, Robert, "Instructional technology and the measurement of learning outcomes: Some questions," *American Psychologist,* **18** (1963), 519–521.

179. Dale, Edgar, "Historical setting of programed instruction," in Lange, Phil C. (ed.), *Programed Instruction,* 66th Yearbook of the NSSE, Part 2, Chicago: U. of Chicago, 1967, pp. 28–54.

180. McNeil, John, "Forces influencing curriculum," *Review of Educational Research,* **39** (June 1969), 293–318.

181. Conant, James Bryant, *The Education of American Teachers,* New York: McGraw-Hill, 1963.

182. Austin, Mary C., *et al., The Torch Lighters: Tomorrow's Teachers of Reading,* Cambridge, Mass.: Graduate School of Education, Harvard University, 1961; Austin and Morrison, *op. cit.;* Professional Standards and Ethics Committee, IRA, *Minimum Standards for Professional Preparation in Reading for Classroom Teachers,* Newark, Del.: IRA, 1965.

183. Bond and Dykstra, "The cooperative research program in first grade reading," *op. cit.,* p. 123.

184. Harris, A. J., and Morrison, C., "The CRAFT project: A final report," *The Reading Teacher,* **22** (February 1969), 335–340.

185. Austin, Bush, and Huebner, *op. cit.*

186. Aaron, Ira E., "What teachers and prospective teachers know about phonics

generalizations," *Journal of Educational Research,* **53** (May 1960), 323–330; Adams, Mary Lourita, "Teachers' instructional needs in teaching reading," *The Reading Teacher,* **17** (January 1964), 260–264; Braam, Leonard S., and Roehm, Marilyn A., "Subject-area teachers' familiarity with reading skills," *Journal of Developmental Reading,* **7** (Spring 1964), 188–196; Ramsey, Z. Wallace, "Will tomorrow's teachers know and teach phonics?" *The Reading Teacher,* **15** (January 1962), 241–245; Smith, Richard J., and Otto, Wayne, "Elementary teachers' preferences for pre-service and in-service training in the teaching of reading," *Journal of Educational Research,* **63** (July–August 1970), 445–449.

187. Austin, Bush, and Huebner, *op. cit.* Also Austin and Morrison, *op. cit.*

188. Professional Standards and Ethics Committee, IRA, *Minimum Standards for Professional Training of Reading Specialists,* Newark, Del.: IRA, 1965. Also, Professional Standards and Ethics Committee, IRA, *Reading Specialists: Roles, Responsibilities, and Qualifications,* Newark, Del.: IRA, 1968.

189. Hall, MaryAnne, "Teacher education in reading," *The Reading Teacher,* **22** (December 1968), 265–270.

190. Austin, Mary C., "Professional training of reading personnel," in Robinson, Helen M. (ed.), *Innovation and Change in Reading Instruction,* 67th Yearbook of the NSSE, Part 2, Chicago: U. of Chicago, 1968, pp. 357–396.

191. Lowry, William C., "Some innovations in the preparation of teachers," *The Education Digest,* **35** (February 1969), 28–31.

192. Hamachek, Don, "Characteristics of good teachers and implications for teacher education," *Phi Delta Kappan,* **50** (February 1969), 341–345.

193. Flanders, Ned, "Interaction and inservice training," *Journal of Experimental Education,* **37** (Fall 1968), 126–133. Also, Flanders, "Teacher influence in the classroom," *op. cit.*

194. Harris, A. J., "The effective teacher of reading," *The Reading Teacher,* **23** (December 1969), 195–204 and 238.

195. Artley, A. Sterl, "The teacher variable in the teaching of reading," *The Reading Teacher,* **23** (December 1969), 239–248.

196. *Ibid.,* p. 247.

197. Austin, Mary C., "Preparing teachers and reading specialists," in Smith, Nila B. (ed.), *Current Issues in Reading,* Proceedings of the Annual Convention, No. 13, Part 2, Newark, Del.: IRA, 1969, pp. 444–451.

198. Robinson, Helen M., "Preparation of reading specialists in the United States," in Staiger, Ralph C., and Andresen, Oliver (eds.), *Reading: A Human Right and a Human Problem,* Second World Congress on Reading, 1968, Newark, Del.: IRA, 1969, pp. 133–140.

199. Robinson, "Preparation of reading specialists in the United States," *op. cit.* And Austin, "Professional training of reading personnel," *op. cit.*

200. Piaget, Jean, "Development of mental imagery," in Ripple, R., and Rockcastle, V. (eds.), *Piaget Rediscovered,* Ithaca, N.Y.: Cornell University, 1964.

201. McNeil, John, *op. cit.*

202. Bond and Dykstra, "The cooperative research program in first grade reading," *op. cit.*

203. Chall, *op. cit.,* p. 94.

204. *Ibid.,* p. 93.

205. Spache, George D., "Contributions of allied fields to the teaching of reading," in Robinson, Helen M. (ed.), *Innovation and Change in Reading Instruction,* 67th

Yearbook of the NSSE, Part 2, Chicago: U. of Chicago, 1968, pp. 237–290.

206. Jenkinson, Marion D., "Sources of knowledge for theories of reading," *Journal of Reading Behavior,* 1 (Winter 1969), 11–26.

207. Gray, William S., *The Teaching of Reading and Writing: An International Survey,* UNESCO Monographs on Fundamental Education, No. 10, Chicago: Scott, 1956.

208. Preston, R. C., "Comparison of word-recognition skill in German and American children," *Elementary School Journal,* 53 (1952), 443–446.

209. Hildreth, Gertrude, "Armenian children enjoy reading," *The Reading Teacher,* 19 (March 1966), 433–445; "Lessons in Arabic," *The Reading Teacher,* 19 (December 1965), 202–210; and "On first looking into a Greek primer," *The Reading Teacher,* 21 (February 1968), 453–463.

210. Husén, Thorsten (ed.), *International Study of Achievement in Mathematics,* Vols. I and II, New York: Wiley, 1967.

211. Penney, Monte, and Hjelm, Howard F., "The targeted research and development program on reading—Part I. History of the U.S. Office of Education's support of reading research," *American Educational Research Journal,* 7 (May 1970), 425–434.

212. Gephart, William J., "Targeted research and development program on reading —Part II: The initial program plan," *American Educational Research Journal,* 7 (May 1970), 435–448.

213. Penney and Hjelm, *op. cit.,* p. 425.

214. *Ibid.,* p. 428.

CHAPTER 24

USSR

D. B. ELKONIN*

TRANSLATED BY R. RAEDER AND JOHN DOWNING

Methods of Teaching Reading

MORE than one hundred years ago, the famous Russian pedagogue, K. D. Ushinsky, introduced into the Russian school system a new phonic method for teaching primary reading and writing. Ever since, prerevolutionary time included, most prominent theorists have been working on the improvement of this method. It has the appearance of being a very consistent and even perfect method. Teachers who employ the contemporary so-called analytic-synthetic sound approach are able to teach children to read in a relatively short time.

Yet, the criticism of this method still does not cease. Censure comes from practical workers, as well as from linguists and psychologists. In fact, experience indicates that this method does not achieve such rapid or satisfactory results in learning to read and write as have been claimed. Linguists assert that the linguistic basis of the method has become obsolete, and that, in order to attain knowledge of language, particularly of its phonemic structure, a revision of the scientific foundations of this method is needed. Psychologists also consider that the underlying conception of the reading process on which this method is based does not correspond with present-day psychological knowledge. Indeed, the adherents of this analytic-synthetic phonic method of teaching literacy lean on atomistic and mechanistic views concerning the sounds of language and ignore all the advances in phonetics that have been made during recent decades. Their outlook also is based on the older empirical psychology of the period at the end of the nineteenth and beginning of the twentieth centuries. Such a psychology causes them to regard the process of learning to read as a simple matter of associations between spoken sounds and alphabetic characters.

An examination of currently used methods of teaching reading in primary schools shows that, although the analytic-synthetic method has been modern-

---

* Editor's Note: In this chapter, Professor Elkonin has chosen to concentrate on one aspect of reading in the USSR: the research on the fundamental psychological processes involved in learning to read Russian that has been conducted over a long period at the Institute of General and Pedagogical Psychology in the Academy of Psychological Science in Moscow. This research provides the basis for a new approach to teaching the beginning stages of reading in Russian and other languages in the USSR.

ized, nevertheless, its original dogmas have not been overcome, and it remains essentially the same as it was many years ago.

These considerations compel one to review the main basic methods of teaching literacy, and to reconsider their linguistic and psychological foundations for a program of research on how to facilitate children's progress in learning to read. Our research on the development of primary reading abilities was based on the following view of the nature of reading, as such.

The final problem of reading is comprehension. In various writing systems, the comprehension of written language occurs as a result of different processes. With pictographic or ideographic writing, where the illustration or symbol marks the concept, comprehension is the result of the direct connection between the symbol and its designated meaning. In alphabetic writing systems constructed on the basis of writing a character for a speech sound, a direct connection between the graphic form of written words and their meaning in the language does not exist. Therefore, to all people with normal hearing, the understanding of reading in such writing systems is realized on the basis of the sound formation of the word, with which the meaning also is connected. In principle, the understanding of the written, as well as the oral language, takes place on the basis of the sound formation of the word. In reading aloud the connection between understanding and the sound formation of the word is obvious. In reading silently, also, understanding depends on the sound form of the word, but only as a sound *image*. No matter how the written word is perceived visually, whether it be perceived as a whole, in syllables, or letter by letter, the understanding is based on the sound formation of the word.

The central importance of exact and correct sound formation leading to the understanding of the word that has been read is demonstrated by a simple and well-known fact: the smallest inaccuracy in the creation of the sound formation on the basis of graphic signs renders the word incomprehensible.

The fact that experienced readers anticipate the material read, on the basis of understanding the preceding text, does not reduce the importance of the part played by the sound formation of the word in comprehension. Such anticipation merely creates the conditions for a quicker rendering. Despite the fact that people often advance the comprehension of a word as a criterion of its correct reading, understanding is not an essential part of the process of reading. It is rather to be regarded as a facilitating or complicating factor. In this view, a word can be read correctly, though not understood. For practical purposes, a reader turns to the dictionary for the meaning of a written word that has been correctly recreated in its sound image (or spoken form) because for the reader there is no meaning associated with that sound image. When all the words in a text are already known, the reader uses his own internal dictionary, in which he finds the meaning of the words read.

Thus, reading is a creation of the sound form of the word on the basis of its graphic representation. Therefore, a good reader is one who knows how to create the correct sound form not only of a known word, but also of any unknown word. It is essential to emphasize that in reading, the sound formation has to be extremely precise. At the smallest distortion, the incorrect choice of a different version of a phoneme, or the incorrect intonation, the form of the word gets distorted, and its understanding is made difficult, or confused. The reader starts to guess and searches for a new sound form.

In the beginning stages of learning to read, comprehension functions for the child as a self-checking device that tells him if he has correctly created the sound form of the written word. For an experienced reader the function of comprehension is different. If he does not understand the material he has read, this signals only that the particular word is an item of the language which he does not know and that he must search for its meaning in dictionaries or other reference books.

This view of the roles of comprehension and the creation of the sound form of a word from its graphic representation provides a model of the processes the child must be taught in learning to read. This understanding of the reading process also permits us to determine the objective of the reader's or learner's behavior. If the chief purpose during the reading act is to create the sound form of words, the sound material of language will be an essential foundation for the reader's work. His basic material must be the sounds of language, for out of them the sound form of words is constructed.

Thus, reading behavior is dependent on the sounds of language. (Of course, not all behavior with language sounds is connected with reading.) This view gives more importance to *auditory* factors than has been accorded to them in much previous work on this problem. More often, *visual* perception has been emphasized.

It is true that, initially, the reader must deal with the graphic signs, with alphabetic characters: he perceives them, distinguishes one from the other, and finds their sound significances. The idea that visual perception plays the most important part in reading gave rise to numerous investigations in which the movements of the eyes during the reading process were studied. (For example, many of these investigations were carried out in the United States.) An especially important result of these investigations was the establishment of the fact that eye movements anticipate pronunciation. However, the perception and discrimination of printed characters are only the external side of the process of reading. Behind it lies hidden the more essential and basic behavior, which the reader produces with the sounds of language. The speed of eye movements does not define the speed of reading. Nor does the so-called span of apprehension determine the speed of reading (that is, the number of graphic symbols perceived simultaneously). Of considerably greater importance than the speed of eye movements and the span of apprehension is the speed of those underlying more central processes concerned with the behavior of creating the sound form of the word and connected with it its comprehension.

Hence, it follows inevitably that the first problem to be solved before teaching literacy is to reveal to the child the sound structure of spoken words; not only the basic sound units of language, but also how language is constructed from them.

Historically, the chief concern of the theorists who fought against the letter-adding conception of the alphabetic method of teaching reading was to divert the child's behavior in learning to read away from the printed characters and toward the sounds of language. However, in the course of the historical development of phonic methods of teaching literacy, the emphasis came to be placed on teaching the sounds of alphabetic characters rather than the letter names. But children are inclined to think that *the sound is the name,* because the character and its name serve to mark the sound. Such a tendency arises in children because, in the course of mastering speech, they have learned that every object has its name. This causes a serious difficulty. If children are not provided with appropriate experiences or training, they will not view the sound as an objective reality. The printed character, on the other hand, will more readily be regarded as a concrete object. This causes children to distort the true relationship between spoken language and written language. Instead of seeing the truth—that the character is a written symbol for the reality of the sound in the primary spoken form of language—they reverse the facts and consider the sound as only the label or name of the character.

Another difficulty frequently reported by teachers of reading is also caused by the child's reversal of the proper relationship between the sound and its symbolic representation in the written language. The so-called blending difficulty arises when children try to construct the sound form of words not out of the sounds of language but from what they think are the names of the characters. In their "blending" difficulties, children demonstrate that their behavior is inappropriately oriented toward the characters they are attempting to name instead of the realities of the sounds of language. This incorrect orientation is facilitated by the fact that often letter names and sounds coincide. Also, in verbally labeling a sound, the label contains the elements directly represented by it. From here arises the displacement of sound names with the sounds themselves. Such a displacement does not help the possibly greater rapprochement of sound names with the sounds themselves, which is distinctly expressed in the contemporary method of teaching literacy and which includes the demand for "clear" pronunciation. This clear pronunciation of a sound is nothing more than giving it a name. Thus, this method only serves to provide more distinctive names, and, as a consequence, unfortunately, the best possible conditions are created for the child to substitute name for object. Then the name impedes the perception of the reality of the sound. Indeed, it is impossible to create the sound form of a word from what are viewed as names of either spoken sounds or written characters.

It is true that not all children who can read when they first come to school are able to hear and discriminate correctly the sounds in words, but there is nothing surprising or incomprehensible about this. One can learn to recognize a combination of single characters for a syllable or a word as a visual pattern without being able to hear and distinguish single sounds in them. This means, therefore, that not every literate child discriminates the sounds of speech. This depends on the method of teaching.

The introduction of prereading activities of auditory discrimination as a preliminary to phonic methods was undoubtedly a progressive step toward acquainting children with the aim of their task in reading—that is, in helping them to understand the sound system of their language. However, until now, insufficient research has been devoted to this matter. A critical examination of these prereading exercises gives one the impression that this practice in sound analysis is only provided to teach children the sounds signified by particular written characters; to help children to understand that a given character is a visual sign for a definite sound; and to assist them in mastering the process of blending a sound with others to make up a syllable.

The usual method goes something like this: From a drawling pronunciation of a syllable by the teacher, the pupils distinguish a new sound, which they pronounce separately; they search for words containing this sound, or they find it in words suggested by the teacher; then the teacher shows them the letter that represents that sound. It is characteristic of the generally accepted method today for each sound of the language to be learned separately. The primary discrimination of the sounds is taught by the teacher's expression of words and syllables. The children must hear only the sound designated by the teacher. The sound thus distinguished becomes the original *standard* on the basis of which the children are to recognize the same sound in other words. As soon as the sound has been discriminated in this way, it is immediately followed by learning the letter that represents it. No other activities are provided to help children master the sound structure of words. As soon as the individual sound has been discriminated and its alphabetic character learned, the pupils go straight on to compose words and syllables with the characters, and all work involving the auditory aspect of language ceases. The result is that the children's attention becomes focused on the characters of written language and not on the sounds of speech.

Thus, the child's study of the auditory aspect of language occurs only to the extent that he works in the initial *alphabet* primer. He distinguishes sounds in words, but only in order to learn the visual *character*. The character becomes the object of his task. It is not surprising that such a method of teaching the operation of sound analysis of words and the related auditory discrimination produces slow and poor results.

It must be admitted that the problem of acquainting children with the sound structure of a language and this objective in reading behavior has not been solved. This applies both to the mastering of reading and to the learning of writing. How essential is it for children in beginning reading to learn the sound structure of the language and to develop their phonematic hearing through auditory discrimination? May it not be sufficient to teach literacy simply by building on the level of phonematic hearing the child developed before entering school in the process of mastering the reception and production of spoken language? This question might be less serious if it concerned only the problem of learning to read and write the characters of the alphabet, but the problem goes far beyond this. It is a matter of helping children to understand the way in which language behaves in spoken and written forms—the sound structure, the grammar, the orthography, and so on.

From practical experience, it is generally accepted that different methods of teaching literacy, grammar, and orthography have varying effects. For example, in the USSR, at one time the whole-word method predominated in the schools. When this method was abandoned because of criticism, the change generally caused a deterioration of literacy in elementary school pupils.

But methods of teaching reading have an even greater influence through transfer effects to other language-learning situations. Therefore, the method of teaching the beginning stages of learning to read and write must be considered not only from the point of view of their immediate direct and practical results in these particular skills, but also from the long-term view of their further effects in the development of other language skills. For this reason, it is very important to use a method from the beginning that will provide the child with a correct orientation to the role of the sounds in language and acquaint him with the correct sound form and structure of words.

Phonematic Hearing

What aspects of the sound material of language in the sound structure of the word must be disclosed to the child before he learns letters and the subskills of reading? Clearly, it must be *phonematic hearing*—that is, the auditory discrimination of separate speech sounds. The child develops the ability to operate with these phonemes at a very early age. The function of this analytic ability seems extremely important because all communication with the people in the child's environment depends on language and, therefore, on this phonematic hearing ability.

Shvatchkin[1] showed that, as early as the end of the second year of life, the child is able to distinguish words that differ from each other by only a single phoneme. In his experiment he presented each child with a pair of words that were the names of objects. Each member of the pair differed from the other by only one phoneme. The criterion for discrimination was the child's ability to react with comprehension to the difference. The difficulty with this method is that one remains uncertain as to whether the child's understanding of words is based on the auditory discrimination of *separate* phonemes, or on whole complexes of sounds in the words. To identify words one uses all the pronounced sounds one hears, and these are perceptible as concrete combinations in the total structure of words. Thus, if one accepts Shvatchkin's data, one must still admit that they provide evidence only on the question of whether very young children can discriminate between *words* that differ only in one of the phonemes that make up their total sound forms.

Apparently, the next stage in the development of phonematic perception occurs as the realization of different functions of phonemes. At this point, as numerous observations of children's speech development have shown, the young child increasingly focuses his attention on the sound aspect of language. He recognizes his inability to pronounce this or that word. This is the first step toward its correct pronunciation. Also, he notices the peculiarities of other children's pronunciation and corrects their errors. He points out homonyms as he becomes aware of them, and so on. All these events show that as early as age 2 to 3 years, the child develops the conscious objective of mastering the sound aspect of language. He is aware of his deficiencies and deliberately practices new sounds in order to master them. He observes how different pronunciations influence the discrimination of words.

The child at a very early age recognizes the existence of what appears to be the standard form of the language in his environment, and he becomes a defender of this standard form, correcting any divergence from it in the pronunciation of other children or adults.

However, in spite of these indications of a relatively high level of development of phonematic hearing, the process of sound analysis of spoken language appears to be incomplete. The full skill involves not only the ability to discriminate between the total sound form of separate whole words, but also the ability to distinguish clearly individual sounds and words as separate units.

Of no less importance is the ability to hear the temporal order of the series of sounds in a word. A word does not consist simply of a complex of sounds. Different words can consist of the same sounds, but differ still in the temporal order in which the sounds occur. It is extremely important not only to be able to detect the presence of a particular sound in a word, but also to have the ability to determine its exact position—that is, which sound occurs before or after another sound as well as the general order of the succession of sounds.

Studies of aphasia provide interesting evidence of the significance of this ability to distinguish a word according to the sounds of which it is composed and the order in which they are arranged in the sound structure of the word. Luria[2] has established that, in cases of injury to the lower sections of the premotor area of the cortex, the disturbance of phonematic hearing takes on a specific character. Such patients who retain phonematic hearing seem to be unable to break down a word into its articulatory units in the ordered series in which they occur. The word as a unitary successive structure in which sound-articulatory units follow one after the other in clear order disintegrates, and the patient cannot analyze its sound succession. Consequently, he confuses the order of sounds or omits them.

In another of Luria's[3] investigations of patients suffering injury to the lower sections of the premotor cortical area, he describes cases where the patient can easily articulate separate sounds when asked to repeat such sounds pronounced for him. Yet, the patient is completely helpless when required to change from the articulation of isolated sounds to the articulation of combinations of speech sounds. Such patients also are incapable of analyzing the succession of sounds of which a syllable or word consists.

These investigations of speech disturbances have provided data that have clarified our understanding of the psychological mechanism of the normal functioning of speech. In the light of these data, it seems essential to review our presentation of the relationships that exist between written language and oral language.

The Writing System

Linguistic historians, describing how the use of written letters as visual symbols for speech sounds emerged, point out that, in principle, the difference between ideographic writing systems and alphabetic ones is that, in the former, meaning was symbolized and, in the latter, the sound units of words were symbolized. They regard the basic merit of the alphabetic writing system to be that separate sounds are distinguished in words. The alphabet characters in a written word provided a visual display that parallels the sound structure of the spoken word. It is important to remember that the purpose of ideographic writing is to directly symbolize meaning, whereas alphabetic writing is aimed at symbolizing the sound forms of words. Therefore, the relationship between the visual stimulus in written language and the object it denotes is entirely different in the various types of writing systems. The pictogram is a simple, direct representation of the object. However, this is not true in the case of the hieroglyph, which instead becomes a written *symbol* for the object. Similarly, the alphabetic character is a written *symbol,* in this case for a sound. There is nothing in common between the sound and the character that marks it. The character neither expresses nor represents directly any real feature of the sound. The written word consists of characters that are symbols for sounds. However, the written word is not simply a symbol for a spoken word, although the former does consist of the symbols that mark the sounds of which the latter is composed. The relationship between the spoken word and its written form is much more complex.

The sound form of a word is not merely a collection of sounds. It is created by a definite successive pronunciation of sounds in time. *Thus, we may define the sound form of a word as a definite organization of sounds in their timely succession.* The alphabetic writing system reproduces these basic relations of succeeding sounds in the form of distances in the spatial succession of characters —the symbols for the sounds. Characters follow one another spatially in the same succession as sounds do in time in the spoken word. *Therefore, it seems appropriate to define the written word not as a symbol, but as a model of the sound form of the word.*

We understand *a model* in this case to be a creation in a new material form— graphic signs—of basic relations existing between the sounds in the spoken word. These relations are relations of successions in time. (It should be noted that it is precisely these relations that give each word its own strong, individualistic, and unique form. Alternative versions of a phoneme that enter into the structure of different spoken words containing the same phoneme arise just because of these temporal relations—that is, the sounds that precede and follow the particular phoneme.)

The Sound Structure of Words

Earlier, we defined reading as the creation of the sound form of the word according to its graphic signs. In the light of the above discussion, we are now in a position to provide a more precise theoretical definition: *reading is the creation of the sound form of the word according to its graphic model.*

It follows inevitably that it is essential to reveal to the child the sound mechanism of language, the sound structure of the word. By this is meant not merely the sounds of which a language consists. In addition, the child must be brought to understand the basic principle of constructing the sound form of words, according to which the sounds in a spoken word are arranged in a certain sequence. In this way, the nature of the skill and knowledge the child is expected to master will be more precisely defined for him. His task, as has been shown, will be not only to hear separate sounds in a word and not only to discriminate them within the word, but also to establish their order in time when the word is spoken, that is, to analyze the sound structure of words.

Present methods of teaching literacy do make use of the sound analysis of words, but only to teach auditory discrimination and the characters of the alphabet that mark the separate sounds. Experimental research shows that children who can hear an individual sound in a word or find it according to a standard example cannot make a sound analysis of successive sounds in a word. In contrast, children who can analyze the sounds as they occur in succession in words, manage very easily to distinguish separate sounds and compare them with one another.

Thus, certain basic experiences with spoken words can enable the child to become acquainted with the structure of the sound form of the word; this facilitates the other sound related tasks usually required in learning to read. It is essential that these experiences with the sound aspect of language *precede* the learning of alphabetic characters as symbols for sounds.

In summarizing this section of this chapter, the following must be stressed. Sound analysis is the operation of arranging the succession of sounds in a spoken word. In the process of accomplishing such an operation, *the child discovers the basic principle of constructing the sound form of words.* This discovery establishes the prerequisite conditions for such correct construction in reading and in making his own models in writing. Whereas learning the arrangement of sound succession includes the definition of the sound units that compose a word, in contrast, the determination of separate sounds contained in a word does not include on its own the arrangement of their succession in a word.

The Problem of Sound Analysis

The arrangement of a succession of sounds in a word, as well as the discrimination of a single sound in a word, seems an extraordinarily simple act for a normal literate adult. This illusion arises from the fact that, at this higher level of development, the operation occurs by then as abbreviated, generalized, perfected, and automatic mental behavior, which requires no effort and causes no problems. But the truth is that this is only the final form of the process of sound analysis of a word. For teaching, this final form is the goal that has to be achieved, progress toward which must follow a certain path for the development of the ultimate process anticipated. The basic position of psychology here is that learning a new skill cannot, and, consequently, must not start from its final form; that mastering the skill does not consist in becoming gradually attached to one or another spontaneously given form, but on the contrary, proceeds by consistent changes of its form from the initial stage to the final mental form.

Where should we begin? How should we lead the child to develop the operation of sound analysis of speech so that it will become entirely mental? In seeking an answer to this question, we have accepted Galperin's[4] thesis that the entirely mental operation can only develop if learning to perform it proceeds in a certain series of stages, namely:

1. Establishing a preliminary conception of the task.
2. Mastering the operation with objects.
3. Mastering the operation at the level of overt oral speech.
4. Transferring the operation to the mental level.
5. Operating at the entirely mental level.

The greatest difficulties arise in finding the child's initial objective form of behavior with the sound form of the word. These difficulties occur, first, with the requirements this initial form of the operation has to satisfy, and, second, with the nature of the actions we want to teach the child—that is, the nature of the sound aspect of language.

What are the requirements to be satisfied in the initial method of learning the operations of sound analysis? First, practical operations with concrete objects must be provided, and, second, these must be operations that will lead the child to discover the basic physical relationships that characterize the sound form of the word—the relationship of the succession of sounds.

These requirements, however, come into conflict with the peculiarities of language with which the child must cope. The sounds of speech can only be either heard or pronounced. Hearing them is the perception of the speech sounds pronounced by another person. In that case, the child does not actively engage in constructing a word from sounds. Thus, only when the child himself pronounces a word and, hence, the sounds of which it consists, do there appear to exist adequate conditions for him to learn the initial form of the desired operation. To compare sounds with one another, to pick them out of words, and to discriminate them is only possible on the basis of pronouncing the words and their component sounds.

But the child runs into great difficulties in analyzing the sound construction of a word. As is well known from classroom experience, on the basis of uttering, children easily divide words into syllables. The syllable appears clearly as a naturally articulated pronounceable unit, in which are merged several sounds into a single articulated act.

It is much more difficult for the child to analyze words into their separate sounds on the basis of uttering them. This difficulty of dividing a word into phonemes is explained by the conflict between the natural word articulation that appears as a unit of pronunciation and the sound as a unit of language. When the individual unit of sound is pronounced, it does not directly coincide with the real unit as it exists in language. Therefore, it often occurs that the child cannot divide a word into sounds on the basis of his own pronunciation, but he is able to discriminate auditorially a discrete sound when he hears the same word pronounced slowly by an adult. However, not even the most precise speech is able to disclose the structure of a word to the child. The most that can be hoped for is to aid the pupil in hearing and discriminating a separate sound.

Now it looks as though we are arriving at an insoluble contradiction. On the one hand, uttering appears to be the only appropriate behavior for dealing with the peculiarities of language described, and, consequently, the development of the operation of sound analysis of words must begin at the level of overt oral speech. But, on the other hand, as experimental evidence shows, such an approach is not very successful.

Fausek[5], on the basis of her many years of experience in teaching literacy to children, noticed that the analysis of something fluid is not possible. Therefore, speech must be materialized—that is, the parts of the word must be represented concretely. This necessity obviously was felt long ago. Alphabet blocks and other devices all provide the child with the opportunity of objectifying the sound.

Present methods of teaching literacy are not alien to this conception. Many children learn to read with the help of cubes and cards that display characters of the alphabet. Indeed, writing itself may provide a basis for the initial materialization of the sound structure of the word. This conclusion is all the more tempting, because, as we explained earlier in this chapter, the written word does not appear as a symbol, but as a model of the spoken word—a model of the word's structure and its principle of construction.

Although this conclusion is very tempting, it is incorrect, because, although the written form of a word must become a model of its spoken form to the child, it does not appear as such to him in the beginning stage. The conclusion is incorrect also because writing requires as prerequisites the subskills of laying out the word into its component sounds in the succession in which they occur in time and of marking the sounds by written characters in the same successive way. Beginners do not possess these subskills.

Furthermore, the materialization of the operation of analyzing a word by means of the characters in its written form is unacceptable because to do this would make the character instead of the sound the focus of the child's attention. Such a writing approach to reading, thus, does not lead the child to master the sound structure of the word in such a way as to lead ultimately to the process of sound analysis at a fully mental level. To this end, apparently, some means must be found to develop the operation of sound analysis *prior* to the presentation of reading itself.

A Method for Materializing the Sound Structure of Words

It seemed to us that the materialized form of the operation must be such that, in the first stage, only the sound structure of the word would be objectified for the child, and that an activity should be provided that would engage the child in modeling only that sound structure. These requirements were met in the following manner.

Figure 24-1 provides examples of the materials used. In these examples the objects illustrated are a balloon, pronounced /ʃar/, in Russian, and geese, pronounced /gúsi/; the first word has three sounds and the second word has four sounds. Below each picture is a diagram of the sound structure of the word that names the object. The diagram consists of a rectangle divided by vertical lines into squares according to the number of sounds in the word represented. In addition, the child was given a quantity of cardboard counters, all in one color. He was instructed to say the words aloud with stressed articulation or to pronounce every sound in succession in a drawl. As he distinguished each sound, he had to place a counter in the appropriate square of the diagram of the word's sound structure and simultaneously call out the sound.

These conditions helped the child in several ways. The picture reminded him of the word that had to be pronounced and analyzed, and the diagram showed how many sound elements had to be found in the word's construction. This led the child to produce behavior that was practical in operation: separating sounds on the basis of specially organized uttering and modeling the succession of sounds in the word. Filling the diagram with counters for the sounds appeared

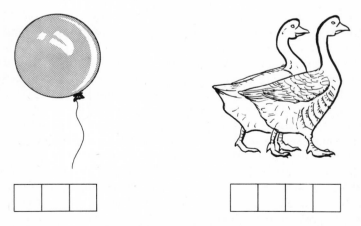

FIGURE 24-1. Apparatus for materializing the sound structure of words.

to the child as a model of the sound construction of the word. It demonstrated in material form the succession and number of sounds in the task word.

Why did we decide to use plain counters and not alphabetic characters for this activity? We rejected characters because they would have diverted the child's attention to the written form of language and the operation of symbolizing, whereas our concern was to focus attention on the building of a spoken word from its component sounds. The use of plain counters prevented any confusion of purpose. Because the abstract counters were the same for all sounds that entered the word's structure, the child's aim was not the symbolizing of separate sounds, but their separation and modeling as a succession. By this method, the temporal succession of sounds was materialized in the form of arranging counters in successive spaces. These appeared before the child distinctly as the sound composition of the word, its structure. It is interesting to note that, by this method of maximally abstract symbolization, it seemed possible to model the general principle of constructing a word, instead of obscuring it with concrete relations between particular sounds of speech and particular characters of the alphabet.

Before going on to report our experiments further, certain preliminary questions we considered need to be mentioned.

In the practice of teaching children to read, it is customary to divide words into syllables out of which the sounds are later distinguished. We questioned this preliminary analysis into syllables and came to the conclusion that not only is this practice unnecessary, but also the uttering of the syllables makes it more difficult to elucidate the sound structure of the word. Firstly, the division into syllables appears as a natural dissection of the word, because the syllable is a pronounceable, but not a linguistic, unit of the word. Secondly, by dividing the sound tissue of the word into syllables, it becomes torn at natural seams, and thereby loses its sound continuity. We accepted that the pronunciation of the word, when one is analyzing its sound structure, must be continuous, but to distinguish the sound elements it must be a more drawled or emphasized pronunciation; for example, *mama* must be pronounced in succession like this: "m-m-mama; ma-a-a-ma; mam-a-a-a." Of course, such pronunciation requires training.

A second preliminary question relates to the naming of the successive sounds as the child distinguished them in the spoken word and marked them with his counters on the diagram. We accepted for these such names as, "be," "ve," "me," and so on.

Thus, in the first stage of its development, the operation should have the following appearance: the child utters the word aloud, separating each successive sound with a drawled or stressed sound, while placing a counter for each in the corresponding square of the diagram below the picture; he names the sound. In essence, the sounds of the word are discriminated and, consequently, they are marked by counters and names.

After working on modeling the sound structure of the word in the complete form of the task, as described above, it was reduced gradually and transferred, first, to the level of overt oral utterance without activities with the counters and diagram, and, later, to the mental level—that is, with no utterance out loud.

Experimental Evidence for the Importance of Materializing the Operation

In our first investigation, conducted by N. A. Khokhlova,[6] the problem concerned the significance of the development of sound analysis in its primary materialized form for mastering the operation. For this purpose three series of experiments were carried out.

In the first series the children learned sound analysis only by means of uttering aloud—that is, without any materialization by the diagrams and counters.

In the second series only partial materialization was provided. The children analyzed the word by uttering it aloud and marked each discriminated sound with counters on a sheet of plain paper. Later, after the same number of words had been analyzed (as by the children in the first series), the children were asked to analyze words without using the counters in order to test the extent to which the operation had been developed.

Finally, in the third series, learning the operation began with the child being shown the picture with the diagram of the sound structure below it. As described earlier, he made the analysis of the word by uttering the successive sounds and by filling the squares in the diagram with the counters for the discriminated sounds. Then, when half the number of words analyzed by the children in the first and second series had been analyzed in this way, these third series children changed over to using counters only—that is, by the same method as had been used in the second series—without the pictures or the sound structure diagrams. This second half was followed by a test of the development of the operation in which words were presented for independent analysis by means of uttering them aloud, that is, at the level of overt oral speech.

The number and types of words were the same in all three experiments. Fifteen 6-year-old children participated in each series. None could read and none was able to carry out a sound analysis of words at the outset of the research. Each child worked in twenty-minute sessions. From five to seven sessions were conducted with each individual.

The results of the first series of experiments confirmed the everyday observation of children's difficulties in the sound analysis of words. Not one child was able to master the operation of the analysis of the sound structure of words, despite all his efforts and in spite of having analyzed some forty words of varying difficulty with the experimenter. No child in this series could cope independently with the analysis of the test words. Because each child was presented with approximately forty words, the fifteen subjects met a total of 620 words. Of these, only ten were independently analyzed. Five of these were analyzed by one child and five other children each analyzed a single word. Clearly, the majority of these children could not independently analyze a single word.

Furthermore, these children's errors did not decrease. Thus, little progress from the beginning to the end of the experiments was discerned.

An analysis of the errors made by the children in the first series confirmed repeatedly that the basic difficulty of sound analysis is separating the vowels from the consonants, overcoming the natural articulatory division of words into syllables.

We conclude from the first series of experiments that the simple exercise of sound analysis on the basis of uttering aloud does not lead to the proper development of the operation of sound analysis.

The general results of the tests conducted at the end of the second series were better than those for the first series, but still the operation did not appear to have been learned. In all, 193 words were presented for analysis. Of these, only 59 or 31 per cent were analyzed independently and without error. Thus, 134 words or 69 per cent were not analyzed. Not one child gave a perfect performance, and only four children were partly successful. Even the analysis of monosyllabic words proved difficult for these children. Of fifty-one cases of such words only twenty-six were analyzed correctly. Of the two- and three-syllable words, 23 per cent were analyzed correctly.

The dynamics of the development of the operation by the method of the experiments of the second series is interesting. The task began with the analysis of monosyllabic words. Comparing the total responses of the group on the first five monosyllabic words with those on the last five one notes improvement: 4 per cent of attempts were correct on the former and 43 per cent on the latter. However, the operation of word analysis seemed to be insufficiently generalized, because these children again experienced great difficulties when presented with two-syllable words and words with adjacent vowels. On the last five words in this series only 19 per cent of the responses were correct analyses. As many as 81 per cent were wrong, despite the use of counters.

Thus, we conclude that the introduction of partial materialization (that is, with counters only) produced better results than in the first series where no materialization was available but the difference was very small. In particular, the operation performed with the monosyllabic words could not be transferred to more complicated types. The operation appears to be neither generalized nor stable.

An entirely different result occurred in the third series. When the test words to be analyzed at the level of overt speech were presented, 82 per cent of the responses were correct. Two- and three-syllable words were managed as easily as monosyllabic ones.

The dynamics of the development of the operation were also different. At first, the responses were the same as in the other two series. Only 7 per cent of responses were correct on the first five monosyllabic words. But, by the end of the series of monosyllabic words, more progress had been made than in the second series. Of the responses, 57 per cent were correct in the analysis of the last five monosyllabic words. On the more complicated words the proportion of correct responses reached 64 per cent on the last five words in this series;

and this was in spite of the fact that the total number of words presented in the third series was less than in the second series (fifteen to eighteen mono-syllabic words per subject in the second series; ten to fourteen in the third series).

In the third series one could see clearly how the operation of word analysis gradually became more developed and stronger. The comparison of these data shows the advantage of the approach used in the third series of experiments.

Per Cent Responses Correct

	2nd series	3rd series
First five monosyllables	4	7
Last five monosyllables	43	57
Last five complicated words	19	64
Transfer test	31	82

Further evidence in support of this conclusion is provided by the data on the number of children who mastered the operation of sound analysis in the three different approaches. One can classify the children into three categories according to their varying success in mastering this operation. The first cate-gory, "Failure," consists of children who were completely incapable of perform-ing the task of sound analysis at the level of overt oral utterance. The second category, "Partial Development," includes children who partly developed the operation. They made many correct responses but a high proportion of errors, too—that is, in more than 30 per cent of the total number of words presented. The third category, "Complete Mastery," consists of those children who com-pletely mastered the task and made only a few accidental errors. The results according to these categories are cited in the table.

Number of Children in Category

Experimental series no.	Failure	Partial development	Complete mastery
1	15	0	0
2	11	4	0
3	1	2	12

This is convincing evidence that the method of developing the operation by which the child produced the model of the sound structure of the word in a developed form is the most effective and rapid.

Although care was taken in selecting the children for these experiments to make sure that in all three series they were equally naïve about the tasks of literacy learning, nevertheless, it might be suspected that the third series accidentally contained children who were more mature. In order to guard against this possible source of error, a fourth series of experiments was conducted as a check on the results reported thus far.

This fourth series included only five children. We began with the development of the operation of analysis on the level of overt utterance. When we had analyzed thirty words with each of these children and were convinced that they had not developed the operation (only 3 per cent of responses were correct), we changed over to the method of the third series (first by picture, diagram and counters, and then by counters only). After these children had analyzed forty more words in this way, a transfer test series was presented for analysis on the level of overt utterance alone. Then 84 per cent of their responses were correct. These results fully confirmed our earlier findings.

In order to understand how to account for the increase in effectiveness and the speed of development of sound analysis in the method of the third series as compared with that of the second series, it is necessary to contrast the second and third methods again and note the nature of their similarities and differences.

In both cases the child utters the word to be analyzed aloud; in both cases he marks the sound with a counter and simultaneously names it; in both cases his behavior results in a row of counters that mark the discriminated sounds of the word. All these events appear to be identical in both methods of analysis.

The essential difference between them is that in the third series the child has a card in front of him with a picture of the object and a diagram of the sound structure of the word, which is the name of the pictured object. Thus, the word presented for analysis is given to the child, first, in the form of a picture, and, second, in the form of a diagram. Then the child fills in the diagram with the counters, which dictate to him the succession of insertion. The child sees the remaining empty squares in the diagram and their successive order. The picture also remains in front of the child constantly, reminding him of the word with which he is reacting. While constructing the spatial model of the sound succession, the child constantly correlates it with the given word. The model constructed by him is, for him, the model of the given word.

Therefore, it seems that effective development of the operation of sound analysis depends not simply on fixing each discriminated sound by means of a counter, but also on the successive filling in of the diagram, which primarily distinguishes for the child the order of succession of the sounds, *the construction of the word*. The main point of the child's behavior, then, is not just to know of what sounds the word consists, but in what order they follow one another. The child's objective is the structure of the word not the determination of sounds. It is important also for the child to apply the model he has composed to the word that had to be analyzed. It appears to him as a pictured word—the name drawn below the picture of the object.

Thus, the outstanding characteristic of the method used in the third series is that the child's objective becomes the understanding of the *succession* of sounds in the word—the sound *structure* of the word. It is this characteristic that determines the successful development of the operation of sound analysis in reading and writing.

Having worked out this principle, it became necessary for us to find out to what extent the behavior of separating sounds becomes generalized. Khokhlova's experiments were based on the development of an operation that originated from a large and varied set of words, which included almost all of the sounds of the Russian language. The possibility could not be excluded that, in the results of such work, standards of sounds had been formed by the children that they later used to recognize already known sounds in new words.

With the aim of elucidating this problem, a special investigation was carried out by Olshannikova[7] in which sound analysis was developed on the basis of a limited number of words that consisted of a small number of sounds. Out of ten sounds nine words were composed—four monosyllabic and five of two syllables each.

Sound analysis was performed by the system of Khokhlova's third series of experiments (by uttering aloud, plus picture, diagram and counters). Then the same task was worked on with the same words on the level of overt utterance alone (without the diagram). After the child had acquired the skill of dividing the nine words faultlessly into their sound structure, the analysis of words was transferred to the mental level. For this purpose, the children were asked such questions as, "How many sounds are in the word? In which position is such and such a sound when you count from the beginning? Which sound is first? Which is last? Which sound comes before (or after) such and such a sound?"

When it was certain that the mental operation in relation to the familiar nine words had been developed, its generalization to new words was tested. The test words were of varying difficulty, including some that were absolutely unknown to the children. All these new words either contained no sound included in the original nine words, or they contained a mixture of new sounds and ones found in the original nine from the first stage of this experiment.

Eight of the ten 6- to 7-year-old children in this study were able to generalize the operation of sound analysis during the nine or ten test sessions. They could analyze any new word, no matter how strange or multisyllabic. At first, these children analyzed the words on the level of overt utterance, but later they progressed to silent analysis, answering questions of the kind mentioned.

Thus, Olshannikova's investigations show that the basis for developing sound analysis by the methods we have devised is not the recognition of sounds against a standard the child has already learned. On the contrary, it is based on the perception of the word as a composition or construction of sounds—that is, *as a sound structure*.

Classroom Evaluation of the Method

After we had determined the real nature of the development of sound analysis, we went on to investigate how it is developed under the everyday conditions of classroom instruction. We adapted the original method to this purpose.

The first experiment was carried out with the older group of kindergarten children in A. A. Venger's class, and in the preparatory class of M. A. Polivanova. All the pupils mastered the task of sound analysis in the course of twelve to fourteen lessons. In the years 1959–1960, a replication experiment was conducted in the first grades of ninety-one schools in Moscow. Also, in 1961, the same experiment was conducted in the first grade of the village school at Mednoye in the Kalininskij district (teacher, A. I. Pavlova) and with a group of 5-year-olds in the kindergarten (teacher L. E. Zhurova) in the same place. In every case the children mastered the operation of the sound analysis of words relatively quickly (ten to twelve lessons) and easily. It was followed by improvements in various aspects of learning literacy.

Let us look in more detail at the data from the work at the village school in Mednoye. The children in the first class there came to school without any knowledge of analyzing the sound structure of the word or of discriminating separate sounds in a word. Altogether, twenty-six students were tested on a list of seven words for analysis. Of the total of 182 words, 74 per cent were analyzed without error. In most cases, the 26 per cent of words with errors arose from omission of vowels. In the kindergarten, twenty children attended the experimental sessions regularly. After fifteen twenty-minute lessons, sixteen children had perfected the operation of sound analysis. Two children missed the vowels when articulating, and two children named syllables instead of sounds. As a test, each child had to analyze two words, one monosyllabic and the other with two syllables. Out of the total of forty words attempted by the whole group, thirty-two were analyzed completely without error. The errors were produced by the four children already mentioned.

This experiment with the 5-year-olds not only confirmed that the approach we had worked out was principally on the correct lines, but it also demonstrated that children of this young age were fully capable of learning the operation of sound analysis and could readily learn literacy under group conditions.

The Psychological Nature of the Operation

At the same time, this experiment with the younger children enabled us to understand the deeper psychological nature of the process. The behavior of the older children already appears abbreviated and the details of the operation are difficult to discern. However, at the younger ages it should appear in a less developed form. It was anticipated that the process would become clearer if one conducted a detailed analysis of words with children of a younger age. Such was the aim of the investigation by Zhurova and Elkonin.[8]

As had been expected, their study did reveal some of the characteristics of the development of sound analysis of words that had been concealed in the experiments with the older children. The importance of stressed intonation of the separate sounds to be distinguished was apparent. This kind of pronunciation must be specially taught. In performing the mental operation of sound analysis, stressed intonation—as well as the method of discriminating sounds—

is necessary for the younger children right through to the end of the teaching sessions. Even then, when they are able to analyze words without the help of the sound structure diagrams and the counters, the removal of the system of intonation leads to errors.

The successive stressed intonation of each sound helps the child to overcome two difficulties. The first problem is connected with the undesirable contradiction existing between the sound unit of language and the unit of speech. The phoneme appears as the unit of language just at the time when the syllable appears as a pronounceable unit of speech. Speech derived from pronouncing the quantum in the form of syllables has to be analyzed in terms of the phonemic units of language—not the articulatory syllabic units. The second difficulty connected with this is that the child has to analyze his own behavior, his own pronunciation.

The solution to this problem is to devise a new task for the child with a word that is different from the original in a way that will make its linguistic structure more distinct and understandable. This procedure must destroy the natural syllabic pronunciation of words and free the child from stereotyped syllabic perception. Uttering the word with stressed intonation and a drawling pronunciation of the separate sounds fulfills the need to orientate the child to the sound structure of the word. Thus, distinguishing the separate sounds by emphasized intonation results in one's hearing them as separate units. Like any behavior, this reaction is performed at first as a highly complex act, but it is gradually abbreviated and is transformed into thought as the silent and unseen articulatory movements of inner speech.

Just as the action of uttering the separate sounds with stressed intonation or drawled pronunciation leads the child to hear the separate sounds in a word, so also does the fixation of each of these sounds, by a counter in the diagram, lead him to discriminate it from other sounds.

The completion of the diagram with the counters has two functions: (1) to separate the sound and (2) to establish the symmetry of the sound structure of the word in relation to the diagram. In filling up the diagram with the counters, the child compares the part he has already completed with what is still unfinished. He searches in the word for just that number of units that remain to complete it. Finally, the completed diagram provides the opportunity to compare different words with each other, not by their meaning, but by their sound structure. The child sees for himself that two words of different meaning can be perfectly equal in respect to the quantity of sounds they contain.

Thus, the operation of sound analysis of the word in its primary developed form consists of several correlated tasks: the drawled pronunciation of the word, by means of which the hearing of the separate sound becomes possible; the fixation of the sounds with counters in the sound diagram, by means of which each sound becomes separated from its adjacent sounds; and the establishment of a simple parallelism between the word's sound structure and its graphic representation in the diagram. All these aspects together comprise the primary developed form of the sound analysis of the word, which, as it becomes abbreviated and generalized, eventually leads to the grasping of the sound structure of a word immediately on the mental level.

The practical sum of these investigations may seem extraordinarily small; the development of a system for teaching the sound analysis of words. Yet, this is the first stage of acquainting the child with the facts of the sound aspect of language, and it is the most important prerequisite for the successful learning of reading and writing. This system has been worked out methodically and is included now in an experimental first primer.

The theoretical significance of this research is that such a complicated aspect of reality as the construction of the sound form of the word can be modeled in concrete materials so that the child can learn to construct such a model of a word's sound structure for himself. This mastering of those aspects of reality expressed in the model raises an interesting question for speculation: Is the general principle of the construction of words from sounds understood by the child who models the sound structure of words under the guidance of the teacher in the manner described?

The Riddle of the Reading Process

The operation of sound analysis and the development of phonematic hearing on that basis seems to be an essential prerequisite to the teaching of reading. However, experimental findings indicate that they are not sufficient. Even if the child has learned the alphabetic characters and their sounds, he is not able to create from them the sound form of a word or a syllable. Why is it that a child who knows the characters and their sounds still cannot read the word or syllable they compose? This, strictly speaking, is the riddle of the reading process. It is not the province of this chapter to trace the history of reading research, but one could demonstrate that the entire history of methods of teaching reading is one of hypotheses about this riddle.

We have based our experimental investigations on the present-day achievements of phonetics, which disclose the phonemic structure of the physical sound basis of language, and on current ideas concerning the relationship between a language's phonemic structure and its conventional writing system (phoneme-grapheme connections).

Without going into this linguistic research, we will just point out three basic considerations from which we derived our hypothesis regarding the nature of the psychological process of reading.

1. *The phoneme and its versions.* Within the phonology one distinguishes between phonemes and versions or graduations of phonemes. By "phonemes" one refers to those types of sounds that differentiate the sound forms of words so that their meaning is distinguished. "Versions of phonemes" are *real* concrete pronounceable sounds of oral speech. A version of a phoneme depends on its place within the complex of other phonemes. They arise automatically in the process of operating the articulatory apparatus. They do not serve to dis-

tinguish the sound form of words or their meaning. Not even people with highly developed phonematic hearing perceive these versions of phonemes. In each language there is a limited and strictly determined number of phonemes that constitute a definite system. But in living speech there exists an endless number of versions of phonemes. In real living language the phoneme exists only in the form of a single version. A phoneme and its version represent in a certain sense one and the same thing: the same sound changes depending on the conditions of its function in speech. Furthermore, different languages discriminate by different phonemic systems. What in one language is a phoneme, can occur in another language only as a version of a phoneme. For example, vowel length in Russian does not produce contrasts, whereas in other languages short and long vowels do represent a contrasting phonemic series. For teaching elementary reading, the principle to be derived from all this is that in living oral speech the phoneme exists only in the form of a concrete variation.

2. *Articulatory anticipation and versions of phonemes.* Zhinkin's[9] investigations have shown that the syllable appears as a pronounced unit; that is, oral speech is divided into syllables. While pronouncing a syllable, the articulatory apparatus anticipates the next sound, and the speech organs are set to produce subsequent sounds. This means that the pronunciation of the first sound of the syllable occurs from the same starting point as the next sound to be produced. Such a mechanism also creates endless versions of phonemes.

3. *Graphemes representing phonemes, not versions.* The writing systems of the majority of Indo-European peoples are based on the phonemic principle: for each grapheme of the particular alphabet there corresponds one or more phonemes. In the ideally constructed alphabet, the number of graphemes should exactly correspond with the number of phonemes. In actual practice there are very few such alphabets. In most languages there is not such a precise correspondence of grapheme-phoneme relations, and usually there are fewer graphemes than phonemes so that one particular grapheme has to stand for not one, but two or more phonemes. In such cases, the phonemic significance of the grapheme is often defined by a subsequent grapheme. But what is most important to stress here is that, even in a perfect system of grapheme-phoneme relations, the grapheme represents only the phoneme and not the versions of phonemes.

These considerations led us to conclude that, even in the ideal alphabet with a so-called perfect one-to-one relationship between graphemes and phonemes, the creation of the sound form of a syllable from its graphic model represents a compound act. We assumed that the mechanism of producing the sound form of a syllable is on the same principle as the mechanism of pronouncing it in oral speech. In oral speech the anticipation of the pronunciation of each sound by setting the articulatory organs to pronounce the next sound takes place automatically and is regulated by the sense of the word to be pronounced. Especially in reading, which is the creation of the sound form of the word, such an anticipatory response must occur. For beginners in learning to read, the graphic model of a word appears to be an original graphic symbol that has to be guessed. The sense of the word, which causes the automatic regulation of articulation in oral speech, is absent in this initial situation in reading. Therefore, it is essential to develop the orientation for the pronunciation of one sound as represented by its letter from the position of the following sound as represented by its letter. We have called this reading mechanism positional. One may conditionally describe the algorythm of the formation of the sound form of the syllable something like this:

> Look at the letter, but do not pronounce the sound determined by it; look at the next letter and be prepared to pronounce the sound it designates (be prepared, but do not pronounce); pronounce the first sound and get into position for pronouncing the second one, and then pronounce the second sound immediately, and so on.

Such is the mechanism of creating the sound form of a word when an ideal phoneme-grapheme correspondence exists. In cases where the reader must choose one phoneme from the alternatives represented by a grapheme on the basis of a subsequent grapheme, the mechanism becomes more complex. Then orientation by the subsequent grapheme determines, not only the pronunciation of the particular version of a phoneme, but also the choice of phoneme—that is, the importance of the *positional* mechanism is doubled.

Orientation to the Russian Writing System

In the course of the historical development of the phonemic structure of the Russian language and the writing system that models it, the correlations between the phonemic and graphemic systems seem to have become rather complicated. The number of characters that mark the consonant phonemes are considerably fewer than the phonemes. Each consonant character, with a few exceptions, marks two phonemes—a hard and a soft one. Thus, a consonant character by itself does not reveal which phoneme it marks. The choice between a soft phoneme or a hard one is determined by the next vowel. Vowel phonemes are marked by a great number of characters. Some characters mark a vowel phoneme plus the hardness of the preceding consonant; others mark the same vowel phoneme but the softness of the preceding consonant phoneme.

Thanks to this peculiarity of Russian consonants and their conventional designation in the graphemic system, the mechanism of creating the sound form of the word involves some complexity. In order to create the sound form of a syllable that consists of a written character marking the sound of a consonant and another marking the sound of a vowel, a complicated preliminary task of positional orientation must be undertaken. The chief problem here is the orientating effect of the next vowel character. It determines exactly which phoneme is designated by the preceding consonant character. At the same time, the vowel phoneme marked by its character determines the position of the articulatory apparatus and, consequently, the concrete version of the phoneme. The beginner at learning to read must solve this problem as a preliminary task before being able to create the sound form of a syllable in the Russian language. Thus, these responses in reading appear to be related in their functioning to those involved in the pronunciation of the syllable.

The main problem in the Russian language is in this orientation through the vowel following the consonant. But in other languages with different systems of phonemes and graphemes and different relationships between them, the content of this orientation will differ.

"Blending Difficulties"

Teaching the skill of creating the sound form of a syllable as a basic unit of reading usually presents great difficulties for children learning to read: these problems are usually referred to as "blending" difficulties and are caused by two factors:

1. A written or printed character may be associated with any one of a number of *versions* of the phoneme. This makes it extraordinarily difficult to choose the essential concrete version.
2. The child is unable to orient himself toward the successive characters that determine the correct choice of the concrete version of the phoneme required in each particular situation. This is what precipitates the blending difficulty.

In attempting to overcome this blending problem, numerous solutions have been proposed and tried out, including the following: (1) the requirement of so-called clear pronunciation of separate sounds upon perception of a character; (2) a special arrangement of characters of the alphabet in the primer, in which the so-called continuant consonants would be learned first, and the "stops" ones, later, as if the blending of the former type of consonants with vowels was in some way easier; (3) a special order of studying sounds and characters such that one would first learn only one sound significance—for example, soft consonants, and then hard ones; (4) a series of techniques, that is, "reading according to fresh tracings of the analysis" or reading after writing, and the like. All these devices of teaching methodology have the single aim of leading the child to discover the essential operation of creating the sound form of the syllable. But all these efforts failed to produce the expected results in the majority of cases. Many children did not arrive at a correct solution in trying to understand what one has to do in order to read a syllable correctly. Instead, they went straight on to a simple recognition of separate syllables as wholes. This was promoted by the frequent repetition of each syllable in the basal reading primers.

Word Changing

Our view was that children can perform the task of creating the sound form of the word even before they learn the consonant characters and their sound significances. It can be accomplished within the special operation of transforming one word into another by changing only one phoneme. There are quite a few such pairs or series of words that differ from one another by only a single phoneme. The process by which the child himself transforms one word into another by replacing only one phoneme in the initial word, we have called word changing. The achievement of this process, according to our theory, must guide the child to the correct creation of the sound structure of the syllable and thus lay the foundation for correct reading.

We have found it necessary to develop this word-changing ability in stages, progressing as soon as is feasible from the developed material operation to the abbreviated mental process.

As has been noted, in the Russian language the chief problem is the orientation toward the position of the vowel phoneme following a consonant. Therefore, we postulated that the child must first master the process of word changing by examples in which this important arrangement of phonemes occurs. A special investigation was conducted to test this aspect of our theory.

In order that the child himself be able to carry out the operation of word changing, he needs to be taught first to differentiate vowel sounds from consonants, and, secondly, the written characters that mark vowel sounds. All this was found easy to teach on the basis of the previously acquired sound analysis of words, described earlier in this chapter.

Method of Materializing Categories of Sound

The experimental teaching was based on the following pattern. After the pupils could easily manage the task of sound analysis and no longer needed the aid of the visual diagram of the sound structure of the word and the counters, the diagram and counters were reintroduced to the children. The pupils were shown how the component sounds varied and their attention was drawn to the vowel and consonant sounds. Now, in analyzing the sound structure of the word, the children filled in the diagram *with counters of two colors;* one designating vowel sounds and the other consonants. Now the word diagram changed into a two-colored one. Six- and 7-year-old children learned very easily to discriminate vowel and consonant sounds in this way.

Our next step was to go on to the discrimination of hard and soft consonants, because this phonemic contrast is of paramount importance in the Russian language. Hard consonants were marked by counters of one color and soft consonants by counters of another color. Now the diagram of the word's sound structure was colored by counters of three colors. (See Figure 24-2.) The children not only filled in the diagram with the counters, but they also called out the names of the phonemic categories. Gradually, they went on to analyzing the sounds without the help of the counters and diagrams, simply naming the phonemes in the succession in which they occurred in the structure of the word and also indicating the phonemic categories to which they belonged.

Only after this did we go on to teach children the written or printed characters that mark vowel phonemes. This teaching was on the basis of the sound structure

FIGURE 24-2. Apparatus for materializing the sound categories: vowel, hard consonant, and soft consonant.

diagrams. The children completed the diagrams with the counters of different colors as described; then they found vowel phonemes common to several such words; the teacher showed the children the written characters for such vowels and distributed individual characters, which the pupils used to replace the vowel counters in the diagrams. At this stage, the schema of the sound structure of the word appeared to the child as a composition of counters that distinguished consonant phonemes of the different categories and letters marking their vowel phonemes. (See Figure 24-3.)

As has been noted, the Russian written language has eight characters to mark

FIGURE 24-3. Sound structure diagram, after the introduction of characters to mark different vowels.

four vowel phonemes, and these serve also to mark the preceding consonant phoneme as either soft or hard. Therefore, the children were taught which character had to be inserted, depending on whether the preceding consonant phoneme was soft or hard. This proved an easy task because this hardness or softness was already marked by the counters of different colors.

Experimental teaching showed that 6- or 7-year-old children very easily managed all these tasks after a series of lessons. We gave ample time for practicing these responses, because we considered that the better the children mastered these phonemic discriminations and the marking of the vowel phonemes, the faster and better they would also master word changing, to which we attached vital importance for reading. Thus, we began teaching the operation of word changing only after the children had completely mastered the sound analysis of words with both differentiation of phonemic categories and the marking of vowel phonemes.

Method of Teaching Word Changing

The children were introduced to the task of word changing in the following manner. They produced the full sound analysis of the word, filling in the word's sound structure diagram with counters marking the various phonemic categories. After this, they replaced the vowel category counters with characters of the alphabet. Then they exchanged one vowel character with another one and determined what new word this produced. In the Russian language, there are very many words that consist of three sounds—that is, two-consonant phonemes with a vowel in the middle. This type of word was most suitable for our purpose in teaching the primary word-changing operation. To facilitate this task of vowel substitution we devised a special apparatus. All the vowel characters were represented on a long, narrow strip of paper. In the sound structure diagram, on each side of the square for the vowel phoneme, a slit was cut through which the strip with the vowel characters was inserted. By moving this strip, the child replaced one vowel with another in succession, changing the sound form of the word and obtaining either new words or nonsense syllables. Very soon, on the average after nine lessons, the child mastered word changing.

To test the effectiveness of word changing as a method of developing the child's understanding of the sound construction of the syllable, when the pupils had completed the word-changing activities we presented them with new syllables and words that they were required to read. These new words and syllables contained consonants they had not met previously in the training examples. A consonant was placed in front of the child and he was told the sound it signified. Then this new consonant was combined with each of the vowels in succession, and the child was asked to read each syllable formed in this manner. The results showed that, in the course of word changing, the children had mastered the process of creating the sound form of a word. Of the pupils, 95 per cent easily managed this syllable reading and progressed to other words.

Conclusion

This research confirmed our hypothesis concerning the psychological mechanism of creating the sound form of the word from its graphic model. Reading is not simply the successive calling of the names of the sounds one after the other. The factors of greatest importance in creating the sound form of a word from its graphic symbols are selecting the phoneme designated by a given character and progressing from the phoneme to its version, which is dependent to a certain extent on positional conditions (the succeeding letter and its sound value). Appropriate orientation to this feature is clearly of vital significance to smooth progress in the initial stages of learning to read.

Current Developments

These researches, which have clarified our theoretical understanding of the psychological process of reading, have also provided a practical basis for the development of a new teaching method, including new materials for elementary reading. Tests of this new method have produced positive results. Currently, further experiments are being conducted with younger children. The method is also being applied to other languages in the USSR. Already, textbooks incorporating the new approach have been produced for teaching children to read in the Armenian and Yakutsk languages, and these are being evaluated in experimental investigations. Thus far, it has been found necessary to make changes in our approach only in regard to the detailed peculiarities of the phonemic structures and the writing systems of these different languages. The basic principles we have described seem to have general validity and therefore remain unchanged.

REFERENCES

1. Shvatchkin, N. Kh., "The development of phonematic perception of speech in young children," *News of the Academy of Psychological Science of the Russian Soviet Federative Socialist Republic,* **13** (1948).
2. Luria, A R., *Traumatic Aphasia,* Moscow: Academy of Medical Science of the USSR, 1947.
3. Luria, A. R., *Psycho-physiological Features of Writing,* Moscow: Academy of Psychological Science of the Russian Soviet Federative Socialist Republic, 1950.
4. Galperin, P. J., "An investigation of the development of mental operations," *Psychological Science in the USSR,* **1** (1959).
5. Fausek, U. I., *Learning Literacy and the Development of Speech by the Montessori System,* Moscow: Gosizdat, 1922.
6. Khokhlova, N. A., *The Comparative Psychological Study of the Sound Analysis of Pre-school Children,* diploma dissertation, Faculty of Psychology, Lomonosov, the Moscow State University, 1955.
7. Olshannikova, A. E., "The development of the generalized mental operation of sound discrimination," *Reports of the Academy of Psychological Science of the Russian Soviet Federative Socialist Republic,* **3,** (1958).

8. Zhurova, L. E., and Elkonin, D. B., "On the question of the phonematic perception of children of preschool age," in the symposium, *Education at the Preschool Age Level,* Moscow: Academy of Psychological Science of the Russian Soviet Federative Socialist Republic, 1963.
9. Zhinkin, N. I., *The Mechanism of Speech,* Moscow: Academy of Psychological Science of the Russian Soviet Federative Socialist Republic, 1958.

Index of Names

Italic numbers refer to entries in the References, which occur at the ends of chapters.

Aaorns, A. C., *242*
Aaron, I. E., *548*
Abernethy, D., 7, *11*
Abiri, J. O. O., 109, *126*,
  233–34, *242*
Abrahams, R. D., 231, *242*
Adams, M. L., *549*
Adams, R. B., 250, *256*
Adiel, S., *439*
Adiseshiah, M. S., 3
Ahmed, M., 66
Allen, J. E., Jr., 504, 513, *545*
Allinsmith, W., *542*
Alonso, A., 259, *281, 282*
Amidon, E. J., *545*
Ammons, H. S., 22, *30*
Ammons, M., 526, *548*
Ammons, R. B., 22, *30*
Ananiev, B., 276
Anderson, C. A., *213*
Anderson, I. H., 153, *167*,
  354, *358*
Anderson, R. H., 494, *540*
Andresen, O., *11, 549*
Anello de Mendolía, I., 281,
  284
Ansari, N. A., 170, *180*
Anzai, E., 458, *464*
Anzako, I., 452, *463*
Arai, Y., *462*
Arbuthnot, M., 376
Arthur, G., 501, *541*
Artley, A. S., 376, 509, 533,
  543, 549
Austin, M. C., vii, 7, *11*, 35,
  38, 163, 179, 525, 536,
  541, 546, 548, 549

Baird, C. L., 368, *381*
Baki, R., *438*
Baleani, V., 281, *284*
Balpuri, S., 170, *180*
Bamman, H. A., 509, *543*
Baratz, J. C., *82, 127, 166*,
  189, *213, 214*, 233, *242*,
  243, 540
Barbe, W. B., 500, *541*
Barrenechea, A. M., 259,
  266, *281*
Barrett, T. C., 209, 210, *215*,
  509, 510, 525, *542, 544*,
  548
Batchelder, M. I., *168*
Belgrano, M., *282*
Ben-Shach, L., *439*
Bentwich, J. S., *438*
Bereday, G. Z. F., 10, *12*,
  54, *64*

Bereiter, C., 187, 230, *547*
Berg, L., *382*
Bergson, H., 274, *284*
Bernstein, B., 187, *213*, 369,
  381
Berra, A., 273
Betts, E. A., 115, *126*
Betzner, J., *168*
Biglmaier, F., vii, 38, 116,
  219, 351, 352, 353, *357*,
  358, 359
Blackie, J., 52, 53, 54, *63, 64*
Blanchard, P., 459, *464*
Bledsoe J., 508, *543*
Block, R., 342, 357
Blom, G. E., viii, 6, 81, 85,
  102, *104*, 105
Bloom, B. S., 502, 511, *542*,
  543, 544
Bloom, S., *439*
Bloomfield, L., 143, *166*, 181,
  213, 217, *240*, 329, *340*
Blum, U., *167, 438*
Board of Education
  (England), *380*
Bobertag, O., 356
Bond, B., *540*
Bond, G. L., 129, *165*, 209,
  215, 504, 530, *542, 548*,
  549
Bosch, B., 355, *359*
Boulay, L., 333, *341*
Braam, L. S., *549*
Bracken, D. K., *11*
Braun, C., *84*
Braverman, S., *439*
Bredsdorff, Aa., 299, *306*
Brickman, W., 287, *305*
Brill, M., *438*
Brimer, M. A., viii, 6, 10, 13,
  30, 32, 46, 60, 157
Brogan, P., 500, *541*
Brown, A. L., *11, 12, 61, 126*,
  341, 489t, *540*
Brown, B. F., *540*
Brückl, H., 355
Bruhns, I., 297, *306*
Bruner, J. S., 74, *83*, 390,
  401, 502, 527, 531, *542*
Brzeinski, J. E., *542*
Burnet, M., *31*, 67, *82*, 170,
  180
Burns, P. C., *547*
Buros, O., 526, *548*
Burt, C., 179, 206, *215*, 248,
  255, 270
Burton, W. H., 334, *341, 544*
Bush, C. L., vii, 525, *542*,
  548, 549

Butler, C., *240*
Butler, N. R., *380*

Cairns, J. C., 253, *256*
Calfee, R. C., 211, *216*
Camilli, E., 279
Capdevila, A., *282*
Carbonell de Grompone, M.,
  266, 275, *282, 284*
Carrigan, P., 516, *546*
Cashdan, A., 379, *282*
Castellan, N. J., 90, *104*
Cattell, J. Mc., 353, *358*
Causey, O. S., *61*
Central Advisory Council for
  Education (England), *63*,
  361, *380*
Central Bureau of Statistics
  (Israel), *438*
Chall, J., 13, *30*, 139, 144,
  166, 209, *215*, 232, *438*,
  519, 538, *542, 546, 549*
Chanson, M., *339*
Chao, Y. R., 35, *61*, 227,
  242, 387, 400, *401, 402*
Chapman, R. S., 211, *216*,
  508, *543*
Chardon, P., 149, *167*, 330,
  335, *340, 341*
Charlier, P. S., 131, *165*, 328t,
  340
Chase, F. S., 38, *62*, 512,
  545
Chatterjee, S. K., *424*
Cheng, C., 105
Chiland, C., 6, *11*, 332, *341*
Chou, E.-L., 106, *126*
Chuang, C. H., 386, 388,
  389t, *400, 401*
Clairborne, J. H., 217, *240*
Clark, M. M., *166, 381*
Cleland, D. L., 509, *544*
Cloward, R. D., 524, *547*
Clymer, T., 520, *542, 546*
Cohen, P., 232, *242*
Cohen, S. A., *547*
Conant, J. B., 530, *548*
Cooper, W. F., 206, *215*
Correll, W., *357*
Cossettini, O., 152, 279, *284*
Critchley, M., 459, *464*
Cromer, W., 294, *305*
Crosby, M., *547*
Cultural Service of the
  French Embassy, *339*
Curry, R. L., 246, 250,
  255, 256

Dale, E., 513, 528, *545, 548*

Daniels, J., 377
Danmarks Statistik, *305*
Dansk Sprognævn, *305*
Darrow, H. F., 500, *541*
Davie, R., *380*
Davis, F. B., 509, *544*
Dawson, M. A., 509, *544*
Dearborn, W. F., 153, *167,*
 354, *358*
Dearden, R. F., 34, *61*
Debiesse, J., *340*
DeBoer, J., 508, *543*
Dechant, E. V., *543*
Decroly, O., 274–75, 325, 335
Defond, M., *167, 340*
de Francis, J., *126,* 384, *400*
de Hirsch, K., 209, *215,* 514,
 545
Delacato, C. H., 515, *546*
Delaunay, E., 276
Department of Education and
 Science (England and
 Wales), *63, 255,* 361, *380*
Deputy, E. C., 74, *83*
Deutsch, M., *547*
Dewey, G., 392, *401*
Dewey, J., 287, 430
Dezeo, E. C., 273, 277, *284*
Diack, H., 377
Diringer, D., 106, *126*
Dixon, W. R., 50, 52, *63*
Dodds, W. J., 488, *539, 540*
Dodge, R., 353, *358*
Doman, G. I., 116, 347
Dottrens, R., 139, *166,*
 331-33, *340*
Douglass, M. P., 245, *255*
Downing, J., vii, *11, 12, 61,*
 84, 108, 109, 117, *126, 127,*
 166, 167, 180, 186, 204,
 213, 215, 222, *241, 255,*
 341, 370, *381,* 489*t, 540,*
 551
Dunn, L. M., *30*
Dunsing, J. D., 546
Durand, P., *167, 340*
Durkin, D., 113, *126,* 501,
 502, *541, 542, 543*
Durrell, D. D., 74, *83,* 209,
 212, *215,* 334, 335, 336,
 341
Dushkin, A. M., *438*
Dykstra, R., 109, *126,* 128–29,
 165, 209, *215,* 504, 505,
 530, *542, 548, 549*

Ebel, R. L., 540, *546*
Edge, S., *104*
Edwards, T. J., *547*
Eisenberg, L., 459, *465*
Eisenstadt, S. N., *438*
Elberling, B. V., 297, *306*
Elkonin, D. B., viii, 32–34,
 67, 70, 81, 124, 149, 154,
 157, *167,* 192, 200, 205,
 211–12, 220, 551*n,* 569,
 579

Elliott, D. L., *546*
Ellis, A. J., 195, *214*
Emans, R., 128, *165*
Emmett, W. G., 54, *64*
Endo, Y., *463*
Englehart, M. D., 525, *548*
Englemann, S., 187, 230, *547*
Enoch, H., *438*
Erdmann, B., 353, *358*
Estruch de Morales, M. M.,
 281, *284*
Evanechko, P., *84*
Ewert, A., *340*

Fagan, E. R., *547*
Farr, R., 525, *548*
Fasold, R. W., 231, 233, 238,
 242, 243
Fausek, U. I., 561, *578*
Featherstone, J., 54, *64,* 159,
 168
Feitelson, D., ix, 70, *82*
 152–54, 203, 204, *215,* 221,
 241, 246, *255, 438, 439*
Feldmann, S., 139, 144, *166*
Fenn, H. C., 392
Ferguson, S., *11*
Fernald, G., 449
Ferreyra, A., 273
Ferry, J., 320, 333
Figurel, J. A., *12, 62, 126,*
 127, 180, 241, 255, 340,
 544, 545
Filho, L., 154, *167,* 272, 276,
 281, *284*
Finck, F. N., 383
Finocchiaro, M., 492, *540*
Flanders, N., 512, 533, *545,*
 549
Fleming, J. T., *214, 401*
Flesch, R., 51, *63*
Florander, J., 297, *305, 307*
Floud, J., *213*
Foshay, A. W., 6, *11,* 43, 44,
 46, 49, 50, 60, *62, 63, 82*
Fox, L. K., 500, *541*
France, N., 366, *380*
Fries, C. C., 34, *61*
Frost, J. L., *11*
Frostig, M., 515, 516, *546*
Führ, C., 344, *357*
Fujii, M., *462*
Fukuzawa, S., 448, *462*

Gagg, J. C., 152, *167, 438,*
 439
Gagg, M. E., 152, *167, 438,*
 439
Gagné, R. M., 527
Gal, R., 131, *165,* 319, 330,
 337, 338, *339, 340, 341*
Galperin, P. J., 560, *578*
Gandolfo, A., *282*
Gann, E., 459, *465*
Gardener, R. C., 493, *540*
Gardner, K., 249, *255*
Garzón, T., *282*

Gaspar, R., 70, *82*
Gates, A. I., 115, 117, *126,*
 161–62, *168,* 370, 387, *401,*
 502, *541, 542*
Gattegno, C., 226, *242,* 377,
 381
Gavel, S. R., 75, *83,* 209, *215*
Genetz, H. M. F., 314
Gephart, W. J., 539, *550*
Geschwind, N., 459, *464*
Gesell, A., 501
Getson, R., *543*
Ghioldi, A., 281, *284*
Gibson, E. J., 70, *82,* 387,
 390, *401*
Gilbert, L. C., 70, *82*
Giles, H. A., 399
Gjessing, H., 7, *12*
Glaser, E. M., 511, *545*
Glaser, R., 528, *548*
Glass, G. V., 516, *546*
Glynn, D. M., 51, *63*
Gobello, J., *282*
Gold, L., *547*
Gooch, S., 162, *168,* 367, *381*
Goodacre, E. J., ix, 51, 52,
 149, 161, 162, 249, *256, 381*
Goodlad, J. I., *540*
Goodman, K. S., 68, *82,* 112,
 123, *126, 127,* 145, *166,*
 186, 187–88, *213, 214,* 230,
 233, 234–35, *242, 401,* 491,
 540
Goody, J., 105–106, *126,*
 193–94, *214*
Gordon, B. Y., *242*
Government of India, *424,*
 425
Grashey, H. v., 353, *358*
Gray, W. S., 4, 5, 6, 7, 8, *11,*
 12, 31, 36, *61,* 65–66, 67,
 82, 116, 120–21, 122, *126,*
 127, 128, 140–42, 146, 147,
 151, 153, 154, 155–56, 158,
 160, 161, 162, *165, 166,*
 167, 168, 170–71, *180,* 182,
 193, 198–99, 206, 208, 209,
 212, *213, 214, 215,* 246,
 251, *255, 256,* 276, *282,*
 311, *318,* 323, 325, 326,
 331, 332, 334, *339, 340,*
 341, 352, 353, *358,* 376,
 383, *400,* 416, *424,* 498,
 500, 538, *541, 544, 550*
Greene, C. B., 509, *543*
Grierson, G. A., 403, 406, *424*
Grimes, J. W., *542*
Groff, P. J., 124, *127*
Grundtvig, N. F. S., 287
Guilford, J. P., 527
Guillemoteau, T., *341*
Guitarte, G., *282*
Gunderson, D. V., 514, *545*
Günther, K. H., *357*
Guszak, F. J., 511, *544*

Hafner, L. E., 509, *544*

Hakulinen, L., 308, *318*
Hall, G. S., 501
Hall, M., *549*
Hall, R. A., Jr., 34, *61*, 154, *167*, 199, *214*, 220, 228, *241*, *242*
Halle, M., 193–94, *214*, 387, *401*
Hallgren, B., 459, *464*
Halsey, A. H., *213*
Hamachek, D., 533, *549*
Hammond, M., *401*
Hansen, E. J., *305*
Hanson, E., 522, *547*
Harman, D., 37, *61*, *62*, 251–53, *256*
Harrington, M. J., 74, *83*
Harris, A. J., 124, *127*, 514, 515, 523, 525, 530, 533, *545*, *546*, *547*, *548*, *549*
Harris, L., 37
Harris, T. L., 515, *546*
Harrison, M., 222
Harrison, M. L., *542*
Hart, J., 208, *215*, *240*
Hartmann, W., 355, *359*
Harvison, A. R., *544*
Hasler, H., 349, *357*
Hayashi, K., *463*
Hayes, A. S., *255*
Hayes, E., 74, *83*
Heimann, A., 354, *358*
Helier-Malaurie, M., *341*
Hellmuth, J., *546*
Helmholtz, H. L. F. v., 353
Henderson, D., *381*
Henry, J. A., 85, *104*
Herber, H. L., 509, *543*
Herdan, G., 383*n*, 391–94, *401*, *402*
Hermann, K., 218, *240*, 301, *306*
Herse, R., 80, *84*
Hildreth, G., 192, *214*, 219–20, *240*, *241*, 539, 550
Hilliard, R. M., 37, *62*
Hinshelwood, J., 459, *464*
Hjelm, H. F., 539, *550*
Hodges, R., *240*
Hoffman, J., 354, *358*
Hogan, U., 509, *543*
Holmes, J. A., 70, *82*, 119–20, *127*, *241*
Horikawa, N., 452, *463*
Horn, T. D., *547*
Horne, D., *546*
Horst, H. M., *547*
Hotyat, F., 43, 48, *62*
Hough, J,, *545*
Howes, V. M., 500, *541*
Huck, C. S., *545*
Hudson, W., 23, *30*
Huebner, M. H., vii, 525, *542*, *548*, *549*
Huelsman, C. B., Jr., 510, *544*
Huey, E. B., 387, *401*, *438*

Hunt, J. M., 502, *542*
Hunt, L. C., Jr., 500, *541*
Hurley, R., 522, *547*
Husén, T., 8, *12*, 16, *30*, 249, *255*, 539, *550*
Huus, H., 509, *543*
Hylla, E. I., 352, *357*

Iglesias, L. F., 278
Imura, T., 458, *464*
Ingenkamp, K. H., *358*
Inhelder, B., 200, *214*
Inner London Education Authority, *380*
International Bureau of Education, *31*, *61*, 65, *82*, 113, 140
Ishii, M., *463*

Jakobsen, G., 299, *306*
Jansen, M., ix, 172, 178, 221, 287, 294, 298, 300, *305*, *306*, *307*
Jansky, J. J., 514, *545*
Jenkinson, M. D., *11*, *12*, 247, 250, *255*, *256*, *305*, *438*, 538, *550*
Jespersen, O., 285, *305*
Johns, E., *380*
Johnson, M. E. B., *380*
Johnson, M. S., 525, *546*, 548
Johnson, R. J., 75, *83*, 210, 211, *215*
Jones, B., 222
Jones, J. K., 226, *242*, 375, 377, *381*
Jung, E., *282*
Junkins, K. M., 74, *83*

Kaga, H., 454, *463*
Kaigo, T., 446, *462*
Kainz, F., 356, *359*
Kamei, M., *463*
Kandel, I. L., 320, *339*
Karlgren, B., 383, 392, *400*
Karlin, R., 509, *543*
Karvonen, J., 317, *318*
Katzenberger, L. F., 355, *359*
Kawai, Y., 203, *215*, 448–49, *462*
Kegel, F. O., *357*
Kellaghan, T. P., 23, *30*
Kennedy, G. A., 384, 386, *400*
Kennedy, J. F., 249
Kephart, N. C., 515, 516, *546*
Keppel, F., 249, 529
Kern, A., 355, *359*
Kern, E., *359*
Ketcham, C. A., *165*, *542*
Khokhlova, N. A., 154, *167*, 564, 568, *578*
Kimball, R. B., *544*
Kimura, K., 202, *214*, 458, *464*
King, E. J., *339*

King, E. M., *542*
King, M. L., *545*
Kirchhoff, H., 352, *357*
Kirchhoff, P., *358*
Kirk, S. A., *30*
Kirste, E., 356
Kleinberger, A. F., *438*
Kleinhans, W. H., 356, *359*
Kleist, K., 458, *464*
Kline, C. L., 383*n*, 395–96, *402*
Klineberg, O., 6, *11*
Kluge, K. F., 355
Kobayashi, Y., 454, *463*
Kochman, T., 231, *242*
Kold, K., 287
Korte, W., 354, *358*
Krakow, I., 426*n*
Krathwohl, D. R., *543*
Kratzmeier, H., *357*
Kress, R. A., 525, *546*, *548*
Krüger, F., 354, *357*
Kunnas, K., 315
Kurasawa, E., 450–51, *462*
Kuratani, M., *463*
Kuromaru, S., 395, 458, *464*
Kutzner, A., 355, *358*
Kyöstiö, O. K., ix, 7, *12*, 208, 209, 218, 309, 310, 317, *318*

Labov, W., 231, 232, *242*
Lado, R., 72, 75, *82*, *83*, 188, 192, 198, *214*, 217, *240*
Lakdawala, U. T., 423, *425*
Lange, P. C., *548*
Langford, W. S., 514, *545*
Lanzelsdorfer, F., *357*
Larsen, A., 298, *306*
Larsen, C. Aa., 302, *307*
Latham, W., *241*
Laubach, F. C., 200, 252, *256*, 329, *340*
Laubach, R., *256*
Lauwerys, J. A., *305*
Lawley, D. N., 41, *62*
Lazar, M., 499, *541*
Leandri, F., 333, *341*
Lebettre, M., 325*t*, 336, *339*, *340*, *341*
Lee, N., 395, *402*
Lee, W. R., 6, *11*, 66, *82*, 143–44, 146, 147, 157, *166*, *167*, 199, *214*
Leerskov, A., 300, *306*
Lefevre, C. A., 146, *166*, 191, 199, *214*, 220, 228, *241*, *242*
Lehtovaara, A., 317, *318*
Leong, C. K., ix, 148, 194, 199, 203, 388, 389*t*, 394, *400*, *401*, *402*
Levy, J., 153–54, *167*, 430–31, 433, *438*
Li, C.-H., *126*
Lietwiler, H. K., 508, *543*
Linder, M., 352, *357*
Livingston, H., *544*
Lloyd, H. M., 523, 524, *547*

Loban, W., 187, *213*
Lobo de Geoghegan, M. A., 281, *284*
Lobrot, M. G., 6, *11*, 338, *341*
Locke, J., 319
López de Nelson, E., 273, *283*
Lorge, I., *544*
Lovell, K., 160–62, *168*, 366, *380*
Lowry, W. C., *549*
Lundahl, F., 291, 298, *305*, *306*
Lunn, J. C. B., *380*
Luria, A. R., 557, *578*
Lynd, H. M., 159
Lynd, R. S., 159

McCarthy, J. J., *30*
McCullough, C. M., x, 33, *61*, *401*, 416, *424*, 509, *543*, *544*
McDavid, R. I., 192, *214*
McDougall, W., 274
McGeeney, P., *180*
MacGinitie, W. H., *542*
McKay, D., 377
McKay, Y., *11*
McKee, P., *542*
McLaughlin, K. L., 74, *83*
McLellan, A., *64*
McLeod, J., *383n*
Macnamara, J., 183, 184, *213*
McNeil, J., *548*, *549*
Mager, R. F., 527
Maguerez, C., 151, *167*
Mainichi Shimbun-Sha, 445, *462*
Maisonny, S. B., 276
Makita, K., x, 38, 107, *126*, 202, 218–19, *240*, 395, *402*, 458, 460, *464*, *465*
Malmberg, B., *282*
Malmquist, E., x, 7, *11*, 74, *83*, 111, 164, 177, 197, 198, *214*, 246, 247, 251, *255*, *487*
Mann, H., 494, 526
Mansion, J. E., *340*
Mao, T.-T., 106
Margairaz, E., 139, *166*, 331–32, *340*
Marksheffel, N. D., 509, *543*, *545*
Marshall, S., 76, *84*
Martin, J. L., 206, *215*
Martinez de Elgorreaga, Y., 279
Maruyama, M., 218, *240*
Masia, B. B., *543*
Mathews, M. M., 488, *539*
Mathews, R. A., 292, 393, *394t*
Matsubara, T., 454, *463*
Matsumoto, R., *464*
Maxwell, S. M., *166*
May, M. M., *241*
Mayer, A., *341*
Mayer-Gross, W., *464*
Mazurkiewicz, A. J., *241*

Meier, H., *357*
Meir, M., *439*
Meltzer, N. S., 80, *84*
Mercante, V., 276, *283*, *284*
Meriam, J. L., 160, *168*
Merrill, M. M., *255*, *256*
Messmer, O., 354, 356, *358*
Metfessel, N. S., *547*
Mezeix, P., 335, *341*
Miles, C., 259
Miller, G. A., 388, 390, *401*
Mills, H. C., *126*
Mills, Q. B., vii, *547*
Minister of Education (Denmark), *306*
Ministry of Education (England and Wales), *63*, 255, 361, *380*
Missildine, W., 459, *465*
Modiano, N., 183, *213*, *540*
Money, J., 395, 396, *402*, *545*
Monroe, M., 74, *83*, 219, *240*, 272, 352, 356, *358*, 376, 460, *465*
Montessori, M., 325, 335
Moore, O. K., 502, 504
Moore, W. J., 509, *543*
Morioka, K., 453, *463*
Morphett, M. V., 115, *126*, 129, 501, *541*
Morris, J., 491, 492, *540*
Morris, J. M., viii, 7, *11*, *63*, 109, 119, 122, *126*, *127*, 134, *166*, 249, *255*, 313, *318*, 371, 376, *380*, *381*, 398, *402*
Morrison, C., vii, 530, *541*, *548*, *549*
Mountcastle, V., 459, *464*
Mountford, J., 71, *82*, 183, *213*
Muehl, S., 211, *216*
Mueller, R. G., 510, *544*
Müller, H., 352, 355, *359*
Müller, R., 352
Müller, W., 355
Muñoz, J. M., 273, 277, *284*
Munro, R., 50, 51, *63*, 376
Muraishi, S., 454, *463*
Murphy, H. A., 74, *83*, 209, 215
Mycock, M., 368, *381*
Mylov, P., 294, 298, *305*, *306*

Nachman, L., 508, *543*
Nakamura, Y., *464*
Nakano, S., 447, *462*
Nance, A. D., 491, *540*
National Advisory Committee on Dyslexia and Related Disorders (USA), *545*
National Society for the Study of Education (USA), 33, *61*
National Union of Teachers (Great Britain), 368, 369, *381*
Navarro, T., *281*

Neale, M., 224
Neijs, K., *31*, 35, *61*, 66, *82*, 182, *213*, 217, *240*
Neisser, U., 390, *401*
Nelson, J., 204, *215*
Newman, H., *547*
Nicholson, A., 74, *83*
Niemi, H., 314
Nyerere, J., 251, 254

Obi, I., 458, *464*
Obonai, T., 454, *463*
Odgers, J., *543*
O'Donnell, M., 50, 51, *63*, 376
O'Gorman, M. B., *64*
Ohanian, V., 51, *63*, 143, *166*
Ohnmacht, D. D., 75, *83*, 210, 211, *215*
Okada, Y., 395, *464*
Okami, S., 456–57, *464*
Olanie, S., *339*
Olds, H. F., Jr., 498, *541*
Oliver, P. R., 204, *215*
Ollila, L., *84*
Olshannikova, A. E., 568, *578*
Olson, W. C., 499, *541*, *546*
Oñativia, O. V., 276, *284*
Oommen, C., x, 121, 150–1, 174, 208–209
Orr, J., 329, *340*
Ortar, G., *438*
Ortego, P. D., 491, 493, *540*
Orton, S., 459, *464*
Osser, H., *401*
Österberg, T., 185, 187, 188, 189–90, *213*, *214*, 225, 237
Otto, W., *549*

Pacolt, E., *357*
Palermo, E., *283*
Passow, A. H., *546*
Pastoriza de Echebarne, **D.**, 279
Pauli, L., viii
Pavlova, A. I., 569
Payet, L., *282*
Penney, M., 539, *550*
Penty, R., 508, *543*
Perelstein de Braslavsky, B., xi, 229, *283*, *284*
Perrot, C., 338, *341*
Personke, C. R., 58, *64*
Pestalozzi, J. H., 319
Peters, M., 226, *241*, *381*
Peterson, R. P., 50–60, *63*, *64*
Pfaffenberger, H., 356, *359*
Piaget, J., 23, 75, 76, 78, 81, *84*, 200, 211, *214*, *216*, 531, 537, *549*
Pick, A. D., *401*
Pidal, R. M., 261
Pidgeon, D. A., 39–43, 44, 48–49, 55, 59, *62*, 368, *381*
Pitman, I. J., 234–35, *242*
Pointud, J., 336, *339*, *340*, *341*
Polivanova, M. A., 569
Postlethwaite, N., 8, *12*

Postman, L., 390, *401*
Powell, W. R., *540*
Prakash, V., *425*
Preston, R. C., 109, *126*, 219, *240*, 342, *357*, 538, *550*
Pringle, M. L. K., 249, *255*, *380*
Professional Standards and Ethics Committee, IRA, *549*
Pumfrey, P. D., 379, *382*
Pylkkänen, L., 314

Rabinovitch, R. D., 459, *465*, 515, *545*
Raeder, R., 551
Rai, A., 455, *463*
Raitio, K., 314
Ramsey, Z. W., *549*
Ranschburg, P., 351, *357*
Ranta, T. M., 218, *240*
Rasborg, F., 302, *307*
Rasch, G., 27, *31*
Rasmussen, G. K., 293, 303, *305*, *307*
Ratz, M. S., 226, *242*
Rauch, S. J., *546*
Rawal, R. T., 423, *425*
Rawat, D. S., 174, *180*, 412, *424*
Raybold, E., 74, *83*
Razik, T., 513, *545*
Reading Project (India), 412, *424*, *425*
Reid, J., 77–78, 80, 81, *84*, 228, 239, *242*, *243*
Reinhard, L., 349, 350, 355, *357*
Reynell, J., 22, *30*
Ricci, M., 399
Rice, J. M., 526
Rickover, H. G., 51, *63*
Riessman, F., 525, *547*
Ripple, R., *549*
Ritsher, C., 494, *540*
Robbins, M. P., 516, *546*
Roberts, G. R., 51, *63*, 155-56, *167*, 366, *380*
Robinson, H. A., 522, *546*, *547*
Robinson, H. M., 7, *11*, *62*, 74, *83*, *241*, 498, 510, 515, 526, 535, 536, *540*, *541*, *542*, *543*, *544*, *545*, *546*, *548*, *549*
Rockcastle, V., *549*
Roehm, M. A., *549*
Rogers, V. R., 54, *63*, 162–63, *168*
Rollins, S. P., 495, *540*
Rordam, T., 287, *305*
Rose, I. M., *241*
Rosen, C. L., 491, 493, *540*
Rosenberger, E., 426n
Rosenblat, A., *214*, 261, *281*
Roth, M., *464*
Rousseau, J. J., 319

Royal Board of Education (Sweden), 483, *487*
Rüdiger, D., *357*
Ruoppila, I., 318
Russell, D. H., x, 509, 510, *544*
Ruthman, P. E., xi

Saadeh, I. Q., *545*
Saarinen, P., *318*
Sakamoto, I., 447, 451, 452, 453, 455, 457, 461, *462*, *463*, *464*
Sakamoto, S., 202, *214*, 458, *464*
Sakamoto, T., xi, 38, 171, 201, 202, 206, *214*, *215*, 443, 445, 454, 461–62, *463*, *465*
Salo, A., 314
Salotti, M., 279
Samuels, S. J., 38, *62*, 64, 75, *83*, 178, *180*, 210–11, *216*, 221, *241*, 328, *340*
Sander, F., 354, *358*
Sanders, N. M., 511, *544*
Sanderson, A. E., 370, *381*
Sandhu, S., 403n
Sapir, E., 187
Sarjeant, I., 50, 51, *63*
Sarmiento, D. F., 268, 273, 275, *282*, *283*
Sartain, H. W., 494, *540*
Sastre, M., 273, *283*
Sato, Y., 454, *463*
Scanlon, D., *305*
Scharfstein, Z., *438*
Schenk-Danziger, L., 352, *358*
Schick, G. B., *241*, *255*, *256*
Schmalohr, E., 355, *357*, *359*
Schmidt, L., 353, *358*
Scholl, G. T., 58, *64*
Schonell, F. J., 50, 51, *63*, 74, *83*, 152, 153, *167*, 224, 374, 376, *438*
Schreiber, J. E., 511, *544*
Schubert, D. G., 456, 461, *464*, *465*
Schultz de Mantovani, F., 279
Schultze, W., 344, *357*
Schüttler-Janikulla, K., *357*
Schwartz, E., 349, *357*
Schwartzberg, H., *541*
Scottish Education Department, *380*
Seashore, R. H., 125, *127*
Sebeok, T. A., *213*
Segovia, L., *282*
Seng, M. W., *547*
Serafica, F. C., 75, *83*
Serdyuchenko, G. P., 253, *256*
Serwer, B. L., *547*
Shah, A. M., *126*
Shane, H. G., 498, *541*
Shaplin, J. T., 498, *541*

Shearer, E., 366, *380*
Sheldon, W. D., vii, 509, *544*
Shell, L. M., *547*
Shiba, S., 453, *463*
Shields, M., 368, *381*
Shimada, S., *464*
Shrodes, C., 457, *464*
Shrof, R. G., *126*
Shuppan Kagaku Kenkyu-Sho, *462*
Shuy, R. W., *82*, *127*, *166*, *213*, *214*, 236, *242*, *243*, *540*
Shvatchkin, N. Kh., 556, *578*
Sigel, I. E., 75, *83*
Simon, J., 330, 331, 336, *340*, *341*
Singer, H., 70, *82*
Singer, M., *126*
Slater, E., *464*
Smith, C. B., *546*, *548*
Smith, D. E. P., 516, *546*
Smith, F., 387, 390, *401*
Smith, N. B., 5, 7, *11*, 488, 513, 517, *539*, *540*, *541*, *543*, *545*, *547*, *549*
Smith, R. J., *549*
Sochurek, H., *357*
Soffietti, J. P., 34, *61*
Solomon, R. H., 74
Somerkivi, U., 317, *318*
Southgate, V., 6, *11*, 51, *63*, 129, 155–56, *165*, *166*, *167*, 224, 226, *241*, *242*, 366, *380*, *381*
Spache, E. B., *541*, *543*
Spache, G. D., 297, 538, *541*, *543*, *549*
Spaulding, S., 66
Spearitt, D., 22, *30*
Spearman, C., 274
Spier, L., *255*
Spolsky, B., 184, 186, 187, *213*, *214*
Srinivas, M. N., *126*
Staiger, R. C., 4, 7, *11*, 31, *61*, 67, *82*, 112, *126*, 151, 158, 163–64, *167*, *168*, 170, *180*, 252, *256*, 488, 489t, *540*, *549*
Stauffer, R. G., 524, *541*, *544*, *547*
Stewart, W. A., 182, 185, *213*, 238, *242*, *243*
Stoff, S., *541*
Stott, D. H., 51, *63*
Strang, R., 174, *180*, 387, *401*, 509, 515, 525, 527, *543*, *546*, *548*
Straub, W., 355, *359*
Stroud, J. B., 74, *83*

Taba, H., 511, *544*
Takagi, K., 461–62, *465*
Tasola, O., 318
Tax, S., 186, *213*, 247, *255*, *464*
Taylor, W. L., 453, *463*

Tewksbury, J. L., 499, *541*
Thackray, D., *61*, 74, *83*, 108, 109, 117, *126*, *127*, 186, *213*
Thompson, B., 377
Thompson, F., *11*
Thomsen, O. B., 287, *305*
Thorndike, E. L., 33, *61*, 430
Thorndike, R. L., 43, 44–45, 46–48, 49–50, 60, *62*, *64*, 71, *82*
Thorner, H., 354, *358*
Tinker, M. A., 33, *61*, 74, *83*, *543*
Tinney, R., 109, *126*
Tordrup, S. A., 301, *306*, 353, *358*
Torres, J. M., 273
Trace, A. S., Jr., 124, *127*, 157
Traxler, A. E., *401*, 509, *543*
Tronchere, J., 336, *339*, 340, *341*
Tsutsumi, Y., *462*
Tulchin, S., 459, *465*
Tyler, R. W., 526, *548*

Uhlig, G., *357*
Uhrskov, M., 298, *306*
UNESCO, *31*, *61*, *62*, 66, 67, *82*, *255*, 444, *462*
Ureña, P. H., *282*
Ushinsky, K. D., 551

Vaherva, T., 310, *318*
Vakil, K. S., 423, *425*
Valdman, A., *340*

Valentine, G., 353, *358*
Valtin, R., 353, *358*
Varela, P. J., 273
Veatch, J., 500, *541*
Venezky, R. L., 184, 211, *213*, *216*, 231, *242*
Venger, A. A., 569
Vernay, L., 325*t*, 336, *339*, *340*, *341*
Vernon, M. D., 72–74, *82*, 174, *180*, 190
Vernon, P. E., 58, *64*
Vidal de Battini, B. E., 260*t*, 261, 263–64, *281*, *282*
Viitaniemi, E., 317, 318
Vikainen, I., 218, *240*, 317, *318*
Vikman, K. O., 309, *318*
Volkelt, H., 354
Vopni, S., 527, *548*
Vormeland, O., 74, *83*
Vygotsky, L. S., viii, 75, 76–77, 78, 81, *84*, 151, *167*, 211, *216*

Wade, T., 399
Waite, R. R., 85, *104*
Walker, D. A., 43, *62*
Warburton, F. W., *63*, 129, *165*, *166*, 227, *241*, *242*, *381*
Warwel, K., 355
Washburne, C. W., 115, *126*, 129, 501, *541*
Webster, S. W., 521, *547*
Wellek, A., 354

Whipple, G., 508, *543*
Whitmore, P., 508, *543*
Whorf, B. L., 187, 245, *255*
Wiberg, J. L., xii, 6, 81, 85, 102, *104*, 105
Wiegand, C. F., 354, *358*
Wiener, M., 294, *305*
Wiley, D. E., 16, *30*
Wing, R. L., *544*
Wiseman, S., 162, *168*, 366, 367, *380*, *381*, 399, *402*
Wittick, M. L., *543*
Wittmann, J., 355
Wittrock, M. C., 16, *30*
Witty, P. A., *543*, *544*, *546*
Wolfram, W., 230, 231, 232–33, 237–38, *242*, *243*
Wolf, W., *545*
Wolfe, L. S., 207, *215*
Wong, S. L., 383
Woodworth, R. S., 390, *401*
Wu, Y.-C., *126*
Wundt, W. M., 353
Wynn, S. J., *547*

Yates, A., 494, *540*
Young, M., 177, *180*

Zazzo, R., 338, *341*
Zeitler, J., 354, *358*
Zhinkin, N. I., 572, *579*
Zhurova, L. E., 154, *167*, 569, 579
Zimet, S. G., 85, *104*

Index of Subjects

Italic numbers refer to substantive notes in the References, which occur at the ends of chapters.

Ability, verbal, 22, 24
Accountability, 112, 158, 159, 371, 529
Achievements, reading, 6, 27, 32–61, 80, 109–10, 119, 209, 210, 244, 337–38
Administration, schools, 9, 54–55, 58, 118, 119, 133–38, 159, 160, 165, 271, 309, 320–23, 343–44, 410, 427–28
Afghanistan, 113
Africa, 20, 426, 427
Age, beginning, reading, 50, 53, 57, 60, 113–18, 119, 158, 272, 290–91, 309–10, 330, 347–48, 369–70, 398, 411, 429, 446–49, 466–70, 500–503, 569
  beginning, school, 9, 14, 16, 27, 57, 60, 111, 113–18, 134, 169, 272, 288–90, 309, 314, 323, 345, 348, 363–64, 411, 448, 466, 475, 494, 500
  level, 49–50, 55, 60, 71, 133, 134, 135, 136, 164, 222, 244
  mental, 114–17, 332, 338, 474, 501-502
Algeria, 252
Alphabets, 20, 21, 106, 141, 181, 195, 208, 217, 226, 266–67, 285, 370, 375, 392, 399, 405, 413, 441, 458, 459–60, 516, 555, 563, 572, 574
Approach, bilingual, 183-84, 493
  child-centered, 132, 142, 147, 155, 158–60, 165, 174, 297, 365, 367, 371, 431, 474, 495, 497, 533
  informal, 53–54, 55, 59, 60, 111, 114–15, 121, 143, 158, 160–63, 165, 174, 366–67, 431, 471, 500, 503, 538
  language-experience, 123, 152, 177, 185, 292–94, 325, 493, 497. See also Experience: spoken language
  linguistic, 123, 227, 236, 374, 504, 516
  progressive, 58, 122, 159, 162, 169, 366–67, 430
Arabic, 20, 21, 69, 219, 405, 406, 539
Araucanian, 261, 262
Argentina, 108, 121, 122, 132, 133, 137, 139, 145, 152, 154, 157, 173, 176, 179, 191, 229, 231, 259–84
Armenian, 192, 219, 539, 578
Asia, 28, 157, 426, 427
Assamese, 403, 404, 405
Atttendance, 109, 287, 288, 344–45
Attitudes, 6, 10, 81, 85–103, 105, 112, 162, 225, 248, 251, 262, 295, 298, 363, 370, 378, 395, 410, 412, 419, 420, 437, 450, 455, 467, 485, 492, 500, 512, 521. See also Reading: interests and attitudes; Teacher: attitudes and beliefs
Australia, 22, 39–43, 48
Austria, 349–50
Autonomy, local, 54, 320, 361, 489–90

Belgium, 43, 48, 60, 328
Bengali, 403, 404, 405, 423

Bible, 112, 428, 429, 432, 437
Bibliotherapy, 112, 452, 456–57
Bilingualism, 107, 182–85, 311, 362, 375, 405, 490–94
Blending, 212, 332, 384, 408, 413, 471, 554, 555, 574
Bolivia, 106
Books, availability of, 67, 121, 122-23, 125, 163, 176, 177–78, 238, 251, 270, 278, 294, 298, 299, 335–36, 362, 363, 368, 419–20, 436, 444, 447, 500, 521, 523
Boundary, grapheme, 204–205, 223
  phoneme, 205, 223, 570
  syllable, 277,563
  word, 80-81, 205–206, 408
Brain damage, 202, 457–58, 515, 525, 557
Brazil, 6, 154, 252, 276
Britain. See Great Britain
Burmese, 69

Canada, 4, 37, 80, 107, 204, 247, 395. See also North America
Categorization, 74–75, 78, 79, 387, 413
Central America, 263
Characters, complexity, 203–206, 389–90, 441, 448–49
  names. See Letter-name
  number of, 20, 21, 193–98, 223, 286–87, 392–94, 408, 429, 440–44, 448–50, 572, 573
  redundancy, 195, 390, 393
  shape, 18, 21, 73, 223, 226, 387, 391, 408–409, 415–16, 429, 434, 440, 441
Cheremis, 308
Chile, 60, 252, 261, 262, 273
China, 106, 192, 193, 195, 386, 396, 399, 441
Chinese, 20, 21, 34, 69, 105–106, 113, 117, 148, 149, 169, 193–94, 196, 199, 203–204, 205, 206, 383–96, 397, 398, 399–400, 441
  characters, phonetic element, 386, 391–92, 395, 398, 400
Clarity, cognitive, 72, 73, 75, 77, 78–80, 150, 151, 160, 171, 174, 178, 182, 191, 198, 202, 205, 207, 211–12, 226, 228, 234, 240
Climate, 114
Clinics, reading, 173, 303, 317, 353, 475, 477-80, 517–18, 524, 535
Cockney, 187, 189
Code, 17, 18, 19, 20, 24, 74, 79, 140, 141, 148, 153, 154, 181, 189, 194–95, 196, 197, 198, 199, 200, 201, 202, 204, 205, 207, 217, 219, 221, 222, 223, 226, 228, 229, 232, 233, 234, 235, 236, 237, 286, 356, 372, 378, 387, 388, 393–94, 396, 400, 416, 429, 434, 458, 459, 491, 506
  color, 226, 227, 275, 372, 375, 377, 504, 516
Communication, 17, 19, 20, 21, 53, 58, 59, 76, 79, 81, 147, 149, 151, 154, 160, 171, 196, 197, 232, 233, 247–50, 293, 393, 493, 506, 522, 531, 532, 556

587

Composition, 52, 59, 152, 197–98, 224–25, 296, 418

Comprehension, listening, 21, 22, 23, 468, 556
reading, 22, 23, 24, 25, 27, 28, 33, 35, 40, 41, 45, 46, 48, 50, 58, 70, 71, 150, 154, 157–58, 162, 173, 190, 197, 210, 224, 232, 279, 281, 294, 295, 297, 330, 333, 336, 338, 352, 355, 365, 367, 379, 397, 398, 415, 417, 423, 437, 450–51, 460, 462, 472, 481–82, 483, 486, 506, 508, 509, 512–13, 518, 528, 534, 552–53

Concepts, abstract, 76–77, 80, 200, 238, 270, 469, 471, 491, 521
linguistic, 67, 68, 72, 75, 76, 77, 78, 79, 80, 81, 113, 150, 160, 174, 176, 191, 200, 205, 206, 211, 469, 561, 567–68, 571

Confusion, cognitive, 72–73, 77, 78, 79, 145, 174, 182, 183–85, 190, 197–98, 202, 203–205, 207, 212, 229, 234, 240, 388, 460

Contracting, performance, 111–12, 529

Conventions, literary, 20, 329, 405

Cooperation, international, 3–5, 15–16, 29–30, 247, 254–55, 539

Creativity in writing. See Composition

Cuba, 490–92

Culture, 85, 87, 98–99, 103, 186, 203, 231, 261, 272, 370, 395, 400, 410, 420, 424, 427, 453, 490, 491–94, 504, 520, 524
importance of reading, 21, 81, 105–108, 111–12, 114, 116, 118, 121–23, 125, 129, 323, 326, 327, 366, 488, 513, 521, 528
purposes of literacy, 184, 268, 528

Cyprus, 362–63

Czech, 21, 217

Danish, 218, 221, 285–86

Decoding. See Code

Denmark, 111, 112, 113, 114, 115, 130, 132, 135, 136, 147, 152, 157, 164, 172, 173, 174, 175, 176, 177, 178, 285–307, 466

Deprivation, linguistic, 187–88

Dialect, 69, 106, 107, 110, 144–45, 149, 153, 185–92, 194, 225, 228–38, 259–65, 285, 308, 350, 384, 403, 404, 405, 406, 491

Differences, individual, 52, 123, 133–36, 164, 291, 315–16, 325, 339, 372, 373, 376, 468, 474–77, 478, 494, 495, 496, 497, 498, 499, 514, 534

Digraphs, 195, 204–205, 332

Disadvantaged, 110–11, 179, 293, 367, 374, 399, 492, 514, 516, 520–25, 534

Discrimination. See Perception

Dropout, 133, 176, 179, 269–70, 297, 410, 491, 524

Dutch, 217

Dyslexia, 158, 202, 218, 272, 274, 280, 301–302, 352, 353, 354, 379, 395–96, 458–60, 514, 515

Ecuador, 113, 252

Education, centralized control, 136, 320, 323, 325–27, 397, 427–28, 451, 489–90
comparative, 10, 15, 16, 30, 41–42, 43, 51, 54

Egypt, 438

Emotion, 112, 182, 184, 185, 186, 218, 275, 290, 295, 303, 339, 348, 459, 466, 478, 486,

Emotion [cont.]
495, 499, 504, 527, 531

England, 24, 39–43, 45, 48, 49, 50–60, 77, 80, 88, 89–98, 103, 106, 117, 119, 122, 131, 134, 137, 138, 147, 149, 155, 156, 158–59, 160, 161, 162, 163, 169, 175, 177, 179, 183, 222, 224, 227, 234, 235, 248–49, 270, 287, 360–82. See also Great Britain

English, 20, 21, 22, 29, 46–47, 48, 66, 69, 87, 88, 106, 107, 110, 115, 117, 124, 137, 142, 143–44, 147, 148, 152–54, 157, 170, 183, 184, 185, 187, 191, 193, 194–96, 197, 202, 203, 204–205, 206, 207, 208, 217, 218, 219, 220–21, 222, 226, 227, 228, 229, 230, 231, 232, 233, 234, 235, 236, 265, 266, 276, 318, 328–30, 342, 362–63, 370, 373, 383, 385, 387–96, 397, 405, 409, 411, 413, 433, 434, 440, 441, 449, 456, 459–60, 470, 475, 490–94, 495, 506
standard, 110, 179, 181, 185, 191, 227, 229, 231, 232–33, 234, 235, 236, 237, 238, 239, 521

Environment, educational, 23, 49, 56, 61, 69, 107, 113, 120, 122, 125, 132, 135, 138, 147, 159, 165, 171, 173, 174, 177, 245, 515, 522–23, 538
linguistic, 11, 61, 67, 68, 123, 181–243, 245, 556–57

Estonian, 308

Ethiopia, 252

Ethnocentrism, 7, 9, 27–28, 71, 105, 148, 185, 245

Europe, 28, 157, 218, 262, 273, 275, 280, 286, 287, 291, 319, 343, 352, 426, 427, 430, 441

Exam, eleven plus, 42, 51, 53, 55

Exliteracy, 170, 252

Expectations of literate responses, 68, 69, 110, 113, 135–36, 165, 174, 180, 181, 182, 185, 188, 205, 225, 231, 232, 236, 239–40

Experience, spoken language, 19–20, 67, 78, 110, 123, 152, 165, 182, 186, 188, 189, 191, 200, 206, 209, 220, 229, 239, 240, 376–77, 468–69, 472, 521, 555
written language, 21, 67, 69, 80, 105, 125, 197, 205, 206, 521

Eye movements, 5, 18, 24, 25, 66, 69–70, 201, 206, 354, 443, 454, 469, 553

Factors, economic, 9, 107, 118, 178–80, 252, 254, 267, 268–70, 279, 286, 343, 360, 362, 366, 369, 410, 419, 422, 436, 446, 490, 505, 520–21, 529, 530, 531
extraneous, 68, 69, 81, 138, 165, 169–80
geographical, 114, 261, 346, 360, 405
historical, 7, 9, 261, 267–68, 319, 343, 363, 367, 405, 426, 494
neurological, 459, 515–16, 531
political, 9, 143, 182, 193, 247, 267–68, 270–71, 286–87, 343, 396
social, 9, 105, 109, 121, 136, 176, 185, 203, 222, 231, 238, 247, 250, 252, 259, 268, 286, 343, 348, 367, 400, 410, 424, 430, 515, 520–25, 531

Failure, reading, 6, 23, 72–73, 75, 81, 108, 133, 150, 172–74, 217, 224, 234, 240, 250, 269, 280, 304, 337–39, 351–53, 432, 435,

Failure, reading [*cont.*]
  438, 505, 519, 529, 538
Family, 67, 175–77, 180, 186, 298, 362, 363, 377, 399, 435, 446, 447, 456, 462, 476, 478, 504. *See also* Parents
Faroe Islands, 285
Faroese, 285
Fashions, teaching, 3, 115, 129, 153, 156, 157, 158, 159, 275, 374, *438*
Fees, school, 179, 290, 411, 412, 446
Finland, 7, 38, 43, 48, 60, 106, 107, 113, 114, 115, 117, 125, 130, 143, 156, 160, 169, 176, 178, 195, 197, 208, 218, 308–18, 466
Finnish, 106, 118, 143, 170, 197, 212, 217, 218, 221, 308, 317, 318
"First Grade Reading Studies," 128–29, 175, 504, 530, 538
France, 6, 43, 45, 48, 87, 89–98*t*, 103, 108, 109, 118, 125, 130–31, 133, 137, 139, 143, 149, 169, 173, 200, 262, 274, 319–41, 343, 353
French, 20, 29, 46–47, 48, 69, 143, 200, 206, 217, 265, 266, 328–30, 392
Furigana, 443

Gaelic, 362
German, 35, 46, 47, 217, 219, 231, 285, 313, 342, 345–46, 348, 349, 351, 392
Germany, 38, 43, 45, 48, 87, 88, 89–98*t*, 103, 106, 107, 109, 110, 115–16, 117, 118, 121, 132, 136, 137, 143, 158, 169, 173, 219, 231, 262, 273, 285, 286, 287, 342–59, 539
Ghana, 182
Gittens Report, 361, 362, 380
Grapheme, 17, 19, 34, 141, 142, 143, 149, 153, 188, 195–96, 200, 204–205, 207, 223, 234, 265, 266, 342, 352, 408, 429, 434, 436, *438*, 553, 554, 555, 558–59, 563, 571, 572–78. *See also* Characters
Great Britain, 6, 50, 51, 58, 59, 87, 108, 109, 111, 113, 115, 118, 120, 122, 123, 125, 131–32, 134, 135, 136, 139, 143, 147, 149, 155, 157, 158, 161–62, 170, 171, 172, 173, 174, 176, 179, 183, 187, 188, 191–92, 193, 194, 195, 204, 222, 224–26, 234–35, 238, 249, 291, 342, 343, 360–82, 426, 427, 466. *See also* England; Scotland; Wales
Greece, 106, 219
Greek, 20, 539
Greenland, 285
Greenlandic, 285
Grouping, age, 496
  grade, 40, 49, 56, 60, 133–35, 270, 337–38, 365, 494–95, 496, 497–98, 500–501
  homogeneous, 42–43, 49, 136, 292, 301, 365–66, 367, 494, 497, 527
  interclass, 136, 498
  multiage, 133, 135–36, 496
  multigraded, 133, 494, 496
  nongraded, 494, 495–96
  vertical (or "family"), 135–36, 368–69, 494, 495. *See also* Teacher: continuity
Guarani, 261–63, 264, 265
Guatemala, 252

Guinea, 252
Gujarati, 403, 404, 405, 423

Hausa, 20
Hawthorne effect, 155, 223
Hazards, literacy learning, 69, 173–74, 180, 212
Health, child, 179, 270, 410, 504
  mental, 111–12, 114, 466–67, 475
Hebrew, 46, 69, 112, 152–53, 176, 193, 206, 208, 218, 427, 429, 430, 433–36, *438*
Heredity, 110, 459
Hindi, 20, 69, 170, 174, 195, 209, 403, 404, 405, 406–409, 411, 413, 415, 416, 423
Hindustani, 404*t*, 406
Hiragana, 195, 201–202, 440–43, 444, 446–48, 454. *See also* Kana
History of reading instruction, 7, 112, 121, 488–89, 554, 571
Home background. *See* Family; Parents
Homework, 169, 175, 295, 335, 398
Hong Kong, 113, 117, 121, 129, 137, 148–49, 164, 169, 170, 175, 192, 193–94, 199, 203, 383–400
Hungarian, 308
Hypothesis, 16, 41, 43, 48, 49, 53–54, 60, 88, 157, 177, 189, 202, 207, 208, 225, 244, 268, 276, 392

Iceland, 285
Icelandic, 285
Ideographs, 17, 106, 201, 204, 383, 385, 393, 395, 441. *See also* Writing system: logographic
Illiteracy, 3, 4, 37–38, 39, 67, 170, 246–47, 250–55, 270, 271, 311, 353, 399, 424, 444, 446, 512
Imagery, 73
Immigrants, 191, 262, 362–63, 365, 426–27, 432, 436, *438*
Incentive, 51, 53
Incompetence, linguistic, 20, 188, 230
India, 20, 60, 67, 87, 89–98*t*, 103, 105, 108, 109, 110, 112, 121, 123, 129–30, 133, 139, 144, 150, 156, 160, 170, 172, 174, 176, 178, 179, 192, 195, 209, 252, 362, 363, 403–25
Individualization, 52, 59, 119–20, 123, 134, 135, 136, 158, 163–65, 291–92, 297, 303, 348, 366, 437, 471, 473, 474–77, 478, 495, 496–98, 499–500, 504, 525, 527, 534, 537–38
Influence, American, 28, 116, 152, 157, 416, 430
Initial Teaching Alphabet (i.t.a.), 17, 52, 143, 173, 175, 196–98, 202, 204, 205, 221–27, 233–35, 238, 367, 372, 375, 377, 440, 442–43, 459, 460, 504
Innovation, 14, 139, 156, 158, 161, 175, 331, 367, 368, 374, 378, 494, 528, 529, 533, 538
Integrated day, 159, 368
Intelligence, 14, 27, 42, 45, 54, 56, 74, 162, 186, 210, 222, 234, 272, 302, 352, 365, 379, 399, 444, 447, 458, 460, 462, 474, 477, 497, 501, 502, 514
International Bureau of Education, 30, 32, 35, 113

International Committee of Experts on Literacy, 36
International Educational Achievements (IEA), 6, 16, 23, 25, 27, 28, 30, 60, 61, 157, 244
International Phonetic Alphabet, 31
International Reading Association (IRA), 4–5, 9, 30, 107, 249, 375, 452, 507, 518, 535
Intonation, 233, 264, 267, 278, 329, 553
Iran, 60, 252
Ireland, 7, 183–84
Irish, 183–84
Israel, 43, 44, 45, 48, 87, 89–98*t*, 103, 112, 113, 136, 139, 152–55, 156, 164, 175–76, 178, 193, 208, 218, 364, 426–39
Italian, 154, 217, 262, 265
Italy, 60, 87, 89–98*t*, 262, 362

Jamaica, 252
Japan, 38, 87, 89–98*t*, 103, 108, 112, 115, 121, 136, 148–49, 154, 169, 175, 178, 179, 181, 193, 195, 201–202, 203, 206–207, 395, 440–65
Japanese, 69, 148, 154, 194, 202, 204, 205, 206,– 207, 227, 383, 390, 392, 395, 441, 452, 453, 458, 459
Japanese Society for the Science of Reading (JSSR), 452, 456
Joplin plan, 136, 498
Jordan, *438*

Kana, 148, 154, 202, 207, 218, 395, 441, 444, 449, 454, 458–60. See also Hiragana; Katakana
Kanji, 136, 148, 194, 195, 201–202, 203–205, 390, 395, 440–43, 444, 447–50, 452, 454, 458–60, 462
Kannada, 403, 404, 423
Kashmiri, 404
Katakana, 195, 202, 440–42, 444, 447–48, 454. See also Kana
Khand, 403
Khasi, 404
Kibbutz, 436
Kindergarten, 9, 45, 80, 111, 113–16, 130, 178, 187, 211, 272, 288–90, 298, 309, 317, 320, 323–25, 338, 347–48, 396, 398, 428, 447–48, 494, 500, 503, 514, 516, 519, 569
Korea, 87, 88, 89–98*t*, 103, 252, 254, 441
Korean, 69
Kota, 403

Labor, child, 179, 410, 446
Language, second, teaching, 27, 169–70, 230, 231, 285, 296, 309–12, 353, 362, 363, 397, 411, 490–94
Languages, differences between, 6, 8, 16, 17, 19, 20–21, 46, 49–50, 66, 68, 69, 70, 142–57, 206, 221, 245–46, 254–55, 276, 362, 394–96, 459, 470, 574, 578
Lebanon, 113
Legasthenie, 351–53
Legibility, 206, 354, 453–54
Letter-name, 75, 80, 141, 150, 208–12, 313, 413, 429, 554
Libraries, public, 177, 238, 251, 297, 298, 299, 363, 420, 436, 485

Libraries, public [*cont.*]
school, 175, 178, 279, 298, 299, 316, 334, 336, 368, 411, 420, 436–37, 485, 490
Linguacentrism, 186, 459
Linguistics, 17, 30, 34, 181, 185, 191, 202, 220–21, 225, 228, 238, 276, 373, 531, 538, 551–52, 571
Literacy, adult, 151, 171, 182, 251–54
definition, 35–38, 112, 247
functional, 4, 36, 151, 171, 246–47, 249–55
hygiene, 164, 254–55, 470, 479, 484, 501, 514, 519, 538
programs, 7, 8, 66–67, 251–54, 377
rate, 37, 38, 39, 108, 121, 175, 178, 179, 193, 218, 246–47, 251, 424, 443–44, 467, 486
restrictions, 105–106, 108
selective, 252
skills, 183
standards, 36, 37–38, 172, 175, 178–79, 246–51, 302, 304, 363, 374, 378, 410, 416, 452, 513

Madagascar, 252
Mainichi Report, 171, 445
Maithili, 404
Malayalam, 403, 404, 405, 413, 415–16
Mali, 252
Manipuri, 404
Manpower, 118, 249–51, 252, 285, 287, 291, 297
Manuals, teachers', 108, 222, 294, 334–35, 416, 418, 473
Marathi, 404, 405, 423
Materials, reading, 4, 6, 9, 51, 52, 65, 66, 68, 80, 85–103, 105, 110, 112, 116, 121, 122–25, 128–29, 132, 136, 137, 138, 151, 155, 160, 163, 172, 178, 210, 222, 226, 227, 232, 234, 235, 237, 238, 239, 270, 275, 276, 277–78, 287, 291, 294, 297, 298–99, 313–15, 323, 330, 331, 332–34, 335, 336, 338, 349, 354, 360, 362, 366, 370, 374, 375–78, 397–98, 416–18, 419–20, 422, 433, 436, 446, 451, 467, 471, 472–73, 475, 484, 488, 490, 491, 492, 493, 494, 499, 502, 504–507, 511, 518, 523, 525, 527, 529, 530, 534, 537, 538, 555, 574, 578
Meaning, reading for, 33, 34, 51, 58, 140–42, 146–47, 148, 150, 153, 155, 273, 295, 332, 351, 365, 371–72, 376, 414, 416, 417, 429, 436, 471
Measure, criterion, 23–27, 162, 165, 175, 246–47, 367, 378, 528, 529, 534, 539
Measurement, 16, 21, 22, 36, 37, 38, 44, 45, 50, 71, 244, 424, 454, 462, 468, 501, 525–29, 531, 535, 536, 538
Mechanics, 52, 141, 149, 150, 155, 199, 333, 365, 484
Memory, 73, 194, 387–90
Method, instructional, 4, 6, 7, 9, 23, 51–52, 58–59, 65, 66, 117, 124, 125, 128–29, 132, 136–38, 139–65, 177, 190, 199, 208, 212, 222, 226, 234, 261, 267, 271, 272–77, 278, 280, 291–96, 300, 311–13, 323, 324, 330–32, 333, 334, 337, 349–51, 355, 361, 366, 370–72, 373, 395, 398, 413–18, 419, 421, 422, 423, 433, 435, 449–51, 452, 467, 470–71, 478, 488, 493, 494, 499, 502,

Method, instructional [cont.]
    504–506, 520, 523, 527, 529, 530, 531, 537, 551–56, 574, 577, 578
  alphabetic, 140, 141, 148, 156, 208, 209, 212, 272, 311, 314, 354, 370–71, 413–15, 429, 449, 554
  analytic, 137, 140, 141, 149, 156, 164, 276, 313, 331–32, 349–50, 355-56, 371, 377, 471
  analytic-synthetic (or "mixed"), 137, 139, 140, 143, 273–75, 278, 331–34, 339, 349, 351, 551
  atomistic decoding, 140–41, 143, 147, 148, 149, 150, 151, 152, 154, 155, 157, 158
  derivation, 450
  eclectic, 51, 55, 140, 142, 294, 416, 471
  5W 1H, 450
  global, 51, 52, 59, 125, 139, 140, 141, 147, 273–75, 277–78, 325, 331, 339, 349–51, 355, 371, 373, 376, 414
  individualized reading, 123, 163–64, 499–500
  kinesthetic, 273, 339
  language restriction, 123–24, 226–27, 236–37
  look-say, 51, 52, 55, 59, 148, 273, 371, 376, 398
  meaningful chunking, 140–43, 146–49, 152, 154–55, 158
  one-step synthesis, 415
  phonic, 34, 50, 51–52, 55, 58–59, 123–24, 125, 139, 140, 141, 143, 145, 147, 149, 156, 157, 188, 200, 209, 212, 219, 226–27, 232, 236, 273, 275–76, 292, 311, 329, 330, 331, 332, 333, 335, 350, 371–72, 373, 374, 376, 377, 378, 413–15, 429, 436, 470–71, 472, 504, 516, 551, 554–55
  phrase, 141, 147, 331, 416
  radical analysis, 148, 398, 449–50
  sentence, 55, 125, 140, 141, 147, 153, 331, 349, 355, 370, 373, 414
  sight, 149, 325, 330
  story, 141, 147
  syllabic, 141, 154, 276, 331
  synthetic, 125, 139–40, 143, 147, 148–52, 156, 157, 164, 208–209, 212, 311, 313, 331–33, 339, 349–50, 355, 377, 413–15, 470–71
  three-step, 450
  word, 124, 139, 141, 147–48, 154, 156–57, 273, 276, 325, 331, 332, 333, 349, 355, 370–71, 376, 414, 416, 449, 556
Mexico, 87, 89–98t, 179, 183
Mismatch, child's language and school's, 19–20, 110, 182–92, 228, 234, 236, 237, 239, 240
  compound, 182, 228–38
  writing system and spoken language, 182, 192–206, 221, 225, 227, 228, 229, 231, 233, 234, 235, 237, 238, 240
Model, literacy learning, 10, 15, 67–69, 81, 160, 165, 174, 180, 181, 294, 538, 539, 553
Mordvinian, 308
Morpheme, 34, 148, 149, 192, 197, 198–203, 206, 228, 261, 263, 330, 383–84, 390–91, 400
Motivation, 10, 21, 76, 81, 85, 105, 114, 115, 121, 129, 138, 142, 151, 154, 159, 160, 161, 165, 171, 179, 184, 185, 252, 270, 275, 279, 315, 370, 376, 378, 416, 431,

Motivation [cont.]
    432, 445, 450, 457, 467, 472, 476, 480, 482, 484, 485, 492, 493, 512, 513, 521, 522, 533, 538
Mundari, 404

National Council of Educational Research and Training (NCERT), 409, 412, 416, 417, 418, 419, 420, 422, 423
National Education Association (USA), 503
National Foundation for Educational Research in England and Wales (NFER), 40, 52, 360, 370, 375, 378
National Reading Center (USA), 519
National Reading Council (USA), 37, 107, 519
National Society for the Study of Education (USA), 164, 499, 528
Navaho, 69, 183
Nepal, 406
Netherlands, 60
New Caledonia, 182
Nicobarese, 404
Nigeria, 20, 23, 109–10, 230, 232, 233–34, 236, 252
"No significant difference," 161, 244
Nongraded plans, 133. See also Grouping
North America, 24, 28, 154, 157, 235, 273, 276, 426
Norway, 7, 10, 74, 87, 89–98t, 103, 107, 111–12, 113–14, 118, 132, 164, 245, 291, 466
Norwegian, 218, 285, 299
Nutrition, 410, 525

Objectives, behavioral, 159
Oraon, 403
Organization, classroom, 135, 159, 164, 292, 334, 366, 374, 497–98, 499, 500, 505, 518
Orientation, literacy, 149–52, 178, 212, 226, 234, 560, 563, 578
  medical, 173, 379
Oriya, 403, 404, 405
Orthography, traditional of English (T.O.), 17, 198, 202, 204, 221–27, 229, 233–35, 442, 459–60, 470. See also Writing system
Overlearning, 170

Pace, learning, 50, 52
Pakistan, 362–63, 405
Pali, 403
Paraguay, 262, 263
Parents, 16, 20, 21, 45, 47, 49, 109, 113, 114, 156, 175–77, 179, 186, 271, 272, 287–88, 290, 291, 292, 301, 309, 310, 311, 336, 338, 344, 348, 349, 361, 362, 363, 369, 370, 395, 410, 412, 432, 435, 438, 444–45, 447, 467–68, 476, 477, 484, 492, 496, 523, 524, 533. See also Family
Perception, auditory, 73–75, 109, 188, 205, 212, 273, 339, 350, 395, 412, 469–70, 471, 501, 514, 522, 554–55, 556, 559
  code's regularity, 217–21, 223, 238
  phonemic, 205, 412, 555, 556–58, 559–72, 575–77
  visual, 17, 18, 21, 70, 73, 74–75, 109, 273, 339, 376, 395, 412, 413, 449, 459–60, 469–70, 501, 503, 516, 552, 553

Persian, 20, 405, 406

Personality, 111, 114, 189, 239, 450, 452, 455, 457, 466–67, 468, 474, 478, 480, 495, 533

Peru, 261

Philippines, 182

Philosophy, educational, 131, 132, 279–80, 289, 293, 300, 365, 367, 368, 395, 442, 531, 538

Phoneme, 17, 18, 21, 34, 35, 74, 78, 79, 106, 141, 142, 143, 146, 148, 149, 153, 188, 192, 194–95, 196, 197, 198, 199, 200, 204, 205, 207, 208, 209, 212, 217, 223, 226, 228, 229, 234–35, 261, 265, 266, 308, 311, 313, 342, 352, 355, 384, 385, 390, 391–92, 395, 399–400, 408, 412, 413, 429, 459, 551, 553, 556–58, 561–68, 570, 571–78

grapheme relation, 6, 17, 18, 21, 34, 35, 107, 141, 142, 143–46, 149, 152, 153, 154, 155, 178, 188, 195–96, 200, 202, 207–208, 217, 219–23, 226–27, 229, 233–37, 265–67, 277, 286, 308, 311, 328–30, 342, 356, 362, 371, 377, 385, 387, 391, 413, 433, 434–36, 471, 551, 571, 572–74

Pictograph, 193, 385, 449, 552, 558

Piteå, 189–90

Plowden Report, 52, 54, 361, 363, 364, 369, 380

Poland, 43, 48, 60

Polish, 46

Portuguese, 154, 275

Posture, inner-directed, 85, 86, 87, 90, 100–101, 103

other-directed, 85, 86, 87, 90, 99–100, 103

Poverty, 20, 179, 247, 270, 362, 520–25

Practice, 169, 170, 173, 379

Prevention, reading disability. See Literacy: hygiene

Problem solving, 33, 72, 73, 76, 79, 117, 150, 151, 162, 182, 183, 191, 225, 229, 234, 240, 511–12

Process, psychological, learning to read, 17–18, 50, 60, 61, 68, 69, 70, 71, 72–81, 113, 141, 174, 201–203, 206, 219, 221, 222, 225, 227, 244, 253, 255, 280, 356, 551, 569–71

reading, 6, 8, 17–18, 50, 61, 66, 70, 71, 72, 75, 81, 201–203, 206, 227, 244, 331, 353, 354, 355, 390, 396, 504, 505–506, 508, 509, 515, 551–53, 560, 571, 578

Psycholinguistics, 4, 8, 22, 69, 181, 244, 253, 255, 318

Punctuation, 21, 228, 278, 286, 352, 405, 409

Punjabi, 404t, 405, 423

Purpose reading, 21, 25, 33, 35, 51, 76, 77, 78, 80, 81, 112, 149, 150–55, 157, 160, 171, 172, 176, 196, 197, 201, 240, 248, 249, 290, 295–96, 398, 480, 481–84, 512

Quecha, 261, 262, 265

Race, 110, 520, 539

Radicals, 148, 149, 386, 391–94, 398, 449–50

Rajmahal, 403

Range, attainments, 41, 42–43, 48–49, 59–60, 161–62, 367

Ratio, pupil/teacher, 45, 118–20, 222, 346. See

Ratio, pupil/teacher [cont.] also Size: class

Readability, 50–51, 52, 296–97, 397, 452–53

Readers, basal, 50, 51, 52, 81, 85–103, 110, 121, 123–25, 137, 140, 164, 190, 197, 222, 294, 332, 334, 349, 376, 378, 397, 436, 437, 472–73, 504, 508

Readiness, reading, 7, 67, 75, 80, 109, 111, 113, 116–17, 119, 129, 164, 165, 174, 186, 209–10, 272, 281, 291, 293, 297, 323, 325, 338, 370, 371, 398, 411–13, 418, 423, 447, 466–70, 475, 476, 479, 491, 495, 500–504, 516, 519, 522, 555, 556

school, 111, 116, 190, 291, 347–48, 475, 523

Reading, beginning, 4, 23, 24, 35, 51, 60, 70, 73, 76, 77, 78, 110, 113, 115, 117, 125, 134, 139, 144, 145, 149, 150, 151, 152, 159, 164, 170, 171, 176, 181, 184, 185, 191, 194, 196, 197, 198, 199, 200, 201, 202, 203, 206, 208, 209, 210, 212, 220, 221, 225, 227, 234, 236, 239, 240, 245, 261, 267, 274, 276, 291, 293, 314, 315, 316, 338, 346, 350, 355, 365, 366, 371, 372, 375, 377, 416–17, 430, 433, 434, 436, 446, 470, 471–73, 485, 502, 503, 524, 539, 551n, 553, 556, 572, 573

centers, 518, 519, 532

comparative, aims, 7–9, 21, 27, 43

courses, 9, 244, 245

in content areas, 481, 483–84, 508–510, 513

corrective, 171, 173, 338–39

creative, 418, 451, 480, 483, 485–87, 509

critical, 251, 295, 418, 480, 483, 505, 506, 510–12

definition, 32–35, 112, 151, 348, 356, 505–506, 513–14, 538, 552

developmental, 132, 171, 508, 512–13, 516, 519, 524, 532

direction, 18, 19, 20, 21, 206–208, 223, 407, 412, 433, 453, 516, 558–59, 561–63, 567, 573

disability, 72–73, 75, 81, 85, 107, 108, 109, 150, 156, 158, 172–74, 207–208, 218–19, 280–81, 298–99, 300, 301–304, 317, 395, 424, 436, 452, 457–59, 467, 477–80, 481, 484, 514–20, 535

flexibility, 295–96, 481–82, 483–84, 512–13

habits, 171, 295, 316, 363, 394, 444–46, 509

integration, 10, 151, 160, 163, 169, 279, 293, 297–98, 315, 420–21, 430, 432, 498

interests and attitudes, 419, 423, 444–45, 447, 455–56, 461, 476, 477, 485, 499, 525, 528

oral, 150, 190, 318, 333, 336, 337, 352, 354, 356, 414, 417, 450, 471, 508, 525

rate, 24, 25, 70, 172, 190, 224, 281, 295, 296, 297, 316, 336, 443, 462, 483–84, 508, 512–13, 553

silent, 23, 24, 25, 150, 197, 274, 278, 281, 318, 333, 337, 338, 398, 414, 415, 417, 552

Reasoning, 73, 76, 204, 221, 225, 415, 417, 511, 513, 528

Rebus, 294

Relevance, 58, 59, 151, 171, 196, 201, 482, 484

Repeating, grade. See Stagnation

Research, cross-national, 4, 5, 6, 8, 9, 21, 23,

Research, cross-national [*cont*.]
    25, 26, 27, 28, 29, 30, 32–61, 69, 71, 85, 120, 132–33, 144, 148, 165, 174, 176, 180, 198, 202, 205, 208, 212, 244–45, 458–60, 538–39
  design, 162, 222, 245, 396, 536
  educational, 30, 115, 116, 148, 156, 162, 175, 245, 318, 409, 412, 422–24, 430, 490, 519, 536–37, 538, 539
  method, 5, 7, 9–11, 13–31, 32, 39, 44, 46, 56, 60–61, 65–67, 85–88, 129, 144, 244–45, 424, 513, 516, 536
    correlation, 209–11
    cross-cultural, 6, 8, 105, 254, 395
    experimental, 14, 15, 479, 520
    sampling, 16, 26, 27, 39–40, 44–45, 47–48, 50, 55–56, 57, 59, 60, 88, 115, 169, 220, 244, 424
    survey, 13, 14, 16, 28, 60, 61, 71, 244, 248
Reversals, 207–208, 352–53
Roma-ji, 440, 441
Russia, 87, 89–98*t*, 103, 308. *See also* USSR
Russian, 20, 29, 124, 192, 193, 308, 393, 551*n*, 568, 572, 573–74, 575–77

Sanskrit, 403, 404, 405, 406, 408, 409, 418
Santhali, 404
Saudi Arabia, 39
Schedule, lessons, 159, 161, 169, 310-11, 325–26, 346, 367, 495, 498
School, buildings, 120–22, 222, 270, 368
  infant, 52, 55, 56, 80, 122, 132, 134, 135, 158, 171, 224, 226, 248, 311, 314, 364–66, 368, 370, 371, 372, 373, 374, 375–76, 378
  junior, 132, 134, 161, 248, 364, 365, 367, 368, 372, 377, 378
  primary, 134, 135, 159, 162–63, 169, 178, 249, 269, 271, 272, 274, 281, 288, 309, 311, 316, 364, 365, 368, 372, 375, 383, 386, 387, 396, 397, 398–99, 410, 411, 421, 422, 436, 455, 551
  rural, 135, 176, 222, 269, 277, 278, 286, 288, 314, 344, 346–47, 362, 367, 371, 410, 412, 422, 477, 478, 521, 569
  secondary, 132, 171, 249, 315, 338, 411, 421, 428, 445, 455, 484, 494, 495, 497, 508–513, 519, 530, 532, 536
Schooling, length, 27, 36, 37, 45, 50, 109, 134, 169, 287, 291, 345, 364–65, 369, 396–97, 409, 411, 427, 444, 446, 480, 494
  segmentation, 133–35
Schools Council (England and Wales), 52, 222, 224–25, 227, 375, 377
Scotland, 43, 45, 48, 49, 58, 60, 77, 149, 176, 235, 360–64, 367, 372, 374. *See also* Great Britain
Scottish Council for Research in Education (SCRE), 360
Script, Devnagari, 405, 406
Self-confidence, 190, 219, 377, 514, 522
Self-expression, 58–59, 76, 159, 160, 171, 196, 197, 247, 274, 279, 293, 316
Semantics, 22, 192, 193, 376, 384, 391
Serbo-Croatian, 46
Sexes, differences in reading attainments, 39, 45, 48, 56, 108–10, 222, 338, 462, 514

Sindi, 404*t*, 405
Size, class, 118–20, 222, 292, 339, 346, 366, 368, 379, 419, 466, 467, 475, 477–78, 498, 518, 523, 524, 530
  school, 135, 223, 362, 368
Slow-learners, 23, 135, 164, 368, 374, 377, 378, 379, 399, 473, 474, 495
Somalia, 39
South America, 154, 263, 426
Spain, 179, 191, 262, 263, 264, 265
Spanish, 21, 29, 69, 143, 145, 154, 183, 185, 191, 206, 217, 228, 231, 259–67, 275, 277, 279, 490–93
Speech, 17, 18, 19, 20, 21, 70, 71, 74, 78, 80, 81, 110, 142, 182, 187, 188, 192, 196–99, 206, 207, 209, 211, 212, 219, 222, 223, 228, 230–32, 235–36, 239, 261–64, 267, 276, 290, 293, 304, 316, 317, 329, 370, 377, 384, 468–70, 472, 515, 531, 552, 553, 554, 555, 556–58, 560–61, 564, 570, 571–72
Spelling, instruction, 50, 52–53, 55, 57, 58, 59, 60, 157, 226, 275–76, 292, 294, 326, 342, 398, 414, 415
  irregularity, 18, 21, 66, 107, 143, 147, 157, 199, 207, 219–20, 223, 225, 230, 233, 236, 276, 286, 308, 329, 391, 460, 470, 572
  reform, 17, 202, 208, 218, 219, 285, 342, 383, 399–400
Sprechspur, 349
Stage, critical, 183, 197, 225, 229, 234, 240, 366
Stagnation, 133–34, 174, 191, 269–70, 337–38, 365, 410, 424, 495
Status, in education, 129–32, 421
  socioeconomic, 16, 20, 54, 55, 78, 161, 187, 192, 193, 222, 232–33, 234, 237, 261, 262, 263, 265, 268, 277, 286, 293, 346, 363, 366, 368, 369, 374, 376, 377, 407, 435, 520–23
Streaming. *See* Grouping: homogeneous
Study skills, 172, 295, 336, 418, 481, 509, 532
Subculture, 110–11, 145, 176, 186–87, 231, 237, 293
  black American, 110, 187, 189, 229–38, 521, 523–24
Subskills, higher order, 9, 171–72, 296–97, 374, 417–18, 508–513
Substitution. *See* Word: changing
Sudan, 252
Sweden, 6, 7, 43, 48, 60, 74, 111–14, 115, 117, 118, 119, 132, 134, 135, 139, 158, 164, 171–72, 173, 177, 185, 189–90, 197, 218, 237, 247, 287, 291, 297, 466–87
Swedish, 46, 190, 218, 225, 299, 308, 311, 473, 475, 483,
Switzerland, 43, 44, 45, 48, 349
Syllabary. *See* Writing system: syllabic
Syllable, 140, 141, 148, 154, 192, 201, 206, 207, 217, 233–34, 238, 264, 265, 267, 273, 276–77, 278, 311, 313, 314, 315, 329, 332, 350, 351, 383–84, 413, 431, 441, 448, 459, 471, 485, 552, 554, 555, 557, 561, 563, 565, 568, 570, 571, 572, 573–75, 577
Symbols, phonetic, used in this book, 31, 383

Syntax, 22, 146, 189, 200, 236–37, 261, 262–63, 316, 330, 342, 376, 378, 385, 390, 392, 398, 405, 406, 418, 556
Syria, 252

Tamil, 403, 404t, 405
Tanzania, 252
Teacher, aides, 495, 532
  attitudes and beliefs, 120, 125, 138, 139–65, 172, 174, 176, 189, 296, 331, 361, 366–67, 370, 372, 378, 412, 414, 430, 477, 525
  autonomy, 54, 55, 58, 136–38, 155, 271, 293, 298, 323, 330, 349, 361, 397, 505, 538
  continuity, 135, 291–92, 301, 476, 496
  selection, 132, 505
  training, 6, 10, 108, 120, 128–33, 134, 138, 139, 155–57, 165, 190, 233, 249, 272, 279–80, 281, 292, 299–300, 303, 309, 316–17, 323, 326–28, 331, 335, 337, 344, 360, 365, 370–74, 376, 396, 398, 411, 413, 414, 418, 421–23, 427, 430, 432, 452, 476, 484, 490, 491, 505, 507, 511, 518, 519, 529–37
  variable, 11, 14, 15, 23, 120, 122, 125, 128–65, 197, 223, 292, 432, 467, 499, 504–505, 523, 533, 538
Teaching, remedial, 6, 10, 108, 158, 171, 172-73, 175, 291, 302–303, 338, 364, 368, 373, 374, 379–80, 423, 452, 460, 473, 477–80, 508, 513, 516–20, 532, 535. See also Treatment: reading disabilities
  team, 494, 495, 498–99, 500
Technology, 163, 173, 280, 336, 378, 397, 500, 507, 528, 533
Telegu, 403, 404t, 405
Television, 21, 108, 123, 171, 209, 248, 251, 297, 378, 397, 444-46, 447, 507–508
Testing, 10, 26, 28, 38, 40, 41, 42, 45–47, 48, 49, 53, 57, 60, 71, 75, 80, 111, 157–58, 161, 162, 164, 173, 174–75, 186, 190, 224, 225, 233, 234, 244, 281, 291, 298, 301, 302, 334, 336–37, 338, 348, 352–53, 366, 378–79, 397, 398–99, 412, 423, 428, 435, 447, 457, 460–62, 466, 468, 479, 480, 492, 501, 514, 516, 517, 518, 519, 525–29, 531, 534
Tests, diagnostic, 26, 164, 318, 378–79, 457, 473, 479, 504, 514, 518, 526, 535
  translation of, 25–26, 46–47, 49, 244
Thai, 21, 69, 206
Thailand, 60
Theory, 3, 4, 8, 10, 13, 17, 41, 49, 60, 75, 76, 148, 198, 212, 244, 253, 254, 272, 280, 294, 300, 352, 355, 356, 390, 392, 493, 498, 504, 515–16, 520, 527, 531, 532, 538, 539, 575, 578
Thinking, 75–77, 78, 81, 200, 211, 413, 451, 462, 485, 509, 510–13, 527
Time, instructional, 113–18, 120, 169–72, 291, 309, 310, 311, 323, 324, 325–26, 327, 330, 332, 336, 345, 367, 397, 428, 437, 449, 475
Timetable. See Schedule: lessons
Todda, 403
Tohan Report, 171, 175, 444–45
Tones, 383, 384, 385, 396, 399

Transfer, learning, 149, 183–84, 225, 560, 564, 565, 568
Treatment, reading disabilities, 164, 173, 280–81, 302, 304, 338–39, 353, 379, 457–62, 477–79, 514, 515–20, 538. See also Teaching: remedial
Tunisia, 252
Turkey, 87, 89–98t, 103, 143, 181, 252
Turkish, 143, 217

Underdeveloped countries, 7, 170
UNESCO, 3, 4–5, 29, 30, 36, 37, 38, 39, 66, 67, 70, 113, 116, 182, 217, 221, 246, 247, 251–52, 253–54, 323, 331, 452
UNIFON, 226, 227
United Kingdom. See Great Britain
United Kingdom Reading Association (UKRA), 5, 249, 375
United States, 4, 6, 7, 28, 33, 34, 35, 37, 38, 39, 43, 45, 48, 50–60, 67, 85, 87, 88, 89–98t, 103, 105, 106, 107, 108, 109, 110–11, 112, 114–15, 117, 118, 119, 123, 124–25, 128–29, 131–32, 133–34, 135–36, 137–38, 140, 143, 148, 149, 157–58, 159, 161, 162–64, 171, 172, 173, 174, 175, 177, 178, 179, 183, 185, 187, 191, 194, 209, 212, 218–19, 222, 224, 226, 229, 230–38, 246, 247, 249, 250–51, 253, 273, 287, 291, 297, 332, 343, 347, 356, 376, 430, 466, 488–550, 553. See also North America
Universals, reading, 49–50, 60, 69–70, 71–72, 73, 117, 149, 239, 396, 398, 578
Universities, reading provisions, 10, 108, 130–32, 172, 280, 300, 317, 327, 374–75, 423, 518, 535–37
Upper Volta, 252
Urdu, 69, 404t, 405, 406, 407
Uruguay, 113, 263, 265, 273, 275
USSR, 6, 32, 67, 70, 81, 87, 89–98t, 103, 115, 124, 149, 154, 157, 192, 193, 200, 211–12, 219, 253, 343, 451, 466, 551–79

Variables, 7, 10, 11, 13, 14, 15, 16, 19, 21, 22, 24, 32, 56, 60–61, 113, 116, 118, 119, 120, 128–29, 138, 169, 176, 177, 179, 180, 221–23, 226, 227, 234, 244–45, 366
Venezuela, 252
Vocabulary, 19, 22, 23, 24, 124–25, 164, 193, 197, 202, 210, 222, 224, 259, 262, 294, 308, 318, 326, 332, 333, 335, 338, 342, 368, 370, 376, 386–87, 389, 393, 397, 403, 405, 406, 412, 413, 417, 423, 441, 453, 460, 468–70, 492, 513
  grading, 50–51, 52, 124–25, 294, 333, 376, 397, 416, 472–73
  technical, of reading, 77, 78, 80

Wales, 39–43, 48, 52, 60, 156, 176, 191, 222, 224, 227, 235, 248, 249, 360–64, 367, 369, 371, 372, 375. See also Great Britain
Welsh, 191, 362–63
West Indies, 362–63
Word, blindness, 158, 218, 301, 304, 352, 379, 457–58, 460, 477
  changing, 350, 574–75, 577
  recognition, 140, 173, 196, 219, 224, 294-95,

Word, recognition [*cont.*]
  354, 376, 378, 379, 414–15
 shape, 73, 152–53, 313, 354, 376, 434–35, 472
World Conference of Ministers of Education
  on the Eradication of Illiteracy, 252
Writing system, alphabetic, 34, 35, 106, 142–44,
  146, 148–49, 153, 155, 188, 192, 194–96,
  198–200, 204–205, 207, 217, 228, 383,
  388, 392, 393, 399–400, 433, 552, 558,
  572
 complexity, 143, 147, 181, 193, 194, 221–23,
  225, 229, 230, 233, 235, 239, 276, 387,
  409, 446, 448, 453, 470, 573
 logographic, 148–49, 192–96, 198–99, 203–
  204, 217, 228, 383, 385–87, 393, 395, 458,
  552, 558

Writing system, logographic [*cont.*]
 syllabic, 148–49, 154, 192, 198, 207, 217, 383,
  390, 395, 440–43, 459
 variable, 6, 9, 17, 18, 19, 20, 21, 50, 66, 72,
  74, 105–107, 117–18, 129, 142–49, 152–
  55, 173, 175, 181, 182, 188, 192–212,
  217–38, 265–67, 276, 285–86, 308, 328–
  30, 342, 370, 387, 390, 399, 407–409,
  433–35, *438*, 440–43, 458, 459, 552, 556,
  558

Yakutsk, 192, 578
Yemen, 39
Yoruba, 69, 109, 229–34, 236
Yugoslavia, 43, 46, 48

Zaubern. See Word: changing